CIVIL WARS
OF THE WORLD

CIVIL WARS OF THE WORLD

MAJOR CONFLICTS SINCE WORLD WAR II

VOLUME II

KARL DEROUEN JR
AND UK HEO, Editors

ABC CLIO

Santa Barbara, California   Denver, Colorado   Oxford, United Kingdom

Library of Congress Cataloging-in-Publication Data

Civil wars of the world : major conflicts since World War II / Karl DeRouen, Jr. and Uk Heo, editors.
    p. cm.
  Includes bibliographical references and index.
  ISBN-13: 978-1-85109-919-1 (hbk. : alk. paper)
  ISBN-10: 1-85109-919-0 (hbk. : alk. paper)
  ISBN-13: 978-1-85109-920-7 (ebook)
  ISBN-10: 1-85109-920-4 (ebook)
  1. Military history, Modern—20th century. 2. Civil war—History—20th century.
I. DeRouen, Karl R., 1962– II. Heo, Uk, 1962–

D431.C54 2007
303.6'409045—dc22

2006039334

11 10 09 08 07   1 2 3 4 5 6 7 8 9 10

Production Editor: Anna A. Moore
Editorial Assistant: Sara Springer
Production Manager: Don Schmidt
Media Editor: Karen Koppel
Media Resources Coordinator: Ellen Brenna Dougherty
Media Resources Manager: Caroline Price
File Manager: Paula Gerard

ABC-CLIO, Inc.
130 Cremona Drive, P.O. Box 1911
Santa Barbara, California 93116-1911

This book is also available on the World Wide Web as an ebook.
Visit http://www.abc-clio.com for details.

This book is printed on acid-free paper. ♾

Manufactured in the United States of America

CONTENTS

VOLUME I

Preface, ix
Contributor Biographies, xi

Introduction, *Paul Bellamy*, 1

Regional Analyses, *Paul Bellamy*

Civil Wars of the World

VOLUME II

PREFACE

Fortunately, interstate war is becoming ever more rare. Civil wars, however, linger on in many parts of the world. Some lead to few deaths (as in various regional wars in Burma and India), but others have high casualty counts. The latter are the focus of this work.

The academic study of civil war onset, outcome, and duration has received great attention of late. Our goal is to provide a useful resource for scholars and the general public alike. These volumes contain a wealth of information and analysis.

The academic community will benefit from our approach, for our essays are organized along lines followed in current research. The general audience will appreciate the historical overviews we provide. The essays are written in a straightforward prose that does not sacrifice content.

The essays consider the onsets of the respective wars. Topics here range from the role of ethnicity to territoriality and economic grievances. Duration is another important consideration. Why are some wars very long and others relatively short? These are important questions because, as the World Bank observes, civil war is the opposite of development. A variety of factors are thought to prolong war: contraband (e.g., diamonds, timber, drugs, gold), youth bulges, low opportunity costs for rebels, and the presence of external intervention.

The essays are concerned with the countries that have experienced the most severe civil wars since World War II. Each essay follows a similar format, making comparison across cases easier.

Several individuals helped make this possible: Scott Bennett, Ashley Leeds, Dave Mason, Terry Roehrig, and Mark Tessler helped us find some of our excellent essayists. We are grateful to Nicolas Sambanis, as we made extensive use of the online data set he provides to accompany his 2000 *American Political Science Review* article with Michael Doyle. Alex Mikaberidze of ABC-CLIO was also a tremendous help in assembling the final product.

Karl DeRouen Jr
Northport, Alabama
Uk Heo
Milwaukee, Wisconsin

CONTRIBUTOR BIOGRAPHIES

Candace Archer is an assistant professor in the political science department at Bowling Green State University in Ohio. She received her MA in international relations and PhD in political science from the University of Delaware. Her research is in international political economy and international organizations. Specifically, her work focuses on global financial issues, global financial crises, and international financial organizations. Her recent work looks at multilateralism surrounding the resolution of financial crisis and the interactions between global credit rating agencies and developing countries. With Glen Biglaiser and Karl DeRouen, she has a forthcoming article in *International Organization* titled "Democratic Advantage: Does Regime Type Affect Credit Rating Agency Ratings in the Developing World?"

Geneviève Asselin pursues her degree at the Norman Paterson School of International Affairs, Carleton University. Her research interests include conflict prevention, human rights, gender, and peacebuilding. Her present research focuses on the role of women in peacebuilding initiatives in Guatemala.

Jessica Atwood, a New Mexico native, is a senior at the University of Alabama. She will graduate with a BA in international relations and Russian in May 2007.

Michael Barutciski, a former Oxford fellow and United Nations consultant, directed the diplomacy program at the University of Canterbury in New Zealand prior to arriving at the Glendon School of Public Affairs at York University. He has carried out research in conflict zones and refugee camps in Asia, Africa, and Europe. His

publications have been cited in leading law and international relations journals as well as in periodicals in geography and anthropology. In April 2005, he accompanied a small group of York students to Rwanda, Congo, and Tanzania, where they spent time with locals and visited UN bodies (UNHCR, MONUC, International Criminal Tribunal for Rwanda), humanitarian nongovernmental organizations, an orphanage, and a refugee camp.

Milica Begovich graduated with a BA in public relations, an MA in political science, and a PhD in political science from the University of Alabama and currently works with the United Nations Development Programme.

Paul Bellamy is a former university lecturer who has worked for various international organizations and has published in a wide range of areas. He is currently a research analyst at the New Zealand Parliamentary Library. The views expressed are those of the author and not necessarily those of his employer.

Chelsea Brown is a doctoral candidate at the University of North Texas. She was recently a visiting lecturer at the University of Canterbury in New Zealand. Her work concentrates on the comparative political economy of financial markets and the effects of economic liberalization programs. Her articles have been accepted in *Journal of Peace Research* (with James Meernik) and *International Political Science Review*.

David Carment is a full professor of international affairs at the Norman Paterson School of International Affairs, Carleton University, and fellow of the Canadian Defence and Foreign Affairs Institute (CDFAI). He is listed in *Who's Who in International Affairs*. In addition, Carment is the principal investigator for the Country Indicators for Foreign Policy project. He has served as director of the Centre for Security and Defence Studies at Carleton University and is the recipient of a Carleton Graduate Student's teaching excellence award, Carleton University's research achievement award, and the Petro-Canada Young Innovator Award.

Daniel Corstange is a PhD candidate in the political science at the University of Michigan, Ann Arbor. He specializes in the politics of the Middle East and has conducted field research in several Arab countries, including Yemen.

David Cunningham is a fellow at the John M. Olin Institute for Strategic Studies at Harvard University. He received his PhD in political science from the University of California, San Diego, in June 2006.

Kathleen Gallagher Cunningham is a PhD candidate in the department of political science at the University of California, San Diego. Her area of expertise is internal conflict, with a focus on self-determination disputes.

Karl DeRouen Jr is an associate professor of political science at the University of Alabama. Some of his recent work appears in the *British Journal of Political Science, Journal of Peace Research, International Organization,* and *Latin American Research Review*. He is currently coauthoring a book on foreign policy decision making for Cambridge University Press.

Beth K. Dougherty is Manger Professor of International Relations and associate professor of political science at Beloit College in Wisconsin. She received her MA and PhD in foreign affairs from the University of Virginia. Her current research focuses on transitional justice in Sierra Leone and Iraq, and her articles have appeared in *International Affairs, Security Studies, Middle East*

Policy, African Studies Quarterly, Active Learning in Higher Education, PS: Political Science, and *International Studies Perspectives*. She and Edmund Ghareeb are the coauthors of *A Historical Dictionary of Iraq,* which was named a Best Reference Source in 2004 by *Library Journal*. Dougherty is the recipient of the 1999 Underkofler Award for Excellence in Undergraduate Teaching (Beloit College) and the corecipient of the 2001 Rowman and Littlefield Award for Innovative Teaching in Political Science.

Peter Finn is a lecturer in political science at the University of Wisconsin–Parkside. His research interests include classical, medieval, and modern political thought, international theory, and the concept of law. He is currently a graduate student at the University of Wisconsin–Milwaukee.

Kenneth Ray Glaudell earned his BA in political science with a minor in Arabic at the University of Illinois (1982) and went on to receive his MA (1987) and PhD (1996) in political science with a minor in Urdu from the University of Wisconsin–Madison, where he concentrated his research on Jamal al-Din al-Afghani, a major source of modern Islamist political thought. He served as a lecturer in the University of Wisconsin system from 1994 to 2004 and is currently an adjunct assistant professor of political science and history at Cardinal Stritch University in Milwaukee, Wisconsin.

Raúl C. González is currently a graduate student in the political science department at Rice University. Although his interests include civil war and other forms of domestic unrest, his present focus of study is the comparative impact of electoral institutions on legislative careers.

Mehmet Gurses is a PhD candidate at the University of North Texas's department of political science. His research interests include democratization, civil wars, post–civil war peace building, political methodology, and Middle East politics.

Cullen S. Hendrix is a PhD candidate at the University of California, San Diego. His research focuses on political economy, with specific interests in civil conflict and public finance in the developing world.

Uk Heo is a professor of political science at the University of Wisconsin–Milwaukee. He is the author, co-author, or coeditor of six books and numerous articles on the political economy of defense spending, international conflict, international political economy, and Asian politics in such journals as *The Journal of Politics*, *The British Journal of Political Science*, *Political Research Quarterly*, *The Journal of Conflict Resolution*, *International Studies Quarterly*, *Comparative Politics*, and *Comparative Political Studies*.

Shale Horowitz is an associate professor of political science at the University of Wisconsin–Milwaukee. His research focuses on ethnic conflict and economic policy making. He is the author of *From Ethnic Conflict to Stillborn Reform: The Former Soviet Union and Yugoslavia* (Texas A&M University Press, 2005) and coeditor of four volumes, including *Identity and Change in East Asian Conflicts: China-Taiwan and the Koreas* (Palgrave Macmillan, 2007). He is the author or co-author of articles in *Communist and Post-Communist Studies*, *Comparative Political Studies*, *Comparative Studies in Society and History*, *East European Politics and Societies*, *Journal of Peace Research*, *International Interactions*, *International Studies Quarterly*, and other journals.

Buddhika Jayamaha, a Sri Lankan native, has an MA in international affairs from Marquette University. He is currently serving in Iraq with the U.S. Army's 82nd Airborne Division.

Neal G. Jesse is an associate professor of political science at Bowling Green State University in Ohio. His research on electoral systems, party systems, and ethnic conflict has appeared in journals such as *Electoral Studies*, *Political Research Quarterly*, *International Studies Quarterly*, *Political Psychology*, and *Representation*. He has chapters in numerous books, including *Elections in Australia, Ireland and Malta under the Single Transferable Vote*, and *The Internationalization of Ethnic Conflict*. He is also coauthor of *Identity and Institutions: Conflict Reduction in Divided Societies* (State University of New York Press).

Tatyana A. Karaman is an assistant professor of political science at Samford University, Birmingham, Alabama. She received her PhD in political science from the University of Wisconsin–Milwaukee. Her primary areas of research are comparative politics and international relations, with a regional concentration in post-Soviet politics.

Joakim Kreutz works at the Uppsala Conflict Data Program, department of peace and conflict research, Uppsala University, Sweden. His main responsibilities include the supervision and delivery of conflict data for the *Human Security Report*, especially concerning estimates of battle deaths, nonstate conflict, and one-sided violence.

Dong-Yoon Lee is a research fellow of the Institute for East Asian Studies at Sogang University in South Korea. He received his PhD in political science from Yonsei University, Korea, in 2002. The title of his dissertation was "Party Politics and Democracy in Southeast Asia: A Comparative Study of the Philippines, Thailand, and Indonesia." Currently his main research agenda includes the political process of Southeast Asian countries and the international relations among those states.

Sharon Lunsford is a PhD candidate in political science at the University of North Texas.

Rodelio Cruz Manacsa is a PhD candidate in political science at Vanderbilt University. He has obtained masters' degrees from the Amsterdam School of International Relations and from Vanderbilt University. He has received numerous scholarships, including those from Fulbright and the European Union. He is also a faculty member of the department of political science at the Ateneo de Manila University in the Philippines.

Eric Pullin is a PhD candidate in the department of history at the University Wisconsin–Madison.

He is writing his dissertation on the role of propaganda in United States–India foreign relations. He is currently working as a curriculum specialist and adjunct faculty member at Cardinal Stritch University in Milwaukee, Wisconsin.

J. Michael Quinn is a PhD candidate in comparative politics at the University of North Texas. His research interests include civil wars, peasant political behavior, political development, and the economics and politics of race and ethnicity.

Marc R. Rosenblum received his PhD from the University of California, San Diego, and is an associate professor of political science at the University of New Orleans, where he teaches courses on U.S.–Latin American relations, U.S. foreign policy, the politics of economic development, and political methodology. His research on the politics of international migration and U.S. immigration policy making has appeared in the journals *Annual Review of Political Science, Comparative Political Studies, Human Rights Review, Journal of Peace Research, Latin American Politics and Society, Migraciones Internacionales,* and *Political Power and Social Theory.* His monograph, *The Transnational Politics of US Immigration Policy,* was published in 2004 by the Center for Comparative Immigration Studies at the University of California, San Diego. He is currently writing a book based on research he completed as a fellow on Senator Ted Kennedy's Judiciary Committee staff. The book is about the U.S. national interest in immigration reform and the current debate over immigration.

Trevor Rubenzer is a PhD candidate at the University of Wisconsin–Milwaukee. His interests include the impact of ethnicity on U.S. foreign policy, international conflict and security studies, and African studies. He has previously published book chapters treating security policy in Nigeria and South Africa.

Idean Salehyan is an assistant professor of political science at the University of North Texas. His research interests include civil conflict, international migration and refugee flows, and human rights. Currently, he is working on a book project that examines the transnational organization of rebel groups. He has recently published articles in the *Journal of Peace Research* and *International Organization.*

Kanishkan Sathasivam received his PhD in political science from Texas A&M University. He also has an MS degree from the University of Tennessee and a BS degree from Saint Louis University. He is an assistant professor at Salem State College, Salem, Massachusetts, where he teaches several introductory and upper-level courses in international and comparative politics. His research interests include the enduring rivalry between India and Pakistan, security and conflict in the Middle East and Central Asia, the proliferation of weapons of mass destruction, and geopolitics among the United States, China, and Russia.

Jonah Schulhofer-Wohl received his BA and MA from Yale University in 2004. He is currently a PhD student in the department of political science and a student associate of the Program on Order, Conflict, and Violence at Yale. His research focuses on the dynamics of political violence against noncombatants. Other areas of interest include economic development and politics in the Middle East and North Africa.

Sahar Shafqat is a specialist in comparative politics. Her main areas of expertise are ethnic conflict, democratization, and gender and development. She graduated from Mount Holyoke College with a bachelor's degree in international relations and economics. She has a PhD in political science from Texas A&M University. She is currently assistant professor of political science at St. Mary's College of Maryland.

Steven Shewfelt is a PhD candidate in political science at Yale University. He received a BA in political science from Northwestern University and an MA in international studies from DePaul University in Chicago. Before joining the program at Yale, he served in the U.S. military, worked at The Carter Center, practiced as a professional mediator, and directed his own conflict resolution consulting firm.

Marc V. Simon is associate professor and chair of the department of political science at Bowling Green State University in Ohio. His research focuses on international and domestic conflict processes and conflict resolution. He has published articles in *The Journal of Conflict Resolution*, *International Interactions*, and *Journal of Peace Research*.

Kristine St-Pierre studies at the Norman Paterson School of International Affairs, Carleton University. Her research interests include conflict prevention, humanitarian intervention, and the nexus between the natural environment and conflict. Her present research focuses on the role of natural resources in the outbreak of interstate armed conflicts in Sub-Saharan Africa.

Jason E. Strakes is a PhD candidate in the department of politics and policy at the School of Politics and Economics, Claremont Graduate University, Claremont, California. His primary research interests are foreign and defense policy, international and intrastate conflict, and the politics of developing nations. Strakes recently published a coauthored article in *Conflict Management and Peace Science* that examines the impact of the 2003 Iraq war on the security perceptions of states in the Persian Gulf region.

Alexander Tan is associate professor/reader and head of the political science program at the School of Political Science and Communications at the University of Canterbury, New Zealand. He is also a research associate with the John Tower Center for Political Studies, Southern Methodist University, Dallas, Texas. He is editor of the *Taiwan Studies Working Paper Series* and an editorial board member of *International Studies Quarterly*, *Electoral Studies*, and *Political Research Quarterly*. He has written widely in the areas of comparative political parties and comparative political econ-omy of the advanced industrial democracies and the nonindustrialized countries.

Clayton Thyne is a PhD candidate at the University of Iowa. His research interests include civil war, interstate war, and Latin American studies. His dissertation examines the effect of signals from the international community on the onset, duration, and outcomes of civil wars.

Jun Wei studies international relations at the University of Chicago. His research focuses on the role of hegemonies in the evolution of international systems and international conflict and explores conflict resolution in Southeast Asia.

John Wilson is a visiting lecturer in the school of government at Victoria University of Wellington, where his teaching interests include international environmental politics and international political economy. He is currently researching security and conflict issues in Iran and Saudi Arabia.

Kyle Wilson received a BA in International Business from the University of Wisconsin–Oshkosh in 2001 and an MA in political science from the University of Wisconsin–Milwaukee in 2004. Currently, he attends Thunderbird, the Garvin School of International Management, in Arizona, where he is pursuing a global MBA.

Jung-Yeop Woo is a PhD candidate in the political science department at the University of Wisconsin–Milwaukee. He received a BA from Seoul National University, Korea, and an MA from Georgetown University in Washington, D.C. His research focuses on international conflict, East Asian security, and Korean politics. His publications include two book chapters, on South Korea's defense policy and on the Korean War.

Min Ye is a PhD candidate in the department of political science at the University of Wisconsin–Milwaukee. He expects to receive his PhD in political science in 2007. His research interests are international crises, Asian politics, and game theory.

CIVIL
WARS
OF THE WORLD

Iraq
(1961–1975 and 1988–1994)

Introduction

The history of many parts of the developing world has often been marred by violent conflict, but particularly intractable are those clashes that result from the arbitrary imposition of political boundaries over ethnically heterogeneous territories in the aftermath of colonialism or major power war. In some instances, the state forms that result essentially represent separate nations trapped within unitary polities. This condition neatly describes the perennial dispute between the Kurds and the minority Arab governments of Iraq. The para-state known as Kurdistan is home to roughly 25 million of the world's Kurdish population, and yet it has only very recently gained a semblance of a representative government. Thus, its existence has been immediately intertwined with that of a country that has experienced much violent contention over competing definitions of statehood. This article examines the past and recent dynamics of the ensuing struggle.

Country Background

The physical composition of the republic of Iraq is a direct consequence of the influence and prolonged involvement of foreign powers in the region. The political geography of the modern Middle East was largely constituted by the European consignment of the territories that were left from the dissolution of the Ottoman Empire after World War I. The British Mandate of 1921 established a new state in the Persian Gulf through the artificial fusion of the three municipalities (vilayets) of Baghdad, Basra, and Mosul. These in turn contained separate ethnic and religious enclaves: the predominantly Sunni minority in the central region; the majority Shi'ite population in the south; and to the north, the territories inhabited by the stateless people known as the Kurds. Although their precise origins are debated, the Kurds are reportedly descended from the Medes, a Persian diaspora with Indo-European linguistic roots. The region commonly identified as Kurdistan is a historical entity that spans five countries, also occupying part of what is now Iran, Turkey, Syria, and the former Soviet Caucasus. Kurdistan's geographical origins can be traced to a province that was created under the Turkish Seljuk dynasty during the twelfth century (Chaliand 1994; Sim 1980, 3, 23). However, the concept of a Kurdish national identity is much more recent, dating to the nineteenth century, when the influence of European nationalism combined with periodic attempts to establish principalities separate from Ottoman control (Chaliand 1994, 26–27). As a result, the political organization of the Kurdish areas became increasingly dependent on the presence of influential sheikhs and tribal leaders (aghas). The 1920 Treaty of Sèvres, which effectively dissolved the Ottoman protectorates, promised to secure an independent Kurdish state but was quickly annulled by a subsequent agreement that divided the remaining territories between France and Great Britain. The area thus separated that lies within the boundaries of Iraq, or Southern Kurdistan, is a highly mountainous region of roughly 80,000 square kilometers, with sparse subsistence farming at high elevations but also fertile plains in which wheat and tobacco are primary crops. Approximately 4–5 million Kurds populate this area, although there has been much migration in past decades due to conditions of instability and economic underdevelopment.

Conflict Background

From its beginnings, the crux of the Kurdish struggle in Iraq has been the popular assertion of a national identity that has never gained the status of an internationally recognized territorial unit. As one author proffers, "[T]he Kurdish people have the unfortunate distinction of being probably the only community of over 15 million persons who has not achieved some form of national statehood, despite a struggle extending back over several decades" (Chaliand 1994, 11). Thus, although the Kurdish–Iraqi conflict is here generically identified as a civil war, it might also be classified along with other, ostensibly intrastate conflicts that are more accurately conceived as warfare between separate political identities—in effect, nations—that occupy the same territorial space and are yet inherently incompatible (Snow 1997, 117).

Yet, in contrast with the ideologically driven policy implemented in Turkey until the early 1990s, that of suppressing or eliminating a separate Kurdish identity, Kurds have not been completely disenfranchised in modern Iraqi society. Citizens of Kurdish descent have occupied elite public offices and have been allowed to communicate and receive education in their own language. However, discrimination and segmentation were certainly prevalent within Iraqi Kurdistan, as the central government sought to forcibly assimilate or suppress Kurdish practices in education and local government that suggested a discrete non-Arab polity.

The armed insurrection pursued by the Kurds in the twentieth century is therefore distinct among ethnic national liberation movements in that its goal was not actual secession but self-government within existing borders. One possible key to understanding this dispute is the manner in which the Ba'ath regime, which ruled Iraq for nearly forty years, understood the rights of the Kurdish nation as a people, not as a territory, because the notion of territory implied literal separation from Iraq. Further, these rights were privileges to be granted by the sovereign state rather than agreed upon by consensus and could thus be withdrawn if deemed necessary. At the same time, Ba'athists did not recognize the concept of a "Kurdistan" but instead saw it as a zone or region, whereas Kurds visualized Iraq as being made up of two polities: an Arab one and a Kurdish one (Gunter 2005, 76). Therefore, the conflict was not simply ethnic and political but also territorial, as it derived from a contested definition of the state and, from the regime's perspective, the potential threat to its cohesion posed by the establishment of an autonomous national identity within the boundaries of Iraq.

The pattern of clashes between the forces of Kurdish opposition and the succession of governments in Baghdad was often cyclical, as the motivation of either side to engage in a war of attrition periodically broke down into efforts to suspend or ameliorate the conflict. This was likely a result of the essential constraints and limitations that affected both parties: Whereas Iraqi regimes have sought to remain in power and maintain control of the state, the primary objective of the Kurdish leadership was to win separate but equal status for the territories it occupied rather than to replace the existing political order as in a classical Maoist insurgency. In particular, Iraqi leaders often called for an end to war, declared amnesties, or falsely promoted the implementation of peace agreements for propaganda purposes. At the same time, Baghdad recognized that although it possessed vastly superior forces and firepower, it could not successfully end the resistance. In contrast, the willingness and ability of the Kurds to continue fighting was affected by the continual shortage of arms and necessary supplies and by the fact that Iraqi counterinsurgency operations inflicted massive casualties among the civilian population.

The historical sequence of the Iraqi–Kurdish conflict can be separated into a series of minor wars or offensives, which include both the Kurdish campaigns initiated to seize territory occupied by national military and security personnel and the Iraqi retaliatory strikes that relied heavily upon aerial bombardment as well as ground forces. These Iraqi actions often occurred in tandem with mass arrests and deportations, massacres, and other scorched-earth activities that underscored the brutality typically associated with much third-world counterinsurgency warfare. The first such skirmish took place on September 11, 1961, when guerrillas led by Sheikh Mohammed and Mustafa Barzani attacked Iraqi convoys, army posts, and police stations, ultimately gaining control of a large section of mountainous area along the Turkish border. These actions precipitated an immediate response by the Qassem regime. The Iraqi air force conducted heavy bombings of villages in the north, leaving hundreds homeless and resulting in many dead and wounded. This action demonstrated to the Kurdish rebels that they would have difficulty withstanding such sustained attacks, as adequate medical provisions were in short supply. A sequel to the initial Kurdish campaign occurred in early spring 1962, when Barzani sought to recapture the positions lost during the Iraqi retaliation. Although the guerrillas were more accustomed to the harsh environment of the mountains during the winter months, these conditions often forced Iraqi troops to withdraw, giving the rebels an element of surprise in targeting bases and convoys.

The second major Iraqi offensive, which lasted from June to October 1963, began a comprehensive mobilization of ground forces (i.e., tanks and artillery) and air strikes to recapture the frontier areas occupied by Kurdish leaders while also suppressing Kurdish bases of support in the mountains. Despite concentrated attacks, Iraqi columns became bogged down by peshmerga resistance, and the offensive gradually lost its momentum. The tactical advantage provided the Kurdish rebels by the mountain environment was demonstrated most clearly on May 11–12, 1966, when troops led by Barzani ambushed and destroyed an entire army column at Mount Handrin, forcing an end to the Iraqi onslaught and deterring Baghdad from engaging in major operations in the far north for the next two years (O'Ballance 1996, 83–84). One of the largest military excursions into the Kurdish strongholds was launched in August 1969, in which all twelve divisions of the Iraqi army were deployed to secure several strategic cities along the northeastern border with Iran. This campaign was pursued in an attempt to conclusively conquer the domestic insurgency in lieu of an expected international confrontation with Tehran. The ultimate failure of the offensive to bring the peshmerga to heel would eventually lead to the secret negotiations that resulted in the historic March 11, 1970, agreement (see "Conflict Management Efforts").

After the breakdown and abandonment of conciliation efforts in the early part of the decade, Baghdad initiated another major assault, which lasted from April to October 1974. With the support of long-range artillery provided covertly by Iran and the United States, the Kurdish forces were able to nearly match the capabilities of the Iraqi army for the first time, leading to a virtual stalemate in which the rebels essentially held their positions rather then making headway in the conflict (O'Ballance 1996, 96–97). The first era of the Kurdish war of resistance came to an end with the collapse of Barzani's forces following the rapid withdrawal of Iranian reinforcements in March 1975 (Chaliand 1994, 62–64). Iraqi columns penetrated far into the northern region of Kurdistan, recapturing territories that had been steadfastly occupied for nearly a decade. The resultant defeat and flight of Barzani and the surrender of his guerrilla forces was followed by a brief "hearts and minds" program, in which the Iraqi regime sought to rehabilitate Kurdistan by building homes, returning confiscated land, and incorporating Kurdish dissident figures into the central government.

Although the guerrilla resistance (albeit under different leadership) continued unabated throughout the remainder of the 1970s, the Kurdish–Iraqi struggle was surpassed by the brutal war that erupted between Iraq and Iran in the autumn of 1980. The Kurdish opposition, however, played an intimate role in a major interstate conflict because of the shared border areas and territories of Iran and Kurdistan, in which many decisive battles took place between Pasdaran (Iranian Revolutionary Guard) troops and Iraqi forces. The nature of the insurgency during this period motivated the formation of a modus vivendi between opposing Kurdish parties that established the Kurdish Front, also known as the Iraqi Kurdistan Front (IKF), with a series of smaller Kurdish political groups in 1987. The new Kurdish forces also received logistic and material support from the Khomeini regime and often fought in conjunction with the Pasdaran (Hyman 1988, 13), which led to the organization of a massive counterinsurgency campaign by the Ba'ath party in 1988 (see "Tactics").

As is true of many aspects of the Iraqi civil wars, the revival of the Kurdish insurrection that took place following the defeat of Saddam Hussein in the 1991 Persian Gulf War was fraught with ambiguity. During the Gulf conflict, some Kurdish factions, such as those led by Massoud Barzani, supported Baghdad against what was perceived as Kuwaiti deceit and Western aggression, whereas others, led by Jalal Talabani, saw the strong international opposition to the invasion as a means to rally against the Iraqi government (Rudd 2004, 22). The uprising against the

regime in Baghdad was therefore galvanized only in the period following the withdrawal of Republican Guard forces from Kuwait and was instigated primarily by the earlier Shi'ite uprising in the southern provinces. The revolt was composed of Kurdish civilians as well as those Kurdish conscripts who defected from the Iraqi armed forces (Rudd 2004, 29–30). It was also largely spontaneous and did not come under the direction of Kurdish political leaders in the IKF until after it had gained control of a significant portion of Iraqi Kurdistan. Improvised attacks against army and security forces were carried out with the aid of captured arms and equipment. Local administrations were set up, and electricity and services were restored. For the first time in its history, the Kurdish movement gained widespread exposure among the general Iraqi population, with dialogues between Kurdish representatives and civilian opponents of the Baghdad regime (U.S. Senate 1991, 3). Many buildings and facilities formerly operated by the security forces were occupied and their contents seized.

However, the initial strength possessed by the uprising gradually subsided as it became overextended owing to its lack of organization; the uprising was crushed in the ensuing weeks by the surviving Republican Guard forces in a series of ferocious tank and air assaults (Rudd 2004, 30; U.S. Senate 1991, 10). The forces of the American-led coalition that had expelled Iraq from Kuwait—adhering to a policy of abstention from penetrating further into Iraq and allowing the Saddam Hussein regime to remain in power—made no move to intervene in the suppression. Between March and April 1991, more than 2 million Kurds fled into the mountainous border regions between Iraq and Turkey in a desperate attempt to escape the retaliation.

What is perhaps most tragic (although not necessarily ironic, given past experience) is that the eventual deescalation of the decades-old conflict with Baghdad in the early 1990s was quickly replaced by internal civil strife within the newly established administration of Iraqi

Kurdistan. The legacy of splits and confrontations within the Kurdish movement came to the forefront in December 1993, when an attack by a pro-Iranian splinter group on a Kurdish Democratic Party base divided the leading Kurdish parties over who should lead a necessary response to the attack (Gunter 1999, 75–77). Criticism of the swift retaliation by militia attached to the Patriotic Union of Kurdistan incited a series of armed confrontations between the rival factions. Violence flared again on May 1, 1994, when a land dispute escalated into prolonged battle between irregular troops allied with either wing of the Kurdish Government. Despite attempts at reconciliation through official meetings, these quarrels persisted through the end of 1994.

The Insurgents

One of the most significant concerns in identifying the combatants in the civil conflict in Iraq is the essential divisions that developed within the Kurdish opposition movement in the period

Table 1: Civil War in Iraq

War:	Kurdish opposition forces vs. Iraqi government
Dates:	September 1961–March 1975; February 1988–December 1994
Casualties:	Total battle deaths unknown; 60,000 civilian deaths from 1963–1975; 180,000–250,000 in 1988
Regime type prior to war:	Military dictatorship (Karim Abdel-Qassem) −5 in 1960 (Polity 2 variable in Polity IV data— ranging from −10 [authoritarian] to 10 [democracy])
Regime type after war:	Autocracy (Ba'ath Arab Socialist Party/Saddam Hussein al-Tikriti) −9 in 1995 (Polity 2 variable in Polity IV data— ranging from −10 [authoritarian] to 10 [democracy])
GDP per capita year war began:	Unknown
GDP per capita 5 years after war:	$2,700 (1999 est.)
Insurgents (combatants):	Kurdish Democratic Party, Kurdish Revolutionary Army (peshmerga), Patriotic Union of Kurdistan
Issue:	Ethnic difference, political autonomy, territory
Rebel funding:	Supported briefly by Iran and the United States, obtained arms and supplies from black market and expatriate Kurdish groups.
Role of geography:	Kurdish guerillas made use of mountain areas to employ hit-and-run tactics, which put Iraqi ground troops at a disadvantage in the early years of the war.
Role of resources:	Control of oil reserves at Kirkuk has been repeatedly contested by the Kurds and Iraqi regimes.
Immediate outcome:	Establishment of Kurdistan Regional Government and National Assembly in 1992, continued internal conflict between Kurdish parties
Outcome after 3 years:	Internal conflicts between Kurdish factions continued despite efforts at reconciliation.
Role of UN:	UN Security Council Resolution 688 adopted on April 5, 1991, condemned Iraqi repression of Kurds as a threat to international peace and security.
Role of regional organization:	Minimal. Regional intergovernmental organizations did not recognize the Kurdish movement and regarded the war as an internal affair.
Refugees:	2 million in 1991
Prospects for peace:	Uncertain. Improved relative to the past but dependent on the outcome of regime change after the U.S. invasion and occupation of Iraq in 2003

Sources: CIA 2006; Doyle and Sambanis 2000; Rudd 2004; estimates of civilian deaths are taken from Human Rights Watch/Middle East Watch 1995.

following the 1958 revolution. This separation would have a considerable impact on the goals and strategies pursued by opposition forces in later years. Ultimately, Kurdish political objectives were often obstructed by the lack of internal cohesion on political as well as ideological levels, which led to open armed conflict within the movement itself. The differences have their roots in the tribal affiliations that form the basis of Kurdish society. The first and most prominent of the groups that made up the Kurdish resistance were the affiliates of the Barzani tribe, led by Mullah Mustafa (known also by his surname, Barzani). Barzani formed the Kurdish Democratic Party (KDP) in 1946; this party would spearhead the resistance movement in Iraqi Kurdistan until Barzani's eventual defeat in the mid-1970s. Although the KDP became organized on a democratic centralist model with a central committee and a politburo, Barzani based his authority largely on personal influence and tribal loyalties. His subsequent ally and oftime rival Jalal Talabani represented the more ideological and modernized wing of the Kurdish cause. Early differences over the direction and leadership of the KDP led to the formation of a rival coalition between minister Ibrahim Ahmad and Talabani, who eventually lent support and assistance to the Iraqi government in carrying out actions against the Barzani-led forces. The split between the Barzani and the Talabani factions also conditioned the relationship between the Kurdish movement and external governments such as Iran. Barzani's sons Idris and Massoud succeeded him in the leadership of the organization after his death in 1979. Talabani founded the Patriotic Union of Kurdistan (PUK) in June 1975 as an alternative wing of the Kurdish opposition, which adopted a more recognizable leftist–Marxist orientation.

As has been the case in numerous insurgencies, some elements of the indigenous Kurdish population did not support the uprising or recognize its leadership, having been largely detribalized or having resided in urban areas where they had been exposed to more modern forms of education and employment. These groups often found themselves caught between Iraqi security forces and the core Kurdish resistance movement. Mustafa Barzani was also ruthless in his policies toward hostile Kurdish tribes in the early years of the war, using isolation and terrorism to consolidate his political influence over local areas (O'Ballance 1996, 51–52). Furthermore, the Kurdish rebels had antagonistic relations with tribal affiliates of other ethnic groups, such as the Assyrians, the Chaldeans, and the Turkomen, who also populated areas of Iraqi Kurdistan.

From the beginnings of the modern Kurdish uprising in the midtwentieth century, the basic military force that carried out the armed resistance against the Iraqi state were the guerrilla fighters known by the term pershmerga, or "those willing to face death." Later organized by the KDP central committee on a "political commissar" model, they became known officially as the Kurdish Revolutionary Army (KRA). However, the consolidation of these troops into professional battle formations was a difficult process. Although the increasing number of Kurdish deserters from the Iraqi national army eventually swelled the rebel ranks and introduced a greater degree of discipline, they were continually deprived of sufficient equipment, weapons, and ammunition, the greater part of which was obtained from captured government arsenals (O'Ballance 1973, 85–87; 1996, 55–57). In addition, they often lacked an effective means of transporting supplies in the field (i.e., logistics) or electronic communications, which hampered their ability to conduct battles across long distances. At the same time, the regular forces under the KDP were essentially held separate from the more tribal militias who answered directly to Barzani.

Iraqi counterinsurgency operations were originally the purview of the standard national armed forces, with the army high command directing ground troops, artillery, tanks, and bombers to advance on peshmerga and KDP positions. However, with the advent of the Ba'ath regime and the creation of elite units and special guards that accompanied the expansion of the security apparatus under Saddam Hussein, the suppression of the Kurdish rebellion became increasingly directed from within the Ba'ath Party itself. The various antiguerrilla campaigns pursued during the 1988–1991 period were carried out predominantly by the main Republican Guard divisions (i.e., the First and Fifth Corps) supported by auxiliary commandos and special forces troops (Human Rights Watch/Middle East 1995, 37–38).

Geography

The Kurdish region of Iraq, or Southern Kurdistan, features highly mountainous terrain with some wooded areas, as well as fertile plains fed by rivers at lower elevations. The peshmerga fighters often made use of the mountain areas to employ hit-and-run tactics, which put Iraqi ground troops at a disadvantage in the early years of the war (O'Ballance 1996, 59). However, the more mechanized, better-equipped Iraqi forces enjoyed tactical superiority in the low-lying regions.

Tactics

Initially, the Kurdish insurgency manifested itself largely in traditional forms of tribal warfare, carrying out attacks with loosely organized bands of fighters. However, the increasing number of Kurdish deserters from the Iraqi national army eventually swelled the rebel ranks (totaling about 20,000 troops in 1961–1963 and 40,000 in 1970), through which they gradually became more disciplined regular forces. The tactical approach pursued by Barzani's forces at this time emphasized disrupting Iraqi army command and control (that is, communications and intelligence) and lines of supply rather than mounting direct attacks on government-held positions (O'Ballance 1996, 51). After a brief period of abstention for fear of damaging vital assets, acts of sabotage and terrorism were eventually employed against oil pipelines as well as military

installations in Kirkuk and other cities occupied by Iraqi troops.

During the early phase of the war, the Baghdad regime relied heavily on aerial bombing directed specifically at tribal areas from which the KDP (Barzani) leadership derived its loyalty. These attacks were conducted separately from ground offensives and were intended to isolate the civilian populace from the guerrilla movement. However, repeated air assaults often had the opposite of their intended effect, as they tended to galvanize and provoke local populations to join and thus strengthen the resistance.

An alternate strategy of internal subversion pursued by Baghdad was the creation of anti-Barzani militias from immediately within the Kurdish areas. These were known as the Jash—paramilitaries recruited by the Iraqi armed forces, composed of Kurdish or non-Kurdish tribes hostile to the KDP leadership. However, these were not professional forces and remained under the control of tribal authorities rather than subject to the Iraqi high command. These militias engaged in traditional acts of terrorism, such as burning crops, damaging buildings, and slaughtering livestock. The Iraqi forces also conscripted a paramilitary unit called the Saladin Force, which was composed of a mixture of Arab and Kurdish troops and was similarly deployed to counter guerrilla actions.

In the late 1980s, the Iraqi regime chose to transfer one of its most fearsome assets—chemical weapons, which it had used against Iranian troops in its eight-year war with Tehran—to the counterinsurgency campaign against the Kurdish rebels. However, it was primarily the civilian population of Kurdistan that bore the brunt of this tactic. This concentration of both conventional and supraconventional military force to quell the resistance in the north during this period was significant in its scope and its level of brutality. The policy was carried out in a series of air attacks, forced relocations, and mass executions that became known as al-Anfal, or "the Spoils." These consisted of eight separate campaigns against several strategic regions that

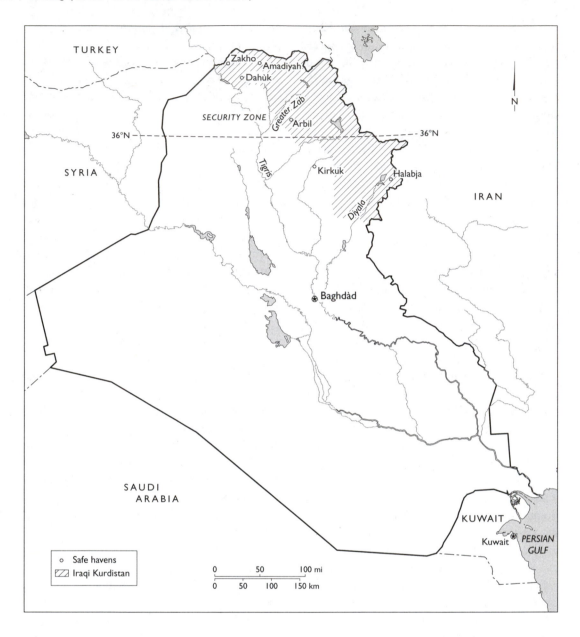

lasted from February to September 1988 (Human Rights Watch/Middle East 1995). Some of the most publicly recognized actions during this time were the air strikes at Halabjah on March 16, 1988, in which cyanide, mustard gas, and nerve gas attacks, directed at villages suspected of serving as bases of support for recently expelled Iranian forces, killed as many as 5,000 civilians. In total, an estimated 200,000 Kurds died as a result of these operations.

The intensive effort undertaken systematically to annihilate the Kurdish opposition at this time was also significant in that it was promulgated from within the ruling Ba'ath Party rather than enacted solely by the military central command. Yet, at the same time, it is arguable that the use of chemical weapons by the Iraqi regime did not represent a fundamental shift in strategy in its war against the Kurds. Rather, the Iraqi leadership resorted to a tactical measure that had already been employed in the context of a major interstate conflict. The willingness of the regime to use poison gas attacks against internal opposition to its rule brought an unprecedented halt to a thirty-year insurgency, as Kurdish forces were unable to retaliate in kind (U.S. Senate 1988, 38).

Causes of the War

The immediate background to the revolt that began in September 1961 was the burgeoning nationalist sentiment that had developed in the Kurdish territories during the period between the end of World War II, and the consolidation of Karim Abdel-Qassem's revolutionary regime in Baghdad. The periodic agitations and minor uprisings that had taken place since the nineteenth century and persisted under the British-installed Faisal monarchy gradually developed into a recognizable movement. At the same time, the Kurds had been allowed to retain an arsenal and relatively independent status. The July 14 revolution of 1958, which overthrew the monarchy of King Faisal and established an Iraqi republic, showed great initial promise for the prospect of Kurdish self-rule. The new government declared the unity of Arabs and Kurds and enshrined the recognition of Kurdish rights in the national constitution. However, as with all modern Iraqi leaders, a primary goal was to defeat internal opposition that endangered stability and threatened coup d'état. Such is exemplary of revolutionary regimes that face both domestic and external challenges to their ability to remain in power.

This condition motivated Qassem to eliminate any potential sources of opposition, which was carried out by banning all outside political parties and interest groups, suppressing independent media, and arresting and imprisoning Kurdish representatives. Further, the president sought to counter the growing political and military influence of Mustafah Barzani by providing support to hostile tribes in the Kurdish region. Thus, when Qassem's government reneged on the promise of greater autonomy for Iraqi Kurdistan, it set in motion a pattern that would repeat itself in decades to come. The precarious nature of Iraqi statehood recurrently forced leaders to impose unitary autocratic rule as a means of consolidating their tenuous political position.

Outcome

The outcome of the second era of the Kurdish–Iraqi conflict was also distinct from other civil wars in that it was resolved neither by means of the combatants reaching a mutually hurting stalemate that convinced both parties to negotiate a settlement nor by means of an externally administered arbitration process. Rather, it ended because the Saddam Hussein regime gradually abandoned its effort to forcibly assimilate Kurdistan into a unitary Iraqi polity, largely because of the constraints it faced from the UN and Allied restricted zones first imposed during the spring of 1991. The continued threat of external intervention that these containment policies posed may have convinced the Saddam Hussein regime that the possible costs of continuing its war against the Kurds far outweighed the value of the objective.

Conflict Status

In October 1991, in conjunction with an economic embargo of Kurdistan, the Iraqi central government withdrew all administration and public services from the Kurdish territories. Although this created an initial period of hardship, general elections were held in May 1992 that established the Kurdish Regional Government (KRG), based in the new capital of Arbil, and a unicameral legislature, the Kurdistan National Assembly (KNA), in July of the same year (Gunter 1999, 67–68). The international community deemed these elections relatively free and fair, although the Allies indicated that they would not extend recognition to a separate Kurdish state (Ofteringer and Backer 1994, 42). A coalition government was then formed that divided power equally between the KDP and the PUK, with each party occupying 50 percent of the 150 seats in parliament.

For the first time, Kurds had achieved the long-standing goal of establishing nominally independent and representative institutions. Yet, this arrangement gradually broke down over the next three years, as the legacy of rivalry and factionalism within the Kurdish movement caused it to degenerate into open combat. The leaders of both parties failed to join the new government, instead exercising power over separate political and territorial entities with adjoining systems of patron–client relations (Leezenburg 2003, 150–51). In December 1993 and May 1994, major battles were fought between militias with ties to the opposing wings of the KRG. As of the end of 1994, the parties had returned to a state of internal civil war, despite mutual efforts at reconciliation.

Duration Tactics

The perpetuation of the Kurdish–Iraqi civil conflict over several decades was the result of an interaction between the opposing agendas, interests, and strategies pursued by both actors, rather than simply the intransigence of either side. Although Iraqi leaders were preoccupied with remaining in power and keeping the Iraqi state intact, the Kurdish elites and insurgent forces maintained their goal of autonomy rather than secession. However, these positions were often incompatible, as they required concessions or compromises to which each party was unwilling or unable to commit. Further, at the level of military confrontation, Iraqi and Kurdish forces introduced no significant tactical innovations during the first decade of the war that would have allowed either side to gain an advantage, which resulted in an ongoing stalemate (O'Ballance 1996, 91).

The second most prominent political activity that fueled the armed Kurdish opposition over several decades was the policy of internal colonialism pursued by the Ba'athist and Aref regimes in the years after the 1963 coup d'état.

This practice is known more generally in Middle East politics as Arabization, or the strategy (pursued by autocratic Arab regimes) of actively assimilating non-Arab ethnicities through tactics such as the forced migration and resettlement of minorities and the repopulation of those areas by members of the dominant ethnic group. In the context of Kurdistan, these policies were directed both at suppressing activities associated with independent governance and at relocating Kurdish populations to areas that were easier for the central government to administer. Thousands of villages and homes were destroyed in the process. Districts and boundaries between provinces were often altered or redrawn to accommodate these relocations as well as to eliminate Kurdish attempts at independent jurisdiction.

External Military Intervention

Until the early 1990s, the involvement of regional governments in the Kurdish insurrection against Baghdad was minimal, the primary concern being to contain the conflict and to prevent it from spilling across contiguous borders. A principal reason for this policy of benign neglect was that the "stateless" nature of the insurgency meant that it was closely linked to the relationship between Kurdish populations in Turkey, Iran, and Syria and their host governments, and threatened to stimulate similar uprisings among dissident Kurds within those countries. During the early Cold War era, Western official opinion was particularly wary of the potential for Iraqi Kurdistan to become a tool of Soviet influence through Moscow's sponsorship of a radical nationalist movement in a key strategic area. Syria briefly provided air and troop support to Baghdad during the era of the United Arab Republic but no substantial backing thereafter. Although the Turkish government planned to mount a joint intervention alongside Iran and Iraq, dubbed Operation Tiger, after a brief uprising in Turkish Kurdistan in 1963, it was quickly aborted when the Soviet Union sent a communiqué that warned against any aggressive action that would interfere in the internal affairs of one its regional beneficiaries. However, as Tehran's relations with Baghdad began to sour in the mid-1960s, limited deliveries of arms were made available to the Barzani rebels, although without any public commitment to direct assistance.

One exception to this standard of noninterference was the covert military support for Barzani's forces arranged by the United States and Iran beginning in 1972. In that year, Washington pursued an intensive bilateral engagement with the government of Shah Reza Palahvi, to foster a strong conservative bulwark against radical Arab states such as Egypt, Iraq, and Syria. The Treaty of Amity and Cooperation concluded between Iraq and the Soviet Union in April 1972 guaranteed increased access to military assistance from Moscow and opened a possible door to greater Soviet influence in the Persian Gulf.

President Richard Nixon and National Security Advisor Henry Kissinger therefore sought to take advantage of a burgeoning revolt against the Iraqi regime to weaken an apparent Eastern bloc ally in the region. In the period from 1973 to 1975, a total of $16 million in U.S. military aid was transmitted to Kurdish forces via Iran through the Central Intelligence Agency (CIA), with some additional assistance from Israel. This arrangement was an obvious artifact of Cold War diplomacy, in which alignments of convenience were often established between state governments as means of "balancing" against the influence of one or another superpower and its allies. Thus, when the shah observed that the Kurdish–Iraqi conflict had reached a virtual stalemate, and that military aid only allowed them to sustain their resistance rather than gain a decisive advantage, the incentives for continued support dwindled. On March 5, 1975, the

An Iraqi Kurd father carries the body of his dead child in a Turkish refugee camp in May 1991. Ethnic Kurds fled their homes in Iraq to the relative safety of the mountains along the Turkish-Iraqi border when fighting intensified between Saddam Hussein's army and the Kurdish peshmerga guerrillas. (Joel Robine/AFP/Getty Images)

governments of Iraq and Iran signed the Algiers Agreement, negotiated with the assistance of Kissinger and Algerian President Houari Boumediene, which temporarily resolved the simmering dispute regarding the Shatt-al-Arab waterway and abruptly ended covert sponsorship of the Kurdish insurgency.

The primary effort at humanitarian intervention in the Kurdish–Iraqi conflict came during the crisis that unfolded during the months following the American cease-fire in the 1991 Persian Gulf War. This was known officially as Operation Provide Comfort (OPC). Following the impetus of UN Security Council Resolution (UNSC) 688, which condemned Iraqi repression in the Kurdish areas, OPC deployed a multinational force of 13,000 troops to establish "safe havens" for the refugees who had fled the massive retaliation against Kurdish towns prosecuted by Republican Guard troops and the Iraqi air force.

It is estimated that as many as 13,000 Kurdish refugees died in the attempted exodus into southern Turkey and Iran. Rather than engage Iraqi forces in combat, these troops were commissioned to delineate a security zone within which civilians and refugees in the Iraqi–Turkish border areas would be protected and provided with food, shelter, and medical support. This zone occupied a triangular, 10,000-square-kilometer space that stretched from the frontier city of Zakho in the north to Amadiyah and Dohuk in the south, and also declared a no-fly zone north of the thirty-sixth parallel, beyond which Iraqi aircraft were forbidden to pass. The refugees who had been trapped in the mountain ranges were gradually resettled within this area. The transfer of responsibility to a UN peacekeeping force was delayed both by Iraqi resistance and by the deployment of a "rapid reaction force" in southern Turkey to intervene in the case of further Iraqi attacks. These forces were eventually withdrawn by the end of October 1991.

At the same time, however, it is a common misperception that UNSC Resolution 688 provided direct authorization for Allied military in-

Zakho

Zakho, a city on the Iraqi-Turkish frontier, was the northernmost point of the triangular "security zone" established by Operation Provide Comfort in April 1991. The deployment of the Joint Task Force, which organized the delivery of aid to resettled refugees, relied upon Zakho as a primary base of operations. The logistics of the humanitarian effort in the following months were heavily dependent upon the availability of strategic transportation and the effectiveness of supply depots established at Zakho in the early weeks of the crisis.

tervention in northern Iraq in the name of protecting human rights. During the spring of 1991, there was significant resistance on the part of representatives of the UNSC permanent member states, particularly the United States, China, and the Soviet Union, who feared that such a ruling would invite future violations of state sovereignty. In fact, the eventual passing of 688 was largely in response to activism on the floor of the General Assembly on behalf of the Kurds by delegates of France, Iran, and Turkey (Malanczuk 1991, 119–20). The text of the resolution therefore makes no reference to Chapter VII of the UN Charter regarding the legitimate use of force or intervention in the internal affairs of a state where human rights violations present a threat to international peace and stability (Malanczuk 1991, 128).

Conflict Management Efforts

The Kurdish–Iraqi civil wars that persisted from 1961 to 1975 were interspersed with a series of cease-fires, negotiated agreements, and false guarantees of Kurdish political autonomy that also influenced the course and intensity of the conflict. These often reflected the recurrent instability in the Iraqi leadership and were therefore linked to efforts to consolidate new regimes. Although provisions that asserted the recognition of Kurdish autonomy were established in writing, the Iraqi government often failed to implement them, as the regime was unable to honestly adhere to these concessions without forfeiting the dominance of the Arab Ba'athist state. In the period after the 1963 coup that overthrew Karim Abdel-Qassem, both the Ba'athist and Aref regimes were weakly institutionalized and lacked broad popular legitimacy.

Thus, these leaderships sought to mobilize indigenous support in an effort to face off the threat to stability posed by a full-blown Kurdish insurgency. One of the earliest such efforts took place on February 12, 1964, when Colonel Aref extended a formal cease-fire after meeting with Kurdish leaders and announced that a provisional national constitution was to be introduced that would decentralize political authority in Kurdistan, although without actual reference to autonomous status. However, the new constitution promulgated on May 3, 1964, declared a pan-Arabist ideal of unity with Nasser's Egypt, which was directly at odds with the Kurdish objective. As no actual amnesties or demobilization of forces had taken place, minor skirmishes between Iraqi troops and peshmerga continued, and open fighting had resumed by the spring of the following year.

On June 29, 1968, the civilian prime minister of the second Aref regime, Abdul Rahman al-Bazzazz, extended the Twelve Point Programme, which essentially reiterated earlier positions on implementing autonomous status for the areas of Kurdistan represented by the KDP (O'Ballance 1973, 129; 1996, 84). Although the plan did not literally introduce a cease-fire, cessation of full-fledged armed conflict prevailed for a brief period. However, any sincere or direct implementation of the agreement was nullified when Marshal Aref was deposed in the second successful Ba'athist coup on July 26, 1968.

The March 11 agreement of 1970 (known also as the Armistice Agreement) was perhaps the most significant attempt at conflict resolution pursued during the first period of the Iraqi civil war. The provisions of this agreement were distinctive in that, despite the manner of their public presentation, they were the result of a long and arduous bargaining process between representatives of the KDP and Iraqi leaders, rather than a stopgap proposal extended by the regime in an effort to reduce the pressures created by an ongoing Kurdish armed opposition. In addition, both sides showed substantial commitment to concluding a peace agreement, as both Iraqi elites and the Kurdish leadership recognized the significant political and human costs of continuing the conflict.

Most importantly, it publicly affirmed, for the first time, the existence of an autonomous Kurdish region. The resulting contract would thus serve as a standard for the extension of concessions by Iraqi leaders in the years to come. The actual peace process was concluded between the Revolutionary Command Council (RCC) of the Ba'ath regime, led by President Hassan al-Bakr and then Vice President Saddam Hussein, and a reorganized KDP central committee. The fifteen articles listed in the document accompanied an amendment of the Iraqi national constitution recognizing the separate and equal status of the Kurds, and most significantly, detailed the administrative structure and function of an independent Kurdistan government, including the delegation of responsibility to members of the legislature. In addition, the final communiqués set a deadline for a complete transition to full Kurdish autonomy by March 1974.

At the same time, however, the agreement failed to resolve several fundamental issues that limited the feasibility and validity of the negotiated provisions. First, it did not establish exactly how the territorial and administrative boundaries of Kurdistan would be drawn. Second, it did not clarify the issue of Kurdish control over budget expenditure and access to government funds. Most important, it intentionally excluded the oil-rich city of Kirkuk from Kurdish jurisdiction, which implicitly demonstrated the intention of the Iraqi government to manage the parameters of the accord in its own favor (Chaliand 1994, 3; O'Ballance 1996, 92).

The gradual breakdown of cooperation that followed in the coming years proved that the treaty had provided only a temporary respite in

Kirkuk

Kirkuk is a city in northern Iraq roughly 250 kilometers north of Baghdad in the foothills of the Zagros Mountains. It is both the center of national oil production (as much as 1 million barrels per day, half of total Iraqi oil exports) and, until the 1980s, was identified by both leading Kurdish parties as the regional capital of Iraqi Kurdistan. Therefore, it has often been the focus of the conflict between successive Iraqi regimes and the Kurdish movement, for both lay claim to its environs as a vital economic and political asset. The campaign of Arabization pursued by the national government since the early 1960s was especially concentrated in the areas adjacent to the city, as they were under the influence of the Kurdish opposition leadership. Kirkuk was also the site of tensions between Allied and Iraqi forces after the 1991 Persian Gulf War, for it lies just south of the "security zone" that was established to prevent further Republican Guard attacks on Kurdish refugees.

an intractable war. Assassination attempts directed at Barzani and other KDP officials, originally suspected of being perpetrated by opposing tribes, were later attributed to the Iraqi regime. The Law on Autonomy (no. 33), which was extended on March 11, 1974, made a unilateral declaration of Kurdish political independence, which largely negated the contents of the 1970 agreement by reneging on the promise to conduct a new population census, by establishing a legislature whose members were directly appointed by Baghdad, and by continuing Arabization policies in the Kurdish region.

The second era of the Iraqi civil conflict saw similar efforts at negotiation, which largely resulted in a period of "neither war nor peace," although the time frame was much smaller. The dialogues that took place between the Kurdish leaders and Saddam Hussein during the spring and summer of 1991 largely reiterated old positions on granting autonomous status (Laizer 1996, 31–32; O'Ballance 1996, 194–95). Yet, both the KDP and PUK leaders took a decidedly prag-

matic route by publicly embracing the terms extended by the Iraqi leadership. It is plausible that they sought to take advantage of any possible deal while Hussein was seriously weakened following his defeat in the Persian Gulf War. Furthermore, they recognized that the protection provided by the Allied troops stationed in the UN-sponsored security zone would not be available indefinitely. By May 1992, these talks had reached a deadlock, and the Kurdish leadership proceeded to hold elections for a new regional government (Ofteringer and Backer 1994, 42).

The final resolution process engaged in by Kurdish leaders during the 1988–1994 period was directed at ameliorating the internal conflict between the main parties that had destabilized the new Kurdistan Regional Government. The Paris Agreement of July 22 1994 was produced by representatives of the KDP and PUK and was overseen by observers from the French government and Kurdish expatriate organizations (Gunter 1999, 77–78). The document was intended to strengthen the institutions and ministerial authority of the government while limiting the power and influence of the old opposition forces. Further, it established an agenda for the pursuit of necessary administrative reforms and restructuring civil–military relations, and it set a date for a new population census and parliamentary elections to be held by May 1995. However, the agreement was not signed as intended, owing to continued fighting in Kurdistan as well as an objection extended by the Turkish government that the establishment of an independent Kurdish regime within Iraq would incite full-scale insurgency in the Anatolia region of Turkey. Although a final strategic agreement was concluded on November 21, 1994, that formally ratified the treaty, the provisions were never implemented, for the rival factions slipped into a renewed Kurdish civil war.

Conclusion

The ultimate resolution of the Kurdish–Iraqi struggle and the status of the Kurdish autonomous regime will lie in the impact of its epilogue—the U.S. invasion and occupation of Iraq, which took place in March 2003—on the future of the Iraqi political system. The Kurdish leadership has extended a proposal to make Kurdistan part of a federated Iraqi republic, thus preserving self-rule while maintaining the cohesion of the present administrative units (Gunter 2005, 74–75). The physical integrity of Iraq as a nation of diverse identities and interests is also of serious concern to the governments of neighboring countries. In particular, Turkey and Iran have long expressed steadfast opposition to the establishment of Kurdish autonomy for fear of disrupting the existing state system in the region (Gunter 1999, 111–26). Although the Iraq war eliminated a regime that had inflicted the most intense suffering on the Kurdish population, it also introduced great uncertainty and ongoing violence in the form of a complex and resilient insurgency, this time against a Shi'ite-dominated transitional government. Thus, although the Iraqi Kurds may have entered a new era of political independence, the country of Iraq continues to be torn by internal conflict.

Jason E. Strakes

Chronology

September 11, 1961   Kurdish revolt begins. Qassem launches first Iraqi offensive in Kurdistan.

February 8, 1963   Qassem regime is overthrown in coup d'état organized by the Free Officers. Ba'ath Party takes power.

November 18, 1963   Ba'athists removed from power in coup led by Colonel Abel Salam Aref.

February 12, 1964   Cease-fire declared by President Aref after negotiations with Kurdish representatives.

May 11, 1966   Ambush by Kurdish rebels at Mount Handrin ends major Iraqi offensives for next two years.

June 29, 1968   Second Aref regime presents Twelve Point Programme for resolution of Kurdish dispute.

July 30, 1968   Aref is overthrown in third Iraqi coup d'état. Ba'ath Party resumes power in Baghdad.

April 1, 1969   Fourth Kurdistan war begins. Major battles in Arbil plain and expulsion and massacre of civilians at Kirkuk.

March 11, 1970   Armistice agreement contains fifteen articles negotiated between Iraqi Revolutionary Command Council and KDP. Promises full autonomy for Kurdish region within four years.

March 11, 1974   Law on Autonomy decreed, which reduces concessions offered in original agreement, imposes provisions that serve the interests of the Ba'ath regime.

March 6, 1975   Algiers Agreement establishes diplomatic rapprochement between governments of Iraq and Iran. Iranian support for KDP ends abruptly.

March 15, 1975   Kurdish resistance collapses. Barzani surrenders to Baghdad and flees to Iran, later seeks asylum in United States.

June 1, 1975   Jalal Talabani inaugurates the Patriotic Union of Kurdistan as an alternative to the KDP.

February 23, 1988   First Anfal campaign begins. Iraqi forces lay siege to PUK headquarters at Segalou.

March 16, 1988   Poison gas attacks at Halabjah kill 5,000 civilian Kurds.

March 5, 1991   Uprisings against the Saddam Hussein regime spread across Iraqi Kurdistan.

April 5, 1991   United Nations Security Council adopts Resolution 688 condemning repression in Kurdish provinces of Iraq.

April 17, 1991   Allied forces begin establishing "safe havens" for refugees and provide food, medical care, and temporary shelter.

May 19, 1992   Kurdish Regional Government is established by general election.

June 4, 1992   One-hundred-fifty-seat Kurdistan National Assembly is established.

December 21, 1993   Outbreak of internal conflict between rival factions within Kurdistan government.

May 1, 1994   Land dispute leads to open civil war between KDP and PUK forces.

July 21, 1994   Paris Agreement is signed by representatives of KDP and PUK but is not implemented. Sporadic fighting continues through end of year.

List of Acronyms

CIA: Central Intelligence Agency
IKF: Iraqi Kurdistan Front
KDP: Kurdish Democratic Party

KNA: Kurdistan National Assembly
KRG: Kurdish Regional Government
KRA: Kurdish Revolutionary Army
OPC: Operation Provide Comfort
PUK: Patriotic Union of Kurdistan
RCC: Revolutionary Command Council
UNSC: United Nations Security Council

Glossary

al-Anfal: "The Spoils," popular title given to a series of genocidal chemical warfare campaigns carried out by the Saddam Hussein regime in Kurdish areas in 1988.

Jash: Paramilitaries made up of Kurds from tribes hostile to the KDP leadership. These were recruited by the Iraqi armed forces to combat the insurgency from within Kurdish areas.

pershmergas: Kurdish guerilla fighters whose name means "those who face death." The main Kurdish forces were made up of pershmergas organized into a regular army by the KDP.

References

Central Intelligence Agency (CIA). 2006. The World Factbook. https://www.cia.gov/cia/publications/factbook/geos/tt.html.

Chaliand, Gerard. 1994. *The Kurdish Tragedy.* London: Zed Books.

Constitution of the Iraqi Kurdistan Region. 1992. www.unpo.org/news_detail.php?arg=34&par=538.

Doyle, Michael W., and Nicholas Sambanis. 2000. Data set supplement to "International Peacebuilding: A Theoretical and Quantitative Analysis." *American Political Science Review* 94: 4.

Ghassemlou, Abdul Rahman, et al. 1980. *People Without a Country: The Kurds and Kurdistan.* London: Zed Books.

Gunter, Michael M. 1999. *The Kurdish Predicament in Iraq: A Political Analysis.* New York: St. Martin's Press.

Gunter, Michael M. 2005. "Kurdish Prospects in a Post-Saddam Iraq." In *The Kurdish Question and the 2003 Iraqi War,* edited by Mohammed M. A. Ahmed and Michael M. Gunter, 71–96. Kurdish Studies Series no. 5. Costa Mesa, CA: Mazda Publishers.

Human Rights Watch/Middle East Watch. 1995. *Iraq's Crime of Genocide: The Anfal Campaign Against the Kurds.* New Haven, CT: Yale University Press.

Hyman, Anthony. 1988. *Elusive Kurdistan: The Struggle for Recognition.* London: Centre for Security and Conflict Studies.

Laizer, S. J. 1996. *Martyrs, Traitors and Patriots: Kurdistan After the Gulf War.* London and Atlantic Highlands, NJ: Zed Books.

Leezenburg, Michiel. 2003. "Economy and Society in Iraqi Kurdistan: Fragile Institutions and Enduring Trends." In *Iraq at the Crossroads: State and Society in the Shadow of Regime Change,* edited by Toby Dodge and Steven Simon. International Institute for Strategic Studies Adelphi Paper 354. Oxford, UK: Oxford University Press.

Malanczuk, Peter. 1991. "The Kurdish Crisis and Allied Intervention in the Aftermath of the Second Persian Gulf War," *European Journal of International Law* 2: 114–32.

O'Ballance, Edgar. 1973. *The Kurdish Revolt: 1961–1970.* Hamden, CT: Archon Books.

O'Ballance, Edgar. 1996. *The Kurdish Struggle: 1920–1994.* New York: St. Martin's Press.

Ofteringer, Ronald, and Ralf Backer. 1994. "Republic of Statelessness: Three Years of Humanitarian Intervention in Iraqi Kurdistan," *Middle East Report* No. 187/188: 40–45.

Rudd, Gordon W. 2004. *Humanitarian Intervention: Assisting the Iraqi Kurds in Operation Provide Comfort, 1991.* Washington, DC: Deptartment of the Army.

Sim, Richard. 1980. *Kurdistan: The Struggle for Recognition.* London: Institute for the Study of Conflict.

Snow, Donald M. 1997. *Distant Thunder: Patterns of Conflict in the Developing World,* 2nd ed. Armonk, NY: M. E. Sharpe.

United Nations Security Council Resolution 688. www.fas.org/news/un/iraq/sres/sres0688.htm.

United States Senate. 1988. *Chemical Weapons Use in Kurdistan: Iraq's Final Offensive: A Staff Report to the Committee on Foreign Relations.* Washington, DC: Government Printing Office.

United States Senate. 1991. *Civil War in Iraq: A Staff Report to the Committee on Foreign Relations.* Washington, DC: Government Printing Office.

Korea
(1950–1953)

Country Background

The Korean War (1950–1953) resulted from the division of Korea into South Korea and North Korea following the end of World War II in 1945. Immediately following this segregation, efforts to reunify the peninsula were attempted. However, when those efforts ended in failure in 1948, the South declared itself the Republic of Korea (ROK), and the North established the People's Republic of Korea (DPRK). In 1949, fighting broke out on the border between the two newly created countries. On June 25, 1950, North Korean forces crossed the divide and invaded the South. An armistice was reached in July 1953. To understand the Korean War, we need also to appreciate how the separation of Korea evolved.

Before 1948 and the subdivision into two political entities, the entire Korean peninsula was one unified country ruled by the Chosun Dynasty. Born in 1392 before dying out in 1910, the dynasty's reign lasted more than half a millennium. In the second half of the nineteenth century, foreign empires sought to increase their influence within the Korean peninsula. Their presence and hopes were met with resistance. South Korea refused to open itself to the world because governing elites, including the king and his immediate subordinates, believed that the society they had achieved through Confucianism needed little or nothing

from foreigners outside China. However, when Japan modernized and opened itself to the Western world, to some extent it inspired Korea and influenced Korean politics. In 1876, the Japanese urged Korea to allow diplomatic relations, thereby opening trade between the two countries. This fledgling relationship with Japan weakened Korea's traditionally close ties to China.

To counter the increasing Japanese influence in Korea, China sought to neutralize its rival by urging Korea to open to the Western countries, which led to the Korea–United States treaty of 1882. But this maneuver failed to slow Japan's impact and growing power in Asia. Even militarily, the Japanese were becoming the dominant players. In 1895, Japan defeated China in the Sino-Japanese War; ten years later, Japan overcame Russia in the Russo-Japanese War. These victories solidified Japan's dominant influence on the Korean peninsula: Korea became a Japanese protectorate in 1895 and in 1910 was formally annexed, marking the end of the Chosun Dynasty.

After thirty-five years under harsh Japanese rule, Korea regained its independence on August 15, 1945, after Japan surrendered to the Allies. This surrender, together with the Soviet Union's landing on the Korean peninsula, would utterly transform Korea. Another important historical incident that shaped Korea's fate occurred in

1943, at the Cairo Conference. The Allies, including the United States, China, and Britain, agreed to strip Japan of all its territories acquired since 1894. In August 1945, on the eve of the collapse of Japan, the Soviet Union (which had joined the fight against Japan in the northern part of Korea a week earlier) agreed to the U.S. proposal that Korea should be divided into two zones across the thirty-eighth parallel for the purpose of acceptance of military surrender.

The intent was merely to ensure that the Japanese north of the line would surrender to the Soviet Union and those south of the line to the United States. In its declaration of war on Japan, the Soviets agreed to this principle. Yet, no precise formula had been agreed to between Roosevelt and Stalin for governing the newly independent Korea. As Blair (1994) notes, Korea was not much known to the world. No one really knew what to do with it, nor did anyone much care. Consequently, the idea of segregating Korea was chosen hastily and casually. On August 15, 1945, fearing Soviet control of the entire Korean peninsula, U.S. President Harry Truman proposed the division of Korea to Joseph Stalin, who agreed the next day. The thirty-eighth parallel was not intended as a permanent dividing line but was simply a practical solution to the vacuum created in Korea by Japan's sudden collapse (Chull Baum Kim 1994). As Gupta puts it, in the context of the developing Cold War, "the 38th Parallel turned into a rigid frontier between two Korean client-states under the influence of the United States and the Soviet Union respectively" (Gupta 1972, 701).

Both great powers used their occupational presence to promote governments friendly to their ideologies and interests. The occupation of Korea by the United States and the Soviet Union was arranged without precise definitions of its nature and duration, thereby greatly reducing Korea's prospects for a smooth transition toward independence and unity (Stueck 1995, 19). The Soviet Union suppressed the moderate nationalists in the north and gave its support to Kim Il Sung, a Communist who had led anti-Japanese guerrillas in Manchuria. In the south, the leftist movement was opposed by various groups of right-wing nationalists. This resistance was due mainly to the U.S. presence, which set up an administration based on the former Japanese colonial structure, in which conservatives held power. Thus, any movements related to socialism or communism were seen as threatening and were suffocated (MacDonald 1996, 47).

The United States found an ally in Syngman Rhee, a nationalist who opposed the Japanese and lived in exile in the United States, and began to support him. During this time, political activity became increasingly polarized between left and right. As Savada and Shaw note, the fate of South Korea was dominated not only by the Cold War antagonism of the two great powers but also by "seemingly irreconcilable political differences among Koreans themselves" (Savada and Shaw 2002, 153).

In May 1948, elections were held in South Korea under the auspices of the United Nations. A national assembly was established according to the outcome of the elections, and this new body elected Syngman Rhee as the first president of the Republic of Korea (South Korea). In the north, a separate regime, the Democratic People's Republic of Korea (North Korea), led by Kim Il Sung, was established in December. It is necessary to remember that the United Nations declared the South Korean government to be the only lawful government on the Korean peninsula.

Conflict Background

Tension escalated in Korea between the formation of the two Korean states in 1948 and the outbreak of the war in June 1950. Each government, North and South, insisted that it was the only rightful government in Korea. Kaufman (1999) contends that the Korean War was part of a continuing civil conflict in Korea that began with the end of World War II, and not merely an isolated event in history. Thus, the development of the ideological struggle among Koreans must

South Korea's Military

South Korea ranked eleventh worldwide in military expenditure in 1999. South Korea's military expenditure in 1999 was $11.6 billion, whereas North Korea spent $4.26 billion. However, if we compare the ratio of military expenditure to gross national product (GNP), North Korea ranked third, spending 18.8 percent of its GNP on its military, whereas South Korea ranked fifty-seventh, spending 2.9 percent of its GNO on its military ("World Military Expenditures and Arms Transfers" 2003).

be further understood. This internal battle over ideas, combined with the Cold War atmosphere, provided the basis for the Korean War.

Socialist and revolutionary ideas had become increasingly popular in Korean intellectual circles in the early 1920s owing to the efforts of certain Koreans who had studied and become radicalized in Japan (Hart-Landsberg 1998). Despite Japan's harsh intervention in and oppression of Korean political life, Communist-inspired resistance continued. Externally, a regional Communist-led resistance movement arose in response to Japanese imperialism in Manchuria and northern China. This continued to influence political consciousness and commitments in Korea. Although Chinese Communists organized and led the main opposition to Japan in Manchuria, Korean Communists also played an important role in the armed struggles there. Some Koreans served as division commanders, Kim Il Sung among them. It was during this conflict that he established his reputation as a liberation fighter in the Second Army. This socialist and Communist movement survived Japan's harsh oppression. It also strengthened and expanded its network in Korea predominantly by creating close ties with farmers, the working class, and student opposition groups upset with Japanese rule.

However, this growing leftist ideology did not reveal serious social problems until the collapse of Japan became obvious. But when collapse became apparent, clashes broke out between the opposing groups, as worker and peasant unions flourished and Communist strength grew. The conservatives (e.g., landowners, businessmen, and manufacturers) who had enjoyed a privileged status under the Japanese rule sought to retain their status after the liberation. Conversely, political leftists, including large numbers of peasants and workers, sought a radical upheaval in the social and political structure of Korea. This political divide and class struggle provided a base of popular support for the regime in the north and, concurrently, political instability in the south.

During the two years following the establishment of a South Korean government, the domestic political conditions were volatile. The UN General Assembly, influenced by the United States, adopted a resolution in November 1947, hoping to resolve the problem of Korea's discord by establishing a new national government to govern all of Korea. The resolution recommended that elections be held no later than March 31, 1948. The Soviet Union, however, refused to cooperate with the United Nations. Despite the Soviet balking, the United Nations Temporary Commission on Korea (UNTCOK) was created in 1947 to sponsor and observe the election of a Korean legislative body, which would be authorized to form a Korean government. The United Nations adopted another resolution on February 26, 1948, to proceed with an election in the South. On May 10, 1948, the UN-sponsored general election was held.

Although it faced strong opposition from the Soviet Union, the United States, given its overwhelming influence in the UN, had little trouble winning approval of its motion. UNTCOK's decision to observe an election in the South alone indicated that their objective was not necessarily a reunification of Korea. Yet, Syngman Rhee and his followers welcomed this resolution, a view not shared by all. In fact, an overwhelming majority of Koreans, including leftists, disputed the election because they feared it would make the separation permanent. Despite the unpopularity of the vote, Syngman Rhee was elected president by the National Assembly on July 20, 1948. U.S. foreign policy had succeeded in dividing Korea and establishing a right-wing government in the South. Yet the violence that continued to spread throughout South Korea undermined the regime's stability. With support from the North, growing numbers joined guerrilla groups fighting to overthrow the Rhee regime and reunite the country. The guerrilla war in the South began on Jeju Island; it is remembered and referred to as 4.3 because it commenced on April 3, 1948. Discontent with the American occupation and with the troops from the central South Korean regime (still in its early stages of formation under Rhee) precipitated the violent outbreak. The South Korean right-wing government was conducting nationwide campaigns to root out Communists and their sympathizers.

As well as being horrified by this brutality, Jeju residents were also upset with the United Nations, which had abandoned its intent to hold elections that would unify the countries; the election of a South Korean government was to take place in May. Many Koreans saw the elections as merely a smokescreen of legitimacy behind which Rhee would be placed in power and kept beholden to the American occupiers (Thompson 2004). Demonstrations against the election were held on March 1, 1948, and many of the protesters were arrested. On April 3, after brutal treatment by police, the people of Jeju struck back. A guerrilla army of nearly 4,000 took control of most of the villages in Jeju (Hart-Landsberg 1998). The South Korean government sent its military forces to the island to suppress the swelling rebellion. Thompson (2004) reports that estimates of the numbers of civilians killed on Jeju during the 4.3 uprisings range from 10,000 to 80,000 (depending on the agency or reporter). Another rebellion broke out in October 1948, this time in the southern port city of Yosu. South Korean soldiers ordered to quell it refused to fight and even turned against the government.

Although the guerrilla war was being fought in the South, tensions between the North and South states were increasing. When a series of Communist-led rebellions in South Korea were suppressed by the South Korean government, the option of unification by insurgency appeared unviable to the Communists (Rees 1988, 93). So Pyongyang was forced to consider more drastic means of achieving its goal. This explains Macdonald's contention that "the Korean War should probably be understood as encompassing an era from 1947 to 1955, with the period of 1950–1953 as its hot phase" (MacDonald 1996, 50).

Incidents along the thirty-eighth parallel began to increase. One of the first major battles between the North and the South took place on May 4, 1949. This skirmishing, initiated by the South, lasted four days and left hundreds dead. Another clash occurred in August, when North Korean forces attacked the ROK units. Starting in September 1949, the military balance of power began to shift in favor of North Korea as additional military supplies began to arrive from the Soviet Union and as North Korean troops returned from China (Hart-Landsberg 1998). As their resources grew, so did their boldness; thereafter, the DPRK frequently initiated the fighting.

The Insurgents

The Korean People's Army of the DPRK crossed the thirty-eighth parallel on June 25, 1950. In the 1970s, however, revisionists began to argue that the war was caused just as much by Western and South Korean provocation (Catchpole 2000, 7). Despite the argument of the revisionists, war-related documents provided by Soviet President Boris Yeltsin in 1994 make it clear that North Korea, operating with major Soviet assistance, was responsible for the invasion (Myers 2001).

Although the Soviet Union and China played an important role in reinforcing the strength of the North Korean People's Army, it appears that they neither ordered nor encouraged Kim Il Sung to initiate a war in Korea (Gye-Dong Kim 1989, 33). Rather, Kim Il Sung was dedicated to

Table 1: Civil War in Korea

War:	South Korea vs. North Korea
Dates:	June 25, 1950, to July 27, 1953
Casualties (KIA):	South Korea: 137,899; North Korea: 520,000; United Nations: 40,670; China: 148,600
Regime type prior to war:	South Korea: Republic (presidential system); North Korea: Communist government
Regime type after war:	Republic (presidential system)
GDP per capita year war began:	US $1,103 in 2002 value for South Korea; no data available for North Korea
GDP per capita 5 years after war:	US $1,509 in 2002 value for South Korea; no data available for North Korea
Insurgents:	North Korea
Issue:	Reunification of Korea, ideological differences
Rebel funding:	Support from Soviet Union, China
Role of geography:	Not applicable
Role of resources:	Not applicable
Immediate outcome:	Stalemate, continued partition of Korea
Outcome after 5 years:	Hostile relationship
Role of UN:	Sent combatants under UNC
Role of regional organization:	Not applicable
Refugees:	More than 7 million separated families
Prospects for peace:	Uncertain in the near future

Sources: Korea Institute for Military History Compilation (n.d.); Groningen Growth and Development Centre (n.d.).

the reunification of Korea and believed that this could only be achieved by the military defeat of the South.

After the Soviet Union agreed to the U.S. proposal—to accept the surrender of remaining Japanese troops north of the thirty-eighth parallel—the Soviets continued to exert influence on the northern part of Korea. Just as the United States did in the South, Soviet forces sought to ensure a political environment in Korea that was favorable to the interests of their country. In this regard, the Soviet occupation favored groups of people strongly inclined to the political left. There were also a number of Korean Communists in the Soviet Far East who were anxious to return to Korea, whose exodus the Soviets encouraged in hopes of building a Communist regime in the North. One of the most famous of these returning Koreans was Kim Il Sung.

There were several differences between U.S. and Soviet policies dealing with the Korean situation at that time. Although the Soviets moved quickly to erase the Japanese presence, the U.S. occupation was based on the structure and personnel of the Japanese colonial government. Although the Soviets supported the work of the Provisional People's Committee, the U.S. occupation had declared their activities illegal throughout the South. This gained popular support for the North Korean regime, at least during its inception. From the Northern perspective, the United States was deliberately destroying the foundation for Korean unity. The North Korean regime also claimed that it held more legitimacy than the regime in the South. As the North moved ahead with its political reforms, the gap between the two Koreas widened.

The North began to implement its land reform program and to nationalize its major industries and firms. Through this process, the Communists gathered popular support; with support from the Soviet command, they built a formidable political and military structure. They expanded and consolidated their party's strength in August 1946 by merging all the left-wing groups into the North Korean Workers' Party. In the same year, the armed forces were organized and reinforced. By June 1950, North

Korean troops numbered between 150,000 and 200,000 and were organized into ten infantry divisions, one tank division, and one air force division. Soviet equipment, including automatic weapons of various types, T-34 tanks, and Yak fighter planes, were provided in early 1950.

With this newfound might, Kim Il Sung made plans to invade South Korea. He had been allowed to build such a force because Moscow viewed North Korea as part of a "security blanket" around its borders (Kaufman 1999, 7). In the spring of 1950, Kim visited Moscow and Peking, where he tried to persuade Soviet leader Joseph Stalin and Chinese leader Mao Zedong to approve his plans for an invasion. Both leaders were reluctant; they feared that an attack on South Korea could lead to an American response. Moreover, the Soviet Union was preoccupied with the West, and China did not want to divert its attention from Taiwan.

Today, there exist different views on who was responsible for the Korean War, even though it is now clear who initiated it. But some maintain that Syngman Rhee was also responsible to some extent. His preparations and announcements of a plan to march toward Pyongyang were probably a determining factor in the outbreak of the war because they hastened reinforcement and strengthening of the North Korean People's Army, as well as advancing the actual invasion date (Gye-Dong Kim 1989, 44). Thus does Gye-Dong Kim (1989) contend that, in fact, both sides in Korea prepared for invasion, although it was the North Koreans who took the initiative.

Geography

Although North Korea's geography did not have strategic importance in the Korean War, an understanding of the land and region is helpful in putting the events in perspective. North Korea is extremely mountainous and marked by deep, narrow valleys. A complex system of ranges and spurs extends across the country in a generally northeast to southwest direction. Most of the soils in the mountainous regions lack organic material and are relatively infertile. Only 18 per-

cent of the land is arable. Nearly all the major rivers arise in the mountains and flow west to the Yellow Sea. Korea's 636-mile boundary with China is formed by two rivers, the Yalu to the west and the Tumen to the east. This abutment of the two countries almost ensured eventual Chinese intervention in the conflict, which China did join in October 1950. The last eleven miles of the Tumen's course separate Korea from Russia. The boundary between the two Korean states is known as the Military Demarcation Line, so designated by the Armistice Agreement of 1953; it replaced the division at the thirty-eighth parallel agreed upon by the United States and the Soviet Union in 1945. The total area of North and South Korea is about 85,300 square miles. North Korea has approximately 47,300 miles, about 55 percent of the total land area, and South Korea has roughly 38,000 square miles.

Tactics

Advised and equipped by the Soviets and with huge reserves of manpower, the North Korean surprise attack was a smashing success. With more than 1,400 artillery pieces and 126 modern tanks from the Soviet Union, the North Korean force of 110,000 soldiers quickly drove through the ill-equipped, outnumbered South Korean forces. By the third day of the invasion, the Northern forces had captured the South Korean capital, Seoul. In contrast to the Soviets' equipping of their North Korean ally with military supplies, the United States refused to aid South Korea in a similar way because it feared that South Korea might use its military strength to invade North Korea, which could lead to a major conflict between the United States and the Soviet Union.

It is believed that Soviet staff officers proffered advice in the drawing of the overall plan for an invasion and conquest of South Korea (Catchpole 2000, 11). The plan's objective was to occupy all of South Korea within fourteen to fifteen days of the invasion and to unify the peninsula under Communist control. Following

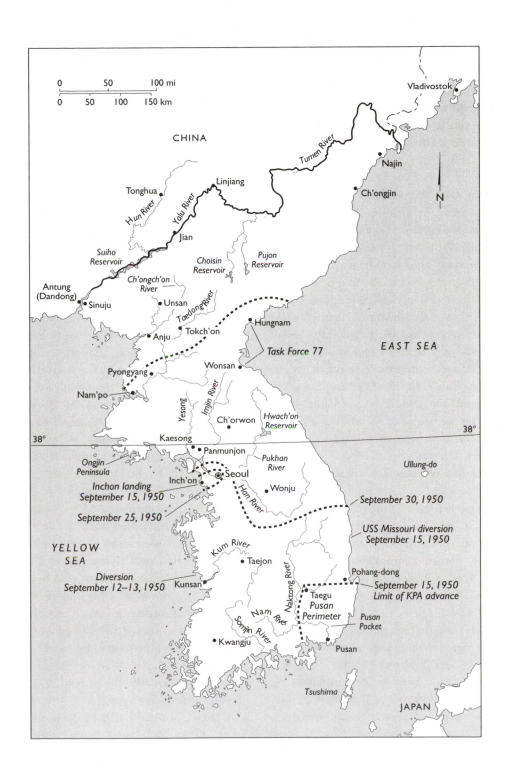

CHINA

Tumen River

Vladivostok

Najin

Ch'ongjin

Tonghua

Linjiang

Hun River

Yalu River

Jian

N

Suiho
Reservoir

Antung
(Dandong)

Sinuju

Ch'ongch'on
River

Choisin
Reservoir

Pujon
Reservoir

Unsan

Taedong River

Hungnam

EAST SEA

Anju

Tokch'on

Task Force 77

Pyongyang

Wonsan

Nam'po

Yesong

Imjin River

Hwach'on
Reservoir

Ch'orwon

38°   38°

Kaesong

Panmunjon

Ongjin
Peninsula

Inch'on

Seoul

Pukhan
River

Ullung-do

Inchon landing
September 15, 1950

Wonju

September 25, 1950

Han River

September 30, 1950

YELLOW
SEA

Kum River

USS Missouri diversion
September 15, 1950

Taejon

Naktong River

Pohang-dong

Diversion
September 12–13, 1950

Kunsan

September 15, 1950
Limit of KPA advance

Taegu
Pusan
Perimeter

Nam River

Pusan
Pocket

Somjin River

Kwangju

Pusan

Tsushima

JAPAN

0   50   100 mi
0   50   100   150 km

Stalin's advice, the North Koreans significantly reduced their activity along the thirty-eighth parallel to lull the South Koreans into a false sense of security. Moreover, the attack was timed for Sunday morning, a time when many South Korean officials and their American advisers were away from their units on weekend passes. This also contributed to the success of the North Korean surprise attack.

Causes of the War

The war cannot be attributed solely to Kim Il Sung's desire to reunify Korea under the Communist regime and the ideological disparity between the two Koreas instigated by the surrounding major powers. The war was also the result of an imbalance of power: The United States failed to study the strategic importance of the peninsula and balance the military strength of the two sides. In this sense, the war was in many aspects a result of the failure of deterrence (Gye-Dong Kim 1989, 45). As Hyung-Kook Kim (1995) points out, the origins and nature of the Korean War are best understood when looked at as two different wars fought in one theater at the same time.

The Korean War has major characteristics of civil war and can be considered as a domestic power struggle between Syngman Rhee and Kim Il Sung. The North Korean leader may well have had aspirations like those of Syngman Rhee—to unify the Korean peninsula immediately (by force if necessary) and then to assume leadership of all Korea—ever since the establishment of his separate regime. Kim Il Sung and Syngman Rhee were fiercely nationalistic, and each was determined to reunite the country under his own rule (Stueck 2002, 69).

Ideological and historical circumstances also contributed to some of the Communists' miscalculations. Kim Il Sung overestimated the prospects for internal disruption in South Korea because his leftist ideology led him to see widespread popular discontent as omnipresent in the capitalist world (Stueck 1995, 355). Re-

cent Communist success in China reinforced this misperception.

The policy of the United States toward Korea also played a role in encouraging Kim's invasion. Had the United States made clear its intention to defend South Korea, the war could probably have been avoided. Despite the instability of the Rhee regime and considerable opposition from the State Department in Washington, which was concerned about the military threat to South Korea from North Korea, the United States hoped to withdraw from Korea as soon as possible. Kaufman (1999) notes that military leaders at that time believed that Korea lacked military and strategic value in a potential war in Asia (Kaufman 1999, 6). They were reluctant to make a military commitment in Asia after the Communist victory in China. Owing to a general manpower shortage in the United States armed forces, the military was reluctant to expand responsibilities. Moreover, they viewed that Europe would be the main area of confrontation with the Soviet Union. They believed that the greatest danger from the Soviet Union would come from a Communist takeover of the economically devastated nations of Western Europe. Prior to 1950, as Kaufman (1999) notes, U.S. officials in Washington perceived the immediate Soviet menace as directed primarily against Western Europe and, to a lesser extent, against the northern tier of Near East countries that included Greece, Turkey, and Iran.

In their view, Moscow sought to achieve its ambitions not through acts of overt military aggression but through subversion of economically destitute governments. Accordingly, the United States planned to protect Western Europe from Soviet expansion by economic assistance (as provided by the Marshall Plan of 1948) and collective security (as embodied in the formation of the North Atlantic Treaty Organization [NATO] in 1949). During the preceding periods, Korea had been a low priority. The military's desire for an early withdrawal stemmed from this low strategic standing and from limited U.S. military resources (Chull

Baum Kim 1994). The withdrawal of U.S. troops from South Korea, combined with the speech by Secretary of State Dean Acheson, encouraged the North Korean leader to pursue his invasion plan (Rees 1988).

In that speech at the National Press Club in Washington in January 1950, Acheson stressed UN protection for places beyond the U.S. "defensive perimeter." The intent of this speech was to alert mainland Communist China that the United States would not act militarily to prevent an invasion of Taiwan and that there was no need to launch an attack on Chiang Kai-shek's Nationalist government there. However, the speech also seemed to indicate that the United States would not act to protect South Korea from attack by its northern neighbor and that the country was outside the sphere of American concern in the Pacific. This omission, albeit unintentional, encouraged North Korea and the Soviets. Combined with the 1948 South Korean elections and the 1949 U.S. military withdrawal from the peninsula, American policy indicated a lack of desire to repel an invasion by North Korea. It was viewed within the United States as unlikely that the Soviet Union would allow such an attack to take place. When the invasion did occur, it dumbfounded the United States.

Outcome
Conflict Status

Early Sunday morning on June 25, 1950, at 4 a.m., North Korea crossed the thirty-eighth parallel and attempted to unify the peninsula using quick and decisive force, believing that a response from the United States and its allies would be delayed or nonexistent. According to MacDonald (1996), Kim Il-Sung seemed oblivious to the possibility that the United States would defend South Korea, that the United States would not tolerate losing South Korea to communism. But this presumption, or failure to presume, proved false: By the end of June, the United Nations had created an international force under the command of U.S. Army General Douglas MacArthur to defend South Korea.

After the UN forces defeated North Korea, the UN General Assembly supported a U.S. proposal to occupy the North until elections could be held for a unified government. But this proposal would not be carried out. The Chinese, alarmed at the UN forces' drive north across the parallel and toward their frontier, intervened. They deployed a large force of the Chinese People's Volunteer Army as support for the North. The combined North Korean and Chinese forces pushed the UN back south of Seoul before a UN counteroffensive finally moved the front lines back to the thirty-eighth parallel in March 1951.

In June, the Soviet representative to the United Nations proposed cease-fire talks. These negotiations went on for two years while Korea continued fighting. The armistice between the UN commander and the combined forces of the North Korean People's Army and the Chinese People's Volunteers would not ultimately be reached until July 1953. South Korean President Rhee disagreed with this move; he insisted on Korea's unification and objected to returning to a policy of containment. In his letter to President Dwight Eisenhower of May 30, 1953, he stated that the Korean question should be solved by punishing the aggressor and by reuniting the country. He even unilaterally released 28,000 prisoners in an attempt to prevent the agreement from being finalized. The United States responded to Rhee's obstinacy by offering a mutual defense treaty: US $1 billion in economic aid over three years and equipment for a twenty-division army. Rhee acquiesced, but South Korea never signed the armistice.

The cease-fire was signed by China and North Korea on the one side and the United States on the other. The armistice agreement was effective without the signature of the South Korean government because international law authorized military commanders to conclude an armistice (Kleiner 2001). This cease-fire has not been converted into any permanent peace settlement. Therefore, the Korean War is not technically over—which makes the Armistice Agreement of 1953 the longest cease-fire in history. The new Military Demarcation Line agreed on by the two sides in the truce was based on natural defenses of water and terrain. To the north and south of the four-kilometer-wide Demilitarized Zone (DMZ) stand North Korean troops on one side and South Korean and American troops on the other. The DMZ is still defended today.

The Korean War, having resolved nothing and ending in a stalemate, left an estimated 1.3 million to 2.4 million Koreans dead. Nearly 37,000 U.S. troops were killed and another 103,000 wounded. An estimated 900,000 Chinese troops were killed and wounded. Turkey, Britain, Canada, France, Australia, Greece, and other UN countries lost between 2,000 and 3,000 troops (Clark 2000).

Duration Tactics

Although more than three years separated the outbreak of the military conflict and the armistice agreement, this superfluous length of time cannot be considered any side's tactic to prolong the war. The reasons for the painful prolongation of the war are twofold: the intervention of China in October 1950 and the lengthy armistice negotiation. The most heated period of the Korean War was from June 1950 through March 1951; the rest of the war involved minor territory change and laborious peace negotiations.

At the end of September 1950, after a successful amphibious landing at Inchon, most South Korean territory was in the hands of UN troops. At this juncture, there was a discrepancy between South Korea's and America's objectives. When the war first broke out, Secretary of State Acheson stated that the fighting had the sole aim "of restoring the Republic of Korea to its status prior to the invasion from the North" (Spanier 1959, 88). As this objective had been achieved, there was no reason for the UN forces to cross the thirty-eighth parallel. However, the South Korean government, which had dreamed of reunification, could not be satisfied with restora-

tion of the status quo that existed before the war. Syngman Rhee felt that the war would remain unresolved unless unity was achieved. The United States eventually converted to Rhee's opinion in the hopes of reducing the Soviet's influence. The United States changed its policy from one of containment to one of rollback (Kleiner 2001), a decision that would profoundly change and greatly prolong the course of the war in Korea.

From April 1951 until the end of the war in July 1953, the war's front remained near the thirty-eighth parallel. In the spring and summer of 1951, the Chinese and North Korean forces tried to retake Seoul. But the front was almost impassable. After this failure, in the spring of 1951, China and North Korea started to reconsider the negotiations (Kleiner 2001). On June 23, the Soviet ambassador to the United Nations revealed a willingness to compromise on a cease-fire and truce. The first negotiation meeting was held on July 8, 1951. But this bargaining proved to be a much more involved process than either side expected. Three main issues in the negotiations were determination of a demarcation line for the cease-fire, establishment of a framework for supervising the armistice, and repatriation of the prisoners of war. Had it not been for the issue of repatriation, an end to the hostilities might have been achieved as early as 1951, two years before the final agreement was reached.

The cause of delay was President Truman's opposition to the repatriation of POWs (prisoners of war) against their will, even though the Geneva Conference of 1949 specifically required all POWs to be repatriated regardless of their consent (Kaufman 1999). On July 8, 1953, it was agreed that those POWs who did not insist on being repatriated would become civilians six months after the conclusion of the armistice agreement. On July 27, 1953, the armistice agreement was finally signed.

External Military Intervention

The invasion of South Korea came as a shock to the United States. Dean Acheson of the State Department had told the U.S. Congress on June 20 that war was unlikely. It was also explicit in his testimony, in 1951, that all agencies of the American government were in accord: An invasion from by North Korea did not appear imminent. However, the CIA reported in early March that such an action was likely and could happen as early as June.

On hearing of the invasion, the United Nations and the American government reacted quickly and decisively. On June 25, the UN Security Council passed the first of three resolutions on Korea that would place the world organization's full authority behind South Korea. During these resolutions, the Soviet delegate to the Security Council was absent in protest of the UN's refusal to recognize the new Communist regime in China. Without the USSR's veto, the motions passed easily. The first Security Council resolution called for a cease-fire, the withdrawal of North Korea forces to the thirty-eighth parallel, and an understanding that all UN members would render every assistance to the UN in the implementation of its decision. On June 27, the Security Council met again and called on the UN members to furnish such assistance. The Republic of Korea needed help to repel the armed attack, and the UN would need assistance to restore international peace and security in the area. With the Soviet's absence and with the Socialist Federal Republic of Yugoslavia abstaining, on June 27 the UN voted to aid South Korea.

Meanwhile, the Soviets claimed that the Korean conflict was an internal affair and therefore

U.S. soldiers pass a line of South Korean refugees near the Naktong River on August 11, 1950. U.S. military intervention reversed North Korean dominance in the Korean War. (Bettmann/Corbis)

outside the Security Council's jurisdiction. They contended, moreover, that because the ruling had been decided in the absence of their delegate, any action taken by the UN would be illegal. Despite the Soviets' accusations, President Truman authorized the use of U.S. naval and air assistance to South Korea. On another front, he also ordered Seventh Fleet to protect Taiwan, both to deter any Communist Chinese aggression toward the island and to dissuade the Chinese Nationalists from military actions toward the mainland. The United States still had substantial forces in Japan, which allowed for such quick intervention. General Douglas MacArthur, in charge of overseeing Japan as Supreme Commander for the Allied Powers and head of American forces in the Pacific, made a trip to Korea to understand the situation there. Following the visit, he asked permission from Washington to use American ground forces from Japan to stop the North Koreans. Truman gave the go-ahead. American combat troops would be sent from Japan to the southeast side of Korea to defend the Pusan area. The first American combat troops from the 24th Infantry Division in Japan arrived at Pusan on July 1, 1950.

The third major policy resolution concerning Korea was made on July 7, 1950. In this, the UN Security Council recommended that UN members providing military assistance under the previous resolutions should make their forces available to a Unified Command (UC) under the United States. The Security Council also authorized the Unified Command to use the United Nations flag concurrently with the flags of the nations participating, in the course of operations against North Korean forces. The United States, asked to designate a commander of the UC, quickly named General MacArthur. Sixteen nations were to send forces to the UNC, another five would send medical units, and forty members would offer aid. Eventually, U.S. forces were joined by troops from fifteen other UN member countries: Canada, Australia, New Zealand, the United Kingdom, France, South Africa, Turkey, Thailand, Greece, the Netherlands, Ethiopia, Colombia, the Philippines, Belgium, and Luxembourg.

After a successful landing at Inchon, the United Nations troops drove the North Koreans back past the thirty-eighth parallel. The goal of restoring the original border between the two Koreas had been achieved, but because of the heady success and the tempting possibility of uniting all of Korea under the government of Syngman Rhee, the Americans decided to continue their drive into North Korea.

This move greatly concerned the Chinese, who worried that the UN forces would not stop at the Yalu River, the effective border between the PRK and Manchuria. Their concern was not without reason, as many in the West, including General MacArthur, thought that spreading the war into China would be necessary. Truman and the other world leaders disagreed. So MacArthur was ordered to be extremely cautious when approaching the Chinese border. Amphibious and airborne operations north of the thirty-eighth parallel could be conducted only if there were no entry or threat of entry by Chinese or Soviet forces. South Korean troops only were to be used near the Soviet or Chinese borders.

The People's Republic of China had issued warnings that if this mandate was not observed, they would intervene. On October 2, 1950, the Chinese Foreign Minister, Chou En-lai, told the Indian ambassador in unambiguous language that although South Korean entry into the North was not significant, American intrusion would be resisted by China. Truman regarded the warnings as a bluff—or worse, blackmail. So, disregarding the threat, U.S. troops crossed the parallel and moved into North Korea.

On October 8, 1950, the day after American troops crossed the thirty-eighth parallel and the UN passed its resolution on Korean unification, Chairman Mao ordered large-scale Chinese military intervention. He issued orders for the deployment of the Chinese People's Volunteer Army to be moved to the Yalu River and to be prepared to cross. On October 15, Truman went to Wake Island to discuss the likelihood of Chinese intervention and his desire to limit the scope of the Korean conflict. MacArthur reassured his commander that there was very little chance of Chinese intervention and that, in any case, his air force was capable of inflicting sufficient destruction on any Chinese ground troops entering Korea.

MacArthur's assurances were misinformed. The Chinese assault began on October 19, just four days after the general's bravado, and was led by General Peng Dehuai in command of 300,000 CPVA troops. The Chinese assault caught the UN troops by surprise, as war between the PRC and the United Nations had not been declared. The Battle of Chosin Reservoir (November 26–December 13) forced the UN deployment to withdraw from the northern part of Korea. The United States X Corps retreat was the longest retreat of an American unit in history. At the end of December 1950, North Korea was back in Communist hands. On January 4, 1951, Seoul was retaken by Communist Chinese and North Korean forces. Both the Eighth Army and the X Corps were forced to retreat.

On April 11, 1951, President Truman relieved MacArthur of his command. The general was seen as having overstepped the bounds of his military responsibilities (Kleiner 2001). These missteps include his meeting with ROC President Chiang Kai-shek in the role of a U.S. diplomat. He had also shown poor foresight at Wake Island when President Truman asked him specifically about Chinese troop buildup near the Korean border. Furthermore, MacArthur had openly demanded the authority to use a nuclear attack on China. He felt it was high time to counter Communism in an offensive, aggressive way. His view, although in perfect agreement with the Republicans, proved his undoing. His successor was General Matthew Ridgway, who managed to regroup the UN forces for an effective counteroffense that slowly but steadily drove back the opposing forces.

Conflict Management Efforts

In imposing military sanctions against North Korea, the United Nations had taken an extraordinary step. The UN also promoted efforts toward a cease-fire to end the Korean conflict and later negotiated a solution to the POW issues. To facilitate the implementation of the armistice, shortly after the agreement to a truce a new Joint Security Area (JSA) was set up in the Demilitarized Zone at Panmunjom. Both parties agreed that a permanent detail of joint duty officers from the United Nations Command and the Communist side would be stationed in the JSA.

Three commissions were created to supervise this cease-fire. The Military Armistice Commission (MAC), which consisted of senior representatives of both sides, would exercise overall supervision of the truce via joint observer teams in the DMZ. The main work of the MAC was to hear the accusations and counteraccusations launched over truce violations in the DMZ.

The second agency created by the armistice was the Neutral Nations Supervisory Commission (NNSC). The NNSC was originally created to inspect for and ensure armistice compliance at locations outside the DMZ. Under the armistice agreement, it originally consisted of delegations from four nations: Sweden and Switzerland (nominated by the United Nations Command and Czechoslovakia and Poland (appointed by the Communists). North Korea declared this body defunct in April 1991 and began boycotting their events. The grounds for this accusation were that the countries they nominated were no longer Communist. When Czechoslovakia split in two in 1993, North Korea refused to accept the Czech Republic as the replacement and forced the withdrawal of their delegation. In February 1995, North Korea forcibly ejected the Polish delegation from North Korea. Today, only the Swedish and Swiss delegations play this role on a full-time basis; the Polish delegation, which never accepted its dismissal, occasionally returns to Panmunjom to participate in NNSC functions.

The third agency was the Neutral Nations Repatriation Commission (NNRC). This agency was to supervise the exchange of POWs, their repatriation, and the eventual disposition of

Mobile Phones in South Korea

It was in 1896 that the first telephones in Korea were installed in the royal palace compound. Public telephone service was introduced in 1902. As of the end of 1979, there were only some 240,000 telephone subscribers, about 6.3 telephones per 100 people (Office of Prime Minister 2006). In 2004, South Korea had more than 33.5 million mobile phone subscribers out of a population of 48.5 million, a mobile phone penetration rate of about 69 percent (Ericsson Market Update: South Korea 2004).

prisoners in neither category. After its initial work on POWs was complete, the NNRC voted to dissolve itself in February 1954.

Conclusion

The border between North and South Korea remains highly armed and tense half a century after the start of the bitter war that divided the peninsula. The Korean War had a profound impact on the fate of Koreans residing in their native land. The war left almost 3 million of their countrymen dead or wounded and millions of others homeless and separated from their families. Globally, the current crisis of North Korea's nuclear threat is also a by-product of the division of the Korean peninsula and therefore a result of the Korean War.

But the debate on the origins of this war continues. Understanding the interplay of domestic and foreign forces is the key to understanding the Korean War (Lone and McCormack 1993). Hyung-Kook Kim (1995) argues that the Korean War must be understood in a wider theoretical framework, not just as a civil war or as American intervention against Communist aggression. As these scholars argue, the origins of the war must be understood in the context of events both inside and outside Korea.

Jung-Yeop Woo

Chronology

August 22, 1910   Japan annexes Korea.

December 1, 1943   Cairo Conference; U.S., U.K., and China state that Korea should become free and independent.

August 15, 1945   Japan surrenders, ending World War II.

September 8, 1945   American occupation forces land in Korea.

September 17, 1947   The U.S. refers issue of Korean reunion and independence to United Nations.

October 1947   The U.S. presents a resolution at UN calling for separate elections in U.S. and Soviet zones. A United Nations Treaty Commission (UNTCOK) would be established to supervise elections for a Korean government.

January 1948   Soviet Union refuses to allow UNTCOK to enter its zone in Korea.

February 1948   UN approves U.S. resolution giving UNTCOK authority to supervise elections in South Korea.

May 10, 1948   National Assembly elected in South Korea.

August 15, 1948   Republic of Korea is officially established.

September 9, 1948   Democratic People's Republic of Korea established in north.

November 1948   President Rhee imposes martial law over most of South Korea after a series of rebellions.

March 1949   National Security Council of UN recommends withdrawal of all American forces by June 30, 1949.

April 8, 1949   Soviet Union vetoes South Korean membership in UN.

January 12, 1950   Secretary of State Acheson delivers speech placing Korea outside the U.S. defense perimeter.

June 25, 1950   North Korea invades South Korea.

June 27, 1950   UN calls for military sanction against North Korea.

June 30, 1950   Seoul falls to North Korean forces. Truman authorizes the use of American ground forces in Korea under the UN command.

July 1, 1950   American task force arrives in Korea from Japan.

July 3, 1950   U.S. troops engage North Koreans for the first time.

September 7, 1950   UN forces successfully defend Pusan perimeter.

September 15, 1950   Amphibious landing at Inchon.

September 27, 1950   Seoul recaptured: Truman approves directive ordering UN forces to cross thirty-eighth parallel.

September 28, 1950   Communist China warns intervention if North Korea is invaded.

October 7, 1950   UN adopts resolution authorizing UN forces to cross into North Korea.

October 19, 1950   North Korean capital of Pyongyang falls to UN forces.

October 27, 1950   South Korean forces reach Yalu River.

November 20, 1950   U.S. forces reach Manchurian border.

November 25, 1950   More than 300,000 Chinese combat troops intervene.

November 26, 1950   Eighth Army is in full retreat.

January 1, 1951   Communist forces advance below thirty-eighth parallel.

January 4, 1951   UN forces abandon Seoul to the Communists.

March 14, 1951   Seoul is reclaimed by UN forces for the second time.

April 11, 1951   Truman relieves MacArthur of his command.

June 23, 1951   Soviet Union calls for cease-fire in Korea.

July 2, 1951   Communists agree to begin armistice negotiations.

July 10, 1951   UN and Communists begin truce talks.

November 25, 1951   Tentative agreement is reached on truce line.

May 7, 1952   Armistice negotiations stall over repatriation of POWs.

May 23, 1953   President Rhee threatens to remove ROK army from United Nations Command in protest over armistice terms.

July 27, 1953   Armistice is signed, ending Korean War.

List of Acronyms

CPVA: Chinese People's Volunteer Army
DMZ: Demilitarized Zone
DPRK: People's Republic of Korea
GNP: gross national product
JSA: Joint Security Area
MAC: Military Armistice Commission
NATO: North Atlantic Treaty Organization
NNRC: Neutral Nations Repatriation Commission
NNSC: Neutral Nations Supervisory Commission

POW: prisoner of war
PRK: People's Republic of Korea
ROC: Republic of China
ROK: Republic of Korea
UC: Unified Command
UNTCOK: United Nations Temporary Commission on Korea

References

Blair, Clay. 1994. "The Korean War: Background and Overview." In *Security in Korea: War, Stalemate, and Negotiation,* edited by Phil Williams, Donald M. Goldstein, and Henry L. Andrews, Jr. Boulder, CO: Westview Press.

Catchpole, Brian. 2000. *The Korean War: 1950–53.* New York: Carroll & Graf.

Clark, Carol. 2000. "Crossing the Great Divide." CNN.com. www.cnn.com/SPECIALS/2000/korea/story/overview/ (accessed September 11, 2006).

Ericsson Market Update: South Korea. 2004. www.ericsson.com/mobilityworld/sub/articles/other_articles/04nov05 (accessed November 4, 2006).

Groningen Growth and Development Centre. No date. www.ggdc.net/dseries/totecon.html (accessed November 4, 2006)

Gupta, Karunakar. 1972. "How Did the Korean War Begin?" *The China Quarterly* 52: 699–716.

Hart-Landsberg, Martin. 1998. *Korea: Division, Reunification, and U.S. Foreign Policy.* New York: Monthly Review Press.

Kaufman, Burton I. 1999. *The Korean Conflict.* London: Greenwood Press.

Kim, Chull Baum. 1994. "U.S. Policy on the Eve of the Korean War: Abandonment or Safeguard?" In *Security in Korea: War, Stalemate, and Negotiation,* edited by Phil Williams, Donald M. Goldstein, and Henry L. Andrews, Jr. Boulder, CO: Westview Press.

Kim, Chull Baum. 1996. "The Korean Scholars on the Korean War." In *The Korean War: Handbook of the Literature and Research,* edited by Lester H. Brune. London: Greenwood Press..

Kim, Gye-Dong. 1989. "Who Initiated the Korean War?" In *The Korean War in History,* edited by James Cotton and Ian Neary. Manchester, UK: Manchester University Press.

Kim, Hyung-Kook. 1995. *The Division of Korea and the Alliance Making Process: Internationalization of Internal Conflict and Internalization of International Struggle, 1945–1948.* New York: University Press of America.

Kleiner, Juergen. 2001. *Korea: A Century of Change.* River Edge, N.J. : World Scientific.

Korea Institute for Military History Compilation. No date. www.imhc.mil.kr/imhcroot/upload/resource/3K28.pdf (accessed November 4, 2006).

Lone, Stewart, and Gavan McCormack. 1993. *Korea: Since 1850.* New York: St. Martin's Press.

MacDonald, Donald Stone. 1996. *The Koreans: Contemporary Politics and Society.* Boulder, CO: Westview Press.

Myers, Robert J. 2001.*Korea in the Cross Currents: A Century of Struggle and the Crisis of Reunification.* New York: Palgrave.

Office of Prime Minister of Korea. 2006. www.opm.go.kr/warp/webapp/content/view?meta_id=english&id=73 (accessed November 4, 2006).

Rees, David. 1988. *A Short History of Modern Korea.* New York: Hippocrene Books.

Savada, Andrea Matles, and William Shaw. 2002. "South Korea: A Country Study." In *Korea: Current Issues and Historical Background,* edited by Edgar V. Connor. New York: Nova Science.

Spanier, John W. 1959. *The Truman-MacArthur Controversy and the Korean War.* Cambridge, MA: Belknap Press.

Stueck, William. 1995. *The Korean War: An International History.* Princeton, NJ: Princeton University Press.

Stueck, William. 2002. *Rethinking the Korean War: A New Diplomatic and Strategic History.* Princeton, NJ: Princeton University Press.

Thompson, William. 2004. "Column: Letters from Korea: Jeju—Shhhhhhh! Don't Ask! (Part 2)." History News Network. hnn.us/articles/7640.html (accessed September 11, 2006).

Whiting, Allen S. 1994. "Collision in Korea: Misperception or Miscalculation?" In *Security in Korea: War, Stalemate, and Negotiation,* edited by Phil Williams, Donald M. Goldstein, and Henry L. Andrews, Jr. Boulder, CO: Westview Press.

"World Military Expenditures and Arms Transfers" (WMEAT). 2003. 28th ed. www.state.gov/t/vci/rls/rpt/wmeat/1999_2000/.

Lebanon
(1975–1978)

Introduction

Although Lebanon gained its independence in 1941 (Rabinovich 1985), "the people of Lebanon have a long and distinctive history" (Bannerman 2002, 197). The Islamic empires of the Umayyad (660–750), the Abbasid (750–1258), and later on the Fatimids, Ayubids, and Memluks of Egypt dominated the area for centuries. From the early sixteenth century, the Sunni Ottoman Turks controlled the whole area, until the dissolution of the empire at the end of World War I (Bannerman 2002).

Through a wartime agreement between Britain and France, Lebanon became a French mandate. France created modern Lebanon on August 31, 1920, by expanding its boundaries to establish a more viable state (Rabinovich 1985). As a result, the northern city of Tripoli, which is a Sunni Muslim center, the southern Shi'ite Muslim centers of Sidon and Tyre, and the Bekaa Valley in the east were added to the Lebanese state. Beirut, the home of all different sects—Maronites and Greek Catholics, Greek Orthodox, Armenians, Sunnis, Shi'ites, and Druze—became the capital city of modern Lebanon. The French mandate came to an end in 1943 as a result of the French political and military decline during World War II and the rise of Syrian and Arab nationalism in the Middle East (Bannerman 2002).

The oral agreement between Christians and Muslims that was reached in 1943 marked the foundations of modern Lebanon. The distribution of power was based upon each community's numerical strength (Rabinovich 1985). As a result, "Christian supremacy" (Rabinovich 1985, 24) in the modern Lebanon was established in the decision that the "president of the republic was to be a Maronite Christian; the president of the Chamber of deputies, a Shi'ite Muslim; the prime minister a Sunni Muslim. The Greek orthodox were to have the vice-prime minister and the vice-president of the Chamber of Deputies" (Deeb 1980, 5). Moreover, "a ratio of six Christian deputies to every five Muslim deputies in parliament" was agreed upon (Rabinovich 1985, 24).

Country Background

Lebanon became one of the most democratic and most stable states in the Middle East after it gained independence. The Lebanese political and economic system attracted deposits and trusts from the oil-rich Arab countries, and "this capital helped fuel the remarkable development during the period of 1955–1975" (Held 2000, 266). The Lebanese economy diversified after independence, and the "manufacturing sector surpassed agriculture in the economic hierarchy" (Held 2000, 267). The share of industry in the gross domestic product (GDP) reached 20 percent in 1974 (Nasr 1990). Lebanon attracted more than 1.5 million tourists before 1975 (Held 2000). Lebanon, with a democratic and highly urban and educated society, was labeled the "Switzerland of the Middle East" before the outbreak of the 1975 civil war (Goldschmidt 2000).

Besides the domestic improvements in the economy, the Lebanese economy took advantage of the regional economic boom, "especially of the growing wealth of the Arab oil states. Beirut supplied a source of entertainment and investment as well as transit points for goods and services" (Bannerman 2002, 206). Nasr (1990, 5) reports that "the average yearly rate of growth was around six percent; the national income per capita increased from $400 in 1965 and $647 in 1970 to $1415 in 1974." The GDP per capita did not decline during the 1975–1978 war. GDP per capita was $3,429 (constant 1985 US dollars) in 1975 (Fearon and Laitin 2003). Parliamentary elections were held with no serious restrictions until the outbreak of the war in 1975. Lebanon received a 5 on the Polity IV scale, which ranges from –10 (least democratic) to +10 (most democratic) in 1975 (Fearon and Laitin 2003).

Conflict Background

The Lebanese 1975–1978 civil war was a resumption of the conflict that took place between the same parties in 1958. The political turmoil in Lebanon during these years was closely related to regional developments. The primary factor that led to the outbreak of conflict between the two major groups, the Christians and the Muslims, was systemic. The Arab-Israeli conflict and Egyptian leader Nasser's nationalistic policies fueled the Muslims' resentment in Lebanon (Rabinovich 1985). The Muslims believed that the political system needed to be altered in such a way that Christians were no longer the dominant element of the system. The conflict broke out between President Chamoun's supporters, Maronite Christians, and the Muslims in February 1958. The Lebanese army remained neutral, and the conflict subsided with U.S. military intervention. The status quo was preserved, yet the 1958

war revealed the shortcomings inherent in the Lebanese political system, on the one hand, and how Lebanese politics is closely related to and affected by regional developments, on the other.

The primary factor underlying the onset of the 1958 and 1975–1978 civil wars should not be characterized as the Christians against the Muslims (Rabinovich 1985). Lebanese society is too complex to be divided into such a binomial dichotomy. Although the sectarian divisions among the groups were the most crucial factor leading to the outbreak of the conflict, "political leaders were the secular heads of prominent families, rather than clerics" (Abu-Hamad 1995, 237). Religious cleavages were used by the leaders to mobilize their communities and differentiate themselves from other groups. Thus, the traditional classification of civil wars as ethnic or religious may not capture the complexity of the Lebanese civil wars.

The first serious indications of impending civil war were the clashes between Palestinians and the Lebanese army in 1969. The conflict over the Palestinian issue served as a catalyst in the 1975 Lebanese civil war. The Palestine Liberation Organization (PLO) and the Lebanese government signed the Cairo agreement in November 1969 (Rabinovich 1985; O'Ballance 1998). This agreement involved ambiguous terms and indeed showed the weakness of the Lebanese government in controlling its own territory.

Events in the late 1960s and early 1970s precipitated the outbreak of the second civil war in modern Lebanon. The war started in April 1975 under the pressure from internal and external forces (Rabinovich 1985). It is common to divide the Lebanese civil war into several phases. For instance, Rabinovich (1985) divides the second civil war into four phases. Similarly, Rasler (1983), based on Hudson (1978), argues that the second Lebanese civil war experienced four distinct phases. Deeb (1980), on the other hand, divides the war into seven phases. These studies conclude that the war started in April 1975 and ended in October 1976 with the Riyadh Conference. Nevertheless, as O'Ballance (1998) argues, the war continued, with severe complications. Although there is no consensus among scholars as to the end date of the second war, this article considers the war to have ended in 1978, when the United Nations Interim Force in Lebanon (UNIFIL) arrived in March 1978, and a six-point national accord was endorsed by the Lebanese parliament and agreed upon by the communities' leaders in April 1978 (O'Ballance 1998; Deeb 1980). Doyle and Sambanis (2000) report that the second civil war in Lebanon lasted thirty-six months, which indicates that the war ended in April 1978.

Therefore, the second Lebanese civil war is divided into five phases. The first four phases are in accordance with Rabinovich's (1985) and Rasler's (1983) classification and analyze the period between the outbreak of the war in April 1975 and the Riyadh Conference in October 1976, at which the fighting parties negotiated a peace settlement. The fifth phase analyzes the post–Riyadh Conference period until the deployment of the UNIFIL and the endorsement of a six-point national accord by the parliament (April 1978). This phase is heavily based on O'Ballance (1998).

The first phase of the war (April–June 1975) was dominated by the clashes between radical Palestinians and the Phalangist militias in Beirut. O'Ballance (1998, 1) reports the incident that marked the outbreak of the civil war in Lebanon:

> . . .on April 13 1975 in the mainly Christian district of Rumaniyeh, outside the Church of St Maron. Pierre Gamayel, leader of Falange (Phalange) Party, sometimes referred to as Kataib, was attending a consecration service. Outside, members of his armed and uniformed militia were diverting traffic away from the front of the church when a vehicle carrying half a dozen Palestinian militiamen—firing their rifles into the air in the customary *"baroud"*—came on to the scene. The Palestinians refused to be diverted from their route, so the Falangists halted their progress and attacked them. In the scuffle the Palestinian driver was killed, as were three Falangists.

The underlying factor, however, was the tension that had been growing within Lebanon. By that time, the Lebanese government had become so weak that each group, both Muslims and Christians, established their own militias to protect their members and to enhance their power. Following the incidents in Beirut, clashes occurred in Tripoli, a Sunni Muslim center, between the supporters of President Franjiyya and ex–prime minister Karami, a Sunni political leader. These incidents resulted in a cabinet crisis. The Muslim members of the Sulh's cabinet, including the prominent Druze leader Junblat, blamed the Phalangists for the clashes and resigned from their posts (O'Ballance 1998; Rabinovich 1985). As Deeb (1980, 1–2) argues, prime minister Sulh's resignation "demonstrated the precariousness and weakness of the prime minister as compared with the president of the republic. Rashid Karami, an ex-prime minister and prominent Sunni leader, reiterated his intention of running in the next presidential elections and maintained that the position of the prime minister in Lebanon had become ineffective and devoid of any real power in decision making."

The second phase (June 1975–January 1976) was characterized by the spread of the war and coalition building among the politically powerful groups. Clashes between mainly Christian and Muslim groups occurred in several large cities, including Beirut, Zahle, Tripoli, and Akkar (Rabinovich 1985). This phase also witnessed the formation of a Shi'ite armed militia—Amal—by the Shi'a leader al-Sadr. Moreover, the Muslims made it clear that they want a revision of the political system. During this period, the Lebanese army disintegrated, and Christian leaders started to discuss the partition of the Christian community.

The third phase (January–May 1976) was marked by Syrian military intervention in the Lebanese conflict. A partition of Lebanon would be consequential for the Syrian regime because it would result in a small Christian state that would make an alliance with Israel and a radical

Arab state that would be supported by Iraq, a bitter rival of Syria. With the consent of the United States and the tacit agreement of Israel, Syria intervened to obstruct a possible partition (Rabinovich 1985). The Syrian direct intervention was expected to stop the violence between the groups. However, the attempts by the Syrian regime to bring about peace and control the fighting groups did not go as planned. The Palestinians, on the one hand, were weary of the Syrian intentions, for Syria was seeking a Greater Syria that would include Palestine land (Rabinovich 1985). On the other hand, Kamal Junblat, a charismatic Druze leader who founded the Progressive Socialist Party, accused the Syrian regime of being corrupt and not genuine in the establishment of "democracy and socialism" (Rabinovich 1985, 52). This resulted in a conflict between the Syrian troops and Muslim groups, primarily the Palestinians and the Lebanese left.

The fourth phase (May–October 1976) was marked by the Riyadh Conference and its consequences. The six parties—Saudi Arabia, Syria, Egypt, Lebanon, the PLO, and Kuwait—convened in Riyadh on October 16, 1976 (Rabinovich 1985). The most important decision made during the conference was to stop the fighting and send an Arab Deterrent Force (ADF) to supervise the normalization process. The ADF, mainly composed of Syrian troops, would be assisted financially by the oil-producing Arab states, primarily Saudi Arabia and Kuwait. Palestinians agreed to retain their pre-1975 positions and restrict their activities in the south. Thus, the Riyadh Conference not only endorsed the right of the PLO to operate in Lebanon, albeit limited to south Lebanon, but also gave Syria the opportunity to establish a political and military hegemony over Lebanese politics (O'Ballance 1998). The fundamental issues between the Muslims and the Christians over the power sharing remained unsolved, however.

The fifth phase of the war was characterized by a decline in violence in Beirut between Mus-

lims and Christians and an increasingly important Syrian direct role (O'Ballance 1998). The ADF failed to disarm the Christian and Muslim militias. The PLO moved back to south Lebanon. However, this caused confrontations with the South Lebanon Army (SLA), Haddad's Christian militia, which was supported by Israel. The relative stability and reduced violence in Beirut, however, were seriously undermined by the assassination of Druze leader Kamal Junblat on March 16, 1977. Junblat was not in favor of the Syrian presence and influence in Lebanon (O'Ballance 1998). In early 1978, Syrian ADF troops clashed with the Christian National Liberal Party (NLP), led by Chamoun. The PLO raids into Israel from south Lebanon finally led to an Israeli invasion of south Lebanon in March 1978. Israel announced that the goal of the operation was to destroy the PLO bases and establish a security zone. Israeli forces, aided by the SLA, did not confront the ADF and did not advance north of the red line, which lay slightly north of the Litani River (O'Ballance 1998). In the same month, the UN authorized the establishment of a UN peacekeeping force to be deployed in south Lebanon. The first UNIFIL troops arrived on March 22, 1978 (O'Ballance 1998). The fifth phase and the civil war ended in April 1978 with a national accord by the groups' leaders that aimed at banning all private militias and reestablishing the Lebanese army.

The 1975–1978 civil war severely impacted the sociopolitical and economic life of the Lebanese. As a result of the war, Lebanon lost its functions "as a financial, cultural, and communication center" in the Middle East (Rabinovich 1985, 57). Thousands of people, mostly Christians, had to emigrate. Sambanis (2004) reports that 285,000 people were displaced during the war period (1975–1990). The war also led to a high number of casualties, 125,892 (Doyle and Sambanis 2000). The war ended in a negotiated settlement (Doyle and Sambanis 2000), yet the country became "divided among external forces and local baronies" (Rabinovich 1985, 57).

Table 1: Civil War in Lebanon

War:	Sectarian conflict among Christian and Muslim groups
Dates:	April 1975–April 1978
Casualties:	125,892
Regime type prior to war:	5 (Polity 2 variable in Polity IV data— ranging from –10 [authoritarian] to 10 [democracy])
Regime type after war:	Not available
GDP per capita year war began:	$3,429 (constant 1985 US dollars)
GDP per capita 5 years after war:	$3,299 (constant 1985 US dollars)
Insurgents:	Christian and Muslim militias
Issue:	Identity and control of the central government
Rebel funding:	Domestic and external sources
Role of geography:	High levels of ethnic and religious concentration in different parts of the country
Role of resources:	None
Immediate outcome:	Negotiated settlement with treaty facilitated by Saudi Arabia
Outcome after 5 years:	War recurred in 1982.
Role of UN:*	Sent peacekeepers into southern Lebanon.
Role of regional organization:	Arab Deterrence Force was active.
Refugees:**	285,000
Prospects:	Contingent on regional political stability

Sources: Doyle and Sambanis 2000, Fearon and Laitin 2003, Nasr 1990, O'Ballance 1998, Rabinovich (1985), Sambanis 2004.

Notes: *Doyle and Sambanis (2000) do not report any UN role in this war. The UNIFIL was primarily deployed in south Lebanon to prevent clashes between the Palestinian groups and Israel.

**These data are for the 1975–1990 period. Abu-Hamad (1995, 241) reports that "750,000 [people] were internally displaced and 930,000 were forced to emigrate." The huge gap between the numbers may be a result of sources they used. Sambanis (2004) data are based on Maksidi and Sadaka (2002), "The Issue of Displaced in Lebanon, 1975–1990: The Movements and Regions of the Displaced." Abu-Hamad's figures are from a 1992 unpublished UN study.

Some features of the war are summarized in Table 1.

The Insurgents

There is no easy way to classify the rebels in the Lebanese civil war. The primary reason for this is that the governmental structure and state apparatus became useless, as it was principally controlled by one group, the Christian Maronites. Although in general the conflict occurred between Muslims and Christians, the temptation to classify the rebels or the fighting parties as Muslims versus Christians should be resisted (Rabinovich 1985). Several clashes occurred among Christians as well as among Muslims during the course of the war; for instance, Syrian troops cooperated with the Christian groups against the Palestinians and the leftists groups in the early years of the war (O'Ballance 1998). Thus, the question of who fought whom is quite complicated in the Lebanese context (O'Ballance 1998).

Despite the fact that the central government almost collapsed, and no central authority was accepted as legitimate by most of the fighting groups, the warring factions could be classified as status quo and revisionist. Generally speaking, Muslim groups sought a fundamental change in the political system, whereas the Christian groups fought to preserve the status quo, in which they were the dominant power (Deeb 1980; Rabinovich 1985).

In the status quo coalition, two groups were most effective. The Phalangist Party was the single most important group in this coalition. The party was founded in the 1930s and became quite influential in Lebanese politics in later decades. In the 1958 civil war, the Phalangists supported President Chamoun (Deeb 1980). The second influential group was the NLP, led by Camille Chamoun. It lacked a coherent doctrine and was primarily based on Chamoun's pragmatic and charismatic personality (Deeb 1980). In the south, the SLA, led by Major Haddad and supported by Israel, was the only effective non-Muslim organization. Despite differences among the Christian groups, they managed to form alliances against the Muslim militias during the 1975–1978 period (Deeb 1980).

Although the government army was composed of both Muslims and Christians, the latter group was in the majority. According to the Doyle and Sambanis (2000) data set, the army size was 55,000. O'Ballance (1998, 14), on the other hand, reports that the government army consisted of somewhere between 15,000 and 18,000 troops. Nevertheless, the Lebanese national army disintegrated in 1976 after the clashes started between Muslim and Christian militias. Hence, the primary combatant force was not the Lebanese national army but rather the militias. The Phalangist Maronites had the largest Christian militia, which was estimated to exceed 10,000 members by the end of 1975. Chamoun's NLP had 2,000 armed militiamen when the war started. In the south, the SLA, led by Major Haddad, had about 2,000 armed militiamen (O'Ballance 1998).

The revisionist coalition was larger and more heterogeneous than the status quo coalition (Rabinovich 1985). The most influential actors were the Palestinian organizations and the leftist militias. Of the leftist organizations and parties, the Progressive Socialist Party (PSP), led by the Druze Kamal Junblat, was the most influential (Deeb 1980; Rabinovich 1985). Fath, led by Yassir Arafat, was the most powerful group among the Palestinian organizations. Syrian intervention produced several pro-Syrian groups during the civil war. The most influential was a Shi'ite organization, Amal, led by al-Sadr. Amal had close ties with Syria and was actively fighting against Israeli forces and their local allies. Of the

Muslim groups, Kamal Junblat's Progressive Socialist Party and the PLO were the most effective. According to O'Ballance (1998), the former group had about 3,000 whereas the latter had about 8,000 well-armed and well-trained men in the late 1970s.

Several scholars (e.g., Collier and Hoeffler 1998; Fearon 2004; Ross 2004) have argued that natural resource wealth has substantial impact on the onset and duration of civil war. However, the debate over the relationship between natural resource wealth and civil wars is not applicable to Lebanese case, for Lebanon has no mineral resources. Nasr (1990) provides a good discussion of the fighting groups' revenue sources in the Lebanese civil war. The Lebanese warring factions benefited from a domestic and regional economic boom in the early and mid-1970s. Consequently, Lebanese expatriates contributed to the Lebanese economy and the continuation of the war. Nasr (1990, 5) reports that "transfers and remittances (wages, savings, benefits) rose . . . from $250 million in 1970 to $910 million in 1975 and 2,254 in 1980. This means that the weight of these remittances in the Lebanese national income rose from 18 percent in 1970 to 35.4 percent in 1980." The external monies received by the PLO contributed to the Lebanese national economy as well. The "Palestine economy" in the late 1970s, as Nasr puts it, "was probably larger than that of the Lebanese state itself" (Nasr 1990, 5). Finally, the Lebanese economy was redistributed among the warring factions. Most of the fighting groups established a de facto rule over some parts of the country and, accordingly, those areas' economic activities. The percent of custom revenues collected by the central government, for instance, declined from 97.4 percent in 1980 to 10 percent in 1986 (Nasr 1990). This gap indicates the increasing power of the locally dominant armed groups and how they were funded throughout the war.

Geography

Geography is a determining factor in the onset and duration of a civil war. Fearon and Laitin

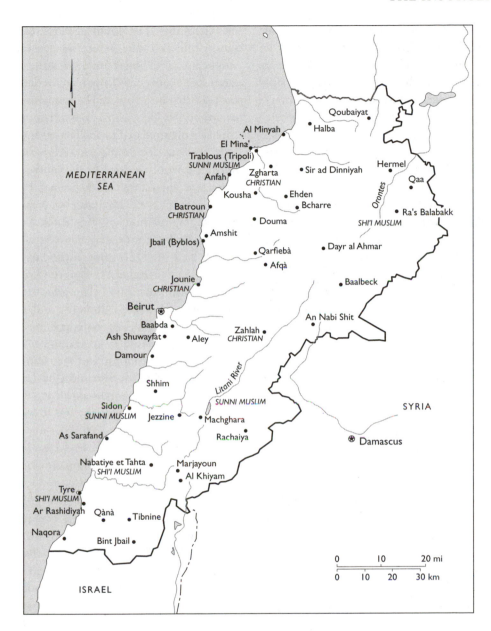

(2003) find that rough terrain increases the probability of a civil war onset. A rugged landscape can provide incentives to the rebel leaders to initiate a conflict with their governments, for mountainous geography makes it harder for the government forces to locate the rebels. Lebanon, unlike other Middle Eastern countries, is mountainous. According to the Doyle and Sambanis's (2000) measure of mountainousness, which ranges from 0 (least mountainous) to 81 (most mountainous), Lebanon receives a score of 57.1. Nevertheless, the effect of such ragged geography is complicated in the Lebanese case. Geography did not serve to hide rebels or warring parties, but it did enable them to carve out small pockets of land in which they became the dominant power. The Christians, for instance, were able to isolate themselves from the rest of the population owing to their geographic location in Mount Lebanon. However, the level of violence was much higher in parts where no sect was dominant. The conflict started in Beirut, a city in which almost all ethnic and religious groups lived and in which the highest number of casualties occurred during the war.

Tactics

The violence between warring factions during the 1975–1978 period took several forms. Because each faction was dominant in some specific areas of the country, most of the violence and killing occurred in areas where members of those sects and groups lived together. Beirut was the most violent place, for almost all sects and groups lived there. Communal violence was the most common form during the first years of the war. The Palestinian refugee camps were among the most common targets of the Christian militias (O'Ballance 1998).

In the following years, car bombs, assassinations, and abductions became widely used by the fighting groups. Abu-Hamad (1995, 241 fn) reports that "17,415 were reported missing and 'presumed dead,' including 13,968 abducted by various factions. During the same period [1975–1990] 3,461 car bombs exploded resulting in 4,386 deaths and 6,784 injuries." The terrorist acts were not confined to the Lebanese borders. The PLO, for instance, was held responsible for several terrorist acts against Israelis during these years in various countries. The Israeli response, however, was mainly to attack the PLO bases in Lebanon, which severely damaged the political and economic infrastructure of the country.

Causes of the War

The causes of the Lebanese civil war are quite complex and numerous. However, the factors that led to the onset of the war can be divided into two broad groups: domestic and external. The domestic factors are closely related to the ethnic and religious composition of Lebanese society. Abu-Hamad (1995) makes a strong argument for the role of local leaders in the onset

of the conflict. The ethnic and religious cleavages within Lebanese society were manipulated and exploited by the community leaders. A sectarian political system helped not only to isolate each sect from the others but also provided the community leaders with a pool of resources that could be manipulated to advance their personal interests. The shift in the numerical strength of the sects, primarily "due to the higher rates of Christian emigration and Muslim birth rates" (Abu-Hamad 1995, 239) over time raised demands for revision of the decision-making process. By 1968, for instance, it was widely acknowledged that Muslims outnumbered the Christians (Abu-Hamad 1995). For political reasons, no official census had been conducted since 1932. However, Gilmour (1983) reports that official estimates of the population divided the sects as follows in 1956: Maronite Catholics, 423,000; Greek Orthodox, 149,000; Greek Catholics, 91,000; Sunni Muslims, 286,000; Shi'a Muslims, 250,000; and Druze, 88,000. Gilmour (1983) also concludes that by 1975 it was widely acknowledged that the Christians were not in the majority and the Shi'a and possibly the Sunni Muslims were more numerous than the Maronite Christians.

The struggle over the Lebanese polity was, however, hastened and worsened by regional developments. The Arab–Israeli conflict was probably the most crucial development that fueled the conflict among the various groups, primarily revisionist Muslims and pro–status quo Christians. The 1948 and 1967 Arab–Israeli wars forced thousands of Palestinians to seek refuge in neighboring countries. A substantial portion of the Palestinians moved to southern Lebanon, Beirut, Baalbak in the Bekaa Valley, and Jordan (Held 2000). After the fighting between Palestinians and Jordan in 1970, the PLO moved its base from Jordan to Beirut, accompanied by another wave of Palestinian refugees.

The rise of Arab nationalism and of Nasserism in particular gave momentum to the conflict between revisionists and status quo groups. The rise of Arabism and Islam as a political alternative, accompanied by the shifting power balances in the Lebanese political system, contributed to the onset of the war. The Muslim community, despite their growing power in terms of population size, was underrepresented in the Lebanese sectarian-based political system. The internal tension among the sects in Lebanon was used by foreign powers, particularly Egypt, Syria, and Israel, to enhance their power either through building alliances with various Lebanese groups or by direct intervention in Lebanese politics. In short, the problems associated with the Lebanese sectarian-based political system were exaggerated by regional developments.

Outcome

The primary conflict between the Christian and Muslim militias ended with a peace settlement signed by the warring factions under the supervision of Saudi Arabia in October 1976. This agreement, although it did not resolve the primary conflict issues among the Muslims and Christians, brought relative stability and peace to Beirut. However, as O'Ballance (1998) reports, the post–Riyadh Conference period was characterized by several important events that led to another wave of violence. The conflict between the Syrian regime and Christian militias, the clash between the Druze and Palestinian militias and Syrian troops, the assassination of the Druze leader Junblat in 1977, the failure of the ADF to bring about order and end violence in Beirut, and the Israeli invasion of south Lebanon in response to the Palestinians' raids into Israel in 1978 worsened the fragile situation in Lebanon. After the UN Security Council's decision to send peacekeepers into south Lebanon, the warring factions agreed on another peace settlement in Beirut in April 1978.

Conflict Status

Several scholars argue that the war did not end in 1978 (e.g., Abu-Hamad 1995; Fearon and Laitin 2003; Nasr 1990; O'Ballance 1998; Samba-

nis 2004). It is not easy to determine when the war ended, mainly because of the number of actors involved. The civil war in Lebanon was fought not only between domestic groups but also between several foreign actors, such as the Palestinians, Syria, and Israel, and to a certain extent the United States, Libya, Iraq, Iran, and several other actors (O'Ballance 1998).

Nevertheless, the fighting between the local groups, mainly Christian militias and Muslim groups, substantially declined after the Riyadh Conference in 1976. After this, the violence continued between Syrian troops and Lebanese groups, between Muslims (PSP and PLO) and Christians in Beirut, and between Israeli forces and Palestinians in the south. Israel's invasion of South Lebanon, as well as Syria's direct control of north and east Lebanon and, to a lesser degree, of Beirut marked the period between the Riyadh Conference and the arrival of UNIFIL in south Lebanon in 1978 (O'Ballance 1998). The conflict, however, continued until 1990s. Following is a brief summary of the events that have occurred since the end of the 1975–1978 war.

The 1978–1980 period witnessed confrontations among the Christian groups. The division between expresident Faranjiyyah, a supporter of Syria, and the other two powerful Christian groups, the Phalangist militia and the NLP, resulted in the killing of several members of the Faranjiyya family, including Suleiman Faranjiyya's son, Tony, and his wife and daughter in May 1978 (O'Ballance 1998). In the following months, Bashir Gamayel, the leader of the Phalangist militia, sought to create a United Maronite Army and clashed with the NLP forces. Meanwhile, the situation in the south was explosive owing to the conflict between Shi'a and PLO militias and Israel. In June 1982, Israel invaded Beirut, and under pressure from the Israeli forces, Bashir Gamayel was elected president. However, on September 14, 1982, he was killed by a bomb. This was followed by Israeli and Phalangist militia forces' attacks on Sabra and Shatila, the Palestinian refugee camps in West

Beirut, which resulted in thousands of deaths. In April 1983, international peacekeeping forces composed mainly of U.S. and French troops deployed to prevent further conflict between the Palestinians and Israeli forces withdrew from Beirut after a huge explosion at the U.S. Embassy (O'Ballance 1998).

The Lebanese civil war became a proxy war between several regional and global forces during the 1978–1990 period. Syria formed alliances with the PLO and other Muslim groups during this period in its fight against Israel. Israel, on the other hand, supported the hard-line Christian militia against Syria and other Muslim groups, primarily the PLO. Hezbollah, supported by the Iranian Islamic regime, became the single most influential Shi'a organization since the early 1980s and remains one of the most powerful groups in Lebanese politics.

The war finally came to an end with a peace settlement signed in Ta'if, Saudi Arabia, in October 1989. The clashes between the supporters of the Ta'if Accord and Syrian forces and the militia of Aoun, a Maronite Christian and an opponent of Syrian involvement in Lebanese politics, came to an end in October 1990, when Aoun sought political asylum in the French embassy (Norton 1991). In August 1991, the Lebanese parliament approved the constitutional reforms laid out in the agreement. The Ta'if agreement discarded the National Pact and called for the disarmament of militias and Syrian withdrawal to positions in Bekaa (Norton 1991). The political dominance of the Maronite Christians came to an end, and the principle of Christian–Muslim equity was accepted (O'Ballance 1998; Norton 1991).

The Ta'if agreement implicitly endorsed the congressional divisions laid out in the National

A woman cries in shock minutes after a car bomb exploded in a crowded Muslim neighborhood in West Beirut, Lebanon, on August 8, 1986, killing thirteen people and injuring at least ninety-two. (Khalil DeHaini/AFP/Getty Images)

Pact. The Maronites' power was reduced in the system, and the Shi'a Muslims, despite their large number, gained only two seats in the parliament. In addition, the Alawis, an offshoot of Shi'a Islam with a close relationship to the Syrian regime, gained two seats in the parliament (Norton 1991).

Duration Tactics

The primary reason for the long duration of the Lebanese civil war was foreign intervention. The war between the domestic groups came to an end in October 1976. But the presence of the foreign powers, especially Syria and Israel, not only internationalized the war but also provided support to the warring factions to continue fighting. The Lebanese civil war became the war for Lebanon among the competing regional states. This is true especially of the post–Riyadh Conference period. From the late 1970s, Syria came to dominate Lebanese politics.

External Military Intervention

The impact of external powers on the Lebanese civil war was immense. The presence of external powers worsened the already delicate balance between the Muslim and Christian groups. After the war began, external powers became involved more directly.

Several countries intervened at one point of the war. Nevertheless, the Syrian and Israeli military interventions were consequential. Syria not only controlled and supported some groups against others but also directly controlled the east and north of Lebanon from 1976 on. Israel invaded South Lebanon and Beirut in 1978 and 1982. Israel withdrew its forces from Beirut in early 1985 but remained in South Lebanon until 2000 (O'Ballance 1998). Syria, through several peace agreements, preserved its influence in Lebanon. Syria withdrew its forces only after strong pressure from the United States and the international community following the killing of former Lebanese prime minister Harriri in February 2005. In short, external military support and intervention not only gave incentives

to the domestic groups to start the war in 1975 but also provided them with financial and military resources to keep fighting.

Conflict Management Efforts

During the 1975–1978 period, conflict management efforts were conducted primarily by Saudi Arabia. A peace agreement was signed by the warring factions in 1976 in Riyadh. This agreement not only endorsed Syria's role in Lebanon but also provided Syria the financial assistance to bring about order in Lebanon. The ADF was mainly composed of the Syrian troops and financed by Saudi Arabia and Kuwait.

UN involvement and mediation efforts came only after Israel became directly involved in Lebanon in 1978. Israel's invasion of the south led the UN Security Council to call for a cease-fire and to establish a peacekeeping force in South Lebanon. Following Israel's invasion of Beirut and increasing violence, the United States pressured Israel to pull back its forces, end the siege in West Beirut, and evacuate the Palestinian militias (O'Ballance 1998). The peacekeeping forces, consisting of U.S., French, and Italian troops, failed to restore order in Beirut and withdrew in 1983 (O'Ballance 1998).

In January 1989, the Arab League delegated the task of finding a solution to the Lebanese crisis to the king of Saudi Arabia, the king of Morocco, and the president of Algeria (Norton 1991). These efforts resulted in the Ta'if Accord, which ended the war and altered the balance of power among the local groups in Lebanon.

Conclusion

Several factors account for the Lebanese civil war. However, the sectarian-based political system and regional factors are the most important. The congressional political system based on the numerical strengths of each community not only exacerbated the divisions among the confessional groups but also hindered the development of cross-sectional political parties. The emergence of cross-sectional parties is more likely in areas where no group is dominant. Beirut, a city that contains roughly 50 percent of the total population, can provide the ground for the emergence of national parties.

One should avoid the common fallacy that the war in Lebanon was a war between Christians and Muslims. Sectarian and religious elements were only markers that differentiated one group from another. Although in the Lebanese context, the Druze and Alawi groups are considered Muslim, these groups are offshoots of Shi'a Islam and are quite secular. Druze, Alawi, and, to a certain extent, Shi'a communities, are considered to be heterodox in the Muslim world; they have been subjected to discrimination and persecution throughout history. Hence, although each group is defined in religious terms, political leaders are not clerics but rather secular heads of prominent families (Abu-Hamad 1995). In a secular, democratic Lebanon, a coalition of Druze and Alawi with Christians would not be surprising. Moreover, O'Ballance (1998, xi) reports that "in a recent brief visit to Lebanon I saw old enemies amicably drinking coffee together and chatting to each other as though little had happened." Hence, Lebanese civil society has persisted, and the probability of reconciliation is high.

Nonetheless, there still remain some problems that are closely related to the probability of war recurrence. The first one is regional. The probability of a sustainable peace in postwar Lebanon is closely related to political developments in the region. The withdrawal of Israel and Syria from Lebanon is good news, but the conflict between these two countries is likely to affect the peace in Lebanon. Moreover, Palestinians account for 9 percent of the Lebanese society (Held 2000), and most of them are still not Lebanese citizens. Hezbollah has close ties to the Iranian Islamic regime and was supported by the Iranian regime during its fight against Israel. Thus, U.S.–Iran relations can also substantially impact the future of Lebanon.

The second and more important problem is systemic. The Ta'if agreement that ended the war in Lebanon implicitly endorsed sectarian divisions and power allocations in Lebanon. As argued earlier, one of the main reasons for the onset of the war in 1975 was the belief that Muslims were underrepresented in the political system. After more than a decade of conflict, the altered system still remains problematic. The single most populous sect, the Shi'a,'i is still underrepresented. Held (2000, 262) reports the estimated percentage of each sect in postwar Lebanon as follows: Shi'ite Muslim, 34 percent; Sunni Muslim, 20 percent; Maronite Christian, 19 percent; Greek Orthodox, 6 percent; Druze, 8 percent; Greek Catholic, 5 percent; Armenian Christian, 6 percent; and other, 2 percent. Despite the overwhelming numerical strength of the Shi'a community (34 percent), they have 22 seats, equal to the Sunni Muslims with 20 percent of the population and fewer than the Maronite Christians' 30 seats with only 19 percent of population (Norton 1991). Therefore, despite their large population, Shi'a Muslims are the most disadvantaged group.

Hezbollah, a militant and fundamentalist Islamic group, has been successful in articulating Shi'a Muslims' demands. Hezbollah is now a political party and represented in the parliament. The incorporation of Hezbollah into the political system is of vital importance. It can provide a guideline for policy makers and especially for the United States in dealing with the rising Islamic movement in the Middle East. The exclusion of Hezbollah or the failure to incorporate it into a democratic political system, however, can be consequential.

Mehmet Gurses

Chronology

August 31, 1920   Modern Lebanon is created by France.

1941   Independence is formally declared.

1943   National Pact, which lays out the basis of power sharing in modern Lebanon, is agreed upon by Maronite Christians and Sunni Muslims.

February 1958   First civil war in modern Lebanon occurs.

November 1969   Cairo agreement is reached between the PLO and Lebanese government after clashes between these two groups.

1970   The PLO transfers its main base from Jordan to Beirut.

April 1975   The second civil war starts.

June 1975–January 1976   The war spreads to other cities.

October 16, 1976   Riyadh Conference is held; warring parties agree to end the conflict; Arab Deterrence Force (ADF) is sent to Lebanon; Syrian role is endorsed.

March 16, 1977   Druze leader Kamal Junblat is assassinated.

March 1978   Israel invades south Lebanon; the UN Security Council authorizes deployment of peacekeepers (UNIFIL) in south Lebanon.

March 22, 1978   UNIFIL arrives in south Lebanon.

April 1978   National accord to end the war is signed by the warring factions' leaders and approved by the Lebanese parliament.

June 1982   Israel invades Beirut.

September 1982   Massacre occurs at Sabra and Shatila camps.

July 1982   International peacekeeping force is deployed in Beirut, consisting of U.S., French, and Italian troops.

April 1983   International peacekeeping force withdraws from Beirut.

January–March 1985   Israel withdraws from Beirut.

October 1989   Ta'if Accord ends the war.

October 1990   General Michel Aoun's militias are defeated; Aoun seeks political asylum in the French embassy.

August 1991   Lebanese parliament approves the Ta'if Accord.

List of Acronyms

ADF: Arab Deterrent Force; mainly composed of Syrian troops and deployed to end the civil war in Lebanon after the Riyadh Conference on October 16, 1976

NLP: National Liberal Party, led by Maronite Christian Chamoun

PLO: Palestine Liberation Organization

PSP: Progressive Socialist Party, led by Kamal Junblat

SLA: South Lebanon Army; General Haddad's Christian militia, supported by Israel in south Lebanon

UNIFIL: United Nations Interim Force in Lebanon

Glossary

Alawi: An offshoot of Shi'a Islam. Most live in Syria.

Amal: A Shi'a political movement that developed in the early 1970s in southern Lebanon.

Druze: An offshoot of Shi'a Islam.

Hezbollah: A militant and fundamentalist Shi'a group and political party. Hezbollah has a strong support from the Shi'a community in Lebanon and is represented in the Lebanese parliament.

Maronites: Members of the largest Christian community in the Middle East.

Phalangist: The most influential Christian–Maronite party in Lebanon.

Shi'a: Literally, "faction"; originates from the clash within the early Muslim community over the right to succeed the Prophet Muhammad. Those who advocated Ali as the rightful successor are known as Shi'a. Today, large populations of Shi'a live in Iran, Iraq, and Lebanon (Godlas 2006).

References

Abu-Hamad, Aziz. 1995. "Communal Strife in Lebanon: Ancient Animosities or State Intervention." *Journal of International Affairs* 49(1): 231–54.

Bannerman, Graeme M. 2002. "Republic of Lebanon." In *The Government and Politics of the Middle East and North Africa,* edited by David E. Long and Bernard Reich. Boulder, CO: Westview Press.

Collier, Paul, and Anke Hoeffler. 1998. "On Economic Causes of Civil War." *Oxford Economic Papers* 50(4): 563–73.

Deeb, Marius. 1980. *The Lebanese Civil War.* New York: Praeger.

Doyle, Michael W., and Nicholas Sambanis. 2000. "International Peacebuilding: A Theoretical and Quantitative Analysis." *The American Political Science Review* 94(4): 779–801.

Fearon, James D. 2004. "Why Do Some Civil Wars Last So Much Longer Than Others?" *Journal of Peace Research* 41(3): 275–301.

Fearon, James D., and David D. Laitin. 2003. "Ethnicity, Insurgency, and Civil War." *American Political Science Review* 97(1): 75–90.

Gilmour, David. 1983. *Lebanon: The Fractured Country.* New York: St. Martin's Press.

Godlas, Alan. 2006. "The Practice and Faith of Islam: Shi'ism." Department of Religion, University of Georgia. godlas.myweb.uga.edu/shiism.html (accessed September 12, 2006).

Goldschmidt, Arthur Jr. 2000. "The Historical Context." In *Understanding the Contemporary Middle East,* edited by Deborah J. Gerner. Boulder, CO: Lynne Reinner.

Held, Colbert C. 2000. *Middle Eastern Patterns: Places, Peoples, and Politics.* Boulder, CO: Westview Press.

Hudson, M. C. 1978. "The Palestinian Factor in the Lebanese Civil War." *Middle East Journal* 32: 261–78.

Nasr, Salim. 1990. "Lebanon's War: Is the End in Sight?" *Middle East Report* January–February (162): 4–8, 30.

Norton, Augustus Richard. 1991. "Lebanon After Ta'if: Is the Civil War Over?" *Middle East Journal* 45(3): 457–73.

Norton, Augustus Richard. 1997. "Lebanon: With Friends like These . . . ." *Current History* (January): 6–12.

Norton, Augustus Richard. 1998. "Hizballah: From Radicalism to Pragmatism?" *Middle East Policy* (January): 147–57.

O'Ballance, Edgar. 1998. *Civil War in Lebanon, 1975–1992.* New York: St. Martin's Press.

Rabinovich, Itamar. 1985. *The War for Lebanon, 1970–1985.* Ithaca, NY, and London: Cornell University Press.

Rasler, Karen. 1983. "Internationalized Civil War: A Dynamic Analysis of the Syrian Intervention in Lebanon." *Journal of Conflict Resolution* 27(3): 421–56.

Ross, Michael L. 2004. "What Do We Know About Natural Resource and Civil War?" *Journal of Peace Research* 41(3): 337–56.

Sambanis, Nicholas. 2004. "What Is Civil War? Conceptual and Empirical Complexities of an Operational Definition." *Journal of Conflict Resolution* 48(6): 814–58.

Liberia
(1989–1997)

Country Background

The Republic of Liberia is located on the west coast of Africa; it is bordered by Sierra Leone, Guinea, and Côte d'Ivoire, and its capital is Monrovia. Liberia is a multiparty republic in which the legislative and judicial branches of government counterbalance the executive branch. It is headed by a president, who elected at regular six-year intervals. The bicameral legislature is modeled on that of the United States and is composed of a twenty-six-seat senate and a sixty-four-seat house of representatives.

A slow process of political freedom and democratic change has characterized Liberia during the last decade. Based on a scale of 1 to 7 (in which 1 is the most free), the 2005 Freedom House scale gives Liberia a score of 5 on political rights and a 4 on civil rights. Liberia has transformed itself from "not free" to "partly free," developing much more political freedom after the civil war through the establishment of proportional representative government (Freedom House 2005). In addition, in terms of regime type and authority characteristics, Polity IV data (2003) allot Liberia a score of 3 on a scale of −10 to 10 (in which −10 represents the most autocratic regime).

Liberia is below the average level of world development in various categories. According to World Bank indicators of 2004, it was ranked as 210th in the world in terms of purchasing power parity (PPP; World Bank 2004b). Among Liberia's population of 3,482,211, 46 percent are below the poverty line, compared to 37 percent for the rest of sub-Saharan Africa. Liberia's education indicator is below world and developing country averages, with a literacy rate of 44 percent (World Bank 2005). The country has recently suffered two civil wars (1989–1997 and 1999–2003) in which the economic and administrative infrastructures were destroyed and law and order ceased to exist. These civil wars devastated the economy. A report released by the World Bank estimates that by the end of the first war in 1996, real gross domestic product was as low as 10 percent of its prewar level. Most multinational corporations (MNCs) left the country during the civil war. Official exports through the government fell from $44 million in 1988 to $25 million in 1997 because of the unrestrained illegal exploitation of natural resources such as iron ore, minerals, and rubber. Real income per capita remained at about one-third of prewar levels (World Bank 2004b). The impact of civil wars on civilians was drastic as well. It was estimated that out of an estimated population of 2.8 million, 150,000 were killed, 750,000 fled the country, and more than 1.2 million were internally displaced (U.S. State Department, 1995). Liberia is currently in the process of recovering from civil wars that have inflicted massive human trauma and caused the collapse of its economic infrastructure.

Conflict Background

The violence in Liberia had its origins in Nimba County, in the December 1989 attack by the National Patriotic Front of Liberia (NPFL) from their bases in the Ivory Coast. The NPFL was led by Charles Taylor, a former official of President Samuel Doe's government. The revolt aimed to topple Doe's government, which was infamous for mass ethnic repression and human rights violations. The attack marked the beginning of eight years of civil war, in which 20,000 people would die and which would make refugees of almost half of the country's population of 2.5 million.

The NPFL's force was made up of the Gios and the Manos, the principal tribes in Nimba County. Both of these groups (constituting about 15 percent of the Liberian population) were motivated by a powerful desire to overthrow Doe's rule because they were suppressed by the Krahn and the Mandingo tribes, which the Doe regime supported. The NPFL insurgents also contained "mercenaries from Burkina Faso and internationalist revolutionaries from Gambia and Sierra Leone" (Ellis 1995). All these groups fought bravely, and by the end of July 1990, Charles Taylor's force had approached the capital and was threatening to overthrow Doe's government. At this time, a new insurgency, the Independent National Patriotic Front of Liberia (INPFL), emerged from the conflict. This splinter group, led by an ally of Taylor, Prince Johnson, broke away from the NPFL. With 500 soldiers, Johnson successfully captured large parts of Monrovia in July 1990 and posed a major challenge to Doe's regime.

From the outbreak of the war, the internal strife in Liberia was characterized by widespread abuse of human rights. The NPFL invaded Krahn Gedeh County and committed atrocities against innocent citizens in revenge for the raid by the Krahn-dominant Armed Forces of Liberia (AFL) of Doe's regime on the Gio and Mano people after the abortive Quiwonkpa coup of 1985 (Alao 1998). In response to the insurgency, the AFL launched a counterattack on civilians in Nimba County. According to reports of the international community, by 1990 at least 200 people, the majority from the Mano and Gio ethnic groups, had been killed by AFL troops in the course of the ruthless campaign (Global Security 2005).

To face the challenge imposed by the overthrow of the legitimate government, and in response to evidence of atrocities committed by the warring factions, a number of West African countries decided to intervene under the leadership of Nigeria. The Economic Community of West African States (ECOWAS) prepared a military intervention force under the command of Ghana's Lieutenant-General Arnold Qainoo. In September 1990, the Economic Community Monitoring Group (ECOMOG) established itself in Monrovia. The situation continued to deteriorate after Doe was captured and mutilated by INPFL's force.

In October 1990, backed by the ECOMOG, the Interim Government of National Unity (IGNU) was established to weaken Taylor's position. It was headed by Amos Sawyer, the former leader of the Association for Constitutional Democracy in Liberia (ACDL). Both INPFL and AFL chose to support Sawyer's regime. However, the NPFL refused to acknowledge IGNU and regarded it as a puppet of the ECOMOG. Taylor's reaction was to establish National Patriotic Reconstruction Assembly Government (NPRAG) in Gbanga. At this time, the NPFL maintained control of large portions of country, in which abundant natural resources such as timber and rubber were exploited and trafficked by Taylor to advance his military and political ambitions.

In November 1990, in response to military and political pressure from the international community, all warlords involved in the conflict met at Bamako, Mali, to discuss the peace process. However, peace talks ended because of disagreement among ECOMOG's member countries over the objective of the intervention.

Charles Taylor, leader of a rebel army during the fighting in Liberia, celebrates a military victory with his troops on July 21, 1990. The Liberian civil war, fueled by the corrupt exploitation of natural resources, ended when Taylor was elected president on July 24, 1997. (Pascal Guyot/AFP/Getty Images)

Consequently, warring factions splintered and proliferated. Seven warring parties emerged from the internal conflict: the NPFL, led by Taylor; the United Liberation Movement of Liberia (ULIMO-J and ULIMO-K), splintered from ULIMO; the Liberia Peace Council; NPFL-Central Revolutionary Council (NPFL-CRC); the Lofa Defense Force; and the remaining forces of the AFL, who were faithful to President Doe. At this time, it became clear that Liberia had devolved into a failed state, in which a legitimate government could not effectively exert its political power within its territory.

From 1993 to 1995, several attempts to impose peace were made by external actors. These efforts involved the signing and implementing a series of peace accords sponsored and monitored by the ECOMOG and the United Nations. However, Liberian warlords continued to fight each other because of the disagreement that ex-isted between Liberian factions and peacekeepers over the composition of a council of state. In September 1995, with the efforts of international community, a Liberian council of state, made up of leaders of the major warring factions, was formed within the framework of the Abuja Peace Accord, accepted in principle by major warring factions. This peace plan led to the final political and military settlement of the civil war.

In accordance with provisions of the Abuja Accord, the disarmament and demobilization of warring factions in January 1997 were followed by democratic presidential and parliamentary elections. The elections were widely monitored and endorsed by international and regional organizations. In July 1997, the National Patriotic Party (NPP) led by Taylor won the election with 75 percent of the vote. This event signified the end of the first civil war in Liberia.

Although in his inaugural address President Taylor promised to devote his efforts to reconciliation, the rule of law, and economic development, his regime was characterized by a "by government militia and security agencies" (United Nations 2003a). In 2001, following an unstable transition period, Liberia engaged in another armed conflict.

Two opposing groups had emerged which together controlled more than two-thirds of the country and which attempted to overthrow Taylor. The Liberians United for Reconciliation and Democracy (LURD), a rebel group supported by the government of neighboring Guinea, emerged in 1999 in northern Liberia. It was composed of excombatants who had been forced into exile as early as 1998, nearly a year after the postwar elections. In 2003, a second rebel group, the Movement for Democracy in Liberia (MODEL) formed in southeastern Liberia. It claimed to "protect the safety and security of all within the borders of Liberia, respect and promote individual human rights" (PBS 2004). In summer 2003, these two rebel groups attacked the capital, Monrovia, and demanded that Taylor resign within three days. President Taylor asked the international community to intervene by way of a peacekeeping force.

In response to the threat posed by the Liberian situation to regional peace and security, the UN Security Council issued a resolution establishing a multinational force to be sent into Liberia to stabilize the situation and to secure the environment for the delivery of humanitarian assistance (United Nations 2003). In addition, at the request of UN Secretary-General Kofi Annan, the United States deployed combat-equipped forces off the coast of Liberia to support Nigerian-led ECOWAS forces entering Liberia.

With the assistance of the international community, Liberia made substantial progress toward peace. In July 2003, peace talks in Akosambo, Ghana, were arranged by the special mediator of the ECOMOG in July 2003. These

were followed by several bilateral meetings of delegations—chiefly the Liberian government, the rebel LURD, MODEL, and eighteen political parties. One important agreement was that a sustainable peace would be achieved in Liberia only if Taylor relinquished the presidency and that his removal from power would ease the path to restoring stability in Liberia and its West African neighbors.

At this time, Nigeria played an important role in resolving the civil strife in Liberia. In particular, it offered an asylum to President Taylor on the condition that he relinquish his power. On August 11, 2003, Gyude Bryant took power as chairman of the Liberia transition authority, with the support of the United Nations and West Africa leaders. The role of the interim government was to create an environment conducive to free and fair elections. On November 11, 2005, after two decades of internal strife, Liberia successfully held presidential elections. Ellen Johnson-Sirleaf became Africa's first elected woman president.

During his exile in Nigeria, Taylor was charged with war crimes by the Special Court, a UN-backed tribunal in Sierra Leone, for his involvement in human rights abuses committed during the civil war in Sierra Leone. The court alleges that "he is among those who bear the greatest responsibility for widespread and systematic rape, murder, physical violence, including mutilation and amputation and other atrocities in Sierra Leone through his support and guidance of the Revolutionary United Front (RUF) rebel movement" (New America Media 2003). In Nigeria, Taylor continued to destabilize the regional peace. More specifically, he was still able to "work through the personal networks of business contacts and 'shadow' market channels of exchange to mobilize mercenaries, influence former allies in the Liberian government and undermine the efforts of other nations and organizations in the region" (Global Witness 2005a). Faced with this situation, the United Nations Security Council passed a resolution empowering the United Nations Observer Mission in Liberia (UNOMIL) to arrest, detain, and transfer Taylor to the UN court in Sierra Leone. According to the resolution, the UN Security Council "decides that the mandate of the United Nations Mission in Liberia (UNMIL) shall include the following additional element: to apprehend and detain former President Charles Taylor in the event of a return to Liberia and to transfer him or facilitate his transfer to Sierra Leone for prosecution before the Special Court for Sierra Leone and to keep the Liberian Government, the Sierra Leonean Government and the Council fully informed" (United Nations 2005).

In March 2006, President Ellen Johnson-Sirleaf submitted a letter formally requesting the extradition of Charles Taylor from Nigeria to face justice. The Nigerian government reacted by stating that Liberia was free to collect Taylor so that he could face war crimes charges in the Liberian courts. Consequently, in April 2006, Charles Taylor was arrested in Nigeria and physically transferred to the UN-backed war crimes court in Sierra Leone. Taylor will face trial in the Special Court for Sierra Leone, where he was indicted on seventeen counts of war crimes and crimes against humanity.

The internal violence in Liberia has destabilized the West African subregion by spilling into neighboring countries such as Sierra Leone and Guinea. During the 1990s, the rebel NPFL stole diamonds in Sierra Leone and attempted to punish its government for sending forces to join ECOMOG units in Liberia to weaken Taylor's position. Specifically, the NPFL became actively involved in the Sierra Leone's civil war by helping the Revolutionary United Front, one of "West Africa's most notorious spoilers" (Adebajo 2004), to destabilize the legitimate government led by President Ahmad Tejan Kabbah. The RUF was infamous for committing atrocities such as cutting off the heads, arms, and legs of defenseless women and children.

Taylor played a major role in supporting the RUF rebels and their leader, Foday Sankoh, with whom he had a close personal relationship that

The Support of the RUF from Liberia

The RUF has received regular training in Liberia, at Gbatala near Gbanga and elsewhere. RUF soldiers have been trained alongside Liberia's Anti-Terrorist Unit (ATU), and President Taylor has frequently used RUF combatants for his own personal security details. Liberian officers and men are also actively assisting the RUF in Sierra Leone, serving as combats, trainers, and liaison officers. Early in 1999, a significant improvement in tactics and use of weapons by RUF rebels was noted in Sierra Leone. Their main base is Camp Najma, where Liberian RUF are trained.

High-level RUF meetings with President Taylor have been noted, along with RUF travel to Monrovia, RUF strategy meetings at the executive mansion, RUF travel on Liberian helicopters, and RUF staging bases at Camp Schefflein, Voionjama, and Foyakama. Liberia has provided the families of many senior RUF officials with a safe haven. Eyewitness accounts speak of RUF fighters treated in Monrovia hospitals, (United Nations Security Council 2000).

can be traced back to their training in Libya, in one of the biggest terrorist training camps in Africa. This relationship can also be traced to Sankoh's support of Taylor's effort to topple Doe's regime in the 1990s (United Nations Security Council 2000).

With the comprehensive support provided by the NPFL of Liberia, the RUF used several international arms brokers to obtain large quantities of weapons imported from Eastern Europe. According to a report of the UN Panel of Experts in 2000, these weapons and supplies included mortars, rifles, rocket propelled grenades (RPGs), satellite phones, computers, vehicles, and batteries (United Nations Security Council 2000). Most of the supplies were sent by road or helicopter to Foyakama, a few miles from the border between Sierra Leone and Liberia, and then transported across the border into RUF territory for onward distribution to the region controlled by the RUF (United Nations Security Council

2000). With considerable logistical support from Liberia's NPFL, RUF evolved from a guerrilla group into a quasi-conventional army, thus leading to Sierra Leone's internal crisis.

In March 1991, backed by Taylor's NPFL, the RUF rebel group launched its first attack on the Sierra Leone government and seized some of the country's territory, beginning one of Africa's most brutal civil wars. During the course of the civil war, the ill-equipped, poorly trained, and logistically deficient Sierra Leone Army (SLA) was unable to defeat the rebels. In later campaigns, RUF firmly controlled large parts of the Sierra Leone countryside.

By 1995, the RUF had gained control of Kono and Tongo, the two most diamond-rich areas in Sierra Leone, and it exploited these resources to sustain its rebellion. During the 1990s, the war in Sierra Leone became a complex conflict with major humanitarian and political disasters. Between 1991 and 1996, the civil war claimed more than 75,000 lives, created half a million refugees, and displaced 2.4 million of the country's 4.5 million people, most of whom were forced into neighboring Guinea and Liberia (Smillie, Gberie, and Hazleton 2000). In 2001, with the efforts of the UN peacekeeping force and other international organizations, the civil war in Sierra Leone ended. National elections were held in May 2002, and the government began to reestablish its authority. At this time, the Liberian government planned to destabilize Sierra Leone by plotting a two-pronged attack, activating cells of well-armed, Liberian-paid operatives already within Sierra Leone, which were later joined by an external force of Anti-Terrorist Unit (ATU) fighters attacking from Liberia. The attack also involved disrupting the UN Special Court's proceedings by releasing ex-RUF leader Sankoh and regaining full access to Sierra Leone's lucrative diamond resources (Global Witness 2003). In sum, by providing support and leadership to RUF, Taylor was directly responsible for fueling and complicating the internal strife and atrocious violations of human rights committed in Sierra Leone.

Civil war in Liberia also spilled over into the neighboring country of Guinea. Since September 2000, the southwest region of Guinea, which is close to the Sierra Leone–Liberia border, had been threatened by a series of border attacks aimed at the Guinean civilians and Sierra Leone and Liberian refugees by the RUF, which was sponsored by the government of Liberia. According to a report by the United Nations High Commission for Refugees (UNHCR 2000), Guinea has Africa's second-largest refugee population, including 130,000 Liberians and 330,000 Sierra Leoneans. Until recently, Guinea's relative stability offered some protection for these refugees; however, these attacks in Guinea caused a major humanitarian crisis (UNHCR 2000). It was estimated that the attacks caused the displacement of 250,000 people from their shelter in Guinea, as well as the deaths of 2,000 people. The United Nations High Commissioners for Refugees, Ruud Lubbers, described the situation as the "world's worst refugee crisis" (Gberie 2001).

Two factors accounted for these attacks. First, the attacks were caused by Liberian President Taylor to retaliate against Guinea for giving refuge to members of the Liberian opposition. In 2003, Taylor argued that "the government of Guinea facilitated the establishment of Liberians United for a Reconciliation and Democracy (LURD) by permitting the recruitment, training and arming of Liberian refugees living in refugee camps in the territory of Guinea" (Allafrica 2003). The second factor was Taylor's pursuit of abundant natural resources. Guinea has diamond reserves estimated at 25 million carats, worth well over $2 billion dollars (Gberie 2001). This was significant motivation for Taylor to plot a series of border attacks in an attempt to acquire diamonds.

In September 2001, when confronted with this dangerous situation, Guinea's prime minister, Lamine Sidime, accused Liberia of destabilizing Guinea by means of the recent attacks, stating that "[e]verything points to the fact that it is an external aggression from Liberia which has, for years, been preparing to engage in war with Guinea" (Afrol 2001). Furthermore, the Guinean government asked for international help to avoid becoming yet another victim of internal chaos caused by Liberia.

In September 2001, members of the United Nations Security Council demonstrated their serious concern over the cross-border attacks on refugees and civilians in southwest Guinea. The council also reconfirmed the military embargo against Liberia. A UN statement made it clear that Liberian-supported Sierra Leonean RUF terrorists and rebels would be held responsible for the attacks. In addition, it called for all states, "particularly Liberia—to abide by its earlier statement, which had called for all UN member States to stop providing military support to the rebels carrying out the attacks" (Afrol 2001). Eventually, with the help of the international community, the sociopolitical crisis in Liberia was solved, and political stability has been restored. In sum, the substantial spillover effects of the Liberian civil war led to the internal turmoil

and the decline of economic development of its neighboring countries.

The Insurgents

The ability of insurgents to fuel armed conflict depends on their capacity to secure access to resources, to procure weapons and materials, and to pay soldiers. In Liberia, the control and exploitation of diamonds, timber, and other raw materials were some of the principal objectives of Taylor's NPFL, which was the main insurgent group in the Liberian civil war. From 1990 to 1994, Liberia exported $300 million worth of diamonds annually, followed by timber at $53 million, rubber at $27 million, iron ore at $43 million, and gold at $1 million. Taylor received approximately $75 million annually from these resources (Cain 1999) to finance the NPFL and gave it the means to sustain the civil war.

Owing to the relatively stable price of diamonds in the global market and the fact that they can be easily seized by individuals or small

Table 1: Civil War in Liberia

War:	NPFL and IPPFL vs. government
Dates:	December 1989–July 1997
Casualties:	150,000
Regime type prior to war:	−4 (Polity 2 variable in Polity IV data— ranging from −10 [authoritarian] to 10 [democracy])
Regime type after war:	3 (Polity 2 variable in Polity IV data— ranging from −10 [authoritarian] to 10 [democracy])
GDP per capita year war began:	$395 (in constant 1990 US dollars)
GDP per capita 5 years after war:	$700 (in constant 2005 US dollars)
Insurgents:	NPFL (National Patriotic Front of Liberia)
Issue:	Ethnic repression, human rights violations, corruption
Rebel funding:	Exploitation of natural resources (diamonds, timber, rubber)
Role of geography:	Rebels hid in rain forest and mountains.
Role of resources:	Diamonds, timber, etc. sold to provide funding for war.
Immediate outcome:	Revolt was victorious; election facilitated by UN and ECOMOG.
Outcome after 5 years:	No fighting
Role of UN:	Facilitated peace talks; sent peacekeeping force.
Role of regional organization:	ECOWAS was active.
Refugees:	779,900
Prospects for peace:	Favorable

Sources: CIA 1990; CIA 2005; Doyle and Sambanis 2000; Polity IV 2004.

What Are Conflict Diamonds?

Conflict diamonds are diamonds that originate from areas controlled by forces or factions opposed to legitimate and internationally recognized governments. They are used to fund military action in opposition to those governments or in contravention of the decisions of the Security Council (United Nations Department of Public Information 2001).

groups of unskilled workers (Ross 2004), diamonds have played an important role in sustaining and advancing Taylor's military and political ambitions and contributed to the prolongation of the civil war in Liberia.

Taylor was attracted to Sierra Leone's diamonds for their high quality and abundance. Diamond reservations were located in the districts of Kenema, Kono, and Bo in the central and eastern parts of Sierra Leone. It was estimated by De Beers in 1998 that diamond production in Sierra Leone was 300,000 carats (worth $100 to $300 per carat) (Global Witness 2000). Official exports through the government of Sierra Leone were estimated at 114,438 carats, whereas in 1999 this figure fell to 9,320 carats (Global Witness 2000). The dropoff in diamond production in 1999 by the government of Sierra Leone could be attributed to the fact that diamond production had fallen under the control of the RUF, which had several diamond mines and was known for producing of gem-quality diamonds (American University 2001).

To sustain the civil war in Liberia with the proceeds from smuggled Sierra Leonean diamonds, Taylor offered comprehensive support to the RUF to increase its control of the diamond fields. With the NPFL's help, the RUF launched its first campaign from Liberia and attacked major diamond mining centers. By 1995, almost all major diamond mining areas had fallen under the control of the RUF in Sierra Leone, giving Taylor a conduit for diamond exports to fuel Liberia's conflict and advance his own personal ambitions. With the combined efforts of Taylor and the RUF, there was a well-established route for diamond production, trading, and smuggling of diamonds in exchange for guns and military hardware. The network originally operated along the long, open border between Sierra Leone and Liberia, which provided a geographic opportunity for Taylor to smuggle diamonds mined by the RUF in Sierra Leone. Millions of dollars worth of diamonds from Sierra Leone were transported from the northern and western areas of Liberia to such ports as Monrovia and Buchanan, where they were shipped to Belgium, Lebanon, and the Netherlands. Weapons, such as AK-47 assault rifles and rocket-propelled grenades, were transported from ex-Soviet and eastern bloc countries, China, and the Balkans into Liberia and Sierra Leone to fuel the civil war. According to an estimate by the Diamond High Council, between 1994 and 1999 Belgium recorded $2.2 billion worth of rough diamond imports from Liberia (Smillie 2002). In addition, the United Nations estimated that the "blood diamonds" that left Liberia in 1999 were worth about $75 million on the open market. Taylor received a commission on each transaction, and Ibrahim Bah Bath, who was a key figure of terrorism in Africa and the Middle East, received the rest (Farah 2001). Thus, an illegal diamonds trade center was established, in which proceeds from diamonds could be used to purchase large amounts of military equipment to fuel the civil war in Liberia.

To combat the illicit traffic in diamonds and to disconnect the link between the illegal diamond trade and internal strife in Liberia, Resolution 1343 of the United Nations Security Council was adopted. It banned the production and transportation of diamonds in the conflict region, and it also banned the Liberian importation of weapons (United Nations 2001b). In addition, the General Assembly would continue an embargo on Liberian diamonds until it could be demonstrated that diamonds no longer led to conflict and that government control met the requirements for lifting sanctions as prescribed in

Security Council Resolution 1521 (United Nations 2003c).

Despite sanctions imposed on the illegal diamond trade, the illegal trading of weapons for diamonds in Liberia has steadily increased. For example, some companies in the diamond business with Liberia have continued to promote illegal arms trade, such as Mano River Resources (MRR) and American Mining Associates (AMA). According to a report by the UN panel of experts in 2005, illegal domestic diamond production generated approximately 350,000 carats per month in 2003 (Global Witness 2005a), and the scale of AMA's operations were "excessive for exploration activity" (Global Witness 2005b). All income from the trade of diamonds was used to buy guns and other military equipment and to prolong the civil strife and destabilize Liberia.

Revenue from the production and trafficking of timber from major timber-producing areas enabled the NPFL to remain militarily active and thus dismiss all efforts toward peace on the part of the United Nations and ECOMOG. Most parts of Liberia were under Taylor's control in 1990. Taylor began to make large profits from timber to sustain his insurgents in Greater Liberia, which included 70 percent of Liberian territory and parts of Guinea and Sierra Leone (Reno 1997).

Millions of tons of timber were produced and transported from Greater Liberia to China, France, and Italy through four ports along the Atlantic Ocean: Monrovia, Buchanan, Greenville, and Cape Palmas. In these ports, logging ships arrived, offloaded arms, and took on loads of logs.

Many multinational corporations involved in timber extraction were associated with smuggling timber from Liberia's resource-rich region and delivering weapons to the NPFL. In the employ of these companies was Gus Van Kouwenhoven, manager of the Oriental Timber Company (OTC), the largest logging operation in Liberia. He had been identified in a series of UN reports as being "involved with the logistical aspects of many of the arms deals" (Global Policy 2001). Specifically, this company controlled 43 percent of what remains of the Upper Guinean Forest ecosystem in Liberia, and was estimated to have paid Taylor $3 million to $5 million for control of the 1.6-million-hectare area (United Nations 2001a). In addition, Leonid Minin, a notorious Ukranian crime figure, was also involved in obtaining logging concessions and providing arms to Liberia. It was reported that in 2000, Minin arranged an import of 10,500 AK 47 rifles, and RPG-26 rocket-launchers and sniper rifles (United Nations 2001). These weapons were used by Taylor to sustain the internal armed conflict.

To cut off Taylor's source of timber, in May 2003 the UN Security Council imposed a ban on all Liberian timber, effective July 7, 2003. In addition, the requirements for lifting of sanctions as set forth in Resolution 1521 reconfirmed that the Liberian government must exercise control over its territory and must have in place the proper accounting and governance mechanisms to ensure that the revenue is not used to fuel conflict (United Nations 2003d). Although measures were taken to this end, Taylor continued to exploit timber to purchase weapons by finding an alternative approach. In 2002, he sold timber concessions inside Sapo National Park, one of West Africa's main woodland reserves. Concession agreements involved a number of stipulations that covered the size and location of the area to be logged, the duration of the agreement, the minimum diameter of trees to be felled, species that can or cannot be taken, environmental safeguards such as maintaining buffer strips along streams, and royalty rates and other fees (Barden 1994). With this alternative, Taylor continued to receive several million dollars from the Oriental Timber Company of Hong Kong. The sum allowed him to buy back, at least temporarily, the loyalty of his senior commanders and arm his troops (Farah 2002). It was obvious that Taylor was still violating the UN arms embargo. Thus, by illegal access to natural resources such as diamonds and timber,

How Is Timber Smuggled?

Containerized Timber

The recent sighting of sawn timber being loaded into a forty-foot shipping container is a new and potentially worrisome development in the handling of sawn timber. The most common form of transporting timber to Monrovia for sale is through large, open-air trucks. Given the increasingly secretive nature of shipments of timber, any moves toward potentially surreptitious means of transporting or even exporting timber deserve further investigation. This particular shipment, spotted near Jenemama in Gbarpolu County, was destined for sale near the Monrovia Freeport, according to workers loading the container.

Although it is not clear that this particular shipment was exported, the use of a sealable container, its transport to Monrovia in the middle of the night, and the lack of adequate customs controls at the port means that similar containers of sawn or raw timber could be exported in violation of the UN timber embargo.

Late-Night Deliveries

From its investigation in October 2004 and before, Global Witness noted that timber deliveries from outlying areas were being made to Monrovia in broad daylight. However, perhaps owing to the increased awareness of the problem of illegally sourced timber, as well as the vigilance of monitors at key entry points to Monrovia, timber transporters have started delivering their loads very late at night or early in the morning, driving up from Buchanan, Tubmanburg, and other sourcing areas to offload their shipments at Freeport and elsewhere, usually before sunrise. This shift in delivery strategy is worrisome if its intent is to evade FDA and independent oversight. Combined with the generally poor oversight of the industry and the potential use of containerized transport, the mechanisms to avoid both Liberian national law and international sanctions are readily exploitable (Global Witness 2005a).

Taylor sustained the civil war in Liberia and played a major role in the destabilization of the region.

Causes of the War

The civil war in Liberia was a product of ethnic hatred and the violation of human rights and systematic corruption of Doe's government. First, internal strife in Liberia can be traced to the country's origins. Historically, Liberia has been divided by two opposing ethnic groups. One group, known as Americo-Liberians, were descended from repatriated slaves who migrated to West Africa from the United States in the nineteenth century under the aegis of the American Colonization Society (ACS). The other group was made up of indigenous tribal Africans. They had a government ruled by kings and village elders. People were bound by "institutional moral rules and laws, and stability was achieved through kinship" (Nmoma 1997). Americo-Liberians regarded this ethnic group as "primitive and uncivilized" and treated them as little more than an abundant source of forced labor (Wippman 1993).

From the founding of the Republic of Liberia in 1847, Americo-Liberians controlled the administrative, fiscal, legal, and military resources of the economy and the government, and the indigenous people became targets of repression. The Americo-Liberians established a "settler oligarchy," which dominated the indigenous people through extreme economic exploitation, including forced labor and brutal repression (Ofuatey-Kodjoe 1993). More specifically, the Americo-Liberians used a policy of "divide and rule" and the practice of recruiting armed forces along ethnic lines and deploying them to brutalize other ethnic groups (Ofuatey-Kodjoe 1993). The Americo-Liberians prevented the indigenous population from receiving education and deprived them of their right to vote by making

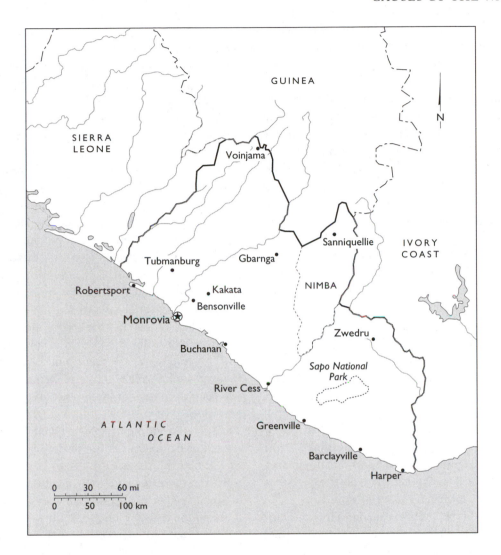

property ownership a prerequisite for education and voting. There was an enormous disparity in the distribution of wealth; the Americo-Liberians heavily taxed the indigenous inhabitants and imposed forced labor for public work projects. Thus, over the course of the nineteenth and twentieth centuries, through control of land and other measures, Americo-Liberians wielded "a monopoly of power over a majority of indigenous peoples" (Khafre 1978).

In the 1970s, the deterioration of the economy caused by the global oil crisis further intensified ethnic repression. During President William Tolbert's reign, various activist groups were formed to demonstrate their concern about the injustices confronted by many Liberians. On April 12, 1980, a group of lower-rank soldiers headed by Master Sergeant Samuel Doe, an indigenous Liberian, seized power through a coup that toppled President William Tolbert's administration. This coup signified the collapse of the political dominance of the Americo-Liberian elite. Initially, Doe tried to present his coup as a victory over an oppressive system. He also promised to curb corruption with effective measures and to realize the equitable distribution of the nation's natural resources and the full participation of all ethnic groups in the political process (Dunn 1998). However, after establishing representation favorable to him, Doe decided to further stabilize his power by continuing the practices of the previous regime. By 1984, a popular slogan justly summarized Doe's Liberia as "Same Taxi, New Driver" (Outram 1997).

Liberia's return to a dictatorial government began with Doe's rapid elevation of members of his own group, Kranh, to high posts in the administration, such as the National Bank and the Department of Defense. Doe filled his administration with Krahn officials, even though Kranh made up only about 5 percent of the Liberian population. Furthermore, Doe offered economic and educational opportunities to the Krahn at the expense of other ethnic groups. This resulted in a disproportionate representation of the Krahn in government. The Krahn dominance was so well established that postcoup Liberia witnessed the emergence of a Krahn–non-Krahn ethnic divide. Many Americo-Liberians felt alienated by the brutal murder of their former leaders, and Gios and Manos felt victimized and marginalized. The deep separation between Krahn and other ethnic groups became wider, and tensions exploded in the wake of the coup attempt during Doe's regime. On November 12, 1985, General Thomas Quiwonkpa, a former officer of Doe in the 1980 coup, invaded Liberia through Nimba County to launch a coup that aimed at toppling Doe's government. The coup failed, and Quiwonkpa was beaten beyond recognition, castrated, and dismembered. The failed coup engendered massive reprisals against the Gio and Mano ethnic groups in Nimba County, the hometown of General Quiwonkpa (Ellis 1999). In sum, the ethnic violence caused by the exclusion of the indigenous majority of the population, along with the imbalance in the distribution of wealth that favored the powerful ethnic groups in the Doe regime, escalated the intergroup tension in Liberia and thus contributed to the outbreak of the civil war.

Apart from ethnic tensions, another underlying cause of the Liberian civil war was the violation and abuse of fundamental human rights during Doe's regime. The killing of President Tolbert and the public execution of thirteen senior officials in 1980 demonstrated the brutality of Doe's regime. During the 1980s, Doe frequently suppressed independent political activities; he charged opponents with treason and often had them executed after summary trials (Human Right Watch 2005). The imprisonment for treason of Gabriel Kpolleh and Caephar Mabande, both leaders of a banned political party, illustrate Doe's efforts to crush all opposition and to impose a de facto one-party state (Human Rights Watch 2005). In October 1989, two people arrested for yet another alleged coup attempt died in custody (Human Rights Watch 2005). The government explained their deaths as a result of natural causes but held no inquest to substantiate this claim.

Furthermore, the Doe government's violation of human rights was demonstrated by its crackdown on the press. In June 1982, the Ministry of Information revoked the license of Radio ELCM, a Catholic station, for reporting a story about several people who were crushed to death at a football stadium. The revocation was done without an administrative hearing as required by the ministry's guidelines (Human Right Watch 1989). Repressive measures included "the closure of newspapers, such as the shutdown of the *Daily Observer* in 1982, summary imprisonment of journalists, harassment of journalists, regulatory edicts, judicial actions, and an actual and unprecedented presidential sanctioning of the murder of a journalist" (Rogers 1996).

Human rights abuses were also committed against students who challenged Doe's rule. When Liberian students became aware of Doe's repressive rule, they began to express their dissatisfaction. The students of the National University of Liberia demanded a return to constitutional civilian rule and became the voice of a disaffected population. On August 22, 1984, 200 soldiers attacked students on the university campus who were protecting a popular professor, Amos Sawyer, from arrest on suspicion of treason. The soldiers arrested, detained, and beat hundreds of students and reportedly raped female students, transforming the University of Liberia into a breeding ground for political agitation and conflict. However, the Doe government denied that any killings had taken place and acknowledged only one case of sexual abuse (Human Rights Watch 2005).

In the late 1980s, as resistance to Doe's government grew, human rights violations became widespread. Torture, disappearances, extrajudicial executions, imprisonment of opposition leaders, and restriction of freedom of expression were all commonplace violations of human rights under Doe's government (Amnesty International 1997). In short, the widespread and organized conflict in Liberia was an expression of dissatisfaction with the violation of human rights committed by the government. The seeds of hate sown by the abuse of human rights took root all over the country, ripened, and bore fruit: the outbreak of civil war in 1989.

Furthermore, the outbreak of civil conflict in Liberia can be explained by examining the widespread corruption in Doe's government of the People's Redemption Council (PRC). Under the dictatorship of Doe, there were no legislative and administrative safeguards to prevent, detect, punish, or eradicate the corruption of public officials. Allegations of high-level corruption among government officials in Doe's administration were frequent. For example, it was alleged that on the day of the coup, the plotters withdrew $200,000 from the national Bank of Liberia; a few days later, $100,000 was stolen from the National Housing Bank, and a further $26,000 was taken from the safe in the executive mansion (Dunn and Tarr 1988). Other corruption was associated with the use of foreign aid.

For example, from 1980 to 1985, the United States gave Liberia nearly $500 million, making Liberia the largest per capita aid recipient in sub-Saharan Africa. The aid money amounted to one-third of Liberia's annual budget. However, the administration and distribution of this aid was under little scrutiny (Adebajo 2002). Corruption became rampant, with much of the aid disappearing into the personal accounts of Doe and other elites in the PRC. By the end of his rule, Doe and his cronies had stolen a reported $300 million in public funds (Berkeley 1992). Adebajo offered this perspective on the corruption: "Doe and his officials illegally acquired wealth and land as blatantly as the True Whigs once did. Revenue from logging concessions and fuel went straight to Doe's private funds; even U.S. food assistance was diverted into private pockets" (Adebajo 2002, 1). Thus, the social inequality and lack of secure personal property rights caused by high-level, systemic corruption contributed to intensified conflict and finally led to the overthrow of Doe's government by internal violence in the 1990s.

Outcome
Conflict Status

The civil war in Liberia ended with an independent democratic election in 1997 as an integral part of the UN's peacekeeping efforts. The electoral process was monitored and assessed by several international organizations: the United Nations, the European Union, and the Carter Center. Sixteen parties registered to take part in the elections. On July 24, 1997, the outcome of the election was announced, and the National Patriotic Party (NPP), led by Charles Taylor, won an overwhelming victory with 75 percent of the vote. The NPP received 468,443 of the 621,888 votes, garnering 49 of 64 seats in the house of representatives and 21 of 26 seats in the senate (Adebajo 2002). The monitors acknowledged that the election was free and fair. Therefore, the Independent Election Commission declared Taylor president of the Republic of

Liberia on July 23. Taylor's victory symbolized the end of the Liberian civil war.

External Military Intervention

Regional organizations and international organizations played a major role in the facilitation of peace and security in Liberia. From the outbreak of the civil war in 1989, the situation in Liberia was characterized by fighting between warlords, a crumbling socioeconomic infrastructure, and extreme violence against civilians. Soon, the crisis in Liberia not only became a threat to its neighboring countries but also destabilized the subregion of West Africa. Therefore, the ECOWAS, a regional organization of West Africa, responded to this situation by establishing the ECOWAS Ceasefire Monitoring Group (ECOMOG) in August 1990 to resolve conflicts among warring factions. It was formed within the framework of ECOWAS's Revised Security Treaty. According to Article 58 of the treaty, the provision of defense and security is one of ECOWAS's objectives, and each member state is obliged to cooperate in the areas of politics, diplomacy, international relations, peace, and security (Malu 2003), thus legitimizing the intervention in Liberia. The objective of the ECOMOG was to stop the fighting among warlords, to monitor the process of the cease-fire, and to integrate the major rivals into an interim administration.

A number of reasons accounted for the ECOWAS's decision to intervene in Liberia. First, the overflow of refugees from Liberia to neighboring countries posed a threat to regional stability (Ero 2000). Armed attacks on civilians had been commonplace since the beginning of the civil war in 1989. A large number of people were forced to flee Liberia to Sierra Leone, Guinea, and Côte d'Ivoire to avoid persecution, imposing a huge economic and political burden on these states. In August 1990, General Emmanuel A. Erskine of ECOMOG argued that, "with the crisis in Liberia creating unbearable refugee problems for Sierra Leone, Ghana, Gambia, Guinea, Nigeria and the Ivory Coast, it is ob-

vious that the situation in Liberia has gone beyond the boundaries of the country and ceases to be an exclusive Liberian question" (Ero 2000, para. 14). Erskine also maintained that this issue "could not be accomplished by the grinding wheels of diplomacy" (Ero 2000).

Furthermore, ECOWAS's decision to intervene was associated with its concern with the major humanitarian crisis caused by the civil conflict in Liberia. According to the Final Communiqué, the ECOWAS's decision to intervene was based on humanitarian consideration. The communiqué stated, "[P]resently, there is a government in Liberia which cannot govern and contending factions which are holding the entire population as hostage, depriving them of food, health facilities and other basic necessities of life" (Ero 2000). ECOWAS further affirmed its commitment to intervene in Liberia, "stopping the senseless killing of innocent civilians nationals and foreigners, and to help the Liberian people to restore their democratic institutions" (Ero 2000, para. 5).

ECOMOG's decision was also related to the protection of citizens of member countries in Liberia. Obed Asamoah, Ghana's foreign prime minister, argued that, "the Liberian situation . . . assumed international dimensions because several thousand Ghanaians, Nigerians and other nationals [had] been holed up in Liberia and [were] suffering because of the fighting" (Adibe 1997, 474). Because of the internationalization of the civil war in Liberia, ECOWAS decided to deploy peacekeeping troops in Liberia to restore peace and security.

Formal ECOMOG involvement in the Liberian civil war began with military deployment near the capital, Monrovia, in September 1990. Specifically, ECOMOG adopted a "limited offensive" strategy, which aimed at driving the NPFL forces, which posed a direct threat to a legitimate government of Liberia, out of Monrovia (Vogt 1997). Consequently, ECOMOG was resisted by the NPFL, and the strategy led to a direct confrontation between peacekeeping forces and the NPFL. However, this strategy succeeded in "containing the conflict, at least for a short period and preventing the situation from degenerating into genocidal proportions like the type of slaughter witnessed between April and July 1994 in Rwanda" (Draman and Carment 2001, 11). To avoid a rapid escalation of the situation, ECOMOG and the NPFL held a series of talks. Based on the official reports of the ministerial conference, there had been substantial disagreement between members of the ECOMOG and the warlords over key elements of the proposed peace plan. Major issues leading to the dispute were: "the desirability and timing of a cease fire, the desirability and composition of an interim government, and the usefulness of deploying a regional peacekeeping force" (Adibe 1997, 473).

However, it was difficult to find common ground on these issues among negotiators. At this time, Taylor's NPFL led the most powerful military force and was committed to controlling the entire country. Therefore, Taylor refused the ECOMOG's request, insisting that the NPFL "took up arms, got rid of Doe, and took more than 98 percent of the country and so had earned the right to rule Liberia" (Adibe 1997, 474). Taylor's objective of capturing the state was destroyed by the engagement of peacekeeping forces of the ECOMOG. Accordingly, in October 1992, Taylor's NPFL launched a major attack named Operation Octopus on ECOMOG positions in Monrovia, aimed at capturing the city and establishing a national government. ECOWAS counterattacked by bombing NPFL's position from air and sea. Backed by units of AFL and INPFL, ECOMOG successfully contained and then turned back the attack (Mackinlay and Alao 1994). This operation illustrated that the Liberia crisis had escalated beyond the negotiating capabilities of ECOMOG. Consequently, the security situation deteriorated rapidly, leading to the continuation of fighting between warlords.

From 1990 to 1993, enormous efforts were made by the ECOMOG to assure that all parties complied with the provisions of a series of peace agreements; however, these efforts failed because of the differences among ECOMOG member states with respect to their strategies. Specifically, Francophone countries of ECOMOG attached much importance to diplomatic strategy, accommodating warlords in a coalition government; however, the Anglophone states stressed launching a military force to contain the rebels and frustrate their aspirations (Armon and Carl 1996). Thus, the lack of consensus among ECOMOG member countries rendered ECOMOG incapable of making the Liberian factions lay down their arms.

In April 1993, Security Council Resolution 856 was passed to send the newly formed United Nations Observer Mission in Liberia (UNOMIL) into Liberia to assist the ECOMOG in monitoring and verifying the peace process—in particular, ensuring compliance with and impartial implementation of the agreement by all parties. UNOMIL was the first United Nations peacekeeping mission undertaken in cooperation with a peacekeeping operation already established by a regional organization (United Nations 2003a). In 1996, with the efforts of ECOMOG and the UN, the Abuja Accord was reached and accepted by all parties involved. This treaty integrated Liberian factions into a unified government following a cease-fire among warlords. In 1997, under the supervision of the UN, a democratically elected government was established, and Taylor was elected president of Liberia. The objective of the peace operation was achieved. In sum, in the Liberian case the conflict resolution process illustrated the effectiveness of the joint intervention strategy of international and regional organizations to address the civil strife in Africa. Specifically, the UN assumed "mainly supervisory roles while regional organizations would carry out the practical aspects of the peace keeping operations" (Alao 1998, 20). The regional organization was familiar with social and economic problems unique to the region; in addition, they were committed to solving the conflict and thus could play a positive role in the mediation process, whereas the United Nations provided abundant capability, resources, expertise, and authority to facilitate the process of disarmament and demobilization.

Conclusion

The civil war in Liberia had a drastic impact on Liberia's economic structure as well as its political structure and claimed the lives of tens of thousands of innocent civilians. About half the country's 2.3 million people fled their homes and are either refugees in neighboring states or displaced inside Liberia. Efforts should be made along domestic and regional dimensions to prevent the recurrence of internal violence in Liberia. First, in a country such as Liberia which has experienced state collapse, efforts should be made to build a strong state that has "ample resources and the administrative and political capacity to control or regulate most economic, social, and political activity" (Gurr 2001, 142). Under this framework, in order to address the issue of ethnic problems and to prevent continuing interethnic revenge, Liberia should include representatives of different ethnic groups in the political process. Specifically, the parliament should be composed of representatives from different ethnic groups.

With this approach, various ethnic groups with different beliefs and backgrounds can live together in harmony without threatening the country's political stability. In addition, the Liberian government should devote resources to socioeconomic development programs to increase "the improvements in the physical quality and dignity of people's lives: access to potable water, safe and sanitary neighborhoods, basic health care, literacy and advanced education, sufficient income to provide at least minimally adequate food and clothing and sufficient income to provide for one's family" (Diamond 1992, 123). With improved living conditions, people would have less motivation to participate in rebel activities against the government. Furthermore, to address the potential threat of internal violence in Liberia, regional organizations such as the Organization of Africa States (OAS) and ECOWAS should establish an institutional mechanism of conflict prevention. Liberia should be integrated into this security framework, in which situations in Liberia would be monitored, potential tension among ethnic groups detected, and ethnic conflicts resolved.

Jun Wei

Chronology

April 12, 1980   Samuel K. Doe, an Army sergeant, overthrows President William Toblert's regime.

May 6, 1985   Doe's National Democratic Party of Liberia (NDPL) wins election.

December, 24, 1989   The National Patriotic Front of Liberia (NPFL), an insurgent of Doe's government led by Charles Taylor, enters Liberia from Côte d'Ivoire, aiming to topple the Doe regime.

August 1990   The Economic Community of West African States (ECOWAS) decides to send ECOMOG, a military intervention force, to stop the fighting.

September 1990   The Independent National Patriotic Front of Liberia (INPFL), a splinter group of the NPFL, captures and kills Doe.

October 1990   The Interim Government of National Unity (IGNU), headed by Amos Sawyer under the auspices of ECOMOG, is established.

August 1993   The United Nations sends the United Nations Observer Mission in Liberia (UNOMIL) to monitor the peace process in Liberia.

1995   Within the framework of the Abuja Accord, an interim state council composed of Liberia's warring factions is established.

August 1997   Charles Taylor is elected president of Liberia with more than 75 percent of the vote.

1999   Liberians United for a Reconciliation and Democracy (LURD), a rebel group that aims to topple Taylor's government, emerges in the northern county of Lofa along the Guinean border.

2001   The United Nations imposes sanctions on Liberian diamonds and issues a travel ban on Liberian government officials in response to Liberia's continued support of the rebel insurgency in Sierra Leone.

August 2003   Taylor is accused of war crimes and exiled.

September 2003   U.S. forces pull out; UN launches peacekeeping mission.

October 2003   Gyude Bryant is sworn in as head of state.

List of Acronyms

ACDL: Association for Constitutional Democracy in Liberia

ACS: American Colonization Society

AFL: Armed Forces of Liberia

AMA: American Mining Associates

ATU: Anti-Terrorist Unit

ECOMOG: ECOWAS Ceasefire Monitoring Group.

ECOWAS: Economic Community of West African States

GDP: gross domestic product

IGNU: Interim Government of National Unity

INPFL: Independent National Patriotic Front of Liberia

LURD: Liberians United for Reconciliation and Democracy

MNC: multinational corporation

MODEL: Movement for Democracy in Liberia

MRR: Mano River Resources

NDPL: National Democratic Party of Liberia

NPFL: National Patriotic Front of Liberia

NPFL-CRC: The National Patriotic Front of Liberia-Central Revolutionary Council

NPP: National Patriotic Party

NPRAG: National Patriotic Reconstruction Assemby Government

OAS: Organization of African States

OTC: Oriental Timber Company

PPP: purchasing power parity

PRC: People's Redemption Council

RUF: Revolutionary United Front

SLA: Sierra Leone Army

ULIMO: United Liberation Movement of Liberia

UNHCR: United Nations High Commission for Refugees

UNOMIL: United Nations Observer Mission in Liberia

UNMIL: United Nations Mission in Liberia

Glossary

Doe, Samuel K.: President of Liberia from 1980 to 1990; came to power by military coup, toppling President William R. Tolbert, Jr.'s government. His regime was characterized by ethnic hatred between Kranh and non-Kranh ethnic groups, violation of human rights, and systemic corruption.

ECOWAS Ceasefire Monitoring Group (ECOMOG): Peacekeeping force, established in August 1990 by ECOWAS, a regional organization of West Africa, to stop the fighting among warlords in Liberia, to monitor the cease-fire, and to integrate the major rivals into an interim administration.

National Patriotic Front of Liberia (NPFL): Rebel force, active from 1989 to 1997, that aimed at toppling Doe's regime; composed of Gio and Mano ethnic groups from Nimba County, who were suppressed by Doe's government in the 1980s.

Revolutionary United Front (RUF): Insurgent force in Sierra Leone, led by Foday Sankoh and supported by Taylor of Liberia; evolved from a guerrilla group into a quasi-conventional army, with near catastrophic consequences for Sierra Leone.

Taylor, Charles Ghankay: Insurgent leader in the Liberian civil war from 1989 to 1997; elected president of Liberia in 1997 and exiled to Nigeria in 2003 after being indicted for war crimes by the United Nations.

References

Adebajo, Adekeye. 2002a. *Building Peace in West Africa: Liberia, Sierra Leone, and Guinea-Bissau.* Boulder, CO: Lynne Rienner.

Adebajo, Adekeye. 2002b. *Liberia's Civil War: Nigeria, ECOMOG, and Regional Security in West Africa.* Boulder, CO: Lynne Rienner.

Adebajo, Adekeye. 2004. "Introduction." In *West African's Security Challenges Building Peace in a Troubled Region,* edited by Adekeye Adebajo and Ismail Rahsid. Boulder, CO: Lynne Rienner.

Adibe, Clement E. 1997. "The Liberian Conflict and the ECOWAS–UN Partnership." *Third World Quarterly* 18(3): 471–88.

Africa Research Bulletin, Economic, Financial and Technical Series. 2004. .41(August 16–September 15). Blackwell.

Afrol. 2000. "Sierra Leone Conflict Spills Over to Guinea?" Available at www.afrol.com/html/News/gui003_conflict_spillover.htm (accessed November 14, 2005).

Afrol. 2001. "UN Blames RUF and Liberia for Attacks in Guinea." afrol.com/News2001/gui001_ruf_liberia.htm (accessed November 14, 2005).

Alao, Abiodun. 1998. *The Burden of Collective Goodwill: The International Involvement in the Liberian Civil War.* Brookfield, VT: Ashgate.

Allafrica. 2003. "Taylor Accuses Guinea to Security Council for Aiding Lurd." Global Policy Forum. www.globalpolicy.org/security/issues/liberia/2003/0226com.htm (accessed November 14, 2005).

American University. 2001. www.american.edu/TED/ice/diamond-sl.htm. (accessed November 9, 2006).

ALO. 2000. "GDP Rankings Current Exchange Rate Method (Numerically by Ranking)." Available at aol.countrywatch.com/includes/grank/gdpnumericcer.asp?TYPE=GRANK&TBL=NUMERICCER&vCOUNTRY=99 (accessed November 14, 2005).

Amnesty International. 1997. "Liberia: Time to Take Human Rights Seriously–Placing Human Rights on the National Agenda." www.amnesty.org/ailib/aipub/1997/AFR/1300597.htm (accessed November 14, 2005).

Armon, Jeremy, and Andy Carl. 1996. "Preface." In The Liberian Peace Process, 1990–1996. Edited by Andy Carl and Jeremy Armon. London. Conciliation Resources.

Asamoah Obed. 1990. quoted in the People's Daily Graphic (Accra), 23 August 1990, See also A Essuman-Johnson. 1990. "The Liberian Refugee Problem and Ghana's Response to It." LECIA Bulletin 2(1) 34–40.

Barden, Clare. 1994. "Combating the Illegal Timber Trade—Is There a Role for ITTO?" In Helge Ole Bergesen and Georg Parmann, eds. Green Globe Yearbook of International Co-operation on Environment and Development. Oxford: Oxford University Press.

Berkeley Bill. 1992. "Between Repression and Slaughter." Atlantic Monthly 270(6): 23-30.

Cain Kenneth L. 1999. "The Rape of Dinah: Human Rights, Civil War in Liberia, and Evil Triumphant." Human Rights Quarterly 21(2): 265–307.

Central Intelligence Agency (CIA). 1990. The 1990 CIA World Factbook. www.gutenberg.org/dirs/etext91/world12.txt. (accessed November 9, 2006).

Central Intelligence Agency (CIA). 2005. The CIA 2005 World Factbook. www.cia.gov/cia/publications/factbook/geos/li.html#Econ (accessed November 9, 2006).

Diamond, Larry. 1992. "Economic Development and Democracy Reconsidered." Reexamining Democracy Essays in Honor of Seymour Martin Lipset, edited by Gary Marks and Larry Diamond. London: Sage Publications.

Diamond Trade in Sierra Leone. 2002. www.american.edu/TED/ice/diamond-sl.htm (accessed November 14, 2005).

Doyle, Michael, and Nicholas Sambanis. 2000. "International Peacebuilding: A Theoretical and Quantitative Analysis." American Political Science Review 94(4): 779–801.

Draman, Rasheed and David Carment. 2003. "Managing Chaos in the West African Sub-Region: Assessing the Role of ECOMOG in Liberia." Journal of Military and Strategy Studies 6(2): 1–31.

Dunn, D. Elwood. 1998. "Liberia's Response to Interventionist Efforts." In K. P. Magyar and E. Conteh Morgan, eds. Peacekeeping in Africa: ECOMOG in Liberia. London: Macmillan.

Dunn, D. Elwood, and S. Byron Tarr. 1988. "Liberia: A National Polity in Transition." Metuchen, NJ: Scarecrow Press.

ECOWAS Standing Mediation Committee. 1990. "Final Communiqué of the First Session." Document 54, Weller, M., Regional Peace-keeping and International Enforcement.

Ellis Stephen. 1995. "Liberia 1980–1994: A Study in Ethnic and Spiritual Violence." Africa Affairs 94(375): 165–97.

Ellis, Stephen. 1999. The Mask of Anarchy: The Destruction of Liberia and the Religious Roots of an African Civil War. London. Hurst and Company.

Ero, Comfort. 2000. "ECOWAS and Subregional Peacekeeping in Liberia." International Peacekeeping 7(2): 95–114. www.jha.ac/articles/a005.htm (accessed November 14, 2005).

Farah, Douglas. 2001. "Al Qaeda Cash Tied to Diamond Trade." Washington Post (November 2).

Farah, Douglas. 2002. "Liberian Leader Again Finds Means to Hang On: Taylor Exploits Timber to Keep Power." Washington Post (June 4).

Freedom House. 2005. "Country Report 2005." www.freedomhouse.org/research/freeworld/2005/Kuwait-PNG.pdf (accessed November 14, 2005).

Gberie, Lansana. 2001. "Destabilizing Guinea: Diamonds, Charles Taylor and the Potential for Wider Humanitarian Catastrophe." Occasional Paper 1, Partnership Africa Canada. International Peace Information Service Network Movement for Justice and Development. October 2001.

Global Policy. 2001. "European Timber Trader Linked with Liberian Arms Trafficking

Companies." www.globalpolicy.org/security/natres/timber/2001/0716gweu.htm (accessed November 14, 2005).

Global Security. 2005a. "Liberia—First Civil War—1989–1996." Available at www.globalsecurity.org/military/world/war/liberia–1989.htm (accessed November 14, 2005).

Global Security. 2005b. "Liberia—Second Civil War—1997–2003." Available at www.globalsecurity.org/military/world/war/liberia–1997.htm (accessed November 14, 2005).

Global Witness. 2000. "Conflict Diamonds: Possibilities for the Identification, Certification and Control of Diamonds. A Briefing Document by Global Witness." www.globalwitness.org/reports/download.php/00036.rtf (accessed November 14, 2005).

Global Witness. 2001. "European Timber Trader Linked with Liberian Arms Trafficking." www.globalwitness.org/press_releases/display2.php?id=117 (accessed November 14, 2005).

Global Witness. 2003. "The Usual Suspects: Liberia's Weapons and Mercenaries in Côte d'Ivoire and Sierra Leone." www.globalwitness.org/reports/show.php/en.00026.html (accessed November 14, 2005).

Global Witness. 2005a. "Timber, Taylor, Soldier, Spy: How Liberia's Uncontrolled Resource Exploitation, Charles Taylor's Manipulation and the Re-Recruitment of Ex-Combatants Are Threatening Regional Security." globalpolicy.igc.org/security/issues/liberia/2005/06timber-taylor.pdf (accessed November 14, 2005).

Global Witness. 2005b. " A Time for Justice." www.globalpolicy.org/intljustice/wanted/2005/06taylor_gw.pdf (accessed June 9, 2006).

Gurr, Ted Robert. 2001. "Minorities and Nationalities: Managing Ethnopolitical Conflict in the New Century." In Turbulent Peace: The Challenges of Managing International Conflict, edited by Chester A. Crocker, Fen Osler Hampson, and Pamela Aall. Washington, DC: United States Institute of Peace Press.

Human Rights Watch. 2005. "Liberia." www.hrw.org/reports/1989/WR89/Liberia.htm (accessed November 14, 2005).

Kandeh, J. D. 1996. "What Does the 'Militariat' Do When It Rules? Military Regimes: The Gambia, Sierra Leone and Liberia." Review of African Political Economy, 23(69): 387–404.

Khafre, K. 1978. "Towards a Political Economy of Liberia." Review of African Political Economy 12: 105–13.

Mackinlay, John, and Abiodun Alao. 1994. "Liberia 1994: ECOMOG and UNOMIL: Response to a Complex Emergency." Occasional Paper Series 2. UNU Publications. www.unu.edu/unupress/ops2.html. (accessed November 14, 2005).

Malu, Linus. 2003. "Collective Peace-Keeping in West Africa." www.monitor.upeace.org/archive.cfm?id_article=61 (accessed November 14, 2005).

New America Media. 2003. "Liberia: Pressure Mounts for Taylor to Face Trial." news.newamericamedia.org/news/view_article.html?article_id=c9c8992416db5e6647fbef719257f848 (accessed November 14, 2005).

Nmoma, Veronica. 1997. "The Civil War and the Refugee Crisis in Liberia." The Journal of Conflict Studies 17(1). www.lib.unb.ca/Texts/JCS/SPR97/articles/nmoma.html (accessed November 14, 2005).

Ofuatey-Kodjoe, W. 1993. "Regional Organizations and the Resolution of Internal Conflict: The ECOWAS Intervention in Liberia." Paper presented at the Workshop on Multilateral Organizations and the Amelioration of Ethnic Conflicts, City University of New York.

Outram, Quentin. 1997. "It's Terminal Either Way: An Analysis of Armed Conflict in Liberia, 1989–1996." Review of African Political Economy 73: 355–71.

PBS. NewsHour. 2004. "Civil War in Liberia." www.pbs.org/newshour/bb/africa/liberia/rebel_groups.htm (accessed November 14, 2005).

Polity IV. 2004. "Polity IV Country Report 2003: Liberia." www.cidcm.umd.edu/inscr/polity/Lbr1.htm (accessed November 14, 2005).

Reno, William. 1997. Humanitarian Emergencies and Warlord Economies in Liberia and Sierra Leone. Helsinki, Finland: UNU World Institute for Development Economics Research.

Rogers, Momo K. 1996. "The Liberian Press Under Military Rule." Liberian Studies Journal. 2(1): 7–32.

Ross, Michael. 2004. "Oil, Drugs, and Diamonds: The Varying Roles of Natural Resources in Civil War." In The Political Economy of Armed Conflict: Beyond Greed and Grievance, edited by Karen Ballentine and Jake Sherman. Boulder, CO: Lynne Rienner.

Smillie, Ian. 2002. "Dirty Diamonds, Armed Conflict and the Trade in Rough Diamonds." Fafo Institute for Applied Social Science. www.fafo.no/pub/rapp/377/377.pdf (accessed November 14, 2005).

Smillie, Ian, Lansana Gberie, and Ralph Hazleton. 2000. "*The Heart of the Matter: Sierra Leone, Diamonds and Human Security.*" www.sierra-leone.org/heartmatter.html (accessed November 14, 2005).

United Nations. 2001a. "Report of the Secretary-General to the Security Council SC/6997." www.un.org/News/Press/docs/2001/sc6997.doc.htm (accessed November 14, 2005).

United Nations. 2001b. "UN Expert Panel on Liberia Report (S/2001/1015)." www.un.org/Docs/sc/committees/Liberia2/1015e.pdf (accessed November 14, 2005).

United Nations. 2002a. "Report of the Secretary-General to the Security Council S2002/470." Available at www.un.org/Docs/sc/committees/Liberia2/470e.pdf (accessed November 14, 2005).

United Nations. 2002b. "Report of the Secretary-General to the Security Council SC 7600." Available at www.un.org/News/Press/docs/2002/sc7600.doc.htm (accessed November 14, 2005).

United Nations. 2003a. "*Liberia—UNMIL—Background.*" www.un.org/Depts/dpko/missions/unmil/background.html (accessed November 14, 2005).

United Nations. 2003b. "Report of the Secretary-General to the Security Council S/2003/769." daccessdds.un.org/doc/UNDOC/GEN/N03/445/30/PDF/N0344530.pdf (accessed November 14, 2005).

United Nations. 2003c. "Report of the Secretary-General to the Security Council S/2003/875." daccessdds.un.org/doc/UNDOC/GEN/N03/491/10/PDF/N0349110 (accessed November 14, 2005).

United Nations. 2003d. "United Nation Security Resolution 1521." daccessdds.un.org/doc/UNDOC/GEN/N03/669/60/PDF/N0366960.pdf (accessed November 14, 2005).

United Nations. 2005. "United Nation Security Resolution 1638." www.globalpolicy.org/intljustice/wanted/2005/1111scres1638.pdf (accessed June 9, 2006).

United Nations Department of Public Information. 2001. "Conflict Diamonds: Sanctions and War." www.un.org/peace/africa/Diamond.html (accessed September 12, 2006).

United Nations High Commission on Refugees (UNHCR). 2000. "UNHCR Office Destroyed in Guinea Fighting." December 7. www.idpproject.org/weekly_news/2000/pdf_files/guin07de.pdf (accessed November 14, 2005).

United Nations Security Council. 2000. "Report of the Panel of Experts of Appointed Pursuant to Security Council Resolution 1306 (2000), paragraph 19 in Relation to Sierra Leone.S/2000/1195." www.un.org.Depts/dpko/dpko/reports.htm (accessed November 14, 2005).

U. S. State Department. 1995. "Liberia Human Rights Practices." Available at dosfan.lib.uic.edu/ERC/democracy/1995_hrp_report/95hrp_report_africa/Liberia.html (accessed November 14, 2005).

Vogt, M. A. 1997. *The Liberian Crisis and ECOMOG: A Bold Attempt at Regional Peace Keeping.* Lagos, Nigeria: Gabumo Publishing.

Wippman, David. 1993. "Enforcing the Peace: ECOWAS and the Liberia Civil War." In *Enforcing Restraint: Collective Intervention in Internal Conflicts,* edited by Lori Fisler Darmrosch. New York: Council on Foreign Relations.

World Bank. 2004a. "Country Brief, Liberia 2004." Available at web.worldbank.org/WBSITE/EXTERNAL/COUNTRIES/AFRICAEXT/LIBERIAEXTN/0,menuPK:356204~pagePK:141132~piPK:141107~theSitePK:356194,00.html (accessed November 14, 2005).

World Bank. 2004b. "GNI per capita, 2004 Atlas Method and PPP. 2004." Available at www.worldbank.org/data/databytopic/GNIPC.pdf (accessed November 14, 2005).

World Bank. 2005. "Liberia at a Glance." Available at www.worldbank.org/data/countrydata/aag/lbr_aag.pdf (accessed November 14, 2005).

Mozambique
(1979–1992)

Country Background

In the last half of the twentieth century, the Republic of Mozambique was among the most conflict-ridden and war-torn nations in the world. After nearly a decade (1964–1975) of violent nationalist rebellion against the Portuguese, the Frente de Libertacao de Mozambique (Frelimo), the anticolonialists who became the first governing party in independent Mozambique, began to combat a growing counterrevolutionary insurgency that called itself the Resistencia Nacional Mozambicana (Renamo). This conflict between the Frelimo government and Renamo rebels, which began only two years after independence, would lead the new country into one of the longest and bloodiest civil wars of the post–World War II era. Before an agreement would be reached in the early nineties to end the war, an estimated 1 million deaths would be attributed to the conflict, with an additional 4 million deslocados, or displaced persons (around a quarter of the entire population) living in refugee camps inside Mozambique or in neighboring Malawi, Zimbabwe, Tanzania, or South Africa (Vines 1991, 1).

It is difficult, however, to determine exactly how many people died as a result of the civil war in Mozambique. The typical distinction between military deaths and civilian deaths is frequently blurred. The United Nations Economic Commission for Africa estimated in 1989 that 900,000 had died from the war. The Correlates of War civil war data file (Sarkees 2000) lists 200,550 state deaths and 1,200,550 total deaths. Sambanis (2000) lists 255,000 total battle deaths, 500,000 total deaths, and 3,500,000 refugees. More than likely, the actual number of deaths occurring from direct combat is much smaller. Throughout most of the conflict, the national military of Mozambique was estimated at approximately 30,000. At its peak, Renamo was even smaller, somewhere between 20,000 and 25,000 men. If both sides had a turnover rate from battle deaths of 100 percent, meaning that every single person who was a soldier at the beginning of the war had been killed and replaced by the end of the war (a nearly impossible scenario), the number of battle deaths would be roughly 50,000 to 60,000. Clearly, the casualty estimates include all civilian deaths blamed on the war. In addition to those killed in military campaigns, the civil war destroyed the economy and prevented aid from reaching people in need during several natural disasters and famines that occurred during the course of the conflict.

A senior U.S. Department of State official referred to the Mozambican civil war in 1988 as "...one of the most brutal holocausts against ordinary human beings since World War Two" (quoted in Finnegan 1992, 5). By the end of the 1980s, Mozambique was reportedly producing less than 10 percent of the food its people needed. When more than three decades of internal war ended in 1992, the life expectancy of the average Mozambican was thirty-seven years, and Mozambique was considered the poorest country in the world, with a gross domestic product per capita around 80 dollars, two-thirds of which consisted of foreign aid (Plank 1993).

Conflict Background

Following independence, conditions inside Mozambique resembled a common scenario in postcolonial states. Conflict began to emerge between societal groups as the new ruling party, dominated by members of the anticolonial opposition, formed what could be called a "backlash" regime (Clement and Springborg 2001, 16). Strong anticolonial and anticapitalist policies were initiated, which in turn helped to mobilize a counterrevolutionary opposition with ties to the former colonial state.

The new ruling party of Mozambique (Frelimo), calling itself Marxist, directed its foreign policy toward alignment with the Soviet Union and Cuba, nationalized industry, outlawed private property, and began the creation of state-run collective farms and communal villages. Frelimo President Samora Machel declared that Mozambique would be "Africa's first Marxist state," and his government's initiatives were said to be strongly influenced by " . . . the historical models for revolution offered by Cuba, Vietnam, the Soviet Union and China . . ." combined with Mozambique's own " . . . long and terrible experience with Portuguese-style capitalism . . ." (Finnegan 1992, 110). As Frelimo's Interior Minister Guebuza described, at independence the regime's immediate goal was to eliminate " . . . the rotten values of the colonial bourgeoisie that had been assimilated by Mozambicans" (Cabrita 2000, 95).

Renamo's makeup, at least initially, came from those with close ties to the former Portuguese security apparatus in Mozambique. This level of assimilation with the former colonial state explains much of the ideological distance between Frelimo and Renamo over what kind of country postindependent Mozambique should become. In 1981, Renamo released its first political manifesto. The rebel group defined itself as a military organization dedicated to ending Frelimo rule in favor of free-market economics and multiparty elections. Renamo's background, as Portuguese-trained soldiers with a free-market political manifesto, provides a vivid example of colonial assimilados coming into conflict with a "backlash" regime.

The Insurgents

Although some debate exists in the literature over the primacy of internal versus external factors in explaining the success of Renamo as an insurgency in Mozambique, the group's origins are generally well-known. Renamo was founded around 1976 by members of the Rhodesian Central Intelligence Organization (CIO) to act as a counterinsurgency force directed against the Zimbabwean National Liberation Army (Zanla), which had based itself in Mozambique after being banned from Rhodesia. Renamo would also retaliate against the Frelimo government for supporting Zanla activities within its territory and for closing Mozambique's border with Rhodesia. According to the rebel group's creator, a Rhodesian military intelligence chief named Ken Flower, Renamo was to be a pseudoterrorist organization (Flower 1987). Recruitment for Renamo came initially from "disgruntled Portuguese" (Vines 1991, 16), many of whom had been associated with the Portuguese General Security Directorate (DGS). Others came from the "crack anti-insurgency units" or "flechas" (Morgan 1990, 605), which were formed and trained by the Portuguese to combat the anticolonial uprising in Mozambique. To escape possible retribution by Frelimo after independence, many Mozambican members of the Portuguese colonial military fled to neighboring Rhodesia, where they were later recruited by the CIO.

Table 1: Civil War in Mozambique

War:	Mozambique (Frelimo) vs. Renamo
Dates:	October 21, 1979–October 4, 1992
Casualties:	1,200,550 (Sarkees)
Regime type prior to war:	−8 Autocracy (Polity 2 variable in Polity IV data—ranging from −10 [authoritarian] to 10 [democracy])
Regime type after war:	6 Democracy (Polity 2 variable in Polity IV data—ranging from −10 [authoritarian] to 10 [democracy])
GDP per capita year war began:	US $1,182
GDP per capita 5 years after war:	US $760
Insurgents:	Resistencia Nacional Mozambicana (Renamo)
Issue:	Ideological struggle for control of central government
Rebel funding:	Aid from Rhodesia until 1980, then South Africa
Role of geography:	Forested center regions were primary areas of rebel activity.
Role of resources:	Limited role; not prominent
Immediate outcome:	Negotiated settlement
Outcome after 5 years:	Stable peace and elections
Role of UN:	7,500 peacekeepers on the ground after settlement
Role of regional organizations:	Not prominent
Refugees:	3–4 million
Prospects for peace:	Very favorable

Sources: Jaggers and Marshall 2000; Sarkees 2000; Sambanis 2000.

Renamo also benefited from a significant splintering of Frelimo at independence between the moderate and democratic Mondlane wing and the more authoritarian pro-Marxist wing, which eventually took power after Eduardo Mondlane's death. Much of Renamo's early recruitment came from Frelimo splinter groups and political dissidents assigned to reeducation camps by the regime's political police and later liberated from those camps by the rebels. Renamo reportedly raised between 1,000 and 2,000 men in the single year of 1979 through "raids on re-education camps" (Finnegan 1992, 32). One of those early recruits was Andre Matsangaissa, a former Frelimo military commander, who, after escaping from a reeducation camp, fled to Rhodesia and became the leader of the new rebel group.

Although initially a rather small unit operating closely under Rhodesian Special Forces units, Renamo's activities expanded in 1978 owing to growing Zanla activity in Mozambique along the Rhodesian border. Counteroffensive bases were set up inside Mozambique to better combat Zanla infiltration routes into Rhodesia and to destabilize Frelimo leadership in Mozambique. Throughout the rest of the 1970s, Renamo did what it was created and trained to do: wreak general havoc in Mozambique in an effort to weaken Zanla and Frelimo in the name of Rhodesian national security. Despite the escalating levels of violence in the 1970s, Renamo expert Alex Vines characterizes Renamo activity at this time as "fairly limited" (1991, 17) compared to what the next decade would bring as Renamo sponsorship shifted from Rhodesia to South Africa.

Control and support for Renamo changed significantly in 1980, when multiracial elections ended white minority rule in Rhodesia (Zimbabwe) and, consequently, CIO support of Renamo. After 1980, Renamo became primarily funded and controlled by South African military intelligence forces to combat increasing activity by African National Congress (ANC) rebels inside Mozambique and to deter Frelimo assistance to the ANC, which reportedly included weapons shipped from the USSR to Mozambique's capital of Maputo (Cabrita 2000, 181).

Thousands of refugees fleeing the civil war in Mozambique crowd a train taking them to Malawi in 1989. Civil war is a leading cause of human displacement. (Peter Turnley/Corbis)

Although Renamo had new South African sponsors, the group's directives in the coming decade would be very similar to what they had been under the sponsorship of Rhodesia: launch counteroffensives against the nationalist rebels, in this case the African National Congress, and weaken the Frelimo regime through the systematic destruction of social and economic infrastructure. With South African support, Renamo's activities reportedly intensified substantially. From 1980 through 1988, Renamo destroyed approximately "1,800 schools, 720 health units, 900 shops, and 1,300 trucks and buses" (Vines 1991, 17). In the Beira corridor alone, an important economic zone stretching from the port at Beira across Mozambique, Renamo destroyed 1,415 pylons (power lines) with an estimated cost of repair of more than $76 million (Vines 1991, 28). In addition to infrastructure, the human loss in Mozambique was becoming monumental. UNICEF, the United Nations Children's Fund, stated that 490,000 children in Mozambique died of starvation between 1980 and 1988. By 1989, the number of both internal and external refugees had "reached over 4.3 million," providing a strong indicator at the time of how devastating the conflict had become (Vines 1991, 17).

Geography

The overall complexity of the Mozambican conflict was greatly facilitated, geographically, by the high number of land borders shared with neighboring countries of Malawi (1,569 kilometers), South Africa (491 kilometers), Swaziland (105 kilometers), Tanzania (756 kilometers), Zambia (419 kilometers), and Zimbabwe (1,231 kilometers). This contributed to interventionists tactics by several of these states and offered temporary safe havens for rebel activity. In addition to the high number of land borders Mozambique shares with neighboring states, the long, narrow

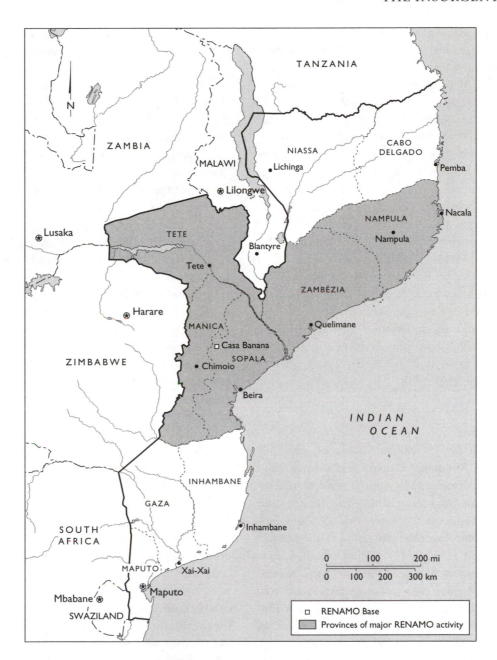

shape of the country may have also contributed to the dynamics of the conflict by allowing the rebels to reach a border with limited effort.

Mozambique, which is roughly twice the size of California, is a very narrow strip of mostly coastal lowlands running along 2,470 miles of the Indian Ocean. Aside from the northern-most regions above Nampula, the country never exceeds 300 miles in width at any one point, providing close proximity to a border at nearly any geographical point. In the Tete province, which served as a major area of rebel activity, the borders of Zimbabwe, Malawi, and Zambia are all within 150 miles and span three sides of the province. Presumably, rebel movement across these borders would go more easily unnoticed or ignored than that of the Mozambique national military. This offered the rebels a unique advantage.

Terrain was also a seen as an important factor in either aiding or limiting the ability of the rebels to expand their territory. The difficulty Renamo had in trying to penetrate the southern regions of Mozambique was, according to some Renamo officials, frequently blamed on the geography and logistics of the area. According to Manning (1998, 168), Renamo officials repeatedly argued that the "absence of dense forests, and the drier, flatter terrain in southern Mozambique provided inhospitable territory for guerrilla bases, in comparison to the geography of the central region." Renamo's most sophisticated base, located at Casa Banana in the Gorongosa mountains, is described as a "dispersed settlement of huts covering several kilometers, under the cover of trees" with only a few entrances through paths "that were closely guarded" (Vines 1991, 85).

Tactics

Despite the transitional phases of Renamo—from a Rhodesian special operations unit, to a South African military proxy, to a self-sufficient domestic insurgency in the Mozambican countryside—its operational tactics remained fairly consistent over the duration of the conflict. Finnegan (1992, 237) describes Renamo's tactics as involving primarily "low-intensity warfare" with an emphasis on the complete devastation of governmental, social, and economic infrastructure in designated "destruction areas." These were zones considered important to the government or thought to be under Frelimo control. According to Alex Vines (1991, 87), the rebel group focused on the complete destruction of all property and facilities in a designated destruction area "so as to make government resettlement utterly unattractive, thereby, maintaining the vacated areas . . . ." Visiting a village that was recently destroyed in a Renamo attack, Finnegan (1992, 12) noted the methodical nature of the destruction: " . . . each tile of a mo-

saic smashed, each pane of a glass block wall painstakingly shattered. It was systematic, psychologically meticulous destruction. The only building in town with its roof untouched was the church." This focus on installations key to the regime also tended to force government resources into a defensive role in which protecting its property took precedence over conducting offensive strikes against rebel areas.

Despite the fact that Renamo tactics have led some scholars to characterize the group as merely "bent on mindless destruction and violence" (Manning 1998, 161), Renamo's "grand" strategy was to force a war of attrition with the government. By engaging in the wholesale destruction of everything important or beneficial to the government and the economy, the Frelimo regime would be weakened to the point of collapse—or, at the very least, forced to negotiate a power-sharing arrangement with the rebels. Finnegan describes Renamo's tactics as a "maximalist strategy, and a pure equation: that whatever weakened Frelimo strengthened Renamo" (1992, 77). In 1988, Renamo President Dhlakama stated frankly in an interview, "Our aim is not to win the war militarily . . . but to force Frelimo to accept negotiations for a democratically elected government" (quoted in Finnegan 1992, 79). As Cabrita (2000, 205) argues, "It was clear from the pattern of Renamo operations that its primary goal was to isolate the government from the rural areas . . . stifling its economic power base . . . ."

Renamo's tactics in target selection, in addition to its effectiveness in weakening and limiting government capabilities, also benefited the rebel group through the creation of a pillage economy. Renamo reportedly took anything and everything of value in a raid before destroying an area and then sold the loot in the markets of neighboring states. Goods included everything from dismantled and later reassembled Land Rover automobiles to smuggled elephant ivory. Touring a communal village destroyed in a Renamo attack, Finnegan noted that "every window, every window frame, every door, every door frame, every piece of plumbing or wiring or flooring had been ripped out and carried away" (1992, 11). A common Renamo practice was to kidnap a large number of peasants during these raids and use them as "porters" to carry the looted items hundreds of miles through the African bush to market, mostly in Malawi. Other abductees were taken back to Renamo camps and used as forced labor. Reportedly, if Renamo planned to stay in an area for any length of time, it would reinstall the local regulos or muenes, the petty chiefs used by the Portuguese as tax collectors and village overseers, who had not been well treated by Frelimo after independence.

The terror of Renamo's often theatrical and ritualized use of violence is itself another operational tactic used purposely to intimidate the civilian population upon which the rebels depended for material support and intelligence. Renamo used violence in ways that have repeatedly been referred to as "cultic" or "ritualized" in order to " . . . instill a paralyzing and incapacitating fear . . . ." in the civilian population and government troops through a " . . . maniacal devotion to the infliction of suffering" (Wilson 1992, 531). Renamo's tactics have been summarily characterized as a "grotesque campaign of terror" against mostly civilians, with a respective lack of any real "political program" (Manning 1998, 161). Such atrocities included the forced participation of relatives in the murder of their own family members, mass rape, and people being crushed in millet grinders or boiled alive. Other unimaginable acts of torture were used, such as facial and bodily mutilation which made the victim a lifelong advertisement for the consequences of resistance (see Wilson 1992).

These tactics led many to consider Renamo the "most brutal rebel army" of their time (Itano 2002, 8). As Vines (1991, 1), argues, "What makes Renamo so different from most successful rebel movements is that the equation between popular support and rebel strength does not generally apply." Renamo's use of violence against noncombatants and their apparent lack of any ideological "hearts-and-minds campaign"

to win over peasant support led to a significantly negative international reputation around the mid-1980s, leading some scholars, such as Geffray (1990, 119), to characterize them as nothing more than a "parasite army" that was only interested in " . . . manufacturing war to subsist by it . . . ." (1990, 120). Nevertheless, the use of widespread violence against civilians was a consistently used and apparently successful operational tactic for Renamo in waging " . . . brutal, but effective, psychological warfare . . . ." (Vines 1991, 90).

Causes of the War

Although the rise of Renamo and the group's early funding can be attributed to interventionist tactics by Rhodesia and South Africa, these external sources of support began to decline in the early 1980s. The Renamo sponsors in Zimbabwe were now out of power, and Frelimo president Samora Machel and South African President P. W. Botha signed the N'komati Agreement in March 1984, halting support to the ANC by one side and to Renamo by the other. It was alleged that South African Special Forces continued some covert support to Renamo after the agreement was signed, but according to postwar interviews with Renamo leaders and officials, the agreement served "as a catalyst to force Renamo to establish itself as an organization in its own right" (Manning 1998, 163) and led to the relocation of rebel headquarters from Phalaborwa (South Africa) to the Gorongosa mountains of Mozambique.

After sponsorship from South Africa had begun to wane, Renamo grew from an externally funded and controlled military surrogate to a pervasive domestic rebellion with support in recruitment, food, and shelter stemming largely from the Mozambique countryside. Alex Vines (1991, 2) notes that "while Renamo was initially trained by Rhodesia, and later by South Africa, it evolved its own style once it operated in the Mozambican bush." Following the N'komati accords, Renamo sought to aggressively expand its operations outside of Sopala and Manica, their central regional heartland, into the northern and southern provinces, to become a self-sustaining force embedded in rural Mozambique. According to interviews with district-level Renamo officials, more than half said they were recruited between 1984 and 1986 to serve as political representatives "in the bush," whereas most of the military leadership was recruited much earlier, in 1979 and 1980 (Manning 1998, 163). By the mid-1980s, Renamo was operating in all ten provinces in Mozambique and had an estimated 20,000 soldiers (Vines 1991, 1).

What accounts for Renamo's success as a rebel group and the resulting protracted civil war against the government of Mozambique? Vines (1991, 74) notes a "paradigm shift" in the scholarly literature on the Mozambican crisis in the mid-1980s "away from the causality... being South African destabilization with the emphases being shifted to a focus on Frelimo's agrarian polices...." By and large, Renamo's expanding levels of support throughout the 1980s is attributed to several largely domestic sources: (a) policies of the Frelimo government, particularly toward traditional agriculture and religion; (b) regional and ethnic divisions within Frelimo and Mozambique; and (c) the attraction of young, impoverished Mozambican boys to the lifestyle of a Renamo rebel.

Renamo was especially apt at maneuvering to capitalize on collective discontent generated by Frelimo policies and orientations that were widely considered disruptive and nontraditional. Frelimo's embrace of socialist projects after independence produced a general disregard for traditional authority figures, such as village chiefs. In an interview in 1988, Mozambique's Minister of Culture Luis Honwana commented on the mistakes the Frelimo government made regarding the indigenous authority structure: "We didn't realize how influential the traditional authorities were; even without formal power.... We will have to restore some of the traditional structures that at the beginning of our independence we simply smashed...." (quoted in Finnegan 1992, 125).

Postindependence Frelimo policies and orientations, especially with regard to agriculture and freedom of religion, brought sudden and radical changes to members of a traditionally bound society. Peasants were forced to abandon their private subsistence plots to work in state-run collective farms and villages. Overall, these collective projects, which were intended to enhance the ailing state sector, were hugely unsuccessful, "marred by misjudgment, misuse and squandering of the large amount of investment put into them." Consequently, they were quite unpopular with the peasants involved (Vines 1991, 115). Renamo made no small effort to exploit these rural grievances by promoting and encouraging angry peasants to resist the state and return to their traditional ways. The governor of Manica province (an area that would later become a Renamo stronghold), commenting on his projects in 1981, stated in frustration that "... peasants are individualistic... they think that all collective life must be bad. The resistance movement [Renamo] has built on this, encouraging people to live in the traditional way... many families have at least one member fighting for MNR" (quoted in Vines 1991, 117).

The government also attempted to widen the agricultural base and decrease urban unemployment in what amounted to a colossal policy mistake called Operation Production, under which approximately 50,000 unemployed city dwellers were forcefully transported to underdeveloped areas of the countryside, dropped off, and told to start farming. Cabrita (2000, 216) notes that five years after Operation Production, there were some people were still trying to locate relatives evacuated in the program. The project was later referred to by Frelimo officials as "a successful recruiting program for the bandits" (Finnegan 1992, 69).

Stemming from its self-perception as a modernizing, leftist regime, the Frelimo government also engaged in considerable repression of religious activity, whereas the majority of the Mozambican population believed in some form of traditional religion. Due to perceived associations with colonialism and indigenous authority structures, the government considered religion a disruptive influence. Party members were not allowed to belong to a church, and traditional spiritual healers were not allowed party membership. According to Finnegan, like the petty chiefs, religious authority figures " . . . were merely pushed aside by the new government" (1992, 64). Cabrita (2000, 121) reports that an estimated 7,000 practicing Jehovah's Witnesses in Mozambique were arrested and sent to reeducation camps for "serving the imperialist powers" with their missionary work.

Renamo, on the other hand, used traditional religious figures extensively in its organization, both to win the support of the peasantry and for protection through spiritual power. The role of spiritual beliefs has been repeatedly emphasized in the literature for its influential role in the Mozambican conflict, particularly in Renamo's identity construction and the belief it was fighting a "war of spirits" against Frelimo (Lauriciano 1990, 9). Much of Renamo's perceived success among the peasantry is said to be rooted in the group's spiritual powers, especially among the ethnic N'dau, who are considered one of the most feared and spiritually powerful tribes in Mozambique. Renamo's embrace of religion also had a very practical side, giving it a psychological advantage in warfare and in attracting support from religious groups. As one local Mozambican preacher stated, " . . . at least Renamo does not stop us from worshipping God . . ." (quoted in Vines 1991, 102). Frelimo's lack of respect for religious belief and lack of support for small farmers generated significant anti-regime sentiment and resulted in an increased presence of Renamo in rural areas.

Much of the sympathy for Renamo is also said to be rooted in "regional/ethnic tensions and imbalances" within Mozambique, dating back to independence and the belief that Frelimo was not truly representative of Mozambican society and that its policies were "ethnically biased as a result" (Morgan 1990, 614). The belief that Frelimo was dominated by Shangaan-speaking southerners of disproportionately mestizo background, combined with Frelimo's tendency to move southerners into positions of authority outside the south, created resentment among many in the northern and central regions of Mozambique.

Ethnic division did exist between the largely southern, Shangaan-speaking Frelimo and the centrally based, Shona-speaking N'dau rebels, but the ethnic divide was largely a by-product of Renamo's founding around the ancestral homeland of the N'dau peoples. Vines (1991, 84) notes that "Rhodesian recruitment of the N'dau, was not, as some commentators have speculated, calculated planning but due to the geographical location of the N'dau along the Rhodesian border." Moreover, several popular data sets used in the study of civil war agree that the Mozambican case was not based primarily on ethnic conflict. Licklider (1995) considers the Mozambican civil war primarily to have been fought over "political/economic" rather than "identity" issues. Similarly, Sambanis (2000) also considers the war as one fought over largely political identities. As in many African conflicts, ethnic politics in Mozambique often reinforced the conflict, although it was not the master or primary cleavage between the rebels and the government.

Last, and perhaps the least studied dynamic explaining Renamo's success, was the attraction of the rebel lifestyle for young, impoverished Mozambican boys. Research discussed by Manning (1998) on Renamo recruitment suggests that the majority of the rank and file who stayed with Renamo throughout most of the war were highly disproportionately poor, uneducated country boys. Those villagers who were economically better off would have been better able to use their resources either to avoid the rebels or to negotiate. For many recruits, the benefits of being Renamo warriors greatly exceeded anything they could have hoped to achieve as peasant farmers in perhaps the poorest country in the world. At the very least they were better fed. Geffray (1990) argues that Renamo made the boys peers and equals in an autonomous, independent social group that provided freedom, fraternity, and social advancement. This lifestyle stood in stark contrast to the dull servitude and domination by tribal elders and petty government officials that characterized life in their former villages. As Finnegan notes, there clearly was talk of the "dirty little secret" that being a Renamo warrior might be fun. Finnegan (1992, 71) describes the account of a kidnapped Angolan mechanic who, after his escape, referred to the rebels he lived with as "having themselves a hell of a time." According to the interviewee, the rebel boys in his camp got high on marijuana, got drunk on beer, and spent most of their days racing stolen motorcycles on homemade racetracks through the African bush.

Outcome
Conflict Status

On October 4, 1992, Frelimo president and Renamo leaders signed the General Peace Agreement (GPA), which effectively ended the civil war in Mozambique. Although 1992 was described as a year of intense fighting, very little

---

Mozambique and Civil War Duration

Only a handful of civil wars in the last fifty years have lasted longer than the sixteen-year conflict in Mozambique. In fact, more than 80 percent of all the terminated civil wars listed in the Correlates of War Project civil war data file (Sarkees 2000) lasted less than 2,000 days (roughly five years). Further, 50 percent lasted less than 500 days (roughly a year and a half), and 25 percent lasted less than a month.

---

violence was reported after the settlement and the start of the UN demobilization and reintegration programs in the same year. Very few cases of general violence have been reported since 1993, giving a strong confirmation of the success of the agreement.

The success of the 1992 accords was perhaps surprising in that the conflict represented, in many respects, an unlikely case for settlement. The two sides had antagonistic roots, reinforced by regional and ethnic hostilities, that went back to colonial rule, and they were engaged in one of the longest, deadliest civil wars of the modern era. There were indicators, however, that motivation and resources were running low in both camps. As early as 1988, officials from the Catholic Church who met privately with Renamo leaders under the auspices of the Peace and Reconciliation Commission thought that Renamo was "serious about wanting to end the war" (Vines 1991, 122). Similarly, Vines argues that, as early as 1983, the Frelimo government had stated in session that it could not defeat the rebels militarily and were going to have to negotiate to end the war and attempted to do just that in the 1984 Pretoria talks. The Frelimo government had nearly abandoned its Marxist ideology by the end of the 1980s and announced in 1990 plans for a liberal democratic constitution that included nearly everything Renamo had supposedly been fighting for: multiparty elections, freedom of religion and association, and an elected executive. Chan and Venancio (1998)

Mozambique and Civil War Deaths

In direct correlation with its length, the civil war in Mozambique is also among the deadliest of modern civil wars. Of the 11,477,830 total battle deaths resulting from civil war since 1945 (obtained by summing the total deaths of every war reported in the Correlates of War Project civil war data file), more than 50 percent (5,800,550) occurred in just five civil wars: Nigeria, China, Mozambique, Sudan, and Afghanistan. Sarkees (2000) reports 1,200,550 total deaths from the Mozambican civil war, making it the third-deadliest conflict in the modern era. In contrast, 80 percent of the post-1945 civil wars experienced fewer than 100,000 deaths per war, whereas 50 percent of the civil wars experienced fewer than 12,000 deaths, and 25 percent of the conflicts experienced fewer than 3,000 deaths.

attribute the timing of the agreement to southern Africa's worst drought in three decades, which seriously affected rebel stronghold areas in central Mozambique. Therefore, as resources for both groups began to dry up, so did the ideological basis of the war.

Walter (1999) argues that the negotiations in the early 1990s not only satisfied the major grievances of both parties but also produced some security guarantees that had not been attainable in prior negotiations. Because Renamo leaders did not trust government officials or view their promises as credible, they wanted such credible guarantees as third-party mediation and dual administrative control of the military to protect themselves during and after the negotiation process. In August 1991, after an initial rejection of outside intervention (particularly United Nations involvement) by the Frelimo government, negotiations resumed in November of the same year, when the government finally agreed to third-party involvement and a new dual national military comprising 15,000 Renamo troops and 15,000 Frelimo troops.

Although the next two rounds of elections from 1992 to 1999, which produced a Frelimo president and parliamentary majority, were considered fraudulent by Renamo, there was no resumption of civil war in Mozambique. As of 2005, thirteen years since the 1992 negotiated settlement laid the structural groundwork for ending the civil war and starting a new multiparty democracy in Mozambique, the prospect for sustained peace remains generally high. Writing on Mozambique's experience with democratic transition, Lala and Ostheimer report that "[t]he outbreak of large-scale violent conflict in Mozambique seems rather unlikely . . . . the ability to mobilize people on a large scale appears to be limited nowadays. Mozambicans are more interested in securing their daily economic survival . . . ." (2003, 65).

Duration Tactics

The civil war between the Frelimo government and Renamo rebels in Mozambique was a particularly long one relative to most civil wars. Worldwide, only a handful of civil wars have lasted longer than the sixteen-year Mozambican conflict. Why did the civil war in Mozambique last so long? Much of the answer has to do with (a) the ability of Renamo to meet its material needs through control of the local peasantry and the creation of a pillage economy, and (b) the inability of the Frelimo state and Mozambican military to penetrate the countryside and effectively target Renamo strongholds.

Renamo is frequently referred to or characterized as a "captive army," made up of a significant number of recruits who were coerced into service after being taken prisoner in civilian raids. This dynamic has been difficult for scholars of revolution and rebellion to understand. How can an effective rebel army be constructed from involuntary members, prisoners, or captives? The literature on Renamo suggests several possible answers to this question. First, Vines (1991) notes that many of Renamo's "coerced combatants" were afraid to escape and go home, for fear of retribution for their participation in the kind of atrocities for which Renamo was famous. Second, it was common for Renamo to relocate coerced recruits away from their homeland in areas of different linguistic dialects; this presumably would make it more difficult to escape. Third, several scholars (see Geffray 1990; Manning 1998; Vines 1991) note that, after their initial involuntary introduction, many recruits—even forced ones—realized that the lifestyle of a Renamo warrior was an improvement over what they had before. Forced recruits, especially children, having little to no education or work experience and thus lacking social networks in civilian life to return to, more than likely served Renamo until the war ended.

There is also the hypothesis that much of Renamo's membership was actually voluntary, rooted in anti-Frelimo activism or selective incentives, and that the high degree of coercion associated with Renamo recruitment may be an exaggeration that explains Renamo's success without attributing it to widespread discontent with the government. Presumably, it would be easier and also perhaps safer for a rebel seeking amnesty and trying to return to a normal civilian life to say, when being interviewed, that he was a forced recruit. One can understand how a reasonable interviewee would expect differential treatment from either the government or society, depending on whether he is viewed as a victim of civil war or a perpetrator of it. That is not to say that Renamo's practice of taking civilian captives was not a regular phenomenon, but that the prominence of forced recruitment absolves both the individual rebel and the government of responsibility for Renamo's success. This theory also goes a long way in explaining how an army of "forced recruits" emerged as a dominant political party after the settlement in 1992, losing the presidency by a small margin and winning 112 parliamentary seats (compared to Frelimo's 129 seats). Obviously, a substantial segment of the population supported the rebels.

The other side of Renamo's prolonged success in rural Mozambique is rooted in the weakness of the Frelimo regime and the inability of its national military to penetrate and control peripheral areas beyond the close reach of the capital. Not coincidently, Renamo made those regions its primary areas of activity. Administratively, the Frelimo government tended to "operate sporadically" outside of major cities, with a limited presence in the countryside (Morgan 1990, 615). More important are the consequences of Mozambique's weak state syndrome for the ability of its national military to deal effectively with the rebel threat. Those efforts have been characterized as seriously lacking in expertise, material support, and troop morale. The national military was described during the conflict as an "undertrained, underequipped, underpaid, and underfed" group of soldiers engaging in irregular seasonal offensives against Renamo areas where the rebels would largely just flee the area (Finnegan 1992, 56).

According to Morgan (1990, 616), the weakness of the military stemmed from its conventional military approach to the war and from

" . . . problems existing at the level of morale and logistics." An aid worker interviewed by Finnegan summarized the situation well: " . . . [I]t's physically impossible for the army to guard this country . . . they say it takes twelve soldiers to guard one kilometer of infrastructure, on average . . . . that would require over a million men just for defense, and that's not to mention going out and fighting" (1992, 95). Touring the Manhica province with a Frelimo official, Finnegan recalled, "It occurred to me that if the entire army were brought to the Manhica district—which constituted less than 1 percent of Mozambique's area—its 30,000 soldiers *might* have a chance of actually securing the district, of making it safe for the people who lived there" (1992, 211). The Mozambique Armed Forces (FAM), despite significant foreign intervention and assistance, were never able to contain Renamo within a particular geographic area or even to keep the group inside Mozambique. This made it very difficult to separate Renamo from the civilian population that nearly always surrounded them. In order to use heavy artillery against Renamo, the national military would attempt to separate the rebels from civilian areas and drive them into evacuated territory. This usually produced poor results and heavy civilian casualties. In short, FAM was unable to sustain a level of combat that could defeat the rebels.

External Military Intervention

A significant degree of external intervention by neighboring states took place in the course of the Mozambican civil war. Although Rhodesia was responsible for Renamo's initial creation, after 1980 the same country, now Zimbabwe, provided the Frelimo government quite a bit of military help in combating the rebel group. In 1982, Zimbabwe assisted Mozambique with the deployment of around 1,000 troops to help the Frelimo regime protect vital government installations and infrastructure along the Beira corridor, an economic zone of roads, rail lines, and pipelines connecting Zimbabwe to the port at

Beira. The corridor was critical to the Zimbabwean economy. As Renamo activities increasingly focused on the destruction of Beira facilities, Zimbabwe increased its troop levels in Mozambique to around 3,000. In 1985, Zimbabwean National Army (ZNA) paratroopers (commanded by former Rhodesian CIO officials) led an assault that captured Renamo's main base in Gorongosa. Throughout 1987 and 1988, Zimbabwean troops gave considerable support to FAM counteroffensive efforts to regain ground in central Mozambique. In 1991, an estimated 10,000 Zimbabwean troops operated on Mozambican soil (Vines 1991, 61).

According to Cabrita (2000, 235), direct intervention by Zimbabwe and Tanzania was "...decisive in containing, and in some instances reversing, the Renamo threat, notably in central and northern Mozambique." The most damaging ZNA tactic was the use of "pseudo guerrillas," who traveled through areas of known Renamo activity locating camps and reporting their locations for air strikes and mortar attacks. According to Cabrita (2000), however, the biggest threat to Renamo from ZNA tactics was the resulting displacement of the villagers living around the Renamo camps, which consequently destroyed the support base the rebels had created among the civilian population.

Several other states either provided military advisors or assisted the Mozambican military in training counterinsurgency units. The Soviets had an estimated 1,000 military advisors in Mozambique as of 1989 and, according to Cabrita (2000, 206), provided most of the planning, ammunitions, and logistical support for FAM counteroffensives in the mid-1980s. Britain's Military Advisory and Training Team (BMATT), also provided military advisorship and helped train at least two Mozambican counterinsurgency battalions from bases in Zimbabwe between 1986 and 1990 (Vines 1991, 51). Although Cuba is mentioned as providing military advisors, Cabrita (2000, 172) reports some combat assistance resulting in the deaths of several Cuban soldiers in June 1980. The Frelimo government also sought considerable assistance from the United States, especially under President Chissano. Despite the Reagan Doctrine, by which the United States would lend support to resistance movements against pro-Soviet, Communist regimes, the Frelimo government and Mozambique were the largest recipients of U.S. economic aid in all of sub-Saharan Africa under both the Reagan and Bush administrations (Cabrita 2000, 250).

Although Renamo received no external assistance on the battlefield, the rebels did have a highly extensive and diversified "external wing" that engaged in international fund-raising. Renamo's external wing was also responsible for the dissemination of propaganda designed to improve the group's image and to advertise their struggle to potential supporters and financial backers around the world. As Finnegan reports (1992, 33), "Pretoria was not Renamo's only source of external support. Portuguese ex-colonials living in South Africa, Portugal, Malawi, and Brazil, including wealthy businessmen who had lost property when independence came to Mozambique, contributed heavily." Renamo leaders visited Europe extensively to meet with right-wing groups in Portugal, West Germany, and France, seeking their support in fighting the Communist threat. By the late 1980s, however, Renamo tactics, made known in the State Department's Gersony Report and in media accounts of such atrocities as the Homoine massacre in July 1987, in which 424 civilians were killed, led to a significant decline in international support. By 1987, Renamo had essentially "lost the propaganda war" (Finnegan 1992, 35).

Conflict Management Efforts

Following the settlement of the war, the bulk of conflict management efforts fell under the jurisdiction of the United Nations. The General Peace Agreement signed by both parties called for a UN supervised cease-fire, election monitoring, demobilization of soldiers, and general humanitarian assistance. In one of his first tasks, Aldo Ajello, the UN's special representative for postwar Mozambique, formed the Supervision and Control Commission (CSC). It was composed of Ajello as chair, along with representatives from Renamo, Frelimo, Italy, Portugal, France, Britain and the United States. The CSC became the central governing body overseeing the implementation of the entire peace agreement. On November 4, 1992, the CSC created several specialized subsidiary groups, including the Cease-Fire Commission, the Commission for the Reintegration of Demobilizing Military Personnel, and the Joint Commission of the Mozambican Defense Force, which would form the core of ONUMOZ (the United Nations Operation in Mozambique; Alden 1995).

In the year following the agreement, Mozambique received more than $1 billion in international aid and more than $700 million from related UN agencies. ONUMOZ consisted of 6,000 military troops from twenty-two countries. Nearly 1,000 official observers governed forty-nine military demobilization sites supervising the transition and conversion of the former combatants into political participants (Msabaha 1995, 224). International observers from many countries helped to monitor the country's first round of elections, which were deemed relatively free and fair. Eighty-five percent of Mozambicans voted in the election, and Frelimo President Chissano beat Renamo's presidential candidate Dhlakama by a close margin. Despite significant delays by some of the subsidiary commissions in fulfilling their tasks and the myriad problems to be expected with such an immense project, the postsettlement management of the Mozambican civil war has since been referred to as the United Nations' "only post conflict success story in Africa" (Manning 2002, 4).

Conclusion

The civil war in Mozambique is an extremely rich case in terms of the unique challenges facing postcolonial societies, the political processes leading to postcolonial civil wars, and the self-perpetuating etiology of structure and agency in lengthy, protracted conflicts. As in most of sub-Sahara Africa, the postcolonial state in Mozambique contained many seeds of internal conflict rooted primarily in postcolonial power struggles and the inability of a new state to control and administer its territory or to consolidate a monopoly on the use of military violence. Once organized by the destabilization efforts of neighboring states, anti-Frelimo opposition in Mozambique, led by Renamo, was sustained and fed by new conflicts and incompatibilities created by a weak state attempting to impose itself on a strong and resisting society. State–society relations under Frelimo reflected nearly mutually exclusive interests (subsistence agriculture versus centralized economic planning; indigenous authority structure versus state power and bureaucracy; traditional religious beliefs versus party ideology), and these cleavages generated significant antistate sentiment, particularly in the countryside.

Renamo's beginnings and growth as a rebel insurgency in Mozambique is an excellent example of the interaction of state behavior and rebel group success. In Mozambique, anti-Frelimo opposition was created when, after independence, significant numbers of Mozambicans became political enemies of the state, based largely on former colonial ties. At the most abstract level, the civil war in Mozambique was caused by a system of dual sovereignty and mutual excludability generated by decolonization and subsequent power struggles, one of the primary causes of civil wars in Africa, according to Zartman (1995). This raises important theoretical implications regarding the extent to which governments create their own resistance movements through policies of political exclusion and repression. Being anti-Frelimo was not only an ideology to be adopted by disgruntled or disillusioned Mozambicans; it was imposed by the Frelimo regime on certain groups or segments of society, many with former military training. Had the Frelimo government, after independence, exonerated those Mozambicans that helped defend the colonial system, presumably there would not have been a mass exodus from Mozambique of those best trained and ideologically predisposed to become Renamo. Probably the largest mistake made by the regime was not allowing those Mozambicans who fought for the Portuguese to join the new (Frelimo) national army after independence.

Cabrita (2000) has suggested that, given the totalitarian nature of the Frelimo regime and its choice to challenge Rhodesia and South Africa by supporting and providing sanctuary to the guerrilla movements that sought to overthrow them, the creation and growth of anti-Frelimo opposition was inevitable. By engaging in mass political exclusion and repression of large segments of its population and by assisting insurgency movements that threatened the national security of neighboring states, the Frelimo government provoked interventionist tactics by neighboring states geared toward the destruction of the regime—goals that happened to mirror those of thousands of Mozambicans who wanted to win back a previous way of life.

The Mozambican case also stands out as a source of optimism and a model for scholars and policy makers interested both in how to achieve an unlikely peace with settlements based on democratization and security guarantees and in how to sustain that peace in the postconflict environment. As a case study, Mozambique is not only one of the few cases in which democratization has been the backbone of a general peace agreement and postwar peace process, it is also one of the few successful ones. Although the initial postwar environment was described as a very "delicate peace" (Alden and Simpson 1993, 1) in perhaps the poorest, least-developed nation in the world, within ten years of the settlement, Mozambique was described as having a "booming" economy with respect to southern Africa. Its postwar rehabilitation effort has been held up as a "model for Afghanistan" and other war-torn states (Itano 2002, 1). In the last decade, Renamo has successfully become a mainstream political party, receiving more than 40 percent of the popular vote in two rounds of general elections and retaining a "high level of popularity, especially among the more isolated rural populations of the north and centre, which feel marginalized by Frelimo policies" (EIU Views Wire 2003, 1).

J. Michael Quinn

Chronology

September 1964   Anticolonial insurgents under Frelimo begin decade-long struggle against Portuguese colonial rule in Mozambique.

April 25, 1974   Military coup in Portugal ends dictatorial rule of Antonio Salazar; new military government begins plans to end Portuguese colonialism.

September 7, 1974   With the signing of the Lusaka Agreement, Portugal signs over the governance of Mozambique to Frelimo transitional government, ending 400 years of colonial rule. Frelimo Mozambique a Marxist-Leninist, one-party state. Thousands of Mozambicans with close ties to the former Portuguese state flee into neighboring Rhodesia and South Africa in fear of retribution by the new government.

1976   In response to Mozambique's support of Zanla rebels and the closing of its border with Rhodesia, members of the Rhodesian military organize Renamo. Andre Matsangaissa, Frelimo military leader sentenced to reeducation camp, flees to Rhodesia and becomes leader of Renamo.

1979   The Mozambique Armed Forces (FAM) attack the Gorongosa mountain bases of Renamo; Andre Matsangaissa is killed. Power struggle begins within Renamo over who will lead the organization. Alfonso Dhlakama prevails, remains leader throughout rest of war.

April 18, 1980   Following multiracial elections ending white minority rule in Rhodesia, state becomes Republic of Zimbabwe, leaving Renamo without a sponsor. South Africa fills this void, becoming primary supporter of Renamo to combat the increased use by the ANC (African National Congress) of infiltration routes into South Africa through southern Mozambique. By 1982, Renamo is operating in nine out of ten Mozambican provinces (Vines 1991, 17).

1982   Zimbabwe sends 1,000 troops to help Frelimo protect Beira corridor, Zimbabwe's vital economic connection to the sea, from repeated Renamo attacks. Increased to 3,000 troops by 1984 and 10,000 by war's end.

March 16, 1984 In the town of N'komati, Frelimo President Samora Machel and South African President P. K. Botha sign Agreement on Non-Aggression and Good Neighborliness, ending South Africa's support to Renamo in exchange for ceased Frelimo support of the ANC.

May 1984 South Africa arranges meeting between Frelimo leaders and Evo Fernades, first secretary general of Renamo, in Frankfurt. Frelimo offers the first of its amnesty programs to the rebels in exchange for peace but does not agree to a multiparty system and top government positions for Renamo leaders.

October 14–18,1984 Further talks between Frelimo and Renamo leaders in Pretoria do not produce an agreement. Renamo's demands include dissolution of Frelimo government, multiparty elections, and withdrawal of all foreign troops from Mozambican soil. Talks end in a Renamo walk-out after South African President "Pik" Botha is accused of favoring the "communist regime." After the talks, Machel takes a significantly tougher public stance toward rebels, stating that he would "wipe them out and that day is not far off" (Vines 1991, 23).

1985–1987 Periods of violence peak as Renamo grows, aggressively expands campaign into northern and southern provinces of Mozambique.

October 19, 1986 Frelimo leader Samora Machel dies in plane crash. Joaquim Chissano becomes new president of Mozambique.

1988 Catholic Church officials with government support from Zimbabwe, Malawi, and South Africa try to start a negotiation process between Frelimo and Renamo leaders.

1989 Renamo and Frelimo have several indirect talks supported by Italy, Portugal, the United States, and United Nations officials.

January 9, 1990 President Chissano announces proposals for constitutional reform and elections for Mozambique. Specifically, a revised and more liberal constitution would be drafted, paving the way for elections in 1991.

November 30, 1990 New Mozambique constitution takes effect, making the country an official multiparty political system.

October 4, 1992 Final negotiations in Rome hosted by the Catholic Church institution of Saint Egidio result in the signing of General Peace Agreement between Renamo and Frelimo, ending sixteen-year civil war. Under the agreement, Mozambique becomes a multiparty state, with Frelimo and Renamo competing in new elections as major political parties.

List of Acronyms

ANC: African National Congress
BMATT: British Military Advisory and Training Team
CIO: Rhodesian Central Intelligence Organization
CSC: Supervision and Control Commission
DGS: Portuguese General Security Directorate
FAM: Mozambique Armed Forces
Frelimo: Front for the Liberation of Mozambique
GPA: General Peace Agreement
ONUMOZ: The United Nations Operation in Mozambique
Renamo: Mozambique National Resistance
UNICEF: United Nations Children's Fund
Zanla: Zimbabwean National Liberation Army
ZNA: Zimbabwean National Army

Glossary

assimilado: A Portuguese word meaning "assimilated native."
regulos: The Portuguese word for the petty chiefs used by the Portuguese and later by Renamo to administer the villages.

References

Alden, Chris. 1995. "The UN and the Resolution of Conflict in Mozambique." *The Journal of Modern African Studies* 33(1): 103–28.

Cabrita, Joao M. 2000. *Mozambique: The Tortuous Road to Democracy.* New York: Palgrave.

Chan, Stephen, and Moises Vanancio. 1998. *War and Peace in Mozambique.* New York: St. Martin's Press.

Clement, Henry M., and Robert Springborg. 2001. *Globalization and the Politics of Development in the Middle East.* Cambridge, UK: Cambridge University Press.

EIU Views Wire. 2003. "Mozambique: Political Forces." December 15. www.viewswire.com/search.asp?action=quick&mode=quick&sService=vw&sText=mozambique&sServiceId=930000293&x=25&y=9.

Fearon, James D., and David D. Laitin. 2003. "Ethnicity, Insurgency, and Civil War." *American Political Science Review* 97(1): 75–90.

Finnegan, William. 1992. *A Complicated War: The Harrowing of Mozambique.* Berkeley, CA: University of California Press.

Flower, Ken. 1987. *Serving Secretly: An Intelligence Chief on Record, Rhodesia into Zimbabwe, 1964 to 1981.* London: Murray.

Geffray, C. 1991. *A Causa das Armas: Antropologia da Guerra Contemporanea em Mozambique.* Edicoes Afrontamento, Portugal: Porto.

Itano, Nicole. 2002. "Lessons for Afghanistan from Mozambique." *Christian Science Monitor* (April 12): 8.

Jaggers, Keith, and Monty G. Marshall. 2000. "Polity IV Project: 2000 Update." www.bsos.umd.edu/cidcm/inscr/polity (accessed December 21, 2006).

Lala, Anicia, and E. Andrea Ostheimer. 2003. "How to Remove the Stains on Mozambique's Democratic Track Record: Challenges for the Democratization Process Between 1990 and 2003." Occasional paper. December. Konrad-Adenauer-Stiftung: South Africa. www.kas.de (accessed July 2005).

Lauriciano, G. 1990. "Spiritual Revolution: Another Revolution in the Countryside." *Domingo (Maputo)* (September 9).

Licklider, Roy. 1995. "The Consequences of Negotiated Settlements in Civil Wars, 1945–1993." *American Political Science Review* 89(3): 681–90.

MacFarquhar, Emily. 1988. "The Killing Fields of Mozambique," *U.S. News & World Report,* May 2: 45

Manning, Carrie. 1998. "Constructing Opposition in Mozambique: Renamo as Political Party."

Journal of Southern African Studies 24(1):161–89.

Manning, Carrie. 2002. *The Politics of Peace in Mozambique: Post-Conflict Democratization, 1992–2000.* Westport, CT: Praeger.

Morgan, Glenda. 1990. "Violence in Mozambique: Towards an Understanding of Renamo." *Journal of Modern Africa Studies* 28(4): 603–19.

Msabaha, Ibrahim. 1995. "Negotiating an End to Mozambique's Murderous Rebellion." In *Elusive Peace: Negotiating an End to Civil Wars,* edited by I. William Zartman. Washington, DC: The Brookings Institute.

Plank, David N. 1993. "Aid, Debt, and the End of Sovereignty: Mozambique and Its Donors." *Journal of Modern African Studies* 31(3): 407–30.

Sambanis, Nicholas. 2000. "Partition as a Solution to Ethnic War: An Empirical Critique of the Theoretical Literature." *World Politics* 52(July): 437–83.

Sarkees, Meredith Reid. 2000. "The Correlates of War Data on War: An Update to 1997." *Conflict Management and Peace Science,* 18(1): 123–144.

Vines, Alex. 1991. *Renamo: Terrorism in Mozambique.* Bloomington: Indiana University Press.

Walter, Barbara. 1999. "Designing Transitions from Civil War: Demobilization, Democratization, and Commitments to Peace." *International Security* 24(1): 127.

Wilson, K. B. 1992. "Cults of Violence and Counter-Violence in Mozambique." *Journal of Southern African Studies* 18(3): 527–82.

Zartman, I. William. 1995. *Elusive Peace: Negotiating an End to Civil Wars.* Washington, DC: The Brookings Institute.

Myanmar/Burma (1968–1995)

Introduction

On May 27, 1989, the official name of Burma was changed to the Union of Myanmar by the ruling State Law and Order Restoration Committee (SLORC). Although the change has been recognized by the United Nations, many ethnic minorities and opposition parties have rejected the new name. In this article, the two names are used interchangeably, but *Burma* is used in reference to events during the period prior to June 1989, whereas *Myanmar* is used for events after that date. Further, this article follows the precedent of the majority of scholars studying the country, for whom *Burman* is an ethnic term identifying a particular group in Burma, whereas *Burmese* is a political term including all the inhabitants of the country—Burman, Karen, Shan, and so forth.

The sparse news coverage from Myanmar in the last decade has largely focused on the weak democracy movement in a country ruled by an authoritarian military government. Following months of political protests, student-led demonstrations were brutally repressed by the armed forces in September 1988. These events and the reluctance of the government to accept the election results two years later have been criticized on a global scale; and sanctions have been imposed by such powers as the United States and the European Union. This has not led to a change in government policy, but the democracy movement, led by Nobel Prize–winner Aung San Syy Kyi, has maintained its struggle by nonviolent means.

The civil war in Myanmar/Burma has been fought between government forces and numerous different rebel forces for decades. The war, which actually consists of several different, intertwined conflicts, has effectively halted the economic development of the country since independence and has affected generations of Burmese people. The complexity of this war can hardly be exaggerated; it has included a socialist government fighting socialist rebels, different rebel groups fighting each other over control of resources while simultaneously trying to establish unified fronts against the government, and local warlords who shift allegiances from rebels to pro-government militias and back to rebels again.

Many of the causes of the civil were evident even before the country became independent in 1949, and several rebel organizations started their armed struggles even earlier, but this article focuses on the period of intense fighting in the years 1968–1995. During that period, it is estimated that at least 267,500 people were killed, and more than 1.3 million Burmese became refugees. It should be noted that these estimates are notoriously unreliable, as the government has deliberately restricted access to information, especially in conflict areas. Fighting has been accompanied by severe atrocities

Drugs, Wars, and "Wars" on Drugs

The production and use of drugs in the Burmese hills have a long tradition. Cannabis has been grown since at least 1000 BC and opiates since the ninth century AD. Commercial production was expanded during the lucrative British–Chinese opium trade in the nineteenth century, especially in the area that later became known as the Golden Triangle. Many ethnic Kokang Chinese began growing opium instead of tea in the territory between Chinese Yunnan province and the Shan state of Hsenwi. Later, the planting of poppies led to colonization of the previously unadministered Wa hills, and by the year 1900, opium had become the official currency of the region. Chinese and international attempts to suppress the international drug trade caused a large number of producers to migrate from Yunnan into the Kachin and Shan hills during the first decades of the twentieth century.

The economic and political power of poppy cultivation in these areas was undisputed—in 1940, opium was more valuable than silver—and the control of the drugs income was significant for rebel and government armies during the war. When the Chinese civil war ended in 1949, the fleeing KMT settled in Burma and developed more institutionalized trade links with outside actors. The Burmese drug trade mainly consisted of local merchants, who bought opium from peasants before transporting it to the Thai border and paying protection tax to different rebel groups and local military officers. On the border, the opium was bought and refined by Chinese crime syndicates allied with local warlords such as Khun Sa. These warlords established substantial armies, which at times claimed to be ethnic rebels and at times government militias. As rebel strength decreased after the breakdown of the CPB in 1989, Burmese opium production soared from 400–600 tons a year to 2,340 tons in 1995. At the same time, new refineries were established closer to the Chinese border, in the Kokang and Wa areas under the control of groups that had signed cease-fire agreements with the government.

The international community, especially the U.S. Drug Enforcement Agency (DEA), has provided aid to the Burmese government in attempts to fight drug trafficking. Starting in 1972, the United States donated helicopters to the Burma Army with the intent of intercepting opium caravans; this type of measure continued until 1988. The resources provided, especially as part of a U.S.-sponsored program in 1985–1988, were used mainly to target food crops, to kill livestock, and to contaminate water for ethnic rebels and their supporters. Indeed, the government has seemed unwilling to act against the drug traffickers and has on several occasions fabricated large-scale operations that have been proven false (Leach 1964; Lintner 2002; Renard 1996; Tucker 2000).

against the civilian population and the fostering of a substantial drugs industry in the hills of the Union of Myanmar.

Country Background

One factor that must be taken into account in any discussion of the conflict's background is that, to a great extent, Burmese people tied their political allegiances to perceived ethnic identities. Interestingly, the different ethnic groups in Burma all share a similar background, tracing their ancestry to different waves of migration from China (Smith 1991, 32–33). Substantial interaction and intermarriages between different ethnic groups have taken place for centuries, but grievances and political activism have often been expressed along ethnic lines. The main division has been between the Burman majority population, which lives on the central plains, and the different ethnic minorities, who live in the surrounding hills. Following centuries of wars between different kingdoms in present-day Myanmar, the Burman Konbaung Dynasty defeated their Mon and Shan rivals and expanded west in the early nineteenth century. This led to conflict with the British colonial rule of India, and in 1886, following a series of wars and alliances with local warlords, Burma became a British colony.

The defeated Burmans became part of British India, whereas the hill tribes became subject to a policy of indirect rule. Local rulers were accorded considerable autonomy concerning customs, religion, and local administration, provided they acknowledged British supremacy and paid annual tribute to the colonial authority (Renard 1996, 26). Other groups, such as the previously enslaved Karen, as well as people living in regions near the present-day border with Bangladesh and India, quickly became loyal to the British and featured heavily in the colonial administration. Furthermore, several ethnic groups converted to Christianity as a result of the activity of missionaries in the late nineteenth century (Po 2001; Tucker 2001, 14–22).

Thus, the anticolonial resistance movement was formed primarily by ethnic Burman nationalists who claimed that the British, the southern Indian immigrants, and the hill tribes all were part of the colonial administration. During World War II, part of the independence movement allied with the Japanese to defeat the British in 1942 (Maung Maung 1990). When the British were defeated, Burman gangs committed atrocities against former British "loyalists," targeting especially the Karen population and Muslims in southern Arakan state. Throughout the war, Karen and Chin forces continued to fight the Japanese occupation as guerrilla forces linked to the British army (Smith 1991, 62–63; Yegar 1972, 95). When it became clear that the Japanese military administration had no plans to actually transfer power to the Burmans, the same independence leaders contacted the British army in India. In secret, different Communist groups linked up with the leadership of the Burma Army and created a unified front as the Anti-Fascist People's Freedom League (AFPFL). On March 27, 1945, the Burmese army defected from the occupation military administration and joined the British forces against the Japanese (Colbert 1977; Koonings and Kruijt 2002, 73; Maung Maung 1990, 145).

After the Japanese defeat, negotiations began between the AFPFL, headed by Aung San, and Britain about the creation of an independent state. The AFPFL remained an unstable alliance, and ethnic riots were common in the years 1945–1947, as several political leaders created

personal armies (*tat*) to strengthen their position. During this transition period, the British organized a new Burma Army, in which the ethnic Burman battalions were separate units from the ethnic forces who became, for example, the Chin, Karen, and Kachin Rifles. As the British–Burman negotiations came to a close, the AFPFL started to disintegrate. A Communist faction had left the alliance and begun to prepare for a Communist revolution, when, in January 1947, an agreement between Aung San and the British Prime Minister Lord Attlee outlined the process for Burmese independence. The plan was immediately met with resistance from Karen leaders, who demanded a separate, independent state, while Shan, Kachin, and Chin ethnic leaders declared that the agreement was not binding on their territories (Tucker 2001, 121). Eventually, the AFPFL negotiated a compromise with the Shan representatives stipulating that their region could secede from the Union ten years after independence. A similar provision was made for the Karenni region, but no such specific agreements were made for territories inhabited by other ethnic groups (Smith 1991, 79).

Following independence, the outbreak of several insurgencies severely inhibited the government's ability to create effective institutions. The instability contributed to the creation of a brief military caretaker administration in 1958–1960, and on March 2, 1962, General Ne Win overthrew the democratically elected government. The new military rulers—officially named the Burma Socialist Programme Party (BSPP)—declared that their main objective was to preserve the unity of the country while introducing the "Burmese Way to Socialism" (Koonings and Kruijt 2002, 279). This was an ideology of mixed Marxist, Buddhist, and nationalist principles that included one-party rule, nationalization of the economy, and measures to make the country the most politically isolated in the world.

As a consequence of the postcoup nationalization programs, the faltering Burmese economy

Forgotten Rebels and Peoples

Not much information is available on the civil war in Burma. However, the information available usually concerns the insurgencies along the borders of China and Thailand. Arguably, even less is known about the rebels in areas of western Burma bordering Bangladesh and India. Several Communist groups had established strongholds in Arakan state even before Burma became independent, and there have also been several movements among the Muslim Rohingya population with the intent of creating a separate state or, since 1971, joining Bangladesh. The region has also experienced much communal violence, in which, typically, Buddhist monks have instigated attacks on Muslims. Large-scale riots in 1978, 1991–1992, and 2001 have forced hundreds of thousands of Rohingya to flee into Bangladesh. The government has been accused of supporting the violence on all these occasions, and the Rohingya have not been recognized as a native population—which means, for example, that they are not allowed to travel freely within the Union of Burma.

North of Arakan state are the Chin hills. The Chin, like the Karen, featured heavily in the British colonial administration, and it was mainly Chin troops that stopped the Japanese advance in World War II. It was connections with Karen rebels that led to the first Chin movements that began to organize in the early 1960s, but the main insurgent forces in the area were Communist units. Another insurgency started up in the area a few years later, but across the border in India, with the goal of creating an independent Chin-Mizoram state. Since the defeat of the Mizo rebellion, the focus has been on the Burmese side of the border, but the Chin rebel forces usually have been very small and poorly equipped. Despite that, they have featured in many rebel alliances, especially linking up with KIO or crossing the border into India for refuge.

Relations between Burma and India have often been strained, partly because each has supported the other's insurgencies in the region. Relations have improved in the last decade, as joint operations have been launched to evict their respective rebels, and India has supported the Burmese government with arms. A major Indian rebel insurgency representing the Naga tribes managed to establish many bases in Burmese territory. There were Naga tribes in Burma as well, and for several decades, the "wild" tribes from the Burmese side kept attacking the villages in India. When the conflict began in India in the mid-1950s, a Burmese Naga leader became inspired and declared the "Sovereign People's Republic of Free Nagaland." The Burma Army did not move against this rebel group, but the Indian Naga began to establish numerous training camps across the border. Eventually, the Indian Naga troops defeated the Burmese tribes, forcing them to end their headhunting practices and focus on supporting their western cousins fighting India (Maitra 1998; Ozturk 2003; Pakim 1992; Pedersen, Rudland, and May 2000; Ramachandran 2005; Soe Myint 2004; Yegar 1972).

suffered further, as the control over an expanded black market trade was virtually handed to ethnic and Communist insurgencies. Twenty years later, this trade was estimated to constitute an annual US $3 billion, or 40 percent of the Burmese gross national product (GNP) (Taylor 2001, 16). Following an intramilitary coup in 1988, the country has invited foreign investments and has established joint economic projects with neighboring countries in several areas. Although the standard of living showed some minor improvements during the 1990s in the major cities, particularly Rangoon, the economy remains one of the least developed in the world. Many inter-

national institutions have complained about the lack of credible statistics for the country, which makes it difficult to correctly assess the economic situation. In 1998, Myanmar remained classified as a least developed country (LDC) and was ranked 131 of 173 countries by the United Nations Development Program (UNDP) Human Development Index. The International Monetary Fund (IMF) estimated a national growth rate of about zero for 2005, while the World Food Program—one of the few UN institutions still allowed in the country—has reported that malnutrition remains a severe and growing problem (Taylor 2001, 85).

Conflict Background

It can be argued that the first Burman civil war began even before the country had become independent. In the months preceding Burmese independence on January 4, 1948, the leader of AFPFL, Aung San, was assassinated by unknown attackers, several communist factions left the AFPFL to prepare for a revolution, the Karen and Karenni political leaders were about to declare independent states, and Muslims in Arakan had pledged themselves ready to fight for an Islamic state (Smith 1991, 87; Tucker 2001, 138–44).

The fighting during the first decade of independence pitted numerous forces against the government, but the Communist Party of Burma (CPB) and the Karen National Union (KNU) soon became the most powerful insurgent groups. Although both of these groups were militarily superior to the government forces, divisions among the different opposition armies, and the sudden appearance of defeated Chinese Kuomintang (KMT) troops in northern Burma in the early 1950s, led to a decrease in conflict intensity (Tucker 2001; Zakaria and Crouch 1985,). The ongoing conflict strengthened the position of ethnic Burman nationalists and the armed forces in the Rangoon government. Any suggestions aimed at appeasing the ethnic minorities through a more federal state were actively opposed by the military leadership. Instead, the government pressured the peaceful ethnic Shan leaders to relinquish their constitutional option to secede from the Union in 1959. These moves fueled a growing Shan nationalism, and in the late 1950s, several groups began to prepare for an armed struggle. In an attempt to unify the country against the Communist rebels, the government of U Nu 1960–1962 introduced efforts to make Buddhism the state religion. This was considered discrimination by the mainly Christian ethnic Kachin, who formed the Kachin Independence Organization (KIO) in 1961.

As the U Nu government declared a willingness to offer some autonomy to the ethnic minorities, the army became increasingly concerned. On March 2, 1962, General Ne Win took power and declared a socialist, one-party state. From 1963 on, the regime arrested political opponents, nationalized key sectors of the economy, expelled "foreigners" (including the substantial Indian and Chinese business communities), and abolished independent media and nonstate-controlled education (Koonings and Kruijt 2002; Zakaria and Crouch 1985). Several measures introduced by the government during the period 1963–1966 had significant implications for the subsequent escalation of the civil war near the end of the decade.

The BSPP's first concern was to eradicate political opposition, and it soon proved willing to use any means necessary. Student activists, political opponents, powerful Buddhist monk organizations, and independent media were attacked, arrested, or closed down by government troops. At the same time, the government invited the insurgents to peace talks. When negotiations failed in November 1963, the BSPP quickly arrested several ethnic political leaders. The most substantial effect was the arrest of the Shan leadership, which led to the collapse of local administrations as the region became subjected to virtual military occupation (Smith 1991, 204–20). But although negotiations had failed, the peace parlay had led given the rural rebel movements a chance to reestablish connections with antigovernment activists in the cities. Furthermore, after a government "demonetization" of the Burmese currency in May 1964, thousands of citizens lost their savings, making rebel recruitment a good deal easier. Although the rebels became stronger as well as more diverse, the new government substantially increased military spending. Further, the army introduced a system of local Ka Kwe Ye (KKY; "defense") militias, especially in the Shan state. The KKY system consisted of government-conferred legitimacy for militias created by local warlords. Many of these militias had first been created as self-defense units against the KMT who settled in the region during the 1950s (Lintner, 1994, 187–88; Smith 1991, 221) Several former KMT forces remained in Shan state and competed for control of drug trafficking with some of the warlords who now joined the KKY program (McCoy 2003, 425–26).

The appearance of KMT troops in northern Burma connected the civil war to the regional security situation in the 1950s. KMT had strong links to Taiwan and U.S.-sponsored anti-Communist operations in Thailand, Laos, and Vietnam. The different insurgencies were also trying to access military resources from abroad. The KNU had suffered an internal split over whether to cooperate with the Chinese-supported Communist Party of Burma or to improve links with the U.S.-allied Thailand (Smith 1991, 214). After the formation of the KIO, explicit requests for military support were made both to India and to the Thailand-based KMT remnants, and the group temporarily joined the World Anti-Communist League (WACL) (Lintner 1994, 190). Despite these alliances, the main outside actor that continued to influence the fighting in the civil war in Burma was China. In 1960, Burma and China signed a border agreement, as the Chinese policy of "peaceful coexistence" was manifested in the early 1960s through aid projects such as construction of bridges and power stations in Burma. Relations remained friendly, despite Beijing's concern following the 1962 coup and the subsequent expulsion of ethnic Chinese. Rather, the downturn of Burmese–Chinese relations followed internal political developments in China. When Mao Zedong initiated the Cultural Revolution in 1966, its primary focus was an internal purge of the Communist Party. However, the nationalism of thousands of ethnic Chinese students in Rangoon provoked communal clashes with the Burman population. Violent riots in late June 1967 led to the destruction of Chinese buildings and property as large Burmese mobs killed hundreds of people and attacked the Chinese Embassy in Rangoon. The Chinese broke off diplomatic relations with Burma, and on August 15, 1967, Beijing radio broadcast a message about the "profound friendship" between China and Burma's Communist rebel movement, CPB. At the same time, preparations had started for an offensive by Chinese "volunteers" into northern Burma (Smith 1991, 226–27).

The Insurgents

Throughout the course of the conflict, numerous insurgent organizations have been active in Burma, although this article focuses on the largest and most significant in the time period covered. The oldest of these was the Communist Party of Burma, originally formed in opposition to the British colonial rule. After the nationalist Student Union at Rangoon University became influenced by Bengali Communists in present-day India, the CPB was formed on August 15, 1939, with Aung San as its first general secretary (Maung Maung 1990, 22; Tucker 2001, 85). In the tumultuous years that followed, the CPB split into several factions, as the original leadership became more concerned with the politics of the independence umbrella organization AFPFL. When Burma became independent in 1948, some Communists had already been outlawed and were fighting the new government. In late March 1948, the main faction of the CPB left the AFPFL and took up arms. Still, it took several years for all the different Communist groups to unify in their opposition to the government (Lintner 1994; Smith 1991, 106)

Somewhat ironically, the first CPB offensive was halted by contributing troops from the Karen Rifles ethnic battalions of the Burma Army. The same troops that saved the first independent Burmese government deserted less than a year later from the Burma Army and became the rebel army of the Karen National Union. Different political Karen parties had unified as the KNU in 1947 after it became clear that the Attlee–Aung San Agreement would not include the most important objective for the ethnic Karen population—an independent Karen state (Tucker 2001). Although the AFPFL had negotiated the conditions for the handover of power, several Karen delegations that had argued for in-

Table 1: Civil War in Myanmar/Burma

War:	CPB, KIO, KNU, MTA vs. government
Dates:	March 1968–December 1995*
Casualties:	267,500 (including 14,000 battle deaths)
Regime type prior to war:	–7 in 1967 (Polity 2 variable in Polity IV data— ranging from –10 [authoritarian] to 10 [democracy])
Regime type after war:	–7 in 1996 (Polity 2 variable in Polity IV data— ranging from –10 [authoritarian] to 10 [democracy])
GDP per capita year war began:	US $415 (constant 1960 dollars)
GDP per capita 5 years after war:	US $1,200 (constant dollars)
Insurgents:	Communist Party of Burma (CPB), Kachin Independence Organization (KIO), Karen National Union (KNU), Mong Tai Army (MTA)**
Issue:	Control of central government; ethnic independence or autonomy
Rebel funding:	Drugs, gems, timber, cross-border trade, support from China
Role of geography:	Very substantial, war characterized by guerrilla warfare
Role of resources:	Very substantial role in onset, duration, and outcome
Immediate outcome:	Conflict continued at lower intensity.
Outcome after 5 years:	Low-level conflict continues.
Role of UN:	None
Role of regional organization:	None
Refugees:	At least 1,333,700
Prospects for peace:	Unclear; armed conflict is barely active, exiled political opposition is strong.

Sources: Doyle and Sambanis 2000; Marshall and Jaggers 2002, Smith, 1991; UCDP 2006.

Notes: * Doyle and Sambanis distinguished between Burma II (1968–1982) and Burma III (1983–1995). According to their data notes, however, this is solely based on previous (COW) literature; Doyle and Sambanis collapse Burma II and III into one observation in their analysis, and this practice has been chosen for this article (Doyle and Sambanis 2000, 25). Furthermore, the substantial conflict escalation began in January 1968, but it is assumed that it took a few months of battle before Doyle and Sambanis's required threshold of 1,000 deaths occurred.

** KNU and MTA are designated as the main insurgent organizations by Doyle and Sambanis (2000). They constitute two of the main ethnic armies, but a description of the conflict would be incomplete without numerous other groups. Of these, at least the CPB and KIO undoubtedly also reached the threshold of war as defined by Doyle and Sambanis.

dependence, or at least an autonomous region within the new country, had been ignored (Smith 1991, 82–87). Throughout 1948, communal violence between Karen and Burman militias escalated; in fact, many of the first KNU military units were created simply to improve the security of local villagers.

The consequences of the different insurgencies, as well as political instability following the murder of Aung San, limited any attempts at state building in the country during the 1950s. The lack of development and security in the hill areas bothered such ethnic groups as the Shan and the Kachin. After a decade of civil war, the government considered the CPB the main threat to national security and focused its efforts on limiting Communist recruitment. An attempt to launch an ideological campaign by projecting the CPB as a threat to Burmese nationalism, as manifested by religion, backfired. When Buddhism was suggested as Burma's official state religion, the Christian Kachin leadership argued that the move was unconstitutional and against the spirit of voluntary membership in the Union. Kachin nationalists already claimed that the Kachin population was not treated equally with the Burmans, citing the example of a border demarcation in 1960 that handed three Kachin villages to China. The Kachin nationalist cause became an armed insurrection on February 5, 1961, when the Kachin Independence Organization (KIO) was formed (Smith 1991, 191).

Likewise, frustration with the government was becoming increasingly common in the neighboring Shan state. The Shan nationalists tied their argument to the government's 1957 declaration that any move toward secession would be tolerated, thus ignoring the provisions agreed on at independence a decade earlier (Lintner 1994, 150). The first Shan rebel force was the Noom Suik Harn (Young Warriors [NSH]), formed in 1958, but from 1959 on, several uprisings broke out across the state. In 1964, the three biggest Shan rebel organizations agreed to join forces as the Shan State Army (SSA) and immediately invited other Shan opposition groups to join an alliance (Smith 1991, 220). Some local militias rejected the SSA offer, for example, the Loimaw Anti-Socialist Army led by Khun Sa ("Prince Pleasant," originally named Zhang Qifu). This militia had formed as one of several local self-defense groups against the KMT forces that settled in Shan state in the 1950s. When the Shan insurgencies grew in strength, the government introduced a tactic that previously had been successful in resisting the KMT invasion: the establishment of local paramilitary forces (Tucker 2001, 172). After a few months of fighting the government, Khun Sa joined the new government-sponsored program in 1964 as one of more than twenty KKY units. The KKY system gave the militias responsibility for policing and trade in their territories, and most of them, including the force of Khun Sa, became important actors in the lucrative drug trade of the Golden Triangle (Lintner 1994, 187; Smith 1991, 221). After the KKY system was abolished by the government in 1973, Khun Sa's forces renamed themselves the Shan United Army (SUA), with the ambition to fight for an independent Shan state. Numerous other rebel groups were active in the region during the following decade; but in 1985, after SUA had been joined by the forces of a rival faction, the Tailand Revolutionary Council (TRC) and changed its name to the Mong Tai Army (MTA), it became the leading Shan insurgent force (Smith 1991, 343).

When the conflict escalated into a full-blown war in 1968, it seemed as though the rebel forces were getting simultaneously stronger and weaker. The most dramatic case was the Communist Party of Burma, which suffered as well as benefited from China's domestic politics during the Cultural Revolution. At the time of the military takeover in Burma in 1962, the rural Communist forces were on the defensive and had lost most of their contacts with like-minded urban movements. The repression of the new military government—officially creating a socialist state—created an exodus of urban activists to join the CPB forces. Furthermore, the 1963 peace talks offered another opportunity for the CPB to strengthen its position as rival Communist groups either joined the CPB or became largely anonymous. By the end of 1967, the CPB had reestablished urban networks, was getting increasing support from China, and was the only opposition army with roots in the ethnic Burman population (Smith 1991, 202, 223). At the same time, the ideas of the Cultural Revolution also inspired the CPB to initiate internal purges to root out "right-wing opportunism." The activity of the Burmese Red Guards changed the CPB leadership, as dozens were killed, including several intellectuals who had joined the party in 1962 (Lintner 1994, 196–97).

It would be incorrect to call the CPB a Chinese proxy, as the policies of the party were specifically Burmese, but the importance of support from its northern neighbor can hardly be underestimated. Even though government offensives in 1968–1975 eliminated all Communist forces in central Burma, the CPB established a strong presence in the north of the country, effectively controlling the Burmese–Chinese border. This presence was based on campaigns against the Burma Army, the ability to make alliances with local warlords to join under the CPB umbrella, and offensives against ethnic Kachin, Shan, and other rebels in adjoining territories. With the support of China, the Communists became the best-equipped rebels, with access to safe bases and hospital resources across the border in Yunnan. Direct Chinese aid to the CPB decreased when the new leader, Deng Xiaoping, announced in 1978 that economic reform and growth would be the prime objective for Beijing. This decision was criticized by the ag,ing CPB leadership who remained staunchly loyal to Maoist principles. Somewhat contradictory to its ideology, the CPB's loss of foreign support was quickly replaced by a free market economy as the organization became increasingly dependent on taxation of border trade (Lintner 1990a, 193). All contraband exported from Kachin areas, as well as much of the black market goods filtering into central Burma, had to pass through CPB-held territory, and the organization established an effective transport network between Yunnan, northern Thailand, and different parts of Burma. Moreover, some CPB commanders received extra income through opium production, even though it never was officially endorsed by the leadership. In 1985, the CPB leadership announced that all party members involved in the drug trade would be severely punished, and it has been suggested that this decision contributed to the sudden breakup of the organization just a few years later (Lintner 1994, 294–95).

In contrast to the Communist insurgents, the ethnic armies received less support from the outside and remained poorly equipped in comparison. The different armies also displayed different characteristics, although there were many similarities between the two biggest ethnic insurgencies, the KIO and the KNU. Both organizations were the leading representatives in the promotion of their respective ethnic causes and were organized as quasi-states with well-developed leadership structures. Although the organizational structure of both groups borrowed much from Communist terminology, the groups remained reserved in their contacts with the CPB. Many prominent members in the KIO had been active in Kachin nationalist student organizations during the 1950s, and although the leadership changed substantially in the mid-1970s, it remained drawn from this intellectual background (Tucker 2000, 88–90). The younger generation of KIO leaders was more moderate in its

approach and replaced the original demand for independence with the goal of Kachin autonomy within the Union of Burma.

The change of leadership also led to a military alliance with the CPB in 1976 after more than eight years of intense clashes between the two rebel groups. This led to an increase in the support the KIO was already receiving from China (Lintner 1990a, 170). Ammunition, however, remained sparse, and the KIO relied on a well-disciplined fighting force based on Kachin conscripts and the efficient use of guerrilla tactics. Despite limited resources, this strategy was so successful that the rebels managed to control almost all the territory in Kachin state for most of the war, with the notable exception of the city of Myitkyina and a small area in the very north, where a local self-defense militia managed to rebuff advancing KIO troops in the mid-1960s. The governments' tactics consisted of aerial bombardment of rebel camps and villages, and temporary short-term offensives with the intent to capture main roads (Lintner 1990a, 138–39) Apart from dropping bombs, Burmese airplanes also sprayed the countryside with herbicide as part of the antinarcotics policy. The Kachin hills have a long history of poppy cultivation, but the KIO had already begun to limit drug production for commercial use in 1964 (Renard 1996). The income from drugs was not necessary for the Kachins, as the region produced the worlds' finest jadeite, as well as gold, rubies, and other precious stones. During the first decade of the war, most of the contraband was sold across the border in northern Thailand with the help of former KMT groups. This link remained but became less important throughout the 1980s as the economic reforms introduced in China made it possible to link up with Yunnanese businessmen (Global Witness 2003, 93; Lintner 1990a, 141, 145).

The Karen National Union managed to establish a quasi-state along the southeastern border with Thailand similar to the territory controlled by the KIO. Rebel-held territory, officially referred to as Kawthoolei, was ruled by the KNU,

Joint Opposition Attempts

Throughout the Burmese civil war, numerous attempts have been made to unify the different rebel armies ever since the CPB created the People's Democratic Front (PDF) with other Communist rebels in March 1949. A year later, disagreements led to heavy fighting between the CPB and other groups. In 1952–1958, some minor, local, joint fronts were established in western Burma, but the CPB became disillusioned and started exploring the possibilities of linking with the ethnic armies instead.

The KNU was split into two competing factions in 1956–1975 mainly regarding the issue of Communist cooperation. The anti-Communist faction established the Democratic Nationalities United Front (DNUF) in 1956–1958 with Mon, Pao, and Karenni rebels. After some of these accepted a government amnesty in 1958, the front ceased to exist. Instead, the pro-CPB KNU faction joined the National Democratic United Front (NDUF) in 1959 with CPB, Chin, Karenni, Pao, and Mon rebel groups. At the same time, the KNU and Karenni leaders were involved in another loose alliance in 1960–1963 that was concerned with helping new groups, such as the KIO and the Shan insurgents, to get organized. When the CPB started an overhaul of its organization in 1975, the NDUF was dissolved, and there was no other Communist participation in the united fronts. An attempt was made in 1989–1991, when some remnants of the CPB formed the short-lived pro-Communist All Nationalities Peoples' Democratic Front (ANPDF).

At the same time, the non-Communist KNU leadership was involved in most attempts to unify the different ethnic armies. An unsuccessful attempt in 1965–1966 was followed by the formation of the Nationalities United Front (NUF) in 1967. The NUF incorporated largely the same members as the previous attempt; namely, the KNU and groups from the Karenni, Kayan, and Zomi rebellions, but also a Shan group and, until 1969, the Mon. The failure of NUF to combat government offensives led to the formation of the Revolutionary Nationalities Alliance (RNA), in which the KNU was joined by Karenni, Kayan, and Shan rebels. Two years later, the Kayan group was replaced by Mon and Arakan rebels in a new alliance, which lasted only a year. This was in turn replaced by the National Democratic Front (NDF) in 1976—this time including all of KNU as well as rebels of Arakan, Karenni, Lahu, Pao, Palaung, and Shan ethnicity. Furthermore, the KIO joined the NDF in 1983, and the organization grew to incorporate Mon, Wa, and Chin ethnic rebels. Following the exodus of student activists in 1988 into rebel-held territories, a parallel united front, the Democratic Alliance of Burma (DAB), was established. It consisted of most NDF members but also incorporated Burman opposition groups. In 1992, the NDF, the DAB, and the exiled opposition established a political alliance called the National Council of the Union of Burma (NCUB), which remains the main political opposition to the Myanmar government (Lintner 1994; National Council of the Union of Burma 2004; Rotberg 1998; Smith 1991).

who maintained good relations with smaller ethnic armies nearby (Rotberg 1998, 141). Indeed, the KNU were directing joint military operations with Mon, Karenni, and student rebels, who otherwise kept their own camps and pursued their own antigovernment struggles. The KNU leader Bo Mya was actively trying to unify all rebel groups through various alliances, even though the central Karen leadership remained cautious concerning any cooperation with the Communists (Rotberg 1998, 142). Several rebel groups, however, were more interested in securing support from the Thai government and possibly the United States. Throughout the war, the KNU was allowed to establish bases on the Thai side of the border, usually in or around the camps set up for Burmese refugees. Thailand also supplied some arms to the rebels but only to a limited extent, as Bangkok was worried that a victory for the ethnic armies could have a destabilizing effect on border relations (Phongpaichit, Piriyarangsan, and Treerat 1998, 129).

The KNU were numerically inferior at all times to the Burma Army troops in the region but managed to establish superiority through the use of guerrilla tactics and intricate defense systems, which depended heavily on intimate knowledge of the terrain and the location of minefields. Furthermore, the KNU generally had a strong support base in the local civilian population, owing to both the history of the movement and the treatment of the villagers by the rebels and the army. The KNU had been founded in part by existing village self-defense militias, whereas the government's counterinsurgency tactics included an element of civilian repression designed to sever the links between rebels and civilians (Tucker 2003). During the years of the government's policy of economic self-sufficiency (1962–1988), territories under Karen control became the most active trading points for black market goods entering and leaving Burma. The KNU were not involved in the drug industry but rather derived their income from taxing the border trade in consumer goods, as well as small-scale logging operations along the border (Global Witness 2003, 59–60).

In Shan state, the situation was quite different from that in Kachin and Karen territories, although government repression of the civilian population was even more common, and some groups received support from Thailand. In particular, three factors contributed to the different characteristics of the war in this territory. First, the influence of the former KMT commanders who remained in the area despite the official transfer of these troops to Taiwan in 1961 led to access to more weapons, owing to their strong links to Thai, Taiwanese, and U.S. security agencies. Second, a main goal for these groups was control of the drug business in the area. In 1994, it was estimated that the profits of narcotics trafficking in Thailand amounted to US $85 billion annually, and the vast majority of these drugs originated in the Burmese part of the Golden Triangle (Phongpaichit, et al. 1998, 86–88). Third, the historical roots of the Shan insurgency, as well as the competition over drugs, led to the establishment of numerous rebel groups, which sometimes unified in alliances but more often used their arms in intrarebel fighting. It was not until 1985 that the Mong Tai Army

managed to become the foremost organized-rebel group promoting the Shan cause. The MTA established such a strong control over the drug trade in the late 1980s that there was severe skepticism both from outside and inside the MTA concerning whether the group had any political or nationalist objectives (McCoy 2003, 438). Local commanders of previously independent rebel groups that had chosen to join forces with MTA declared that the best chance for the insurgents was to unify, and as the MTA was military strong, it made sense to accept the leadership of Khun Sa. It has been implied, however, that there were few direct clashes between the Burma Army and the forces of MTA directly under Khun Sa's command, as these were more concerned with protecting the opium convoys (Lintner 1994, 264; Uppsala Conflict Data Program 2006).

Geography

At the time of conflict escalation in 1968, some areas of Burma had been outside government control ever since independence. Even when the Burma Army captured rebel territory in the conflict, there were few areas in the hills where the government permanently replaced the insurgents. By 1968, both the CPB and the KNU had established a strong presence on the central plains and in the Irrawaddy River delta southwest of Rangoon. After a series of large-scale government offensives in the early 1970s, these areas were lost, which effectively cut off the rebel armies' links to the urban population and also frustrated future attempts to initiate cooperation between different rebel movements.

The geographic features of Burma can be said to resemble a huge basin surrounded by hills. After the Burma Army's successes, the lowlands remained controlled by the government, as the rebels used the surrounding steep hills and thick jungles to set up protected bases. Furthermore, the country is divided by three main rivers—the Irrawaddy, the Chindwin, and the Salwan—as well as the smaller but strategically important Sittang, which flow from north to south. Into

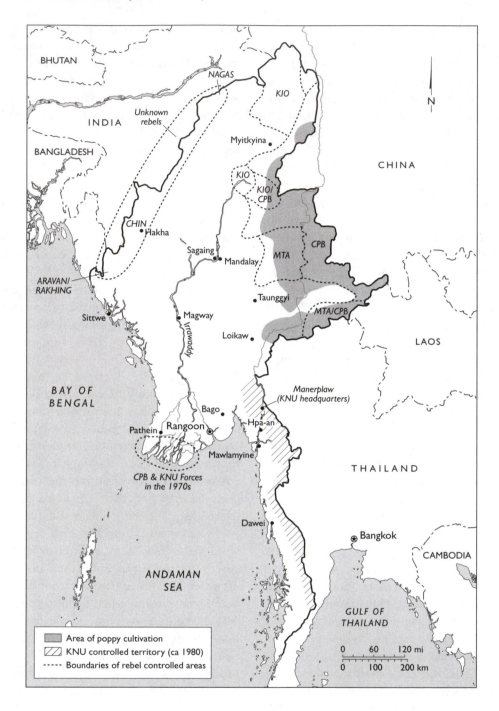

these rivers feed thousands of others, and during the monsoon, which lasts from May to October, almost all watercourses in Burma become impassable. According to Tucker (2001), "This [the monsoon] too has tended to the isolation of Burma's hill minorities, for no commander, whatever the size and power of his forces, would commit them to expeditions extending into the monsoon" (Tucker 2001, 9).

The conflict has been fought almost exclusively in rural areas and hillsides, and the rebels have often relied on their superior knowledge of the terrain in their military planning. Apart from the geographical features, which have made it relatively easy for smaller rebel units to avoid direct confrontation, abundant natural resources and relations with neighboring countries have influenced the dynamics of the conflict. Apart from the drug trade, Burma is also famous for its gemstones, especially rubies, sapphires, and jade, as well as numerous mineral resources, including oil and natural gas. Other such resources include tin, lead, silver, and zinc; marble is quarried in the western part of the country, and logging is common in the northern and eastern regions. During the first twenty years of the conflict, the isolationist policies of the Burmese government made it possible for the different rebel groups to receive income from the export of these resources. Since the intramilitary coup in 1988, the new government of Myanmar has actively sought to establish business links with foreign firms to capture the rents from these resources, which have played an important role in affecting the outcome of the conflict.

Tactics

The capabilities and, indeed, the tactics have been different for the rebel armies, with the ethnic organizations KIO, KNU, and MTA all focusing on small-scale guerrilla tactics, while the CPB chose a different approach. A short description of the characteristics of the respective groups is followed by a more thorough look at government counterinsurgency tactics, as these have received international condemnation. The ethnic rebel armies mainly used guerrilla warfare against the government, although some more substantial military installations were built at times, especially around the KNU headquarters at Manerplaw. Most of the fighting consisted of clashes with small arms or mortars, as the KNU artillery often discouraged the government from using its aerial superiority (Carey 1997b, 131). Most of the arms used by KNU and MTA were smuggled from Thailand. The majority of these were either bought legally with the

income from cross-border trade or illegally through contacts within the Thai armed forces. Another important source of arms was stockpiled weapons from previous conflicts in the region, such as those in Vietnam, Laos, Thailand, and Cambodia (Phongpaichit, et al. 1998, 127).

The KIO received almost all its weapons from China, especially after the alliance with the Communists in 1976. The KIO had already established cross-border connections as part of a network in which China had provided military training to ethnic and Communist rebels in northeast India since the mid-1960s (Lintner 1990a, 82; Maitra 1998, 68, 71). By far the best-equipped rebel organization was the CPB. It received substantial official support from China in 1968–1981 and could still import arms through Yunnan in the period that followed. With more advanced military capabilities available, the CPB were more inclined to use "traditional" military tactics in their offensives. The leadership was also influenced by Chinese military strategy, which largely focused on strength in numbers, and thus the CPB "human wave" attacks usually led to high casualty figures for both the government and the rebels (Lintner 1990a, 198–200).

Focusing on the government forces, increased resources were directed toward the army from 1962 on, as the government initiated an offensive strategy against the different insurgents. Apart from a direct increase in military expenditure, the army also benefited from indirect allocation of resources, as different army organizations became increasingly important business actors in the Burmese state-controlled economy (Koonings and Kruijt 2002, 279). With regard to military strategy, the army has used a dual approach. In the distant border areas, alliances were sought with local militias to attack rebel bases, whereas the main military machinery would be deployed against one area at the time. This was visible through the KKY system during the period 1964–1973, as well as in the ceasefires offered to rebel groups after 1990. Also, since 1966 the military has focused on a counterinsurgency tactic known as the Pya Ley Pya

(Four Cuts). The four cuts strategy consists of cutting the four main links (food, funds, intelligence, and recruits) between insurgents, their families, and local villagers. Details have been provided by Smith (1991):

> To begin with, selected rebel areas, just 40 to 50 miles square, were cordoned off for concentrated military operations. Army units then visited villagers in the outlying fields and forests and ordered them to move to new "strategic villages" (byu hla jaywa) under military control on the plains or near the major garrison towns in the hills. Any villager who remained, they were warned, would be treated as an insurgent and ran the risk of being shot on sight. After the first visit, troops returned periodically to confiscate food, destroy crops and paddy and, villagers often alleged, shoot anyone suspected of supporting the insurgents. (Smith 1991, 259)

In 1979, the first major offensive was launched in Shan state, and soon thereafter, fighting intensified closer to CPB bases (in 1982) as well as those of the KNU (in 1984) (Lintner 1990a, 210; Lintner 1994, 267).

The expansion of the military in the period of the BSPP (1962–1988) remained marginal in comparison to the military buildup that followed the intramilitary coup in 1988. During the first six years of the new government, the army grew from 180,000 to some 300,000 troops. At the same time, the government announced a new political outlook, referred to as "peace through development." It consisted of several aspects, both military and political, and took into account relations with neighboring countries. The military was expanded and modernized; several large arms deals were secured from China and—more recently—India; and efforts were made to improve the infrastructure of army positions rather than withdraw during the monsoon (Rotberg 1998, 203–204). The new policy further escalated the human rights abuses of the army, as forced labor became more common in these infrastructure and agriculture projects (Soe Myint 2004, 17). Several nongovernmental organiza-

tions (NGOs)—as well as UN agencies—have collected statements about army harassment, torture, rape, and extrajudicial killings from Burmese refugees in Thailand, accusations that have been denied by the government.

Apart from strengthening the military positions, the government started offering cease-fire agreements to rebel groups under which they would be allowed to keep their arms and remain responsible for policing and developing their respective territories. One common provision of these agreements obligated cease-fire groups to help the government fight remaining rebels in the area, which further increased the pressure on the insurgent organizations (Rotberg 1998, 205). The final aspect of the government's new political outlook was improving relations with neighboring countries. In the mid-1980s, the army had managed to capture some strategic trading locations on the Chinese and Thai borders, which led to a significant loss of revenue for the KNU and the CPB. Starting in 1989, Burma initiated joint infrastructure projects with neighboring states and offered concessions in logging and resource development to foreign firms. The consequence was a strengthening of Burmese military presence in border areas and a decrease of foreign support for the rebels (Carey 1997a, 80–82, 117, 149; Taylor 2001, 142–243)

Causes of the War

Besides the background causes just described, some additional factors contributed to the sudden escalation in 1968. For the ethnic rebel armies, the attempted peace negotiations in 1963–1964 had provided evidence of the military government's unwillingness to compromise on issues of autonomy for the hill tribes. At the same time, it had also become clear that opposition to the government was widespread. The demonetization of currency in 1964 and severe shortages of rice and other foodstuffs in Rangoon in 1967 contributed to an increase in rebel supporters and recruits, while the growth of black market trade provided more funding for the insurgencies (Lintner 1994, 197; Zakaria and Crouch 1985). By the end of 1966, the ruling BSPP government had managed to establish its one-party rule, remove opposition parties, and nationalize the economy. It then started preparing for a large-scale offensive against the insurgents, utilizing the four cuts strategy with the intention of focusing all capabilities on one area (Smith 1991).

The third—and possibly most influential—causative factor was the breakdown of Burmese–Chinese relations in 1967 following the Cultural Revolution and ethnic riots in Rangoon. In the Yunnan province of China, just across the Burmese border, a substantial invasion force was assembled to support the CPB. Although most of the Chinese support was administered through the Yunnanese regional government and thus was not official policy, the Communist rebel forces were boosted by thousands of Chinese "volunteers." The CPB plan was a large-scale offensive to push the Burma Army out of present-day Shan state and continue south until the invasion forces linked up with the pockets of CPB guerrillas in central Burma. On New Year's Day 1968, the Chinese-backed forces attacked and initiated an offensive that would not halt for five more years. As the CPB forces also became entangled in fighting local warlords and other rebels such as the KIO, the government concentrated on the Karen forces in the Irrawaddy Delta and the Communists in central Burma (Lintner 1990a, 209–10).

Outcome

The four cuts campaigns in the early 1970s were successful in expanding government control over territory in central Burma, but the different rebel forces remained in charge of the border and hill areas. During the 1980s, the situation stabilized; annual dry-season hit-and-run offensives were conducted by the government troops, while the rebels remained in control of their respective territories. The government was employing the four cuts strategy all over Burma,

and the insurgents were desperately trying to bring the human rights violations to the attention of the international community (Lintner 1990, Tucker 2000). Although intense fighting continued until 1995, a series of events in 1988–1989 eventually determined the outcome of the conflict.

As the cost of fighting the insurgents continued to increase, with as much as 40 percent of the Burmese budget spent on defense services, economic problems became evident in the mid-1980s (Koonings and Kruijt 2002). In 1987, Burma was accorded least-developed country (LDC) status by the UN, for the country was unable to cope with payments of its US $3.5 billion foreign debt. The government's decision to demonetize the three highest denominations of bank notes in September 1987 provoked an outcry from the business communities and student unions—as it happened, just days before annual university fees were due to be paid in cash (Lintner 1990b; Steinberg 2001).

Riots erupted outside Rangoon universities; as discontent among the general public continued to grow, more student-organized antigovernment rallies were held from November 1987 through June 1988. All protests were met by violent repression by the police. Demonstrations spread during the summer of 1988, and martial law was declared as the student movement began to mobilize the entire Burmese population (Lintner 1990b; Steinberg 2001). On August 8, 1988, the biggest public protest in decades was organized; several hundred thousand Burmese participated in strikes and antigovernment protests throughout the country. When night fell on the demonstrations, the government response began. After interviewing eyewitnesses, Lintner (1990b) described the scenes in Rangoon: "[A]t 11:30, trucks loaded with troops roared out from behind the City Hall. These were followed by more trucks as well as Bren-carriers, their machine-guns pointed straight in front of them . . . . Two pistol shots rang out—and then the sound of machine-gunfire reverberated in the dark between

Students and fellow members of the opposition protest the government's antidemocratic policies in a demonstration in Rangoon, Burma, on September 1, 1988. A brutal government crackdown ensued that sent protesters into hiding in the countryside. (Sandro Tucci/Time Life Pictures/Getty Images)

the buildings surrounding Bandoola Square. People fell in droves as they were hit" (Lintner 1990b, 97).

Army suppression in the days that followed killed an estimated 3,000 people in Rangoon and countless others throughout the country. The international community condemned the regime, and antigovernment demonstrations continued. On September 18, the government announced over state-run radio that the military had assumed power to "bring a timely halt to the deteriorating conditions . . ." (Lintner 1990b, 131). The newly appointed government, calling itself the State Law and Order Restoration Council, announced forthcoming elections but acted principally to repress the continuing demonstrations. Machine-gun fire and mass arrests cleared the streets, and order was reestablished within a few days of the intramilitary coup. In the weeks that followed, 8,000–10,000

student and urban activists fled to the border areas to join the rebel armies against the government (Fink 2001; Lintner 1990b).

The new SLORC government quickly focused its attention on reforming the socialist economy. The state remained the main economic actor, but a concerted effort was made to increase official foreign trade and limit the opportunities for rebel income. Following offensives in 1984, the Burma Army had established bases along parts of the Moei River, which constitutes the Burmese–Thai border, making the KNU-controlled cross-border trade more difficult. In January 1987, the army captured Pangshai, the main trading post on the border to China, and in May 1987, the KIO headquarters at Na Hpay and Pa Jau fell into government hands (Lintner 1994, 267–71). In 1989, the government began to give concessions to Thai timber firms, and these were soon followed by projects to exploit

Myanmar's fish and mineral resources. Since 1993, the number of joint Thai–Burmese projects has continued to increase and has included energy production through hydroelectricity and gas pipelines in border areas (Carey 1997a, 117, 149; Rotberg 1998, 136; Taylor 2001, 121). Similar agreements were made in the northern part of the country; six Sino-Burmese trade and economic agreements were signed in November 1989. These agreements were accompanied not only by Chinese military aid but also by investments and beneficial loans that made it possible for Myanmar to improve its infrastructure (Carey 1997a, 80–82). As a consequence of increased foreign investment in the area, both Thailand and China tried to influence the Burmese rebels to end their armed struggle and sign cease-fire agreements (Taylor 2001, 129).

After 1988's turmoil in the cities, it seemed as though the rebel armies were in an ideal position to launch a decisive strike in the civil war. However, the rural-based rebels were hardly aware of the opportunity, for the government's four cuts tactics had severed links between the rebels and the urban populations. Thousands of students fled into the jungle with the expectation, based on government propaganda, that the rebels were substantially stronger than they actually were. Many quickly became disillusioned and returned to the cities or continued into exile. However, the years 1988–1990 established a link between the student-led democracy movement and the ethnic armies, especially at the KNU headquarters at Manerplaw (Lintner, 1990b).

Regardless, the key event for the outcome of the conflict occurred a few months later and had no connection at all to the democracy movement. The strongest rebel movement in early 1989 was the CPB, which controlled substantial territory in northern Shan state, coexisted peacefully with the KIO in the areas bordering China and India, and also controlled some pockets of territory along the western border with Bangladesh and India (Lintner 1990; Tucker 2001). Within the CPB, some discontent was growing. The politburo's aging leadership, mainly ethnic Chinese who adhered strictly to Maoist ideology, had never really become popular among their forces. The military strength of the CPB had been based on Chinese support and the ability to defeat or incorporate local militias as part of the CPB structure, usually by providing them with military equipment. This arrangement was most obvious with the ethnic Wa population, which made up nearly 80 percent of the Communist army. The Wa—based mainly in the northeastern part of Shan State—had declared at Burmese independence their intent to withdraw from any type of state formation. In the early 1970s, some Wa tribes formed a rebel movement to fight for autonomy, whereas other tribes remained focused on self-sufficiency and traditional customs (which included head-hunting) for another decade. The independent Wa had been defeated in the CPB offensives during the 1970s and then had enlisted as CPB troops. After the Chinese withdrew their support of the CPB in 1981, the benefits to local commanders decreased, the more so when the Communists lost some control over the cross-border trade in 1987. The human cost of the conflict was felt mostly by the Wa tribes, as the "human wave" military strategy preferred by the CPB leaders created substantial fatalities in each offensive. Additionally, most local Wa commanders also depended on income from drug trafficking, and so another reason for concern was the CPB leadership's 1985 edict that all involvement in the opium trade would be severely punished.

All these factors can help explain the sudden implosion of the Communist insurgency in Burma. In March 1989, some Kokang Chinese CPB troops rebelled, and the mutiny quickly spread into all Communist areas in the northeast. The Wa units joined the mutiny in April, the CPB split into several ethnically based forces, and the party leadership fled into exile in China. When news of the events spread, the Myanmar government reacted quickly, making contact with the newly formed groups and offering them agreements whereby they would remain in autonomous control of their respective territories (Lintner 1994). Several groups quickly signed the cease-fire agreements, including the largest army formed from the remains of the CPB, the United Wa State Army (UWSA). One of the provisions for the ceasefire with the 20,000 troops strong UWSA was that the organization would help the government defeat other rebels in their vicinity (Carey 1997b).

After the signing of the agreement, the UWSA declared it had no intention of fighting against the KIO, as it had no grievance with the Kachins, but it quickly launched an offensive against its main competitor in the drug trade, the Mong Tai Army. Repeated UWSA offensives against the MTA, with logistical support of the government, led to an upsurge in fighting in Shan state in 1990–1993 (Lintner 1994; McCoy 2003). After substantial battlefield successes, in 1993 the UWSA began to suggest the formation of an autonomous Wa state in the north, which led to the deployment of more government troops for a final push in the region (Lintner 1994). Following years of constant retreat, the MTA commander, Khun Sa, invited 1,500 Burma Army troops to occupy his headquarters on New Year's Day 1996, where he quickly negotiated surrender (Rotberg 1998, 188). Khun Sa was moved into a luxurious villa in one of Rangoon's nicest areas, where he continued to pursue his business interests in gambling and tourism (Lintner 2002; McCoy 2003; Tucker 2001). The remaining MTA troops were demobilized, but the rebel army had weakened considerably during the prevous year—only 1,800 troops participated in the surrender (out of the prior year's estimate of 10,000). Many had defected to continue the insurgency on a lower scale in several newly formed Shan organizations.

Another aspect of the cease-fires in 1989 was their influence on the fighting ability of the KIO. The new agreements led to the isolation of a KIO brigade in Shan state, in territory controlled by cease-fire groups; this unit also signed a cease-fire with the government in 1991. Nego-

tiations were opened with the KIO leadership as their contacts in China began to promote the idea of a settlement as beneficial to cross-border trade and Kachin economic development. After a de facto cessation of hostilities in 1993, a permanent cease-fire between the KIO and the government of Myanmar was agreed to in early 1994, in which the Kachin were allowed to keep their armed force and develop their region. The KIO still maintain, however, that they remain an armed insurgency organization and that the cease-fire should not be considered an acceptance of the Myanmar military government (Global Witness 2003; Tucker 2001).

The joint effect of the cease-fires in the north and the modernization of the government forces combined to increase the military pressure against the KNU. In 1992, it was reported that Myanmar forces deployed along the western border had increased from 5,000 to more 55,000 men in a few years. Military spokespersons claimed that the KNU would be defeated within months as a new offensive was launched in the first months of 1992. After months of heavy fighting, in which government troops allegedly even attacked from the Thai side of the border, the fighting came to a standstill. Then, on April 28, 1992, the government announced a unilateral cease-fire. Although smaller skirmishes continued, attempts were made by Thailand to initiate negotiations; these quickly broke down (Carey 1997a, Tucker 2001), fueling feelings of discontent that had been growing among the Buddhist part of the Karen population for a few years. Although the leadership of the KNU remained mainly Christian, some 70–80 percent of the field soldiers were Buddhist. Generally, these soldiers had been recruited from among the poorer, less educated Karen villagers, who felt excluded from the income provided by taxation and from promotions to high-ranking positions in the army (Gravers 1999, 89). The sense of discrimination among the Buddhists was further enhanced when U Thuzana, a leading monk in the Myaing Gyi Ngu monastery, and the KNU leader, Bo Mya, disagreed over the construction of a new pagoda. U Thuzana become a popular leader among the war-weary population after predicting in the late 1980s that peace would follow after fifty pagodas had been built in Karen state. The KNU leadership agreed to the building of a new pagoda according to U Thuzana's plan but did not allow the pagoda to be painted white or a monastery to be established in it, for it was located on a mountaintop overlooking KNU headquarters (Gravers 1999, 90–96).

It is believed that the growing discontent among the Buddhist KNU was fueled by government agents. In December 1994, a few hundred soldiers mutinied and declared the formation of the Democratic Karen Buddhist Army (DKBA). Almost immediately, the DKBA announced a cease-fire with the government and helped guide Burma Army troops through the minefields and other obstacles into the KNU headquarters of Mannerplaw. After a few weeks of intense fighting in January 1995, the KNU retreated across the border into Thailand; joint DKBA and government offensives continued, even into refugee camps in Thai territory (Carey 1997b; Fink 2001; Rotberg 1998, 203–205) The KNU lost most of the territory it previously had controlled, but it continues to fight against the Myanmar government on a lower scale. During the last decade, the KNU political leadership has become closely linked to the exiled democracy movement, and KNU troops still launch guerrilla strikes on government forces from time to time (UCDP 2006).

Conflict Status

Of the four rebel organizations discussed herein, only the KNU remains active a decade later. The intense fighting has subsided, and the influence of the rebel groups has decreased substantially, but the main grievances remain and are significant to the political future of the Union of Myanmar. The present ethnic insurgent groups have created a common front with the former student movement and are unified in their demands for a democratic state with ethnic minority rights. Even though some fighting occasion-

ally is reported, there is great uncertainty concerning the amount of conflict activity in Myanmar. Several NGOs are active among refugees on the Thai–Burmese border, documenting continuous abuse—rape, forced labor, torture, and killings—by Myanmar government troops as part of counterinsurgency operations (Soe Myint 2004, 17).

The Kachin areas under KIO control have received increased income from the logging industry, and there has been an influx of ethnic Chinese into all of northern Myanmar (Global Witness 2003, 84–85). It is a sign of strength that the KIO can maintain the cease-fire while also officially acting as an opposition organization in criticizing the government. By far the most powerful cease-fire group is the UWSA, which formed after the mutinies of the CPB. It has established control over two Wa regions with such military strength that Myanmar government officials need permission to enter. Originally dependent on income from the drug trade, the group has ventured into other business activities and have also launched crop substitution initiatives in their areas. However, the group has also clashed with the Myanmar government a few times, and when the army recently suggested disarming the cease-fire groups, both the KIO and the UWSA declared unwillingness to comply (UCDP 2006). The actual reasons for the conflict remains, along with several political organizations, but the governments' combination of strong military rule and economic development has limited armed activity during the past decade.

Duration Tactics

The events following the military coup of 1962 set the stage for the outbreak of intense fighting and provided the basic structure that led to the long duration of the conflict. Arguably, the ethnic armies benefited from the support of their local populations, but events of the last decade have shown that this could only influence duration to an extent. The economic program of radical nationalization initiated in the name of the

"Burmese way to socialism" increased the capabilities of the rebels, as official trade with neighboring countries was discontinued. The rebels, who controlled the resource-rich border regions, quickly established links with China and Thailand and benefited immensely from the upsurge in black market trade. It should be noted that, while resources such as drugs, gems, and timber were being transported out of Burma, consumer goods in large quantities were imported through rebel-held areas. In the mid-1970s, one of the busiest markets in Rangoon became unofficially renamed the Yodaya Zei ("Thailand market") for its abundance of imported goods in a country largely closed off from the world (Renard 1996, 47).

However, one might argue, if the rebels received support from neighboring countries and controlled the income of almost half of the Burmese economy, why did they not succeed in defeating the government? The reasons have to do with the counterinsurgency tactics of the government as well as the relations between the dozens of rebel armies active in Burma throughout the conflict. Even though Burma became, and remains, a police state where abuse of human rights continues to be reported, the government's tactics were successful in one important aspect: Possible political links were cut between the Burman opposition, the urban activists, and the rural insurgents. The geographic and cultural barriers that made it difficult for the government to defeat the rebels also made it difficult for the rebels to find opportunities for decisive offensives. At the same time, the numerous reasons for fighting against the government often made the insurgencies less a threat than the sum of their parts. Throughout the civil war, the different rebel groups have fought among themselves, thus limiting their ability to defeat the government. With regard to the time period and the groups covered here, the most serious incidents were the full-scale war in 1968–1976 between the KIO and the CPB, and the intra-Shan fighting in the early 1980s,

which eventually made the MTA the strongest group. Later, this fractionalization among the rebels was exploited by the Myanmar government, contributing in a major way to the outcome of the conflict.

External Military Intervention

The conflict did not see any outright external military intervention, although it is suspected that Chinese troops were involved in the great CPB offensive that began in 1968. No official acknowledgement was made; however, it has been argued that the CPB's ranks were boosted by Chinese "volunteers" following the reports of attacks on ethnic Chinese in Burma in the preceding year.

Conflict Management Efforts

As mentioned in the introduction, international concern with Burma has centered on the situation between the democracy movement and the government since 1988. During recent years, the international community has become more concerned with the treatment of ethnic minorities, as shown, for example, by the appointment of a UN special envoy to Myanmar in 2000. However, during the period covered in this article, little attention was given to the civil war. In the last decade of the conflict, both China and Thailand tried to influence rebel groups to accept a cease-fire with the government; however, it is arguable that this effort had much to do with these countries' ambition to improve economic interaction across the border. Although there have been several proposals for negotiations from both sides of the conflict, these hardly led to anything more than exploratory talks. The cease-fires with different rebel groups since 1989 have not led to any outright attempts to manage the issues of the conflict. Indeed, the conditions set for former fighters "returning to the legal fold" are very strict, and many choose to flee to Thailand. According to one former soldier, the terms of his amnesty stipulated that he had to report to the nearest police office on a daily basis, which in effect meant he could not settle on his family's farm (conversation with the author, 1999).

Conclusion

Two military takeovers influenced the increase and decrease of fighting in the Burma civil war. Both were followed by military buildup and increased repression, but different approaches to economic development created strikingly different outcomes. To claim that it was all about money would be to oversimplify the complex political landscape of Burma, but economic issues have certainly had a substantial impact on the war. In writing about the civil war in Burma/Myanmar, one is strongly tempted to begin almost every sentence by introducing yet another ironic turn of events. The government tried to build a Soviet-style, isolationist, Communist state while predominantly fighting Communist rebels. The Communist rebels became dependent on the development of a large-scale capitalist economy. Different rebel groups have spent as much energy fighting each other as they have fighting the government, and so on. After more than fifty years as insurgents, the rebel groups have become increasingly unified in the last decade, since government offensives have ended the large-scale fighting. The very same issues that were disputed when the Burmese leader Aung San demanded independence from the British colonial empire at the end of World War II remain unsolved and have further exaggerated the divisions within the Burmese society. After one of the most intensely fought civil wars for decades, with millions of refugees, the international community is starting to focus on the problems in Myanmar—following government repression of a nonviolent political movement.

Joakim Kreutz

Chronology

August 15, 1939   Communist Party of Burma (CPB) is formed in Rangoon.
February 5, 1947   Karen National Union (KNU) is formed.

January 4, 1948   Burma becomes independent.
March 28, 1948   CPB starts fighting the government.
January, 1949   KNU starts fighting the government.
January–March 1950   Some 2,000 Kuomintang (KMT) troops cross the border from China, settling in Burmese Shan state following Maoist victory in the civil war. Several Shan villages begin setting up self-defense militias to protect themselves from KMT and Burma Army.
February 5, 1961   Kachin Independence Organization (KIO) is formed.
March 2, 1962   General Ne Win overthrows the democratic Burmese government and installs a military dictatorship, the Burma Socialist Program Party (BSPP).
1964   Government introduces the KKY self-defense militia program in Shan state. Many local warlords join, including Khun Sa.
June–July 1967   Violent riots break out in Rangoon; Burmese attack Chinese interests.
January 1, 1968   Large-scale military offensive is launched by the CPB across the border from China.
January 1968   Fighting begins between KIO and CPB after Communist forces invaded Kachin-held territory.
September 1968   Government offensive is launched against Karen and Communist insurgents in the Irrawaddy delta.
October 20, 1969   Khun Sa is arrested and jailed in Mandalay.
October 1971   CPB and Karen forces are driven out of the Irrawaddy delta by government offensives.
January 1973   The KKY system is abolished, principally because of international criticism about its involvement in the drug trade.
September 7, 1974   Khun Sa is released from prison after his troops had held two Soviet doctors hostage since April 1973. He remains in Mandalay until February 1976 before returning to the hills.
May 10, 1976   Leaders of approximately a dozen different ethnic rebel armies meet at KNU headquarters, form the National Democratic Front (NDF).
July 6, 1976   KIO and CPB leaders meet and agree to a military alliance.
March 3, 1985   Shan United Army joins forces with the Tailand Revolutionary Council to

become the Mong Tai Army, led by Khun Sa.

January 1987 Government offensives capture several positions from the CPB on the Burma Road and the border with China.

May 26–30, 1987 Government offensives capture KIO headquarters and strategic positions on the border with China.

March–September 1988 Antigovernment demonstrations break out across Burma and are brutally suppressed by the army.

September 18, 1988 The military take over government as the State Law and Order Restoration Council (SLORC).

November 18, 1988 Ethnic rebel armies of the NDF join forces with twelve Burman opposition parties in the Democratic Alliance of Burma (DAB).

March 12, 1989 The CPB began to disintegrate as ethnic Kokang leave the organization. Mutinies quickly spread; by April 20, the CPB no longer exists.

May 27, 1989 SLORC announces that the country's name is officially changed from Burma to Myanmar.

December 15, 1989 The last of the groups formed after the CPB mutinies signs a cease-fire agreement with the government.

January–April, 1990 Government offensives capture several KNU positions and push thousands of Karen into Thailand as refugees.

May 27, 1990 First multiparty elections since 1960 are held; more than 70 percent of population votes for the opposition National League for Democracy.

June 19, 1990 General Saw Maung declares power will be handed over as soon as new constitution is written.

January–March 1992 Government offensives capture positions only ten kilometers from KNU headquarters.

April 8, 1993 KIO signs cease-fire agreement with the government.

December 1994 Buddhist Karen mutiny against the leadership of KNU, form Democratic Karen (Kayin) Buddhist Army (DKBA).

January 1995 DKBA guide government troops in attack on KNU headquarters. KNU withdraw across border into Thailand.

January 1, 1996 Following a year of large-scale government and UWSA offensives, Khun Sa invites government troops into MTA headquarters and surrenders.

List of Acronyms

AFPFL: Anti-Fascist People's Freedom League
ANPDF: All Nationalities People's Democratic Front
BSPP: Burma Socialist Programme Party
CPB: Communist Party of Burma
DAB: Democratic Alliance of Burma
DEA: (U.S.) Drug Enforcement Agency
DKBA: Democratic Karen (Kayin) Buddhist Army
DNUF: Democratic Nationalities United Front
GNP: gross national product
IMF: International Monetary Fund
KIO: Kachin Independence Organization
KKY: Ka Kwe Ye (government defense militia)
KMT: Kuomintang (Chinese nationalist forces)
KNU: Karen National Union
LDC: least developed country
MTA: Mong Tai Army
NCUB: National Council of the Union of Burma
NDF: National Democratic Front
NDUF: National Democratic United Front
NGO: nongovernmental organization
NSH: Noom Suik Harn, Young Warriors
NUF: Nationalities United Front
PDF: People's Democratic Front
RNA: Revolutionary Nationalities Alliance
SLORC: State Law and Order Restoration Council
SSA: Shan State Army
SUA: Shan United Army
TRC: Tailand Revolutionary Council
UNDP: United Nations Development Program
UWSA: United Wa State Army
WACL: World Anti-Communist League

References

Carey, Peter, ed. 1997a. *Burma: The Challenge of Change in a Divided Society*. London: Macmillan.

Carey, Peter. 1997b. *From Burma to Myanmar: Military Rule and the Struggle for Democracy*. London: Research Institute for the Study of Conflict and Terrorism.

Colbert, Evelyn. 1977. *Southeast Asia in International Politics 1941–1956*. Ithaca, NY: Cornell University Press.

Doyle, Michael W., and Nicholas Sambanis. 2000. "Data Set Notes, November 6, 2000." www.nyu.edu/gsas/dept/politics/faculty/cohen/codebook.pdf. (accessed March 1, 2005).

Fink, Christina. 2001. *Living Silence: Burma Under Military Rule*. London: Zed Books.

Global Witness. 2003. "A Conflict of Interests: The Uncertain Future of Burma's Forests." Briefing Document. www.globalwitness.org/reports/

index.php?section=Burma (accessed July 27, 2005).

Gravers, Mikael. 1999. *Nationalism as Political Paranoia in Burma,* 2nd rev. ed. Richmond: Curzon Press.

Koonings, Kees, and Dirk Kruijt, eds. 2002. *Political Armies: The Military and Nation Building in the Age of Democracy.* London: Zed Books.

Leach, Edmund R. 1964. *Political Systems of Highland Burma: A Study of Kachin Social Structure.* London: Athlone Press.

Lintner, Bertil. 1990a. *Land of Jade: A Journey Through Insurgent Burma.* Edinburgh, UK: Kiscadale.

Lintner, Bertil. 1990b. *Outrage: Burma's Struggle for Democracy.* Bangkok: White Lotus.

Lintner, Bertil. 1994. *Burma in Revolt: Opium and Insurgency Since 1948.* Boulder, CO: Westview Press.

Lintner, Bertil. 2002. *Blood Brothers: Crime, Business and Politics in Asia.* Chiang Mai, Thailand: Silkworm Books.

Maitra, Kiranshankar. 1998. *The Nagas Rebel and Insurgency in the North-East.* New Delhi: Vikas Publishing.

Mansingh, Surjit, ed. 1998. *Indian and Chinese Foreign Policies in Comparative Perspective.* New Delhi: Radiant Publishers.

Marshall, Monty G., and Keith Jaggers. 2002. *Polity IV Dataset.* College Park, MD: Center for International Development and Conflict Management, University of Maryland. www.cidcm.umd.edu/inscr/polity/polreg.htm (accessed July 27, 2005).

Maung Maung, U. 1990. *Burmese Nationalist Movements 1940–1948.* Honolulu: University of Hawaii Press.

McCoy, Alfred W. 2003. *The Politics of Heroin: CIA Complicity in the Global Drug Trade,* 2nd rev. ed. Chicago: Lawrence Hill Books.

National Council of the Union of Burma. 2004. www.ncgub.net (accessed September 12, 2006).

Ozturk, Cem. 2003. "Myanmar's Muslim Sideshow." *Asia Times* (October 21).

Pakim, B. 1992. *India-Burma Relations.* New Delhi: Omsons Publications.

Pedersen, Morten B., Emily Rudland, and R. J. May, eds. 2000. *Burma-Myanmar: Strong Regime, Weak State?* Adelaide: Crawford House.

Phongpaichit, Pasuk, Sungsidh Piriyarangsan, and Nualnoi Treerat. 1998. *Guns, Girls, Gambling, Ganja: Thailand's Illegal Economy and Public Policy.* Chiang Mai, Thailand: Silkworm Books.

Po, San C. 1928. 2001. Reprint. *Burma and the Karens.* Bangkok: White Lotus Press.

Ramachandran, Sudha. 2005. "Indian Troops to Enter Myanmar." *Asia Times* (July 21).

Renard, Ronald D. 1996. *The Burmese Connection: Illegal Drugs and the Making of the Golden Triangle.* Boulder, CO: Lynne Rienner.

Rotberg, Robert I., ed. 1998. *Burma: Prospects for a Democratic Future.* Washington, DC: Brookings Institution Press.

Silverstein, Joseph. 1977. *Burma: Military Rule and the Politics of Stagnation.* Ithaca, NY: Cornell University Press.

Smith, Martin. 1991. *Burma: Insurgency and the Politics of Ethnicity.* London: Zed Books.

Soe Myint. 2004. *Burma File: A Question of Democracy.* Singapore: Marshall Cavendish International.

Steinberg, David I. 2001. *Burma: The State of Myanmar.* Washington, DC: Georgetown University Press.

Taylor, Robert H. 2001. *Burma: Political Economy under Military Rule.* London: Hurst.

Tucker, Shelby. 2000. *Among Insurgents: Walking Through Burma.* London: Flamingo.

Tucker, Shelby. 2001. *Burma: The Curse of Independence.* London: Pluto Press.

Tucker, Mike. 2003. *The Long Patrol: With Karen Insurgents in Burma.* Bangkok: Asia Books.

Uppsala Conflict Data Program (UCDP). 2006. Uppsala Conflict Conflict Database. www.pcr.uu.se/database (accessed November 7, 2006).

Yegar, Moshe. 1972. *The Muslims of Burma.* Wiesbaden, Germany: Otto Harrassowitz.

Zakaria, Haji Ahmad, and Harald Crouch, eds. 1985. *Military-Civilian Relations in South-East Asia.* Singapore: Oxford University Press.

Nicaragua
(1978–1979 and 1980–1989)

Introduction

Nicaragua's geographic location in the middle of Central America has magnified the importance of conflicts within the country to its neighbors and the United States. The two civil wars discussed here—one in the 1970s and one in the 1980s—had domestic roots but were heavily influenced by these other countries. The civil war that resulted in the 1979 overthrow of the Somoza dictatorship had its beginnings in the early 1960s when the Sandinista rebels first organized. The Sandinistas and Somoza owed their origins to the U.S. occupation, which, except for a few months in 1925, lasted from 1912 to 1933. The civil war between the Contra rebels and the Sandinista government, which lasted from 1980 to 1989, was largely a result of U.S. policies aimed at overthrowing the Sandinistas. This article provides a summary of both civil wars, with emphasis on the causes of the conflicts and the factors that contributed to the rather unique outcomes of each. For convenience, throughout the article the first civil war is referred to as the Sandinista revolution and the second as the Contra war.

Country Background

Before the civil wars, Nicaragua was a poor country of 3 million people (Defronzo 1991, 189) plagued by a repressive, authoritarian government. With the rest of Central America, it obtained independence from Spain in the 1820s. Afterward, its politics were dominated by elite families centered in Leon (the liberal party) and Granada (the conservative party). The United States was interested in the country mainly as a possible location of a transisthmian canal, for the San Juan River and Lake Nicaragua covered all but fifteen miles between the Atlantic and Pacific oceans. Most inhabitants of Nicaragua lived on the Pacific side of the country and had a Spanish or mixed ethnic heritage; on the east side of the country lived a small minority of Native Americans and descendents of former African slaves.

The first Somoza (Anastasio Somoza Garcia) came to power based on his control of the National Guard, a military body organized and trained by the United States to facilitate U.S. withdrawal from occupation in 1933. After 1926, during the second half of the U.S. occupation, a nationalist rebel group organized by Augusto Cesar Sandino fought to oust the U.S. marines and the National Guard. After the United States withdrew in 1933, Sandino was assassinated by members of the National Guard, and his rebellion died out. Somoza ruled the country until he was assassinated by a young poet in 1956. After this, power passed to his two sons—first to Luis Somoza Debayle until his death in 1967, then to Anastasio Somoza Debayle. The Somoza family used its position to accumulate enormous wealth. The Somozas pursued policies designed to repress and buy off their domestic rivals, and they sought the unqualified support of the United States as their external guarantor of power. Ultimately, the poverty of ordinary Nicaraguans, combined with the greed, corruption, and repression of the dictatorship, created the basis for a revolution led by the Sandinistas, a rebel group with historical and ideological roots in Sandino's earlier rebellion.

Conflict Background

The first civil war under consideration, the duration of which is often listed as 1978–1979, had it origins in a guerrilla movement founded in 1961 (Booth 1985; Christian 1985; Crawley 1984; Diederich 1981; Walker 1986). The Sandinista rebels sought to overthrow the Somoza dictatorship and control the government. The conflict had an ideological component in that the rebels supported Marxist-oriented policies that aimed to redistribute wealth, whereas Somoza was staunchly anticommunist and promoted an elite-dominated market economy. There was little, if any, ethnic dimension in the conflict. In addition to the tradition of Sandino, the Sandinistas were inspired by the example of Fidel Castro, whose guerrillas overthrew the government of Cuba in 1959. Until the final stages of the conflict in 1978–1979 there was little intervention except for military support provided to the Somoza regime by the United States. The Sandinista forces grew rapidly from about 500 in 1978 to a final 1979 level of about 5,000 (DeFronzo 1991, 202). Somoza's National Guard had approximately 7,500 troops in September 1978 and had grown to 11,000 by March 1979 (Pastor 2002, 101). Casualty estimates from the Sandinista war vary, but a conservative approximation is 30,000 dead.

The Contra war from 1980 to 1989 was similar in that the Contra rebels aimed to overthrow the Sandinista government and, at least initially,

restore the old order. This was also a classic Cold War stalemate, with the United States supporting the anti-Communist Contras and the Soviet Union and Cuba among the main supporters of the Sandinista government. The Contra forces were formed from elements of the National Guard who fled after the Sandinista victory. With U.S. funds, training, and organization, they grew to a force of about 30,000 in the mid-1980s (Pastor 2002, 27). The largest Contra faction, the FDN (Nicaraguan Democratic force), had 6,000–12,000 soldiers in the latter half of the 1980s (DeFronzo 1991, 211). They faced a Sandinista military force of 25,000 in 1981 (Dickey 1987, 140), which grew to 60,000 soldiers and 200,000 local militia units in the late 1980s (DeFronzo 1991, 215)

The Contra war was the more internationalized of the two conflicts. It produced about 40,000 casualties and had important effects on neighboring Honduras, which hosted most of the U.S.-funded Contra bases, and El Salvador, which received increased aid from the United States to counter its own leftist rebels, who received support from the Sandinista government. The military regime in Argentina was a strong backer of the Contras; initially, the Argentine presence helped the United States conceal its involvement. Costa Rica, although it tried with some success to remain neutral, was another country where Contras organized against the Sandinistas.

In the early 1980s, it appeared that the Contra war could be an ongoing, low-intensity conflict of long duration. The end of the Cold War in 1989 was one of several factors that contributed to a speedier end to the Contra war. And in the United States, the 1986–1987 Iran–Contra scandal undermined what little domestic support there was for the war. Finally, the change of administration from Reagan to Bush brought a desire to "take Nicaragua off the agenda" and create a stronger working relationship between the new president and Congress (Pastor 2002). The mediation and peace efforts of other countries in the region, specifically the Arias plan, were in-

Table 1: Civil War in Nicaragua

War:	FSLN vs. government; government vs. Contras
Dates:	1978–1979; 1980–1989
Casualties:	1978–1979, 50,000; 1980–1989, 43,000 (Doyle and Sambanis 2000), 160,000 wounded (Pastor 2000, 161)
Regime type prior to war:	–8 from 1946 to 1979 (Polity 2 variable in Polity IV data— ranging from –10 [authoritarian] to 10 [democracy])
Regime type after war:	–6 to –1 between 1982 and 1989; +6 in 1991 (Polity 2 variable in Polity IV data— ranging from –10 [authoritarian] to 10 [democracy])
GDP per capita year war began:	US $2,215.30 (2006 dollars; from PWT 1978)
GDP per capita 5 years after war:	US $2,432.82 (2006 dollars; from PWT 1984)
	US $1,711.63 (2006 dollars; from PWT 1994)
Insurgents:	FSLN (Sandinistas); Contras (FDN, ARDE, others)
Issue:	1978–1979: Repression and corruption in government
	1980–1989: Ideological struggle for control of central government
Rebel funding:	1978-1979: From rebel activities (ransom), aid from Argentina, Chile, Panama, Costa Rica, Cuba
	1980–1989: United States, Saudi Arabia, Brunei, Taiwan, Israel, Argentina, Colombian drug traffickers, wealthy individuals
Role of geography:	Rebels hid in forest and mountains; porous borders helped all sides obtain arms.
Role of resources:	Not applicable
Immediate outcome:	1978–1979: Rebel victory
	1980–1989: Negotiations, elections, peaceful transfer of power
Outcome after 5 years:	1978–1979 (1984): New civil war
	1980–1989 (1994): Stable peace
Role of UN:	Provided election monitors in 1990 and peacekeepers to disarm Contras after election
Role of NGOs:	Carter Center instrumental in mediating and monitoring 1990 election.
Role of regional organization:	1978–1979: OAS was involved at the end, encouraged dictator to step down.
	1980–1989: Governments in region made peace initiatives (Contadora; Arias plan).
Refugees:	Remnants of Somoza government and National Guard fled in 1979.
Prospects for peace:	Good

Sources: Doyle and Sambanis 2000, DeFronzo 1991, Heston et. al. 2002 (PWT), Pastor 2002.

strumental in providing the opportunity for a nonviolent solution to the conflict once the U.S. support for the Contras waned. In the end, the Sandinistas lost power in an election but remained active as an opposition party.

The Insurgents
The Sandinistas

Though they began with about twenty poorly trained, poorly equipped guerrillas and little support from moderates in the populace, by 1979 the Sandinistas led a coalition that overthrew the Somoza regime. Like most rebel groups, the Sandinista National Liberation Front (FSLN) began as a group of weak resisters who, throughout most of the 1960s, barely avoided total defeat. After repeated cycles of confrontation, defeat, retreats, and regrouping, they achieved an enduring but low-level resistance in the early 1970s (Booth 1985, 138–41). The guerrilla core of the group was well-organized, and it learned to become integrated with the peasant communities in the countryside for support. Yet the Sandinistas were not very effective in mobilizing the masses who resented Somoza's rule until after the 1972 earthquake in Managua. The consensus among analysts of this postquake period of the Nicaraguan conflict is that the naked greed shown by Somoza and the Guard in the aftermath of the quake cost the regime the support of middle- and upper-sector business elites that had been the core of Somoza's internal legitimacy (Booth 1985, 81–85; Crawley 1984, 150; Diederich 1981; Lake 1989, 19–20; Walker 1986, 32).

In response to Sandinista growth after the earthquake, Somoza increased repression by imposing a "state of siege," or martial law, from 1974 to 1977; this repression caused internal debates that split the Sandinista organization while at the same time stimulating more mobilization among the masses. The Sandinistas were also unique in their willingness to use women in combat roles in the movement; at the end, up to a quarter of their soldiers were women (Booth 1985; Pastor 2002). Also, in the end the Sandinistas benefited from their willingness to ally with progressive Catholics who embraced "liberation theology." Finally, by making alliances with moderates, democrats, and disillusioned economic elites after 1977, the Sandinistas were able to garner support from an unusual array of sources that were united in their desire to depose Somoza.

The Contras

Initially, the Contras were composed of former members of Somoza's National Guard who fled the country after the revolution and whose skill set made soldiering their best method of earning a living. The former guard members certainly had intense grievances against the Sandinistas and the Carter government. Yet, had they been left to their exile in Honduras, Costa Rica, and the United States, they would not likely have organized a coherent guerrilla resistance. It was the U.S. government funds, weapons, organization,

and training that created this rebel force. Once organized, the Contras appeared to be a credible force because of the continuing support of the United States. This credibility encouraged others who shared or developed their own grievances against the Sandinista government (such as Miskito Indians, economic elites, and alienated members of the Sandinista government), to decide to rebel. They were also supported by the hierarchy of the Catholic Church, which disapproved of liberation theology and the participation of priests in the Sandinista revolution.

Geography

Nicaragua is well-suited to guerrillas who wish to use mountainous and jungle terrain for cover and retreat zones. The northern border with Honduras is mountainous, making it easily permeable. The Atlantic (Miskito) coast is sparsely populated and contains jungle and rain forest. About 90 percent of Nicaraguans live on the Pacific side of the country; those on the Atlantic side include about 70,000 Miskito Indians, other indigenous peoples, and a number of descendants of African slaves who fled to Nicaragua from other countries. The Atlantic side was dominated by Britain until the 1890s, and many people in the region speak English instead of Spanish (DeFronzo 1991, 190).

Only 15 percent of the country is arable land (CIA 2006); in 1998, 26 percent was forested (Wilkie, Aleman, and Ortega 2002). Deforestation is an increasingly significant problem in Nicaragua. The country has been the victim of countless natural disasters and is vulnerable in particular to hurricanes (Mitch killed 3,800 in 1998 ([National Climatic Data Center 2006]), earthquakes (one centered in Managua on December 23, 1972, killed 5,000), landslides, and volcanoes (Wilkie, Aleman, and Ortega 2002).

Nicaragua's urban centers include the capital of Managua (population 1.1 million in 2003), whose central district was destroyed by the 1972 earthquake and was not rebuilt. Smaller cities include Leon (population 124,000 in 1995), Granada (population 72,000 in 1995), and Chi-

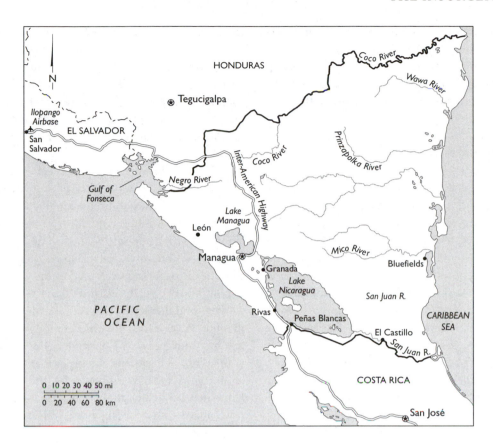

nandega (97,000 in 1995) (Europa World Year Book 2005).

Tactics

The Sandinistas

A strength of the Sandinistas was the variety of tactics they used to mobilize followers (Simon 1991). In their early days, they pursued the standard rural guerrilla tactics preached by Mao Zedong and Che Guevara. Owing to the small size of the movement in the 1960s, the Somoza regime was able to defeat these efforts. However, as the rebels regrouped in the early 1970s, three factions formed, each pursuing a different set of tactics (Booth 1985, Pastor 2002). The first, the "prolonged peoples' war" (guerra popular prolongada) faction, led by Tomas Borge and Henry Ruiz, maintained rural guerrilla tactics, with less emphasis on political indoctrination and more on the development of small groups of guerrillas,

or foco, that could strike at the regime. A second faction, the proletarios, led by Jaime Wheelock, pursued an urban strategy that sought to mobilize unions, poor city neighborhoods, and urban workers against the regime. Principal tactics of this faction included strikes and demonstrations. The third, the Tercerista faction, led by Daniel and Humberto Ortega, sought to build broader-based coalitions, including moderate regime opponents and religious people who were not attracted to Marxism. They employed a variety of high-profile acts of resistance and terrorist tactics, such as hostage taking, designed to gain maximum publicity for the cause and to demonstrate to potential recruits that the regime could be successfully resisted. The most famous example was the August 1978 seizure of 1,500 hostages in the national palace. The raid, led by Eden Pastora, ended with the release of fifty FLSN prisoners, payment of $500,000 in ransom, and safe passage out of the country for the hostage takers (Diederich 1981). The raid also validated the Tercerista strategy as the most effective for mobilizing dissent. Soon afterward, the three factions reunited to jointly pursue the final overthrow of Somoza.

The Somoza Government

Anastasio Somoza Garcia fit the stereotype of a kleptocratic leader, but like most dictators, he developed a great deal of political skill in dividing and buying off moderate opponents. With Communist rebels, however, he had no qualms about using indiscriminate force, and this would contribute greatly to his downfall. Although at times it gained him some temporary advantage, such as during the "state of siege" imposed from 1975 to 1977, in the longer term it inflamed the opposition and allowed the FSLN to grow stronger and draw in more moderate allies.

Researchers generally note two important turning points in the conflict: the Managua earthquake of 1972 and the assassination of *La Prensa* editor Pedro Joachim Chamorro in 1978. Both led to serious tactical errors. As noted above, Somoza and his cronies stole earthquake aid; this greatly intensified the grievances among the urban poor in Managua and created the opportunity for the broad-based mobilization under an anti-Somoza banner that the FSLN eventually achieved. The Chamorro assassination alienated elites in the country; had Somoza been able to prevent it, or had he taken steps to punish those responsible, he might have avoided this elite division, which theorists of revolution assert is a crucial factor in the overthrow of governments (Goldstone 1982).

The Contras

Because the first groups of Contras consisted of former National Guard members who were known for their brutality, it is not surprising that the tactics of the Contras involved a considerable amount of terrorism in addition to the standard hit-and-run guerrilla tactics. After the initial Contra forces were established and trained, the United States increased aid, providing higher-quality weapons and more pay for the fighters (Dickey 1987). Although many Contra fighters believed that they were pursuing a guerrilla strategy similar to that by which the Sandinistas succeeded in the first civil war, in fact the U.S. strategy was one of "low-intensity conflict." This strategy allowed the United States to use the Contra forces as proxies to keep pressure on the Sandinista government without committing U.S. troops. This pressure would cause the Sandinistas to become militaristic and repressive and would eventually drive the population away from supporting the regime.

This low-intensity conflict strategy explains some of the terrorist tactics used by the Contras; they attacked civilians such as teachers, coffee workers, and literacy workers sent by the regime to poor rural areas, in order to prevent the regime from providing tangible gains to the population. The strategy was supplemented by a total trade embargo imposed by the United States in 1985, which took away a trading partner that accounted for 30 percent of Nicaraguan trade (DeFronzo 1991, 210).

The Sandinista Government

The Sandinistas pursued a variety of tactics to resist the Contras. They tried to pursue policies aimed at reversal of social and economic inequalities as a means of maintaining popular support and delegitimizing the Contras. This includes their early literacy campaign, which mobilized thousands of Nicaraguans and sent them to rural villages to teach others to read. However, the Contra attacks on teachers, coffee workers, and government officials led the Sandinistas to pursue an increasingly militarized response, which in the end proved costly and sometimes counterproductive.

The Sandinistas received arms from the Soviet Union and Cuba and built their standing army to a size that, on paper, was larger than all of their neighbors' armies combined. They also militarized society with the creation of local militias; the goal here was to prevent Contras from making gains at the village level that could not be identified and quickly countered. Such militarization led to many abuses, such as the jailing of Miskito dissidents, but Sandinista abuses were less frequent and less severe than those of the Contras, according to international human rights organizations (DeFronzo 1991, 213).

The Sandinistas combined militarization with cooperative acts designed to counter the arguments of the United States that they were a brutal Communist dictatorship. They eliminated the death penalty, offered amnesty to former National Guard members and Contras at various times during the conflict, and were credited with generally humane treatment of prisoners. Most significantly, they held a national election in 1984 that was validated as reasonably fair by international observers although dismissed by the United States as a sham.

Some tactical mistakes of the Sandinistas included programs that ostensibly protected the Miskito Indians from the Contras but instead required them to move away from their home villages. Also, at the outset of their revolutionary government, the Sandinistas insisted on supporting rebels in El Salvador, with the hope that they, too, could succeed. However this support led President Jimmy Carter to cut off U.S. aid and provoked the Reagan administration to begin organizing the Contras. Just as Castro occasionally told the Sandinistas that the best help he could give them was no help at all, the Sandinistas might have considered that their policies would, as Pastor (2002) eloquently describes, bring about the very things they wanted to avoid—a war with the United States and dependence on the Soviet Union. The Sandinistas decided that the United States would likely fabricate provocations anyway; hence the potential benefit of a revolution in El Salvador was worth the risk. This turned out to be incorrect.

Causes of the War
The Sandinista Revolution

The central cause of the first civil war was similar to dozens of others in Latin America and the developing world—a corrupt, economically ineffective, repressive, and illegitimate dictatorship that created vast grievances among the masses of poor people but eventually even among elites in the country. Of course, grievances are a necessary precondition to rebellion but hardly sufficient. Those with grievances could pursue many means of redress. The 1956 assassination of Somoza Garcia showed that an isolated dissident could not create effective change. The 1959 Cuban revolution revealed another, more effective strategy. But the first group of Sandinista rebels who attempted a rural guerrilla resistance was largely unsuccessful; the coercive power of the regime was too strong. The Sandinistas achieved success only when they expanded their narrow ideology to embrace moderate regime opponents. Once they had demonstrated that they had a significant chance of success (Lichbach 1994), they were able to mobilize effectively as well as attract external support.

Just as important to the success of the Sandinistas were conditions affecting the Somoza regime. The regime was weakened by a natural disaster (the 1972 earthquake), a loss of support from its international patron (with the election of Carter as U.S. president in 1976), and finally by its own tactics of indiscriminate repression in response to growing Sandinista strength. It is easy to speculate, in hindsight, that a leader less greedy and more creative than Somoza could have made the compromises necessary to maintain U.S. support and that of the economic elite in the country.

The Contra War

The desire of the United States to create an armed resistance to the Sandinista government was the most important factor in the creation of the Contra war. Remnants of Somoza's National Guard would no doubt have mounted attacks on their own, but without U.S. funds, weapons, and training, this would not have constituted an ongoing civil war. Still, the Contras were able to attract additional groups and leaders who had become disenchanted with the Sandinista government (for

Rattlesnakes

One of the most notorious Contra fighters, Pedro Pablo Ortiz Centeno (nom de guerre: El Suicida), nearly died while attempting to flee after the 1979 Sandinista revolution. El Suicida was made famous in the United States by the writings of Christopher Dickey of the *Washington Post* (Dickey 1987). As a member of Somoza's National Guard, El Suicida had been trained by the United States at the School of the Americas in Panama. After the fall of Somoza on July 20, he and others in his unit (the Rattlesnakes) hijacked a boat and attempted to make it to El Salvador. However, they ran out of food and water after one day, and on the second day the boat ran out of fuel. They drifted until July 23, when they were saved from certain death by the appearance of a commercial fishing boat. The fishing boat's crew attempted to help the drifting vessel, but the Rattlesnakes overpowered the crew and took their boat to La Union, El Salvador. Within a few weeks, the Rattlesnakes were in Honduras, forming the beginnings of the Contra forces that would challenge the Sandinistas for the next decade (Dickey 1987).

example, Eden Pastora); thus they were able to recruit in both urban and rural areas.

Outcome
Conflict Status

The Sandinista revolution ended with the breakdown of the Somoza government and the Sandinista takeover on July 20, 1979. The Sandinistas installed a junta that consisted of guerrilla leaders (including Daniel Ortega as the spokesperson of the group) and moderates Alfonso Robelo Callejas and Violeta Barrios de Chamorro, widow of Pedro Joachim Chamorro, the assassinated editor of *La Prensa*. The new government stated its intention to develop a "mixed" economy and to pursue policies aimed at helping the poor. However, Somoza had left only $3 million in the treasury, and the Sandinistas inherited a $1.6 billion debt (Booth 1985;

Walker 1986). By 1980, tensions had developed between the Sandinistas and their moderate allies; Robelo and Chamorro resigned from the junta in April, and opposition developed among business elites, Catholic bishops, and even former guerrilla leaders such as Eden Pastora in 1982 (Dickey 1987, 149). Within six weeks of its inauguration in January 1981, the Reagan administration signed an intelligence "finding" that allowed it to begin organizing the bands of former National Guard members into what became the Contras (Dickey 1987; Pastor 2002).

The Contra war was resolved by an election that brought to power Violeta Chamorro and the Nicaraguan Opposition Union (UNO) coalition. The election was the result of the Arias peace plan, which brought pressure from the Central American governments who supported it, and of long negotiations between the Sandinistas and their opponents, mediated by former President Jimmy Carter. After the election, Chamorro decided to retain Humberto Ortega (brother of Daniel) as head of the armed forces. This and other gestures helped the Sandinistas accept their electoral defeat and make the transition to an opposition political party and political movement. They remain a strong force in Nicaraguan politics. In the elections, Daniel Ortega finished second with 42 percent of the vote (Anderson and Dodd 2002). In 2006, a more moderate Ortega was elected president.

Duration Tactics

Using 1961 as a starting point, the Sandinistas took quite a long time to achieve their final victory, and the odds were against them most of the way. They received little external help in the first decade and had little success in generating popular mobilization. They benefited from the brutality and unpopularity of Somoza, which gave them an enemy they could use to mobilize. Ironically, it was when the guerrillas grew strong enough to split into factions that they were able to make tactical innovations that helped them in the end. The three FSLN factions each pursued

Daniel Ortega, the charismatic leader of the Sandinista rebels, addresses his supporters in Managua, Nicaragua on July 19, 1979. Ortega was elected president of Nicaragua in 2006. (Patrick Chauvel/Sygma/Corbis)

different tactics; while this competition could have been destructive, in the end it was constructive. The success of the Terceristas in achieving popular mobilization led the Sandinistas to reunify and eventually defeat Somoza's National Guard. Guerrilla tactics usually take a long time, and as noted earlier, they usually fail when used against a government that is not colonial or a foreign occupier.

The lack of military intervention to aid Somoza also shortened the conflict. At the very end, in June 1979, it became apparent to all that the Somoza government would lose. Yet, despite desperate mediation attempts by the United States, Somoza stubbornly refused to turn power over to a successor in the National Guard and seek exile. According to Pastor (2002), this prevented a solution that might have kept the Sandinistas from controlling the entire government. Had the United States succeeded in getting Somoza to step down, to leave the Guard intact,

and to find a replacement leader, the conflict would have been substantially longer.

Several factors prolonged the Contra war, but three stand out as important. First, the bipolar Cold War system quickly led both sides in the conflict to receive aid from rival superpowers. A second factor is that the U.S. administration and the Sandinista government deeply distrusted each other, and as a result both chose to pursue a military solution to the conflict rather than a diplomatic one. The Carter administration initially offered aid to the Sandinista government but ended it after evidence surfaced that the Sandinistas were arming the rebels in El Salvador. The election of Ronald Reagan, who came to power with a mandate to pursue a more confrontational policy toward the Soviet Union, effectively ended U.S. efforts to pursue a diplomatic solution. As Robert Pastor (2002) convincingly argues, the policies of the United States and the Sandinistas were driven by their leaders' mutual obsession with each other as enemies. Ironically, this obsession led each side to take actions that brought about the very outcome that they said they feared. The United States wanted the Sandinistas to become more democratic, less dependent on Moscow, and less likely to spread revolution in the region. The reverse occurred. The Sandinistas wanted to maintain relations with moderate supporters in Nicaragua, diversify their foreign relations, and be free from U.S. attack; instead, they became dependent on the Soviets and the Cubans, alienated moderate supporters, and faced a Contra rebellion that was well-funded by the United States.

A third factor in prolonging the conflict is the rather high level of armaments (by Central American standards) provided by interveners. However, when conditions changed to prevent this level of armament, the war came to an unexpectedly quick ending. The conditions that ended the war were the Iran-Contra scandal (which nearly eliminated support in the U.S. Congress for continued armament of the Contras); the end of the Cold War in 1989 (which diffused the superpower conflict that was the basis of the U.S. and Soviet provision of arms); and finally, the Arias peace plan (which was there when all sides needed a way out of the conflict).

External Military Intervention

The FSLN was supported by Venezuela, Panama, Costa Rica, and Cuba in 1978–1979. Before this period, Costa Rica had provided sanctuary for the FSLN. Panama provided asylum for the guerrillas who raided the Nicaraguan national palace, and later transferred arms to the FSLN. The help from Cuba came very near the end, in the form of arms shipments through Costa Rica (Christian 1985; Diederich 1981). This was a departure from Castro's previous position that the best help he could provide the Sandinistas was "not to help at all" (Booth 1985, 134). His fear was that Cuban aid would provide the pretext for U.S. intervention.

The Somoza government was supported by the United States until September 1977, when President Carter, who had embraced human rights as the "soul" of his foreign policy, essentially told Somoza that support was no longer unconditional. This caused Somoza to lift the state of siege. Somoza had the diplomatic support of some right-wing governments in the region, such El Salvador and Argentina, but was opposed in the end by all members of the OAS except Paraguay (on June 23, 1979, the OAS voted seventeen to two to demand that Somoza resign). To influence Somoza to moderate his policies, the United States used economic incentives tied to human rights, eventually pursuing the meditation effort described following to encourage Somoza to leave before the Sandinistas won.

The United States funded the Contras and supported Honduras for hosting their bases. The Contras were also funded by the royal family of Saudi Arabia; the sultan of Brunei; Taiwan; Colombian drug traffickers; and private individuals recruited by the Reagan administration during the period from October 1984 to June 1986, when the United States was prevented by the Boland amendments from legally supporting the Contras. Costa Rica initially permitted Contra bases, but this ended after Oscar Arias was elected in 1986. The United States imposed a total trade embargo in May 1985 (Pastor 2002).

The Sandinistas initially received humanitarian aid from the United States, but Carter cut this off in January 1981 after evidence of Sandinista support for Salvadoran rebels came to light (Pastor 2002). The sources of weapons for the Sandinistas were the Soviet Union and Cuba (Regan 2002). Their goal was to prevent a Contra victory, but they were also careful not to provoke direct U.S. military intervention into the conflict. They provided helicopters and other weapons that were very helpful for fighting the Contras, who were using the hilly, forested regions near the Honduran border to conceal their bases.

Conflict Management Efforts

By 1977, there was growing awareness in the United States, on the part of Central American governments, and among elites in Nicaragua that in order to prevent a Sandinista victory, Somoza needed to leave power. The question was, when and how could this be done? As the fighting intensified in 1978, many efforts were made to convince the dictator to leave. From October to December 1978, the United States led an OAS-sponsored mediation effort that sought, through negotiations with Somoza and the Broad Opposition Front (FAO), to find a way for the dictator to leave power before his term of office ended in 1981. After consideration of many ideas, including a national plebiscite on Somoza's rule, the mediation ended in failure (Lake 1989, ch. 8). Somoza did not want to leave office and was concerned for his life and his assets should he be forced out. The Sandinistas were suspicious that the mediation was a deliberate attempt to weaken the revolution and to install some form of "Somocismo without Somoza" by retaining the National Guard in a new government (Pastor 2002). Had the mediation succeeded, the war would have been shortened, and a more moderate coalition would likely have governed. Because it failed, the Sandinistas went on to military victory seven months later.

Because it appeared that the United States and the Sandinistas were not likely to make any progress on what had become an important regional problem, the leaders of several Central and South American countries took a variety of initiatives to fill the diplomatic vacuum. The first effort was called the Contadora plan; it was launched at a meeting of the foreign ministers of Mexico, Venezuela, Colombia, and Panama on the Panamanian island of Contadora in January 1983. As Pastor (2002, 198) notes, it was the first time in the century that the United States was excluded from such a negotiation in the Americas. Over the next two years, the group wrote four drafts of a treaty, and though Nicaragua agreed to sign the final (June 6) draft, the United States, Costa Rica, Honduras, and El Salvador refused, and the process petered out.

However, with the 1986 democratic elections of Vinicio Cerezo in Guatemala and Oscar Arias in Costa Rica, a new peace plan began brewing. In February 1987, Arias proposed a ten-point peace plan, building on the Contadora proposal. This would eventually become the basis for negotiations that led to the 1990 election that ended the conflict. The Contras agreed to the election and applied lessons that it had learned from its electoral defeat in 1984—namely, not to boycott an election that could be fair and bring them legitimacy, if not political power. The Sandinistas agreed to the election partly because they believed that they would indeed win a free election, and that if the election were validated as free by international observers, U.S. funding of the Contras and the war would end.

The Organization of American States (OAS) and the UN both provided election monitors (DeFronzo 1991, 218), and the UN helped to disarm the Contras after the election. Former U.S. President Jimmy Carter played a central role in negotiating the detailed terms of the election itself. Without his mediation, it is likely that the whole effort would have failed. Carter insisted upon several mechanisms to make sure that voter intimidation would not be tolerated, that the vote would be accurate and credible, and that both sides would accept the result.

Conclusion

The two civil wars in Nicaragua provide much to consider for those interested in the dynamics of civil war and rebellion. The Sandinista revolution was one of a very few that used guerrilla tactics to overthrow a nonoccupation government. Was their success due to their innovation and effectiveness or to the poor strategies pursued by Somoza? The lack of a moderate alternative to the Somoza regime combined with the Sandinistas' willingness to expand their coalition to include moderates to provide the Sandinistas with the political and military strength

Guerrilla War

The Sandinista revolution in Nicaragua is one of a very small number of civil wars in which local rebels used guerrilla war tactics to defeat an independent, noncolonial government. After 1945, the only other examples are China in 1949 and Cuba in 1959 (Iran in 1979 did not involve guerrilla tactics). As Dyer (2004, 396) notes, the rural guerrilla war technique was most effective against foreign occupiers and colonial governments, for reasons stressed by many scholars (e.g., Mack 1975). The guerrillas needed only to continue fighting, and eventually the costs to the colonial power would outweigh the benefits of fighting away from home. However, an independent government and its army are already home and thus more inclined to fight on indefinitely against the insurgency.

to win the civil war. Still, Somoza had a loyal military force behind him, and had he been more willing to compromise to divide his opponents, he might have been able to survive.

The Contra war was one of the first successful uses of a low-intensity conflict strategy, and it is one of a rare number of civil wars that have resulted in stable, democratic outcomes. Are these cases unique, or are there lessons here that can be applied elsewhere? The end of the Cold War created an international context that made the Contra war likely to end; however, the fact that it ended in democracy has a lot more to do with the active role played by states and nongovernmental organizations (NGOs) committed to peaceful conflict resolution. In particular, the efforts of states in the region to create and implement the Arias plan, plus the availability and willingness of Jimmy Carter to act as mediator, were necessary for democracy to prevail.

Marc V. Simon

Chronology

1893   General Jose Santos Zelaya, a liberal, seizes power and establishes dictatorship.

1909   U.S. troops help depose Zelaya.

1912–1925   United States establishes military bases.

1926–1933   After a nine-month absence, U.S. troops return to Nicaragua during civil war, train and support the National Guard against guerrillas led by Augusto Cesar Sandino.

1934   Sandino is assassinated on the orders of General Anastasio Somoza Garcia, National Guard commander.

1937   General Anastasio Somoza Garcia is elected Nicaraguan president.

1956   General Somoza is assassinated but is succeeded as president by his son, Luis Somoza Debayle.

1961   Sandinista National Liberation Front (FSLN) is formally organized.

1967   President Luis Somoza dies in office.

February 1967   Anastasio Somoza Debayle is elected president.

December 1972   Powerful earthquake hits Nicaragua, killing 10,000.

September 1974   Somoza Debayle is re-elected president.

December 1974   FSLN guerrillas hold hostage a handful of leading government officials; exchange hostages for eighteen jailed Sandinistas, $5 million, and safe passage to Cuba.

1975   Government imposes a state of siege; lasts until September 1977.

1975   FSLN splits into three factions: Proletarians, Prolonged Popular War, and the Terceristas (Insurrectional Faction).

September 1977   United States makes military assistance conditional on improvements in human rights.

January 1978   Pedro Joaquin Chamorro, editor of *La Prensa* and moderate critic of the Somoza regime, is assassinated; this triggers a general strike and brings together moderates and the FSLN in a united front to oust Somoza.

February 1978   United States suspends all military assistance.

March 1978   Nicaraguan Democratic Movement is formed.

September 1978   Group of the FSLN Terceristas led by Eden Pastora take over the National Palace and hold 2,000 government officials hostage; hostages are freed in exchange for $500,000 ransom, the release of fifty FSLN members, and safe passage out of the country.

March 1979   Three factions of the FSLN formally unify.

1979   The National Patriotic Front is formed.

February 1979   Sandinista guerrillas formally unify.

July 17, 1979   President Somoza flees.

July 19, 1979   Managua falls to Sandinistas.

May 1980   Council of State is formed.

1980   Somoza is assassinated in Paraguay.

January 1981   United States suspends all aid to Nicaragua.

March 1981   Reagan administration authorizes support for groups trying to overthrow the Sandinistas.

1981   Groups of former members of the National Guard form what is known as the Contras.

July 1981   United Nicaraguan Opposition is formed.

1982   State of emergency is declared by Sandinista government in response to Contra attacks.

December 1982   U.S. Congress passes Boland amendment, which prohibits use of funds to overthrow Sandinistas.

January 1983   Contadora peace initiative lauched by Mexico, Venezuela, Colombia, and Panama.

May 1983   Reagan cuts Nicaraguan sugar quota.

October 1983   United States invades Grenada.

October 1984   Second Boland amendment bans all U.S. funding for Contras.

November 1984   FSLN wins 67 percent of the votes in national election; Daniel Ortega becomes president.

1984   U.S. mines Nicaraguan harbors and is condemned by World Court for doing so.

April 1985   United States imposes a total trade embargo on Nicarargua.

June 1986   Sandinistas agree to sign Contadora peace treaty; U.S. Congress votes to resume aid to the Contras.

February 1987   Peace plan is proposed by Costa Rican President Oscar Arias.

August 1987   Arias plan is signed (commonly known as Esquipulas II).

January 1988   President Ortega holds direct talks with Contras, lifts state of emergency, and calls for national elections.

February 1988   U.S. Congress bans all military aid to Contras.

March 1988   A cease-fire is negotiated between the Contras and the Sandinista government.

December 1989   United States invades Panama to capture leader Manuel Noriega.

February 1990   Violeta Barrios de Chamorro wins presidency in election; FSLN hands over power.

List of Acronyms

FAO : Broad Opposition Front

FDN : Nicaraguan Democratic Force

FSLN : Sandinista National Liberation Front

NGO: nongovernmental organization

OAS: Organization of American States

UNO: Nicaraguan Opposition Union

Glossary

Boland amendments: A series of laws sponsored by U.S. representative Edward P. Boland, chairman of the House Intelligence Committee, by which the U.S. Congress placed limitations on U.S. aid to the Contras. The first, in 1982, limited the U.S. to overt funding aimed at interdicting arms shipments to El Salvadoran rebels; it prohibited military support the purpose of which was the overthrow the government of Nicaragua. The most important one, passed in 1984, made it illegal for the United States to provide any funds to the Contras. This ban was lifted in 1986.

Contras: The counterrevolutionary rebels who fought the Sandinista government; derived from the Spanish *contrarevolucionario*.

elite-dominated market economy: An economy in which private ownership and free markets are dominant but in which a few politically connected individuals, families, and corporations control an inordinate amount of the capital and production of the country. The elites often engage in monopolistic behavior that reduces economic competition.

foco: The Spanish word for "focus." A foco insurgency is one that is organized into small bands of fast-moving, rurally based guerrillas that can attack government forces. This method does not stress the political indoctrination of the population, but hopes to ignite popular support for the guerrillas by winning military victories over state forces.

intelligence finding: Beginning with the 1974 Hughes-Ryan Act, the U.S. Congress required that the president sign a written statement to inform Congress of any important covert action that the president desires to initiate. The statement indicates that the president "finds" that the covert action is important for U.S. national security.

Iran–Contra scandal: To circumvent a congressional ban on funding for the Contras between 1984 and 1986, officials in the Reagan administration used several creative and illegal means to provide funds. The one that caused the scandal involved the creation by members of Reagan's National Security Council of an entity outside the U.S. government, dubbed the Enterprise, which could carry out Reagan's foreign policy objectives without using congressionally controlled U.S. government funds. Using the Enterprise, Reagan sold weapons to Iran with the hope that the Iranians would use their influence to secure the release of several U.S. citizens who were being held hostage by terrorists in Lebanon. (One hostage was released.) The scandal emerged in 1986 when the U.S. public learned that Reagan had violated his stated policy of not negotiating with terrorists. Soon they also learned that the weapons had been sold at inflated prices and that profits from the arms sale were diverted to the Contra rebels in Nicaragua, all in violation of U.S. law.

kleptocrat: A government leader, usually a dictator, whose primary motivation in governing seems to be the pursuit of wealth for family and friends through graft, theft of government funds, and general misuse of authority.

legitimacy: The ability of a government authority to generate compliance from its people without the use of coercion.

liberation theology: A movement in the Roman Catholic in the early 1970s. Advocates of liberation theology wanted the Church to become more actively involved in attacking the political, economic, and social causes of poverty and injustice. The movement was especially strong in Latin America, where the church had accepted dictatorship and economic exploitation for decades.

mixed economy: An economic system that allows some government control mixed with some private enterprise. It contrasts with a pure centrally planned Communist economy, in which the government owns virtually all productive enterprises, and a pure free-market economy, in which private citizens and corporations own productive enterprises.

necessary condition: In formal logic, a cause that must exist for a particular effect to occur. Without the existence of the necessary condition, the consequence cannot occur. A *sufficient condition* is a cause that, if present, will always produce the particular effect.

plebiscite: A vote by an entire electorate to decide a question of importance. Synonymous with *referendum.*

terrorist tactics: The use of violence or threats of violence, usually directed at innocent civilians, that seeks political change by generating fear. Terrorist tactics are not aimed at influencing the direct victims of violence, but rather the public and government audience watching the violence. Terrorist tactics can be used by individuals, groups, or governments. Typical examples include bombing, hijacking, hostage taking, and armed assault.

trade embargo: The reduction or end of exports and imports by one country with another country. Embargoes are usually imposed to protest either political or economic policies in the targeted country

References

Anderson, Leslie, and Lawrence Dodd. 2002. "Nicaragua Votes: The Elections of 2001." *Journal of Democracy* 13(3): 80–94.

Booth, John A. 1985. *The End and the Beginning: The Nicaraguan Revolution,* 2nd ed. Boulder, CO: Westview Press.

Booth, John, and Thomas Walker. 1989. *Understanding Central America.* Boulder, CO: Westview Press.

Central Intelligence Agency (CIA). 2006. *The CIA World Factbook 2006.* www.cia.gov/cia/publications/factbook/ (accessed January 3, 2006).

Christian, Shirley. 1985. *Nicaragua: Revolution in the Family.* New York: Random House.

Crawley, Eduardo. 1984. *Nicaragua in Perspective.* New York: St. Martin's Press.

DeFronzo, James. 1991. *Revolutions and Revolutionary Movements.* Boulder, CO: Westview Press.

Dickey, Christopher. 1987. *With the Contras: A Reporter in the Wilds of Nicaragua.* New York: Simon & Schuster.

Diederich, Bernard. 1981. *Somoza.* New York: E. P. Dutton.

Doyle, Michael W., and Nicholas Sambanis. 2000. "International Peacebuilding: A Theoretical and Quantitative Analysis." *American Political Science Review* 94(4): 779–801.

Dyer, Gwynne. 2004. *War,* 2nd ed. Toronto: Random House Canada.

Eich, Dieter, and Carlos Rincon. 1984. *The Contras: Interviews with the Anti-Sandinistas.* San Francisco: Synthesis Publications.

Europa World Book. 2005. London: Europa Publications.

Gilbert, Dennis. 1986. "Nicaragua." In *Confronting Revolution: Security through Diplomacy in Central America,* edited by Morris Blachman, William LeoGrande, and Kenneth Sharpe. New York: Pantheon.

Goldstone, Jack. 1982. "The Comparative and Historical Study of Revolutions." *Annual Review of Sociology* 8: 187–207.

Heston, Alan, Robert Summers, and Bettina Aten. 2002. "Penn World Table, Version 6.1," Center for International Comparisons at the University of Pennsylvania (CICUP), October.

LaFeber, Walter. 1993. *Inevitable Revolutions: The United States and Central America,* 2nd ed. New York: W.W. Norton.

Lake, Anthony. 1989. *Somoza Falling.* Boston: Houghton Mifflin.

Lichback, Mark I. 1994. *The Rebel's Dilemma.* Ann Arbor: University of Michigan Press.

Mack, Andrew. 1975. "Why Big Nations Lose Small Wars: The Politics of Asymmetric Warfare." *World Politics* 27(2): 175–200.

Millet, Richard. 1977. *Guardians of the Dynasty: A History of the U.S.-Created Guardia Nacional de Nicaragua and the Somoza Family.* Maryknoll, NY: Orbis Books.

National Climatic Data Center, U.S. Department of Commerce. 2006. "Mitch: The Deadliest Atlantic Hurricane since 1780." lwf.ncdc.noaa. gov/oa/reports/mitch/mitch.html (accessed January 3, 2006).

Pastor, Robert. 1988. *Condemned to Repetition: The United States and Nicaragua.* Princeton, NJ: Princeton University Press.

Pastor, Robert A. 2002. *Not Condemned to Repetition: The United States and Nicaragua,* 2nd ed. Boulder, CO: Westview Press.

Regan, Patrick M. 2002. "Third Party Interventions and the Duration of Intrastate Conflict," *Journal of Conflict Resolution* 46(1): 131–53.

Selser, Gregorio. 1981. *Sandino.* Trans. Cedric Belfrage. New York: Monthly Review Press.

Simon, Marc V. 1991. *A Dynamic Model of Civil Conflict: Implications for Intervention.* Ph.D. dissertation, Indiana University.

Somoza, Anastasio, and Jack Cox. 1980. *Nicaragua Betrayed.* Boston: Western Islands.

Walker, Thomas. 1986. *Nicaragua, the Land of Sandino.* Boulder, CO: Westview Press.

Wilkie, James W., Eduardo Aleman, and Jose G. Ortega, eds. 2002. *Statistical Abstract of Latin America,* vol. 38. Los Angeles: UCLA Latin American Center Publications, University of California.

Nigeria (1967–1970)

Introduction

The Nigerian civil war will be always be remembered as a significant humanitarian tragedy that took place within a state struggling with the political nature of ethnic identity. Though blessed with significant natural resources; Nigerian statehood was plagued by patterns of colonial administration, a federalist system based largely on ethnic identity, local and national corruption, and the uneven distribution of natural resources. Each of these factors resulted in the attempted secession of several territories in the southeast, which collectively referred to themselves as the Republic of Biafra.

Country Background

On October 1, 1960, more than seventy years after the formation of the first British protectorate in what was to become known as Nigeria, the country gained formal independence. Although Nigeria enjoyed a brief period of democratic rule from 1960 to 1965, a military coup in January 1966 brought down the First Republic and ultimately resulted in a military dictatorship under the leadership of Major General Aguiyi Ironsi. A countercoup in July of the same year left Lieutenant Colonel (later General) Yakubu Gowon in power (Falola 1999, 119). As a result, in the period immediately before the civil war, Nigeria was a military dictatorship operating under what was designed as a federal system of government. In the aftermath of the Nigerian civil war, the country remained a military dictatorship until a brief period of democratic rule began during the period 1979–1983. After a series of military dictatorships ruled the country from 1983 to 1999, Nigeria made the transition to democracy and at present is a democratic state.

At independence, Nigeria's gross domestic product (GDP) per capita was approximately US $1,000 (constant) (Heston, Summers, and Aten 2002). The discovery of oil in the Niger Delta in the 1950s provided a key source of national income. From that point forward, Nigeria has existed as a rentier state. In the final full year before the civil war, GDP per capita had fallen to approximately US $800 (constant). In 1971, the first full year after the civil war, GDP per capita stabilized at around US $1,200 (constant). Although these figures are not the lowest in Africa, it is important to recognize that poverty has always been a significant obstacle to Nigeria's political development. Even today, nearly two-thirds of Nigerians live below the poverty line (Van Buren 2002, 829).

Conflict Background

The ethnic and religious heterogeneity that characterizes Nigeria has been one of the primary sources of three civil wars since Nigeria gained independence in 1960. This article primarily treats the civil war that occurred between July 1967 and January 1970. However, smaller-scale intrastate wars took place within Nigeria in both 1980 and 1984 (Sarkees 2000). Other scholars treat the events of 1980 and 1984 as part of a single continuous event (Doyle and Sambanis 2000). Regardless of how one counts the number of civil wars in Nigeria, it is clear that religious tensions are a major and persistent source of instability.

The genesis of the religious conflict that resulted in civil war is the basic religious divide in Nigeria between Islam on the one hand and Christianity and indigenous beliefs on the other. The religious divide is in part a legacy of Nigeria's colonial administration by the British. In northern Nigeria, the British relied on a system of indirect colonial administration that left Islamic religious practices intact. Christian missionaries were not allowed to operate in the major portion of the Northern Protectorate unless they were granted permission by the local emir (Niven 1971, 22). In the south, where Christian missionaries operated freely, major portions of the population converted from their existing beliefs to Christianity. As a result, approximately 50 percent of Nigerians practice Islam, whereas approximately 40 percent practice Christianity (CIA 2005). Christians who live in the north and Muslims who inhabit the south, as well as citizens who live in areas where religious boundaries overlap, often live in fear of religious violence.

In 1980, followers of Muhammad Marwa, also known as Maitatsine, united in Kano in opposition to the secular government. The Maitatsine movement gained momentum as a result of the government's poor economic performance and efforts to partially control religious practices in the north (Falola 1999, 169). A series of riots erupted in Kano, and the government dispatched military forces to quell the unrest. Approximately 5,000 deaths occurred during the ensuing clashes between religious extremists and government forces. Ultimately, the Nigerian government reestablished some degree of control over the Kano area. However, religious tension remained high in various portions of northern Nigeria. In 1981 and 1982 the military responded with force to the razing of several government buildings in Kano and other northern cities.

In February 1984, members of the Maitatsine sect launched another offensive in and around the city of Yola (Wunsch 1991). Approximately 1,000 people died as a result of the Maitatsine violence and the government counteroffensive. In addition, approximately 30,000 people became internally displaced as a result of the violence around Kano and Yola. Though government forces were ultimately victorious, religious violence remains a significant problem in Nigeria. The fact that several states in northern Nigeria have adopted Shari'a law alongside Nigerian common law is a continued source of tension between Muslims and Christians.

As devastating as the various religious-based conflicts in Nigeria have been, they pale in comparison to the results of the civil war that took place between 1967 and 1970. The Nigerian civil war (also called the Biafran Secession, the War of Nigerian Unity, and the Biafran War) resulted in more than 100,000 battle deaths (Sarkees 2000). Estimates of the total death toll vary widely, with some estimates as high as 2 million (Doyle and Sambanis 2000). Many of the civilian fatalities were from starvation as a result of the shortages that occurred during the war and the government blockade of insurgent-held areas. Relief agencies did their best to provide aid to those in need (see sidebar, "The Relief Effort: Highs and Lows"). In addition, more than 500,000 civilians became refugees or internally displaced persons (IDPs) as a result of the war.

As is the case with the civil wars of the 1980s, Nigeria's deadliest conflict has its roots in the colonial era. The formally distinct territories, amalgamated under colonial rule, that make up present-day Nigeria are among the most ethnically diverse in the world. Many of these territories possessed an administrative apparatus strong enough to exist as states for hundreds of

The Relief Effort: Highs and Lows

The effects of both the war itself and the blockade imposed by the Nigerian government took a heavy toll on civilians in Biafra. As the war lingered on, the UNHCR estimated that more than 3 million children in Biafra were in danger of starving (Goetz 2001). In response to the crisis, several international relief organizations attempted to deliver food and supplies to civilians in Biafra. The relief effort had mixed results.

On the positive side, relief organizations delivered as much as 500 tons of food and supplies into Biafra daily in what became known as the Biafran Airlift. The size and scope of the relief effort was the largest undertaken since World War II (De St Jorre 1972, 238). Catholic and Protestant relief organizations, at times in coordination with the International Committee of the Red Cross (ICRC), were involved in the relief effort. It is clear that these supplies saved countless civilians from starvation.

At the same time, owing to both a lack of funds and a lack of supplies, smaller relief agencies were often forced to book space on the same aircraft that were smuggling arms into Biafra. The Nigerian government believed that arms shipments disguised as humanitarian aid shipments were a boon to the rebellion. The government placed a ban on nighttime flights in Biafra and shot down a Swedish ICRC aircraft. The ICRC made the critical mistake of sending the same negotiator to both sides of the dispute in an attempt to secure safe passage for relief flights. Each belligerent party suspected the ICRC of working for the other side (De St. Jorre, 1972; Goetz, 2001).

ethnic groups tends to dominate in one portion of the country. The Ibo tend to dominate the east, the Yoruba the west, and the Hausa–Fulani the north.

In addition to the fact that the British indirectly ruled northern Nigeria and directly ruled southern Nigeria, the politicization of identity under colonial rule helped to create an ongoing rivalry between the three principal ethnic groups. For example, the MacPherson constitution, introduced in 1951, militated against future stability by creating a federation with a Northern Region larger than the Eastern and Western Regions. Even before the various constitutional conferences that took place in Nigeria, attempts by Christian missionaries to identify and cultivate distinct language patterns in Nigeria created more unified ethnic in-groups in areas with formerly distinct languages (Wunsch 2003, 17). In addition, the British arbitrarily assigned population figures to each region in a fashion that once again favored the north (Nwachuku 2004, 14). Intense regionalism, cultivated by the British but also favored by the Hausa–Fulani, ensured that it would be very difficult to unite Nigeria politically in the postcolonial era.

At the onset of the Nigerian civil war in July 1967, the government was able to call on more than 150,000 troops (Niven 1971, 131). By the end of the war, the Nigerian Armed forces consisted of over 250,000 troops. Though the total rebel military strength is more difficult to calculate, it is estimated that the Biafran Army may have reached a maximum strength of around 100,000 troops (Niven 1971, 131). In addition to its numerical superiority, the Nigerian government also possessed superior arms and equipment. For example, the Biafran army relied on but two aircraft, a B-26 and a B-25 (De St. Jorre 1972, 150). Although the government air force was not at the pinnacle of modernity, it did possess a larger number of newer aircraft. Pilots from Egypt, as well as mercenary pilots, tilted the air advantage even more in the government's favor.

years before the British arrived in the 1800s. Today, Nigeria is made up of more than 250 distinct ethnic groups, none of which can claim majority status (Badru 1998, 2). The three most populous ethnic groups are the Hausa–Fulani, who constitute approximately 29 percent of the population, the Yoruba, who make up 21 percent of all Nigerians, and the Ibo (also called Igbo) who make up about 18 percent of the Nigerian population (CIA 2005). Each of the three major

Table 1: Civil War in Nigeria

War:	Biafran separatists vs. government
Dates:	July 3, 1967–January 13, 1970
Casualties:	100,000 (military); more than 1 million (civilian)
Regime type prior to war:	–7 (military dictatorship). Polity 2 variable in Polity IV data—ranging from –10 (authoritarian) to 10 (democracy)
Regime type after war:	–7 (military dictatorship). Polity 2 variable in Polity IV data—ranging from –10 (authoritarian) to 10 (democracy)
GDP per capita year war began:	US $820 (constant 1967 dollars)
GDP per capita 5 years after war:	US $1,066 (constant 1975 dollars)
Insurgents:	Biafran separatists (most from Ibo ethnic group)
Issues:	Ethnic identification; regional autonomy; oil revenues
Rebel funding:	Internal donations; limited arms support from France, Côte d'Ivoire, Gabon, Israel, Spain, and Portugal
Role of geography:	Rebel coastline vulnerable; wet conditions slowed government forces; little topographic shelter from air attack
Role of resources:	Oil blockade of Biafra region by government naval forces
Immediate outcome:	Government military victory
Outcome after 5 years:	Lingering tension, but rebel army and civilian integration
Role of UN:	Not applicable
Role of regional organization:	Limited reconciliation attempts by the OAU and commonwealth
Refugees:	500,000 total refugees and IDPs
Prospects for peace:	Uncertain (two other civil wars based on religion)

Sources: Doyle and Sambanis 2000; Heston, Summers, and Aten 2002.

The Insurgents

It is common, in the context of civil war, to think of insurgents as groups of guerrilla warriors fighting an unconventional war while holding little, if any, significant territory. In the case of the Nigerian civil war, however, it is much more accurate to think of the insurgents as regionally based military and political elites. Lieutenant Colonel (later General) Chukwuemeka Odumegwu Ojukwu, who led the Biafran secession, was a regional governor. As a result of his regional base of power, Ojukwu enjoyed significant control over media in the Eastern Region—access to resources and a level of popularity seldom enjoyed by insurgent leaders (Aborisade and Mundt 2002, 17). In this sense, General Ojukwu's position could be more closely associated with that of General Robert E. Lee in the American Civil War rather than the "classic" African civil war that pitted government troops against guerrilla forces (as in Angola or South Africa, for example).

In addition to Ojukwu, several other key figures played roles in the Biafran secession. Many of these individuals were among Nigeria's intellectual elite. One of the legacies of direct colonial rule in the east and west is that the Nigerian bureaucracy tended to be dominated by Ibos, who had access to European-style education during the colonial period. For example, Chinua Achebe, an Ibo novelist, was one of the chief architects of the effective Biafran propaganda machine.

The Ibo also attempted to win the support of other ethnic minority groups by appointing regional minorities to Biafran government and important military posts. N. U. Akpan, an Ibo, was appointed chief secretary of the Biafran government (De St. Jorre 1972, 13). Victor Banjo, a Yoruba, led the Biafran military in the midwest. Although the Biafran secession is often thought of as an Ibo secession, it is important to recognize that Biafra was as ethnically diverse as the remainder of Nigeria. For example, the strategic Niger Delta is inhabited primarily by the Kalabari and Ogoni ethnic groups (Niven 1971, 25). Although these groups were part of Biafra when it seceded from Nigeria, the perception, even within Biafra, that the Ibo had the most to gain from the civil war had an adverse impact on the secessionist movement.

Ojukwu's position as the leader of a regional military government and, later, of a declared independent state provided the Biafran movement with other advantages as well. Because the area controlled by the secessionists included the bulk of Nigerian oil reserves as well as Nigeria's only oil refinery, Biafran control over millions of dollars in oil revenues was a distinct possibility. Royal Dutch Shell, the petroleum concern with the greatest stake in Biafra, was much more interested in keeping the oil flowing than in taking sides in the conflict (De St. Jorre 1972, 139). The Nigerian government, however, was concerned both with the potential source of revenue to the breakaway region and the legitimacy that the receipt of oil royalty payments would confer on the Biafran secessionist movement. As a result, the government used its limited naval forces to blockade the Biafran coast and launch an attack on the oil city of Bonny.

Despite the blockade, Ibo-dominated Biafra was able to take advantage of its border with Cameroon and the dearth of government naval capability to smuggle goods onto the international market and arms into Biafra. Although estimates of the amount of revenue generated by smuggling are unavailable, it does appear that black market activity generated enough revenue to sustain the secessionists during much of the war (De St. Jorre 1972, 142). In addition, it is important to recognize that the Nigerian civil war cut off the government-controlled areas of the country from their major supply of coal (which was in Biafran territory).

In addition, to the revenue generated from smuggling activities, Biafra received the armaments necessary to fight the war from France, South Africa, Israel, and Portugal (Falola 1999, 122). As the conflict intensified and the effects of the government blockade began to show, Biafra relied on aid from the International Committee of the Red Cross (ICRC) and other international relief organizations to secure necessary food, medicines, and resources for the general population. In addition, many of these resources were funneled to the military to sustain the secessionist movement.

Geography

The Eastern Region of Nigeria, which was proclaimed the Republic of Biafra in 1967, has a diverse geography. The western boundary of Biafra was defined by the Niger River and its delta in the south. The most populous city in the south central portion of the republic was Port Harcourt. To the southeast of Port Harcourt, the city of Bonny on the Gulf of Guinea was the home of Nigeria's only oil refinery. To the east, Biafra was defined by its border with Cameroon. A government publication from 1967 lists the northern border as roughly corresponding to 7 degrees north latitude (Government of the Republic of Biafra 1967). The total population of the Republic of Biafra at the outbreak of the civil war in 1967 was approximately 13 million (De St. Jorre 1972, 15).

The geography of Biafra played a key role in the Nigerian civil war. Recall that Nigeria's oil reserves, by far the country's most lucrative resource, are concentrated in the area around the Niger Delta. Had the Biafran secession been successful, these resources would have been primarily in the hands of the new republic. At the same time, the concentration of oil near Nigeria's coast made it essential for the winning side to have naval superiority. Since the government was the only participant in the civil war with naval capabilities, it was able to take advantage of Biafran geography by employing a blockade from the sea.

In 1967, the network of roads and railways in Biafra was more developed than in any other part of Nigeria (Niven 1971, 108). This fact had both positive and negative consequences for the Biafran armed forces. On one had, it is easier to conduct resupply missions when there is a well-developed transportation infrastructure. Conversely, it was also easier for government forces

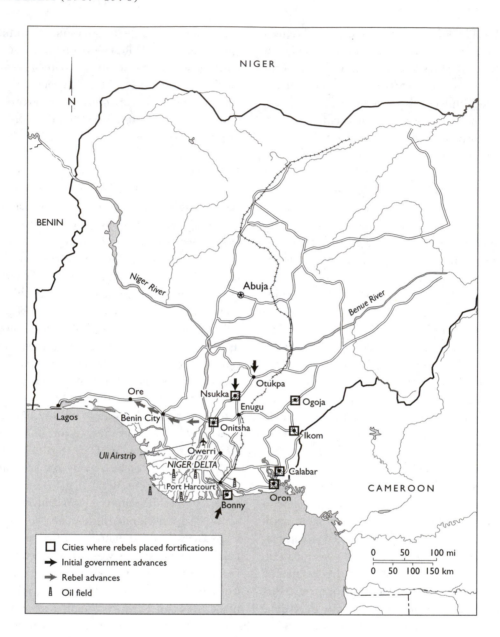

Cities where rebels placed fortifications
Initial government advances
Rebel advances
Oil field

to gain ground once they had advanced beyond the initial Biafran defenses. Like many road networks in Africa, however, many of the roads in Biafra were subject to washout during periods of heavy rain.

Tactics

Conventional tactics dominated the strategies employed by both the government military and the Biafran military during early stages of the Nigerian civil war. Later in the war, as the government forces asserted their conventional dominance, the rebel army adopted guerrilla tactics. The secessionists' initial preference for conventional tactics is not surprising, given the secessionist nature of the conflict. In addition, military leaders in the east were not convinced that the government army would have the discipline, training, and leadership necessary to win. Preparation for the impending war accelerated rapidly in August 1966 after the government withdrew all noneastern members of the armed forces from the city of Enugu (Atofarati 1992).

Biafran military leaders deployed their armed forces to counter a direct frontal assault by government forces. The main initial goal of the Biafran armed forces was to defend key cities, resources, and transportation infrastructure. The secessionists took up a major position on the rail line that runs from the northern border to the city of Port Harcourt. In addition, the rebels took positions around the cities of Nsukka and Ogoja in the north, Calabar and Oron in the east, and Onitsha on the Niger River in the west. Overall, the Biafrans placed three infantry battalions in the north, one in the central portion of the country, and three more in the south and southwest (Atofarati 1992). Finally, the Biafran army used intelligence gained from various sources to determine the most likely routes that the Nigerian armed forces would use to attack.

The secessionists also attempted to develop the human infrastructure necessary to engage in a conventional war. The rebel military government created departments to maintain the distribution of food and clothing to the military and civilians during the war. They collected donations from the populace to finance food, equipment, and arms purchases (Atofarati 1992). The rebels also trained women as spies to infiltrate government territory and gain critical intelligence. Unfortunately, food shortages during the war led to mass starvation in many areas of rebel-held territory.

The rebel deployment at Onitsha was to lead to one of the major turning points in the war. On August 9, 1967, after more than a month of defensive skirmishes in which the Biafran forces seemed to be giving ground and regrouping deeper in Biafran territory, General Ojukwu ordered a surprise attack across the Niger River at Onitsha and into government territory in the midwest (Niven 1971, 115). By the end of the day, much of what had been the Midwest Territory was under the control of Biafran commanders. It had taken approximately 1,000 soldiers to accomplish the task (De St. Jorre 1972, 154). In addition, the Biafran forces used their limited air-strike capability to bomb Lagos on the same day as the invasion of the midwest. After advancing into the Midwest Territory, the Biafran forces advanced from Benin City to Ore, where they stopped for an unknown reason. This provided the government with enough time to mobilize a counteroffensive. The government sent several battalions from Lagos, which was a little more than 100 miles away. Ultimately, the government forces drove the rebels back into Biafran territory.

The midwest offensive was a wake-up call for the government forces, which had not anticipated the move. From that point forward, the government forces continued to tighten their naval blockade. In addition, the government widened its offensive and was quickly in control of several key cities. Had the Biafran forces succeeded in the midwestern offensive, it may well have changed the dimensions of the entire conflict by endangering the capital city of Lagos (Niven 1971, 118). However, the failure of the Biafran forces to consolidate their gains resulted in renewed fervor on the part of the government forces.

Although military tactics were important to the Biafran secessionist movement, it was clear at the outset that diplomatic tactics would be the key element in a successful rebellion. If the Biafran military could hold out long enough to gain sympathy and recognition, the government might be forced to the negotiating table by international pressure. Ojukwu and other Biafran leaders believed that the oil companies would rapidly pressure their home governments into pushing for a negotiated settlement (Falola 1999, 122). The basic plan was to force private firms operating in Biafra to declare their allegiance to one side or the other in the war. The secessionists were convinced that basic greed would convince the oil companies to support Biafra, especially since the Biafrans were prepared to offer more favorable deals to the oil companies.

Biafrans wait for aid in July 1968. Widespread famine gripped the area during the civil war between Nigeria and the secessionist region of Biafra. (Kurt Strumpf/AP/Wide World Photos)

Besides the oil companies, the separatists attempted to forge relationships with some of Nigeria's enemies. Many West African nations feared Nigeria's size and potential power. The white minority-rule regimes in Southern Africa might be convinced to take steps that would weaken the hegemony of one of the most outspoken critics of apartheid in South Africa and white majority rule in Rhodesia. The fact that the Soviet Union was a major supporter of the government might convince the British and the United States to reconsider or at least soften their position on Nigerian unity. Israel was another target of Biafran attempts to gain diplomatic legitimacy and access to the arms necessary to continue fighting. Biafran leaders hoped the Egyptian involvement on the side of the government would entice Israel to offer recognition and support to Biafra. Finally, Biafra heavily courted French diplomatic recognition and military support. France had been one of the major players in

the scramble for Africa and had competed vigorously with Great Britain for colonial holdings. In addition, many of the Francophone states of western and eastern Africa were targets of the Biafran diplomatic machine for the same reason.

Unfortunately for the secessionists, foreign support of the Nigerian government has been cited as a key reason for the failure of the separatist movement in Biafra (Nwachuku 2004, 36). The oil companies, although they may have been able to extract more favorable terms from a successful Biafran government, were concerned above all with maintaining their oil revenues. Since the government forces had an effective blockade of the Biafran coast, it was clear that the only way to keep the oil flowing was to cooperate with the government. The most the Biafran movement received was a stated policy of neutrality from the oil companies.

The secessionists were slightly more successful in gaining some level of diplomatic recognition. Tanzania, Zambia, Gabon, Côte d'Ivoire, and Haiti all recognized the Biafran declaration of independence from Nigeria (Falola 1999, 123). However, many countries in Africa were concerned about, granting recognition to a breakaway republic that was dominated by a single ethnic group. The Organization of African Unity (OAU), which is currently called the African Union (AU), holds as one of its key principles the maintenance of colonial borders. Because Africa is ethnically diverse, many countries view the maintenance of colonial boundaries in the postindependence era as vital to avoid the breakdown of African countries into territorially insignificant states. France was also unwilling to formally recognize Biafra, though it did provide a sort of quasi-recognition through its surrogate, Côte d'Ivoire.

Recall that one of the principal tactics of the rebels was to attempt to force the government to the negotiating table to sue for peace. The Biafrans were able to convince the OAU to take up the issue of Biafra in September 1967. The OAU formed a consultative committee to discuss the conflict. However, only one of the members of the committee, Ghana, had any sympathy for the Biafran cause (De St. Jorre 1972, 191). In May 1968, the two belligerent parties also met at a conference in Kampala, the capital city of Uganda. There is evidence that some countries, most noteworthy Zambia, recognized Biafra in advance of the Kampala talks in order to force Nigeria to seek a peaceful solution to the conflict (De St. Jorre 1972, 199). As it turned out, however, Biafra's diplomatic victories only served to inject false hope into the secessionist movement.

The ability of Biafran diplomats to secure access to international arms transfers was also mixed and limited. France supplied a small number of Panhard armored cars to the rebels (De St. Jorre 1972, 215). Gabon sent light armaments, which were in turn replaced by France. Southern Rhodesia (now Zimbabwe) also provided light armaments as well as rockets for the B-26 bomber. The rockets were subsequently used in the air raid of Lagos. Israel provided So-

viet guns that it captured during the Six Days' War (De St Jorre 1972, 219). Spain and Portugal also provided limited assistance. The secessionists also resorted to building their own armored vehicles out of industrial equipment and farm machinery.

It is widely known that, in addition to arms transfers, mercenaries were a source of potential military strength for the secessionists. In the final analysis, however, mercenaries played a relatively small role in the war. Part of this was because the Biafran forces were suspicious of mercenaries after having fought against many of them as part of the Nigerian military contingent dispatched to fight in the Congo. In addition, many mercenaries were reluctant to come to Biafra because there was a distinct possibility that they would be called on to fight against "brothers in arms" hired by the government (De St. Jorre 1972, 313). Ironically, the main role played by mercenaries during the war may have been the failure of government mercenary pilots to destroy the makeshift Uli Airstrip, which was located about halfway between the cities Onitsha and Oguta (see sidebar, "The Relief Effort: Highs and Lows").

At the same time, the Nigerian government enjoyed more direct, more tangible success on the diplomatic front. The key Nigerian ally during the conflict was the Soviet Union. The Soviets had been displeased with General Ironsi's decision to arrest those responsible for the original 1966 coup (Matusevich 2003, 109). General Gowon, who took power in the subsequent countercoup, recognized that Soviet support would be vital if the east ever seceded. As it became increasingly clear to Gowon that the east would revolt, he attempted to solicit Soviet support directly by dispatching diplomats to Moscow to "inspect the embassy" (De St. Jorre 1972, 181). In fact, of course, the Nigerian delegation was there to discuss an arms deal.

The Soviets responded with more support than the Biafrans were to receive from any of their allies. First, the Soviets provided two Czech Delphin L-29 jet fighters. Soon, the Soviets provided

Mercenaries, the Uli Airstrip, and the Prolonged Civil War

The Uli Airstrip was the most important link between Biafra and the outside world during the Nigerian civil war. Most of the major airfields in Biafra were captured by government forces early in the war. Had the Nigerian government destroyed the Uli Airstrip, the war and the humanitarian catastrophe that accompanied it probably would have ended very quickly. Unfortunately, the government was dependent on mercenary pilots who were skilled enough to target the airport at night. When mercenaries working for the government refused to destroy the airport, Biafra was able to continue its resistance (De St. Jorre 1972, 318).

Why were the mercenary pilots unwilling to strike an obvious military target? There are two basic reasons. First, the mercenaries working for the government knew that relief planes would be flying into the Uli Airstrip at night. It was not the cargo of these planes that concerned the mercenaries; instead, it was the pilots. Many of the pilots who transported relief supplies to Biafra were also mercenaries hired by various relief organizations. As many of the relief mercenaries had worked with the government mercenaries in the Congo, there was a gentlemen's agreement that mercenaries would not intentionally target each other.

In addition, there was a basic financial incentive not to destroy the airport. Mercenaries from both sides knew that the end of the Uli Airstrip would mark the end of the rebellion. In this context, the destruction of Uli would have been bad for business. In the end, the rebels used the Uli Airstrip successfully until the last days of the war. Although the airstrip allowed valuable assistance to reach starving people, it also was a key factor in allowing the rebellion to last well beyond what most observers expected. The irony of Uli, as critical as it was to the final outcome, is one of the more poorly documented events of the war (De St. Jorre 1972).

six more L-29s, along with more than ten MiG-15 and MiG-17 fighter trainers (Matusevich 2003, 114). Soviet proxies in Eastern Europe also provided technical assistance and additional equipment. Eventually, the Soviets supplied the Nigerian military with a wide variety of armaments, including "MiG-17 fighters, Ilyushin bombers, heavy artillery, vehicles and small arms" (De St. Jorre 1972, 182). Finally, the Soviets provided Egyptian pilots to fly some of the aircraft and technical assistance to improve Nigerian industrial development.

In spite of their successes with the Soviets, the United States and Great Britain were not as directly supportive as the Nigerian government had hoped. The United States almost immediately imposed an arms embargo on both sides, and the British refused to sell arms to the government. It was clear, however, that the British ultimately supported the idea of Nigerian unity. As it turned out, the fact that many states declared official neutrality in the conflict hurt the Biafrans far more than it hurt the government.

Given its diplomatic and military advantage, the government announced its belief that the war would be over within a month. The basic military strategy was to capture first the city of Nsukka and then the cities of Ogoja, Abakaliki, and finally Enugu (Atofarati 1992). These victories would be enough to force the capitulation of secessionist forces. In July 1967, the Nigerian armed forces began their offensive by advancing on the main roads toward the fortified cities of Nsukka and Ogoja. Though the Biafrans had initial success in defending these cities, the government forces used intelligence gathered from local sources to refine their strategy (Atofarati 1992). As a result, government forces quickly overran the cities of Nsukka and Ogoja. When the Nigerian First Infantry Battalion took the city of Enugu in October 1967, the government assumed that the rebellion would collapse. By the end of the same month, government forces had also occupied the key city of Calabar.

As the government army advanced deeper into Biafran territory, the rebels began to draw on more unconventional tactics. They began to use their superior knowledge of the terrain to temporarily cut government supply lines when they became overextended. The rebels also began to use improvised land mines made from scrap metal placed in milk cartons with small amounts of explosives (De St. Jorre 1972, 206). The rebels also booby-trapped oil tanker trucks to explode at the approach of government forces. Each of these measures, while successful in slowing the Nigerian military advance, also created dangerous conditions for Biafran civilians. In May 1968, General Ojukwu formally announced that the rebels would now fight the war using guerrilla tactics rather than conventional ones. In the same month, it a speech commemorating the first anniversary of Biafran independence, Ojukwu declared, "For these values and principles we are willing to endure our present hardship. Let us individually resolve to shape our own lives to accord with these objectives of our nation" (Government of the Republic of Biafra 1993, 235).

Causes of the War

It would be easy enough to argue that the Nigerian civil war was little more than an ethnic conflict between Ibos and non-Ibos (especially the Hausa–Fulani). Although it is true that Nigeria's ethnic diversity played a role in causing the conflict, it is also apparent that other factors were involved. One need only examine the relatively rapid reintegration of Ibo military personnel and civilians into Nigerian economic, social, and political life to understand that the Biafran secession was much more than an ethnic war. Although there were several key historical events that pushed Nigeria toward civil war, it is argued here that there were three key proximate causes of the conflict. The first of these was the politicization of ethnic identity, first by the British and then by independent Nigeria. The second proximate cause was the militarization of Nigerian politics. The third proximate cause of the war was the unequal distribution of resources, especially oil, within the country.

As mentioned at the beginning of this article, the British played a key role in the politicization of ethnic identity in Nigeria. The combination of the British protectorates into a single political entity in 1914 resulted in a mix of indirectly ruled and directly ruled territory. The results of direct colonial rule provided ethnic groups in the south, especially the Ibo, with superior education and health care. It is not surprising, in this context, that the Ibo came to dominate the Nigerian civil service in the postindependence era. At the same time, the failure of the British to adjust administrative boundaries after the protectorate merger gave the Hausa–Fulani control over more territory than all the other ethnic groups combined.

Politicization of ethnic identity emerged in the developing Nigerian political party system before independence. The National Council of Nigeria and the Cameroons (NCNC), formed in 1944, was designed to be a national party aimed at securing independence for Nigeria. However, the Yoruba and Ibo members of the party quickly began to suspect each other of attempting to dominate the NCNC (Amoda 1972, 19). A civil war between the two rival ethnic groups was narrowly averted. The Yoruba responded by forming the Action Group (AG) to coordinate policy in the Western Region. The Hausa–Fulani-dominated Northern Region formed the Northern People's Congress (NPC). The NCNC remained the key party in the Ibo-dominated Eastern Region.

In 1959, elections were held under British observation to determine the political makeup of government in the postindependence era. The NPC won 134 seats, the AG seventy-three, and the NCNC eighty-nine. Although the NCNC could have formed a coalition with the AG based on the north–south divide, the NCNC instead became the junior partner in coalition with the NPC. The NCNC made this decision in part because Ibo party leaders viewed political payoffs in the south as a zero-sum game between the Yoruba-led AG and NCNC (Falola 1999, 102). The fact that no strong national party ever emerged in prewar Nigeria, coupled with the ethnic character of the three dominant parties, is clear evidence of politicized ethnic identity.

One of the first postindependence manifestations of ethnic politicization was the census crisis of 1962. Nigeria's first Prime Minister, Abubakar Tafawa Balewa, announced that there would be a new census, designed to update the British figures of 1953. The completed census suggested that the population in the Northern Region had grown by 30 percent, while the Western and Eastern Regions had grown by more than 70 percent (Nwankwo and Ifejika 1970, 47). Had the census results stood, there would have been a major shift in power within Nigeria toward the south. However, the government, which was controlled by the NPC, recalculated the growth rate for the Northern Region at 80 percent, placing the Hausa–Fulani in a position of dominance once again. After the AG and NCNC threatened a parliamentary walkout, all census results were annulled. A subsequent census produced similar results. The census figures ensured both political dominance by the north and a revenue allocation formula that would benefit the north at the expense of the east, west and midwest.

Politicized identities, however, are but one of the causes of the Nigerian civil war. The militarization of Nigerian politics is another critical factor. Beckett and Young (1997) refer to a "permanent transition" to democracy in Nigeria. In the permanent transition, the military reluctantly intervened to rid Nigeria of the problems of corrupt civilian government. However, it is never clear exactly when the military intends to go back to the barracks. Whenever there is actual or perceived instability in the country, the threat of military intervention looms large.

In Nigeria, the politicization of the military began before independence. Because of direct colonial rule in much of the south, well-trained Ibo officers occupied a majority of officer positions. In the postindependence era, the Northern Region worried about Ibo domination of the armed forces. As a result, the government instituted a quota policy designed to redress the inequities in the armed forces. Before the quota, the Eastern Region accounted for approximately 45 percent of all officers, and the Northern Region accounted for roughly 32 percent. After the imposition of the quota, the proportions reversed (Peters 1997, 80). Although the quota created a national military that was more reflective of census figures, it also resulted in a less professional, more politicized armed forces. The perception in the Eastern Region was that the Northern Region was attempting to erode one of the few areas of Ibo breathing space in Nigerian politics.

One of the roots of the Nigerian civil war can be traced to the military intervention in Nigerian politics that occurred in 1966. An earlier crisis in the Western Region had resulted in a split within the AC and, ultimately, the formation of the Midwest Region. The Midwest Region struck a political bargain with the Northern Region and agreed to certify the disputed census figures in exchange for government aid. Irregularities in the 1964 general election and the 1965 regional election in the west created a constitutional crisis (Falola 1999, 106). All these factors weakened the Nigerian state and created conditions that were ripe for a military takeover. In January 1966, a military coup led by junior officers (code-named Operation Leopard) ultimately resulted in the assumption of power by General Ironsi (De St. Jorre. 1972, 30–40). It was this military intervention that started a series of tragic events that led to the Nigerian civil war.

Most military coups, of course, do not lead to civil wars. In the case of Nigeria, however, the politicization of ethnicity combined with the politicization of the military and the subsequent militarization of Nigerian politics to produce deadly results. In spite of evidence to the contrary, the Northern Region saw the January 1966 coup as an attempt to achieve Ibo domination of Nigeria. Ironsi's decision to declare Nigeria a unitary republic, as well as his decision not to harshly punish the coup instigators, did little to allay this fear. In addition, the political and military officials who were killed in the coup were predominately non-Ibo.

In July 1966, Lieutenant Colonel Gowon launched a successful countercoup. However, the Ibo military, led by Ojukwu, was able to maintain control in the Eastern Region. At the same time, groups of loosely organized northern militia began hunting down and killing Ibo who happened to live in the north. It is estimated that more than 30,000 Ibo were killed during the reprisals, and another 2 million Ibo were permanently displaced (Waugh and Cronjé 1969, 37). Most of those who were displaced fled to the Eastern Region. Political intervention by the Nigerian military, coupled with the politics of ethnic fear and hatred, had left Ojukwu in a position of power in the Eastern Region. Ojukwu could claim, with some accuracy, that he was the only person capable of protecting the east. He could also claim that the only way for the Eastern Region to avoid a repeat of the events of 1966 was to secede.

In addition to the roles played by militarization and politicization of ethnic identity, the uneven distribution of resources in Nigeria was also a major factor in the Eastern Region's decision to withdraw from Nigeria. As noted earlier, the results of the disputed Nigerian census enabled the Northern Region to justify the redistribution of wealth in ways that would tend to benefit the Hausa–Fulani. The Ibo and Yoruba, of course, were aware of this. Royalties from the Dutch and French oil companies operating in the Niger Delta pumped millions of dollars into the Nigerian economy. Ojukwu clearly believed that control of the oil resources in the southeast could make Biafra a viable independent state.

Oil was not the only economic factor to contribute to the war, however. During the 1950s and 1960s, one of the most attractive career paths for university-educated students was the Nigerian civil service. Since the south tended to be more educated than the north, southerners, especially Ibo, tended to dominate the civil service. After independence, however, the quota system used to achieve balance in the military was

also applied to the Nigerian civil service. As a result, there was widespread discontent among young southern intellectuals, who felt as though they were being passed over in favor of less-qualified northerners (Nafziger 1982, 77). This, in turn, forced those who were university educated to seek regional positions. It is no surprise, then, that many of the key figures in the Biafran secession where young, well-educated elites. Given the three major factors highlighted previously, it is evident that the Nigerian civil war was much more than a product of simple ethnic grievances.

In January 1967, Ojukwu and Gowon met in Aburi Ghana in a last attempt to resolve their differences. Ojukwu argued that the existing federal arrangement should be replaced with a loose confederation. Gowon proposed maintaining the existing federal structure. In addition, Gowon proposed the addition of eight new states. Two of these states, located in what was the Eastern Region, in effect would have diluted Ibo power and removed Ibo influence over the oil reserves (De St. Jorre 1972, 142). This was more than Ojukwu would stand for. On July 3, 1967, the Nigerian civil war began.

Outcome
Conflict Status

Without the groundswell of international recognition and support that the rebels had hoped for, it was clear that the Nigerian government forces would ultimately prevail. In the period from December 1969 through January 1970, government forces began to converge on the last rebel strongholds around the cities of Oguta, Orlu, and Nnewi in the western portion of Biafra. The First Division of the government army converged with the Third Division on the Uli Airstrip (De St. Jorre 1972, 394–95). The key city of Owerri, which had been the fallback capital of Biafra, fell on January 8. Finally, General Ojukwu fled Biafra for Côte d'Ivoire via the Uli Airstrip just before it was seized by government forces. On January 12, 1970, Major General

Philip Effiong, acting in place of General Ojukwu, called upon the Biafran rebels to end the fighting. The Nigerian civil war formally ended the following day, when Effiong surrendered to General Gowon. The final result of the war was a complete government victory. Although the war ended with the unconditional surrender of the rebels, the Nigerian government opted for a strategy of reconciliation rather than punishment (De St. Jorre 1972, 407). There were no mass trials of rebel military leaders, and many members of the Biafran military were reintegrated into the Nigerian army.

Refugee repatriation was a more difficult matter. The conflict created more than 500,000 refugees and internally displaced persons. As the government army advanced deeper into rebel-held territory, people living in threatened cities usually withdrew deeper into Biafra with the secessionist army. According to the United Nations High Commissioner for Refugees (UNHCR), more than 30,000 children were displaced as a result of the conflict (Goetz 2001). By February 1971, those children who had been forced to flee Nigeria were effectively repatriated (Goetz 2001). Many Ibo who lived in Port Harcourt, where Ibo were a minority, left or were forced out during the war and never returned (Nwachuku 2004, 40). However, most IDPs in Ibo-majority areas were able to return to their cities and villages after the war. Soldiers or people simply searching for food, however, had pillaged many of their homes.

Duration Tactics

The Nigerian civil war lasted much longer than the one month originally anticipated by the government. Several factors combined to prolong the war. First, the rebel army, as mentioned above, was well prepared for the initial government advance. Although government forces were successful in their initial military objectives, the rebels simply fell back to established rendezvous points. Nigerian supply lines were also spread thin by the rebel incursion into the Midwest Region. This enabled rebel forces periodically to cut the government's supply lines by vanishing in the face of direct attack and reappearing behind government lines.

The switch from conventional to guerrilla tactics also probably prolonged the war. The makeshift land mines and booby traps mentioned earlier almost certainly slowed the government advance. The government was prepared to fight a conventional war based on controlling key cities and pieces of territory. The government was not as prepared to fight an enemy that seemed to vanish in front of them after the initial phases of the war. Knowledge of terrain also benefited the rebels in their efforts to slow the government advance.

External Military Intervention

There was no blatant external intervention in the Nigerian civil war by other states. The Soviets chose to aid the Nigerian government indirectly, providing Egyptian pilots to fly Soviet MiGs. No country chose to dispatch troops directly to Biafra. Mercenaries from various states participated in the conflict but without sanction from a specific state. Material support from the Soviets, coupled with a general lack of international support for Biafra, tipped the scales even further in the government's favor.

Conflict Management Efforts

Conflict management efforts were unsuccessful in limiting or shortening the Nigerian civil war. The OAU eliminated its ability to be an effective mediator by endorsing a status quo policy (De St. Jorre 1972, 192). Although there were several attempts by potential mediators to bring the two parties to the negotiating table, only the talks held in Kampala, Uganda, in May 1968 had any chance of success. The talks were arranged by Arnold Smith, a Canadian diplomat and secretary-general of the commonwealth (De St. Jorre 1972, 193). Almost immediately, it became clear that the two belligerent parties were too far apart to reach a political settlement. The rebels enumerated three basic demands: (1) immediate cessation of all fighting, (2) immediate removal of the economic blockade by the government, and (3) withdrawal of all troops to their prewar positions (Government of the Republic of Biafra 1993, 231). The rebels also proposed an international monitoring force to oversee compliance with their terms.

The government countered with its own twelve-point proposal. The following is a summary of each point, based on Government of the Republic of Biafra (1993, 232–33).

1. A cease-fire day would be set.
2. A cease-fire hour would be set.
3. Before the cease-fire, the rebel army would renounce secession in exchange for the cessation of government hostilities.
4. Troops would be frozen in their current positions as of the cease-fire hour.
5. The federal army would accompany observers and Ibo police officers to supervise rebel disarmament.
6. Within seven days after the cease-fire, the rebels would turn over the administration of the breakaway region to the federal government.
7. The federal government would appoint a commission to temporarily administer rebel-held territory. The rebels would have input regarding the membership of a minority of commission members.
8. The police would be responsible for law and order.
9. The federal government would recruit Ibos and integrate them into the federal army.
10. An easterner would be appointed to the Federal Executive Council.
11. The federal government would grant amnesty to rebellion leaders in appropriate cases and general amnesty to other rebellion participants.
12. Both sides would exchange prisoners of war.

The inclusion in the rebel proposal of an immediate military withdrawal, as well as government insistence on renunciation of the secession, effectively eliminated the possibility of a compromise.

Conclusion

The immediate political result of the Nigerian civil war was a clear victory for the government forces and the maintenance of Nigerian unity. Although it appears unlikely that another state will actually attempt to secede, it would be an overstatement to argue that the Nigerian civil war produced enduring stability in Nigeria. Gowon's decision to add eight states to the federal system set in motion a process that ultimately led to the creation of thirty-six states in Nigeria. The problem is that most of these states were created in an effort to satisfy the desires for increased autonomy of Nigerian ethnic minorities. This strategy has been successful in that no region has attempted to secede from Nigeria since the civil war. However, the strategy also produces state-level policies that once again are often based on the politicization of ethnic identity (Suberu 2001, 81). Statehood also provides ethnic minority groups in Nigeria with new opportunities to make redistributive demands on the central government. The recent series of oil-related kidnappings around Port Harcourt demonstrate, in part, the pressures that result from state and local redistributive demands.

It is worth noting that the two smaller-scale civil wars that have occurred since the end of the Biafran secession have been based on the politicization of religion. Nigerian federalism is designed in part to defuse national-level religious conflict by allowing states to integrate aspects of religious law into their judicial processes (Suberu 2001, 4). Many northern states have taken advantage of this by establishing Shari'a courts to preside over Muslims. However, both of the smaller civil wars resulted from a combination of religious conflict between fundamentalist Muslims and more moderate Muslims, or between fundamentalist Muslims and non-Muslims. One of the keys to maintaining peace in Nigeria is finding a way to protect the rights of non-Muslims in the north. The majority of Muslims in Nigeria appear to favor the application of Islamic law for Muslims only. There are those, however, who would prefer to eliminate the secular legal system entirely.

Nigeria's size, relative military strength, and natural resource base create a great deal of potential for political and economic development. To this point in history, Nigeria has failed to fulfill its enormous promise. The key to avoiding future conflict will be balancing the power of federalism to dilute conflict with ethnic and religious-based federalism's tendency to atomize Nigerian politics. One reason for guarded optimism is the fact that Nigeria made the transition from the kleptocracy of Sani Abacha to a fledgling democracy under Olusegun Obasanjo in 1999. Obasanjo had the military credentials that may be necessary to keep the military from attempting to dominate the political process. Because the militarization of Nigerian politics was one of the three key causes of the civil war, maintaining civilian leadership is almost certainly in the country's best interest.

Trevor Rubenzer

Chronology

October 1, 1960   Nigeria gains independence from Great Britain.

1963   Nigeria becomes a federal republic.

1964   Disputed census results finalized; Northern Region's gains allow it to retain redistributive advantage over other regions.

1965   Elections in the Western Region turn violent. Midwest Region forms.

January 1966   General Aguiyi-Ironsi takes power as the result of a coup originally launched by junior officers. Many non-Ibo leaders are killed in the violence.

May 24, 1966   Ironsi abolishes federal system and replaces it with a unitary republic.

May 27, 1966   Riots begin in the Northern Region, resulting in the death of Ibo civilians.

July 28, 1966   A successful countercoup orchestrated by General Gowon leads to the death of Ironsi and many Ibo officers; original federal form of government is restored.

September 29, 1966   Violence against Ibos in the Northern Region leaves 30,000 dead; surviving Ibo flea to Eastern Region; central government fails to halt the slaughter.

May 27, 1967   Eastern Region proposes that Nigeria be reorganized as a confederation; Gowon rejects and creates eight new states, bringing the total to twelve; this dilutes Ibo power by creating two new Ibo minority states in what was the Eastern Region.

May 30, 1967   Eastern Region secedes; takes the name Biafra.

July 3, 1967   Nigerian civil war begins.

July 25, 1967   Government forces capture southern coastal city of Bonny.

August 9, 1967   Rebel troops take key city of Benin in Midwest Region. Biafran armed forces gain control over most of region over the next several days. Federal troops scramble to protect Lagos and plan counteroffensive.

August 17, 1967   Battle of Ore (a strategic city in the Midwest Region). After several days of fighting, government troops repel rebel advance. Rebels never advanced farther than Ore and were subsequently driven back into Biafra.

October 1, 1967   Nigerian army occupies strategic Biafran city of Enugu.

October 18, 1967   Nigerian army occupies the city of Calabar.

March 21, 1968   Nigerian army occupies city of Onitsha.

April–May 1968   Tanzania, Gabon, Côte d'Ivoire, and Zambia recognize Biafra.

May 1968   Peace talks in Kampala, Uganda, fail to produce a peaceful settlement.

May 18,1968   City of Port Harcourt falls to Nigerian army.

September 30, 1968   Provincial headquarters in Okigwi captured by Nigerian First Division.

April 15, 1969   Nigerian army takes city of Bende; rebels defeat federal army at Owerri; Ojukwu makes Owerri the new administrative capital.

June 1969   Government forces shoot down ICRC relief aircraft at Uli Airstrip. Government argues that relief aircraft are also carrying arms to the rebels.

July 12, 1969   Relief aircraft downed at Uli Airstrip by Nigerian forces.

August 1969   Nigerian troops capture city of Ebocha, one of the main rebel refineries.

December 25, 1969   Federal army establishes corridor between Enugu and Port Harcourt, enabling improved coordination in strategy. Biafra is effectively cut in two. Final rebel offensive.

January 8, 1970   Owerri falls to Nigerian forces.

January 10, 1970   Ojukwu flees Biafra for Côte d'Ivoire.

January 12, 1970   New rebel leader General Effiong calls on the rebels to stop fighting.

January 14, 1970   Formal surrender by Effiong on behalf of the rebels ends Nigerian civil war.

List of Acronyms

AG: Action Group
AU: African Union
GDP: gross domestic product
ICRC: International Committee of the Red Cross
IDP: internally displaced person
NCNC: National Council of Nigeria and the Cameroons
NPC: Northern People's Congress
OAU: Organization of African Unity
UNHCR: United Nations High Commissioner for Refugees

Glossary

direct colonial rule: A policy under which the colonial power assumes near total responsibility for the administration of its colonial dominion. In Nigeria, the Southern Protectorate was administered via a more direct form of colonial rule. As a result, people in the south had more access to the British educational and health systems. This in turn led to domination of the Nigerian bureaucracy by citizens from the south, especially Ibo citizens.

guerrilla warfare: Borrowed from the Spanish word for war (guerra), guerrilla warfare is a technique that uses small, mobile combat units. Instead of fighting with reference to a front line, guerrilla cells try to attack whenever an opportunity arises. The goal is not to hold territory but to make it costly for the opposing military to continue fighting. In Nigeria, the rebels partially switched to guerrilla tactics after it became clear that they could not win a conventional war.

indirect colonial rule: A policy that allows indigenous authorities to administer their territories directly. Local authorities took direction in turn from the colonial authorities. Colonial power usually does not interfere in day-to-day administrative issues. The British used indirect colonial rule to administer northern Nigeria.

internally displaced person (IDP): Someone who has fled his or her home due to a well-founded fear of persecution for reasons of race, religion, nationality, membership in a particular social group, or political opinion or because of armed conflict but who has not crossed an internationally recognized border. During the Nigerian civil war, there were far more internally displaced persons than refugees.

federalism: A form of political organization in which governmental power is divided between a central government and territorial subdivisions. Powers reserved for territorial subdivisions are guaranteed in the country's basic law. Except for a brief period under the rule of General Ironsi, Nigeria has operated as a federal republic. Federalism in Nigeria is designed to defuse conflict, but it also tends to encourage demands based on ethnicity and religion.

Maitatsine riots: Followers of Muhammad Marwa, also known as Maitatsine, initiated riots designed to reject secular government in Nigeria in favor of Shari'a. The resulting violence led to Nigeria's second civil war.

rentier state: A state that derives most or all of its revenue from the sale of oil or other key natural resources. The fact that Nigeria is a rentier state creates tension because oil is not evenly distributed in the country.

Shari'a: Traditional Islamic law, drawn from the Koran and the teachings of the prophet Mohammed. Several northern states have adopted Shari'a law as part of their systems of jurisprudence. Two of Nigeria's three civil wars have been fought over religious issues relating to the application of Shari'a.

References

Aborisade, Oladimeji, and Robert J. Mundt. 2002. *Politics in Nigeria*, 2nd ed. New York: Longman.

Amoda, Moyibi. 1972. "Background to the Conflict: A Summary of Nigeria's Political History from 1914 to 1964." In *Nigeria: Dilemma of Nationhood, An African Analysis of the Biafran Conflict*, edited by Joseph Okpaku, 14–75. New York: The Third Press.

Atofarati, Abubakar A. (Major). 1992. "The Nigerian Civil War: Strategies and Lessons Learnt." Nigerian Young Professionals Forum Web site. www.ypforum.org/history_civilwar2 (accessed May 29, 2005).

Badru, Pade. 1998. *International Banking and Rural Development: The World Bank in Sub-Saharan Africa.* Broofield, VT: Ashgate.

Beckett, Paul, and Crawford Young. 1997. "Introduction: Beyond the Impasse of 'Permanent Transition' in Nigeria." In *Dilemmas of Democracy in Nigeria,* edited by Paul Beckett and Crawford Young. Rochester, NY: University of Rochester Press.

Central Intelligence Agency (CIA). 2005. *CIA World Factbook.* www.cia.gov/cia/publications/factbook/ (accessed May 31, 2005).

De St. Jorre, John. 1972. *The Nigerian Civil War.* London: Hodder and Stoughton.

Doyle, Michael W., and Nicholas Sambanis. 2000. "International Peacebuilding: A Theoretical and Quantitative Analysis." *American Political Science Review* 94(4): 779–801.

Falola, Toyin. 1999. *The History of Nigeria.* Westport, CT: Greenwood Press.

Goetz, Nathaniel H. 2001. "Humanitarian Issues in the Biafra Conflict." *Journal of Humanitarian Assistance.* Working Paper No. 36. www.jha.ac/articles/u036.htm (accessed May 31, 2005).

Government of the Republic of Biafra. 1967. "Introducing the Republic of Biafra." Available at www.biafraland.com/Biafra percent20 history.htm (accessed May 28, 2005).

Government of the Republic of Biafra. 1993. *Crisis and Conflict in Nigeria: A Documentary Sourcebook 1966–1970.* Vol. II, July 1967–January 1970. Edited by Anthony Kirk-Green. Hampshire, UK: Gregg Revivals.

Heston, Alan, Robert Summers, and Bettina Aten. 2002. "Penn World Table Version 6.1," Center for International Comparisons at the University of Pennsylvania (CICUP). October.

Matusevich, Maxim. 2003. *No Easy Row for a Russian Hoe: Ideology and Pragmatism in Nigerian Soviet Relations, 1960–1991.* Trenton, NJ: Africa World Press.

Nafziger, E. Wayne. 1982. *The Economics of Political Instability: The Nigerian-Biafran War.* Boulder, CO: Westview Press.

Niven, Rex. 1971. *The War of Nigerian Unity, 1967–1970.* Totowa, NJ: Rowman and Littlefield.

Nwachuku, Levi A. 2004. "A Survey of Nigerian History Since Independence." In *Troubled Journey: Nigeria Since the Civil War.* Edited by Levi A. Nwachuku and G.N. Uzoigwe, 21–43. Lanham, MD: University Press of America.

Nwankwo, Arthur Agwuncha, and Samuel Udochukwu Ifejika. 1970. *Biafra: The Making of a Nation.* New York: Praeger.

Peters, Jimi. 1997. *The Nigerian Military and the State.* New York: I.B. Tauris.

Sarkees, Meredith. "Correlates of War Data on War: An Update to 1997." *Conflict Management and Peace Science* (18)1: 123–144.

Sarkees, Meredith Reid. 2000. "The Correlates of War Data on War: An Update to 1997." *Conflict Management and Peace Science,* 18(1): 123–144.

Suberu, Rotimi T. 2001. *Federalism and Ethnic Conflict in Nigeria.* Washington, DC: United States Institute of Peace.

Van Buren, Linda. 2002. "Nigeria: Economy." In *Africa South of the Sahara,* 829–937. London: Europa.

Waugh, Auberon, and Suzanne Cronjé. 1969. *Biafra: Britain's Shame.* London: Michael Joseph.

Wunsch, James S. 1991. AllRefer.com Website. "Nigeria Country Study and Guide: Religious Sectarianism." reference.allrefer.com/country-guide-study/nigeria/nigeria158.html (accessed May 28, 2005).

Wunsch, James S. 2003. "Nigeria: Ethnic Conflict in Multinational West Africa." In *Encyclopedia of Modern Ethnic Conflicts,* edited by Joseph R. Rudolph, 169–182. Westport, CT: Greenwood Press.

Pakistan (1971)

Introduction

Pakistan, like most postcolonial societies, has struggled to define its national identity. This struggle and its attendant uncertainties have created structural conditions ripe for civil war. During its independent history, Pakistan has experienced subnational challenges from nearly all of its various major ethnic groups. This article focuses on the most violent instance: the secession of East Pakistan to form the independent nation of Bangladesh. The civil war has been the most violent event in Pakistan's history, but it is not the only attempt by a subnational group to claim autonomy.

Country Background

Pakistan is a very diverse and multiethnic country. The major groups in the country are as follows:

Bengalis, who constitute most of the population in East Pakistan and a numerical majority in the former federated Pakistan

Punjabis, who are concentrated in Punjab province, represent a numerical majority in contemporary Pakistan and are the most dominant group politically.

Sindhis, the third-largest group, live in Sindh province and have a fairly active nationalist movement, which was involved in violent conflict with the government in the 1980s.

Pathans, the fourth-largest group, are concentrated in Pakistan's North-West Frontier Province (NWFP) and have significant representation in the Pakistani military; Pakistani Pathans also have ethnic ties to Pathans in Afghanistan.

Muhajirs, the fifth-largest group, consist of Muslims who moved from India to Pakistan after partition; they are concentrated mostly in urban Sindh.

Baluchis, the smallest group numerically, are concentrated in Baluchistan province; Baluchis have a fairly active nationalist movement, which was involved in violent conflict with the government in the mid-1970s and has been active again under the Musharraf military government. At the time of writing, the civil unrest in Baluchistan threatens to become the biggest challenge of General Musharraf's rule; there are daily reports of attacks by Baluch insurgents and frequent skirmishes between Baluch and government forces.

Conflict Background

The Pakistan civil war lasted from March to December 1971 and claimed very high casualties: an estimated 1 million dead and as many as 10 million displaced refugees. (Estimates of fatalities range from 300,000 to 3 million; Pakistan claims that only 26,000 people died.) The war also witnessed widespread atrocities against women. The war eventually drew Pakistan's archrival India into the conflict, and India's intervention played a decisive role in ending the war in favor of the secessionists. Pakistan's military, which until then had projected a powerful image as national defender and efficient administrative organization and had been in power before the war, suffered a massive blow both militarily as well as in terms of its prestige. Not surprisingly, the humiliation of the Pakistani military allowed a democratic civilian government to be ushered in after war's end.

The Insurgents

Three main groups resisted the Pakistani central government: political leaders, disaffected soldiers, and guerrilla activists. Eventually, these were joined by Indian military personnel, but this was much later when the war had expanded beyond Pakistani borders.

The Bangladeshi independence movement was always guided by the political leadership. Political parties covered the ideological spectrum in East Pakistan and included Communists, Islamic parties, liberals, and conservatives. But the nationalist (and secular) Awami League assumed dominance in the political sphere very early, under the leadership of the populist Sheikh Mujibur Rahman. Mujib introduced his Six Points demand on March 23, 1966:

1. The Constitution should provide for a Federation of Pakistan in the true sense on the basis of the Lahore Resolution and for a parliamentary form of government based on the supremacy of a directly elected legislature on the basis of universal adult franchise. The representation in the federal legislature shall be on the basis of population.

2. The federal government shall be responsible only for defence and foreign affairs, and currency subject to the conditions provided in (3) below.

3. There shall be two separate currencies mutually or freely convertible in each wing for each region, or in the alternative, a single currency, subject to the establishment of a federal reserve system in which there will be regional federal reserve banks, which shall

Table 1: Civil War in Pakistan

War:	East Pakistan vs. government
Dates:	March 25, 1971–December 16, 1971
Casualties:	300,000 to 3 million estimated
Regime type prior to war:	Military junta
Regime type after war:	Parliamentary democracy
Insurgents:	Mukti Bahini–Mitro Bahini
Issue:	Secessionist movement for territorial independence
Rebel funding:	India
Role of geography:	Rebels hid in neighboring India.
Role of resources:	Negligible
Immediate outcome:	Bangladeshi independence
Outcome after 5 years:	Slide toward military rule
Role of UN:	Negligible
Role of regional organization:	None
Refugees:	10 million, almost all returned within a year
Prospects for peace:	Secessionist movement was successful, ending conflict.

devise measures to prevent the transfer of resources and flight of capital from one region to another.

4. Fiscal policy shall be the responsibility of the federating units. The federal government shall be provided with requisite revenue resource for meeting the requirements of defence and foreign affairs, which revenue sources would be automatically appropriable by the federal government in the manner provided and on the basis of the ratio to be determined by the procedure laid down in the Constitution. Such constitutional provisions would ensure that the federal government's revenue requirements are met consistently with the objective of ensuring control over fiscal policy of the governments of the federating units.

5. Constitutional provisions shall be made to enable separate accounts to be maintained of the foreign exchange earnings of each of the federating units, under the control of the respective governments of the federating units. The foreign exchange requirements of the federal government shall be met by the governments of the federating units on the basis of a ratio to be determined in accordance with the procedure laid down in the Constitution. The regional governments shall have the power under the constitution to negotiate foreign trade and aid within the framework of the foreign policy of the country, which shall be the responsibility of the federal government.

6. The government of the federating units shall be empowered to maintain a militia or para-military force in order to contribute effectively towards national security (Sisson and Rose 1990, 20).

The Six Points crystallized East Pakistanis' resentment and sense of exploitation in national affairs and were soon adopted as the battle cry of the Bengali political leadership, which became unified in the face of an increasingly aggressive West Pakistani government.

Pakistan remained under authoritarian rule for most of its independence until December 1970, when the first national competitive elections were held. Not surprisingly, Mujib's Awami League emerged as the single largest winner in East Pakistan and the overall winner as well; it garnered 167 of 169 seats in East Pakistan (167 out of a total of 313 seats in the combined national parliament). Mujib insisted that his Six Points be accepted as a condition for forming the government.

This was unacceptable to the military ruler, General Yahya Khan, as well as the other civilian politicians. Most notably, the other major contender to power, the Pakistan People's Party, led by the charismatic Zulfikar Ali Bhutto, refused to accept an Awami League government. Certainly, this had to do with basic power politics, in which every party was pushing for maximum advantage. But the psychological and cultural barriers to West Pakistan's acceptance of an East Pakistani government cannot be underestimated (Sisson and Rose 1990).

The failure to form a government produced a protracted period of wrangling and negotiation. On March 3, 1971, Mujib and Bhutto, along with Yahya Khan, met in Dhaka to negotiate a settlement of the political impasse. They failed to reach an agreement, and Mujib called for a general strike. This unleashed a period of popular agitation, which was coupled with a buildup of military personnel in the province (most of them non-Bengali). On March 25, 1971, the Pakistani military moved in to begin a campaign of repression called Operation Searchlight. Sheikh Mujibur Rahman was arrested, and masses of people were killed, particularly students and professors. This began a period during which numerous massacres were carried out. (Some observers have argued that

Was It Genocide?

One of the most controversial issues regarding the Pakistani civil war is whether or not genocide occurred during it. Few would deny that the loss of Bangladeshi lives was grievous. Pakistan still maintains that only 26,000 people were killed, but most experts believe that many more died; the estimates range from 300,000 to 3 million. The higher figure probably comes from a statement attributed to General Yahya Khan, who said, "Kill three million of them and the rest will eat out of our hands" (Payne 1973, 50). But that figure is considered too high to be logistically feasible. A more widely accepted figure is about 1 million.

Whatever the real figure, it is clear that the Pakistani army committed planned acts of atrocity in East Pakistan. Initially, the army targeted intellectuals, but the scope of the massacres was soon expanded. One of the Pakistan army's last acts in East Pakistan was on December 14, 1971, when it systematically eliminated a large number of Bengali intellectuals.

these massacres constituted genocide; see sidebar, "Was It Genocide?"

Mujib declared Bangladeshi independence, which was announced to the world on March 26, 1971. A number of Awami League leaders had fled to India and formed a Bangladeshi government-in-exile on April 17, 1971.

The first and earliest military actors were Bengali soldiers and officers in the Pakistani military. As noted earlier, Bengalis were severely underrepresented in the military, a fact that was one of the main East Pakistani grievances. This fact, in addition to the West Pakistanis' racist constructions of Bengalis in general, had already severely strained relations within the military. There was only one Bengali unit in the Pakistani Army, the East Pakistan Rifles. Martial law had been imposed by General Yahya Khan in March 1969, immediately after he took control of the country from the erstwhile dictator, Ayub Khan. Yahya Khan instituted a policy of doubling Bengali representation in the military (which was

only seven infantry battalions at the time). But this was probably too little and too late, and the policy was not well received among military leaders in any case.

As early as March 1971, Bengali soldiers refused to heed orders to fire on demonstrators, setting in motion a small-scale mutiny. Therefore, it is not surprising that the first official salvo of the civil war was fired by a Bengali military officer. Major Ziaur Rahman, commander of the East Bengal Regiment, broadcast the first international announcement of Bangladeshi independence. Rahman read the declaration of independence penned by Sheikh Mujibur Rahman on March 26, 1971. This is considered the official start of the civil war.

The main rebel force was the Mukti Bahini. It had originally been generated as a sort of paramilitary–security wing of the Awami League, but it soon grew in size and acquired a guerrilla nature. It was led by a retired Pakistan Army officer, Colonel Muhammad Ataul Gani Osmani. As more and more Bengali soldiers defected, they swelled the ranks of the Mukti Bahini as well as adding to its store of weaponry. In addition, the Mukti Bahini received material support from the government in neighboring West Bengal state in India. West Bengal consists primarily of Bengalis, so the state shared ethnic ties with East Pakistan. It became part of India at partition because a majority of its people were Hindu.

In response, the Pakistani military raised a paramilitary force, the Razakars, who were loyal to the central government. Many of these were from the Bihari community, a small Urdu-speaking minority in East Pakistan. The Razakars, along with military action, were able to keep the revolt in check for the monsoon months of June and July. But Mukti Bahini was constantly regrouping in India. In addition, the Indian government was planning to intervene further in the conflict. As many as 10 million refugees from East Pakistan had fled to India to escape the violence, which gave India a pretext for intervention.

Mukti Bahini guerrilla troops prepare to bayonet men who collaborated with the Pakistani army during East Pakistan's fight to secede from Pakistan. The third India–Pakistan war resulted in the creation of the independent nation of Bangladesh. (AFP/Getty Images)

Geography

Undoubtedly, geography played a factor in the war; at the very least, the rebels were much more familiar with the lush terrain. The Pakistani army was much better equipped to control urban areas, and rebels were able to retreat relatively safely into the countryside after setbacks. Moreover, the war itself was far away from military and political headquarters in West Pakistan, which presented the most daunting challenge, and made it nearly impossible to move personnel and equipment quickly and efficiently to the theater of war. Movement was especially difficult because Pakistan could not fly over Indian airspace, and its ability to use its ports in Karachi and Dhaka was limited.

East Pakistan's border wth India provided a ready-made site for rebels to regroup and train, and they had considerable Indian support. After refugees began flooding into India, the Indian government set up refugee camps in the states of West Bengal, Bihar, Assam, Meghalaya, and Tripura. These camps became training grounds for the Mukti Bahini.

Tactics

The Mukti Bahini's tactics consisted of conventional guerrilla activities, including small strikes in urban and rural settings (especially in Dhaka, the capital of East Pakistan). The Mukti Bahini received considerable resources from the Indian government. In addition, the Indian military provided cover for the Mukti Bahini by shelling Pakistan army positions inside East Pakistan from Indian territory. The Indian government provided weapons to the Mukti Bahini as well, although these are largely considered to have been obsolete; the majority of

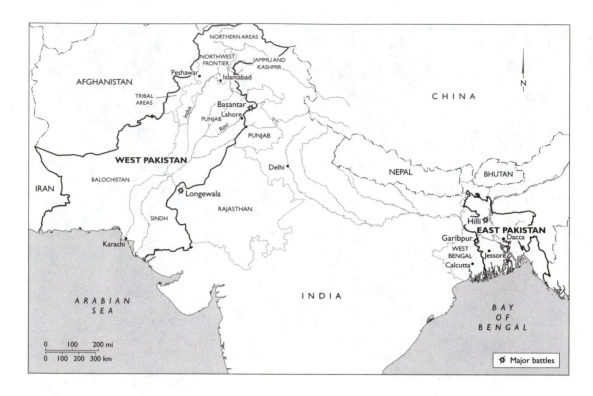

modern weapons were obtained by guerrilla forces on the international arms markets (Sisson and Rose 1990, 185).

Causes of the War
The Formation of Pakistan

To understand how the secession of East Pakistan came about, it is essential to first examine the historical background of Pakistan. Pakistan was created in 1947 when British India was partitioned into the majority-Hindu state of India and the majority-Muslim state of Pakistan. But Pakistani independence was by no means inevitable. The struggle for independence in British India was initially dominated by Hindus and led by the Indian National Congress, and the movement was focused on the independence

of a united India; the division of India never occurred to leaders such as Nehru and Gandhi. But Muslims, who had not been very politically active in British India, especially after the uprising in 1857, began to feel increasingly alienated from the independence movement, fearing that their interests were not being addressed. In 1906, the All-India Muslim League was formed. At the same time, most Muslim members of the independence movement felt increasingly marginalized from the Hindu-dominated congress, which was the organization leading the mainstream independence movement. Most of these Muslim members left congress and joined the Muslim League; eventually the League came to be led by secular and Western-educated activists such as Muhammad Ali Jinnah, who was to eventually become the founder of Pakistan.

The idea of Pakistan as an independent country was first articulated by Muhammad Iqbal in his "two nation" theory, which argued that the Muslim and Hindu communities in India were two separate and distinct nations. It was as late as 1940 when the explicit demand for Pakistan was first made, in the Lahore Resolution. The group at the helm of the Pakistan movement lacked the overtly religious component that one associates with Pakistan today and was committed to a secular state. Indeed, as Hamza Alavi has put it, "the Pakistan movement was not a movement of Islam but of Muslims" (Alavi 1986, 22). And within the Muslim community in India, the groups that were overtly religious (Islamic) were distanced from the Pakistan movement, such as the Jama'at-i-Islami Party, or people associated with the Deobandi movement. Indeed, somewhat ironically, the Islamists in India were fiercely opposed to the division of British India. Thus, the Pakistan movement remained dominated by a group that has been called the "salariat": secular, urban professionals in the Muslim community (see Alavi 1986). But the movement's leaders were eager to attract members of the ulema (the ulema are roughly equivalent to the clergy in the Christian context but are much less formalized in the Islamic context), some of whom eventually joined the movement, but the consequence was a struggle over the nature of the new state (i.e., whether it was to be secular or Islamist).

Most Hindu Indians (and the British) remained strongly opposed to the idea of partition, but massive civil disobedience campaigns eventually forced the hands of the leaders. It became clear that independence from the British would come only with partition. According to many estimates, approximately 7–8 million people moved across the newly created India–Pakistan border at partition (in both directions). There were violent riots associated with this movement of people, resulting in massive dislocation, injuries, rapes, and the deaths of as many as 1 million people. Today, Pakistan is approximately 95 percent Muslim.

When Pakistan did become independent, it inherited a geographically divided state. West Pakistan, consisting of the Muslim-majority regions of the northwest of British India, and East Pakistan, consisting of the Muslim-majority portion of Bengal, were separated by almost 1,000 miles, with the newly independent India lying between them. The new country was not only difficult to maintain and defend militarily, it faced considerable logistical challenges from the start. And the geographical divide did little to help existing ethnic tensions between East and West Pakistan, which would eventually worsen to lead to a civil war and the secession of East Pakistan to form Bangladesh in 1971. The new nation was born with a sense of being besieged by the larger and more powerful India. Many Pakistanis continue to believe that most Indians have never reconciled themselves to the reality of partition, which leads to even greater suspicion between the two countries (Sathasivam and Shafqat 2003).

The Ethnic Dimension

Although the new nation had successfully gained independence both from the British and from India, it was by no means united. In fact, Pakistan was composed of various ethnic groups that supported the new country in varying degrees. The Muslim salariat, which was the vanguard of the Pakistan movement, was drawn most heavily from two ethnic groups: the Punjabis and Urdu-speaking Muslims in the United Provinces (UP), who were to form the Muhajir group in an independent Pakistan. Additionally, support for Pakistan was strongest in these regions as well. These were the two groups that would come to dominate independent Pakistan, which would lead to increased resentments and tensions between the various ethnic groups that constituted Pakistan. There were six primary ethnic groups in Pakistan: Punjabis, who dominated the political and economic systems as well as the military; Pashtuns (this community is referred to variously as Pashtuns, Pathans, and Pakhtuns), who were also well represented in the military; Baluchis, who were perhaps the least enthusiastic supporters of Pakistan; Sindhis, who were also aligned with a Sindhi nationalist movement; Muhajirs, who were refugees from India who had migrated to Pakistan at partition; and Bengalis, who historically had a very strong sense of Bengali (as opposed to Muslim) nationalism.

The biggest challenge to Pakistani nationhood was from Bengali nationalism. Bengalis dominated East Pakistan and were the biggest ethnic group in terms of population in all of Pakistan. But Punjabis and Muhajirs dominated the administrative, political, and military arms of the country, and Bengalis were marginalized in the new country; their sense of alienation was only underscored by the fact that their region was located on the other end of the subcontinent from West Pakistan, the nucleus of the country. Emblematic of the ethnic tensions were the political struggles over the language issue, namely, declaring a national language for Pakistan. The language chosen was Urdu, which was the native language only for the Muhajir community but was widely spoken by many other Pakistanis. However, Urdu was not spoken widely by the Bengalis, and the conflict over the institution of Urdu as the exclusive national language in 1952 was an early harbinger of the tensions between East and West Pakistan that were to eventually result in civil war.

Although Bengalis in East Pakistan constituted a numerical majority in the country, they were a marginalized group. In addition to cultural and political alienation, Bengalis also experienced a high degree of economic exploitation by the western segment of the country. Central government expenditures in West Pakistan were much higher than in East Pakistan. Moreover, East Pakistan was an important source of export earnings for the country—from its textile mills, jute products, tea, and other agricultural products—but it saw disproportionately little development. This economic relationship is not enough to qualify the East Pakistan revolt as a "sons of the soil" case (Fearon 2004). Economic exploitation in this case really served to reinforce the sense of alienation that Bengalis already felt.

Another important event that complicated the ethnic dimension of Pakistani politics was the Soviet invasion of Afghanistan in 1979. The Afghanistan war had tremendous fallout for Pakistan, which continues to the present day. Most notably, Pakistan was faced with a humanitarian crisis as millions of Afghan refugees streamed into Pakistan after the Soviet invasion. This humanitarian crisis was coupled with a more delicate political one, for the presence of the refugees stirred the complicated stew that is Pakistani ethnic politics. The majority of the Afghan refugees were Pashtuns, an ethnic group that is about equally divided across both sides of the Afghan–Pakistan border. The border itself is based on the British-era Durand line, which Afghanistan has never officially accepted as the international boundary between Pakistan and Afghanistan. Additionally, Pashtuns are an important ethnic minority group within Pakistan—for example, they are well represented in the military—but there is a strong Pashtun nationalist movement, which has posed threats to the Punjabi-dominated central government. The threat such a nationalist movement poses becomes even greater if the movement spreads across international boundaries, leading to calls for an independent Pashtunistan. Greater ethnic tensions were not the only fallout of the Afghan war. The effort against the Soviets also led to a huge arms buildup within Pakistan, which served to further militarize Pakistani society in what has been called the "Kalashnikov culture." In addition, the Afghan war led to an increase in the narcotics trade.

The Military in Pakistani Politics

A critical factor in explaining the civil war in Pakistan is the dominant role played by the military in Pakistani politics throughout its history. Pakistan has been under military rule for approximately half of the time it has been independent. As was the case with many postcolonial countries, Pakistan inherited weak civilian political institutions from British colonialism. The military, dominated by the Punjabis and to a lesser extent by the Pashtuns, has styled itself as the only real guarantor of Pakistani national unity. The military has stepped in to take control in response to many crises in Pakistani history, but even when the military has not been in direct control, it has exerted enormous influence on the polity. Consequently, the Pakistani military has seen itself as being charged not only with *external* security but also with *internal* security.

Given that the military has assumed the role of national uniter, it has responded most energetically to threats from ethnic nationalist movements. For example, in 1970, when civil unrest in East Pakistan was at its peak, General Yahya Khan declared martial law, which eventually led to civil war. The Pakistani supreme court later declared this imposition of martial law illegal. It should be noted that ethnic unrest is not the only condition that has prompted the Pakistani military to act. For example, in 1977, when Islamist parties were leading the civil unrest in opposition to alleged electoral rigging by the Bhutto administration, General Zia ul Haq declared martial law yet again. But it has been usually (although not exclusively) during periods of military rule that the most brutal repression of ethnic nationalist movements has occurred. For example, the civil war in East Pakistan in 1971 was marked by widespread rape and killing by Pakistani military personnel of the local Bengalis. And during the Zia government in the 1980s, the military was involved in the forceful suppression of uprisings by Baluchi and Sindhi nationalists (Harrison 1981a, 1981b; Rakisits 1988).

The Language Movement

Within Pakistan, ethnic identity revolves around language. Therefore, language has played a critical role in fomenting nationalism. Urdu, the mother tongue of a small minority in Pakistan, had become linked with the Pakistan nationalist movement. The Muslim League had

---

The Rape of Women in Wartime

The wartime rape of women has been an unfortunately common occurrence in modern times. The Bangladesh liberation war is often asserted to be one of the most grievous examples of wartime rape. According to one widely quoted estimate, between 250,000 and 400,000 girls and women were raped in East Pakistan, resulting in 25,000 pregnancies.

After the war, the Bangladeshi leadership attempted to rehabilitate these women. In February 1972, the Bangladesh War Rehabilitation Board was created. Sheikh Mujibur Rahman and other leaders attempted to remove the stigma under which these women were living. War victims were declared biranganas, or heroines, and were to be considered honorable, courageous women who had made the ultimate sacrifice for their nation. This strategy was not entirely successful.

---

promoted Urdu as a language of unity among Indian Muslims in the run-up to independence. In the newly independent country, Urdu emerged as a front-runner for "official" language status. This was true even though Urdu was spoken as a first language by a small minority, most of whom were refugees from north India (mostly from the UP). Various explanations can be given for this. Perhaps the most convincing theory is that Urdu had acquired the status of an "intellectual" language and had considerable cultural cachet.

It is no surprise, then, that the introduction of Urdu as the national language aroused considerable resentment and animosity among non-Urdu–speaking groups. Among these, the largest group were the Bengalis, who comprised the vast majority in East Pakistan; indeed, they were the majority ethnic group in federated Pakistan as a whole. Even though Bangladeshi independence would not come until 1971, it is accurate to say that the roots of the Bangladeshi nationalist movement lie in the momentous events of 1952, when the Bangla movement first mobilized to oppose Urdu as the national language.

The political center of gravity in the new nation was in the western region, in West Pakistan, even though Bengalis constituted a majority of the population. Culturally, Bengalis had been constructed in the west as somewhat less "pure" Muslims and Pakistanis. This image was linked to language, for Bengali was the only Pakistani language not written in the Persian–Arabic alphabet. It was also linked to a notion of Bengali inferiority that was deemed almost essentialist and was racialized.

The language issue arose soon after independence. In Pakistan, Urdu, although spoken by a small minority, was the language of the cultural and political elite. (However, most of the elite also spoke English, which became a de facto official language.) Elevating Urdu to the status of sole official language (as was suggested as early as 1948 by Jinnah) was bitterly resented by East Pakistanis. The matter came to a head in 1952, as the East Pakistan-based Awami League political party launched a popular campaign to have Bengali recognized as an additional official language along with Urdu. A coalition of political organizations declared February 21, 1952, a general strike day. On that day, police fired on unarmed students protesting outside the Provincial Assembly in Dhaka, killing five. Over the next few days, mass civil unrest took hold in the city. Although this wave of unrest was quickly brought under control through strong repressive measures (including the closing of college campuses), the language movement spread quickly to other parts of East Pakistan. The language riots of 1952 radicalized East Pakistanis more than any other issue. It also allowed a strong nationalist political leadership to emerge in East Pakistan, notably the Awami League. The immediate impact of the riots was that the central government eventually conceded and granted Bengali the status of official language as well as Urdu. But the long-term implications were to unify and politicize Bengalis in East Pakistan.

Of course, the language issue has been most prominent in the case of East Pakistan. But language has been an important mobilizing force in other cases as well, including uprisings by Sindhis and Baluchis. The current uprising in Baluchistan, beginning in 2003, demonstrates this well.

Accommodating Regional Autonomy

Another important backdrop to the civil war was the succession of attempts to accommodate regional autonomy for the various provinces of Pakistan. The language movement and other events continued to demonstrate the fragility of the Pakistani federation, and the country was involved in various attempts to fashion a workable constitutional framework that would reasonably represent the interests of different communities. Throughout the 1950s, various constitutional frameworks were proposed, but none was acceptable to the military and bureaucratic establishment. In 1958, martial law was imposed, and General Ayub Khan took control. Ayub Khan's rule would last until 1969, when he was forced from power by another military junta, that of General Yahya Khan. Ayub Khan was a proponent of the One Unit Scheme, introduced in 1956, and continued to maintain it. This scheme was designed to neutralize the numerical majority of East Pakistan. It merged the existing provinces of Punjab, North-West Frontier Province, Baluchistan, and Sindh, and all federal territories into a single administrative unit to achieve greater parity with East Pakistan. The scheme aroused great suspicion in East Pakistan and was also met with considerable resentment on the part of the smaller provinces in West Pakistan, who feared Punjabi dominance.

Ayub Khan consolidated power after a referendum in 1960 and presidential elections in 1962. These elections were held using the basic democracies structure, which was an indirect form of elections with a limited number of electors (based on regional representation). This framework was viewed with great suspicion by many, including the Bengalis in East Pakistan. Moreover, the election was fraught with irregularities. All this served only to heighten the anxieties and resentment that Bengalis felt. Although Dhaka (East Pakistan's capital) was designated the legislative capital of the country, the legislature had no power, and this continued to marginalize Bengalis.

After the 1965 war with India, Ayub Khan and the military suffered a blow, as they were perceived to have been weak, especially in the negotiations for the cease-fire agreement. The postwar period was marked with increasing opposition activity and civil unrest in both East and West Pakistan. Ayub Khan was ultimately forced out of power by his military chief, General Yahya Khan, in March 1969. Yahya Khan called for elections in December 1970. The results of this election provided the immediate backdrop to the civil war, as discussed earlier.

Outcome
Conflict Status

The Pakistan civil war is one of the very few to have resulted in a successful secessionist movement. The rebel forces, supported by India, were successful. The immediate outcome of the war was the creation of a new independent nation, Bangladesh. Pakistan signed an unconditional surrender on December 16, 1971. The surrender was signed by General Niazi (see sidebar, "Instrument of Surrender"), upon which all 93,000 Pakistani soldiers were taken as prisoners of war. At the time, this was the biggest surrender since World War II. Refugees began to be repatriated soon after the surrender.

Duration Tactics

The war was relatively short, lasting approximately nine months. But the war might have been even shorter had several factors not existed. The secessionist nature of the war meant that the central government was even more keen to hold onto East Pakistan. The loss of East Pakistan would directly call into question the identity and existence of Pakistan itself as a home-

land for the Muslims of India. It would also mean an implicit victory for Pakistan's archrival India, which was untenable. External assistance from India was instrumental in prolonging the war. Without Indian assistance, the Mukti Bahini would probably have been defeated in short order.

Following are the major battles of the war.

> Battle of Hilli (aka Bogra), November 22, 1971–December 13, 1971
> Battle of Garibpur (aka Boyra), November 20, 1971–November 21, 1971
> Battle of Longewala, December 5, 1971–December 6, 1971
> Battle of Basantar (aka Barapind), December 4, 1971–December 16, 1971

External Military Intervention

The major external military actor was India, whose role was decisive in the war. India played a role in three main ways: as provider of material aid to the rebels, especially Mukti Bahini; as principal military opponent; and as diplomatic actor.

India announced full support of the Bangladeshi struggle on March 27, 1971; indeed, it had been actively arming and training members of the Mukti Bahini from the very start of the war. For example, in June 1971 the Indian army started a program to train Mukti Bahini recruits. Recruits were sorted by their education—science graduates were given two months' technical training, undergraduates were given training in small arms, and others were trained in sabotage techniques, such as the use of explosives. Estimates suggest that approximately 70,000 recruits had been trained (Sisson and Rose 1990, 184–85).

As the civil war stretched into the summer of 1971, refugees from East Pakistan began flooding into India. This not only presented an urgent humanitarian crisis for India, it also provided legal and diplomatic cover for India's intervention in the war. Pakistan, realizing that formal Indian military intervention was imminent, launched preemptive air strikes in India on December 3, 1971. The Mukti Bahini now joined forces with the Indian army to form the Mitro Bahini. At this point, the war took a decisive turn in favor of the rebels. India was far superior to Pakistan militarily and played its hand cleverly. In particular, India had a larger, better-armed army and superior naval forces.

In addition, India had the advantage of being able to attack Pakistan on both its eastern and western fronts. The portion of the war in which India was formally engaged with Pakistan was mostly conducted on the western front. Of the major battles in the war, perhaps the most decisive one was the Battle of Longewala (Shorey 2005). This battle lasted from December 5 to December 6, 1971. The Pakistan army launched an attack inside India in Rajasthan state (on the western front in the war). The Pakistan army had the advantage in number of troops; it fielded approximately 2,000 soldiers, whereas India only had about 120 soldiers defending the position. But Pakistan failed to provide air cover for the attack, and the battle was ultimately a humiliating defeat for the Pakistani forces. India was also able to blockade the Pakistani navy, headquartered in Karachi in West Pakistan, which made the navy a nonfactor in the war.

India also played a critical role as a diplomatic actor. Pakistan could expect to depend on two countries for support: China and the United States. Pakistan had developed a close alliance with China, which was greatly strengthened after the Indo-China war of 1962. The United States, too, was an important ally in the Cold War, as it was able to depend on the Pakistani military to fight communism. Pakistan also provided a useful regional counterweight to India, which was allied with the Soviet Union. Pakistan and the United States were members of CENTO (Central Treaty Organization) along with Iran, Turkey, and Britain. This organization was modeled along the lines of NATO and provided for mutual defense and cooperation. The goal of the treaty was to contain the Soviet Union by establishing a strong line of defense along the Soviet Union's southern perimeter. Although CENTO was relatively weak, it did establish a formal military link between the United States and Pakistan.

But India was able to skillfully manipulate international actors to limit the extent of support from Pakistan's allies, as a result of Indian Prime Minister Indira Gandhi's diplomatic efforts. Gandhi signed a twenty-year friendship treaty with the Soviet Union, which ensured that China would play a limited role in the conflict. As a result, China continued to support Pakistan through the civil war but provided little material aid and did not move its troops to the Indian border to engage Indian forces away from the civil war.

Gandhi also undertook a tour of Europe during the fall of 1971 in which she was able to persuade France and the United Kingdom to break with the United States and block any pro-Pakistan actions in the United Nations Security Council. (Gandhi also visited the United States in November 1971 and rejected U.S. advice on the conflict.) As a result, the United Nations played little role in the conflict, and the United States was able to provide only limited unilateral support to Pakistan. As a symbolic gesture, the United States dispatched a task force headed by the nuclear-armed carrier *Enterprise* from the Gulf of Tonkin to the Bay of Bengal on September 10, 1971. But U.S. forces never entered the war. The Soviet Union responded by sending two groups of ships from Vladivostock on December 6, 1971; these remained in the area until January 7, 1972.

Conflict Management Efforts

As mentioned previously, outside actors were limited in their influence on the conflict (except for India). Therefore, it remained essentially a trilateral affair between Pakistan, the Bangladeshi rebels, and India. No other parties were involved in the surrender.

Pakistan and India held a bilateral summit, the Shimla Summit, from June 28 to July 3, 1972. Representing Pakistan was its new leader, Prime

Minister Zulfikar Ali Bhutto. Bhutto and Indian Prime Minister Indira Gandhi were able to fashion a permanent cease-fire as well as a political resolution of some of the war's issues. The main political issues were recognition of Bangladesh as an independent nation, the return of Pakistani POWs, and the Kashmir issue. The last was the most intransigent issue. India wanted the cease-fire line in Kashmir to be a permanent international border, but Pakistan was understandably reluctant to concede this point. The two nations did agree, however, to withdraw all forces to pre-1971 borders. The Shimla Summit agreement has been controversial because India has interpreted it to mean that all issues, including that of the status of Kashmir, will be settled in a bilateral manner. Pakistan disagrees with this interpretation, because it has historically been keener to involve international actors in the dispute, as it perceives such involvement to favor Pakistan's position. India agreed to release Pakistani POWs, but only after a period of three months. Pakistan eventually recognized Bangladesh on February 22, 1974.

Conclusion

The Pakistan civil war resulted in the creation of Bangladesh. It also had lasting effects on regional dynamics as well as domestic politics within Pakistan. In the region, the war deepened the rivalry and animosity between Pakistan and India, a conflict that dominates the regional dynamic. Interestingly, although there is still considerable tension between Pakistan and Bangladesh, the two countries have been able to develop a fairly amicable relationship.

In some ways, there is little possibility of the recurrence of a civil war like the Bangladesh war because it was such a unique case, owing both to geography and to the strong nature of Bengali nationalism from a very early stage. However, other cases of subnational nationalism have continued to confront the Pakistani state: Baluchistan in the 1970s (and currently), Sindh in the 1980s, and many other cases of demands

for autonomy. These challenges are fairly common in most postcolonial societies and to some extent may be considered "natural" by-products of colonialism. But the Pakistani state may be considered responsible to some extent as well. By repressing all demands for regional autonomy, often very brutally, the Pakistani state has been unable to accommodate the interests of all its various ethnic groups.

The secession of Bangladesh led to greater anxiety on the part of the the Pakistani establishment about subnational challenges. One consequence has been to strengthen the military (after a short period of national disgrace in the early to mid-1970s). The military, always distrustful of civilian politicians, has stepped in twice since the 1971 war to safeguard what it sees as national interests, including protecting the national integrity of the country.

Another consequence has been the growing Islamization of Pakistani society. The trend toward using Islam for political expediency reached a new high under the government of Zulfikar Ali Bhutto. His main constituency consisted of the landed rural classes, peasants, and the laboring classes, and he had to find a way to reach out to other groups. According to Anita Weiss,

> Bhutto adopted Islamic slogans, particularly those stressing egalitarianism and social justice as a means of legitimating his economic policies, thereby increasing his popularity. There was no attempt to include specific Islamic laws in the legal system until it became politically expedient to do so in early 1977 when drinking, gambling, and night clubs were banned. This was soon followed by the replacement of Friday for Sunday as the weekly holiday (Weiss 1986, 9).

Besides trying to appeal to a broader cross-section of society, Bhutto and others introduced such measures in response to Islamist activists. One of the truisms of Pakistani politics has been that Islamist parties control no more than 10 to 15 percent of popular support. Although that is true, it is also true that Islamists have generally been very successful and efficient at mobilizing popular support and organizing civil unrest. This was very much the case during the Bhutto administration, and in fact it was the civil unrest generated by the Islamists (and others) that became the pretext for the military to move in again in 1977 under General Zia. The most dramatic imposition of Islam on public life occurred under Zia with the Islamization program.

With the Bhutto administration, Pakistan first began to seek closer relations and cooperation with actors in the Muslim and Arab world, a trend that has continued to the present day. After the humiliating defeat of Pakistani forces in 1971 and the nuclear test by India in 1974, Pakistan's security establishment was in a major crisis, and the Middle East connection was perceived to be an extremely useful counterforce to India, one that could be more dependable than the United States. W. Howard Wriggins (1984) writes that many in the Pakistani foreign policy establishment felt that the United States had "let them down" in the 1965 and 1971 wars with India and could not be considered a reliable ally (Sathasivam and Shafqat 2003).

The loss of Bangladesh and India's nuclear test in 1974 gave urgency to Pakistan's plans for a nuclear weapons program. Bhutto endeavored to acquire assistance from the Middle East for this project, and certainly emphasizing common religious and cultural ties helped the effort. In particular, Saudi Arabia emerged as a crucial ally in terms of material support (Rizvi 1983; Tahir-Kheli and Staudenmaier 1982). Pakistan became an official nuclear nation in 1998 when it tested as many as six nuclear devices. In some circles, the proposed product of a Pakistani nuclear program even came to be known as the Islamic bomb.

The lasting lesson of Bangladesh for the Pakistani establishment should have been that violent secession can only be avoided by peacefully accommodating regional demands. But, unfortunately, that has not been the pattern in post-1971 Pakistan. A diverse, multiethnic society such as Pakistan requires a genuine federal framework. Unless such a framework is implemented, with meaningful power for the various provinces of Pakistan, true peaceful coexistence of Pakistan's ethnic groups will be impossible.

Sahar Shafqat

Chronology

March 25, 1971   Mujibur Rehman is arrested in Dhaka. Operation Searchlight begins with the massacre of masses of people, particularly intellectuals.

March 26, 1971   East Pakistan declares independence. Official start of civil war.

April 17, 1971   Exiled leaders of Awami League form a provisional government in India.

December 14, 1971   Systematic elimination of Bengali intellectuals is begun by Pakistani Army and local collaborators.

December 16, 1971   Lieutenant General A. A. K. Niazi, supreme commander of Pakistani Army in East Pakistan, surrenders to Mitro Bahini (allied forces of Mitro Bahini and Indian army), represented by Lieutenant General Aurora of the Indian army.

December 16, 1971   Bangladesh gains independence.

January 12, 1972   Sheikh Mujibur Rahman is released from prison in Pakistan and returned to independent Bangladesh to become prime minister.

June 28–July 3, 1972   Shimla Summit between India and Pakistan negotiates postwar situation.

February 22, 1974   Pakistan recognizes Bangladesh.

List of Acronyms

CENTO: Central Treaty Organization, a Cold War–era military alliance that replaced the Baghdad Pact. Its membership consisted of the United Kingdom, the United States, Pakistan, Iran, and Turkey.

NWFP: North-West Frontier Province

UP: United Provinces

References

Alavi, Hamza. 1986. "Ethnicity, Muslim Society, and the Pakistan Ideology." In *Islamic Reassertion in Pakistan: The Application of Islamic Laws in a Modern State,* edited by Anita Weiss. Syracuse, NY: Syracuse University Press.

Brownmiller, Susan. 1975. *Against Our Will: Men, Women, and Rape.* New York: Simon & Schuster.

Fearon, James D. 2004. "Why Do Some Civil Wars Last So Much Longer than Others?" *Journal of Peace Research* 41: 275-301.

Harrison, Selig S. 1981a. "Baluch Nationalism and Superpower Rivalry." *International Security* 5(3): 152–63.

Harrison, Selig S. 1981b. *In Afghanistan's Shadow: Baluch Nationalism and Soviet Temptations.* New York: Carnegie Endowment for International Peace.

Payne, Robert. 1973. *Massacre: The Tragedy of Bangladesh and the Phenomenon of Mass Slaughter throughout History.* New York: Macmillan.

Rakisits, C. G. P. 1988. "Centre-Province Relations in Pakistan Under President Zia: The Government's and the Opposition's Approaches." *Pacific Affairs* 61(1): 78–97.

Rizvi, Hasan-Askari. 1983. "Pakistan: Ideology and Foreign Policy." *Asian Affairs* (Spring): 48–59.

Rummel, R. J. 1997. *Death by Government.* Somerset, NJ: Transaction Publishers.

Sathasivam, Kanishkan, and Sahar Shafqat. 2003. "In India's Shadow? The Evolution of Pakistan's Security Policy." In *Conflict in Asia: Korea, China-Taiwan, and India-Pakistan,* edited by Uk Heo and Shale Horowitz. Westport, CT: Greenwood.

Shorey, Anil. 2005. *Pakistan's Failed Gamble: The Battle of Laungewala.* New Delhi: Manas.

Sisson, Richard, and Leo Rose. 1990. *War and Secession: Pakistan, India, and the Creation of Bangladesh.* Berkeley: University of California Press.

Swiss, S., and J. E. Giller. 1993. "Rape as a Crime of War—A Medical Perspective." *Journal of the American Medical Association* 270: 612–15.

Tahir-Kheli, Shirin, and W. O. Staudenmaier. 1982. "The Saudi-Pakistan Military Relationship: Implications for U.S. Policy." *Orbis* 26(1).

Weiss, Anita. 1986. "The Historical Debate on Islam and the State in South Asia." In *Islamic Reassertion in Pakistan: The Application of Islamic Laws in a Modern State,* edited by Anita Weiss. Syracuse, NY: Syracuse University Press.

Wriggins, W. Howard. 1984. "Pakistan's Foreign Policy after the Invasion of Afghanistan." *Pacific Affairs* 57(2).

Peru
(1980–1996)

Introduction

The Sendero Luminoso's civil war in Peru marked a sixteen-year period of increasing terror for civilians and havoc for the Peruvian government. The bulk of this dispute showcased how an internal war of attrition can undermine legitimate government, the effectiveness of guerrilla tactics, and the ineffectiveness of many counterinsurgency techniques. It also demonstrated the power that one charismatic individual can have on a conflict and on its chances for peace. This chapter explains the path taken by the Peruvian conflict, its underlying causes, its intractability, and the way in which it finally ended.

Country Background

Peru gained independence from Spain in 1824 and subsequently fell into a number of armed disputes with its Latin American neighbors. Despite serious border disputes with both Ecuador and Chile, Peru was not troubled by serious internal conflict until the 1980s. The Shining Path insurgency (or Sendero Luminoso) constitutes the greatest internal challenge Peru has faced since independence.

In the decades preceding the Sendero Luminoso civil war, Peru experienced two dramatic changes in regime type. The 1950s and early 1960s were marked by increasing levels of democracy (moving from 4 to 5 on the Polity scale). However, in 1968 the country changed course when General Juan Velasco Alvarado assumed power through an armed coup d'état. In 1975, Alvarado was removed from power in a second coup, led by General Morales Bermudez, who ruled through a military government until 1980, when the country returned to civilian rule and democracy. Former President Fernando Belaundé was reelected to the position in 1980. This oscillation between democracy and military rule set the stage for insurgency in the countryside and eventual civil war. In addition to the return to democracy, 1980 also marked the beginning of the long and bloody Sendero Luminoso civil war.

Somewhat remarkably, Peru remained democratic throughout most of the Sendero Luminoso civil war. Between 1980 and 1991, Peru functioned as a democratic polity, even increasing its level of democracy over time. However, in 1991, President Alberto Fujimori returned the country once again to military rule. President Fujimori abandoned democracy and succeeded in taking control of the government. The tenure of Fujimori's military rule outlasted the Sendero Luminoso civil war, which lost momentum in the mid-1990s. Fujimori eventually went into self-imposed exile, and in 2001 Peru once again became a democracy.

In addition to the tumultuous changes in regime type, alternating between democracy and military rule, Peru's economy experienced major swings before and during the course of this conflict. Macroeconomic indicators show that the state of Peru's economy worsened in the five years before the war. Beginning in 1975, prior to the outbreak of war, Peru's per capita gross domestic product (GDP) declined steadily. The overall wealth of the nation was decreasing year by year. Moreover, in the years preceding the war, the military government attempted to implement major land reforms. These reforms were designed to alleviate inequality between landholders and peasants but were unable to make significant headway (McClintock 1984). The reforms did not provide substantial benefits to much of the peasant class and did little to ease the effects of the mounting economic crisis (see Mason 1998 for a discussion of the reasons these reforms were ineffective).

In the wake of economic downturn and land reform, there was a slight economic recovery in 1981, but this was followed by the subsequent plummeting of national wealth (measured by GDP) in 1983. The El Niño weather phenomenon contributed significantly to the hardship through its effect on crop growth. The country saw another economic high point in 1987, where it appeared that the economy had recovered to levels like those reached in the 1981 recovery (based on comparable GDP levels). However, there was another dramatic drop in economic performance between 1987 and 1990, where national GDP reached a 30-year low at $3,584 per capita (measured in 1996 U.S. dollars). From 1991 on, the road to economic recovery was steady, if bumpy; nevertheless, by the year 2000 Peru had still not reached its prewar level of prosperity (Gleditsch 2002).

Prewar Peru was characterized by volatility in terms of both its economy and its government. The instability of both government and economic performance were exacerbated by the conflict during the subsequent sixteen years of fighting.

Conflict Background

Although the Sendero Luminoso war posed the largest threat to Peru in recent history, the country faced three other significant militarized conflicts during the Sendero civil war. Peru engaged in two minor armed conflicts with Ecuador and simultaneously dealt with an insurgency led by the Tupac Amaru Revolutionary Movement (MRTA). Both conflicts with Ecuador (in 1981 and 1995) were border disputes and were resolved relatively quickly with international involvement (United States, Argentina, Brazil, and Chile facilitated the end of the disputes). The MRTA movement (a Marxist insurgency) was active between 1983 and 1993. The group used terrorist tactics aimed at ridding the country of imperialism and establishing a Marxist regime (Gleditsch, Wallensteen, Eriksson, and Hårvard 2002). The MRTA movement gained notoriety with a number of terrorist acts, the most famous of which was the 1996 attack on the Japanese ambassador's residence and the subsequent hostage situation. However, the influence of this movement was largely overshadowed by the scope of damage caused by the Sendero war.

The Sendero Luminoso war was first and foremost an ideological dispute. The rebels' primary aim was the overthrow of the state, which they envisioned would then be replaced by a peasant revolutionary regime (Gleditsch, et al. 2002). The armed conflict began in early 1980 and lasted until the mid-1990s; by 1996 it had lost significant momentum. Although the rebels clearly identified with communism internationally and with Maoism specifically, they followed their own brand of ideological thinking. They wanted to understand communism in the Peruvian context, and this isolated the group somewhat from other such movements around the world, particularly after the death of Mao (Palmer 1986). Sendero maintained connections with China and international Communist organizations at the early stages of the conflict but tended to view other Communist organizations as revisionist, especially after the end of the Cold War.

This immensely violent conflict began with few deaths but spiraled out of control in the mid- and late 1980s. At the initial stages of the struggle, conflict-related deaths numbered less than 100 a year, with a sharp jump to nearly 2,000 deaths in 1983, when Sendero engaged in more intense and far-reaching operations. A decade into the conflict, an estimated 20,000 had been killed in Peru in political violence. This estimate reached approximately 28,000 by 1996, when the conflict finally petered out (Gleditsch, et al. 2002; Mason 1998). These initial estimates of the death toll were eclipsed, however, by the report of the Peruvian Truth and Reconciliation Commission (TRC) in 2003 (see sidebar, "The Unknown Magnitude of the Conflict"). After years of investigation, the TRC estimated the total number of lost lives between 1980 and 2000 at 69,280 people (TRC 2003).

During the conflict, the Peruvian military was made up of 264,000 troops (Doyle and Sambanis 2000). Government troops fought the Sendero Luminoso fighters with both conventional military units and sinchis, which were specially trained paramilitaries (Mason 1998, 222). By 1991, the Sendero Luminoso fighters numbered as many as 15,000 by some estimates and as few as 3,000 by others (Mason 1998, 223).

The Insurgents

Although the Sendero Luminoso armed struggle began in earnest in 1980, its foundations were laid in the 1960s and 1970s in the context of severe economic challenges for the peasant and indigenous populations of Peru. Sendero Luminoso was founded by Abimael Guzmán in the 1960s, but the organization only began its People's War, with the goal of complete overthrow of the Peruvian state, in 1980. The movement began at the National University of San Cristobal de Humanga in the Ayacucha department in the mountains of Peru. Guzmán's initial political organizing included recruiting students and founding an outreach program in the community surrounding the university. The Sendero ideology developed from Guzmán's synthesis of Maoist thought and the work of Mariategui (a Peruvian intellectual and founder of the Com-

The Unknown Magnitude of the Conflict

Like other contemporary civil wars, the Sendero Luminoso war produced an extremely high death toll among both combatants and noncombatants. Peruvians in the combat zones were subject to violence from all sides—from government troops, from Sendero guerrillas, and even from civil defense groups set up in local communities for self-defense. The magnitude of the deaths and disappearances during the conflict was difficult to assess, in part because the government was unable to provide a reliable count at the time.

When the Truth and Reconciliation Commission released its final report in 2003, one of the most shocking findings for Peru as well as the international community was the size of the death toll it reported. Earlier estimates place the number of deaths caused by the conflict at around 28,000 between 1980 and 1996 (Gleditsch, et al. 2002). However, the TRC reports that it could account for nearly 70,000 individuals who had been killed or who disappeared between 1980 and 2000—more than double previous estimates. Table 1 illustrates the initial estimates of change in the cumulative death counts based on several sources. The TRC finding is also marked for the year 2000, although the TRC does not provide a yearly account of when the estimates of the deaths took place.

munist Party of Peru). From its early stages, the Sendero movement was designed to be a long-term program for social change, one that involved the destruction of the contemporary state through civil war and its eventual replacement with a peasant-based revolutionary regime.

Sendero Luminoso was made up primarily of educated mestitos who were recruited from universities. They also drew from the indigenous population in Ayacucho, where the movement was based. The Ayacucho department is inland from the coast and was extremely isolated from the rest of the country due to the difficulty of travel on underdeveloped roads. The majority of

Table 1: Civil War in Peru

War:	Sendero Luminoso vs. government
Dates:	May 1980–1996
Casualties:	69,280
Regime type prior to war:	3 (polity 2 variable in Polity IV data ranging from –10 to 10)
Regime type after war:	1 (polity 2 variable in Polity IV data ranging from –10 to 10)
GDP per capita year war began:	US $4,831 (constant 1996 dollars)
GDP per capita 5 years after war:	US $4,589 in 2000 (constant 1996 dollars)
Insurgents:	Partido Comunista del Peru en el Sendero Luminoso de Mariategui (Communist Party of Peru in the Shining Path of Mariategui), known as Sendero Luminoso
Issue:	Ideological struggle for control of central government
Rebel funding:	Drugs and looting
Role of geography:	Rebels developed and operated in an extremely remote part of the country.
Role of resources:	Coca production and related economic activity funded rebels.
Immediate outcome:	Government victory though capturing rebel leader and rooting out the remaining rebels
Outcome after 5 years:	Military government
Role of UN:	None
Role of regional organization:	None
Refugees:	200,000 IDPs; no indication of large-scale repatriation
Prospects for peace:	Favorable since Peru's return to democracy in 2001

Sources: Doyle and Sambanis 2000; Gleditsch 2002; Gleditsch et al. 2002; Marshall and Jaggers 2003; McClintock 1984

peasants in Ayacucho lived and worked communally in indigenous communities.

Between 1980 and 1982, Sendero Luminoso engaged in numerous attacks against the state, in particular against government functionaries. This strategy aimed at delegitimizing the state by forcing individual government members to abandon their duties or be killed. In 1983, the group progressed to the next stage of their revolutionary plan: generalizing violence to a larger population and with greater intensity.

Sendero gained initial support within the local population by providing benefits to them, such as education, farming, and medical services. However, the generalization of violence extended Sendero's attack to the indigenous and local communities in Ayacucho as well as to a geographically larger area. Peasants were subject to attacks from both the government sinchis (paramilitaries) and the Sendero Luminoso's senderistas (fighters). These opposing pressures on peasants collided to create drastically increasing death tolls throughout the conflict area.

In the mid-1980s, Sendero Luminoso expanded geographically to the Huallaga River Valley, which had become a primary location for coca growing. Coca farming and the exploitation of producers constituted the major source of revenue for the group. Sendero's profits from the exploitation of drug production were estimated to be between US $20 million per year to US $550 million per year (McClintock, 1998, 72). Coca was grown and processed into paste in Peru, but transported out of the country for the final production of cocaine. Much of these Sendero profits came from charging drug runners to use Sendero-controlled airstrips in the region (McClintock 1998, 72).

The greatest strength—and subsequently the greatest weakness—of the Sendero Luminoso movement was the singular importance of Abimael Guzmán. The founder and leader of

Sendero was revered as godlike by many of his followers. He was called both the Fourth Sword of Marxism (the other three being Marx, Lenin, and Mao) by party members and Doctor Puka Inti (Red Sun) by the Ayacucho indigenous communities (McClintock 1998, 63). Not only did Guzmán dominate the movement as a quasi-spiritual–ideological leader, he dominated nearly every aspect of planning and tactical decision making throughout the war.

Guzmán's primacy in Sendero allowed the movement to be one of the most cohesive and efficient rebel organizations in the world. The organization was strictly hierarchical, with Guzmán as the head. Guzmán personally oversaw the allocation of nearly all of the organization's funds (McClintock 1998, 72). Sendero scholars and historians identify only one major instance of dissension within his party during Guzmán's tenure. This took place in 1988, when Guzmán made the executive decision to expand the guerrilla campaign into the Peruvian capital, Lima. Guzmán's wife (a member of his inner circle and an important party functionary), as well as several top Sendero officers, believed this move to be premature and openly opposed it in the 1988 Sendero conference (McClintock 1989, 66). Guzmán prevailed, and the expansion to Lima went forward.

Ironically, it was at his safe house in Lima that Guzmán was finally caught in 1992. Following his capture, the organization split into two factions. This split is identified by many historians as the beginning of the group's downfall. One faction remained loyal to Guzmán and became known as the pacifists—so named because they supported Guzmán's plea for a cease-fire and a peace agreement, which he made from prison. The second faction rejected Guzmán's promotion of peace and was known as the hardliners (sometimes referred to as Sendero Rojo). Oscar Ramírez Durand (alias Feliciano) led the hardliners from the time of their break with the Guzmán supporters in 1994 through the rest of the insurgency. He was captured in 1999 (Gleditsch, et al. 2002).

Democracy and Civil War: The 1992 Coup

When President Alberto Fujimori came to power in 1990, Peru was in the midst of civil war and economic crisis. Fujimori was elected as an outsider, a relatively unknown economist who promised to implement much-needed economic reforms and help the country find a resolution to the Sendero Luminoso war. These two tasks constituted a significant challenge, one that led Fujimori to work outside the government and eventually subvert democracy in pursuit of his goals.

Two years after he assumed the presidency, Fujimori faced mounting resistance to his economic policy from the parliament and intensified attacks on Lima by Sendero. In response to the parliament's opposition to his policies, Fujimori suspended the constitution and dissolved the legislature in April 1992. He cited both economic crisis and the inability of the government to effectively combat Sendero as justification for his bold move. There was little popular resistance to the Fujimori takeover, which can be attributed in part to the success of Sendero's campaign to discredit the government.

The 1992 coup marked the second failure of democracy for Peru within thirty years. Bowing to international pressure, President Fujimori did consent to new elections and the drafting of a new constitution, which was passed in 1993. However, Fujimori's government never passed legislation to implement the constitution. Despite periodic elections, the international community heavily criticized Fujimori for his autocratic rule. Fujimori remained in power until 2001, when he fled the country to self-imposed exile in Japan.

Geography

The Sendero Luminoso movement began in the remote and isolated Ayacucho department, located in the southern Sierra region of the country. The country is divided into twenty-four departments and one constitutional province. Approximately 47 percent of the country is covered by mountainous terrain, and Ayacucho lies within this area (Fearon and Laitin 2003).

Although eastern Peru is heavily forested, the Ayacucho region is not densely forested (Food and Agriculture Organization of the United Nations n.d.).

The two most important geographical features of the conflict are the isolation of Ayacucho and the people's reliance on subsistence agriculture in the department. As mentioned above, the relative isolation of the region al-lowed Guzmán to develop the movement over time with little interference from the state. Once Sendero began its campaign for domination within the Ayacucho regional base, government forces had difficulty reestablishing control in the remote region.

The second important feature of Ayacucho's geography is the effect of mountainous terrain on the livelihood of the peasants. The land in

Ayacucho and the surrounding regions was not suitable for traditional agriculture (McClintock 1984, 59). Most peasants in the mountainous Sierra region relied on subsistence agricultural production for their livelihood. This reliance on subsistence agriculture was a product of several things: the terrain, the structure of the communal farming culture, and the encroachment of hacienda farming on the better lands (Mason 1998, 209–210). The limited options for food and commercial activity in Ayacucho meant that the peasants were vulnerable to a subsistence crisis, which began in the 1970s and continued into the 1980s, when the El Niño caused a drought in the southern Sierras (McClintock 1984, 61). The tenuous position of rural peasants in Ayacucho proved a fertile and protected ground for Sendero activists to recruit members and set up a base of operations. Peasant dissatisfaction with the government, both for the failure of the land reforms of the 1970s and neglect during an ongoing subsistence crisis, provided an opportunity for Sendero to make significant inroads in the community.

Tactics

Sendero Luminoso engaged primarily in guerrilla tactics during the armed struggle from 1980 to 1996. Sendero's overall revolutionary strategy was comprised of six planned stages, only four of which were accomplished (Manwaring 1995). Prior to the initiation of armed conflict in 1980, Sendero engaged in stage one, which included the political organization of the movement. Following this initial stage, Sendero engaged in stages two through four successively. These were (2) moving into offensive combat, (3) generalization of violence to a wider population, and (4) consolidation of control in geographic areas of expansion. Each of these three stages was achieved through guerrilla violence and broad terror campaigns. Stage five included attacks on cities to bring about the fall of the government, and stage six entailed engendering state collapse and preparation for world revolution (Manwaring 1995, 163). Although Guzmán initiated stage

five by expanding their campaign of violence to Lima, the group never successfully consolidated power in major cities.

Sendero relied almost exclusively on guerrilla tactics and seldom mounted large-scale operations. They attacked a variety of targets and locations, focusing on government and commerce. Sendero was able to engage in a number of attacks with a minimum of equipment and weapons. Many of their supplies were obtained though raids on government facilities and commercial mining projects (Gorriti Ellenbogen 1990, 108–109). An example of one of the larger operations that Sendero completed was an attack on a prison facility. This attack was aimed at gaining arms for future operations and freeing Sendero prisoners. Sendero's goal was to obtain just enough weapons to carry out the guerrilla campaign, not to amass arms for any conventional war (Gorriti Ellenbogen 1990, 108). Additionally, some arms were purchased, including G3 and FAL automatic rifles and U.S.-made hand grenades (McClintock 1998, 73).

During the course of the conflict, the change in Sendero's tactics—in particular, increasing the scope of targets attacked—had an important effect on their ability to maintain support for their movement. Although the movement started with a strong base of supporters in the peasant community of Ayacucho, the progression of strategy to stage two (the generalization of violence) alienated and killed many people originally sympathetic to the movement. Any individuals who opposed Sendero as the sole legitimate authority were punished or eliminated. One Sendero member is quoted as saying, "This is a revolution, and anyone who opposes it will be crushed like an insect" (McClintock 1998, 68). In fact, the vast majority of those targeted for violence between 1980 and 1992 were peasants, followed by urban residents, then government officials. Additionally, within this timeframe a large number of teachers, businessmen, and social activists were killed by Sendero, as well as several aid workers and clergy (McClintock 1998, 63).

Sendero Luminoso also looked to the future of the movement by training children and youth members, desensitizing them to killing at an early age. For example, children were taught to kill chickens at an early age to prepare them for the violent nature of the movement. Among the more vindictive and horrific acts aimed at limiting all other social organization among the population was the murder of grassroots leader Maria Elena Moyano, whose body was later blown up in front of her children (McClintock 1998, 63–68). In addition to targeting the government officials, Sendero also targeted leftist politicians working within the legal system in order to prevent a moderate leftist movement from gaining mass appeal. Guzmán, who argued that his path was the only legitimate course for change, branded Peru's legal leftist parties as "revisionist" (Gorriti Ellenbogen 1990, 123). Moreover, Sendero came into direct armed conflict with the Tupac Amaru Revolutionary Movement, a more moderate leftist insurgency group (National Memorial Institute for the Prevention of Terrorism 2006).

The Peruvian government's response to Sendero attacks tended to be incoherent and somewhat indiscriminate in its reprisals during most of the conflict. In 1982, President Belaúnde conceded that the rebellion in Ayacucho was indeed out of their control and called for military penetration into the area. Belaúnde declared a "military emergency zone" in Ayacucho as well as a number of provinces into which Sendero had expanded, which limited the freedoms of civilians in these areas (McClintock 1984, 52).

The government used specially trained paramilitaries (sinchis) to route out senderistas. Initially, only 1,500 sinchis were sent to Ayacucho, but this number was quickly increased to 7,000 (McClintock 1998). Government troops had difficulty engaging the senderistas, given the nature of Sendero's tactics (small guerrilla attacks) and the group's organization (members worked in cells of three to four individuals). Moreover, it was difficult to distinguish senderistas from members of the local population—a fact that led to an incredible number of civilian deaths. The government carried out systematic campaigns, attacking villages and individuals suspected of collaboration with Sendero. This strategy had the detrimental by-product of alienating any local support for the government in Sendero-controlled regions, even in the face of increasing violence from Sendero as well. Recently, the Truth and Reconciliation Commission found that the government's use of sinchis "led to an increase in human rights violations, generated resentment and distanced the police from the population" (TRC 2003, Item 43). This strategy undermined the ability of the government to gain support, and possibly information on Sendero, from the peasant population, which itself was coming under increasing scrutiny from Sendero. Moreover, the disunity among government forces exacerbated the potential for human rights violations perpetrated against peasants. In the first half of the 1980s, three separate police organizations engaged in counterinsurgency operations without well-coordinated sharing of information about the local populations (TRC 2003).

In 1989, the government forces began to shift their strategy from somewhat indiscriminate hunting for Sendero supporters and operatives to attempting to discern friendly, neutral, and enemy populations. The government also shifted its focus to the capture of key leaders in the movement in order to decapitate the organization (TRC 2003). The strategy paid off immensely when Guzmán was captured in Lima in 1992. Guzmán's capture and subsequent treatment in custody may have been the single most important action the state took to end the war. Guzmán's position as the logistical and ideological leader of Sendero exposed the movement to a power vacuum after his capture. Initially, Guzmán argued from prison that the movement would continue on its course without his individual contribution. However, Guzmán later called for an end to the conflict, leading to the first major split in Sendero and a weakening of the movement. One of the most politically savvy tactics the government pursued was to demon-

Abimael Guzmán, founder of the Shining Path and leader of the Maoist revolution in Peru, raises his fist as he speaks at a press conference from his jail cell in Lima on September 24, 1992. With Guzmán in captivity, the war decreased in magnitude but did not end. (Reuters/Corbis)

strate publicly that Guzmán was in fact an ordinary and vulnerable person. They did this in an effort to deconstruct his revered persona among his followers. After his capture, Guzmán was displayed in black-and-white-striped pajamas in his jail cell carrying out ordinary tasks. Footage of Guzmán following guard's orders was also released to the public, which further contributed to the deconstruction of Guzmán's public persona (McClintock 1998).

Causes of the War

Understanding the emergence and relative success of Sendero Luminoso can be broken down into two interrelated questions: Why did this organization begin the war, and why did the peasant population support them? To understand the causes of this conflict, we need to understand both the choice to begin an armed insurgency and the ability of that insurgency to thrive among the Peruvian population. Thus, we need to examine the motivation of the organization and leaders like Abimael Guzmán, as well as reasons for large-scale support from the population during the beginning of the conflict.

The Sendero Luminoso conflict was first and foremost an ideological battle for the rebel organization and its leaders. When Sendero began the conflict, they were not attempting a quick overthrow of the government. The civil war was a long-term strategy designed to change Peruvian society by toppling the government and replacing it with a Communist state. The Sendero rebels were trying not simply to take gain control of the government, but to change the regime (or type of government) in Peru. Abimael Guzmán was motivated by the Communist thinkers Mao and Mariategui. He relied upon the work of these men to develop his own views that communism was the only legitimate form of government. His own rigid adherence to Maoism is generally accounted for by personal proclivities; however, a number of changes that took place in Peru are likely to have made communism more attractive to intellectuals and activists (McClintock 1998).

The social, economic, and political conditions in Peru prior to the Sendero war created a fertile ground for the insurgency. The Peruvian government's vacillation between military rule and democracy could easily be interpreted as a failure of both types of governance. When Peru transitioned back to democracy in the late 1970s, there was a large amount of support both from political elites and from the populace for legitimate leftist political parties. The primary leftist parties garnered more than 29 percent of the vote in 1978 constituent assembly elections (trailing the victorious center party, with 35 percent). Yet, the legitimate (or legal) leftist parties were unable to maintain popular support. After the reinstatement of democracy, the parties of the left were mired in infighting and fractionalization (Roberts 1996). Due to their inability to consolidate power, the legal organizations representing the political left (or more socialist-oriented parties) lost momentum. Leftist intellectuals were confronted, on one hand, with the inability of the legal leftist parties to capitalize on strong popular support and, on the other hand, with the incredibly cohesive and disciplined Sendero organization. Sendero Luminoso had a clear, if more radically leftist, mission and a concrete logistical plan. Given this comparison, Sendero was a clear and viable option for pursing political change for many young political elites.

Although the appeals of communism and of Sendero as a political entity were likely to attract educated elites seeking social change, Sendero could not have developed or succeeded without its base of support in Ayacucho. Sendero Luminoso grew to a substantial size (estimated between 3,000 and 15,000 members), but it began as a small collective of intellectuals seeking to change the way Peru was governed. Instrumental to Sendero's campaign was their ability to draw members and cooperative support from the peasant population and to secure a base in the Ayacucho region.

Peasants in this region provided a fertile ground for Sendero for several reasons. First, the relatively impoverished population suffered from a history of neglect and experienced a subsistence crisis during Sendero's organizing stage. Most of the peasants in the Ayacucho region worked the land communally for subsistence farming and leased out additional labor to hacienda owners. The haciendas typically used the best land in the area and benefited more substantially from the land reform of the 1970s (Roberts 1996). The ability of individuals to sustain their livelihood dictates, in part, the moral view of peasants about the legitimacy of governance (Scott 1976). When peasants are able to provide for themselves, they are unlikely to rebel or, in this case, support the Sendero insurgency. Gurr (1970) also argues that economic hardship is an incentive to rebel. It is clear that there were significant decreases in the ability of rural peasants in Ayacucho to provide for themselves and their families at the time that Sendero became active in the region. Moreover, Sendero provided important relief and social services to the peasant population at the outset of the movement. In contrast, the government was largely unable or unwilling to help the peasant population.

A number of scholars argue that, in addition to the role of economic grievance, perception of relative wealth is an important factor in the decision to rebel (Hechter 1975). People will be more likely to rebel not when they are destitute, but when they are disadvantaged relative to other people (Gurr 1970). McClintock reports that living conditions in the Ayacucho area fell to lower levels than other regions throughout the country in the years leading up to the civil war (McClintock 1984, 59–60). Moreover, although the Ayacucho compared unfavorably to nearly all other regions, it was particularly less well off than the coastal regions in which the capital was located. The relative deprivation of the Ayacucho people may have played an additional role in their willingness to support the Sendero movement and ultimately contributed to the success of the insurgency.

Outcome
Conflict Status

The war did not decisively end with a treaty or military victory, although by 1994 the rebels had split into two factions, and approximately 6,000 Sendero rebels had surrendered (TRC 2003). After the split in 1994 between the pacifists and the hardliners, the number of Sendero attacks decreased steadily. Oscar Ramìrez Durand continued to lead the hardliners until 1999, when he was captured. However, Sendero's level of activity was so low that some estimates place the war's end in 1996. The government forces were able to capture many of the Sendero leadership after the arrest of Guzmán, and this appears to have been the blow that pushed the rebels into a downward spiral.

Duration Tactics

The extreme length of the war (approximately sixteen years) can be attributed to two general issues: an inability of either side to achieve military victory and the unwillingness of either side to pursue negotiated settlement. The rebels' guerrilla war tactics and their ability to loot resources from the cocaine trade made Sendero a difficult target with reliable and lucrative funding. Moreover, the inability of the government to effectively combat the guerrilla war allowed the rebels' campaign to delegitimize the government to succeed in large measure, weakening the government (and possibly contributing to the collapse of democracy in 1992).

The guerrilla nature of this conflict meant that the Peruvian military never faced the rebel troops in a conventional battle and in fact needed to combat the group on several fronts—violent attacks on all types of targets, thefts of supplies from mines and government installations, and territorial expansion of the group. The primary objective of the government, therefore, was to capture or eliminate Sendero operatives and leaders, not necessarily to engage the group during any specific attack. This was a difficult feat for the government for three reasons. First, the Sendero movement was based in a geographically strategic area. Government troops could not mount a quick-response offensive deep into the mountains. Second, the Sendero rebels were extremely well organized and secretive. The small-cell structure of the group allowed senderistas to operate knowing only a few other members. When the government succeeded in capturing one rebel, he or she was unlikely to lead to many others. Third, the relative secrecy of the organization necessitated that the government use information from the rural population, who would know which individuals were active in the movement from the rebels' work in the community or connections to family and friends. However, the government's strategy of indiscriminate attacks and killing of civilians turned the population against the state.

Moreover, Sendero did not prepare for or attempt to win the war through military victory. Sendero's strategy from the outset of the conflict was to delegitimize the state and cause it to collapse. Guzmán and the Sendero elites were not looking to gain control of the government but to create a wholly different political entity based on Communist ideals. Only after the government had lost control and credibility would Sendero step into the power vacuum left by the government's fall. The Sendero strategy was one of attrition—the slow wearing down of one's enemy—that necessitates a long war. Sendero planned for a long conflict and was careful not to overstep its reach throughout the dispute. As noted before, the group sought to acquire only the military means necessary to inflict terror and disrupt the ability of the Peruvian administration to govern.

Sendero fought a war to delegitimize the government, not to cripple it strategically. The turning point of the war was the capture of Guzmán, which reestablished, to some extent, the effectiveness of the government.

In addition to a military victory, the conflict could have ended with a negotiated settlement. However, the likelihood of a successful treaty being signed was low for two reasons. First, parties at war will be likely to settle through negotiations when there is little else to gain through fighting. Yet the rebels in this conflict saw both present and future gains in fighting. They engaged in violence not to obtain any particular goods or concessions from the state but to decrease its effectiveness and perceived competence.

Second, parties to the conflict will sign a settlement when they are relatively certain that they cannot get a better deal by continuing to fight a while longer. One critical way parties to a civil war assess this is by learning from the battlefield (Smith and Stam, 2004). However, the Sendero Luminoso civil war never produced large-scale battles between rebel and government forces. The Truth and Reconciliation Commission of Peru finds that " . . . the limitations of the police intelligence services hindered their ability to adequately understand what was occurring. This, along with the lack of knowledge of the nature of the PCP-SL [Sendero], caused them to underestimate the magnitude of the developing phenomenon" (TRC 2003). The tit-for-tat nature of Sendero attacks and government reprisals did not reveal a great deal of information to either side about how the conflict was likely to develop and who was likely to get the upper hand in the future.

External Military Intervention

There was no direct military intervention on the side of the Peruvian government or Sendero Luminoso during the conflict. The United States put pressure on the government to curtail coca production, as they did with a number of Latin American countries during the American War on Drugs. It is not clear that this pressure had any impact on the conflict.

Conflict Management Efforts

There were no mediation or conflict management efforts from the international community or external states.

Conclusion

The conflict in Peru between the government and Sendero Luminoso proved to be the most devastating time period in the country's history. More people died in this war than in all other conflicts in Peru since independence (TRC 2003). However, the potential for renewed conflict is low for several reasons. First, Sendero as a political and military organization has been significantly dismantled. Second, the general population is likely to be more resistant to the appeals of such movements as a result of experience with this war. Finally, the Truth and Reconciliation Commission has produced a detailed account of the factors that allowed the insurgency to reach such destructive levels and has proposed a plan for reparations to those most affected by the conflict. The likelihood of a return to conflict will decrease further if Peru can implement the recommended steps for reconciliation. However, there are significant challenges to this, both in terms of bringing the perpetrators and planners of violence to justice (particularly those on the government side) and in terms of distributing adequate reparations to victims.

One major policy implication to be derived from this conflict is that governments challenged by rural insurgencies need to go to great lengths to differentiate rebels from civilians in their efforts to combat the challenge. This policy is central to both the minimization of violence and effectiveness of counterinsurgency. Only after the Peruvian troops changed their strategy to minimize attacks on innocents and focused on locating the Sendero leadership did they succeed in their counterinsurgency efforts.

There are also two important general lessons from this conflict, both for Peru and for other nations. The first lesson is that there are significant risks to neglecting entire segments of a population. The destitution and isolation of Ayacucho peasants, many of whom were ethnically distinct form the majority of Peruvians, had serious consequences for the country as a whole. This lesson has become a prominent issue for American politics today as concern grows about the terrorist and insurgency organizations developing in failed states and regions outside of government control in other countries.

The second lesson that we should draw from Peru's experience is one that has reappeared time and time again. The neglect and persecution of a small population should concern the majority of the population in a country. One of the TRC's general findings was that many Peruvians outside the main conflict zone felt disconnected from the conflict; educated and urban citizens in particular were indifferent to the struggle while it was confined to the mountains. However, the conflict had enormous implications for all Peruvians, including its contribution to the failure of democracy and the 1992 coup. Popular complacency regarding the suffering of minority populations has led to disastrous outcomes in the past, such as the Jewish holocaust and the Rwandan genocide and is likely to do so in similar situations in the future.

Kathleen Gallagher Cunningham

Chronology

1980   Sendero Luminoso begins its armed resistance.

1981   Border conflict with Ecuador ensues over Cordillera del Condor.

1982   El Niño weather phenomenon occurs. President Belaundé declares state of emergency in several regions (called military emergency zone) and sends 1,500 sinchis to Ayacucho.

1983   El Niño weather phenomenon occurs.

January 1983   Eight journalists are massacred by residents of Urchuraccay who thought the journalist were senderistas; incident is heavily publicized, leads to government's restriction of access to the region.

June–July 1984   Violence escalates sharply as Sendero begins stage three of its plan, the generalization of violence.

1985   Alan Garcia Perez of the American Popular Revolutionary Alliance (APRA) wins the presidential election—the first exchange of power from one democratically elected leader to another in forty years.

1986   Sendero Luminoso begins to profit from coca growth and production.

1989   Government changes its strategy to distinguish among friendly, neutral, and enemy populations and to target political-administrative organizations (OPAs) of Sendero Luminoso. Peru's economy experiences hyperinflation. Sendero controls about 28 percent of municipalities (McClintock 1998, 73)

1990   Alberto Fujimori is elected president.

1991   Sendero Luminoso comes into armed conflict with MRTA in the central Andean Huallaga region.

April 5, 1992   President Alberto Fujimori seizes power in an army-backed coup, suspending those sections of the constitution and dissolving the congress.

September 12, 1992   Sendero leader Guzmán is captured in Lima. Within weeks, more than 1,000 more Sendero members are captured, including twelve of nineteen central committee members.

December 1993   New constitution for Peru is passed, although it is never implemented.

September 15, 1993   Guzmán sends a written peace offer from prison, which is rejected by the government.

April 5, 1994   Operation Aries begins, the last big government military offensive against Sendero. By this year, nearly 6,000 rebels had surrendered.

June 17, 1994   Moises Simón Limaco Huayuscachi, whom security forces described as the co-coordinator of the Central Directorate of Sendero Luminoso, is captured in Lima along with Mario Vasquez, another prominent leader.

June 16, 1995   President Fujimori announces passage of a law offering amnesty to members of the military involved in the war since 1980. Border conflict with Ecuador.

List of Acronyms
APRA: American Popular Revolutionary Alliance
GDP: gross domestic product
MRTA: Tupac Amaru Revolutionary Movement
OPA: political-administrative organization
TRC: Truth and Reconciliation Commission

Glossary
Communists: Individuals who believe in an ideology that dictates that political and economic means should be controlled through an equal share of power.

Guerilla tactics: Using varied methods of attack, focused on small attacks to incite terror or disrupt daily life.

Hardliners: A faction of Sendero that continued fighting after the capture of Guzmán.

Maoism: Political ideology espoused by Mao Zedong that promoted communist revolution.

Mestistos: People of mixed ethnic heritage, which was typically a combination of Spanish and indigenous peoples: Mestistos were also called Creole.

Pacifists: A faction of Sendero that advocated peace after the capture of Guzmán.

Revisionist: A term for communists or socialists who departed from the original thinking of communist leaders.

Sendero Rojo: Another name for the Hardliners faction.

Sinchis: Government paratroopers, or units specially trained to pursue rebel and guerrilla fighters.

Senderistas: Fighters for Sendero Luminoso.

References

Bermeo, Nancy. 1997. "Myths of Moderation: Confrontation and Conflict during Democratic Transitions." *Comparative Politics* 29(3): 305–322.

Doyle, Michael, and Nicholas Sambanis. 2000. "International Peacebuilding: A Theoretical and Quantitative Analysis." *American Political Science Review* 94(4): 779–801.

Fearon, James D., and David D. Laitin. 2003. "Ethnicity, Insurgency, and Civil War." *American Political Science Review* 97(1): 75–90.

Food and Agriculture Organization of the United Nations Maps. No date. www.fao.org/forestry/site/6452/en/per (accessed March 19, 2005).

Gleditsch, Kristian S. 2002. "Expanded Trade and GDP Data." *Journal of Conflict Resolution* 46 (October): 712–724.

Gleditsch, Kristian S., and Michael D. Ward. 1997. "Double Take: A Re-examination of Democracy and Autocracy in Modern Polities." *Journal of Conflict Resolution* 41(June): 361–382.

Gleditsch, Nils Petter, Peter Wallensteen, Mikael Eriksson, Margareta Sollenberg, and Håvard Strand. 2002. Armed Conflict 1946–2001: A New Dataset." *Journal of Peace Research* 39(5): 615-637

Gorriti Ellenbogen, Gustavo. 1990. *The Shining Path: A History of the Millenarian War in Peru*, translated by Robin Kirk. Lima, Peru: Editorial Appoyo.

Gurr, Ted. 1970. *Why Men Rebel*. Princeton, NJ: Princeton University Press.

Hechter, Michael. 1975. *Internal Colonialism*. Berkeley: University of California Press.

Manwaring, Max. 1995. "Peru's Sendero Luminoso: The Shining Path Beckons." *Annals of the American Academy of Political and Social Science* 542 (Small Wars): 157–66.

Marshall, Monty G., and Keith Jaggers. 2003. *Polity IV Project: Political Regime Characteristics and Transitions, 1800–2002*. Maryland: University of Maryland.

Mason, T. David. 1998. "Take Two Acres and Call Me in the Morning: Is Land Reform a Prescription for Peasant Unrest?" *Journal of Politics* 60(1): 199–230.

McClintock, Cynthia. 1984. "Why Peasants Rebel: The Case of Peru's Sendero Luminoso." *World Politics* 37(1): 48–84.

McClintock, Cynthia. 1989. "The Prospects for Democratic Consolidation in a 'Least Likely' Case: Peru." *Comparative Politics* 21(2): 127–148.

McClintock, Cynthia. 1998. *Revolutionary Movements in Latin America: El Salvador's FMLN and Peru's Shining Path*. Washington, DC: United States Institute for Peace.

Moore, Will H. 2000. "The Repression of Dissent: A Substitution Model of Government Coercion." *Journal of Conflict Resolution* 44(1): 107–27.

National Memorial Institute for the Prevention of Terrorism (NMIPT). "Terrorism Knowledge Database." www.tkb.org/Home.jsp (accessed March 12, 2005).

Palmer, David Scott. 1986. "Rebellion in Rural Peru: The Origins and Evolution of Sendero Luminoso." *Comparative Politics* 18(2): 127–146.

Roberts, Kenneth. 1996. "Economic Crisis and the Demise of the Legal Left in Peru." *Comparative Politics* 29(1): 69–92.

Scott, James C. 1976. *The Moral Economy of the Peasant: Rebellion and Subsistence in Southeast Asia.* New Haven, CT: Yale University Press.

Smith, Alastair, and Allan C. Stam. 2004. "Bargaining and the Nature of War." *Journal of Conflict Resolution* 48(6): 783–813.

Truth and Reconciliation Committee (TRC). 2003. "General Conclusions." www.cverdad.org.pe/ ingles/ifinal/conclusiones.php (accessed March 14, 2005).

U.S. State Department, Bureau of Western Hemisphere Affairs. 2005. "Country Profile on Peru." www.state.gov/r/pa/ei/bgn/35762.htm (accessed March 4, 2005, updated June 2006).

The Philippines (1972–1996)

Introduction

States in plural societies have the arduous tasks of maintaining internal order and defending the integrity of its borders. To survive, they must find effective ways to reconcile interests, regulate domestic behavior, and eliminate external threats. However, interests and capabilities change over time. Ethnic communities may come to believe that their interests are best served by having their own state (Brown 1994; Stavenhagen 1996).

Individuals and organizations can articulate that ethnic yearning and give it shape. In the process, history is given a new frame. Symbols are created, and heroes celebrated. However, identities are not pliable entities. They must find some deep resonance within the community (Azar 1986). It is in this context that we study the struggle of the Bangsa Moro in the Philippines.

Country Background

The Philippines is an archipelago of approximately 7,107 islands situated in the Southeast Asian region. About 21.3 percent of the country is mountainous terrain. The topographical fragmentation of the Philippines makes national governance and security very problematic; the vast maritime border makes barring illegal entries difficult, and the forested mountains provide hiding places for rebels and lawbreakers. As of July 2006, the country had approximately 89 million inhabitants (CIA 2006). The majority are Christians (91.5 percent), and 4 percent of the population are Muslims, who live mostly on the island of Mindanao. The political and administrative center is Manila.

Upon receiving political independence in 1945, the Philippines had been a democratic polity, except for the years 1972–1986, when it was interrupted by Ferdinand Marcos's dictatorial rule (Lande 1996; Wurfel 1988). Marcos was deposed in 1986 by the People Power Revolution, led by Corazon Aquino and Jaime Cardinal Sin. The Philippines has since reconstituted its democratic institutions.

Conflict Background

The history of the Philippines is laden with violent challenges to the administration of the central government based in Manila. Right after World War II, deteriorating conditions in the countryside led to peasant uprisings, the most serious of which was headed by former guerrillas who fought the Japanese during the war, the Hukbong Mapagpalaya ng Bayan (Huks). It was largely a localized revolt brought about by the oppressive conditions in the countryside (Kerkvliet 1977). The uprising was effectively contained in Central Luzon, and it was decisively beaten in 1954. Casualties from the revolt were estimated at around 9,000 people (Fearon 2004). Out of its ashes came the Partido Komunista ng Pilipinas (PKP), which eventually chose the aboveground, electoral way as its mode of struggle (Saulo 1990).Nevertheless, the deleterious condition of the peasantry was fertile ground for a new challenge to the state. In 1968, a professor from the University of the Philippines, Jose Maria Sison, and some other young activists "reestablished" the Communist Party of the Philippines (CPP). They contended that the "old guard" (the PKP) had strayed from the Communist way by choosing to participate in the "farce" called elections (Chapman 1987; Jones 1989). The objective of the CPP was the seizure of the state through armed struggle. They believed that the best way to attain their goal was to follow the Maoist strategy of a protracted people's war: encircling the cities from bases in the countryside, and then seizing the cities and the administrative center when the time was ripe (Guerrero 1979; Weekley 2001). In 1969, Sison met Bernabe Buscayno, a Huk leader, and the party's military arm, the New People's Army (NPA), was formed.

The CPP–NPA was committed to an armed struggle intended to establish an alternative polity in the Philippines based on Maoist-Leninist ideology. Its greatest support was in the early 1980s, when it had an estimated 18,000–23,000 armed supporters (Dolan 2003). However, its leaders made the tactical mistake of boycotting the 1986 presidential elections, which marginalized the party, depriving it of any meaningful role in the postauthoritarian transition (Rocamora 1996). The removal of Marcos also deprived the party of a clear target to oppose. In the 1990s, support for the party declined in consonance with the gradual erosion of support for communism worldwide (Weekley 2001). Support for the insurgency was also weakened by the growing disenchantment with leaders who lived comfortably abroad while their cadres suffered on the field. There was also bitter infighting within the party over the continued viability of the Maoist strategy (Abinales 1996; Rocamora

1996). Casualties from both sides stand at around 40,000 (Fearon 2004). The insurgency is still ongoing, though conflict intensity lessened considerably in the 1990s.

Finally, the Philippine state has also confronted challenges to its internal sovereignty on the island of Mindanao. In 1968, Nur Misuari, Salamat Hashim, and other young Muslim intellectuals secretly established the Moro National Liberation Front–Bangsa Moro Army (MNLF–BMA) with the objective of establishing a separate state in Mindanao (Chalk 2002). This was in reaction to two events: the Jabidah massacre of 1968 and the declaration of martial law on September 21, 1972. It was primarily an ethnic uprising to assert Moro historical rights to their "homeland," as well as to reverse Moro marginalization in political affairs and economic development.

The MNLF came into the open in 1972 with a series of offensives against the Philippine military. It had an estimated 6,000 armed supporters at that time (Political Instability Task Force 2006) confronting the national armed forces, which was 55,000 strong in 1972. The "struggle of the Bangsa Moro people" has been the Philippines' most violent conflict, with casualty estimates ranginge from 75,000 (Fearon 2004) to 120,000 (Gutierrez 2000b). It is this particular internal conflict that is the subject of extensive analysis in this article.

The Insurgents

To get a full picture of the MNLF and the Moro Islamic Liberation Front (MILF) as rebel organizations, it is imperative to understand the different ethnic communities in Mindanao and how the Moro nation came to be imagined. In early Philippine history, the primary instruments of group identification were language and blood relations (Patanne 1996; Scott 1994). The introduction of the Islamic and Christian faiths to the islands provided another mechanism for distinguishing among the various communities in the south. Currently, there are four major Muslim ethnic groups in Mindanao: the Tausugs, the

Table 1: Civil War in the Philippines

War:	Bangsa Moro vs. Government of the Republic of the Philippines
Dates:	November 1972–September 1996
Casualties:	75,000–120,000
Regime type prior to war:	–9 (Polity IV data; ranging from –10 [authoritarian] to 10 [democracy]) 6 (Freedom House)
Regime type after war:	8 (Polity IV data; ranging from –10 [authoritarian] to 10 [democracy]), 2 (Freedom House)
GDP per capita year war began:	US $2,544.5 (PPP, constant 1996 prices)
GDP per capita 5 years after war:	US $3,122.9 (PPP, constant 1996 prices)
Insurgents:	Moro National Liberation Front (MNLF), Moro Islamic Liberation Front (MILF)
Issue:	Struggle for a separate state for Moros
Rebel Funding:	Local support, funding from Arab states (e.g., Libya, Malaysia, Saudi Arabia) and groups such as al-Qaeda
Role of geography:	Rebels build camps in deeply forested and mountainous terrain.
Role of resources:	Mindanao is the last undeveloped region in the Philippines.
Immediate outcome:	GRP and MNLF signed peace agreement on September 2, 1996.
Outcome after 5 years:	MNLF resumed armed struggle against GRP in November 2001. Misuari was arrested in Malaysia and turned over to the Philippines in 2002. New leadership abided by agreement. MILF–GRP hostilities are ongoing.
Role of UN:	Minimal
Role of regional organization:	Organization of the Islamic Conference (OIC) facilitated talks and negotiations.
Refugees:	200,000
Prospects for peace:	Favorable

Sources: Fearon 2004; Gutierrez 2000b; Polity IV Project (n.d.); Freedom House 2006; Heston, Summers, and Aten 2002; U.S. Committee for Refugees 2004.

Sama, the Maguindanaos, and the Maranaos (Abbahil 1984).

The Tausugs mostly reside in the Sulu archipelago, in the provinces of Sulu, Basilan, Tawi Tawi, Zamboanga del Sur, Palawan, Zamboanga del Norte, and Davao. The name *Tausug* can be roughly translated as "People of the Current." A substantial number also reside in Sabah, where they answer to the name *Orang Suluk.*

The Sama reside in certain localities in the Zamboanga peninsula, although they consider the Sulu archipelago their home. Initially, students of Philippine cultural history referred to them as Samals, a name that is now considered repugnant by the Sama. This is because the word *Samal* means "dirty" in Tausug and was derisively employed by the Tausugs to distinguish themselves from the Sama (Horvatich 1993; Stone 1974). The majority of those who pledge allegiance to the cause of the Moro National Liberation Front (MNLF) are Tausugs and Sama. Nur Misuari, the best-known leader of the MNLF, is a Tausug. The Maguindanaos live primarily in the Cotabato region. They can be found residing in substantial numbers in four provinces: Maguindanao, North Cotabato, South Cotabato, and Sultan Kudarat.

Finally, the Maranos populate the area of North Central Mindanao, near Lake Lanao (the name *Maranao* means "People of the Lake"). Most of the members of the MILF, which split off from the MNLF in 1984 under the leadership of Salamat Hashim, were Maguindanaos and Maranaos (Vitug and Gloria 2000). Hashim is a Maguindanao.

These four ethnic communities are fragmented by their different traditions. Any organization seeking to mobilize these communities for collective action must develop a powerful rationale that can overcome the inherent tensions extant among them. The founders of the MNLF found such a rationale in the common history of the Muslim communities: a long narrative of suffering and destitution under the colonial and postcolonial regimes based in Manila, involving the coercive expropriation of Moro lands and political marginalization in the formulation of state policy. These grievances were harnessed by the MNLF as the cognitive and emotive underpinnings of Muslim solidarity. The leader of the MNLF, Nur Misuari, framed the cause for a Bangsa Moro (Moro Nation) as a *nationalist* struggle against the "gobirno a sarwang tao" (foreign government) based in Manila (Kamlian 1995).

The MNLF ideology was founded on two key concepts: gaosbaugbug and kaadilan. The first term is a compound of two words: *gaos*, meaning "ability," and *baugbug*, which can be translated as "commitment." Thus, the MNLF rebel is someone who has the capacity to commit. Commit to what? To kaadilan, a utopic vision that is the complete opposite of what the Moro experience in their present state. In kaadilan, they shall recover their land, shall be politically influential, and shall be prosperous. That will be the state of affairs in the Moro's bangsa, or "homeland" (Tan 1993, 38–40).

However, a basic ideological difference emerged between the MNLF and the MILF as to the nature of the rebellion. The content of the ethnonational discourse of the MNLF was primarily cultural–historical and not religious. Although there was an attempt to deploy Islamic

An armed member of the Moro Islamic Liberation Front (MILF) guards a mosque in Zamboanga city in southern Philippines on November 20, 2001. The MILF is one of several separatist groups intent on securing independence of parts of the southern Philippines on behalf of the minority Muslim population of the region. (AP/Wide World Photos)

concepts such as jihad and ummah, the separatist project of the MNLF sought to gain adherents by promising the recovery of the Moros' ancient homelands (Macansantos 1996).

Although the MNLF considered the fight for the Bangsa Moro a nationalist project, the MILF, led by Hashim, came to consider the armed conflict as essentially a religious struggle (Kamlian 1995; Lingga 1995). "If the Moros fought for anything related to their perceived racial distinctness, it was peripheral; the main point always was religion" (Jubair 1999, 15). The various communities indeed shared a collective historical suffering, but the ground of the rebellion is Islam. The reason for seceding is to establish a state that will be guided by Islamic law, one in which Muslim values and beliefs can be practiced in their fullest sense (Gutierrez and Guialal 2000).

Logistically, the MNLF was funded by domestic and foreign sources. The MNLF prided itself as an internally funded secessionist movement, although it quickly came to realize the importance of foreign support. The Malaysians trained the earliest set of leaders and combatants in Sabah (Gutierrez 2000b). Throughout most its struggle against the government of the Republic of the Philippines (GRP), the MNLF has received support from Arab countries, notably Libya and Saudi Arabia. Meanwhile, there is also some evidence that the MILF was funded not only by Arab states but by organizations such as al-Qaeda. The MILF was linked to Osama Bin Laden when some of its forces trained and fought in Afghanistan as mujahideen. Bin Laden reciprocated by providing funding for the MILF cause (Abuza 2003; Ressa 2003).

Geography

The MNLF's base of operations is located in Southern Mindanao, where it can take advantage of the mountainous terrain and the support of their fellow Muslims. Tawi-Tawi, for example, is a major base in the struggle because it is one of the few remaining province in the Philippines in which the population is predominantly Muslim. Currently, the MNLF and the MILF actively operate in Jolo, Basilan, Maguindanao, Lanao del Norte, Lanao del Sur, Sulu, Tawi-Tawi, and North Cotabato (Gutierrez 2000a; Kamlian 1995).

Tactics

The MNLF and the MILF have adopted the rudiments of conventional warfare. They establish bases for supplies, training, and ammunition and engage the enemy in planned offensives. The goal is to increase the number of these bases and consolidate control province by province. These bases are built in areas where the rebel group has ethnic support. Thus, MNLF bases are established in Tausug areas, whereas MILF bases are built in Maranao or Maguindanao areas. For example, the MILF's central base, Camp Abubakar As-Siddique, is located at the heart of Maguindanao province (Vitug and Gloria 2000).

This is very much unlike the protracted war strategy adopted by the CPP-NPA. The latter avoids frontal face-offs with government forces and relies instead on ambushes and quick retreats. They are usually on the move and do not have fixed bases (Weekley 2001). The intent of those who adopt the guerrilla strategy is to be "invisible from the enemy" and wear him down.

Most of the arms of the MNLF and MILF are stolen or purchased from the Philippine military (Gutierrez 2000b). This means that they still operate with antiquated M-16 rifles and AK-47s. Field commanders have complained about their lack of effective antitank weaponry. However, the MILF has been able to purchase such weaponry with funding provided by the group of Osama Bin Laden. But their gains were greatly dissipated by their crushing loss at the hands of the military in 2000, when they lost Camp Abubakar (Vitug and Gloria 2000).

Causes of the War

The literature on ethnic mobilization contends that common experiences of discrimination or

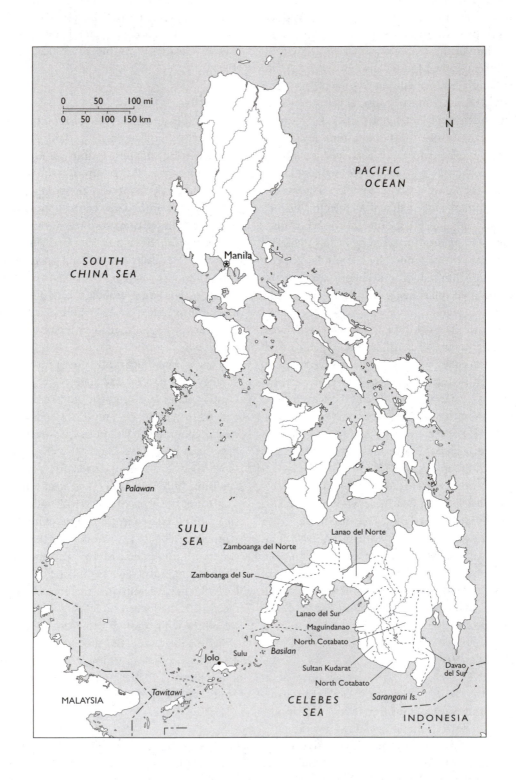

SOUTH
CHINA SEA

PACIFIC
OCEAN

N

0   50   100 mi
0   50   100   150 km

Manila

Palawan

SULU
SEA

Lanao del Norte

Zamboanga del Norte

Zamboanga del Sur

Lanao del Sur

Maguindanao

North Cotabato

Jolo   Sulu   Basilan

Sultan Kudarat

North Cotabato

Davao
del Sur

Tawitawi

MALAYSIA

CELEBES
SEA

Sarangani Is.

INDONESIA

possession of valid grievances do not necessarily translate to collective undertakings (Carment 1994; Olzak 1983). The onset of ethnic violence is usually preceded by a period of incubation in which such experiences or grievances are articulated, nurtured, and thereafter acted upon by social movements. Rodolfo Stavenhagen (1996) posits two types of factors that generate collective action among ethnic groups: Predisposing factors constitute the fundamental causes of the struggle, whereas triggering factors are the immediate causes of mobilization.

Muslim grievance against the Philippine state can be attributed to three factors: (1) the pejorative treatment Muslims have received from Christians; (2) the loss of the Muslims' homeland through discriminatory colonial policy; and (3) the "integration" policy of the state, which threatened their identity and way of life.

The Muslims in the Philippines have considered their rebellion a struggle for independence that goes all the way back to their resistance against the Spanish invaders in 1521. When the Spaniards came, they initially used the name *Moro* to refer to Muslims in Manila and later to refer to the people who resided in the southern part of the archipelago (Jubair 1999). The name *Moro* could have been derived from the word *Moor,* used by the Spaniards to designate a Berber of North Africa (Abubakar 1973).

Majul (1973) claims that a negative connotation was later inculcated in the minds of Christian Filipinos by the Spanish clergy to incite them to fight their brothers in the South; the Christian Filipinos were told that the Muslims were the enemies of their new religion (Dery 1997; Marohomsalic 2001). In this view, Morohood was forged in the fight against the Spaniards and Christianization. The political scientist Michael Mastura contends that Moro identity originated as a "reaction against the imposition of a monolithic colonial administration, nurtured with . . . missionary activities" (1976, 8). The Moro historian Jamal Kamlian claims that it was the "high degree of unity and cooperation" among the Moros that was re-

sponsible for their long and successful resistance against Spain (1995, 51).

The debate is contentious over whether the notion that the Muslims were united by a sense of Morohood in their struggle against Spain has a historical basis or was simply a framing imposed by the MNLF to provide some rationale for their secessionist project. The political scientist Thomas McKenna contends that Muslim resistance against Spain could be best characterized as disjointed and differentiated (1998). "Throughout their history a lack of unity has characterized the Moros: an inability of Maranao, Maguindanao and Tausug to join together in a common cause" (Gowing 1979, 238). There is also a dearth of historical evidence linking the resistance in Sulu to the armed opposition in Lanao and Cotabato. Bangsa Moro, the project of the Islamic political movements, may be a fairly recent construct—a notion that makes sense only when located within the MNLF's nationalist ideology (McKenna 1998).

Although the literature is divided over whether or not the struggle against Spanish rule developed a sense of unity among the different ethnic communities, there seems to be agreement that the American period brought a greater awareness among the Muslim groups of their common identity. The Americans categorized the people living in the islands as Christian Filipinos, pagans, or Moros. A 1903 statute (Act No. 1787) established a Moro province with provisions for its own governor and legislative council. These political bodies were empowered to formulate and enact policies autonomously, independent of the government in the Christian north.

The distinction between Christians and Moros eventually became sharp. The American use of the religion-based categories sensitized Muslims to their "separate identity" and led them to more aggressively pursue self-governance. Initially, the American colonizers undertook to placate the Moros so they could concentrate on subduing the Christian Filipinos, who continued to resist the colonizers in Luzon. It was critical to the consolidation of American rule that the Sultan of Sulu be prevented from entering into an alliance with Filipino nationalists, because that would mean fighting a war in the north and the south with the rather thin U.S. force (Gowing 1983, 37). However, when U.S. rule became consolidated in Luzon and the Visayas in 1901, they implemented a "pacification" campaign against the Moros to fully exploit the natural resources of Mindanao. "The Moros had to be tamed or pacified so that 'Moroland' would be safe for capitalism" (Muslim 1994, 57).

The United States instituted a system of land titling in Mindanao, with the "official" objective of enabling the administrators to identify lands without owners that could then be given to tenants and small agricultural workers. However, the system ran directly counter to the Filipino Muslims' conception of land. In their worldview, the communities' lands are pusaka, a collective inheritance. No one "owned" the land itself. Not even Muslim leaders, the datus, could "own" the land, although they could identify who may use it. "Only the produce of land can be truly possessed" (Fianza 1999, 29). The system displaced the ethnic communities from their ancestral lands, as most Muslims did not register their land. Christian–Muslim land disputes led to the rise of violent gangs such as the Barracudas (mostly Maranaos) and the Ilagas (predominantly Ilongos), ostensibly to defend Christian and Muslim properties (Gomez 2000, 156–73). Their plight became worse when the U.S. land reform code distributed their traditional lands to multinational companies. Many Muslims came to support the armed campaign of the MNLF because of the belief that their victory meant recovery of their ancestral lands.

In 1907, American policy with regard to the Moro changed with the establishment of the Philippine Assembly. This political body quickly became "the forum for nationalist views demanding that Mindanao be fully incorporated into the Philippines" (Abinales 2000, 30). Manila politicians were of the belief that Mindanao is

Juramentado and Kristyano

The historical, deep-seated animosity between Christians and Muslims in Mindanao is perpetuated by social conditioning. Christian children are told to be wary of the Muslim, who is depicted as irrational and violent, someone who "quickly loses his mind" (juramentado) and thus should be avoided as much as possible. On the other hand, Muslims are told to be careful in their dealings with kristyanos (Christians) who are portrayed as callous property grabbers. Gutierrez (1997, 94) tells the story of a foreigner who saw that people entering a mosque simply left their shoes and sandals outside. He inquired whether it was possible that someone might steal them. The Moro replied, "only if a kristyano passes by" (Gutierrez 1997).

Philippine territory and that any policy that entailed the dismemberment of the country was unacceptable. In line with President Woodrow Wilson's directive to prepare the Filipinos for self-rule and under pressure from assembly members, Governor Frank Carpenter decided to integrate Mindanao into the same system of governance that existed in the rest of the country.

Two policies were enacted to bring the Muslims into the "mainstream." First, Christians in Luzon and the Visayas were relocated to Mindanao. The policy was justified by the contention that the presence of the Christians would have a "civilizing influence on wild tribes" (Abinales 2000, 17–67; Rodil 1994). Second, the Muslims were made to attend the public schools run by the Americans. The official objective for the establishment of these schools was to develop a civic consciousness among the different peoples in the Philippines. However, Filipino Muslims eventually came to realize that the colonizers were employing the schools to impart the message that foreign and Christian cultures were "mainstream" and "superior" (Gowing 1983, 134).

The policy of integrating the Muslims into the mainstream was carried out by successive

Filipino administrations after independence was granted to the colony in 1946. From Roxas to Marcos, the Philippine state simply continued the policy of integration. If the root of the problem was the incapability of the Muslims to adjust to modernity because of their rigid beliefs and practices, then the solution was to develop their consciousness and welfare through education and to provide them with housing, health facilities, and industries. The Filipino envisioned by the integration project was a Muslim who looked and thought like a Christian (Muslim 1994; Thomas 1971).

The policies were met with deep hostility and anger. The Muslims had lost their ancestral lands, they were minoritized in their own homeland (because of the resettlement policies), and now their identity was threatened by the school system. These were the grievances Muslims carried within themselves. These deep-seated resentments would explode into the open with Jabidah in 1968.

One event has been pointed out by almost all scholars of the Bangsa Moro rebellion as the triggering cause of the mobilization for the creation of a separate Islamic state: the 1968 Jabidah massacre (Majul 1985; Noble 1976;). It involved the murder of around twenty-eight Muslim recruits on Corregidor Island after they allegedly resisted their deployment to Sabah (Glang 1969). It was described as part of a Marcos plan to send soldiers to incite ferment that would strengthen the Philippines' claim to the territory being held by Malaysia. However, upon learning the real objectives of the mission, the Muslim recruits mutinied and were executed (George 1980). Jabidah fomented widespread resentment among many Muslims who saw the event as the final straw in their long history of suffering.

Historically, leaders of traditional families provided the initial framing of the Filipino Muslims' grievances. A member of congress, Omar Amilbagasa, filed a bill in the lower house calling for the creation of the independent state of Sulu in 1961. In 1968, Udtog Matalam led the formation of the Muslim Independence Movement (MIM), the

objective of which was to push for the separation of Mindanao, Sulu, and Palawan from the Philippines. In 1974, the Bangsa Moro Liberation Organization (BMLO) was formed under the leadership of Rashid Lucman, who eventually crowned himself paramount sultan of Mindanao and Sulu in 1974. The solution to the sad state of Filipino Muslims may involve secession, but this objective was initially pursued through aboveboard, constitutional means (Chalk 2002).

Jabidah seemed to demonstrate to the Muslim students that the legal approach was futile, that the approach had not worked in the past and would almost certainly founder against a dictatorship. The core of the political movement that would eventually advocate armed separatism was composed of young intellectuals who had studied in Manila or abroad (e.g., Egypt, Libya, Qatar). They developed a strategy more aggressive that those initiated by their "untrustworthy, aristocratic, and egocentric" elders (Gutierrez 2000b, 311). For Nur Misuari, Salamat Hashim, and Mohagher Iqbal, the end goal was an independent state. And the means to be used was armed force.

Misuari and his group realized that if they were to win the support of Muslims to engage the state militarily, they would need an identity that would sharply distinguish them from Bangsa Filipino. They would need symbols powerful enough to unite the fragmented Muslim communities and sustain a protracted struggle against the machinery of the state. They found their symbol in the historical figure of the Moro. The designation was extremely useful to the purposes of the students. First, colonizers employed the term as a derogatory sense, but it would now be employed as a symbol of pride. The image of the Moro conjured up images of valor, defiance, and determination—qualities critical for recruiting members to their side. "Moro was equated with valor and resistance, and to be called one fueled yearnings for a unique, historically different nation all the more" (Gutierrez 2000b, 312). As Moros have always been the masters of their own destiny, it was only fitting that they should have their own state: the Bangsa Moro Republik (Kamlian 1995).

Second, the students emphasized that the Moros had never been conquered. The colonial regimes of Spain and the United States had been unable to bring the Moros to their knees. Moros have an indomitable spirit and have always found ways to avert defeat. Morohood was seen as a powerful symbol sustaining the spirit of the movement's members after the commencement of armed confrontations with the state.

Finally, in the Moro they found a symbol that could potentially unite the fragmented Muslim ethnic communities. They contended that the Tausugs, Samas, Maguindanaos, and Maranaos all shared a single history of oppression (by alien colonizers and by the Manila government). Their message was that the sorry condition of the Filipino Muslim could only be reversed if they came together, just as their ancestors had done before them. It made the argument for unity quite compelling.

The MNLF came out into the open two months after the declaration of martial law, although it had actually started as the underground movement of the youth sector of the Muslim Independence Movement (MIM) (Balacuit 1994). Its objective was clear and unequivocal: to found a separate state for Moros through armed struggle against the predominantly Christian Philippine state. Misuari did not mince any words, charging the Philippine government with "low intensity ethnic cleansing." He contended that the state sought "to destroy the national consciousness and Islamic identity of the Bangsa Moro people," and that justified a call for a jihad ("holy war") against the state (Balacuit 1994, 8). With that pronouncement, the Muslim resentment that had been kindled by a massacre was successfully framed into a noble cause for war.

Outcome
Conflict Status
The rebellion spearheaded by the MNLF held the GRP to a military stalemate in the 1970s, but support for the rebellion declined in the 1980s as the movement proved incapable of dealing with three critical problems: (1) how to deal with the traditional Muslim structures, (2) how the Bangsa Moro Republik should be governed, and (3) how to deal with the interethnic tensions within the Bangsa Moro movement.

The MNLF based their rebellion on collective memory of a past uncorrupted by colonialism and Christianization. However, such appeal to history had the unintended effect of legitimizing the traditional political structures that they denounced as feudal and exploitative. The MNLF once contended that the cause of the Moros' economic destitution was not only the perverse governance by colonialists and Manila-based rulers but also the corruption of the traditional elite. Thus, the Bangsa Moro struggle was framed as not only anticolonial but also anti-elite (Majul 1985; Molloy 1988).

However, the MNLF realized that if they continued to denounce the traditional Moro elite, they risked losing the resources that the local lords and their private armies could provide. Thus, the leaders of the MNLF were faced with the choice of either to continue their ideological diatribe against the traditional elite or to enter into an uneasy alliance with them for tactical reasons. Eventually, facing considerable losses on the battlefield, the MNLF leadership found it more expedient to jettison their ideological beliefs to keep the money and manpower flowing in from the elite. According to Molloy (1988, 69), this decision "restricted the Front's ideological platform to simple demands for secession and a vague notion of an Islamic state."

In hindsight, the MNLF's alliance of convenience with the elite was quite beneficial to the rebellion in the short term, but its long-term consequences for the uprising were severely damaging. The Moro elite supported the cause of the MNLF at the beginning but comfortably shifted their allegiance to the Marcos dictatorship when they realized that such move would bring greater rewards and rents. The elite's shift of allegiance drained the MNLF of vital manpower when the clan leaders pulled their private armies from the field. Even more tellingly, the elite repudiated the MNLF's belief in a tawhidi society. The MNLF held the notion that a Moro state should be devoid of any political, social or economic segmentation, that society must reflect the divine oneness, or tawhid (Owen 1992). However, the elite soon realized that such a concept threatened their inherited preeminence in their respective ethnic communities.

Another factor that led to the decline of support for the MNLF's cause was its inability to present a clear and coherent redistributive agenda. The Bangsa Moro rebellion presented itself as an armed struggle for social justice, but the MNLF was unable to offer any ideas to promote social equity or to propose an alternative economic model. The MNLF position on the economy was framed in very vague terms. Its manifesto stated that the movement shall "never tolerate any form of exploitation and oppression of any human being by another or of one nation by another" (Gutierrez 2000b, 326). The absence of a clear-cut economic policy direction eroded the MNLF's ideological hold on its adherents. It opened the movement to the criticism that a victory for the MNLF would result not in a tawhidi society unsegmented by class but in the domination of economic life by the Tausugs.

Finally, the decision of Salamat Hashim to split from the MNLF and establish the MILF shook Misuari's nationalist project to its very base. The antipathies of the ethnic communities with each another proved too formidable to be overcome by a project based on the invocation of a common historical past. The quest for a Bangsa Moro nation was effectively scuttled by ethnic antagonism. The MNLF came to be seen as the Tausug branch of the Moro movement (headed by Misuari), whereas the MILF was linked with the Maguindanaos (under the leadership of Hashim). (The split produced a third group, the so-called MNLF-Reformist wing, which was composed mostly of Maranaos and was led by Abul Khayr Alonto. It is no longer active.) The MILF tried to disabuse the notion that

> ## Lineages to the Divine
> The leadership of the Bangsa Moro struggle comes from the Tausug and Maguindanao ethnic communities. The word *Tausug* (who lead the MNLF) means "People of the Current." The Tausugs believe that their designation was also ascribed to them because of their bravery and courage. Thus, they are Tau Maisug, or "brave people." The Tausug claim their noble lineage from Tuan Masha'ika, a son of two gods, Jamiyum Kulisa and Indira Suga.
>
> Meanwhile, the name *Maguindanaos* means "People of the Flood Plain" because they live near a delta that is prone to overflow, flooding the plains. They claim lineage from Rajah Indarapatra, a child from the seventh layer of heaven who agreed to accept mortality. It was said that Indarapatra taught the Maguindanaos the arts of farming, healing, and sword making. The tensions between these two groups seem to suggest that godly descent is insufficient for peace (Abbahil 1984).

it was a Maguindanao clique, but its most prominent leaders were Maguindanaos, as those at the top of MNLF were Tausugs (Vitug and Gloria 2000). Furthermore, as Gutierrez has pointed out, an authentic multiethnic leadership or a notable pan-Moro army have never emerged. "The Maguindanaoans would generally choose to fight alongside other Maguindanaoans [rather] than with Tausogs or Maranaos" (Gutierrez 2000b, 325).

The MNLF and the GRP negotiated a peace agreement on September 2, 1996, after a series of talks in Jakarta, Indonesia. In the agreement, an executive body was created, the Southern Philippines Council for Peace and Development (SPCPD). In the agreement, the head of the body would have the capacity to administer the economic development of the thirteen provinces stipulated in the Tripoli Agreement, with the addition of Sarangani. It also stipulated the integration of MNLF combatants into the police and military. Nur Misuari, the chairman of the MNLF, was appointed head of SPCPD in 1996.

However, it became apparent that Misuari lacked the necessary administrative and managerial skills to govern. Revolutionaries are often very inept administrators. His terms as SPCPD chairman and governor of the Autonomous Region of Muslim Mindanao (ARMM) were riddled with charges of corruption and failed programs. In 2000, the Philippine government sought to provide a graceful exit for Misuari by rescheduling the elections for ARMM governor to 2000, giving him the opportunity to step aside in favor of Parouk Hussin, the MNLF's foreign minister (Vitug and Gloria 2000).

Misuari resisted the government's schemes to marginalize him. In 2001, he and his followers mounted an attack on government facilities in Jolo as a demonstration of force and to reignite the MNLF's struggle for true autonomy. However, the putsch was quickly contained and crushed, forcing Misuari to flee to Sabah, where he was captured by Malaysian authorities in November 2001. Misuari was turned over to the Philippine government in 2002, and he is being tried for sedition.

As for the MILF, they distanced themselves from the GRP-MNLF agreement as well as the SPCPD and entered into their own negotiations with the state. However, when talks broke down in 2000, President Joseph Estrada launched an all-out assault against the MILF on the pretext that the group was harboring members of the Abu Sayyaf, a terrorist group trained and funded by al-Qaeda. The MILF was defeated in the confrontation, losing their historical and spiritual center, Camp Abubakar As-Siddique. In 2003, Salamat Hashim, the MILF's founder and spiritual leader, passed away; the leadership passed to Al-Haj Murad. Without Hashim, it is questionable how long the MILF will last as a rebel organization. They have since resumed negotiations with the GRP.

Duration Tactics

The Bangsa Moro struggle can be categorized as an example of a rebellion based on grievance (Collier and Hoeffer 2004). The predisposing factors of the rebellion are historically rooted and deep-seated. This sense of injustice was the emotive reason the MNLF was able to rapidly recruit combatants in the 1970s and can explain how they were able to sustain their resistance for two decades thereafter. A rebellion framed in an ethnic context provides a clear lens through which to identify enemies and to explain the causes of one's destitution (Esman 1989; Fearon and Laitin 2003). Support for the Bangsa Moro cause is likely to continue, given the deterioration of the socioeconomic situation of the Muslims in Mindanao.

Another factor that enabled the rebels to sustain their rebellion in Mindanao was the topographic fragmentation of the Philippines. It proved difficult for the central government to mount campaigns in deeply forested, mountainous terrain. To this was added the fact that the rebels established their bases in the provinces where particular ethnic communities supported them. For example, the MNLF was active in Tawi-Tawi, a province dominated by Tausugs. Meanwhile, the MILF had most of its bases in Maguindanao, home of the Maguindanaos.

The rebel cause was also aided by the limited capacity of the state to fully engage the rebels. The central government could not throw the full weight of its military might against the MNLF or the MILF, because it had to allocate its limited resources to containment of other threats to national security. The Armed Forces of the Philippines (AFP) had to deal with the attacks and incursions of the CPP-NPA in Luzon and in several parts of the Visayas. Currently, the AFP and the PNP also have to contend with the terrorist activities of the Abu Sayyaf.

Finally, the MNLF and the MILF also received financial support from the outside. Such countries as Saudi Arabia, Libya, and Iran had channeled monetary and logistical support to the rebellion since the outbreak of violence in 1972. In the case of the MILF, training and financing were also received from groups such as al-Qaeda (Ressa 2003). This external support was vital to the insurgency, especially when support for its cause began to decline as Marcos's authoritarian regime collapsed in 1986 and the country reverted to democracy. However, when the Organization of the Islamic Conference (OIC)—especially the MNLF's main supporters (Libya, Saudi Arabia, and Indonesia)—began to back the initiatives of President Ramos in 1992, the MNLF faced the possibility that its financial well was drying up. The MNLF finally signed a peace agreement with the GRP on September 2, 1996.

Conflict Management Efforts

The case of the MNLF was described as the only "success story of the OIC in its record of dispute settlement" (Vitug and Gloria 2000, 70). This success may be due to the fact that the MNLF was able to sustain its rebellion largely with the support of the OIC. Thus, when the OIC finally declared that it was time for the MNLF and the GRP to "further the peace process," the MNLF took the bargaining table more seriously.

The MNLF initially obtained its financing from within but immediately saw the benefits of financing from without. Both Islamic tenets and international law were utilized to legitimize this procurement of external intervention. In the Islamic political imagination, all the believers of Islam constitute one undivided community; the term *ummah* refers both to the Muslim society contained within a state and to the broader "community of the faithful" (Decasa 1999; Roy 1994). Thus, the 1974 MNLF manifesto declared that the Bangsa Moro struggle is "part of the Islamic World as well as of the Third World and the oppressed colonized humanity everywhere in the world" (cited in Santos 2001, 57).

In 1974, the MNLF charged the Marcos administration with undertaking what it referred to as "low intensity ethnic cleansing" in Mindanao because of the administration's support of armed Christian gangs (e.g., the Ilagas) and its policy of driving Muslims off their ancestral lands. Clearly, the tactic was crafted to demonstrate to the international community that the MNLF was a national liberation movement (NLM) fighting to preserve its identity against a racist state; see, for example, the United Nations' Declaration of Friendly Relations Declaration (1970), as well as the Aalands case (1920). The claim had the effect of allowing third states to come to the movement's aid, which was very important for the resource-strapped MNLF. As a national liberation movement, the MNLF was also empowered to enter into treaties with other countries (Cassesse 2001, 76–77).

States such as Libya, Saudi Arabia, and Iran gave the MNLF much-needed financial, logistical, and diplomatic support. The interest of the OIC was also credited with restraining the Marcos administration from committing gross violations of human rights in the Mindanao region. In the jargon of international law, the Moro rebellion had become an "internationalized non-international armed conflict": a dispute that has not yet reached the character of interstate conflict but in which external intervention is present (Gasser 1983).

The OIC provided much-needed support for the Moro cause in the international arena but also acted to restrain the MNLF from pursuing its secessionist intentions aggressively. Some members of the OIC, such as Libya and Malaysia, expressed public support for the objectives of the MNLF rebellion, whereas others, such as Iran, Syria, and Saudi Arabia, never took public positions but provided clandestine funding. However, some states within the OIC were also engaged in struggles against separatist movements, most notably Indonesia and Iraq; these states blocked full OIC recognition of the MNLF because they feared that it would embolden other separatist groups.

It can be reasonably averred that the OIC was very much responsible for the decision of the Moro groups to reduce their claims to autonomy. With regard to the Philippine case, it adopted the very conservative position that the conflict between the GRP and the MNLF must be resolved "within the framework of Philippine sovereignty and territorial integrity," effectively shredding the separation option from the table. Eventually, the Tripoli Agreement, which was signed by the GRP and the MNLF in December 1976, entailed the formation of an autonomonous regional system in Mindanao, not a separate state. Although the MNLF attempted to place the secession option back on the table at various points afterward, they were never able to really step out of the shadow of the Tripoli Agreement. That aagreement was the framework upon which the Peace Agreement of 1996 was negotiated, the document that brought the MNLF back into the fold of the law. The MNLF's decision left the MILF the only Muslim group currently in armed engagement with the state.

Conclusion

Plural societies face the perpetual dilemma of maintaining internal order and preserving their borders. Historical grievances of ethnic communities can suddenly explode into the open, triggered by some event that crystallizes their perceived disadvantaged situation. This rage can be articulated and given form by an organization toward the goal of greater political participation, autonomy, or separation (Esman 1989). Enemies are identified, causes enumerated, and courses of action mapped.

Such was the case with the Philippine Muslims. Although recognized for their valiant resistance of the Spanish invaders, they have since been marginalized in Philippine socioeconomic and political life. Colonial administrations forcibly dispossessed them of landed properties, and Mindanao remained undeveloped because of the concentration of government decision making in Manila. The Muslims' discontent exploded into the open after the Jabidah massacre in 1968 and was given political form by the MNLF.

It can be reasonably asserted that the 1996 agreement was tailored to bring the MNLF back into the fold of the law. However, negotiating with the MNLF alone could not achieve peace in the Southern Philippines. For most of the Muslims, the MNLF had come to be considered the Tausug component of the Bangsa Moro struggle. The claims of the Maguindanaos and the Maranaos have been lodged with the MILF, and it would take the state the same amount of political creativity that the government showed in the MNLF negotiations to convince the MILF to lay down their arms. However, the death of Salamat Hashim provided the GRP and the MILF with a more flexible window for negotiations. Hashim, like Misuari, was not fully convinced of the autonomy alternative to secession. With his towering presence absent from the table, the peace process may be advanced more fully.

The MNLF no longer has the political or military organization to restart an armed resistance against the state, and for this reason it can be expected that the 1996 peace agreement will hold. But given the continued marginalization of Muslims in their own region, and the continued underdevelopment of provinces with large segments of Muslim population, a trigger event is likely to galvanize Muslim resistance anew. The autonomy alternative having failed to provide a solution to the problems of the Muslims, a more viable path to peace would be the formation of a federal system in the Philippines. With much local government power devolved, the Muslims would finally get the chance to govern themselves or to learn to govern with the Christians and the Lumads. Such would be difficult, but in the end, the vigor of societies can only be preserved, said an eminent philosopher, "by the widespread sense that high aims are worthwhile" (Whitehead 1933, 371).

Rodelio Cruz Manacsa and Alexander Tan

Chronology

March 1968   Jabidah massacre occurs; twenty-eight Muslims mutiny and are executed. Filipino Muslims protest and prepare for armed rebellion.

1969   The Moro National Liberation Front (MNLF) is secretly founded under the leadership of Nur Misuari.

September 21, 1972   Ferdinand Marcos places the country under martial law.

November 1972   Bangsa Moro rebellion breaks out with offensives against the Philippine military in Sulu, Lanao del Norte, Lanao del Sur, and Jolo.

1973   Marcos creates the Southern Philippine Development Administration (SPDA) to "bring development" to Mindanao while continuing military operations.

1974   Muslim secessionist movement gains international recognition. The Organization of the Islamic Conference (OIC) recognizes the MNLF as the representative of the Moro people.

December 23, 1976   The MNLF and the government of the Republic of the Philippines (GRP) enter into the Tripoli Agreement, in which the MNLF agrees to reduce its claims to an autonomous region of thirteen provinces and nine cities. The GRP grants the claim as long as "constitutional processes" are followed. MNLF splinters when a faction related to Salamat Hashim disagrees with the reduced claim.

1977   Negotiations break down; the MNLF insists that immediate autonomy be granted on the thirteen provinces and nine cities, but the GRP insists on plebiscites.

1979   The MNLF reverts to secession as the goal of the Bangsa Moro struggle.

1984   The Moro Islamic Liberation Front (MILF), an MNLF splinter group, is formed under Salamat Hashim.

1986   President Marcos calls for an emergency presidential election, which is held but with fraudulent results. Marcos is deposed in a spontaneous, nonviolent uprising called the People Power Revolution, headed by Corazon Aquino and a Church prelate, Jaime Cardinal Sin. Aquino is installed as president.

1989   The Philippine legislature crafts the Autonomous Region of Muslim Mindanao (ARMM), bestowing autonomy on any province or city that votes for the scheme in a plebiscite. Only four of the thirteen provinces select autonomy.

1993   Emissaries of Aquino's successor, President Fidel V. Ramos, and the MNLF meet in Jakarta.

1994   President Ramos grants amnesty to Muslim rebels.

September 2, 1996   Peace agreement is signed by the MNLF and the GRP. Misuari is elected governor of the ARMM and is also named chairperson of the Southern Philippines Council for Peace and Development

(SPCPD). MILF rejects the agreement and pursues its own negotiations with GRP.

2000   Ramos's successor, Joseph Estrada, launches a full assault against the MILF and captures Camp Abubakar, the MILF's central lair.

January 2002   Upon receiving news that he will not be reappointed head of the SPCPD nor supported as ARMM governor, Misuari leads an armed attack against Philippine forces in Jolo. Violence breaks out between the MNLF and the GRP.

November 2002   Misuari is captured in Pulau Jampiras, Malaysia. He is eventually turned over to the Philippines, where he is being tried for sedition. Parouk Hussin succeeded Misuari as MNLF head.

July 13, 2003   MILF founder Salamat Hashim dies; Al Haj-Murad is named head of the MILF.

List of Acronyms

AFP: Armed Forces of the Philippines
ARMM: Autonomous Region of Muslim Mindanao
BMA: Bangsa Moro Army
BMAF: Bangsa Moro Armed Forces
BMLO: Bangsa Moro Liberation Organization
CPP: Communist Party of the Philippines
GRP: government of the Republic of the Philippines
MILF: Moro Islamic Liberation Front
MIM: Muslim Independence Movement
MNLF: Moro National Liberation Front
NLM: national liberation movement
NPA: New People's Army
OIC: Organization of the Islamic Conference
PKP: Partido Komunista ng Pilipinas (Communist Party of the Philippines)
SPCPD: Southern Philippines Council for Peace and Development
SPDA: Southern Philippine Development Administration

Glossary

Bangsa Moro: The "nation" envisioned by MNLF leaders in the 1960s to unify the different Islamic communities. *Bangsa* means homeland, and *Moro* is an epithet first employed by the Spanish colonizers to refer to Muslims but later appropriated by MNLF leaders in 1960s as a symbol of their struggle. They claimed that, despite the diversity among them, they shared a common past: a history of defiance and resistance that dated as far back as the Spanish period. They transfigured the negative epithet bestowed by colonizers into a symbol of pride and freedom.

gaosbaugbug: One of the two pillars of MNLF's ideology. *Gaos* can be roughly translated as "ability" and *baugbug*, "commitment." A Muslim can be a member of the MNLF only if he has the capacity to commit to the realization of kaadilan.

jihad: Roughly translated as "holy war," which, according to the MNLF ideology, can be waged against a regime that has become gobirno a sarwang tao (a government alien to the people).

kaadilan: The endpoint of the Bangsa Moro struggle, a state in which supposedly all the wrongs committed against the Muslims shall be rectified and their way of life forever protected.

Moro: The designation used by the Spaniards to refer to the Muslims in Manila and later to the Islamic peoples in the south. Moro was derived from the term *Moor,* which the Spaniards used to mean a Berber of North Africa; the Berbers conquered Spain in 711.

tarsilas: Genealogies of the different ethnic communities in Mindanao, where their divine lineages can be supposedly traced.

tawhid: The oneness of the divine that should be reflected by any Muslim order.

ummah: The worldwide brotherhood of Muslims.

References

Aalands case. 1920. *LNOJ Special Supplement* No. 3: 18.

Abbahil, Abdulsikkik. 1984. "The Bangsa Moro: Their Self-Image and Inter-Group Ethnic Attitudes." *Dansalan Quarterly* 5: 197–250.

Abinales, Patricio. 1996. *The Revolution Falters.* Ithaca, NY: Southeast Asian Program, Cornell University Press.

Abinales, Patricio. 2000. *Making Mindanao.* Quezon City, Philippines: Ateneo de Manila University Press.

Abubakar, Asiri. 1973. "Muslim Philippines: With Reference to the Sulus, Muslim-Christian Contradictions, and the Mindanao Crisis." *Asian Studies* 11: 112–28.

Abubakar, Carmen. 1983. "Islamization of Southern Philippines: An Overview." In *Filipino Muslims,* edited by F. Landa Jocano. Quezon City, Philippines: Asian Center.

Abuza, Zachary. 2003. *Militant Islam in Southeast Asia.* Boulder, CO: Lynne Rienner.

Ahmad, Aijaz. 2000. "The War Against the Muslims." In *Rebels, Warriors and Ulama: A Reader on Muslim Separatism in Southern Philippines,* edited by Kristina Gaerlan and Mara Stankovich. Quezon City, Philippines: Institute of Popular Democracy.

Balacuit, Jimmy. 1994. "Muslim Rebellion in Southern Philippines Revisited." *Mindanao Forum* 9: 1–29.

Brown, David. 1994. *The State and Ethnic Politics in Southeast Asia.* NY: Routledge.

Carment, David. 1994. "The Ethnic Dimension in World Politics: Theory, Policy and Early Warning." *Third World Quarterly* 15: 551–82.

Casino, Eric. 1972."Integration and the Muslim Filipinos." *Philippine Sociological Review* 20: 360–62.

Cassese, Antonio. 2001. *International Law.* Oxford, UK: Oxford University Press.

Central Intelligence Agency (CIA). 2006. *World Factbook: Philippines.* www.cia.gov/cia/publications/factbook/geos/rp.html (accessed May 24, 2006).

Chalk, Peter. 2002. "Militant Islamic Extension in the Southern Philippines." In *Islam in Asia,* edited by Jason Isaacson and Colin Rubenstein. New Brunswick, NJ: Transaction Press.

Chapman, William. 1987. *Inside the Philippine Revolution.* London: L. B. Tauris.

Che Man, W. K. 1990. *Muslim Separatism: The Moros of Southern Philippines and the Malays of Southern Thailand.* Quezon City, Philippines: Ateneo de Manila University Press.

Collier, Paul, and Anke Hoeffler. 2004. "Greed and Grievances in Civil War." *Oxford Economic Papers* 56: 563–95.

Coronel Ferrer, Miriam. 1997. *The Southern Philippines Council for Peace and Development: A Response to the Controversy.* Quezon City: Center for Integrative and Development Studies, University of the Philippines.

Decasa, George. 1999. *The Qur'anic Concept of Umma and Its Function in Philippine Muslim Society.* Rome: Gregorian University Press.

Declaration on Principles of International Law Friendly Relations and Co-Operation among Sates in Accordance with the Charter of the United Nations. 1970. In *Basic Documents in International Law,* edited by Ian Brownlie. New York: Oxford University Press.

DeRouen, Karl, and David Sobek. 2004. "The Dynamics of Civil War Duration and Outcome." *Journal of Peace Research* 41: 303–20.

Dery, Luis. 1997. *The Kris in Philippine History.* NP: privately printed.

Dolan, Ronald. 2003. "Philippines: A Country Study." In *The Philippines: Current Issues and Historical Background,* edited by Harry Calit. New York: Nova.

Esman, Milton. 1989. *Ethnic Politics.* Ithaca, NY: Cornell University Press.

Fearon, James. 2004. "Why Do Some Civil Wars Last Longer than Others?" *Journal of Peace Research* 41: 275–301.

Fearon, James, and David Laitin. 2003. "Ethnicity, Insurgency, and Civil War." *American Political Science Review* 97: 75–90.

Fianza, Myrthena. 1999. "Conflicting Land Use and Ownership Patterns and the 'Moro Problem' in Southern Philippines." In *Sama-Sama: Facets of Ethnic Relations in South East Asia,* edited by Miriam Coronel Ferrer. Quezon City, Philippines: Third World Studies Center.

Freedom House. 2006. *Freedom in the World Comparative Rankings: 1973–2005.* 65.110.85.181/uploads/FIWrank7305.xls (accessed May 24, 2006).

Gasser, Hans Peter. 1983. "Internationalized Non-International Armed Conflicts." *American University Law Review* 33: 145–157.

George, T. J. S. 1980. *Revolt in Mindanao: The Rise of Islam in Philippine Politics.* Kuala Lumpur, Malaysia: Oxford University Press.

Glang, Alunan. 1969. *Muslim Secession or Integration?* Quezon City, Philippines: privately printed.

Gomez, Hilario. 2000. *The Moro Rebellion and the Search for Peace.* Zamboanga, Philippines: Silsilah Publications.

Gowing, Peter. 1964. *Mosque and Moro: A Study of Muslims in the Philippines.* Manila, Philippines: Philippine Federation of Christian Churches.

Gowing, Peter. 1979. *Muslim Filipinos: Heritage and Horizon.* Quezon City, Philippines: New Day.

Gowing, Peter. 1983. *Mandate in Moro Land: The American Government of the Muslim Filipinos 1899–1920.* Quezon City, Philippines: New Day.

Guerrero, Amado. 1979. *Philippine Society and Revolution.* Oakland, CA: International Association of Filipino Patriots.

Gutierrez, Eric. 1997. "Scenes from a Conflict." In *Roots of Conflict,* edited by Rosalita Tolibas-Nunez. Makati, Philippines: Asian Institute of Management.

Gutierrez, Eric. 2000a. "In the Battle Fields of the Warlords." In *Rebels, Warlords and Ulama: A Reader on Muslim Separatism in Southern Philippines,* edited by Kristina Gaerlan and Mara Stakovich. Quezon City, Philippines: Institute of Popular Democracy.

Gutierrez, Eric. 2000b. "The Reimagination of the Bangsa Moro: 30 Years Hence." In *Rebels, Warlords and Ulama: A Reader on Muslim Separatism in Southern Philippines,* edited by Kristina Gaerlan and Mara Stankovich. Quezon City, Philippines: Institute of Popular Democracy.

Gutierrez, Eric, and Abdulwahab Guialal. 2000. "Unfinished Jihad: The MILF and Peace in Mindanao." In *Rebels, Warlords and Ulama: A Reader on Muslim Separatism in Southern Philippines,* edited by Kristina Gaerlan and Mara Stakovich. Quezon City, Philippines: Institute of Popular Democracy.

Heston, Alan, Robert Summers, and Bettina Aten. 2002. *Penn World Tables Version 6.1.* pwt.econ.upenn.edu/php_site/pwt_index.php (accessed July 22, 2005).

Horvatich, Patricia. 1993. "Keeping Up with the Hassans: Tradition, Change and Rituals of Death in a Sama Community." *Pilipinas* 21: 51–71.

Jones, Gregg. 1989. *Red Revolution.* Boulder, CO: Westview Press.

Jubair, Salah. 1999. *Bangsamoro: A Nation Under Endless Tyranny,* 3rd ed. Cotobato City, Malaysia: Marin Press.

Kamlian, Jamail. 1995. "MNLF Identity and Attitudinal Perspectives." *Mindanao Forum* 10: 1–28.

Kerkvliet, Benedict. 1977. *The Huk Rebellion.* Berkeley: University of California Press.

Lande, Carl. 1996. *Post-Marcos Politics.* Manila, Philippines: De La Salle University Press.

Lingga, Ahoud. 1995. "Salamat Hashim's Concept of Bangsamoro State and Government." *Dansalan Quarterly* 15: 49–60.

Macansantos, Rosello. 1996. "Building the Culture of Peace in Southern Philippines: Retrospect and Prospects." *Mindanao Forum* 11: 47–60.

Majul, Cesar. 1973. *Muslims in the Philippines.* Quezon City, Philippines: University of the Philippines Press.

Majul, Cesar. 1985. *Contemporary Muslim Movements in the Philippines.* Berkeley, CA: Mizan Press.

Marohomsalic, Nasser. 2001. *Aristocrats of the Malay Race: History of the Bangsa Moro in the Philippines.* Marawi City, Philippines: M.S.V. Press.

Mastura, Michael. 1976. "Administrative Policies Toward the Muslims in the Philippines." *Dansalan Papers* 5: 1–20.

Mastura, Michael. 1984. *Muslim Filipino Experience*. Manila, Philippines: Ministry of Muslim Affairs.

McKenna, Thomas. 1998. *Muslims, Rulers and Rebels*. Berkeley, CA: University of California Press.

Molloy, Ivan. 1988. "Decline of MNLF in Southern Philippines." *Journal of Contemporary Asia* 18: 59–76.

Muslim, Macapado. 1992. "Historical Roots of the Contemporary Moro Armed Struggle in the Philippines." *Dansalan Quarterly* 12: 3–58.

Muslim, Macapado. 1994. *The Moro Armed Struggle in the Philippines: The Nonviolent Autonomy Alternative*. Marawi City, Philippines: Mindanao State University.

Noble, Leila. 1976. "The MNLF in the Philippines." *Pacific Affairs* 19: 405–24.

Noble, Leila. 1981."Muslim Separatism in the Philippines 1972–1981: Making of a Stalemate." *Asian Survey* 21: 1097–1114.

Olzak, Susan. 1983. "Contemporary Ethnic Mobilization." *Annual Review of Sociology* 9: 355–63.

Opinion upon the Legal Aspects of the Aalands Islands Question, LNOJ, SS (October 1920), No. 3, 5, 198.

Owen, Roger. 1992. *State Power and Politics in the Making of the Modern Middle East*. New York: Routledge.

Patanne, Eufemio. 1996. *The Philippines in the 6th to16th Century*. Quezon City, Philippines: privately printed.

Political Instability Task Force. 2006. *State Failure*. globalpolicy.gmu.edu/pitf/ (accessed July 18, 2005).

Polity IV Project. No date. *Political Regime Characteristics and Transitions, 1800-2004*. www.cidcm.umd. edu/polity/ (accessed July 18, 2005).

Ressa, Maria. 2003. *Seeds of Terror: An Eyewitness Account of Al-Qaeda's Newest Center of Operations in Southeast Asia*. New York: Free Press.

Rocamora, Joel. 1996. *Breaking Through*. Metro Manila, Philippines: Anvil Publishing.

Rodil, Rudy. 1994. *The Minoritization of the Indigenous Communities in Mindanao and the Sulu Archipelago*. Davao City, Philippines: Alternate Forum for Research in Mindanao.

Roy, Oliver. 1994. *The Failure of Political Islam*. Cambridge, MA: Harvard University Press.

Saber, Mamitua. 1974. "Maranao Social and Cultural Transition." In *Muslim Filipinos*, edited by Peter Gowing and Robert McAmis. Manila, Philippines: Solidaridad.

Santos, Soliman. 2001. *The Moro Islamic Challenge: Constitutional Rethinking of the Mindanao Peace Process*. Quezon City, Philippines: University of the Philippines Press.

Saulo, Alfred. 1990. *Communism in the Philippines: An Introduction*. Quezon City, Philippines: Ateneo de Manila University Press.

Scott, William Henry. 1994. *Barangay: 16th Century Philippine Culture and Society*. Quezon City, Philippines: Ateneo de Manila University Press.

Stavenhagen, Rodolfo. 1996. *Ethnic Conflicts and the Nation State*. New York: St. Martin's Press.

Stone, Richard. 1974. "Intergroup Relations among the Tausugs, Samals and Badjaos of Sulu." In *Muslim Filipinos*, edited by Peter Gowing and Robert McAmis. Manila, Philippines: Solidaridad.

Tan, Samuel. 1993. *Internationalization of the Bangsa Moro Struggle*. Quezon City: University of the Philippines Center for Integrative and Developmental Studies.

Thomas, Ralph. 1971. *Muslim but Filipinos: The Integration of Filipino Muslims 1917–1946*. Ph.D. dissertation, University of Pensylvania.

Tolibas-Nunez, Rosalita. 1997. *Roots of Conflict: Muslims, Christians, and the Mindanao Struggle*. Makati, Philippines: Asian Institute of Management.

United States Committee for Refugees. 2004. *World Refugee Survey*. Washington, DC: U.S. Committee for Refugees.

Vitug, Maritess Danguilan, and Glenda M. Gloria. 2000. *Under the Crescent Moon: Rebellion in Mindanao*. Quezon City, Philippines: Ateneo Center for Social Policy and Public Affairs and Institute for Popular Democracy.

Weekley, Kathleen. 2001. *The Communist Party of the Philippines 1968–1993*. Diliman, Philippines: University of the Philippines Press.

Whitehead, Alfred North. 1933. *Adventures of Ideas*. New York: McMillan.

Wurfel, David. 1988. *Filipino Politics: Development and Decay*. Quezon City, Philippines: Ateneo de Manila University Press.

Russia
(1994–1996)

Introduction

The Chechen quest for independence began in 1991, when Chechen nationalists came to power in Chechnya and declared its sovereignty from the Russian Federation. In 1994, after several unsuccessful attempts to unseat the nationalist government, Russian president Boris Yeltzin resorted to what hoped to be a quick and victorious war. Contrary to these expectations, however, the Russian troops met fierce resistance from the Chechen fighters and from the Chechen population. After almost two years of continuous fighting and approximately 30,000 in casualties, the Russian administration ended the conflict by agreeing to withdraw its troops and to postpone a final decision on the Chechen independence until December 31, 2001. Despite the agreement, however, the Chechen nationalists continued their demands for independence supported by a series of terrorist attacks. In retaliation for terrorist attacks, on October 1, 1999, Russian ground troops entered Chechnya for another military campaign that became known as the Second Chechen war.

Country Background

The Russian Federation entered the First Chechen war (1994–1996) as a newly established democracy overwhelmed by economic hardship, political instability, and the rise of nationalist feelings. On August 24, 1991, the Russian Federation proclaimed its independence from the Soviet Union and started the process of forming a democratic political system and market economy to replace the socialist political institutions and planned economy of the Soviet era. By the outbreak of the war, Russia had emerged as a presidential republic characterized by a strong executive branch, a weak parliament, and a multiparty political system. President Boris Yeltsin, who was popularly elected by more than 57 percent of the electorate in the first democratic presidential election on June 12, 1991, headed the executive branch. The legislative powers of Russia were vested in the two newly formed chambers of the Federal Assembly: the Federal Council (upper chamber) and the State Duma (lower chamber). In accordance with the new Russian Constitution (1993), Yeltsin's presidential powers were significantly greater than those of the Russian legislature. However, it did not prevent the legislature from providing opposition to Yeltsin and his cabinet.

The 1993 parliamentary elections were contested by thirteen political parties, eight of which passed a 5-percent threshold and received seats in the State Duma. None of the parties had a clear majority in the parliament. Russia's Choice, the major reformist coalition and Yeltsin's supporter, performed better than any other party in single-mandate districts and received a total of

66 seats in the Duma (more than any other party); however, it lost the party-list election and could hardly compete with the conservative opposition. As a result, an odd coalition of ultranationalists (the Liberal Democratic Party of Russia), Communists (the Communist Party of the Russian Federation), and agrarians (the Agrarian Party) took control of the legislature and posed a real threat to Yeltsin and his reforms.

Many experts attribute the good performance of the conservative parties in the 1993 parliamentary election to a general disillusion among the Russians with economic reforms undertaken by Yeltsin and his cabinet. Wishing to transform Russian socialist planning into a market economy, Boris Yeltsin enlisted help of one of his supporters, young economist and politician Yegor Gaidar. In June 1992, Yeltsin appointed Gaidar acting prime minister, and Gaidar's team started one of the most ambitious economic reforms, known as a "shock therapy." It included liberalization of prices, legalization of private business and private ownership of land, introduction of free trade and commercial banking, massive privatization of state-run enterprises, and radical cuts in military spending. The impact of these changes on the public was severe. By the end of 1992, real income had fallen by 47 percent; the inflation rate reached an unprecedented 2,600 percent; and GDP declined by 14 percent. Absolute poverty and unemployment, practically unknown during Soviet times, became a fact of everyday life. As a result, economic reform and its advocates became extremely unpopular with the majority of Russians.

In addition to economic devastation, Yeltsin and his cabinet had to deal with the rise of nationalist feelings among the members of the federation. In 1991, when the Russian Federation declared its independence from the Soviet Union, it comprised 89 constituent units populated by more than 100 various nationalities. By 1993, several of those units had either openly declared their independence from Russia (for example, Chechnya and Buryatia) or expressed a

desire to secede from the federation (for example, Tatarstan). Initially, the Yeltsin administration, overwhelmed by the difficulty of economic transition, decided to ignore the problem of rising nationalism. However, by the end of 1994, the conservative opposition openly criticized the president for mishandling the situation, charging him with ruining the federation. In response, Yeltsin decided to get tough on attempts to secede, hoping that he could fight a quick, popular, and victorious war against the breakaway republic.

Conflict Background

Officially, the Chechen war started on December 11, 1994, and lasted until August 25, 1996. Overall, it was a disastrous war, with 30,000 casualties, most of them civilian. The Russian forces accounted for approximately 48,000 troops. Estimates of the Chechen forces vary widely (from 1,000 to 10,000 fighters). The Russian government fought the Chechen war to stop Chechnya from seceding from the Russian Federation. The Chechen separatist forces fought the war in an attempt to establish an independent Muslim state of Ichkeria (Chechnya).

At the end of the Soviet era, Chechnya was a part of the Chechen-Inquish Autonomous Soviet Socialist Republic. In 1991, after the collapse of the Soviet Union, Chechen nationalists came to power in Chechnya and declared sovereignty. However, their proclamation was not supported by the Inguish part of the republic. As a result, the Chechen-Inquish Republic split into two parts: Chechnya and Ingushetia. Ingushetia remained a part of the Russian Federation, whereas Chechnya declared its full independence from Russia in 1993.

In November 1991, Boris Yeltsin sent federal troops to Chechnya to stop the secession. However, the Supreme Soviet (the legislative branch of the Soviet era) did not support Yeltsin's decision, and the troops had to withdraw. Unable to deploy federal troops, the Yeltsin administration made several attempts to unseat the nationalist

Table 1: Civil War in Russia

War:	Chechen separatists vs. government
Dates:	December 1994 to August 1996
	October 1999–present
Casualties:	1994–1996: 30,000 (1994–1996];
	1994–2004: 50,000–250,000 estimated
Regime type prior to war:	4 (ranging from –10 [authoritarian] to 10 [democracy])
Regime type after war:	4 (ranging from –10 [authoritarian] to 10 [democracy])
GDP per capita year war began:	US $7,687.77 (1994)
GDP per capita 5 years after war:	US $9,995.91 (2001)
Insurgents:	Chechen separatists
Issue:	Secession
Rebel funding:	Drugs, Soviet aid
Role of geography:	Rebels used urban combat in cities and guerrilla warfare in mountains.
Role of resources:	Russian oil pipelines in Chechnya made Chechnya vital to Russian Federation.
Immediate outcome:	Government defeat with postponement of resolution of independence for five years
Outcome after 5 years:	Continuous conflict, pro-Russia government
Role of UN:	No peacekeepers; condemned terrorism
Role of regional organization:	OSCE was active.
Refugees:	365,000
Prospects for peace:	Unfavorable

Sources: Human Development Report 2002; Marshall, Jaggers, Gurr 2004; World Bank 2004

government of Chechnya, but none was successful. As a result, the Russian administration lost control of the situation in Chechnya, whose nationalist government gained popularity and strength. By 1992, according to the Russian Interior Ministry, 250 Russians had been killed in Grozny (the capital of Chechnya), and about 300 had disappeared without a trace (Yanchenkov 2000). By 1994, thousands of Russians had abandoned their homes in Chechnya and fled to Russia.

The Insurgents

The Chechens are one of more than forty ethnic groups that have historically populated the Caucasus (Kavkaz), a predominantly mountainous territory expanding from the mouth of the Kuban River on the Black Sea to the Apsheron peninsula on the Caspian Sea. Chechens are the largest ethnic community of the North Caucasus. They account for about 2 million people,

approximately 900,000 of whom live in the territory of present-day Chechnya. Together with the neighboring Inquish, the Chechens constitute the Vainakh people (*Vainakh* means "our countrymen"). The first written records of Chechens, who called themselves the Nokhchi, go back to the early Middle Ages. During that time, together with other Vainakh tribes and Caucasus peoples, Chechens attempted to establish two independent states. The territory of the Chechen and Dagestani mountains comprised the Sirir kingdom, and the North Caucasian plains and foothills were part of the Alanian state. However, in the thirteenth and fourteenth centuries, the territories of the Northern Caucasus were repeatedly invaded by the Tatar–Mongol troops, and Chechens were forced to retreat to the mountains, where they remained until the fall of the Golden Horde.

The highlander legacy left an important mark on the Chechen culture. On the one hand, living in mountain communities prevented an emergence of different classes among the Vainakh. They have never known either slavery or serfdom, and every man was a warrior. Local rule by feudal lords was limited in scope and based on popular support by essentially free people. On the other hand, the long history of mountain life proved to be an obstacle to establishing a state once the Chechens repopulated the plains. The primary loyalty of Chechens was to their families and clans, and none of the clans wanted to see members of another clan rise to power. As a result, the Vainakh people resorted to inviting princelings of their highland neighbors to rule them and have never had a ruler of their own.

The first close association between the Chechens and the Russians took place in the mid-sixteenth century. During this time, the Russian tsar's policy focused on a peaceful colonization of the region. This was successfully accomplished by the end of the seventeenth century, when Chechen communities officially recognized Moscow's rule. However, in the mid-eighteenth century, Russia changed its policy, choosing an open military expansion to the North Caucasus. This change led to widespread resistance among the Chechen population. The resistance movement was led by Sheikh Mansur, who hoped to establish a single Muslim state in the North Caucasus.

Although Sheikh Mansur never achieved his main goal, his armed resistance to Moscow's colonial rule served as an aspiration for many future generations of the Chechens. It took the tsarist army more than a century of active conflict before they were able to suppress the Chechen resistance and bring Chechnya under Russian administrative rule. In the late nineteenth century, as a part of the tsar's policy, the Russian administration began to deport Chechens from their homeland to Turkey, starting another wave of active resistance.

Soviet rule of the twentieth century was just as alien to the Chechens as the earlier rule of the Russian tsars. The Bolsheviks took control of the North Caucasus in 1921, creating the Chechen Autonomous Region in 1922. In 1934, the Soviet regime unified Chechnya and Ingushetia in the Chechen-Inquish Region. In 1936, the Soviet Federal government granted the Chechen-Inquish Region the status of autonomous republic. However, Soviet domination of the Chechens did not last. In 1942, the republic was occupied by Nazi Germany. The Chechen and Inquish units of the Soviet Army defected and collaborated with the Nazis against the Soviets. The Soviets treated this collaboration as an act of treason and dismantled the Chechen-Inquish Republic once it was back under Soviet control in 1944. The inhabitants of the dismantled republic were deported to the Kazakh Soviet Socialist Republic (Kazakhstan) and to Siberia. It was not until 1957, four years after Stalin's death, that the republic was reestablished and Chechens were allowed to return to their homeland. However, a total reconciliation between the Russians and Chechens has never taken place. The Russians continued to believe the Chechens to be treacherous and unreliable people, while the Chechens continued to believe the Russians to be colonial invaders and continued their hopes for independence.

The collapse of the Soviet Union seemed to open a window of opportunity for Chechen nationalists, who declared independence on November 1, 1991. Dzhokhar Musayevich Dudayev, the leader of the movement for Chechen independence and the first separatist president of the Chechen Republic of Ichkeria, was a child of the Chechen deportation who spent his first thirteen years in Kazakhstan. In 1957, he and his family returned to Chechnya, where he finished night school and qualified as an electrician. To continue his education, Dudayev entered the Tambov Higher Military Aviation School for Pilots, which he finished in 1966. In 1968, Dudayev joined the Communist Party of the Soviet Union and continued to advance steadily in his military career. In 1987, he received the rank of major general and assumed command of the strategic Soviet air base at Tartu, Estonia. In May 1990, Dudayev retired from his military career

Chechen Currency

Early in 1997, the Chechen separatist government decided to pursue a policy of greater economic independence from Russia by issuing new Chechen currency, the nakhar. The currency was modeled on the U.S. dollar and barred essential elements, including watermarks, to prevent counterfeiting. It was printed at a secret press in Britain and then delivered to the vaults of the Chechnya's central bank. The new currency was issued in Soviet-style denominations, starting with one-, three-, and five-nakhar notes and going up to a one-thousand-nakhar note, which bore a portrait of Chechen folk hero Sheikh Mansur galloping on horseback.

In his interview with a Reuter's correspondent, bank chairman Nazhmudin Uvaisayev stated, "I want our nakhar to be a hard currency, respected by all. It will be tied to currencies like the dollar and the German mark and pegged to the dollar at a rate of one to one." However, his hopes for the nakhar were based more on national pride than on a sound monetary policy. Because there were no gold reserves in Chechnya to support their new currency, even Chechen petty traders were wary of the nakhar. The currency remained sealed in the vaults of the bank until Grozny was taken over by federal forces in 1999 (*Daily Turkish News* 1996).

and returned to Chechnya, devoting himself to politics and to establishing a sovereign Chechen state. Dudayev's aggressive nationalist views earned him recognition among other proponents of Chechen independence, placing him at the head of the movement.

Although Dudayev and his supporters were unanimous in their strong anti-Russian sentiments and in their desire for an independent Chechnya, they were much less unified on the role of Islam in the future state. Even though Islam came to the region in the fourteenth and fifteenth centuries, it was not widespread in Chechnya until the late eighteenth and the early nineteenth centuries. During that period, Islam served as a unifying force among the mountain peoples in their resistance of Russian rule—most notably in 1834, when Imam Shamil was able to unite a part of the North Caucasus region, including Chechnya, in gazavat (a holy war of Muslims against infidels) against the Russian troops. Since that time, Islam has remained an important part of the Chechen culture, and not even Soviet rule could eradicate Muslim beliefs among the Chechens. However, of the many forms of Islam, only its modern Sunni version has been adopted in Chechnya. In addition, many pre-Muslim customs have retained their importance in the Chechen culture. As a result, even though Dudayev and his supporters declared that they sought to establish an independent Muslim state of Chechnya, there was little effort to make everyday life conform to Islamic standards. Furthermore, in his interview with *Time* magazine, Dudayev stated that, by starting a military campaign against Chechnya, Russia forced Chechens into Islam, even though they were not ready to accept Muslim values (Zarakhovich 1996).

Geography

Chechnya is situated on the northern slopes of the Caucasus Mountains. Its total territory is only about 5,800 square miles (approximately three-quarters the size of New Jersey). However, the republic encompasses topographically distinct regions. The southern part comprises densely forested mountains. By contrast, the northern part of Chechnya is composed of plains and lowlands. The western part of Chechnya comprises the Terek and the Sunzha valleys. It is the main agricultural region of the republic. Grozny, the capital of the republic, lies in the central part of Chechnya. Gudermes, the second largest city, is located on the Sunzha River 22.3 miles east of Grozny.

By virtue of Chechnya's topography, the war involved urban warfare as well as mountain warfare. The Russian army, heavily armed with tanks, artillery, and aircraft, was at a disadvantage in both types of warfare. In contrast, it allowed the Chechen separatist troops to compensate for

⊛ Moscow

N

UKRAINE

•Novorossiysk

STAVROPOL
KRAI

BLACK
SEA

• Budenovsk

• Pervomaiskoye

• Mozdok
Vladikavkaz • Barsuki   • Kizlyar
                • Groznyy
CHECHNYA
GEORGIA   • Khasavyurt

TURKEY   DAGESTAN

ARMENIA

CASPIAN
SEA

KAZAKHSTAN

AZERBAIJAN

Baku •

0   100   200 mi
0   100   200   300 km

their small numbers and lack of artillery by engaging in predominantly infantry combat.

In urban combat in Grozny and other major cities, the Russian army needed a manpower advantage of at least 5:1 (mostly infantry) to secure every building they took and to continue to advance. However, this had not been foreseen by the Russian general staff. As a result, the first assault on Grozny lasted for two months instead of the estimated two hours. The successful use of antiarmor ambushes allowed the Chechens to inflict heavy loses on the Russian troops and force them to retreat repeatedly to the outskirts of the city to regroup. In a single New Year's Eve attack, the Russians lost about 70 percent of their 230 tanks. By destroying the first and last tanks in a column, Chechen guerrillas trapped the rest of the column in the city's narrow streets and then showered them with gasoline and petrol bombs.

In mountain warfare, the Chechen separatists were also at an advantage. Superior knowledge of the terrain allowed them to compensate for their lack of heavy artillery. In thickly forested mountain regions, they made effective use of booby traps and the mining of roads. At nighttime, separatists would sneak between two Russian units stationed opposite each other and start firing, causing the Russians to fire at each other. In addition, the local population provided the rebels with food and shelter out of sympathy or fear.

Tactics

The Russian troops were not only more numerous but also more technologically advanced than the Chechen fighters. For example, in the December 31, 1994, attack on Grozny, the Russians employed 230 tanks, 454 armored infantry vehicles, and 388 artillery pieces. By contrast, the Chechen rebels had only 50 tanks, 100 armored infantry vehicles, and 60 artillery pieces (Cassidy 2003). To compensate for their disadvantes in manpower and weapons, the Chechens employed guerrilla warfare tactics against the Russian troops. Here, their main objective was to avoid a direct battle and to draw the Russians into the center of the city, where their rear could be attacked and destroyed. In addition to guerrilla warfare at home, the Chechens used terrorist tactics outside Chechnya, where hostage taking attacks became their most common tactic.

The first serious terrorist attack took place in June 1995, when the Chechen separatists led by Shamil Basayev carried out a hostage-taking raid in the southern Russian town of Budyonnovs (Stavropol Krai). During the raid, the Chechens rounded up several hundred civilians and moved them to a busy local hospital, where they were held hostage along with the hospital staff and patients. After securing their positions, the separatists demanded that the Russian government withdraw federal troops from Chechnya and begin direct negotiations with Dzhokhar Dudayev. The siege lasted for almost a week, despite the Russians' attempts to seize the hospital and free the hostages, of which there were more than 1,000. Finally, direct negotiations between Russian Prime Minister Victor Chernomyrdin and Basayev resolved the situation by allowing the Chechens to leave the hospital using 150 hostages as cover. In the course of the standoff, 129 civilians were killed, and 415 were wounded. In January 1996, Chechen separatists under the command of Salman Raduev raided the town of Kizlyar, taking hostage more than 2,000 civilians and, under their cover, retreating to the village of Pervomaiskoye in Dagestan. The attackers held their positions for two weeks, executing forty-one hostages and completely destroying the village (*Pravda* 2002).

In response to the Chechen tactics of guerrilla warfare and terrorism, the Russian force employed massive aerial and artillery bombardment of Grozny (Chechnya's capital) and other population centers, as well as isolated air strikes of smaller rebel units in the mountains. However, this strategy was unsuccessful against the widespread rebels. In addition, massive aerial and artillery bombardment of Grozny resulted in extensive civilian casualties and destruction of property, which in turn led to a significant increase in anti-Russian sentiment among the civilian population. Angered by the indiscriminate Russian attacks, many of the civilian sympathizers, including women and teenagers, either joined the rebels or willingly helped them. As a result, the Russian troops could not rely on the support and loyalty of the local population and in many cases suspected them of collaboration with the rebels. The so-called white stockings, all-female sniper units, became especially infamous among the Russian troops. They were armed with sniper rifles and were said to shoot exclusively Russian officers. The Russian press often claimed that, alongside the Chechen women, those units contained female snipers from the Baltic States, Ukraine, Azerbaijan, and Russia. However, no official data support either the existence of the units or their multiethnic makeup (Nikulina 2000).

In addition to antagonizing the local population, Russian heavy bombardment of Chechen population centers led to the critical reaction of the international community. An especially tense situation developed between the Russian Federation and Turkey, which Russia suspected of providing direct financial and military aid to the Chechen separatists (Daniszewski 2002). Although Turkish officials have never publicly denied or confirmed these accusations, members of Turkish extremist groups were open about their sympathies and even engaged in terrorist activities on the Chechen side. On January 16, 1996, a group of Chechen rebels and pro-Chechen Turkish gunmen led by Turkish extremist Mohamed Tokdzhan hijacked the Russian ferryboat *Avrasiya* in the Turkish port of Trabzon on the Black Sea, taking hostage more than 150 passengers, most of whom were Russians. The hostage takers stated that their actions were in support of the hostage-taking operation carried out by the Chechen rebels in the Dagestan village of Pervomaiskoye and demanded that the Russian federal government stop the war and start negotiations with the Chechen separatists. After three days, the hostages were released unharmed, and the attackers surrendered to the local authorities.

Shortly after the declaration of independence, Dudayev issued a decree creating a new Ministry of Defense of the Chechen Republic. According to the decree, all military personnel and weaponry located in the territory of the republic were transferred to the direct command of President Dudayev. In May 1992, the Russian Federation agreed to transfer to Dudayev's command 50 percent of all weaponry remaining in the territory of Chechnya (Kop'ev 1997). However, the Russian Ministry of Defense failed to evacuate the remaining weaponry and military equipment quickly; as a result, by the summer of 1994, the newly formed Chechen military had control of more than 80 percent of all weaponry and equipment located in Chechnya's territory (Kop'ev, 1997). This included 42 tanks, three MiG-17s, and two MiG-15 jet fighters, more than 250 low-flying aircraft, 139 artillery systems, about 50,000 rifles, and more than 150,000 grenades.

To protect Chechnya's newly proclaimed independence, mandatory military service for all male Chechen citizens ages 19–26 was established in 1992. In addition, the presidential directive of February 17, 1992, offered amnesty to any Chechen citizen who would desert from the Russian army and join the Chechen forces. Altogether, six military drafts took place in the period from 1991 to 1994. By 1994, the Chechen military included 2,000 men in the Presidential Guards, 3,500 men of the joint forces of the Ministry of Internal Affairs and the Department of State Security, and about 13,500 enlisted personnel, of which 1,500 were in fighting readiness and the rest in various stages of military training.

Causes of the War

The causes of the Chechen war are numerous and complex. It is commonly suggested that the war was the outcome of long-standing animosity between the Chechens and the Russians. Indeed, the history of the relationship between these two peoples is characterized by continuous

Chechen attempts to free themselves from Russian domination and by Russian efforts to suppress these attempts. As a result, once the collapse of the Soviet Union presented another opportune moment, the Chechens attempted to secede from the Russian Federation. However, at the end of 1980s, tensions between Moscow and Grozny were at their lowest, at least on the surface. In 1989, for first time in the Chechen history, a Chechen native, Doku Zavgaev, became a first secretary of the Chechen-Inquishen regional committee of the Communist Party of the Soviet Union. In 1991, another Chechen, Ruslan Khasbulatov, was elected speaker of the Supreme Soviet of the Russian Federation, while Salambek Khadjiev became soviet minister for the chemical and oil-refining industry.

The Chechen-Inquish Autonomous Soviet Socialist Republic was growing and becoming more industrialized. In little more than thirty years after the reestablishment, the population of the republic had risen to 1,275,500 people (USSR Population Census 1996). There are no separate data for people residing in the territories of Chechnya and Ingushetia, but the estimates for 1989 were 1.1 million and 170,000, respectively (Cherkasov, 2004). The ethnic composition of the permanent residents of the Chechen-Inquish Autonomous Soviet Socialist Republic in 1989 was as follows: Of the total population of 1,274,000, 734,000 were Chechen, 163,800 Inquish, 293,800 Russian, 14,800 Armenian, and 12,600 Ukrainian (USSR Population Census, 1989). Although there are no exact data on the specific ethnic composition of Chechnya in 1989, it can be estimated that "of 1,984 thousand permanent residents, about 715 thousand were Chechens, 25 thousand were Inquish, and 269 thousand were Russians" (Cherkasov 2004). Grozny, the capital of the Chechen-Inquish Republic, grew into a major industrial city with almost 490,000 residents, of whom approximately 260,000 were Russians, the second-largest ethnic group after the Chechens.

The rural areas of the Chechen-Inquish Republic remained predominantly underdeveloped, however. Always suffering from the lack of arable land, the rural population had a much lower standard of living than the urban population, who were employed predominantly in the chemical and oil-refining industries. According to Soviet statistics, by the mid-1980s there were already tens of thousands of unemployed in the rural areas of the republic (Chechnya.Ru n.d.). In 1989, Doku Zavgaev promised to reduce the level of unemployment among the rural population by developing new jobs in food and food processing; however, this promise remained unfulfilled, and in August 1991 the number of unemployed in the republic reached 100,000 people, or approximately 20 percent of the population (Chechnya.Ru n.d.)

This economic stagnation caused many rural residents to move to Grozny, where they fueled increasing nationalist sentiments. In addition to the impoverished rural population, the Chechen nationalist opposition was supported by emergent black market elites, lured by the possibility of privatization of the Chechen oil refining industry after secession from the Russian Federation. The final source of support of the nationalist movement came from the Muslim clergy, who hoped that secession from the Russian Federation would lead to the establishment of an Islamic state.

In 1990, Dzhokhar Dudayev, a politician and former Soviet air force general, headed the Chechen nationalist movement. In 1991, he became a chairman of the executive committee of the National Congress of the Chechen People, a nationalist opposition organization. Shortly after that, on August 22, 1991, Dudayev carried out a successful coup against the Communist government of the Chechen-Inquish Autonomous Republic. In October, he was elected president of the newly declared Chechen Republic. Within one month of the election, Dudayev unilaterally declared absolute Chechen independence.

In response, the legislature of the Russian Federation refused to recognize either the legitimacy of the Chechen presidential election or the republic's independence. Moscow's unwillingness to grant Chechnya independence was based on its fear of a domino effect as well as the strategic importance of the republic for Russia. Beginning in October 1991, crushing separatist aspirations became one of the main concerns of the Russian administration, as Tatarstan, Bashkortostan, and Buryatia also claimed independence. As a result, allowing Chechen independence would encourage a further disintegration of the Federation. In addition, its geographical location made Chechnya of extreme importance to the Russian Federation, for two reasons. First, access routes to both the Black Sea and the Caspian Sea run from the center of the federation through Chechnya. Second, vital Russian oil and gas pipeline connections with Kazakhstan and Azerbaijan also run through Chechnya.

In November 1991, President Yeltsin issued emergency rule in Chechnya and sent Russian Interior Ministry troops to Grozny in hopes of deposing Dudayev. However, Yeltsin's actions were not supported by the Russian Supreme Soviet, and the troops had to be withdrawn soon thereafter. From that point until the summer of 1994, the Russian Federation adopted a policy of support and cooperation with the opposition of Dudayev. In January 1993, a Russian delegation visited Grozny to discuss power delineation between the Russian Federation and the Chechen Republic; however, Dudayev was not invited to participate. In late 1993, the Chechen Provisional Council, led by Avturkhanov, Mayor of the Nadteretnyj District of Chechnya, emerged as the opposition leader. Other groups opposing Dudayev's policies joined with the council. Although the Provisional Council lacked any real power outside of the Nadteretnyj district, the Russian Federation saw it as a new partner and refrained from any further negotiations with President Dudayev. In negotiations with Moscow, Avturkhanov agreed to reintegrate Chechnya into the Russian Federation and to overthrow Dudayev. Armed with the military and financial support of the Russian government, the Chechen Provisional Council attempted an

---

National Anthem of the Chechen Republic of Ichkeria

We were born at night when the she-wolf whelped,
In the morning, to lion's deafening roar, we were named.
There are no gods save Allah.
In eagles' nests our mothers nursed us,
To tame wild bulls our fathers taught us.
There are no gods save Allah.
Our mothers raised us to dedicate ourselves to our sacred land,
And if they need us we're ready to fight the oppressive hand.
There are no gods save Allah.
We were born and grew up free as the mountain eagles,
With dignity and honor we always overcome hardship and obstacles.
There are no gods save Allah.
Granite rocks will sooner fuse like lead,
Than we will lose our honor in life's struggles.
There are no gods save Allah.
Earth will sooner be swallowed up by the broiling sun,
Than we emerge from a trial in life without our honor!
There are no gods save Allah.
Never will we submit and become slaves,
Death or freedom, for us there's only one way.
There are no gods save Allah.
Our sisters' songs will cure our wounds,
Our beloved's eyes will supply the strength of arms.
There are no gods save Allah.
If hunger weakens us, we'll gnaw on roots,
And if thirst debilitates us, we'll drink dew.
There are no gods save Allah.
For we were born at night when the she-wolf whelped.
God, Nation and Vainakh homeland.
There are no gods save Allah.
(www.chechenpress.org; English version at www.kavkazcenter.com)

unsuccessful coup in Grozny, in November 1994. Once it was clear that the opposition would not be able to overthrow Dudayev, Yeltsin and the Russian Security Council resorted to direct military involvement.

Outcome
Conflict Status

Officially, the first Chechen war ended on August 31, 1996, when Alexander Lebed, the head of the Russian Security Council, and President Aslan Maskhadov signed the Khasavyurt Agreements. According to the agreements, the Russian side had to withdraw all federal forces from Chechnya by December 31, 1996, and a final decision on the question of Chechnya's independence was postponed until December 31, 2001. However, owing to continuing terrorist attacks, demands for independence, and the inability or unwillingness of the Maskhadov administration to enforce the rule of law in the republic, the relationship between Chechnya and Russia has not been normalized. Paramilitary forces led by warlords continued to operate freely in the territory of the republic, kidnapping Russians and foreigners for ransom. In December 1998, one New Zealand and three British telecommunications engineers working in Chechnya for a British company were abducted and killed. In addition, Chechen warlords carried out a number of incursions into Dagestan and Stavropol Krai, abducting and killing civilians.

Finally, on August 2, 1999, a group of Islamic extremists led by Shamil Basayev and Jordanian-born militant Khattab crossed into neighboring Dagestan and in five days captured the villages of Rahata and Ansolta in the Botlikhsky district. During this attack, some 108 Dagestani civilians were killed, and hundreds more were wounded. More than 31,000 civilians were forced to evacuate, and 4,236 families lost their homes. Basayev called the attack the opening act of a crusade to liberate the entire North Caucasus region. In response, the Russian Federation carried out a counteroffensive, quickly recapturing the villages. In September 1999, a series of middle-of-the-night explosions took place in Moscow, Volgograd, and Buinaksk apartments, killing more than 300 people. The Russian government attributed the attacks to the Chechen separatists, and the public demanded retaliation. In late September, the Russian air force began bombing targets within Chechnya; on October 1, Russian ground troops entered Chechnya and marched toward Grozny. In response, President Maskhadov declared a ghazevat (holy war) against the Russian troops, issued a martial law, and drafted all eligible men. This started the military campaign that became known as the Second Chechen war.

The Second Chechen war was much more successful for the Russian side, whose initial objective was to create a pro-Russian security zone in the northen part of Chechnya. By October 5, federal forces had taken contol of about two-thirds of the northern Chechnya, securing its positions up to the Terek River. On October 15, the commander of the federal forces in the Caucasus, General Viktor Kazantsev, announced that the security zone had been successfully created and that his forces would move to the second objective of the operation, the elimination of militant forces throughout Chechnya. In late October, Russian troops started a surface-to-surface missile strike on Grozny and air bombing of the second largest city in the republic, Gudermes, heavily fortified by the Chechen forces. On November 12, 1999, Gudermes fell to the Russian troops. By the end of November, the Russian forces had almost completely encircled Grozny, taking under their control all but the southern approaches to the city. On November 26, 1999, Valery Manilov, deputy chief of staff of the federal army, announced that the second phase of the operation was almost complete and that the final phase—the elimination of Chechen paramilitary groups in the mountains and restoration of law and order—was about to begin. In December, Russian authorities issued a warning to all residents of Grozny to leave the city by December 11—the starting day of a full-scale attack on the city. Intense fighting over Grozny lasted until early February 2000, when federal troops forced the Chechen fighters to leave the city and retreat to the southern mountains.

On June 8, 2000, President Putin issued a decree imposing direct rule of Chechnya and appointed Akhmed-hadji Kadyrov to head the temporary administration of the republic. In response, President Maskhadov returned as a guerrilla leader and denounced Kadyrov as a traitor. Until his death in 2005, Maskhadov was viewed as a primary leader of the Chechen separatist movement, who carried out organized resistance against the Russian forces and orches-

trated several assassination attempts on Kadyrov. The Russian authorities named Maskhadov the second–most-wanted terrorist and placed a $10 million bounty on his capture.

On October 23, 2002, a group of 50 Chechen militants, 32 men and 18 women led by Movsar Barayev, occupied a Moscow theater in the Dubrovka area of Moscow, taking hostage about 900 theatergoers and theater staff. After securing the building, the hostage takers demanded the complete withdrawal of the Russian troops from Chechnya within a week. They also agreed to free the child hostages if they (the militants) were allowed to meet with the press. The reporters were allowed in, and the attackers released 200 people, most of whom were women,

A video still of a Russian news broadcast shows members of a Chechen rebel group speaking to journalists inside the theater building they captured in Moscow on October 23, 2002. Russian special forces stormed the theater in the early morning of October 26, 2002, bringing an end to the crisis. Of over 800 hostages taken, 129 died, most of whom succumbed to the gas used by rescuers. (AFP/Getty Images)

children, and Muslims. However, the further negotiations with the rebels attempted by several members of the Duma were not successful, and no clear official policy was determined by the Putin administration. Finally, on the early morning of the third day, Russian special forces stormed the building, suspecting that the hostage takers had started executing hostages. During the storming, an unidentified narcotic gas was used to subdue the hostage takers, all of whom were killed.

Altogether, 129 hostages died in the takeover; 2 were shot by terrorists, and the others died through a combination of the gas, lack of food and water, and lack of adequate medical treatment following the raid. On the afternoon of the same day, in a televised address President Putin publicly apologized for the hostages' deaths, asking forgiveness for not being able to save everyone, thanked the special forces for their bravery in rescuing almost 750 people, and stated that the siege "proved that Russia cannot be brought down to its knees" (Glassner and Baker 2002). However, the public reaction to the storming was mixed. Public polls conducted in Moscow showed that city residents were split over the support of the use of force, whereas people living outside the city limits mostly supported the government's actions (Public Opinion Foundation 2002). Also, a number of anti-Chechen–war demonstrations took place in Moscow during the siege. In response, in a joint effort, President Putin banned antiwar protests, and the Duma passed a bill limiting press coverage of antiterrorist operations. In addition, the Duma rejected a proposal to create an independent commission to investigate the handling of the crisis.

On March 23, 2003, a new Chechen constitution was passed in a referendum. The Russian authorities claimed that the referendum commanded almost 88 percent turnout, with more than 96 percent voting in favor of the constitution. The new constitution firmly declared Chechnya part of the Russian Federation, stating specifically in Chapter 1, Article 1, that "[t]he territory of the Chechen Republic is one and indivisible and forms an inalienable part of the territory of the Russian Federation" (Constitution of the Chechen Republic 2003). On March 24, 2003, President Putin praised the referendum as a positive step toward normalization of the situation in Chechnya and added that it "resolved the last serious problem relating to Russia's territorial integrity" (BBC 2003). Following the referendum, a new presidential election was held. The result of the election was that Kadyrov became the new Chechen president, reaffirming his commitment to preserving the territorial integrity of the Russian Federation.

External Military Intervention

There has been no external military intervention by any state. The Russian Federation insisted that the war in Chechnya was a matter of Russian internal affairs and strongly opposed any third side's intervention in the conflict. However, foreign mercenaries, mainly from Arab countries, and Wahhabi volunteers took an active part in the conflict. Arab mercenaries appeared in Chechnya as early as 1994, when the Jordanian commander Khattab brought approximately 200 ex-Afghan fighters to train newly recruited Chechen forces. Khattab quickly earned the rank of second in command and became known as "the king of mercenaries." During the Second Chechen war, Russian officials attributed to the Arab mercenaries and Wahhabi volunteers the operation of a large set of training camps in Chechnya and in Dagestan, Azerbaijan, and Georgia. According to Russian officials, these training camps included suicide bomber camps and were financed by radical Islamic organizations such as the Muslim Brotherhood and al-Qaeda (Allenova 2004). However, other sources argue that the Russian government heavily exaggerated the degree of involvement of Arab mercenaries and Wahabbi volunteers in the conflict (Dunlop 1998).

Conflict Management Efforts

Although the international community mainly ignored the Chechen problem prior to the war, it made several attempts to monitor and manage the conflict once it started. In March 1995, the Organization for Security and Cooperation in Europe (OSCE) reached an agreement with the Russian government to establish a permanent OSCE presence in Chechnya. The OSCE's assistance group in Grozny existed from late April 1995 until late October 1999, when it pulled out for security reasons. During this period, the group was actively involved in documenting abuses of human rights, providing humanitarian relief, and taking part in negotiations between the sides.

Conclusion

Although by ratifying the constitution of 2003, the Chechen electorate confirmed the republic's status as an inalienable part of the Russian Federation, fighting between the federal troops and the Chechen separatists continued, and terrorist attacks carried out by Chechen militants remained a major threat to Russian national security. On May 12, 2003, two suicide bombers drove a truck full of explosives into a government administration and security complex in Znamenskoye, in northern Chechnya, killing 59 people and wounding many others. Only two days later, on May 14, 2003, two female suicide bombers killed at least 16 people and wounded 145 in a suicide bomb attack during a religious festival in the town of Iliskhan-Yurt, east of Grozny. On June 5, 2003, a female suicide bomber ambushed a bus carrying Russian air force officers and pilots in Mozdok (North Ossetiya), near Chechnya, and blew up the bus, killing herself and 18 other people.

To appeal to Chechen militants and to prevent further terrorist attacks, on June 6, 2003, the Duma approved a partial amnesty for Chechen separatists who were willing to disarm. President Putin stated that this measure would stabilize the situation inside the Chechen Republic as well as reduce the threat of further terrorist attacks (*Duma News* 2003). However, two parties in the Duma, the liberal opposition

Yabloko and the ultranationalists, opposed the amnesty. Sergei Mitrokhin, the deputy chairman of Yabloko, publicly called the amnesty a public relations stunt and stated that, under the condition of continuous fighting, the amnesty had no chance of promoting peace (Gazeta.ru 2003). The West's reaction to the amnesty was negative as well, mostly due to the fact that the amnesty provided protection to Russian solders accused of committing crimes against civilians in Chechnya.

Only a month after the Duma passed the amnesty, on July 5, 2003, two women suicide bombers killed 15 and injured 60 people at an open-air rock festival at Moscow's Tushino airfield. On August 1, 2003, another terrorist attack took place in Mozdok in North Ossetiya. This time, a suicide bomber killed at least 50 people at the town's military hospital. Starting in December 2003, Chechen militants increased their activity in Moscow and other Russian cities. On December 5, 2003, Chechen militants were tied to an explosion on a commuter train in the Stavropol region that killed at least 36 people and injured more than 150. On December 9, 2003, a female suicide bomber exploded her bomb in the center of Moscow near Hotel Natsional and the State Duma building, killing at least 6 people and injuring 11 others. On February 6, 2004, a deadlier attack took place in Moscow's subway—a rush-hour explosion on a commuter train killed 41 and injured 70. The situation inside the Chechen Republic remained highly unstable, with Maskhadov continuous attempts to overthrow Kadyrov's pro-Kremlin administration. Finally, on May 9, 2004, Akhmedhadji Kadyrov was killed and Russia's top military commander in the North Caucasus critically injured by explosive devices detonated under their seats on Grozny's Dinamo stadium during a military parade celebrating the 59th anniversary of the Russian victory in World War II. Following Kadyrov's death, Aslan Maskhadov announced in a radio interview that his forces were ready to switch to offensive tactics, specifically the targeting of Russian military sites. On

June 22, 2004 (the sixty-third anniversary of the beginning of the Great Patriotic War, when the Soviet Union was occupied by Nazi Germany), open fighting erupted between separatist forces and federal troops in Ingushetia (bordering Chechnya in the south) after Chechen militants launched coordinated attacks on security, administrative, and policy buildings in the cities of Nazran, Ordzhonikidzevskaya, and Karabulak.

On August 29, 2004, a presidential election was held in Chechnya. The participation was 85 percent, with 73.48 percent of the votes cast for Alu Alkhanov, a Russia-supported candidate. Maskhadov and other Chechen rebels refused to accept the results of the election and vowed to assassinate the new president. Just two days after the election, the Chechen separatists carried out one of their cruelest attacks. On the morning of September 1, the first day of school throughout the Russian federation, a group of 30 armed Chechen terrorists seized Beslan's Middle School Number One, taking 1,300 hostages, most of whom were schoolchildren seven to eighteen years old. The terrorists moved all hostages to the school gym, mined the gym and the rest of the school building with explosive devices, and threatened to execute 50 children for every one of their own killed in a rescue operation. The Russian officials said that they would not use force to free the hostages and agreed to start negotiations with the attackers. The Russian side was represented by pediatrician Leonid Roshal, for whom the hostage takers asked specifically. However, on September 2, negotiations between Roshal and the attackers reached a stalemate, with the hostage takers refusing even to allow food and water to be delivered to the children. To support the Russian side in negotiations, Ruslan Aushev, a former president of Ingushetia, volunteered to talk to the hostage takers. As a result of his negotiations, the attackers agreed to release to him 26 nursing mothers and their infants but refused to make any further concessions. Soon after that, two explosions took place in the school, but the federal forces were given orders not to fire. The next day, the hostage takers al-lowed federal security troops to remove bodies from school grounds. However, when medical workers and security troops arrived at the agreed-upon pickup point, the attackers fired, and two large explosions took place in the school. One of the explosions broke the gymnasium's wall; a group of about 30 hostages tried to escape while being fired upon by the hostage takers. At this point, the Russian troops were given orders to storm the building. The assault lasted for more than two hours, during which the hostage takers activated the rest of the explosives, completely destroying the gym and setting the rest of the building on fire. In the siege, 331 civilians died, including 156 children and 11 solders. Shortly after the siege, Shamil Basaev claimed responsibility for it and stated that he personally had trained the hostage takers. He also stated that the bloody outcome and the death of so many children was on Putin's hands and that the attackers would have let the hostages go if their demand for an immediate end to the war in Chechnya had been met (BBC News 2004).

Even among the separatist leadership, not everyone was willing to accept the blame for the Beslan tragedy. In his official statement, on September 23, 2004, Aslan Maskhadov unconditionally declared that neither he nor separatist forces under his command had anything to do with the Beslan attack. However, he noted that the Beslan tragedy and similar acts came as "a consequence of and reaction to the genocidal war of the Russian government against the Chechen nation, during which the Russian army has killed 250,000 people, including 42,000 children" (Maskhadov 2004). In addition, Maskhadov called on the international community to create an international tribunal to investigate crimes committed by both sides during the war.

In its turn, the international community uniformly condemned the terrorists' actions. On the first day of the attack, President George W. Bush offered "any form" of support to Russia. In addition, the Russian Federation asked for an emergency meeting of the United Nations Security Council on the evening of the same day. The members of the council condemned the attack and demanded "the immediate and unconditional release of all hostages of the terrorist attack" (Utro.ru 2004). German Chancellor Gerhard Schröder publicly stated that the sole responsibility for the tragedy should be placed on the terrorists. However, many other European leaders did not agree with Schröder and demanded an explanation from the Russian government on the handling of the situation. Specifically, it was believed that the use of flamethrowers by the Russian security forces and shelling by Russian tanks led to the high number of casualties among the hostages. In response, Putin rejected any allegations against the federal security forces and promised to get even tougher in the fight against terrorists. The results of the domestic investigation of the Beslan events, however, confirmed the use of tanks and flamethrowers in the assault. Nevertheless, according to the deputy prosecutor general of the Russian Federation, Vladimir Kolesnikov, neither the flamethrowers nor the shelling caused any casualties among the hostages (Kommersant 2005).

Although the Beslan tragedy shocked the Russian public and the international community and caused disagreement within the leadership of the Chechen separatist forces, it did not put an end to the conflict. Fighting between the federal troops and the Chechen militants led by Aslan Maskhadov continued, especially in the southern region of the republic. On March 8, 2005, the Alfa and Vympel special force units of the Federal Security Service (FSB) carried out an operation in the village of Tolstoi-Yurt, located twenty miles north of Grozny. According to Ilya Shabalkin, spokesman for the federal forces in the North Caucasus, during the operation the special forces exploded a bunker, killing Aslan Maskhadov (Jamestown Foundation 2005). Chechen First Deputy Prime Minister Ramzan Kadyrov, son of the assassinated president, welcomed the news, stating that with Maskhadov's death the separatist forces would lose their potency and popular appeal (Kommersant 2005).

However, Shamil Basayev called on all Chechens to continue their resistance and announced that Abdul-Khalim Sadulayev, a field commander and former head of Chechnya's Islamic Court, was elected the new leader of the separatist forces.

In August 2005, in his interview with Polish newspaper *Gazeta Wyborcza* (Kavkaz Center 2005), Abdul-Khalim Sadulayev stated that, indeed, Aslan Maskhadov's death was a great loss to the Chechen resistance; however, in no way did it signify an end of that resistance. On the contrary, it would serve as an inspiration to those who are alive in their struggle against the Russian occupiers. When asked about the prospects for the end of the war, Sadulayev stated that the Chechens would never end their resistance and submit to the Russian rule; that instead they would continue to fight until the total independence of the republic was attained (ChechenPress 2005). This unyielding position of the Chechen separatist leadership, combined with the equally unyielding resolve of the Putin administration to preserve the territorial integrity of the Russian Federation, leaves a little hope for a complete end to the conflict in the near future.

Indeed, as this article was written, pro-Chechen militants launched another major attack. On October 13, 2005, they targeted the city of Nalchik, the capital of the Kabardino-Balkar Republic in Southern Russia. During the attack, the militants occupied the policy and other governmental buildings and took civilian hostages. In response, President Putin sent 1,500 regular troops and 500 special forces to retake the city. At least 90 people were killed, including 72 rebels, 12 police, and 12 civilians.

Tatyana A. Karaman

Chronology

November 30, 1994   Boris Yeltzin issues presidential decree, *About Measures to Return Constitutionality and Law and Order on the Territory of the Chechen Republic,* which stipulates immediate disarmament and liquidation of all military formations in the territory of Chechnya.

December 1, 1994   Air strike on Grozny begins.

December 6, 1994   Russian Minister of Defense Pavel Grachev and Chechen President Dudayev meet in the Republic of Ingushetia (Russia).

December 11, 1994   Boris Yeltzin signs presidential decree, *About Measures to Provide Law and Order and Public Safety on the Territory of the Chechen Republic.* Russian troops enter Chechnya.

December 31, 1994   Russian forces begin assault on Grozny.

January 18, 1995   Chechen Presidential Guards leave the Presidential Residency.

March 6, 1995   Russian troops take complete control of Grozny.

March–April 1995   Fighting continues over rural and mountainous regions of Chechnya.

April 27, 1995   Yeltzin signs decree, *About a Unilateral Armistice for the Period from April 28, 1995 to May 12, 1995.*

May 18, 1995   Russian troops renew fighting for control over mountainous regions of Chechnya.

June 14, 1995   Separatists under Shamil Basaev take hostages in Budenovsk, Russia.

June 19, 1995–July 20, 1995   Three rounds of negotiations take place in Grozny between the Russian and Chechen delegations.

August 1, 1995   Maskhadov, Chechen army chief of staff, issues order for immediate voluntary disarmament of Chechen military formations and cease-fire.

October 9, 1995   Russian Federation unilaterally withdraws from the cease-fire negotiations and renews military operations.

January 1, 1996–January 18, 1996   Chechen separatists take hostages in Kislyar and Pervomayskoe.

January–May 1996   Fighting continues over rural and mountainous regions of Chechnya.

May 27, 1996   Negotiations take place in Moscow between Boris Yeltzin and a Chechen delegation headed by Yandarbiev. Cease-fire agreement is signed by both sides.

June 4, 1996–June 11, 1996   To continue the Moscow agreement, negotiations take place in Nazran, capital of Ingushetia, between a Russian delegation headed by Ivan Rybkin, Security Council secretary, and a Chechen delegation led by Movladi Udugov, acting first vice premier. Agreement is reached for phased withdrawal of all federal forces from Chechnya, complete disarmament of all separatists' military and paramilitary groups, and end of all military actions by August 30, 1996.

August 2, 1999   Islamic extremists led by Shamil Basayev and Jordanian-born militant Khattab cross into neighboring Dagestan and in five days capture the villages of Rahata and Ansolta in the Botlikhsky district.

September 1999   A series of middle-of-the-night explosions take place in Moscow, Volgograd, and Buinaksk apartments, killing more than 300 people.

September 30, 1999   Second Chechen war begins.

November 12, 1999   Gudermes falls to Russian troops.

December 1999–February 2000   Intensive fighting over Grozny continues.

February 1, 2000   Grozny falls to Russian troops.

June 8, 2000   President Putin issues decree imposing direct rule of Chechnya and appoints Akhmed-hadji Kadyrov to head temporary administration of the republic.

October 23, 2002   Chechen militants occupy a Moscow theater in the Dubrovka area of Moscow, taking hostage about 900 theatergoers and theater staff.

March 23, 2003   New Chechen constitution is passed in a referendum.

June 6, 2003   Duma approves partial amnesty for Chechen separatists.

October 5, 2003   Akhmad Kadyrov is elected president of Chechnya with 82.5 percent of votes.

May 9, 2004   Akhmad Kadyrov is assassinated.

August 29, 2004   New pro-Russian president, Alu Alkhanov, is elected. Ramzan Kadyrov, son of the former president, becomes vice president.

September 1, 2004   Chechen terrorists take hundreds of children and adults hostage in a school in the North Ossetian town of Beslan (Russian Federation). Russian special forces storm the school after a three-day siege; 331 civilians, including 156 children, are killed.

March 8, 2005   Russian special forces assassinate former separatist president, Aslan Maskhadov.

October 13, 2005   Chechen militants occupy Nalchik, capital of the Kabardino-Balkar Republic in Southern Russia.

List of Acronyms
FSB: Federal Security Service
OSCE: Organization for Security and Cooperation in Europe

References

Abubakarov, Taymaz. 1998. Rezhim Dshokhara Dudaeva: Pravda i Vymysel; Zapiski Dudaki.

Allenova, Olga. 2004. "Terrorist Act Contract." *Kommersant: Russia's Daily Online*. www.kommersant.com (accessed February 24, 2004).

BBC News. 2003. "What Comes After the Referendum (in Russian)." March 25. news.bbc.co.uk/hi/russian/news/newsid_28860 00/2886183.stm (accessed January 12, 2006).

BBC News. 2004. "Excerpts: Basayev Claims Beslan." June 17. news.bbc.co.uk/1/hi/world/europe/3665136.st m (November 16, 2006).

Bennet, Vanora. 1998. *Crying Wolf: The Return of War to Chechnya*. London: Picador.

Blank, Stephen J., and Earl H. Tilford, Jr. 1995. *Russia's Invasion of Chechnya: A Preliminary Assessment*. Carlisla Barracks, PA: Strategic Studies Institute.

Bloed, Arie. 2000a. "The OSCE and the Conflict in Chechnya," *Helsinki Monitor* 11(2): 58–59.

Bloed, Arie. 2000b. "The OSCE Returns to Chechnya?" *Helsinki Monitor* 11(3): 83–84.

Busygina, Irina. 1997. "The OSCE in Chechnya." In *Balancing Hegemony: The OSCE in the CIS*, edited by Neil S. MacFarlane and Oliver Thränert, 115–21. Kingston/Ontario: Queens University Centre for International Relations.

Cassidy, Robert. 2003. "Russia in Afghanistan and Chechnya: Military Strategic Culture and the Paradoxes of Asymmetric Conflict" (monograph). www.strategicstudiesinstitute. army.mil/Pubs/people.cfm?q=96 (accessed November 16, 2006).

ChechenPress. 2005. Interview with Abdul-Khalim Sadulayev. (accessed June 12, 2005).

Chechnya.Ru. No date. "Chechnya: Historical Overview." www.chechnya.ru/view_all.php? part=hist&offset=17 (accessed November 30, 2006).

Cherkasov, Alexander. 2004. *Book of Numbers, Book of Loss* [Kniga chisel. Kniga utrat]. In Russian. www.mhg.ru/publications/370D65E (accessed November 30, 2006).

Constitution of the Chechen Republic. 2003. www.oefre.unibe.ch/law/icl/cc00000_.html (accessed November 16, 2006).

Curran, Diane, Fiona Hill, and Elena Kostritsyna. 1997. *The Search for Peace in Chechnya: A Sourcebook 1994–1996*. Cambridge, MA: Harvard University Press.

Daniszewski, John. 2002. "Moscow Says Turkey and Qatar aiding Chechens."

www.smh.com.au/articles/2002/11/01/1036027 036824.html (accessed November 16, 2006).

Dudaevskogo Ministra Ekonomiki i Finansov [The Regime of Dshokhar Dudayev: Truth and Fiction; Notes of Dudayev's Minister of Economics and Finances]. Moscow: INSAN.

Duma News. 2003. "New Chechen Amnesty." duma.hro.org/2003/06/04.htm (accessed November 23, 2006). June 6. In Russian.

Dunlop, John. 1998. *Russia Confronts Chechnya: Roots of a Separatist Conflict*. Cambridge, UK: Cambridge University Press.

Furman, Dmitrii Efimovich. 1999. *Chechnia i Rossiia: Obshchestva i Gosudarstva* [Chechnya and Russia: Societies and States]. Moscow: Polinform-Talburi.

Gall, Carlotta, and Thomas de Waal. 1997. *Chechnya: A Small Victorious War*. London: Macmillan.

Gall, Carlotta, and Thomas De Waal. 1998. *Chechnya: Calamity in the Caucasus*. New York: New York University Press.

Gazeta.Ru. 2003. "Amnesty Bill Approved Amid Security Fears." www.gazeta.ru/2003/06/06/ Amnestybilla.shtml (accessed 11/16/2006). June 6.

Glassner, Susan, and Peter Baker. 2002. "Russian Seizes Theater from Militants in Bloody Battle." *Washington Post*, October 26, A01.

Goltz, Thomas. 2003. *Chechnya Diary: A War Correspondent's Story of Surviving the War in Chechnya*. New York: Thomas Dunne Books.

Hansen, Greg. 1996. *War and Humanitarian Action in Chechnya*. Providence, RI: Thomas J. Watson Institute for International Studies.

Henze, Paul B. 1995. *Islam in the North Caucasus: The Example of Chechnya*. Santa Monica, CA: RAND.

Human Development Report. 2002. "Deepening Democracy in a Fragmented World." hdr.undp. org/reports/global/2002/en/.

Iskandarian, Aleksander. 1997. "War and Social Change in Chechnya." In *Balancing Hegemony: The OSCE in the CIS*, edited by Neil S. MacFarlane and Oliver Thränert, 111–15. Kingston/Ontario: Queens University Centre for International Relations.

Jamestown Foundation. 2005. "Maskhadov Killed." March 9. jamestown.org/publications_ details.php?volume_id=409&issue_id=3256& article_id=2369385 (accessed November 16, 2006).

Kavkaz Center. 2005. "Russia's Tactics Make Chechen War Spread Across Caucasus." 72.14.

209.104/search?q=cache:ylIBNdABBfYJ:www.
kavkaz.org.uk/eng/content/2005/09/16/4074.
shtml+Sadulayev+interview+Polish&hl=en&
gl=us&ct=clnk&cd=2 (accessed November 30,
2006).

Knezys, Stasys. 1999. *The War in Chechnya.*
College Station: Texas A&M University Press.

Kommersant. 2005. "Prosecutor General Reached
the Approved Conclusion." October 21.
kommersant.com/p619765/ Prosecutor_
General_Reached_ the_Approved_Conclusion/
(accessed November 16, 2006).

Kommersant. 2005. "Aslan Maskhadov Killed. "
March 9. www.kommersant.com/p552963/
Aslan_Maskhadov_Killed/ (accessed November
16, 2006).

Kop'ev, Andrei. 1997. *Chechensky Kapkan* [The
Chechen Trap]. Moscow: Rodina.

Kulikov, Anatolii S., and Sergei A. Lembik. 2000.
*Chechenskii uzel: khronik vooruzhennogo
konflikta 1994–1996* [The Chechen Knot:
Chronicle of the Armed Conflict 1994–1996.].
Moscow: Dom Pedagogiki.

Lieven, Anotol. 1998. *Chechnya, Tombstone of
Russian Power.* New Haven, CT: Yale University
Press.

Lohman, Diederik. 2000. "The International
Community Fails to Monitor Chechnya
Abuses." *Helsinki Monitor* 11(3): 73–82.

Marshal, Monty, Keith Jaggers, and Ted Robert
Gurr. 2004. Polity IV www.cidcm.umd.edu/
polity/.

Maskhadov, Aslan. 2004. "Official Statement by
President of the Chechen Republic of
Ichkeria." Ministry of Foreign Affairs of the
Chechen Republic of Ichkeria. www.
chechnya-mfa.info/print_news.php?func=
detail&par=123.

Mulvey, Stephen. 2000. "Analysis: Chechen War on
the Web." *BBC News Online.*
news.bbc.co.uk/1/hi/world/europe/619180.stm
(accessed June 12, 2005).

Muzaev, Timur Magomedovich. 1999.
*Chechenskii Krizis—99: Politicheskoe
Protivostaianie v Ichkerii: Rasstanovka Sil,
Chronika, Fakty* [The Chechen Crisis—99:
Political Confrontation in Ichkeria: The
Arrangement of Forces, Chronicle, Facts].
Moscow: Informatsionno-Ekspertnaia Gruppa
Panoram.

National Anthem of the Chechen Republic of
Ichkeria. Chechenpress State News Agency.
Official Web page of Chechen separatist forces.
www.chechenpress.org. English version

available at www.kavkazcenter.com (accessed
October 16, 2005).

Nikulina, Natal'ya. 2000. "Poolya v Sninoo
[Bullet in the Back]." *Slovo*
(February)129–142.

Orlov, Oleg Petrovich. *Rossiia—Chechnia: Tsep'
Oshibok i Prestuplenii* [Russia—Chechnya: A
Chain of Mistakes and Crimes]. 1998.
Moscow: Zvenia.

Pravda. 2002. "Chechnya: Information" English.
pravda.ru/hotspots/2002/11/14/39481.html
(accessed December 1, 2006). November 14.

Public Opinion Foundation. 2002. "The Actions of
the Authorities: The 'Only Right Move'"
(Report). bd.english.fom.ru/report/map/
presnyakova/ed024433 (accessed November 16,
2006).

Panico, Christopher. 1995. *Conflicts in the
Caucasus: Russia's War in Chechnya.* London:
Research Institute for the Study of Conflict and
Terrorism.

Politkovskaia, Anna. 2001. *A Dirty War: A
Russian Reporter in Chechnya.* London:
Harvill.

Politkovskaia, Anna. 2003. *A Small Corner of Hell:
Dispatches from Chechnya.* Chicago: University
of Chicago Press.

Seely, Robert. 2001. *Russo-Chechen Conflict,
1800–2000: A Deadly Embrace.* London:
Frank Cass.

Smith, Sebastian. 2001. *Allah's Mountains: The
Battle for Chechnya.* London: I. B. Tauris.

Tishkov, Valery A. 1997. *Ethnicity, Nationalism and
Conflict in and After the Soviet Union: The Mind
Aflame.* London: Sage.

Tishkov, Valery A. 2004. *Chechnya: The Making of
a War-Torn Society.* Berkeley: University of
California Press.

Troshev, Gennadii. 2002. *Moia Voina: Chechenskii
Dnevnik Okopnogo Generala* [My War: The
Chechen Diary of a Trench General]. Moscow:
Vagrius.

USSR Population Census 1989. [Itogi Vsesoiuznoy
perepisi naseleniia 1989 goda]. 1996.
Minneapolis: East View Publications.

Utro.ru. 2004. "Putin Accepts Condolences
[Putin prinimaet soboleznovaniya]." www.
utro.ru/articles/2004/09/02/346709.shtml
(accessed November 30, 2006). In Russian.
September 2.

World Bank. 2004. The World Bank Group: Data
& Statistics. www.worldbank.org/data/.

Yanchenkov, Vladimir. 2000. "Outcasts in Their
Own Land [Izgoi na rodnoi zemle]." *Trud.*

www.trud.ru/trud.php?id=200002170300502. In Russian. February 17. 5.

Zarakhovich, Yuri. 1996. "Terms of War and Peace: Chechen Leader Jokhar Dudayev." *Time* (March 4): 43

Zelkina, Anna. 2000. "The Chechen Future in the Russian Federation." *Helsinki Monitor* (March): 42–52.

Zorin, Vladimir. 1997. *Chechhnya: Difficult Road to Peace.* Moscow: Violanta.

Rwanda
(1990–1994)

Introduction

The Rwandan civil war, which lasted from October 1, 1990, until 1994, was by far the most intense conflict Rwanda has experienced. Between 3,025 and 5,500 people died in the midst of the conflict in addition to the 800,000 killed during the genocide (Jones 1999a). An estimated 10 percent of the total population lost their lives during the last three months of the conflict, and 30 percent were forced into exile (Prunier 1999).

The "October War" began when a Tutsi refugee rebel group, the Rwandan Patriotic Front (RPF), launched a surprise attack from Uganda on October 1, 1990. The conflict lasted four years and was characterized by different phases of escalation and deescalation. Efforts at mitigating the conflict were put forward as early as fifteen days after the outbreak of the war. These efforts led to the Arusha peace agreements, brokered by the Organization of African Unity (OAU), signed on August 4, 1993. However, on April 6, 1994, Habyarimana's plane was shot down by unidentified assailants. The event triggered wide-ranging massacres by Hutu militias of Tutsi and Hutu moderates sympathetic to the peace process, thus renewing the civil war. Large-scale fighting continued for another 100 days and culminated in the capture of Kigali by the RPF on July 19, 1994 (Jones 1999a). Soon afterward, exiled Hutu militias in Zaire (now named the Democratic Republic of the Congo,

DRC) would work to resuscitate the civil war engulfing the Great Lakes region in regional crisis (Kuperman 2000; Prunier 1995).

This article focuses on the underlying causes of the civil war in Rwanda and the process through which the war culminated in genocide in 1994 (The Convention on Genocide defines *genocide* as "acts committed with the intention to destroy, wholly or in part, a national ethnic, racial or religious group," according to the United Nations General Assembly 1948, article 2). Subsequent conflict management efforts are examined, as are some basic lessons learned from international intervention during the civil war.

Country Background

Rwanda is a landlocked country located in East Central Africa, in the Great Lakes region. The country, whose capital is Kigali, extends over 26,338 square kilometers, a size comparable to that of Belgium. The total population is 8.4 million, of which 84 percent are Hutu, 14 percent are Tutsi, and 1 percent are Twa. More than half of Rwandans are Roman Catholic (56.5 percent); other religions include Protestant (26 percent), Adventist (11.1 percent), and Muslim (4.6 percent). Official languages include Kinyarwanda, the universal Bantu vernacular, as well as French and English (CIA 2005).

Rwanda attained independence from Belgium on July 1, 1962, when the Hutu, after having won the parliamentary elections in 1961, installed the first Hutu-led republic. For the first time in Rwandan history, the Hutu majority in Rwanda was taking the reins of power from a Tutsi minority, which had been the ruling elite since pre-colonial times. Although the Hutu claimed a multiparty regime, the country soon became a de facto single-party system under President Kayibanda (1962–1973) and later under Habyarimana (1973–1994). Both regimes were described as autocratic (Doyle and Sambanis 2000; Polity IV 2003). Executive power was purposely selected from a small political elite (the akazu), political opposition was suppressed, and a policy of Tutsi exclusion was carefully implemented.

Economically, the country attained an enviable position in comparison with its neighbors. Gross domestic product (GDP) per capita rose steadily from US $514 in 1960 to US $731 in 1985, mostly owing to coffee exports. By 1985, Rwanda was considered a successful African economy and an "oasis of progress" in sub-Saharan Africa (Heston, Summers, and Aten 2002; Sellström, Wohlgemuth, and NAI, 1996; Smith 2002, 150). However, after the collapse of coffee prices in 1986, the Rwandan economy suffered considerably (Prunier 1995). Between 1989 and 1993, the decline averaged about 40 percent. In September 1990, one month prior to the RPF invasion, structural adjustment programs (SAPs) were implemented. For many scholars, these structural factors—economic and political—became permissive conditions that contributed to the weakening of the regime's legitimacy, capacity, and authority and favored insurgency (Des Forges 1999; Fearon and Laitin 2003; Smith 2002).

Conflict Background

The RPF invasion of 1990 is closely interconnected with repeated Tutsi refugee invasions from Uganda and Burundi following Rwanda's independence (Sellström, et al. 1996). In fact, persist-ent Tutsi repression by Hutu governments in post-colonial Rwanda and the subsequent movement of tens of thousands of Tutsi refugees in neighboring countries paved the way for the creation of a rebel movement (*inkotanyi*, "refugee warriors") in Uganda and Burundi, which would later become the Rwandan Patriotic Front. Inkotanyi were fighting not only for Tutsi protection but also for repatriation to their homeland. From 1961 until 1990, inkotanyi periodically invaded Rwanda from Uganda and Burundi in response to pogroms against domestic Tutsi in Rwanda (Jones 1999a; Lema 2000; Otunnu 1999a). The RPF invasion in Rwanda in 1990 was aimed not only at refugee repatriation of Tutsi but also at destabilizing the regime to ultimately bring about political change (Lema 2000). Most agree that by 1990 the civil war had become ethnically based because it involved the Tutsi-led RPF against the Hutu-led government forces (Doyle and Sambanis 2000; MAR 2000; Uppsala Conflict Database Project 2003). The civil war is also characterized as a "communal contender," since the two groups were struggling for a hold on power. The Minorities at Risk (MAR) project defines *communal contenders* as "culturally distinct peoples, tribes, or clans in heterogeneous societies [that] hold or seek a share in state power" (2000).

Although the RPF used Uganda as a launching pad for the invasion, the Rwandan civil war was an internal or intrastate conflict because it was organized and launched by Rwandan Tutsi against the Rwandan Hutu government. Uganda, Zaire, and Burundi all contributed to the conflict, providing arms or human resources to the rebels, the Hutu militias, and the government forces, but this involvement was, at most, irregular and unofficial, and no regular troops were provided (Doyle and Sambanis 2000; Uppsala 2003; IISS 2005).

The Insurgents

The rebel force in Rwanda was known as the RPF and its military wing as the RPA (Rwandan Patriotic Army). The RPA was the "official"

Table 1: Civil War in Rwanda

War:	RPF vs. government forces (Rwandan Armed Forces)
Dates:	October 1, 1990–July 19, 1994
Casualties:	3,025–5,500 battle-related deaths (and 800,000 deaths during genocide)
Regime type prior to war:	Autocratic; high
Regime type after war:	Autocratic; medium-high
GDP per capita year war began:	US $870.04 (1990)
GDP per capita 5 years after war:	US $944.86 (1999)
Insurgents:	Rwanda Patriotic Front (RPF)
Issue:	Tutsi refugee repatriation; power struggle
Rebel funding:	Uganda; Tutsi diaspora
Role of geography:	RPF invades from Uganda; hides in highlands.
Role of resources:	Collapse of coffee prices, scarcity of arable lands contributes to conflict.
Immediate outcome:	RPF military victory; continued raids carried out by ex-RAF/Hutu militias in refugee camps in DRC
Outcome after 5 years:	Two invasions by RPF in DRC (1996, 1998); periodic invasions by AliR militias in Rwanda; conflict between DRC and Rwanda
Role of UN:	Peacekeeping force of 2,500 from October 1993; withdrawal of major contingents in 1994; Opération Turquoise in June 1994; UNAMIR extended until March 1996.
Role of regional organization:	Peace negotiation brokered by OAU from 1990; Arusha Peace Agreements signed August 4, 1993.
Refugees:	1.91–3.2 million (1995 estimate); 2 million(1998 estimate)
Prospects for peace:	Internal peace: Uncertain and elusive; Tutsi-led RPF retains hold on power. Regional peace: Cease-fire agreement signed in July 1999 between DRC, Uganda, and Rwanda; 8,000-15,000 FDLR members (2005) still hiding in DRC, to be disarmed and demobilized by MONUC.

Sources: Harff and Gurr 1998; Heston, Summers, and Aten 2002; IISS 2005; MAR 2000; Polity IV Project 2003; UNHCR 1995.

name of the armed branch of the RPF, although in practice the name *RPF* referred to both the political and the military wings of the movement (Prunier 1995). The RPF was created in 1987 in Kampala, Uganda, by Rwandan exiles, mainly Tutsi who had been living in Uganda for three generations. The rebel movement was led first by Major General Fred Rwigyema and later by General Paul Kagame.

The RPF was, in fact, an extension of the Rwandan Alliance for National Unity (RANU), which was created in 1979 by Tutsi radicals who were behind earlier inkotanyi invasions (Prunier 1995). Foreseeing in the mid-1980s that refugees would never return to Rwanda except through the use of force, many RANU members joined forces with the Ugandan National Resistance Army (NRA) to help General Museveni overthrow the Obote regime in Uganda in January

1986. This strategy would then allow the RPF, mainly composed of NRA soldiers, to reinforce its military capability to launch a stronger attack on the Hutu regime in Rwanda (Otunnu 1999a).

The RPF received most of its funding from Ugandan President Museveni and the Tutsi diaspora living abroad. Once the decision to attack Rwanda was made by July 1990, Rwigyema went on a fund-raising mission throughout the communities of Tutsi émigrés in Europe and North America. Financial contributions came from exile communities in Canada, the United States, and Europe, for they were the wealthiest, but also from larger communities of Tutsi in Africa (Prunier 1995; Sellström, et al. 1996).

Geography

Geography played a crucial role in the development of rebel tactics and strategies. Located in

Rwandan Patriotic Front leader Paul Kagame tours a rural area with his troops in 1993. Kagame became president of Rwanda in April 2000. (Joel Stettenheim/Corbis)

the Great Lakes region, Rwanda is bounded by four neighbors: Uganda in the north, Tanzania in the east, Burundi in the south, and Lake Kivu and the DRC in the west (Varga, Draman, Marriott, and Carment 2002). Not only do these countries share geographical boundaries, they also share culture and ethnic geography that influences rebels' strategic organizing (Gachuruzi 1999). Before the invasion in 1990, Tutsi-friendly regimes in Uganda and Burundi allowed the RPF to use their territory "as a sanctuary for the planning of attacks, stockpiling of weapons, raising funds and movement of troops" (Otunnu 1999b, 43).

The geography of the Great Lakes region is also conducive to guerrilla-style warfare (Varga, et al. 2002). Rwanda's mountainous and volcanic region along its northwest border with Uganda provided the RPF with easy access to Rwanda while at the same time allowing them to take refuge and hide when necessary. In general,

they used the cold, volcanic highlands for two reasons: to buy time and regroup, and to prepare for the next attack (Prunier 1995).

Tactics

The RPF's most important sources of arms were Uganda and to a lesser extent China, Libya, and Iraq. When the RPA was created in 1987, 3,000 Rwandans from the NRA defected, taking their personal weapons and ammunitions with them. Their weapons included heavy machine guns, mortars, BM-21 multiple rocket launchers, recoilless rifles, Russian ZUG light automatic cannons, land mines ranging from World War II–vintage mines to modern, nonmetallic, antipersonnel, and antitank types. Arms were also purchased from independent arms dealers in Africa and Eastern Europe, where the collapse of the former Soviet Union had been accompanied by a sharp drop in international weapon and ammunition prices

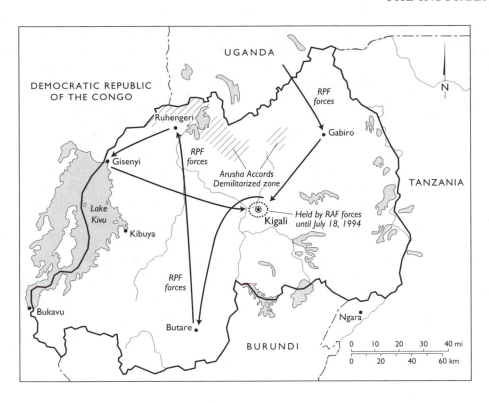

(Otunnu 1999b; Prunier 1995; Sellström, et al. 1996, Sislin and Pearson 2001).

Evidence also indicates that the RPF was supported by the Tutsi diaspora with regard to recruits. Émigrés in North America and Europe constituted an important part of the fighting forces. As Prunier argues, "[T]he émigré component of the early RPF recruitment gave it a very high average standard of education ... making it probably the best educated guerrilla force the world had ever seen" (1995, 117). This high level of education would contribute greatly to the RPF's efficiency as a fighting force. As the war extended, the RPF was frequently reinforced with child soldiers. As a result, prior to the invasion in 1990 the RPF numbered around 4,000 men. By early 1991, the RPF had grown to 5,000, by the end of 1992 to 12,000, and in April 1994, force size exceeded 25,000 (Sellström, et al. 1996). In terms of field operations, the RPF conducted what is referred to as a "typical guerrilla hit-and-run pattern of operations," which the Rwandan government

forces, even on the offensive, could not prevent (Prunier 1995, 135).

By contrast, the Rwandan government had, prior to the RPF invasion in 1990, an army of 5,000 men equipped with small arms (Kakwenzire and Kamukama 1999). France was the first to supply the Rwandan Armed Forces (RAF) and its Presidential Guard, providing heavy artillery and Gazelle helicopters. During the conflict, the RAF acquired its arms mainly from Egypt, South Africa, and the United States (Sislin and Pearson 2001). Financing of the RAF's war effort is believed to have come from neighboring Zaire through the illegal trade of the mantrax drug and from public enterprises such as Rwandex, Sonarwa, and Rwandatel (IISS 2005). In short, the internal economy was a main engine for the government's war effort, and the military consumed 38 percent of Rwanda's budget (Reyntjens 2000; SIPRI 2005; Uvin 1998). By mid-1992, the RAF had increased its human capability dramatically and boasted a total of 50,000 soldiers (Prunier 1995).

In addition, the Presidential Guard, as well as extremist forces within the Coalition pour la Défense de la République (CDR) and Mouvement Révolutionnaire National pour le Développement (MRND) political parties, used the same training techniques it had learned under French guidance to train paramilitaries and youths militias—known as Interahamwé and Impuzamugambi—"in extremist killer tactics" to prepare for the genocidal killings (Kakwenzire and Kamukama 1999, 78). The Interahamwé was attached to the MRND political party, and the Impuzamugambi was attached to the CDR party (Des Forges 1999). Beyond machetes, the RAF distributed automatic rifles and hand grenades to the militias (IISS 2005). It is estimated that, at the onset of genocide in 1994, militia size was between 15,000 and 30,000 (Kuperman 2000).

Causes of the War

Causes of protracted conflicts such as the civil war in Rwanda are numerous, complex, and, in many cases, cumulative. The following three sections document the factors that triggered the onset of civil war and genocide. The first and second sections examine permissive and proximate causes that prompted the RPF invasion in 1990, and third section examines the causes of the genocide.

Permissive Causes

Four main clusters of factors help explain the causes of internal conflict: cultural, political, economic, and environmental–demographic (Brown 1996). All four illustrate important permissive causes of the civil war in Rwanda.

Cultural Factors

Colonialism played a significant role in affecting perceptions between Hutus and Tutsis in Rwanda. The impact of European interaction with Rwandan society was important in defining social relations within the country's borders and in emphasizing ethnic differences (Jones 2001).

In precolonial times, the word *Tutsi* referred to a person rich in cattle, and the word *Hutu* referred to the mass of peasants who worked for them. Tutsis were thus the elite group (and represented the monarchy in precolonial Rwanda) and Hutus the subjects (Des Forges 1999). As in Burundi, Hutus and Tutsis were ordered in a social hierarchy in which there were a superordinate group, the Tutsis, and a subordinate group, the Hutus (Horowitz 1985). During colonial rule, German and Belgian rulers alike consolidated this power structure, reinforcing Tutsi superiority over Hutu (e.g., through the introduction of ethnic cards). This emphasis on ethnic difference in the allocation of power would be perpetuated following independence in 1962.

Group perceptions were also influenced by regional tensions, especially in neighboring Burundi, where both Hutus and Tutsis lived. Atrocities perpetrated against Hutus in Tutsi-led Burundi had a contagious effect in Hutu-led Rwanda following the independence, providing incentives to reproduce violence against Tutsis in Hutu-led Rwanda (Utterwulghe 1999). Violence against Hutus in Burundi and against Tutsis in Rwanda reinforced the fears of extinction and sentiments of mistrust on both sides. These fears would be strengthened in October 1993 following the coup d'état against Burundi's first Hutu government.

Political Factors

Ethnic discrimination and exclusionary politics against Tutsi in postcolonial Rwanda are other important factors that help to explain the motivations for rebel invasion in 1990. Following independence, the two Hutu regimes began implementing policies of ethnic ratios and regional quotas all over Rwanda, voluntarily excluding Tutsis from political power as a means of securing their own grip on power. They used methods of political mobilization that included using Tutsis as scapegoats. "Racism was propagated among Rwandan youth at school, through radio and theater," and the history syllabus portrayed Tutsis as "natural enemies of the Hutu" (Kakwenzire and Kamukama 1999, 72). Over and above such discrimination, the Hutu elite also used "targeted violence" against Tutsis, that ranged from individual assassination to limited massacres (Jones 2001, 16). Overall, the number of lives lost in anti-Tutsi riots between 1959 and 1973 is estimated to fall between 250,000 and 600,000 (Lema 2000; Prunier 1995; Utterwulghe 1999). Ethnic scapegoating as carried out by the Hutu government displaced and drove millions into exile (Payne and Dagne 2002).

Economic Factors

Discriminatory economic policies combined with the economic misfortunes of the 1980s constitute a third cluster of permissive factors motivating the rebel invasion of 1990. From 1973 onward, policies biased against Tutsi at the expense of a specific group of Hutu from the northwest region of Rwanda (affiliated with Habyarimana's akazu) in accessing land or capital slowly began to generate discontent in Rwanda. Wealth and power imbalances were not due to the "usual urban-rural disparities;" economic imbalances were due to a systematic discrimination that was becoming increasingly evident (Des Forges 1999, 46). When the economy slumped following the collapse in coffee prices in 1986, the popularity of Habyarimana's regime further declined. Discontent was echoed not only among Tutsi but also from within Habyarimana's Hutu party, especially among Hutu southerners who were increasingly victimized under Habyarimana's rule. By the end of the 1980s, intra-Hutu tensions had formed a widening cleavage (Kuperman 2000; Sellström, et al. 1996). This sent a signal to the RPF that the Habyarimana's authority was increasingly challenged and had weakened.

Demographic Pressure

Several authors argue that overpopulation and land scarcity played a key role in the outbreak of the Rwandan civil war and genocide (Prunier 1995; Renner 1996). In Rwanda, every square kilometer of arable land supported, on average,

> # The Rise and Fall of the Habyrimana Regime
>
> A "Tutsi overlord image" was used by both the Kayibanda and Habyarimana regimes as a means "to consolidate power for their own Hutu group" (Kakwenzire and Kamukama 1999, 72). When Tutsis invaded in 1961–1966, they were referred to as *inyenzi*—meaning cockroaches. These invasions are said to have radicalized politics, especially as Habyarimana made no attempts to redress the mounting ethnic problem. The unparalleled promotion of ethnic ideology is what helped keep alive and strengthen interethnic hatred, culminating in the genocide.
>
> By the late 1980s, the legitimacy of Habyarimana's regime was in sharp decline. "The leaders of the RPF in Uganda judged that time was ripe to declare war against the regime. In an interview broadcast by the Voice of America in the week of the outbreak of the October 1990 War, a spokesperson of the RPF rebellion justified the choice of this particular timing referring to the convergence of conditions, citing [among other things] the appropriation of national resources by the ruling elite and famine in the country . . ." (Gasana 2002, 219–20).

more than 400 people (Utterwulghe 1999). As Prunier argues, "[T]here was an increase in competition for access to that very specialized resource [agricultural lands], which could only be appropriated through direct control of government power at high levels" (1995, 84). On the other hand, other authors, such as Homer-Dixon, believe that "land scarcity played at most a peripheral role by reducing regime legitimacy in the countryside" (1999, 17). Although the overpopulation and land scarcity arguments remain very influential in current debates about the conflict, it is reasonable to say, rather, that a combination of factors prompted the civil war and genocide in Rwanda (African Rights 1995).

Proximate Causes

This section examines the proximate, or immediate, factors that triggered the onset of civil war.

First, the Ugandan and Rwandan policies regarding Tutsi refugees in exile in Uganda played a significant role in prompting the RPF invasion in Rwanda in 1990. In the 1980s, the Obote regime in Uganda and its continuous attacks on Rwandan refugees had motivated many to seek repatriation in Rwanda. Tutsi refugees further felt betrayed by Uganda when, after they had helped Museveni's NRA overthrow the Obote regime in 1986, Museveni vacated their position in the new government. In Rwanda, from 1987 until 1989 the issuance of government statements refusing to allow the immigration of large numbers of Tutsi refugees back into Rwanda was another proximate factor that prompted the RPF invasion. Back in 1990, 600,000 Tutsis (who constituted half of Rwanda's Tutsi population) lived outside of the country (Des Forges 1999; Prunier 1995; Sellström, et al. 1996). The massive repatriation of all Tutsi refugees was perceived as a threat to the fragile Rwandan economy and to the political authority as well (Kakwenzire and Kamukama 1999).

In addition, prior to the invasion Rwanda was on the verge of collapse both economically and politically (Prunier 1995). Economically, conditions within the state were deteriorating, leaving as the sole option a request for assistance from financial institutions, notably the International Monetary Fund (IMF) and the World Bank (WB). Introduced a month before the invasion, the reforms imposed a 67 percent devaluation of the national currency, and the SAPs' policies included privatization and cuts in public spending (Utterwulghe 1999). As Prunier notes, "[B]etween the coffee price decline and the war economy crisis, the SAPs merely contributed to weakening further an already exhausted economy" (1995, 160). When the RPF finally decided to cross the border into Rwanda on October 1, 1990, the Hutu regime was perceived as financially, organizationally, and politically bankrupt. To quote Fearon and Laitin, the regime's weakness was rendering "insurgency more feasible and attractive" (2003, 75–76). In short, "[t]ime was ripe to declare war against the regime" (Gasana 2002, 219). In Rwanda, the Hutu government was aware of such inevitability. The visible presence of high-ranking and armed Rwandan refugees within the ranks of the Ugandan NRA, the RPF's intense fund-raising campaign in Uganda and among émigrés, and the unsuccessful RPF invasion in 1989 were indicators signalling that it was only a matter of time before an organized invasion took place. This forced the Hutu government to mobilize military support from its allies Egypt, France, and Zaire. In return, "these responses sent an unequivocal message to the RPF: invade while you still stand a good chance of destabilizing the government or stay in Uganda and disintegrate into oblivion" (Otunnu 1999b, 36). Not coincidentally, the invasion erupted when Ugandan President Museveni and Rwandan President Habyarimana were attending a UNICEF meeting outside their respective countries. On October 1, 1990, 4,000 soldiers defected from the Uganda army, including former army Commander and Ugandan Defence Minister Fred Rwigyema, joined the RPF ranks and crossed the Rwanda border. By October 4, 1990, the RPF was within seventy kilometres from Kigali.

The Genocide

From the start, the genocide was entangled with the civil war, and the escalation of the civil war further complicated the attempts to halt the genocide. The following three factors help to explain what prompted the genocide in April 1994.

The Rise of Extremism

Extremism played a significant role in the lead-up to the genocide in 1994. Extremism was set into play when, in 1990, as a result of international pressure for democratization by donor countries, President Habyarimana announced that he would end the single-party system and allow rival parties to compete for power. In June 1991, a new constitution was signed, accompanied by a new political parties law. Soon after, five new political parties made up of both

Hutus and Tutsis were legally registered, and by the beginning of 1992, this figure had risen to twelve. These included the Mouvement Démocratique Républicain (MDR), the Parti Social Démocrate (PSD), the Parti Libéral (PL), the Parti Démocrate Chrétien (PDC), the Mouvement Républicain National pour la Démocratie et le Développement (MRNDD), and seven smaller parties (Des Forges 1999; MAR 2000). Created by Habyarimana, these seven smaller parties, composed primarily of Hutus, were a "deliberate attempt to make a sham of multipartyism" (Kakwenzire and Kamukama 1999, 69). In fact, these small parties, especially the CDR were extremist Hutu parties. The creation of small Hutu factions was considered to be, according to Habyarimana, "the 'best' way to face the challenge caused by the rebirth of political party activities in the country" (Kakwenzire and Kamukama 1999, 70).

Habyarimana's way of dealing with political activity by creating extremist factions significantly increased extremism in Rwanda. During the peace negotiations in 1992, radical forces from within Habyarimana's party used the same strategy of splintering as a means of avoiding the power-sharing provisions proposed by the OAU. When Habyarimana realized the danger of such a strategy of factionalism and extremism, it was too late. Extremist forces had already begun to train paramilitary militias and propagate anti-Tutsi hate in all parts of Rwanda (Kakwenzire and Kamukama 1999; Kuperman 2000).

Elite Manipulation of Ethnic Hatred and Propaganda

As a way to mobilize the general populace in his favor, Habyarimana used the invasion of October 1990 as an opportunity to revive ethnic sentiments. Elite manipulation of ethnic hatred became evident when, in September 1992, a government commission set up to identify the real enemy in Rwanda's civil war, explicitly recognized that "Tutsi inside or outside Rwanda who are extremist and nostalgic for power [and] who want to take power in Rwanda by force"

were enemies of the state (Kakwenzire and Kamukama 1999, 74). The elite also worked at redefining the conflict as one between "Rwandans," who supported the president, and "ibyitso," those believed to be accomplices of the enemy, including the Tutsi minority and Hutus opposed to the regime.

From then on, extremist sentiments were reinforced and hardened. Habyarimana began to implement an ideology he referred to as the "Union of the Bahutu," the objective of which was basically to unite Hutus to wipe out Tutsis (Kakwenzire and Kamukama 1999). Through the Radio Télévision Libre des Mille Collines (RTLM) and its countrywide outreach, the Hutu government organized campaigns to create fear and hatred of the Tutsi, playing "upon memories of past domination by the minority and on the legacy of the revolution that overthrew [Tutsi] rule . . . in 1959" (Des Forges 1999, 3). RTLM journalists, who were members of the extremist CDR and MRND parties, "spent all day broadcasting intoxicating propaganda based on ethnicity" (Kakwenzire and Kamukama 1999, 76). The population of Rwanda was being psychologically prepared and conditioned to extremism. Meanwhile, Habyarimana was providing military training to the youth of his party (the MRND); they would be known as the Interahamwé during the genocide.

The civil war, which at its origins in 1990 pitted the RPF against government forces, was slowly transformed by the Hutu elite in Rwanda into a war between Hutu Rwandans and Tutsi refugees and eventually led to genocide in April 1994. As Des Forges states, "[t]hrough attacks, virulent propaganda, and persistent political manoeuvering, Habyarimana and his group significantly widened divisions between Hutu and Tutsi by the end of 1992" (1999, 4).

The Burundi Effect

On October 21, 1993, Tutsi soldiers in Burundi seized and murdered President Ndadaye, the first Hutu to be elected president in Burundi's history. The assassination sparked a series of massacres in which tens of thousands of Burundians died and some 70,000 Burundian Hutus poured into southern Rwanda. Ndadaye's death "at the hands of an all-Tutsi army" had "an immediate and powerful demonstration effect on the Hutu of Rwanda . . . The message came clear and loud: 'Never trust the Tutsi!'" (Sellström, et al. 1996, 45). This served as a powerful tool of Hutu mobilization in Rwanda.

In sum, the genocide was not a manifestation of "ancient hatreds," nor was it a case of uncontrollable rage or of a "people gone mad." The genocide resulted from "the deliberate choice of a modern elite to foster hatred, and fear, to keep itself in power" (Des Forges 1999, 1).

Outcome
Conflict Status

The war ended on July 19, 1994 following the "military" victory of the RPF. The RPF captured Kigali on July 6, thus forcing the government forces and extremists into exile. Although some argue that "since there was no capitulation by the ousted government the event does not qualify as a victory" (Uppsala 2003), in reality, the conflict ended because the RAF and Hutu militias sought refuge in neighboring Zaire. By forcing government and militia forces away from the country, the RPF could declare victory even with no clear capitulation. This contested end of the civil war has brought some, such as Utterwulghe (1999), to argue that conflict remains *latent* because the underlying causes were unresolved and the conflict unsettled between the RAF and the RPF. This section further explores some of the outcomes of the civil war as it ended in 1994.

Since 1994, the RPF has managed to end large-scale violence, to establish a new regime inspired by the power-sharing arrangement of the Arusha Accords, where Hutus have reserved seats in the government coalition, and to engage in the activities of the International Criminal Tribunal for Rwanda (ICTR) (Doyle and Sambanis 2000).

However, by mid-1995, the government coalition had already begun to crumble. Five Hutu ministers, including the prime minister, left the coalition, complaining that the "real" power remained in the hands of an authoritarian Tutsi leadership (Longman 2004). In early 2000, the Hutu president of the republic, Pasteur Bizimungu, left the country for similar reasons. As a result, Hutu are now underrepresented in government, and a Tutsi-dominated RPF holds all political and military power (MAR 2000).

Although the RPF was acclaimed for ending large-scale violence and genocide in July 1994, they are not blameless. In the days and weeks after combat ended, RPF soldiers massacred unarmed civilians in a number of communes, killing several hundreds in refugee camps and assassinating political and military leaders who were close to Habyarimana's political party. It is estimated that, between April and August 1994, 25,000 to 45,000 were killed by the RPF (Des Forges 1999). Similarly, in 1996 and in 1998, the RPF invaded Zaire with the aim of curbing suspected Hutu militias and rebel supporters. The RPF also contributed to the ousting of Zairian President Mobutu in 1996, significantly intensifying the tensions between Zaire and Rwanda up to the present day (Payne and Dagne 2002).

In addition, the civil war and the genocide in Rwanda generated an enormous spillover effect. Only a few months after the outbreak of hostilities, thousands of refugees fled Rwanda to Tanzania, Zaire, and Burundi. Estimates in 1995 place the figure between 1.9 and 3.2 million refugees (Adelman and Suhrke 1999; Prunier 1999). Internally displaced persons (IDPs) in March 1995 were estimated at close to 800,000; in 1998, in excess of 2 million (Adelman and Suhrke 1999; Cohen-Deng 1998 in Doyle and Sambanis 2000). This refugee outflow impacted significantly the internal and external situation of these countries, imposing heavy economic, political, and geopolitical burdens.

Moreover, the civil war in Rwanda created a contagion effect in neighboring Zaire. Following the capture of Kigali by the RPF, 1.7 million people, most of them Hutu extremist militias and government forces, fled Rwanda to Zaire. With the military support of President Mobutu Sese-Sekou, ex-RAF forces and Hutu militias in exile reorganized their forces from Zaire. By December 1994, refugee camps in Zaire had been transformed into training camps for militias, and the defeated Rwandan interim President Sindikubwabo (who had replaced Habyarimana after his death) had installed and proclaimed its government in exile, and regrouped under the banner of the Armed Forces for the Liberation of Rwanda (ALiR) (which would become the Democratic Forces for the Liberation of Rwanda (FDLR) in 2000). This shows the extent to which the civil war had not completely ended. Periodic raids were carried out in northwest Rwanda by Hutu militias from Zaire. This contagiously ignited a conflict between Rwanda and Zaire (Sellström, et al. 1996). The refugee spillover of Hutu militias in Zaire thus played a definitive role in leading the two countries into overt war in 1996 and again in 1998, and in destabilizing regional security by drawing in neighboring Zimbabwe, Angola, Namibia, Uganda, Rwanda, and Burundi.

Duration Tactics

Four aspects of the civil war in Rwanda had notable effects on the duration and escalation of the civil war. First, the access to arms, equipment, and resources enabled both the RPF and the RAF to rearm intensively, not only during the conflict but also following the signing of the Arusha peace agreement on August 4, 1993, thus contributing to the country's outburst on April 6, 1994 (Prunier 1995). As Sellström et al. argue, "the influx of weapons from foreign sources" greatly influenced the duration and intensity of civil war and the massacres (1996, 67). For instance, in 1991–1992, France provided US $6 million worth of war material to the government forces. Second, the RPF's superiority to the RAF in fighting skills, higher morale, and discipline significantly affected the military balance between the two parties, thus influencing the

duration of the conflict. Third, the media (especially the RTLM), which played a crucil role in fueling political hatred and inciting violence against Tutsis and moderate Hutus, also had an important effect on the escalation of the conflict in 1994 (African Rights 1995; Sellström, et al. 1996). Fourth, the lack of international response when the civil war and the massacres against Tutsis began in 1990 had a huge impact on the duration and the escalation of the conflict. According to Des Forges, the international community "overlooked the systematic discrimination against Tutsi" and most were satisfied with the explanation that "the killings were spontaneous and uncontrollable" (1999, 17). Furthermore, the lack of international response to the massacres in Burundi following the president's death in October 1993 sent the signal to the Rwandan extremists "that they too could slaughter people in large numbers without consequence" (Des Forges 1999, 17).

External Military Intervention

No country sent regular troops in aid of the government or the rebels. France actively supported the Rwandan government by sending 370 and 670 men in October 1990 and February 1993, but this support did not last and was, at best, irregular. Officially, the French government has denied its active participation in the war since their withdrawal in December 1993, when UN forces were deployed (Human Rights Watch/ Arms Projects 1994; Prunier 1995).

Zaire also played a significant role in the conflict. Since 1965, Mobutu has supported actively the Rwandan Hutu government and in 1990, Zaire intervened to help Habyarimana's armed forces. Overall, Zaire sent 500 troops and allowed Hutu militias to take refuge in Zairian territory, to set up camps and conduct training both before and after the RPF capture of Kigali. Arms continued to flow to the ex-Hutu government in exile in Zaire, despite the UN arms embargo of 17 May 1994 (Human Rights Watch/Arms Project 1995; IISS 2005; Sellström, et al. 1996).

Conflict Management Efforts

From the onset of conflict, there were various attempts to mitigate the civil war, from informal to formal negotiation, peacekeeping, and crisis management. Yet these measures were not sufficient to terminate the war completely or to prevent the ensuing extreme mass killings.

Fifteen days after the RPF invaded, the OAU, along with Belgian and Tanzanian officials, were the first to pursue negotiation. From 1990 to 1992, six cease-fires were concluded and renewed after consecutive violations. These negotiations are referred to as the preliminaries of the negotiation process and would become the basis for the Arusha peace process (Sellström, et al. 1996; Jones 1999b).

A formal negotiation process with the OAU, Belgium, and Germany began in Arusha, Tanzania, on June 12, 1992, and it took more than a year to reach a mutual settlement. The power-sharing agreement between all parties was hard to achieve. Members of Habyarimana's party (the MRND) viewed the provisions as "political victories by the RPF" and posed a threat to Hutu power (Jones 1999b, 140). Also, the exclusion of the CDR party from the political arrangements because of its extremist nature was another point of contention. American, French, and Tanzanian diplomats backed the Rwandan government, recalling that "it was better to have extremists on the inside of the tent, pissing out, than on the outside of the tent, pissing in" (Jones 1999b, 139). Nonetheless, in January 1992, when the OAU offered the remaining seats of the power-sharing arrangement to the CDR on the condition that the CDR signed a code of ethics committing them to peace, it was too late; they had refused. Within days, the CDR and MRND organized demonstrations against the peace talks. More than 300 Tutsi civilians in the north of Rwanda were murdered (Jones 1999b). The rejection of the Arusha accords by the CDR and MRND parties would soon be the precursor of greater violence.

The "Peace Agreement Between the Government of the Republic of Rwanda and the Rwandese Patriotic Front," known as the Arusha Accords, was finally signed on August 4, 1993. The Accords included five main protocols signed at different stages of the negotiation: (1) a protocol on the rule of law; (2) a power-sharing arrangement and the creation of the Broad-Based Transitional Government (BBTG); (3) the repatriation of Rwandan refugees and the resettlement of displaced persons; (4) the integration of armed forces; and (5) miscellaneous issues (Jones 1999a, 1999b).

An observer mission for the Uganda-Rwanda cease-fire, the United Nations Observer Mssion to Uganda-Rwanda (UNOMUR), was created in June 1993 with a mandate to regulate the flow of arms along the Ugandan border. After the Arusha Accords were signed, UN Security Council Resolution 872 (October 5, 1993) authorized the UN Assistance Mission in Rwanda (UNAMIR). UNAMIR was a 2,538-person "neutral international force" led by Canadian Brigadier General Roméo Dallaire. UNAMIR's mandate was to provide for security in Kigali, oversee the creation of the BBTG, and monitor the cease-fire in the new demilitarized zone along with UNOMUR (Jones 1999b; Laegreid 1999; Sellström et al. 1996). More importantly, the mission was adopted under Chapter VI authority, which meant it could only use force if UNAMIR was directly attacked (Laegreid 1999). In the case of civil violence or genocide, UNAMIR did not have the mandate to retaliate.

In retrospect, these efforts proved to be less than optimal. The BBTG was never fully established. Parties that did not agree began to splinter, further dividing moderates and extremists. By the time the BBTG was supposed to convene in January and February 1994, assassinations of moderate political leaders had already begun. A special envoy from the United Nations High Commissioner for Refugees (UNHCR) at the time predicted that "a bloodbath of unparalleled proportions" was under way; similar warnings were made by the head of UNAMIR, Lieutenant General Roméo Dallaire (Jones 1999b, 145).

UNAMIR's lack of trained personnel, equipment, and financial resources prevented the mission from effective peacekeeping. The UN Department of Peacekeeping Operations (DPKO) in New York was also reluctant to take any offensive action, given UNAMIR's limited Chapter VI mandate. In the first weeks of April 1994, members of the Security Council were questioning whether UNAMIR should remain in place or be withdrawn. No Western states were willing to send troops. By April 19, Belgian troops—the strongest and best-equipped unit—were withdrawn after ten Belgian peacekeepers were killed by extremists. On April 21, the Security Council reduced UNAMIR's role to a "political presence" (Laegreid 1999, 239). There were final attempts by Tanzania to save the Arusha Accords at the beginning of April 1994, but it was too late. Subsequent efforts also failed, and "the jaws of genocide closed around the peace process in Rwanda" (Jones 1999b, 146).

From April 29, 1994, after 200,000 Tutsis had already been killed, UN Secretary General Boutros-Ghali appealed to the Security Council for measures to protect the civilians. It was several weeks before the international community responded. UNAMIR "became increasingly involved in self-protection tasks [and] within a week, 14,000 civilians had gathered under UN protection" (Laegreid 1999, 237).

The first measure was officially launched on June 23, 1994, when France, faced with public opinion criticizing the French army for "having trained the killer militias," dispatched 2,200 soldiers to Rwanda (Prunier 1999, 283). The mission, known as Opération Turquoise, was to create a Safe Humanitarian Zone in southwest Rwanda to protect civilians. Although Paris was acting unilaterally in this humanitarian intervention, it was granted a military force by the Security Council and a Chapter VII mandate (allowing the use of force) for two months. In retrospect, the mission, which arrived very late in the conflict, was able to save an estimated 12,000–15,000 Tutsi and prevented a profound refugee crisis in Burundi. Yet it was criticized for having provided relief mostly to Hutu IDPs, Interahamwe militias, and ex-RAF troops and

their families (Prunier 1999; Sellström, et al. 1996), which in return allowed "the retraining and rearming of large numbers of former government troops" along Rwanda's frontiers (Freedom House 2000).

A second relief operation was initated in August 1994, when the U.S. government unilaterally deployed troops in Central Africa. An estimated 2,000 Americans took part in Operation Support Hope (Payne and Dagne 2002). Efforts were coordinated with humanitarian organizations and UNAMIR to create safe corridors for returning IDPs and refugees.

The postwar situation was aggravated by the large number of refugees and IDPs (between 1.9 and 3.2 million) in neighboring Zaire (DRC), Burundi, and Tanzania, and by the return to Rwanda of former Tutsi refugees (about 600,000) who had been in exile in Uganda for more than three generations (Prunier 1995; Sellström, et al. 1996). By August 1994, 115,000 had returned from DRC, but operations were halted because ex-RAF forces began terrorizing refugees in Zairian camps (Halvorsen 1999). Until 2002, many have been forced to return by the governments of Burundi, Uganda and Tanzania. In 2002, a change in UNHCR policy regarding Rwandan refugees stated that future repatriation would be voluntary. In 2004, a report from Amnesty International Canada stated that, since 2002, an estimated 55,756 Rwandese refugees had been repatriated, and another 60,000 Rwandan refugees were still to be repatriated (2004).

The ICTR was created in November 1994 in Arusha under the presidency of Richard Goldstone, a South African judge, but the first indictments did not take place until November 1995. As Des Forges points out: "[e]stablishing the responsibility of *individual* Hutu is ... the only way to diminish the ascription of *collective* guilt to all Hutu" (1999, 736). Considering the common assumption that all Hutus killed Tutsis, and that very few considered the role of Tutsis and the RPF in the civil war, the ICTR decided to prosecute both Hutus and Tutsis responsible for crimes against humanity committed between January 1, 1994, and December 31, 1994.

Since then, thousands have been arrested and await trial, often in inhumane conditions. By 1996, only 1,500 of the 135,000 detainees had been tried (Des Forges 1999; Sellström, et al. 1996). In response, some regional authorities have recently encouraged the local settlement of claims by survivors through a customary process known as gacaca, in which trials take place before a community gathering, and only those accused of causing injury or death during the genocide are judged (Des Forges 1999). While many agree that the gacaca process is not perfect—many believe the process may end up doing more harm than good by opening up old wounds and by further polarizing Hutus and Tutsis rather than reconciling them—it is regarded as "the best available solution, [which] could yet succeed if the government remains vigilant and flexible" (Wolters 2005, 19).

Conclusion

To recapitulate, the civil war in Rwanda was rooted in a pattern of Tutsi refugee invasions that followed discriminatory and exclusionary policies against Tutsis in postcolonial Rwanda. By the time of the invasion in 1990, the rebel movement had gained strength and was highly militarized and disciplined, mainly because of Uganda's Museveni's support. The political and economic conditions in Rwanda were declining, which signaled regime weakness and created an opportunity to launch a surprise attack.

Since the RPF had a military superiority over the RAF, the war took three years to settle. The RAF received significant militarily support from France and Zaire, which greatly influenced the duration of the conflict. After a year of formal negotiation, the Arusha Accords were finally signed in August 1993, leaving the UN peacekeeping force in charge of implementing its protocols. However, Arusha was soon undermined by extremist forces in disagreement with the accords, propelling the country into civil chaos

The RPF's Invasion Versus Rwandan Armed Forces

"At the time of the RPF invasion, Rwanda had an army of only 5,000 men, equipped with light arms including Belgian-made FAL, German-made G3 and AK automatic rifles . . . eight 812 mm mortars, six 57 mm anti-tank guns, French AML-60 armored cars, and 16 French M. armored personnel carriers" (Kakwenzire and Kamukama 1999, 78). By mid-1991, the RAF had grown to 15,000 men, reaching 30,000 by the end of the year, and 50,000 by mid-1992 when the Arusha negotiations began.

and genocide after Habyarimana's death in February 1994.

Overall, as a means of preventive diplomacy, the Arusha process was admirable in a number of respects: It brought to the table an appropriate balance between regional and international players, neutral elements, and members of the majority of political organizations in Kigali. However, Arusha was a failure in terms of ending the conflict. As Jones points out, "the Arusha process was sophisticated and well managed, but the outcome was flawed. The outcome reflected the inherent difficulties in achieving a stable transition bargain in the context of civil war" (1999b, 132).

This raises important questions with regard to conflict resolution and peacekeeping in civil war contexts. First, should conflict resolution include or exclude extremists? Whereas in South Africa all political elements were included in the peace process with apparent success, in Rwanda the peace negotiations excluded hardliners and failed to prevent the ensuing genocide. Some argue that providing a stronger role for hardliners in Rwanda could have contributed to securing their power and perhaps could have avoided the tragic events of April 1994 (Jones 1999b).

Second, what role should international actors play in conflict resolution? In Rwanda, the agreement was negotiated under great international pressure. By forcing the two sides to adopt untenable positions, the intervention of the Arusha participants (the OAU, France, Belgium, and the United States) did not alleviate the already tense situation and resulted in tragic consequences (Jones 1999b).

Third, the case of Rwanda's peacekeeping force also raises questions about United Nations intervention and its rapid-reaction force capacity. Some argue that providing a greater role and more robust force for UNAMIR, including a Chapter VII mandate allowing the use of force, could have improved the declining security situation in Kigali. Dallaire (2003) claimed that a robust contingent of 5,000 could have prevented the genocide and dissuaded extremists. Indeed, it is increasingly being recognized that, in an era characterized more and more by internal conflicts and civil wars, there is a need for the UN, or any other regional organizations such as the African Union (AU), to develop a rapid-reaction capability, or a stand-by force, that would be ready to rapidly intervene when massive human rights abuses are perpetrated against a population.

In conclusion, prospects for peace in Rwanda remain uncertain and elusive. Between 8,000 and 15,000 ex-Hutu militia members and Rwandan Hutu refugees, now organized under the banner of the FDLR, continue to operate from east DRC and oppose Tutsi rule in Rwanda. Last March 31, 2005, following peace talks in Rome with representatives from the Congolese government, the FDLR finally agreed to put an end to their hostilities against Rwanda, to stop terrorizing Congolese civilians, and to demobilize and return to Rwanda where the FDLR would become a political party (International Crisis Group 2005). The United Nations Mission in the Democratic Republic of the Congo (MONUC) was mandated to disarm, demobilize, repatriate, resettle, and reintegrate FLDR members in Rwanda before September 2005. However, as of July 2006, the FDLR had not yet abandoned the DRC and many commanders were still hiding in the bush in the Kivu province "ready to carry on fighting" (BBC News 2006). The degree of Hutu mobilization in the DRC, as well as DRC support for the Hutu rebellion, both create opportunities and incentives for the renewal of conflict in the future (Harff and Gurr 1998).

In Rwanda, the Tutsi-led RPF who retains its hold on power and allows little autonomy for Rwandan Hutu, seems to reproduce the ethnic politics that they were trying to avoid when they came to power. A major obstacle to the establishment of a durable peace in Rwanda remains the way the Tutsi-led government in Rwanda will reconcile with the Hutu majority not only within the country but also within the region, and how the Rwandan government will reintegrate the Hutu militias who are to return to Rwanda. Durable peace will also depend on the ability and willingness of Rwanda's population to move beyond divisive distinctions between Hutus and Tutsis, and to view all members of society as Rwandans.

Geneviève Asselin, Kristine St-Pierre, and David Carment

Chronology

October 1, 1990   RPF invades northeast Rwanda from southern Uganda.

November 1, 1990   RPF is pushed back into Uganda. For two years, they will launch periodic invasions into northern Rwanda.

July 22, 1992   Cease-fire negotiated at Arusha, Tanzania. OAU provides a fifty-member Neutral Military Observer Group (NMOG I) in Rwanda.

February 8, 1993   RPF launches an attack against the Rwandan government in response to the massacre of 300 Tutsis by CDR and MRND. The RPF doubles size of its occupied territory—reaching as far as twenty-three kilometers from Kigali—forcing Habyarimana to resume peace talks.

June 22, 1993   UNOMUR is deployed along the Rwanda–Uganda border to prevent Ugandan aid to RPF.

August 4, 1993   President Habyarimana and RPF sign the Arusha Peace Accords, establishing a provisional multiparty government.

October 5, 1993   UNAMIR is deployed to help implement and monitor the Arusha Accords. UNAMIR's mandate ends March 8, 1996.

October 21, 1993   Tutsi soldiers in Burundi seize and murder newly elected Hutu president. The assassination sparks a series of massacres; tens of thousands of Burundians die, both Hutu and Tutsi.

April 6, 1994   President Habyarimana's plane is shot down, killing him along with Burundian President Ntaryamira. Hutu are urged to seek revenge by killing Tutsis and moderate Hutus.

April 7, 1994   Extremist Hutus take over government. Hutu militia and the RAF begin the massacre; the civil war with RPF is renewed.

April 21, 1994   Ten UN Belgian officers are killed. Security Council (SC) Resolution 912 reduces UNAMIR's strength from 2,548 to 270.

May 17, 1994   SC Resolution 918 imposes an arms embargo against Rwanda. UNAMIR's strength is increased to 5,500 troops; full deployment of troops takes nearly six months.

June 22, 1994   SC Resolution 929 establishes a Chapter VII multinational humanitarian operation. French-led Opération Turquoise delimits a humanitarian protection zone in the southwest region of Rwanda.

July 6, 1994   RPF capture Kigali and call for immediate cease-fire.

July 19, 1994   RPF military victory; new multiparty government is formed. Pasteur Bizimungu, a Hutu, is appointed president.

November 8, 1994   International Criminal Tribunal for Rwanda is established.

List of Acronyms

ALiR: Armed Forces for the Liberation of Rwanda

BBTG: Broad-Based Transitional Government

CDR: Coalition pour la Défense de la République

DPKO: Department of Peacekeeping Operations (UN)

DRC: Democractic Republic of the Congo

FDLR: Democratic Forces for the Liberation of Rwanda

GDP : gross domestic product

ICTR : International Criminal Tribunal for Rwanda

IDPs: internally displaced person

IMF: International Monetary Fund

MDR: Mouvement Démocratique Républicain

MONUC : United Nations Mission in the Democratic Republic of the Congo

MRND: Mouvement Révolutionnaire National pour le Développement

MRNDD: Mouvement Républicain National pour la Démocratie et le Développement

NMOG: Neutral Military Observer Group

NRA: National Resistance Army (Uganda)

OAU: Organization of African Unity (now African Union, AU)

PDC: Parti Démocrate Chrétien

PL: Parti Libéral

PSD: Parti Social Démocrate

RAF: Rwandan Armed Forces

RANU: Rwanda Alliance for National Unity

RPA: Rwandan Patriotic Army

RPF: Rwandan Patriotic Front

RTLM: Radio Télévision Libre des Mille Collines

SAP: structural adjustment program

UNAMIR: United Nations Assistance Mission in Rwanda

UNHCR: United Nations High Commissioner for Refugees

UNICEF: United Nations International Children's Fund

UNOMUR: United Nations Observer Mission to Uganda-Rwanda

WB: World Bank

References

Adelman, Howard, and Astri Suhrke. 1999. *The Path of a Genocide: The Rwandan Crisis from Uganda to Zaire.* New Brunswick, NJ: Transaction.

African Rights. 1995. *Rwanda: Death, Despair, and Defiance.* London: African Rights.

Amnesty International Canada. 2004. "Rwanda: Protecting their Rights: Rwandese Refugees in the Great Lakes Region." December 15. www.amnesty.ca/resource_centre/reports/view.php?load=arcview&article=2076&c=Resource+Centre+Reports (accessed November 12, 2006).

BBC News. 2006. "Congo Election Reporters' Log: Thursday." July 27. news.bbc.co.uk/2/hi/africa/5219668.stm (accessed November 12, 2006).

Brown, Michael. 1996. "The Causes and Regional Dimensions of Internal Conflict." In *The International Dimensions of Internal Conflict,* edited by Michael E. Brown. 571–601. Cambridge, MA: MIT Press.

Carment, David, and Patrick James. 2002. *Escalation of Ethnic Conflict: A Survey and*

Assessment. http-server.carleton.ca/~dcarment/papers/escalati.html (accessed August 11, 2005).

Central Intelligence Agency (CIA). 2005. *World Factbook: Rwanda.* Washington DC: Central Intelligence Agency. www.cia.gov/cia/publications/factbook/index.html (accessed January 9, 2006).

Dallaire, Roméo. 2003. *Shake Hands with the Devil: The Failure of Humanity in Rwanda.* Toronto: Random House Canada.

Des Forges, Alison. 1999. *Leave None to Tell the Story: Genocide in Rwanda.* New York and Washington, DC: Human Rights Watch.

Doyle, Michael W., and Nicholas Sambanis. 2000. "Dataset Notes. Supplement to International Peacebuilding: A Theoretical and Quantitative Analysis." *American Political Science Review* 94(4).

Fearon, James D., and David D. Laitin. 2003. "Ethnicity, Insurgency, and Civil War." *American Political Science Review* 97(1): 75–90.

Freedom House. 2000. *Freedom in the World: Rwanda.* www.freedomhouse.org/research/freeworld/2000/countryratings/rwanda.htm (accessed April 28, 2005).

Gachuruzi, Shally B. 1999. "The Role of Zaire in the Rwandese Conflict." In *The Path of a Genocide: The Rwandan Crisis from Uganda to Zaire,* edited by Howard Adelman and Astri Suhrke, 51–61. New Brunswick, NJ: Transaction.

Gasana, James. 2002. "Natural Resource Scarcity and Violence in Rwanda." In *Conserving the Peace: Resources, Livelihoods and Security,* edited by Richard Matthews, Mark Halle, and Jason Switzer, 199–246. Manitoba, Canada: IISD and IUCN.

Halvorsen, Kate. 1999. "Protection and Humanitarian Assistance in the Refugee Camps in Zaire: The Problem of Security." In *The Path of a Genocide: The Rwandan Crisis from Uganda to Zaire,* edited by Howard Adelman and Astri Suhrke, 307–320. New Brunswick, NJ: Transaction.

Harff, Barbara, and Ted Robert Gurr. 1998. "Systematic Early Warning of Humanitarian Emergencies." *Journal of Peace Research* 35(5): 551–579.

Heston, Alan, Robert Summers, and Bettina Aten. 2002. *Penn World Table Version 6.1.* Center for International Comparisons at the University of Pennsylvania (CICUP). pwt.econ.upenn.edu/php_site/pwt61_form.php (accessed April 28, 2005).

Homer-Dixon, Thomas.1999. *Environment, Scarcity, and Violence.* Princeton, NJ: Princeton University Press.

Horowitz, Donald L. 1985. *Ethnic Groups in Conflict.* Berkeley, CA: University of California Press.

Human Rights Watch. 2003. "Preparing for Elections: Tightening Control in the Name of Unity." (May). www.hrw.org/backgrounder/africa/rwanda0503bck.htm (accessed May 8, 2005).

Human Rights Watch/Arms Project. 1994. "Arming Rwanda: The Arms Trade and Human Rights Abuses in the Rwandan War." *Human Rights Watch* 6(1).

International Crisis Group. 1999. "Five Years after the Genocide in Rwanda: Justice in Question." April 7. www.icg.org//library/documents/report_archive/A400224_07041999.pdf (accessed May 8, 2005).

International Crisis Group. 2001. "Consensual Democracy in Post-Genocide Rwanda. Evaluating the March 2001 District Elections." October 9. www.icg.org//library/documents/report_archive/A400453_09102001.pdf (accessed May 8, 2005).

International Crisis Group. 2002. "Rwanda at the End of the Transition: A Necessary Political Liberalization." November 13. www.icg.org/home/index.cfm?id=1555&l=1 (accessed May 8, 2005).

International Crisis Group. 2005. "The Congo: Solving the FDLR Problem Once and for All. May 12. www.crisisgroup.org/home/index.cfm?id=3426&l=1 (accessed November 12, 2006).

International Institute for Strategic Studies (IISS) Armed Conflict Database. 2005. *Burundi, The DRC, Rwanda, Uganda.* www.iiss.org/ (accessed April 13, 2005).

Jones, Bruce D. 1999a. "Civil War, the Peace Process, and Genocide in Rwanda." In *Civil Wars in Africa: Roots and Resolution,* edited by M. Ali Taisier and Robert Matthews, 53–86. Montreal, Canada: McGill-Queen's University Press.

Jones, Bruce D. 1999b. "The Arusha Peace Process." In *The Path of a Genocide: The Rwandan Crisis from Uganda to Zaire,* edited by Howard Adelman and Astri Suhrke, 131–56. New Brunswick, NJ: Transaction.

Jones, Bruce D. 2001. *Peacemaking in Africa.* Boulder, CO: Lynne Rienner.

Kakwenzire, Joan, and Dixon Kamukama. 1999. "The Development and Consolidation of

Extremist Forces in Rwanda 1990–1994." In *The Path of a Genocide: The Rwandan Crisis from Uganda to Zaire,* edited by Howard Adelman and Astri Suhrke, 61–93. New Brunswick, NJ: Transaction.

Kuperman, Alan J. 2000. "Rwanda in Retrospect." *Foreign Affairs* (January/February): 94–118.

Laegreid, Turid. 1999. "U.N. Peacekeeping in Rwanda." In *The Path of a Genocide: The Rwandan Crisis from Uganda to Zaire,* edited by Howard Adelman and Astri Suhrke, 231–51. New Brunswick, NJ: Transaction.

Lema, Antoine. 2000. "Causes of Civil War in Rwanda: The Weight of History and Socio-Cultural Structures." In *Ethnicity Kills? The Politic of War, Peace and Ethnicity in Sub-Saharan Africa,* edited by Einar Braathen, Morten Boas, and Gjermund Saether, 68–86. UK: Macmillan Press.

Lemarchand, R. 1994. "Managing Transition Anarchies—Rwanda, Burundi, and South-Africa in Comparative Perspective." *Journal of Modern African Studies* 32(4): 581–604.

Longman, Timothy. 2004. "Obstacles to Peacebuilding in Rwanda." In *Durable Peace: Challenges for Peacebuilding in Africa,* 61–85. Toronto, Canada: University of Toronto Press.

Mamdani, Mahmood. 2001. *When Victims Become Killers: Colonialism, Nativism, and the Genocide in Rwanda.* Princeton, NJ: Princeton University Press.

Marshall, Monty G., and Keith Jaggers. 2002. *Polity IV Project: Political Regime Characteristics and Transitions, 1800–2002. Dataset User Manual.* College Park, MD: Center for International Development and Conflict Management (CIDCM).

Minorities at Risk Project (MAR). 2000. *Assessment for Hutus in Rwanda.* Center for International Development and Conflict Management (CIDCM). www.cidcm.umd.edu/inscr/mar/assessment.asp?groupId=51702 (accessed April 28, 2005).

Otunnu, Ogenga. 1999a. "Rwandese Refugees and Immigrants in Uganda." In *The Path of a Genocide: The Rwandan Crisis from Uganda to Zaire,* edited by Howard Adelman and Astri Suhrke, 3–30. New Brunswick, NJ: Transaction.

Otunnu, Ogenga. 1999b. "An Historical Analysis of the Invasion by the Rwanda Patriotic Army (RPA)." In *The Path of a Genocide: The Rwandan Crisis from Uganda to Zaire,* edited by Howard Adelman and Astri Suhrke, 31–51. New Brunswick, NJ: Transaction.

Payne, Donald M., and Ted Dagne. 2002. "Rwanda: Seven Years After the Genocide." *Mediterranean Quarterly* 13(1): 38–43.

Polity IV Project. 2003. *Political Regime Characteristics and Transitions, 1800–2003.* www.cidcm.umd.edu/inscr/polity/ (accessed May 2, 2005).

Prunier, Gérard. 1995. *The Rwanda Crisis: History of a Genocide.* New York: Columbia University Press.

Prunier, Gérard. 1999. "Opération Turquoise: A Humanitarian Escape from a Political Dead End." In *The Path of a Genocide: The Rwandan Crisis from Uganda to Zaire,* edited by Howard Adelman and Astri Suhrke, 281–305. New Brunswick, NJ: Transaction.

Renner, Michael. 2002. *The Anatomy of Resources Wars.* Worldwatch Paper 162. Washington, DC: Worldwatch Institute.

Reyntjens, Filip. 2000. "Small States in an Unstable Region—Rwanda and Burundi, 1999–2000." *Current African Issues* no. 23. Uppsala, Sweden: Nordiska Afrikainstitutet.

Sellström, Tor, Lennart Wohlgemuth, and the Nordic Africa Institute (NAI). 1996. *The International Response to Conflict and Genocide: Lessons from the Rwanda Experience. Study 1: Historical Perspective: Some Explanatory Factors.* Uppsala, Sweden: Steering Committee of the Joint Evaluation of Emergency Assistance to Rwanda.

Sislin, John, and Frederic S. Pearson. 2001. *Arms and Ethnic Conflict.* Lanham, MD: Rowman & Littlefield.

Smith, David Norman. 2002. "Globalization and Genocide: Inequality and Mass Death in Rwanda." In *On the Edge of Scarcity: Environment, Resources, Population, Sustainability, and Conflict,* edited by Michael N. Dobkowski and Isidor Wallimann, 149–172. Syracuse, NY: Syracuse University Press.

Stockholm International Peace Research Institute (SIPRI). 2005. www.sipri.org/ (accessed April 28, 2005).

Tekle, Amare. 1999. "The OAU: Conflict Prevention, Management and Resolution." In *The Path of a Genocide: The Rwandan Crisis from Uganda to Zaire,* edited by Howard Adelman and Astri Suhrke, 111–31. New Brunswick, NJ: Transaction.

United Nations. 2001. *UNAMIR.* www.un.org/Depts/dpko/dpko/co_mission/unamir.htm (accessed May 5, 2005).

United Nations. 2003. *UNOMUR*. www.un.org/Depts/dpko/dpko/co_mission/unomur.htm (accessed May 5, 2005).

United Nations General Assembly. 1948. *Convention on the Prevention and Punishment of the Crime of Genocide*. December 9. www.hrweb.org/legal/genocide.html (accessed December 26, 2005).

United Nations High Commissioner for Refugees (UNHCR). 1995. *The State of the World's Refugees: In Search of Solutions*. Oxford University Press. www.unhcr.ch/ (accessed May 7, 2005).

Uppsala Conflict Database Project. 2003. *Rwanda*. www.pcr.uu.se/database/conflictInformation.php?years=1990&bcID=92&variables%5B%5D=6&button=+Search+ (accessed April 28, 2005).

Utterwulghe, Steve. 1999. "Rwanda's Protracted Social Conflict: Considering the Subjective Perspective in Conflict Resolution Strategies." *The Online Journal of Peace and Conflict Resolution* 2.3 (August). www.trinstitute.org/ojpcr/2_3utter.htm (accessed May 5, 2005].

Uvin, Peter. 1998. *Aiding Violence: The Development Enterprise in Rwanda*. West Hartford, CT: Kumarian Press.

Varga, Sonja, Abdul-Rasheed Draman, Koren Marriott, and David Carment. 2002. *Conflict Risk Assessment Report: African Great Lakes*. Ottawa, Canada: Country Indicators for Foreign Policy (CIFP), Carleton University. www.carleton.ca/cifp (accessed April 25, 2005).

Wolters, Stephanie. 2005. "The Gacaca Process: Eradicating The Culture of Impunity in Rwanda." Situation Report, Institute for Security Studies. August 5. www.iss.co.za/AF/current/2005/050805rwanda.pdf (accessed November 21, 2006).

World Bank Group. *The Economics of Civil Wars, Crime and Violence*. www.worldbank.org/research/conflict/civil.htm (accessed May 16, 2005).

Somalia
(1988–1991 and 1992–Present)

Introduction

Somalia, a country synonymous with civil war, failed state syndrome, and anarchy, suffers from chronic clan warfare stimulated by Cold War rivalries and failed humanitarian intervention. Since independence, the people of Somalia have suffered regular civil and international conflict. This history defines Somalia, and its future will be a function of this history. More than a decade after the fall of Siad Barre, the country remains without an effective central government. The civil war affected all of Somalia's neighbors, as each one was the subject of irredentist claims on its territory. Somalia claimed Kenya's Northern Frontier district, Ethiopia's Ogaden region, and Djibouti. These irredentist claims complicated regional dynamics and led to a lack of political support for settlement of the disputes involved in the civil war. Not until the regional and international powers realized that a civil war in Somalia affected them all did they support peace in Somalia.

Country Background

The peoples now known as Somalis come from an ancient people called Berberi. Evidence suggests they have lived in the region since 100 AD. Somalis, a derivation of Samaal, are pastoral nomads and followers of Islam. Six major clans compose the Somali ethnic group. The Dir, the Daarood, the Isaaq, and the Hawiye follow pastoral lifestyles; the Digil and the Rahanwayn follow an agricultural life. Islam, introduced in the eighth century, has strongly influenced the legal and cultural identities of the Somali people. Initially, the Somali people created outposts on the coasts in the ancient cities of Seylac, Berbera, Merca, and Mogadishu to trade with other cultures. The Somali people possess a strong identity and show a fierce independence. A central part of Somali life and central to their identity are their clan affiliations (Metz 1992, xxi).

Present-day Somalia began as two different entities, one administered by Italy and the other by the United Kingdom. The United Kingdom controlled the northern area to maintain a strategic supply area for its important colonies in Yemen and India. This area of Somalia contained substantial animal resources to feed the United Kingdom's people across the Red Sea. Southern Somalia became part of Italy and allowed Italians to resettle in the region to relieve population pressures in Italy. An important historical aspect of the two entities rests with the differences in the colonial administration of the two zones. As Italians migrated to Somalia to make a new life, southern Somalia benefited from additional educated administrators who improved education, commerce, infrastructure, and sanitation systems in the region. In the north, the United Kingdom used the region to extract resources and did little to empower its inhabitants.

Somalia was formed by the merger of British and Italian Somaliland, whereas French Somaliland became Djibouti, and the Somalis in Kenya and Ethiopia remained part of those countries. Although the Somali identity forms the majority of these areas, Somalis also live outside these areas in other neighboring countries throughout the region. After independence, Somalia followed a policy of nonalignment and chose to receive support from the United States, the Soviet Union, and the Peoples' Republic of China.

Mohamed Siad Barre came to power in a coup d'état on October 21, 1969, after the death of President Shermaarke. He garnered the support of the military and the police and proclaimed a new Somali Democratic Republic. This new entity proclaimed its goal as the unification of all Somali peoples and the end of all clannism in Somalia. Although Somalia initially maintained a nonaligned foreign policy, when Siad Barre came to power, he shifted Somalia's allegiance to the Soviet sphere of influence. In exchange, the Soviet Union sent small arms and light weapons, tanks, aircraft, and advisors to train the Somali National Army (SNA).

As a believer of "scientific socialism," Siad Barre made efforts to bring development to his people. Unfortunately, his irredentist claims on his neighbors' Somali populations created turmoil throughout the region. The idea of a greater Somalia that joined Somalis from Ethiopia, Djibouti, and Kenya consumed the government of Siad Barre. This led to the unsuccessful invasion of the Ogaden region of Ethiopia and both tacit and direct support of Somali rebel groups in the surrounding countries.

Somalia's military buildup during the 1970s allowed the government to field one of the largest and best-trained militaries in Africa. With the assistance of Soviet advisors, equipment, and material, Somalia began to consider means of achieving its stated intention of uniting all Somalis into a Greater Somalia. Histori-

cally, Somalia's irredentist claim on the Ogaden of Ethiopia emanated from Ethiopia's seizure of the area after the defeat of Italy in World War II. The Ogaden contained a large population of Somalis under foreign domination and became the focus of Somalia's military buildup. In 1977, Somalia sent its forces into Ethiopia and initially made substantial gains. As Somalia succeeded in capturing territory in the Ogaden, the Soviet Union pulled its support from Somalia and began reinforcing Ethiopia. This transition led to a reversal of Somalia's gains and forced Somalia to withdraw in defeat. (See also Lewis 2002.)

Conflict Background

Somalia's unsuccessful war against Ethiopia over the contested Ogaden region initiated a long period of rebellion against the leadership of Siad Barre. After Somalia's loss in the Ogaden, several groups challenged his leadership and formed in opposition to his rule. This sparked a coup attempt in April 1978 by military members of the Majerteyn clan. Barre and his supporters prevailed and unleashed a vicious campaign against military and civilian members of the Majerteyn clan. This reprisal began a cycle of violence against those groups that challenged his leadership. An insurgency began with this coup attempt. Although the initial coup failed, it put in motion a chain of events that led to his overthrow. After Barre realized that members of the Majerteyn clan were responsible for the coup attempt, he began a campaign against the entire clan. Later, as more clans realized that his tactics included manipulating clan differences, the rebellion grew to include the Isaaq clans of the north. Both groups experienced the wrath of Siad Barre as his secret police massacred their people (Lyons and Samatar 1995, 17).

Because of Barre's campaign of violence against the Majerteyn clan, thousands of people fled to the relative safety of Ethiopia. While in Ethiopia, Colonel Abdullahi Yusef formed the Somali Democratic Salvation Front (SSDF) with material and tacit support from the government of Ethiopia. Although the SSDF initially received support from Somalis, it eventually lost support because of its ties with the Ethiopian government (Adam 1995, 76; Lyons and Samatar 1995, 17).

The goal of the Ogaden war was to unite the Somali people. Ogadeni Somalis lost their independence when Ethiopia seized the region during the colonial period. After Somalia's loss to Ethiopia, many of the Ogadeni Somalis fled Ethiopia, fearing reprisal from the Ethiopian government. As they fled, Siad Barre offered sanctuary in Somalia; however, this gesture came at the expense of the northern Isaaq clan displaced by these arriving Ogadenis. This calculated move by Siad Barre drew the scorn of the Isaaq clan and sparked the creation of the Somali National Movement (SNM), a movement primarily focused on the overthrow of the Siad Barre regime (Adam 1995, 76; Lyons and Samatar 1995, 18).

The SNM operated out of Ethiopia, just like the SSDF, until the governments of Ethiopia and Somalia agreed that it was in their mutual interest to end support of each other's rebel movements. Ethiopia found itself in the midst of the civil war against Eritrean separatists, while Somalia increasingly found itself embattled by various clan-based Somali groups. The treaty of nonaggression and noninterference obliged Ethiopia to end support of all Somali groups; accordlingly, the SNM and other groups changed strategies with the loss of their bases in Ethiopia. The peace accord between Ethiopia and Somalia triggered the decline of Somalia. With the loss of its bases in Ethiopia, the SNM began a military campaign against the Siad Barre regime. The SNM captured Burao and Hargeisa in May 1989. Barre sent a full contingent of soldiers and equipment, including the air force. The air force began an indiscriminate aerial bombardment of Hargeisa and destroyed more than 50 percent of the city. The bombardment spared no one and became another crime against humanity, recognized but practictly ignored by the international community (Adam 1995, 76; Lewis 2002, 262; Lyons and Samatar 1995, 18).

With instability mounting throughout north and central Somalia, Siad Barre's government began to unravel, continuing its descent into the status of a failed state. Other groups that were upset about the policies and practices of the Barre regime sensed the weakness of the central government and began to organize against the regime. Disaffected Ogadenis formed the Somali Patriotic Movement (SPM) and began attacks on the government at Afmadu in March 1989. Rebel groups now covered the majority of the country from the north, throughout the central region, and into the south, including parts of Juba and Benadir (Lyons and Samatar 1995, 18).

At this point, the Majerteyn, Ogadeni, and Isaaq clans now openly rejected the leadership of Siad Barre, and the Hawiye clan joined in the open struggle against the government to protect its interests. Members of the SNM had created the United Somali Congress (USC) in 1987 in Rome. Although they shared a common distrust and hatred of the Barre regime, they realized his wrath when Hawiye clan members in the Somali Army mutinied in Galkayo, triggering a murderous response from the military. Despite the shared resolve against the government, factions within the USC differed on how to cooperate with other groups, including the SNM. These factions included General Mohammed Farah Aideed, who believed the USC should cooperate with the SNM (Adam 1995, 77; Lyons and Samatar 1995, 19).

The trend of clan-based rebel movements weakened the fabric of Somali society, and people began to turn to the clans for protection and welfare. As Barre retaliated against the various clans, the Marehan clan dominated the military because it was the only clan loyal to Barre. This accelerated the perception of the other clan groups that regime change was the only way to end the reprisals by the Barre regime and bring stability back to Somalia. Although all the clan groups agreed that the Barre regime should be overthrown, cooperation between the clan groups remained limited and difficult (Lyons and Samatar 1995, 19).

In January 1991, Siad Barre fled Mogadishu after the combined forces of the USC (jointly led by Mohammed Farah Aideed and Ali Mahdi) entered the capital. After the fall of Mogadishu, neither Aideed nor Mahdi could agree on how to share power. Aideed, who was of the Habar Gidr subclan, and Mahdi, who was of the Abgal subclan, each received support from their clans to lead the country. Aideed's clan enjoyed the support of the SNM in the north. Mahdi's clan were the original inhabitants of the Mogadishu area, whereas Aideed's clan settled in the area later. While Aideed pursued Barre south of Mogadishu, Mahdi declared himself the head of the new government of Somalia. Aideed did not recognize the proclamation, and this led to a division of Mogadishu between the Habar Gidr and the Abgal subclans. After fleeing the capital, Barre made one last attempt to reclaim power. He gathered his forces south of the capital and made one last push to take the city back from the USC. His attempt failed, and Barre fled into exile. This led to further bloodshed, a failed UN intervention, and additional years of suffering for the people of Somalia (Lewis 2002, 264).

Before meetings to discuss a cease-fire, Aideed (representing the United Somali Congress), Ahmed Omar Jess (representing the Somali Patriotic Movement), Mohamed Nur Aliyow (representing the Somali Democratic Movemement [SDM]), and Abdi Warsame (representing the Southern Somali National Movement [SSNM]) came together to formulate a common strategy for the discussions. The parties signed the cease-fire agreement on March 3, 1992, in which all parties agreed to end hostilities and maintain the status quo (Clarke and Herbst 1997, 7).

As the world witnessed the human tragedy of the famine in Somalia, pressure mounted on the international community to intervene to halt the fighting and facilitate the delivery of humanitarian assistance. The end of the Cold War opened the way for the United Nations to take a stronger role in dealing with international peace and security as envisioned in its charter. With the support of the United Nations, the United States launched an invasion of Somalia with the primary purpose of bringing about the conditions necessary to deliver humanitarian assistance to those areas in the south most devastated by famine (Lewis 2002, 267–75; Lyons and Samatar 1995, 29–35)

After Somalia descended into violence, the United Nations, the Organization of African Unity (OAU), the Arab League, and the Organization of the Islamic Conference (OIC) all discussed the situation in Somalia. The United Nations actively participated in Somalia after the collapse of the Barre regime but could not fully operate in the lawless environment. Due to the violence, the United Nations removed its personnel from the country on several occasions. On January 23, 1992, the United Nations began its official involvement by passing Security Council Resolution 733. The resolution urged all the parties to cease hostilities, created an arms embargo, and requested humanitarian assistance.

During the early 1990s, at the height of the post–Cold War euphoria for United Nations involvement, Somalia became the testing grounds for UN and member state humanitarian intervention. On April 24, 1992, the UN Security Council passed Resolution 751, creating the United Nations Operation in Somalia (UNOSOM) to monitor a cease-fire between the Somali factions headed by Ali Mahdi and Mohammed Farah Aideed. Gradually, the mission grew from fifty members to more than 4,000 as the mission transitioned between a peacekeeping mission and a humanitarian mission to provide food to those suffering from a famine. Cooperation between the United Nations and its specialized agencies escalated to mitigate the suffering of the Somali people. Unfortunately, the Somali factions decided to continue the civil conflict, which led to a considerable escalation in international involvement.

Because of the deteriorating security situation, the UN Security Council authorized the use of force in its Resolution 794. The Unified

Task Force (UNITAF), led by the United States, was deployed to Mogadishu on December 9, 1992, in response to Security Council Resolution 794. UNITAF's primary responsibility was to secure the capital and provide a safe environment for the distribution of humanitarian assistance. Upon the realization of these mandates, the United Nations began the transition between UNITAF and UNOSOM II (as embodied in Security Council Resolution 814).

UNOSOM II attempted to continue the successes realized by UNITAF by maintaining security and continuing the humanitarian work started earlier. However, General Aideed escalated the violence by directly attacking UNOSOM II forces. In June 1993, Aideed's forces attacked Pakistani soldiers, and in October 1993, U.S. soldiers supporting UNOSOM II died in a protracted battle with Aideed's forces. The attack on the U.S. soldiers started the gradual withdrawal of peacekeeping forces, and UNOSOM II completely withdrew in March 1995 (Howe 1996; United Nations Operation in Somalia, n.d.).

The Insurgents

This section discusses the clan-based groups and attempts to provide insight into their creation, leadership, composition, and goals. The three core rebel groups are the United Somali Congress, the Somali National Movement, and the Somali Salvation Democratic Front. These groups played a crucial role in the overthrow of Siad Barre. They also competed for leadership within Somalia after the fall of his government.

The United Somali Congress, composed of members of the Hawiye clan, initially formed from two conferences, one held in Rome (1987) and one in Ethiopia (1989). The USC formed at a time when the state had ceased to function properly. Since its inception, USC suffered from internal divisions, and when Jiumale died in mid-1990, a bitter conflict ensued between the USC's military wing leader, General Aidid (of the Habir Gedir subclan) and its Manifesto

representative, Ali Mahdi (of the Abgal subclan). The USC seized control of Mogadishu in 1991 and expelled Barre. Once Barre had left Mogadishu, conflict between the two leaders for control of the USC and national leadership led to internecine wars, in June and September 1991 and March 1992, between the two subclans. The competing groups destroyed large parts of the capital city. Mohamed Farah Aideed (also allied with the SNM) maintained control over southern Mogadishu and some regions in central Somalia, whereas self-proclaimed interim president Ali Mahdi Mohamed maintained control of northern Mogadishu. The inability of any one group or person to fill the leadership vacuum paved the way for creeping warlordism in southern Somalia. A third faction of the USC continued to exist in Mogadishu—a nonviolent opposition called the Manifesto Group. The weakening military power of the Barre regime had allowed a loyal opposition to issue a manifesto during his last year. However, the rapid success of the USC, facilitated by the success of the Manifesto Group, left the USC without a developed, politically mature party program and organization. To maximize support, Aideed's group created the Somali National Alliance (SNA), which included the USC, the SPM, the SDM, and the SSNM (Adam 1995, 77; Ahmed 1999, 242; Lyons and Samatar 1995, 79; Woodward 2003, 71).

The Somali National Movement, composed of a group of businesspersons, religious leaders, intellectuals, and former army officers drawn from of the Isaaq clan, led the opposition of Siad Barre in the late 1980s. The SNM formed in 1981 with support from Ethiopia during much of the 1980s. In 1988, the SNM occupied much of northern Somalia and suffered brutal reprisal attacks from Siad Barre. The SNM won control of the north (former British Somaliland) in 1991 and declared the territory the independent (but as yet unrecognized) Republic of Somaliland. Drawing support primarily from the Isaaq clans of the Togdher region, the SNM was launched in

Table 1: Civil War in Somalia

War:	Rebel alliance (SNM-USC-SPM) vs. government
Dates:	1988–1991 and 1992–present
Casualties:	500,000
Regime type prior to war:	–7 (ranging from –10 [authoritarian] to 10 [democracy])
Regime type after war:	Collapse of central authority (Interregnum –77)
GDP per capita year war began:	US $170 (1989; GNP)
GDP per capita 5 years after war:	US $500 (2003)
Insurgents:	SNM, USC, SPM, and others
Issue:	Ideological struggle for control of central government
Rebel funding:	Neighboring countries, Soviet Union, United States
Role of geography:	Rebels destroyed agricultural sector, causing famine.
Role of resources:	Land played a significant role in clan politics.
Immediate outcome:	Overthrow of government, failed humanitarian intervention, ongoing
Outcome after 5 years:	Anarchy, no central government
Role of UN:	Facilitated humanitarian intervention, peacekeeping mission
Role of regional organization:	IGADD, OAU involved in peace talks
Refugees:	800,000 refugees, 2 million IDPs
Prospects for peace:	Unlikely in the near future

Sources: Institute for Security Studies (n.d.); Metz 1992, 134; Polity IV Project 2003; United States Committee for Refugees 1997.

London (political) and Ethiopia (military) and had announced it would coordinate efforts with the SSDF. The SNM expressed several Isaaq grievances, which included inadequate political representation, neglect in development, and economic controls that adversely affected trade with the Gulf states. Following the formation of the SNM, the Barre government intensified its repressive policies against the Isaaq. To create animosity between clans, Barre posted senior military officers in the Somali army from Isaaq clans in Majerteyn regions as the government waged war against the Isaaq people (Ahmed 1999, 242; Lewis 2002, 252; Lyons and Samatar 1995, 78; Woodward 2003, 69).

The Somali Salvation Democratic Front, mainly composed of members of the Majerteyn subclan of Darod clan, was led by General Mohamed Abshir Musse, and its regional stronghold was in northeastern Somalia. The SSDF was formed in 1979 by Colonel Yusuf Abdullahi, following Siad Barre's attacks on the Majerteyn in retaliation for the coup attempt, and was supported by Ethiopia in the 1980s. Tensions with Aideed led the SSDF generally to side with the Ali

Mahdi's Somali Salvation Alliance (SSA). A smaller SSDF group is based in Kismayu, among the Hert subclan, and is found there with the SPM faction under Colonel Jess. Those mainly Mudugh-based Majerteyn clansmen associated with the unsuccessful attempted coup of 1978 had by late 1981 formed the SSDF, a guerrilla organization that transferred its operational headquarters to Ethiopia and set up a powerful radio transmitter in the following year to spread propaganda. In June of that year, with military support, SSDF forces pushed across the Ethiopian border and seized control of a small area inside Somalia. The government's reaction to the coup attempt, the formation of the SSDF, and other incursions into government-held territory was repression and vicious reprisals against the Majerteyn clan (Ahmed 1999, 242; Lewis 2002, 251–52; Lyons and Samatar 1995, 78; Woodward 2003, 69).

Several smaller groups also participated in the Somali civil war. Many of the following groups participated in the various peace conferences. The Somali Patriotic Movement, a grouping of Ogadeni subclans (of the Darod clan), attempted to lay claim to the region around the southern port of Kismayu, thereby triggering conflict with other Ogadeni sub-clans. Ahmed Omar Jess led one faction, which was allied with Aideed's SNA. Adan Abdullahi Nur (Gabiyo) led another faction, allied with Ali Mahdi's SSA and with General Mohamed Siad Hersi (Morgan). A group of Ogaden clan soldiers and officers defected from Siyad's army in 1989 and formed the SPM. A splinter SPM faction headed by Umar Jess and based in the Kismayu area allied with the Aideed faction of the USC. The Ogadeni-led SPM also worked with the SNM, formed in 1989 following the arrest of General Nur (Gabiyo), then minister of defense and the highest-ranking Ogadeni in government (Adam 1995, 77; Ahmed 1999, 242; Lyons and Samatar 1995, 78; Woodward 2003, 71).

The Somali Democratic Movement is an organization based among the Rahanwein people (the agriculturalists of Somalia, who suffered some of the worse consequences of the famine), active around the town of Baidoa; the organization split and reformed a number of times in the period 1992–1994. At different times, various factions have been associated with the SSA and the SNA. The Southern Somali National Movement is a Dir clan movement based among the Bimaal subclan in southern coastal Somalia. The movement split into factions, one allied with Aideed's SNA and the other with Ali Mahdi's SSA. The Somali African Muki Organization (SAMO) represents minority populations (mainly farmers) of Bantu origin in the southern riverine regions, the most vulnerable victims of the war and famine. These farmers operated outside the clan system. One faction allied with the Somali Salvation Alliance, and another allied with the Somali National Alliance. The Somali Democratic Alliance (SDA) is a Gadabursi (Dir clan) organization from the northern Somaliland region around Boroma. Originally formed in 1989, it initially opposed the SNM's policy of independence and participated in the Addis Ababa talks. The SDA allied with the Somali Salvation Alliance and now controls Somaliland with the United Somali Front (USF) and the SNM (Adam 1995, 77; Lyons and Samatar 1995, 77–78; Institute for Security Studies n.d.).

The Somali National Democratic Union (SNDU) is a Darod Faction allied with the SSA. General Omar Haji Mohamed Siad Hersi (Morgan) led the Somali National Front (SNF), which is composed of Marehan (part of the Darod and Siad Barre's clan) and allied with the SSA. The Somali National Union (SNU) is a Reer–Hamar group supported by many coastal, urban Somalis (outside the clan system). Historically these urbanized groups have weak clan links to the rest of Somalia but strong trading links to the Indian Ocean. As a relatively wealthy minority, they suffered greatly during the civil war and from banditry. Different factions of the SNU allied with the SSA and SNA. The United Somali Front is an Issa group (Dir Clan) based in the far northwest (Somaliland). The Issa broke with the SNM in 1991 and has had close relations with the government of Djibouti. The United Somali Party is a Dolbahante–Warsangali subclan (of the Darod clan) movement. This subclan straddles the border between northern Somaliland and southern Somalia, and the USP has been in conflict with the SNM. The party allied with the SSA (Adam 1995, 77; Lyons and Samatar 1995, 77–79).

Geography

Somalia is located in eastern Africa, also known as the Horn of Africa. Somalia borders the approach to the Bab el Mandeb, the strategic area near the opening to the route through the Red Sea to the Suez Canal. Due to its strategic importance, the United States and its allies maintain a naval presence in the region. This presence is predicated on the fact that Somalia has a weak central government and no organized naval contingent to protect the approach. In light of increased terrorist threats and the bombing of the USS *Cole* in Yemen, it is clear that the areas off the coast of Somalia have become a haven for terrorists. Continued concern that Somalia and

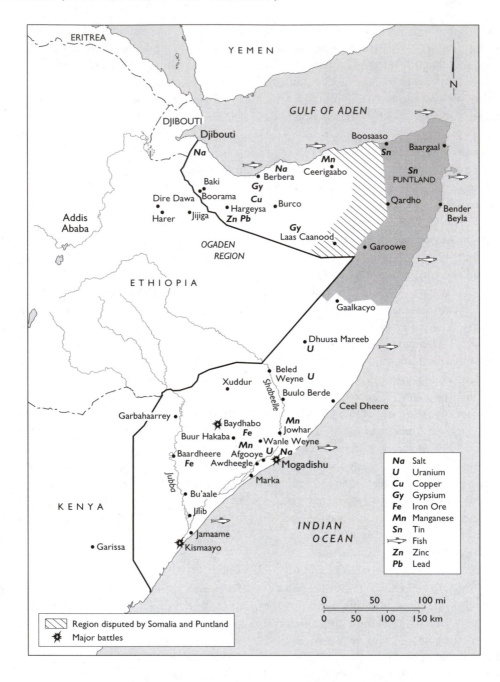

Map legend:

Na	Salt
U	Uranium
Cu	Copper
Gy	Gypsium
Fe	Iron Ore
Mn	Manganese
Sn	Tin
⟹	Fish
Zn	Zinc
Pb	Lead

Region disputed by Somalia and Puntland

✹ Major battles

its territorial waters are a risk to international peace and security has made it necessary for international monitoring of the region.

Somalia has a population of about 8.6 million, a July 2005 estimate derived from an official census taken in 1975 by the Somali government. Due to the lack of a fully functioning central government, the presence of nomads, and the movement of refugees owing to famine and clan warfare, population numbers are only estimates. Although the majority of the Somali population identifies themselves as Somalis, clan-based designations caused many of the conflicts within Somalia. Clan-based rivalries escalated throughout the conflict and continue to the present day.

The climate and geography of Somalia affect the distribution of economic resources, which contributed to the civil conflict. In the northern part of the country, the people relied on animal husbandry for their survival. They would raise cattle, camels, and other animals and export them to regional markets, including those in Yemen and Saudi Arabia. In the south, especially between the Jubba and Shabeelle rivers, the people relied on agriculture to support their economy. The war devastated both economies. In the south, Barre's supporters destroyed the crops during their retreat from Mogadishu, creating a famine. In the north, the livestock industry suffered from low commodity prices after Saudi Arabia barred Somali animals from its territory because a disease was found among its stocks. Low livestock prices and increasing conflict after the signing of the nonaggression treaty with Ethiopia contributed to the escalation of the conflict.

Somalia possesses many natural resources: uranium and largely unexploited reserves of iron ore, tin, gypsum, bauxite, copper, salt, natural gas, and probably oil reserves. Somalia also contends with recurring droughts, frequent dust storms over the eastern plains in summer, and floods during the rainy season. The natural resources and environmental hazards in Somalia contributed to the vulnerability of the regimes in Somalia. Droughts limited the amount of food the country could produce. The regime's destruction of crops as they fled the capital magnified the natural hazards. Although Somalia is a large country with natural resources, it had not been able to benefit from these resources because of lack of capital and other problems related to lack of development.

Tactics

Tactics in the civil war ranged from conventional warfare to guerrilla warfare. The rebels initially received support from Ethiopia; however, when Siad Barre made peace with Haile Mengistu Miriam, the rebels lost their patron. Without the support of Ethiopia, the rebels began an all-out attack on the Barre regime. To maintain their momentum. they used confiscated and abandoned military equipment. Due to the patronage of the United States and the Soviet Union and its war with Ethiopia, Somalia possessed a large quantity of military hardware. Also, the rapid demobilization of the Ethiopian military after its war with Somalia provided a large, inexpensive supply of weapons for rebel forces. Rebel groups relied on the availability of second-hand weapons, as well as weapons smuggled into the country in violation of the United Nations weapons embargo.

All sides in the conflict used tactics to terrorize the civilian population. Clan-based rivalries fueled murder, torture, rape, and destruction throughout Somalia. These tactics forced clan groups to organize militia and other military-style organizations to defend their interests. Without these protections, their people suffered the murderous rage of the various ethnic groups. Somalia's system of compensation for crimes committed against other Somalis complicated the civil war. When a Somali of one clan dies by the hand of another, Somali heritage requires monetary compensation or retribution by the same crime. The civil war stretched this system to the limit because a shortage of blood money increased the cycle of violence, leading to system collapse.

The regions (Somaliland and Puntland) achieved peace because they put aside this cycle of violence through concerted efforts at reconciliation among the inhabitants. Conciliation efforts, such as using a council of elders to settle disputes, led to a more stable situation, in which state institutions reappeared to run services that the central government had operated in the past.

Causes of the War

First, the Cold War rivalry between the United States and the Soviet Union provided Somalia with ample foreign aid and weapons to conduct inter- and intrastate conflict. Initially, Somalia received foreign and military aid from the Soviet Union. During its war with Ethiopia, Somalia severed its ties with the Soviet Union because the latter would not provide the assistance Somalia requested to defeat Ethiopia and unite the Ogaden Somalis with their homeland. The United States filled the vacuum created by the Soviet Union's departure. Although the United States did not provide foreign and military aid at the same level as the Soviet Union had, Somalia was still able to purchase the military equipment it needed to destabilize the region.

Second, ethnic and clan cleavages contributed to the civil war in Somalia. Although Somalia is the most homogeneous state in Africa, the Somali people subdivide into several clans, subclans, and clan groups. These divisions exist down to the family level. The unification of British and Italian Somaliland forced the various clans to work together to create a common Somali identity; however, clan rivalries require all disputes to be settled with blood, if necessary. Therefore, when one clan achieves superiority over another or all others, it is possible to manipulate clan sensitivities. Siad Barre chose to manipulate the fragile peace between the clans to benefit his own. What ensued was a deadly civil war that pitted Somali against Somali for superiority and leadership.

Third, artificial borders contributed to the civil war in Somalia. At independence, Somalis lived in Somalia, Ethiopia, Djibouti, and Kenya. An ethnic boundary across sovereign boundaries, especially in Africa, where the sanctity of colonial boundaries was part of the Organization of African Unity charter, creates temptations to preserve unity. Africa decided during the creation of the Organization of African Unity that colonial borders are inviolable, despite their limitations; otherwise, interstate war would continually exist. Therefore, states acceding to the charter agreed to a higher prevalence of internal conflict rather than interstate conflict. Somalia, one of the worst cases of internal strife, maintained its continuity partially be-cause of its ethnic homogeneity and partially because of its desire to realize pan-Somali unity. Although the people of Somalia did not create this idea, the leaders of the country never forgot their Somali brethren in neighboring Ethiopia, Djibouti, and Kenya. Somalia's irredentist claims caused the death of millions and threatened the stability of the entire region. The Congress of Berlin, which partitioned Africa, clearly did not take into consideration the delicacies of African lineage. Their lack of insight led to catastrophic consequences not only in Somalia, but in all of Africa.

Fourth, despotic rule contributed to the civil war in Somalia. After Somalia's devastating loss to Ethiopia in the Ogaden war, Siad Barre chose to maintain his control over the country by using tactics that discriminated against other clans. His brutality in dealing with the Isaaq and the Majerteyn clans led to animosity among the clans and destroyed the concept of Somali unity. Because of his manipulation of clan and subclan identity, the country descended into anarchy.

Fifth, external intervention by the United States and the Soviet Union contributed to the civil war in Somalia. Both countries provided substantial military and financial assistance. During the years following independence, the Soviet Union provided millions of dollars in military assistance. Not only did the Soviet Union train the Somali military, it also provided substantial equipment and material. With this infusion of military resources, Somalia began to realize that pan-Somali union might be possible through the use of force. Rather than negotiating autonomy for its Somali brethren in Djibouti, Ethiopia, and Kenya, Somalia possessed the military resources to annex these regions militarily. In 1977, Somalia began a campaign to annex the Ogaden region of Ethiopia, the largest concentration of Somalis outside Somalia. This action was counterproductive to Soviet interests because the Soviets also supported Ethiopia; therefore, the Soviets began to limit the ability of Somalia to continue to build its military. Siad Barre was infuriated that the Soviet Union would limit its military support at the very moment Somalia needed it the most. Thus strained, the relationship between Somalia and the Soviet Union ended. To fill the void left by the termination of the Somali–Soviet relationship, Somalia sought out the assistance of the United States. The United States gladly accepted a patron–client relationship with Somalia; however, it did not provide the same level of military assistance, choosing to focus on humanitarian and development-related assistance instead. The United States would not become a party to Somalia's war with Ethiopia, even though Ethiopia was part of the Soviet sphere of influence in Africa. The Cold War rivalry facilitated the conflict between Ethiopia and Somalia, a conflict that led to the civil war in Somalia (Lyons and Samatar 1995, 26).

Finally, decolonization from the United Kingdom and Italy occurred rapidly and did not allow for adequate transfers of sovereignty. The indigenous population did not possess the skills to maintain the bureaucracy that the colonial powers had created. Throughout the period of decolonization in Africa, colonial powers notoriously refused to adequately prepare their subjects for independence. The main colonial powers in Africa were the United Kingdom, France, Portugal, and Italy. Throughout the colonial period, the colonial powers subjugated the indigenous peoples to treatment as second-class citizens who could not rise above a certain level in their own countries. Citizens from the metropolis, educated at home, ran the civil service, the economy, and the military. Indigenous peoples participated in these institutions but did not run them, nor did they receive training to run them. Many colonial powers believed that they would have ample time to make the transition from subjugation to autonomy and eventually to independence. However, the indigenous peoples determined the timeline for independence with their resolve, and the colonial powers left without providing a means of efficient self-rule. Somalia suffered the same fate to which many of its fellow African nations succumbed. During the period of decolonization, Italy, France and the United Kingdom tried to determine how best to deal with independence. Italy and the United Kingdom agreed that Italian and British Somaliland might fare better as one independent state. Before this could be arranged, both entities declared independence and shortly thereafter agreed to form a union of their two polities. This rapid transition left no time for training the military, the civil service, or the health care and education sectors. The lack of training and the rapid transfer of sovereignty contributed to the weak nature of the Somali state and allowed a despotic rule to rise to power, eventually committing the country to a war that would begin the slow collapse of the Somali state (Ahmed 1999, 239).

Outcome
Conflict Status

Since October 8, 2004, and the release of the UN secretary-general's report S/2004/804, the situation in Somalia continues to transform as the Transitional Federal Government attempts to relocate in Mogadishu. Despite attempts to relocate the government from Kenya to Somalia, the security situation in the former capital remains insecure. Because of the danger, several members of the government recommended relocation to a safer city such as Hargeisa or Kismayu. This option received little support, for the majority agree that Mogadishu must be the capital of Somalia to ensure legitimacy in the eyes of all Somalis.

The Somali National Reconciliation Conference concluded on October 14, 2004. Colonel Abdullahi Yusef Ahmed won the vote for president. He chose as prime minister Ali Mohammed Gedi, who proceeded to create the Transitional Federal Government (TFG) of Somalia. The prime minister formed a cabinet, but the members of conference who chose the leadership rebelled against his choice, believing that he had not followed the formula devised for fairly representing all clans and subclans. The

The Transitional Federal Government

The Transitional Federal Government, formulated during peace talks in neighboring Djibouti, continues to guide the country from war to peace. Unfortunately, the TFG fails to make substantial progress toward asserting their legitimate role as the sole government in Somalia. Warlordism continues to limit its ability to relocate to Mogadishu and perform its duties. In October 2004, Abdullahi Yusuf Ahmed was elected transitional federal president of Somalia for a five-year period. In December 2004, Ali Mohamed Gedi became prime minister. The cabinet, consisting of ninety ministers and deputy ministers, was appointed in January 2005. The Transitional Federal Assembly, established in August 2004, elected Shariff Hassan Sheilh Adan as speaker of the assembly. These organizations were established during long negotiations and represent the hopes of the Somali people for peace.

After fourteen attempts to make peace, Somali factions finally are optimistic that the current Transitional Federal Government can lead the transition from war to peace. Unfortunately, thirteen other attempts failed to lead the country to peace, prosperity, and sustainable development. In addition, the current Transitional Federal Government does not encompass Somaliland and Puntland, which complicates peace efforts. Because of security concerns, the central government does not function out of the former capital of Mogadishu. Instead, it operates out of a small city not threatened by instability. This decision has strained relations between various factions. Although this new Transitional Federal Government began to take responsibility for state institutions, such as its seat at the United Nations, negotiation of natural resource contracts with multinational corporations, formation of a military, and signing of free trade agreements, the people of Somalia have not experienced the benefits they expect from a central government.

The tsunami of December 26, 2004, as it did in Southeast Asia, destroyed poor coastal areas of Somali. Despite being thousands of miles away from the epicenter near Indonesia, Somalia felt the impact of the tsunami. Without an operational central government, the only assistance to coastal communities was from international organizations and nongovernmental organizations (NGOs). The new Transitional Federal Government must rise up from the ashes of Somalia and bring hope to its people (United Nations Security Council 2005a, 2005b; United States Department of State 2005).

prime minister capitulated and submitted a larger cabinet that included additional members to meet the requirements of fair distribution of personnel.

Due to the deteriorating security situation in Mogadishu, the TFG's relocation plan to move from Nairobi to Mogadishu initially failed. The TFG proceeded to petition the Intergovernmental Authority on Development (IGAD) for military support in reclaiming Mogadishu from the warlords. IGAD was actively involved in the peace process through the IGAD Facilitation Committee. With the realization of peace, the TFG believe IGAD could bring about the realization of a Somalian central government seated in Mogadishu. The "troika" of IGAD, the United Nations, and the IGAD Partners Forum began the process of planning a support mission to create the conditions necessary for the TFG to relocate to Mogadishu. On October 14, IGAD held a Special Summit on Somalia where the Facilitation Committee became the Coordination and Monitoring Committee for Somalia to spearhead the peace support mission to Somalia. On October 25, 2004, the president asked the African Union Peace and Security Council to also commit troops to a peace support mission to relocate the TFG to Mogadishu. On February 7, 2005, the African Union authorized IGAD to deploy a peace and support mission to Somalia. To this point, the political will has not materialized, as many donor countries will not fully commit their forces until the TFG has an agreement with the warlords who do not support a peaceful transition. As evidence, an armed group has been operating inside Somalia with the goal of assassinating all leaders in the country who support the TFG. In 2005, General Mohammed Abdi Mohamed, Colonel Mahamond Batar, and Muhammed Hassan Tako, supporters of the TFG, were assassinated (United Nations Security Council 2005a, 2005b).

Also complicating issues in Somalia was the devastating tsunami of December 26, 2004. Although most of the world's attention was focused on Southeast Asia, the area of Somalia called Puntland declared a state of emergency in response to the disaster. More than 150 lives were lost, 18,000 households affected, and 54,000 people displaced. Because it was the peak fishing season, many families' only livelihood was destroyed when their boats were lost. In addition, many fishermen never returned. To assist relief efforts and to help realize the TFG, the United Nations supports the country through its focal point for activities in Somalia, the United Nations Political Office for Somalia (UNPOS) (United Nations Security Council 2005a, 2005b).

The TFG is attempting to normalize the situation in Somalia by taking on the more traditional roles of the state. To accomplish what experts thought impossible, the TFG returned to Somalia, to the city of Jowhar, because the leaders of the government believed Mogadishu lacked adequate security. In addition, the TFG began recruiting a security force, prepared to negotiate natural resource contracts, and signed a trade pact with Kenya. These activities provide a glimmer of hope for the future of Somalia (Reuters 2005a, 2005b, 2005c; CNN 2005).

The year 2006 brought additional challenges to the fragile peace in Somalia. Famine returned to the southern regions, creating another humanitarian disaster. The UN estimates that 2.1 million Somalis depend totally on international aid; without a functioning central government, the people of Somalia remain vulnerable to human and natural disasters. Additional UN estimates reveal that as many as 250,000 internally displaced persons reside in and around Mogadishu, and 370,000–400,000 internally displaced persons reside in Somalia as a whole. With these challenges facing the people of Somalia, security, no matter who provides it, becomes a valuable commodity. In the face of theses challenges, the Islamic Court Union (ICU) provided security to the people of Somalia. By providing a functioning legal system and security based on Shari'a law, the ICU gained many supporters. However, many outsiders question the means by which security has been provided. The ICU maintains a well-armed militia supplied by those who abrogate the UN arms embargo on Somalia that has been in place since the initial conflict. These militias police the jurisdictions of the eleven courts forming the ICU and are known for their brutality in enforcing Shari'a law. Stories of killings, amputations, and other violent sentences remind observers of the root causes of the rise of the Taliban in Afghanistan.

Despite significant progress in forming a transitional government, Somalia again reverted to violence in early 2006. In some of the most intense fighting since the beginning of the civil war, the Alliance for the Restoration of Peace and Counterterrorism (ARPCT), a grouping of secular clans of Somalia, many of whom participated in the earlier fighting, clashed with the Islamic militias of the Islamic Court Union, who provided stability within Mogadishu and the surrounding areas through the provision of Shari'a law in eleven jurisdictions. The Islamic Court Union provides basic services to the impoverished slums of Mogadishu, bringing security through the provision of Shari'a law and by the creation of Islamic Court militias. This provision of services threatened the position of the ARPCT, as the people of Mogadishu saw the Islamic Court Union militias as providing the security that the ARPCT could not. The poor of Mogadishu traded their secular leaders for religious groups who brought stability through the provision of services and Shari'a law. The ARPCT, which initially formed in February 2006 in an attempt to destroy terrorism, could not provide the same level of security. Despite unsubstantiated reports of support from the United States, ostensibly to capture al-Qaeda terrorists wanted for the 1998 bombings of the U.S. embassies in Kenya and Tanzania as well as the suicide bombings of an Israeli hotel in Kenya, the ARPCT has lost several bloody battles with the Islamic Court Union militias. Making the situation worse in Somalia is yet another famine in southern Somalia. Years of war have made the southern parts of Somalia particularly vulnerable to famine. The ongoing violence in the capital makes it difficult to deliver needed humanitarian aid to the peoples in the south. The continuing suffering of the people of Somalia serve no one's interests as Somalia slips farther away from the prospects for peace.

On May 31, 2006, the United Nations Security Council demanded a cessation to hostilities in Mogadishu for the second time in a month. The council urged the parties to the dispute to reach a negotiated settlement to the dispute within the framework of the Transitional Federal Charter. To achieve this, the disputants must finalize the national security and stabilization plan. Before the violence, the disputants had made progress toward reconciliation. For example, they had agreed on a transitional charter, and parliament was functioning in an attempt to draft a constitution. These were the first signs of a functioning centralized government in the more than fifteen years since the civil conflict began. With the active participation of IGAD and the AU, the region and world were optimistic that peace was forming in Somalia. The arms embargo on Somalia since 1992 remains in force despite its inability to stop the flow of arms across the border. Despite calls by the Security Council for member states to cease the flow of arms, the embargo continues to be violated. Somalia again finds itself at a critical moment in its history, in which the parties to the dispute must address their differences in order to realize peace, prosperity and sustainable development. Without peace, the future of Somalia remains uncertain, and the continuation of conflict threatens the progress toward peace

gained over the past fifteen-plus years (United Nations Operation in Somalia n.d.).

Duration Tactics

Throughout the conflict in Somalia, the clans used animosity between themselves to fuel rivalry and prolong the conflict. Despite multiple efforts to manage the conflict, violence continues. Those clans that do not find peace to be in their interests stifle peace efforts through fear and intimidation. These clans contribute to the existence of a stateless society. Lack of cooperation and continued violence prevent the realization of peace throughout Somalia. The autonomous regions, Puntland and Somaliland, maintain peace and security and enjoy moderate economic growth because of organic peace initiatives formed from traditional methods of reconciliation. Somali culture respects the role of elders, as does much of sub-Saharan Africa, so it is no surprise that those clans who wanted peace would turn to their elders to realize it.

After fourteen attempts at peace, the current TFG represents the transition between warlord-based politics and business-related politics. The years during which warlords controlled Somalia did not provide business interests with the security necessary to operate efficiently. Although business interests enjoyed the nonexistent regulatory environment, to realize larger gains these interests require minimal government services. The availability of electricity, roads, and security only improve the business climate, as long as the government does not begin regulating business activities. In the post–civil war era, peace did not provide motivation to end conflict, as the parties to the dispute would not benefit from peace. Warlords and business interests both benefited from the status quo. As business interests evolved, they realized that the warlords did not provide the environment necessary for them to realize the full potential of their business activities. As this realization grew, the warlords' tactics of promoting anarchy no longer benefited the business sector. These events changed the duration tactics within Somalia and led to increased

Black Hawk Down

The popular movie *Black Hawk Down,* based on the book written by Mark Bowden, depicts the chaotic events of June 19, 1992, in which seventeen Americans died after a failed operation. The movie depicted not only the bravery of the American soldiers but also the role of the international community in rescuing the troops from their situation. International forces quickly organized their troops, APCs, and tanks into a column and went to rescue the surrounded Americans. At great risk to their personal well-being, these international troops extracted the Americans and brought to an end this deadly event.

America's support for Somalia in the 1980s prolonged the inevitable collapse of the Barre regime and the total collapse of the Somali state. Somalia's descent into anarchy continued despite the unprecedented response of the international community. America's role in the humanitarian intervention was to provide food to a country beset by famine created by its ongoing civil war. Unfortunately, humanitarian success did not translate into military success when mission objectives changed to focus on long-term security. At this point, many realized that certain Somali factions would not support peace unless they remained in power. Once Mohammed Farah Aideed's network was identified as a threat to the peace and stability, the United States began to dismantle the network's infrastructure. In a battle immortalized in newspaper, book, and film, the world saw Task Force Ranger battle Aideed's forces in the center of Mogadishu. American casualties mounted as they fought through the night. When the sun rose, American soldiers realized the magnitude of the battle as an international force fought their way to the center of Mogadishu to rescue the Americans. The full impact of the event was visible on American foreign policy into the new millennium.

Although Task Force Ranger accomplished its mission, Americans awoke to the realization that Somalia was no longer a humanitarian intervention but a military operation to influence the outcome of a civil war. After the events depicted in *Black Hawk Down,* President Bill Clinton made the decision to withdraw U.S. forces from Somalia. Shortly after the withdrawal, the UN force found itself in a downward-spiraling situation and withdrew as well, leaving Somalia in the hands of warlords uninterested in peace. A Somalia Syndrome settled over American foreign policy, and U.S. inaction in Rwanda, Zaire, Liberia, and other African hot spots led to the death of millions (Bowden 2000; Lewis 2002).

support for peace and the installation of a new government (Lortan 2000, 1–3).

External Military Intervention

The United States and the United Nations intervened in Somalia to address conditions caused by the civil war, including famine, disease, and desertification. Although the mandate of the U.S.-led United Nations intervention defined the delivery of humanitarian assistance as the primary concern of the mission, those involved understood that the humanitarian disaster stemmed from human causes, not natural ones. Although the United Nations and the United States intervened in Somalia for noble reasons, the intervention plunged the country deeper into chaos. After the international community withdrew from country, official external military intervention stopped. During the period following the failed humanitarian intervention, warring clans continued fighting, with no clear successor to the Barre regime.

Although Somalia's neighbors did not officially intervene in the conflict, the collapse of the Somali state prevented an accurate accounting of the actions of its neighbors. Each neighbor suffered from Barre's irredentist claims on its territory and did not initially respond to assist its neighbor. During the Ethiopia–Eritrea war, the two sides not only fought over territory but also fought a proxy war between rival Somali factions. This extension of their war complicated the situation in Somalia and led to the deaths of hundreds of Somalis. As time elapsed, Somalia's

Somali refugees crouch beside the body of a person who died at the refugee camp in Baidoa, Somalia, in 1992. Drought, famine, and civil war contributed to widespread starvation in Somalia and the death of hundreds of thousands of people. (Peter Turnley/Corbis)

neighbors realized that the collapse of the Somali state affected their security. Somalia's neighbors, along with the international community, became concerned that the lawless nature of Somalia created a security vacuum in the region. Nonstate actors often shift their operations to collapsed states because of the lack of a central authority to police their activities. The United States and its allies began to patrol the coast off the Horn of Africa in response to the bombing of the USS *Cole* in Yemen and the increase of terrorist operations globally. Djibouti houses U.S. and allied troops in response to the increased terrorist operations in the region (Lortan 2000, 1–3).

Ethiopia is the central actor in external intervention in Somalia despite its involvement in reconciliation efforts. Ethiopia supports a weak decentralized government in Somalia that cannot threaten Ethiopia's security. Ethiopia intervened in Somalia by capturing three districts in

the Gedo region. Egypt is interested in a strong centralized government in Somalia to distract Ethiopia from developing its Nile River assets. The development of these resources would impact the downstream resources Egypt relies on for its economic survival. The war in Ethiopia–Eritrea led to proxy battles in Somalia. Eritrea supported anti-Ethiopia groups, whereas Libya and Sudan supported anti-U.S. groups. Yemen has strong commercial ties with various factions (Farah, Hussein, and Lind 2002, 327).

Conflict Management Efforts

Organizations at the international, regional, and subregional levels attempted to manage the conflict in Somalia. Despite active participation by the United Nations, the Organization of African Unity (now the African Union), and the Intergovernmental Authority on Development, a peaceful settlement to the dispute did not materialize.

The United Nations sponsored national reconciliation talks between the warring parties in 1991. Fifteen factions attended these conferences in Addis Ababa, Ethiopia, in January and March 1991. These conferences produced the Addis Ababa accords, which the parties never implemented, owing to distrust between the warlords who controlled Somalia. Complicating matters was Somaliland's declaration of independence and Puntland's autonomy from Southern Somalia (Farah, Hussein, and Lind 2002, 328).

As the parties to the dispute failed to implement the first Addis Ababa accords, they decided to hold another reconciliation conference, Addis Ababa II. The conference occurred in March 1993 (Lyons and Samatar 1995, 49–53).

The United Nations began its involvement with Security Council Resolution 733, which provided for a general embargo on Somalia to help bring about conditions necessary to the peaceful settlement of the dispute. Later, Security Council Resolution 751 created UNITAF, led by the United States. The UN Security Council designed the mission to bring peace to Somalia and stem the famine affecting all of Somalia. This mission led to UNOSOM I and UNOSOM II (Farah, Hussein, and Lind 2002, 328; Lewis 2002, 267–75).

Djibouti, Eritrea, Ethiopia, Kenya, Somalia, Sudan, and Uganda constitute the Intergovernmental Authority on Development. The IGAD replaced the Intergovernmental Authority on Drought and Development in 1996. The organization formed in 1986 to determine a united approach to the problems of Eastern Africa (IGAD website). The IGAD plays a central role in the reestablishment of a recognized, central government in Somalia. Djibouti hosted the conference where Somalis negotiated the creation of the Transitional Government. The IGAD plans to send in a stabilization force to bring peace to the capital. Uganda and Sudan plan to lead this aspect of the mission.

The heads of state and government of the Organization of African Unity proclaimed on September 9, 1999, their intention to create an African Union (AU) as outlined in the Sirte Declaration (AU website). During the active phase of the civil conflict in Somalia, the OAU played an important role in the implementation of Security Council resolutions. Today, the AU actively supports the efforts of the IGAD in Somalia. At the regional level, these two African organizations facilitated the peace effort at every step. The African Union agreed to provide a peacekeeping force upon the successful deployment of an IGAD force. Continued violence and the inability of IGAD to deploy its forces delay plans to deploy these troops. Also, the front line states, Djibouti, Kenya and Ethiopia, offered to contribute the bulk of the AU force. This composition created substantial debate among the TFG, for many do not trust these states to deploy their forces throughout Somalia.

Conclusion

Somalia's ethnic homogeneity initially created strong bonds between the clans of Somalia; however, when Siad Barre decided to exploit the differences between the clans through the use of retribution and murder, the identity of Somalis crumbled under the weight of hatred and animosity. Many predicted that ethnic homogeneity meant that Somalia was destined for stability and economic prosperity, but for a variety of reasons the state collapsed and spiraled into obscurity. Despite good intentions, the international community failed to address the root causes of the conflict, and anarchy continues to define Somalia. With the creation of a new government, a new chapter of Somali history begins. The future of Somalia remains bleak; however, the success or failure of the new government will determine whether prospects for peace will improve.

After decades of civil war, the people of Somalia see new hope on the horizon. Through the efforts of countless diplomats, civil servants, academics, politicians, soldiers, elders, and regular civil servants, a new government exists. Although it will be difficult to maintain momentum (the first attempt failed), this new government will strive to create a presence in Mogadishu, to reach out to its people, including Somaliland and Puntland, and to bring civility back to Somalia. This grand achievement will be for naught without the strong political, economic, and, if necessary, military support of the entire international community.

Kyle Wilson

Chronology

1887   Great Britain establishes a protectorate over Somaliland.

1889   Italy establishes a protectorate over south-central Somalia.

June 26,1960   British Somaliland becomes independent.

July 1, 1960   Italian Somaliland and Somalia become independent.

October 21, 1969   Siad Barre seizes power.

October 21, 1972   Written script for Somali language is established.

July 23, 1977   War with Ethiopia begins.

April 8, 1978   Coup attempt against Siad Barre.

December 1990   Uprising begins against Siad Barre regime.

May 18, 1991   Former British Somaliland declares independence.

January 27, 1992   Siad Barre leaves Mogadishu.

April 24, 1992   UNOSOM I peacekeeping mission begins.

December 3, 1992   UNITAF mission begins.

March 26, 1993   UNOSOM II peacekeeping mission begins.

May 2, 2000   Arta Peace Conference is held in Djibouti.

February 26, 2003   Nairobi Peace Conference is held in Kenya.

August 22, 2004   Current transitional government forms.

October 10, 2004   Abdullahi Yusef Ahmed is elected president.

November 3, 2004   Ali Muhammad Gedi is appointed prime minister.

October 25, 2005   Yusef requests African Union troops.

February 7, 2005   African Union approves IGAD peace support mission.

February 2006   Alliance for the Restoration of Peace and Counterterrorism created to combat terrorism in Somalia.

May 31, 2006   UN Security Council calls for a cessation of hostilities between the Alliance for the Restoration of Peace and Counterterrorism and the Islamic Court Union.

List of Acronyms

ARPCT: Alliance for the Restoration of Peace and Counterterrorism

ICU: Islamic Court Union

IGAD: Intergovernmental Authority on Development

NGO: nongovernmental organization

OAU: Organization of African Unity

OIC: Organization of the Islamic Conference

SAMO: Somali African Muki Organization

SDA: Somali Democratic Alliance

SDM: Somali Democratic Movement (Somali National Alliance)

SNA: Somali National Army

SNA: Somali National Alliance

SNDU: Somali National Democratic Union

SNF: Somali National Front

SNM: Somali National Movement

SNU: Somali National Union

SPM: Somali Patriotic Movement (Somali National Alliance)

SSA: Somali Salvation Alliance

SSDF: Somali Salvation Democratic Front

SSNM: Southern Somali National Movement (Somali National Alliance)

TFG: Transitional Federal Government

UNITAF: Unified Task Force (UN)

UNOSOM: United Nations Operation in Somalia

UNPOS: United Nations Political Office for Somalia

USC: United Somali Congress (Somali National Alliance)

USF: United Somali Front

USP: United Somali Party

References

Adam, Hussein M. 1995. "Somalia: A Terrible Beauty Being Born?" In *Collapsed States: The Disintegration and Restoration of Legitimate Authority,* edited by I. William Zartman. Boulder, CO: Lynne Rienner.

African Union. Website. www.africa-union.org/home/Welcome.htm (accessed June 28, 2005).

Ahmed, Ismail. 1999. "Understanding Conflict in Somalia and Somaliland." In *Comprehending and Mastering African Conflicts,* edited by Adedeji Adebayo, 236–56. New York: St. Martin's Press.

Allard, Kenneth. 2002. *Somalia Operations: Lessons Learned.* Honolulu, HI: University Press of the Pacific.

Ayittey, George B. N. 1998. *Africa in Chaos.* New York: St. Martin's Press.

Bowden, Mark. 2000. *Black Hawk Down: A Story of Modern War.* New York: Signet.

Central Intelligence Agency (CIA). *World Fact Book 2005: Somalia.* www.odci.gov/cia/publications/factbook/geos/so.html (accessed September 20, 2005).

Chapin-Metz, Helen. 1993. *Somalia: A Country Study.* Washington, DC: Library of Congress.

Clarke, Walter, and Jeffrey Herbst, eds. 1997. *Learning from Somalia: The Lessons of Armed Humanitarian Intervention.* Boulder, CO: Westview Press.

CNN. 2005. "Somalia Signs Historic Trade Pact with Kenya." September 6. edition.cnn.com/2005/WORLD/africa/09/06/kenya.somalia.reut/ (accessed September 6, 2005).

Farah, Ibrahim, Adbdirashid Hussein, and Jeremy Lind. 2002. "Deegan, Politics and War in Somalia." In *Scarcity and Surfeit: The Ecology of Africa's Conflicts,* edited by Jeremy Lind and Kathryn Sturman. Pretoria: African Centre for Technology Studies and Institute for Security Studies.

Green, Reginald Herbold. 1999. "Towards a Macro-Economic Framework for Somaliland's Post-War Rehabilitation and Reconstruction." In *Comprehending and Mastering African Conflicts,* edited by Adedeji Adebayo, 257–81. New York: St. Martin's Press.

Howe, Jonathan T. 1996. "Somalia: Frustration in a Failed Nation." In *Soldiers for Peace: Fifty Years of United Nations Peacekeeping,* edited by Barbara Benton, 158–85. New York: American Historical Publications.

Institute for Security Studies. No date. Website. www.iss.co.za/AF/profiles/Somalia/SecInfo.html (accessed May 21, 2005).

Institute for Security Studies. No date. Website. www.iss.org.za/AF/profiles/somalia/Table_Economy.html (accessed August 21, 2005).

Intergovernmental Authority on Development. Website. www.igad.org/ (accessed June 28, 2005).

Lewis, I. M. 2002. *A Modern History of the Somali: Revised, Updated and Expanded.* Athens: Ohio University Press.

Lortan, Fiona. 2000. "Rebuilding the Somali State." *African Security Review* 9(5/6). www.iss.org.za/Pubs/ASR/9No5And6/Lortan.html (accessed April 23, 2005).

Lyons, Terrence, and Ahmed I. Samatar. 1995. *Somalia: State Collapse, Multilateral Intervention, and Strategies for Political Reconstruction.* Washington, DC: The Brookings Institution.

Metz, Helen Chapin, ed. 1992. *Somalia: A Country Study.* Washington, DC: Library of Congress.

Polity IV Project. 2003. *Political Regime Characteristics and Transitions, 1800–2003.* www.cidcm.umd.edu/inscr/polity/ (accessed May 20, 2006).

Reuters. 2005a. "Somalia Minister Returns to Moagadishu Amid Fresh Row." August 14. www.alertnet.org/thenews/newsdesk/L14614522.htm (accessed September 6, 2005).

Reuters. 2005b. "Somali Troop Move Has Peaceful Intention–PM." August 19. za.today.reuters.com/news/NewsArticle.aspx?type=topNews&storyID=2005–08–19T131140Z_01_BAN947460_RTRIDST_0_OZATP-SOMALIA-TROOPS–20050819.XML (accessed September 6, 2005).

Reuters. 2005c. "Somalia Says Ready for Oil, Mineral Deals in Months." August 28. za.today.reuters.com/news/newsArticle.aspx?type=businessNews&storyID=2005–08–28T131351Z_01_BAN847544_RTRIDST_0_OZABS-SOMALIA-RESOURCES–20050828.XML (accessed September 6, 2005).

United Nations Operation in Somalia. No date. Website. www.un.org/Depts/dpko/dpko/co_mission/unosom1backgr2.html (accessed August 31, 2005).

United Nations Security Council. 2005a. *Report of the Secretary-General on the Situation in Somalia. S/2005/89.* New York: United Nations.

United Nations Security Council. 2005b. *Report of the Secretary-General on the Situation in Somalia. S/2005/392.* New York: United Nations.

United States Department of State. 2005. *Somalia.* www.state.gov/r/pa/ei/bgn/2863.htm (accessed September 20, 2005).

United States Committee for Refugees. 1997. *World Refugee Survey 1997.* Washington, DC: United States Committee for Refugees.

United States Library of Congress. *Country Studies: Somalia.* lcweb2.loc.gov/frd/cs/cshome.html (accessed September 20, 2005).

Woodward, Peter. 2003. *The Horn of Africa: Politics and International Relations.* New York: I.B. Tauris.

Zartman, I. Willam, ed. 1995. *Collapsed States: The Disintegration and Restoration of Legitimate Authority.* Boulder, CO: Lynne Rienner.

South Africa (1976–1994)

Introduction

The struggle to end white minority rule in South Africa and the accompanying policy of apartheid lead to one of the most protracted civil conflicts in African history. Unlike most civil wars, however, the conflict evolved from one of peaceful protest into guerrilla warfare over a period of several years. The persistence of various rebel groups was largely due to the international isolation of South Africa during the apartheid era. Isolation provided a basis for support of the rebels, both from within the region and as part of the broader Cold War. Ultimately, the persistence of the rebels and important national and regional political changes led to the end of apartheid and the advent of majority rule.

Country Background

On May 31, 1910, the Union of South Africa became an independent state within the British Commonwealth. In 1961, South Africa left the Commonwealth and became the Republic of South Africa (RSA) (Saunders 2002b, 966). Afrikaner nationalists, who had fought both British rule and competition from blacks, formed the National Party (NP) in 1912. After more moderate members of the NP allied themselves with the South Africa Party (SAP), eventually forming the United Party (UP), a

group of ultranationalists under the leadership of Daniel Malan formed a more reactionary NP. When the NP took power in 1948, it began to institute the policy of apartheid (which means separateness in Afrikaans). Apartheid ultimately led to civil war.

In the years immediately before the civil war began, the level of democracy in South Africa depended directly on the color of one's skin. South Africa's polity score was +4 on a scale of −10 to +10 (Marshall and Jaggers 2002). South Africa had a relatively high polity score, for an authoritarian state, before the civil war because of the broad range of civil and political rights granted to whites. Blacks, by contrast, were denied suffrage, whereas Indians and coloreds were progressively stripped of their limited freedoms. During the course of the civil war, South Africa's polity score remained +4. After the advent of majority rule in 1994, the country's polity score increased to +8. Today, the polity score stands at +9.

From an economic standpoint, South Africa has always been one of the most developed states in sub-Saharan Africa. In 1976, the year the guerrilla war began, the gross domestic product (GDP) per capita was US $7,536 (Heston, Summers, and Aten, 2002). Early in the civil war, the South African economy continued to grow, in part because the government initiated import substitution industrialization (ISI)

in anticipation of international sanctions. However, international pressure eventually began to
take its toll. Although economic sanctions
against the South African government were
often ineffective, international lending institutions began to consider South Africa a poor
credit risk in 1985 (Lieberfeld 1999, 34). As a result, GDP per capita five years after the civil war
ended stood at US $7,460 (Heston, Summers,
and Aten, 2002). One of the major factors that
prevented real GDP from falling even further
was the presence of valuable natural resources
in South Africa, especially diamonds (Harsch,
1987, 54).

Although GDP per capita is comparatively
high in South Africa, it is important to recognize
that, during the apartheid era, the vast majority
of material wealth was concentrated in the
hands of the white population. In the era of
black African majority rule, income disparity is
a lingering problem. Whites in South Africa continue to earn more than 50 percent of available
income (Van Buren 2002, 976). As a result, the
level of income inequality in South Africa is
among the highest in the world (Doyle and
Sambanis 2000).

Conflict Background

There is some degree of debate over how to classify the South African civil war. Some scholars
classify the war as an ethnic conflict (see Doyle
and Sambanis 2000). Other authors point out
that the African National Congress (ANC) was
founded on principles of nonracialism (see
Davis 1987, 4). Although black nationalism was
a contending force in rebel politics, it was certainly not the only, or even the primary, political
force in play. In addition, classification of the
South African civil war as an ethnic war ignores
the ethnic diversity among blacks and whites in
South Africa.

Perhaps the most intuitive way to classify the
South African civil war is to consider the primary goal of the rebels. The Freedom Charter,
adopted in 1955, became the official political

platform of the ANC. The preamble to the Freedom Charter reads as follows:

> We, the People of South Africa, declare for all
> our country and the world to know:
> that South Africa belongs to all who live in
> it, black and white, and that no government can
> justly claim authority unless it is based on the
> will of all the people;
> that our people have been robbed of their
> birthright to land, liberty and peace by a form of
> government founded on injustice and
> inequality;
> that our country will never be prosperous
> or free until all our people live in brotherhood,
> enjoying equal rights and opportunities; that
> only a democratic state, based on the will of all
> the people, can secure to all their birthright
> without distinction of colour, race, sex or
> belief;
> And therefore, we, the people of South
> Africa, black and white together equals,
> countrymen and brothers adopt this Freedom
> Charter;
> And we pledge ourselves to strive together,
> sparing neither strength nor courage, until the
> democratic changes here set out have been won
> (ANC Website, 2005).

As the Freedom Charter indicates, the principal goal of those who rebelled against
apartheid was liberation from white rule and
democracy. As a result, this article treats the
South African civil war as a struggle between
two contending ideologies: the supremacist
ideology of apartheid and the liberation ideology of the rebels.

In addition to the debate over classification
of the South African civil war, there is some
question as to when the war began. The main
rebel group, Umkhonto we Sizwe (Spear of the
Nation), formed in 1961 (Motlhabi 1988, 73).
Umkhonto we Sizwe, sometimes called MK
after a group of earlier volunteers known as
Amadelakufe (those who do not fear death),
carried out its first attacks against government
installations in December 1961. The early portion of MK's history, however, was characterized by infrequent attacks that tended to focus
strictly on economic targets. It was not until

June 16, 1976, in the wake of the Soweto massacre, that the MK began to target political infrastructure, including police stations and other government buildings. On April 26, 1994, the civil war ended with the first free elections in South Africa.

The South African civil war is also unique in the number of battles fought in neighboring countries. One of the best examples of direct South African military intervention is Angola. South Africa intervened on the side of the União Nacional para a Independência Total de Angola (UNITA) in order to counter the Soviet Union, who backed the Movimento Popular de Libertacão de Angola (MPLA). In addition, the ANC had offices in the capital city of Luanda (Garztecki 2002, 35). Mozambique, Lesotho, Botswana, Tanzania, Zambia, and Zimbabwe were all subject to South African military incursions (Davis 1987, 42–46). Finally, South Africa

attempted to dominate Namibia as an illegitimate trust territory (Saunders 2002a, 727).

The Insurgents

In reality, several groups in South Africa attempted in one way or another to undermine the apartheid system of government. By restricting the definition of *rebel* to "one who takes up arms against the government," it is possible to narrow the discussion to three main groups. The best-known of these groups is the African National Congress. Once called the South African Native National Congress (SANNC), the ANC was founded in 1912 with the primary goal of advancing the interests of nonwhite elites. In its early history, the ANC preferred a constitutionalist approach, choosing negotiation with the South African government over confrontation (Davis 1987, 5). After the NP initiated apartheid,

Table 1: Civil War in South Africa

War:	ANC–MK vs. government
Dates:	June 1976–April 1994
Casualties:	100,000
Regime type prior to war:	Polity score of 4 (ranging from −10 [authoritarian] to 10 [democracy])
Regime type after war:	Polity score of 8 (ranging from −10 [authoritarian] to 10 [democracy])
GDP per capita year war began:	US $7,536 (constant 1996 dollars) significantly lower for nonwhite population
GDP per capita 5 years after war:	US $7,460 (constant 1996 dollars); significantly lower for nonwhite population
Insurgents:	ANC (African National Congress), Umkhonto we Sizwe
Issue:	Ending white minority rule, apartheid
Rebel Funding:	Soviet aid (for military operations), international fund-raising (for overall ANC mission)
Role of geography:	Rebels used rain forest cover in bases outside South Africa.
Role of resources:	Gold, diamonds, and strategic resources helped government resist multilateral sanctions.
Immediate outcome:	Transition to majority rule, elections
Outcome after 5 years:	Democracy, lingering violence
Role of UN:	None within South Africa; monitoring of Cuban and South African withdrawal from Angola
Role of regional organizations:	OAU supported ANC; SADCC attempted to achieve economic independence from South Africa.
Refugees:	Not applicable, although forced displacement of blacks was common
Prospects for peace:	Favorable

Sources: Doyle and Sambanis (2000); Heston, Summers, and Aten (2002); Marshall and Jaggers (2002).

the ANC turned to nonviolent protest in an attempt to alter government policy. It was at this time that a founding member of the ANC Youth League, Nelson Mandela, rose to prominence within the organization.

It was not until the formation of Umkhonto we Sizwe in November 1961 that the ANC became a true rebel group in the sense that it sought to use controlled violence to bring down the existing government. Ironically, it was the results of a protest led by a rival group called the Pan Africanist Congress (PAC) that played a major role in the ANC decision to take up arms against the government. The PAC organized a protest against the pass laws, which prohibited travel outside of racially segregated areas without a government-issued pass. In Sharpsville, the police responded to the protest by killing sixty-seven blacks (Thompson 1995, 210). In response to a large demonstration in Cape Town, the army and the police jailed more than 17,000 protesters. Soon afterward, the government banned both the ANC and the PAC.

On December 16, 1961, MK attacked several government installations in Johannesburg, Port Elizabeth, and Durban. At the same time, the organization distributed leaflets announcing the MK and explaining its decision to take up arms.

The second rebel group in South Africa was the aforementioned PAC. The PAC formed April 6, 1959, as the Africanist alternative to the ANC (Davis 1987, 10). The basic ideological divide between the ANC and the PAC centered on the issue of "racial purity" within the anti-apartheid movement. Africanists argued that freedom required the development of strong black nationalism. The ANC, by contrast, considered itself a "big tent" movement, willing to accommodate coloreds, Indians, and even whites.

The PAC launched its own guerrilla organization called Poqo (Pure). Initially, Poqo participated in several bombing campaigns in the early 1960s. However, the PAC suffered a series of setbacks that also harmed Poqo. The ANC's major advantage was that it had been at least partially prepared to reorganize underground well before the PAC and the ANC were outlawed in 1960. The PAC, by contrast, had been in existence only since 1959. In addition, Poqo demonstrated more initial willingness to attack white civilians directly (Muthien 1990, 81). This decreased the legitimacy of Poqo among moderates.

A third rebel organization is the South African Communist Party (SACP). Forced underground by the 1950 Suppression of Communism Act, the SACP formed well-developed covert networks (Davis 1987, 9). In addition, members of the SACP sought to coordinate protest activity with the ANC, which was still legal at the time. Although many ANC members were quite suspicious of the Communists, they also recognized that they could benefit from SACP know-how if the ANC were ever forced underground. As a result, members of the SACP took on many important leadership roles within the ANC and MK. For example, Joe Slovo, SACP chairman, was a respected member of the ANC Revolutionary Council (Ellis and Sechaba 1992, 56). For its part, the apartheid government used the SACP–ANC alliance for its own ends, claiming that South Africa was a target of the world Communist revolution. The validity of the government's assertion, however, was probably overstated (see sidebar, "The SACP and the ANC").

Of course, no rebel group can exist without an adequate source of funding. The ANC did not have access to South Africa's mineral wealth. Money to support day-to-day (nonmilitary) operations came from a variety of sources. First, the ANC raised some money and supplies from its own projects, including fund-raising cultural tours and ANC-owned farms in Zambia (Davis 1987, 73). Several of the Nordic countries provided funding for education, including scholarships for study abroad. International organizations pledged additional support.

Most of the money for the US $50 million annual military budget came from the Soviet Union and its satellites in Eastern Europe (Davis

The SACP and the ANC

One of the National Party's most powerful arguments against the economic isolation of South Africa was the idea that the government was one of the final lines of defense against communism in sub-Saharan Africa. The NP fanned anticommunist flames by pointing out the cozy relationship between the ANC and the SACP. Upon closer examination, however, the extent of this relationship seems to have been greatly exaggerated.

First, documentary evidence suggests that Nelson Mandela sought Soviet support only after he recognized that it had been previously given to noncommunist and anticommunist states (Meli 1989, 149). In fact, most of the members of the ANC Youth League, which Mandela helped to found, were initially highly suspicious of Communists (Kempton 1989, 156).

Second, the ANC and the SACP shared a common enemy. Common hatred of the NP formed one of the primary bases of the ANC–SACP relationship (Ellis and Sechaba 1992, 26). The fact that the ANC became more radicalized in the 1960s and 1970s can be traced as easily to its response to reactionary NP policy as it can to SACP influence. In fact, the Suppression of Communism Act that forced the SACP underground also forced it directly into league with the ANC. Finally, many members of the SACP recognized that the transition to socialism might not be the only acceptable goal in South Africa. Multiracial democracy was also an acceptable goal (Kempton 1989, 162).

Although the NP may have exaggerated the amount of power held by the SACP within the ANC, there certainly was a relationship between the two groups. The SACP played a strong role in drafting the Freedom Charter and held important positions on the ANC Executive Committee and within MK. It is even possible that the SACP held a level of influence within the ANC disproportionate to its numbers. The overall evidence, however, suggests that the relationship between the ANC and the SACP was based much more on common interest than common ideology (Ellis and Sechaba 1992; Kempton 1989; Meli 1989).

1987, 74). In addition, the ANC was able to raise significant amounts of cash from wealthy South African expatriates. The ANC also conducted fund-raising activities among South African blacks and sympathetic whites. Finally, the ANC often funneled international donations of food and equipment to Umkhonto we Sizwe.

Geography

Both political and physical geography played an important role in the South African civil war. As the ANC was charged with the task of setting up an entire government in exile, it would be impossible to use physical geography to completely obscure the location of all critical ANC centers. As a result, political geography played a key role. Given the ability of South Africa to project its military might into other states, the rebels needed to choose their base locations carefully. Namibia was under direct South African control for portions of the war. Botswana, Zimbabwe, and Mozambique provided tempting targets for direct South African raids. Lesotho was completed surrounded by South African territory, and Swaziland was almost completely engulfed.

As a consequence of these geopolitical concerns, most of the key ANC military and non-military bases were located in Angola, Tanzania, and Zambia. For example, MK operated twelve training and transit camps in Angola between 1976 and 1989 (ANC 1997). The main political headquarters of the ANC was located in Lusaka, Zambia. A major MK operations base was located near Dar es Salaam, Tanzania (Davis 1987, 48–49). Even at this distance from South Africa, many ANC and MK bases were destroyed by ground or aerial attack.

The ANC had a political presence in Botswana, Zimbabwe, Mozambique, Swaziland, and Lesotho. These political offices were often unofficial and carefully hidden, for they were within easy range of attack by the South African

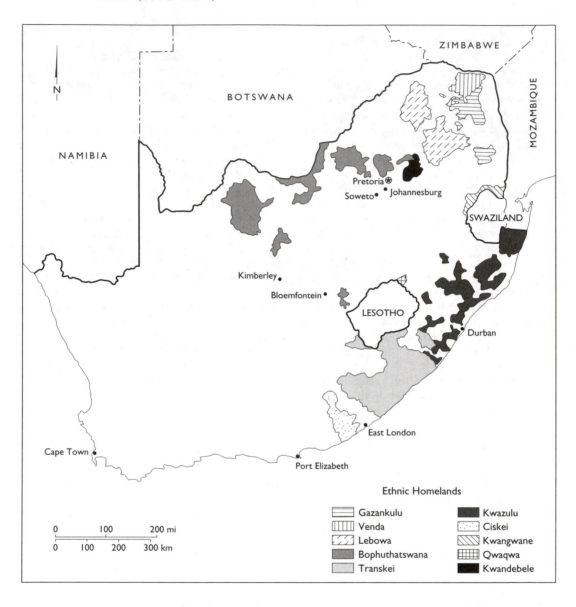

Ethnic Homelands

Gazankulu   Kwazulu
Venda   Ciskei
Lebowa   Kwangwane
Bophuthatswana   Qwaqwa
Transkei   Kwandebele

Defense Force (SADF). Collectively, these states were also the principal transit points for MK rebels making their way from Angola, Zambia, or Tanzania to South Africa. ANC leaders had learned the hard way that it was necessary to trade convenient access to South Africa for relative safety. In 1963, South African police raided an MK camp in the suburb of Rivonia near Johannesburg. Rivonia, at the time, was MK's national headquarters (Davis 1987, 17). Several critical ANC leaders, including Nelson Mandela, were captured in the raid.

Physical geography was also very important to the rebels. Several years after the civil war ended, the MK highlighted the importance of physical geography in the conflict by revealing that MK training camps taught courses in military topography (ANC 1997). Because government security forces had an advantage in technology, rebels attempting to return to South Africa had to take advantage of the rough, bushy terrain that lies on the frontier between South Africa and many of its neighbors. Working in small units allowed the MK to cross the border with less chance of detection (Feit 1971, 236).

Tactics

Umkhonto we Sizwe's basic strategy focused on four principal types of targets. One of these was key government installations and infrastructure, including South African Police installations and personnel (Muthien 1990, 83). MK also attacked and damaged government-owned railways and power stations. The goal of these "challenge attacks" was to demonstrate to the white populace that the government could not protect them from the rebel movement (Davis 1987, 121). The overall hope was that pressure from white citizens for protection would force the government to the negotiating table.

Economic targets were also frequently subject to guerrilla attacks. There is overlap here with the government infrastructure category, as the ANC considered the railways economic targets. However, the rebels also attacked white South African businesses. Most of these attacks were carried out at night to minimize the potential for white civilian casualties. The ANC was committed enough to avoiding civilian categories that it became the first national liberation movement to sign the Geneva Convention and its Optional Protocol of 1977 (ANC 1980). However, because many of the preferred economic targets were located in heavily populated areas, it was not uncommon for civilians to die in ANC attacks.

A third popular set of MK targets were those designed to gain direct support among South African blacks. These "linkage attacks" were direct responses to popular protest against elements of white rule (Davis 1987, 151). For example, on October 15, 1980, MK targeted and destroyed a railway line in the Dube area. The ANC considered this attack part of its support of community resistance, as Soweto community leaders had called for a boycott of the rail line in response to rent increases in the area (ANC 1997). Because whites possessed a virtual monopoly on South African media, linkage attacks were one of the few ways that the ANC–MK could inform community leaders that the rebels were working on their behalf.

Linkage attacks became even more important as the South African government attempted to drive a wedge between blacks, coloreds, and Indians by establishing a tricameral parliament that included the latter two groups. The United Democratic Front (UDF), which originally formed in an effort to block the tricameral parliament, became a key coordinating actor in the township revolts that began in the mid-1980s (Seekings 2000, 121). The various groups organized under the UDF would work to foster a popular uprising. MK would ensure that protests were buttressed by guerrilla force. In addition, the UDF directly aided MK by increasing the size and number of safe havens within the townships (Davis 1987, 89).

The fourth common target set consisted of those individuals whom the ANC considered to be collaborating with the apartheid regime. Former members of the ANC, as well as prosecuting attorneys and other prosecution witnesses, became targets of MK attacks. One example of an attack on collaborators was the assassination of Abel Mthembu on April 14, 1978. Mthembu, a former ANC deputy president, had turned states evidence at a key trial of ANC members (ANC 1997).

If the overall strategy was to attack infrastructure, people, and institutions associated with apartheid, the dominant tactic was guerrilla warfare. Given the sophistication of South African border security, it was possible for MK rebels to return to the country from the various training camps only if they traveled in small groups (often five or fewer). Similarly, the rebels attacked their targets in small groups as well. By attacking in groups of between three and five members, the rebels had a better chance of avoiding detention and capture. When possible, MK planted timed explosives and land mines to allow the rebels to return to the underground before the government became aware of the attack.

As is the case with most guerrilla movements, the ability to obtain adequate supplies of small arms was critical in Umkhonto we Sizwe's effort to end apartheid. MK relied on two basic sources of weapons. The most reliable source of small arms for the rebels was the Soviet Union. The Soviets provided Skorpion VZOR 61 machine pistols from Czechoslovakia, Tokarev T-33 pistols, Makarov SL pistols, and AK-47 rifles (Davis 1987, 71). The Soviets also supplied hand grenades, antitank land mines, and antipersonnel land mines.

Armed with Soviet weapons, the rebels were no match for the conventional superiority of the government forces. In addition, MK experienced severe weapons shortages because of the difficulty in smuggling small arms across the border. After 1985, MK officers were instructed to recruit their own resistance cells from among the general population rather than attempting to reconnect with other foreign-trained rebels (Davis 1987, 124). This created further weapons shortages, since a single foreign-trained rebel possessed only the weapons that he was able to smuggle into the country.

With restricted access to Soviet weapons within South Africa, the rebels turned to theft as a second source of small arms. South African history has produced a society where gun ownership is very common. Often, black domestic workers were able to gain access to caches of small arms that subsequently found their way into MK hands. Local police departments, especially in those areas where blacks had access to weapons, were also very popular targets.

For its part, the government used a variety of demographic, legal, and military tactics in an attempt to maintain the political status quo in South Africa. First, it is necessary to recognize that the apartheid system itself was part of the South African government's attempts to quell any potential rebellion. A series of pass laws made it very difficult for most blacks to gain access to white urban areas. Only blacks who carried a specially endorsed urban pass were allowed to remain in the cities, under the terms of the Urban Areas Act (Beck 2000, 128). The Promotion of Bantu Self-Government Act of 1959 essentially eliminated political rights for blacks outside of the land reserved for blacks under the 1936 Land Act. The ultimate goal of the South African government was to confer independence on the ten Bantustans (homelands) that occupied approximately 13.7 percent of South African land (Beck 2000, 134). From a military perspective, the Bantustans served as a form of buffer between the black and white populations.

Second, the South African government used destabilization techniques on neighboring countries to make it more difficult for MK and the ANC to find sanctuary. South Africa supported the UNITA in the Angolan civil war in an attempt to thwart the MPLA. As the MPLA supported both South African and Namibian rebels, its defeat would have been a significant victory for South Africa. South Africa also supported rebel movements in Mozambique, Zimbabwe, and Lesotho. The strategy of destabilization was at least partially successful. Mozambique agreed in 1984 to expel the ANC from its territory in exchange for a cessation of South African support of the Resistência Nacional de Moçambique (RENAMO). South Africa successfully included ANC expulsion from Angola in the terms of its final withdrawal in 1989 (Garztecki 2002, 36).

The destabilization policy, although partially successful, was also self-defeating. By fostering instability in neighboring states, the government effectively made it more difficult for those states to comply with South African desires to deny asylum to the ANC. Weak political and military institutions in South Africa's neighboring countries made them attractive transit routes for MK. In addition, South Africa did not always keep its side of the bargain. For example, the RSA continued to support Renamo in Mozambique even after the 1984 agreement. As a result, there was little incentive for the Mozambican government, which sympathized with the Marxist and liberation components of ANC thought, to actively root out rebels from its territory.

The RSA augmented its destabilization strategy by fostering economic dependence on the part of South Africa's neighbors. Lesotho, which is entirely surrounded by South Africa, required access to transportation infrastructure, electricity, and food from the RSA. Almost all of Swaziland's trade traveled through South Africa, and remittances from Swazi laborers in the RSA were a critical source of income. Mozambique required the use of South African ports. Each of these states was also dependent on food imports and technical expertise from South Africa. South Africa used threats of withdrawal of this assistance to encourage more favorable policies in the neighboring states (Davis 1987, 41).

When destabilization efforts failed to eliminate the ANC as a threat, the SADF was willing to use force directly against the ANC in the sanctuary states. Several ANC bases in Angola were destroyed by SADF air raids (ANC 1997). The SADF also raided ANC offices and MK bases in Mozambique, Lesotho, Zambia, Botswana, and Zimbabwe. South African military superiority, coupled with weak foreign governments, made it difficult for the RSA's neighbors to resist incursions.

In addition to the RSA's ability to project its military power abroad, South Africa made the protection of its own border a key element of its antirebel strategy. Combining numerical and technological superiority, the SADF and the SAP (South African Police) were often successful in capturing MK recruits as they attempted to flee South Africa. Many fully trained rebels were also captured as they attempted to reenter the country. The RSA's border strategy also made it difficult for the rebels to smuggle arms into South Africa.

The South African military also used human intelligence to supplement its military might. Especially in the early days of MK, the Bureau of State Security (BOSS) found it relatively easy to infiltrate the ranks of rebel organizations. Thousands of arrests occurred inside South Africa as a result of these efforts. Infiltration of MK units outside of South Africa also provided the South African National Defense Force (SANDF) with the location of several rebel bases. Eventually, the ANC adapted to government tactics by giving more autonomy to smaller localized units and limiting the amount of critical information held by any single resistance cell.

The NP government realized over time that military action alone would not be sufficient to quell the rapidly spreading rebellion in South Africa. As a result, the government instituted a series of reforms of the apartheid system that were designed to pacify the disenfranchised while maintaining white authority. For example, the government allowed the formation of African trade unions in the early 1980s. The government also relaxed some of the provisions of the Group Areas Act by allowing blacks and their families to reside permanently in African townships within white urban areas. The RSA also relaxed restrictions on interracial marriage.

The success of apartheid reforms in muting rebel opposition, however, was limited for two reasons. First, most of the government's reforms did little to alter "grand" apartheid. For example, the government attempted to grant artificial independence to the Bantustans at the same time that it allowed some Africans more freedom of movement. Most Africans recognized that independence for the Bantustans would result in permanent subjugation of blacks in South Africa. Second, incremental reforms raised expectations for further changes to the apartheid system.

The government also altered apartheid in an attempt to thwart the rebels by pitting various disenfranchised groups in South Africa against each other. One example of this tactic is the tricameral parliament mentioned earlier. By giving Indians and coloreds a limited voice in RSA policy, the government hoped that these groups would turn against black South Africans. This strategy had limited success, in part because of the limited nature of colored and Indian representation and in part because of the efforts of the UDF to discredit government policy.

Somewhat more successfully, the central government also attempted to pit various black groups against each other. The roots of this strategy date to the very beginning of apartheid, when Indians and coloreds were treated as homogeneous groups, but blacks were subdivided into smaller groups for classification purposes. One primary example of this strategy was the formation of Inkatha "hit squads" under the partial direction of the SAP. Fortunately for the MK, the government strategy was limited in part by the unity fostered by the UDF. Although it would be erroneous to suggest that all disenfranchised groups were united by a common strategy, organizations like the UDF and the ANC were able to draw on the existence of a common enemy to partially unify opposition to apartheid.

Causes of the War

In general terms, the principle cause of the South African civil war was the National Party's apartheid policy. The word *apartheid*, which means separateness in Afrikaans, took on two principal forms. Petty apartheid consisted of those policies that affected the day-to-day lives of nonwhite South Africans. Grand apartheid, by contrast, concerned the distribution of political rights and territorial relations in South Africa (Beck 2000, 126). The apartheid system relied on a basic racial classification system. The NP divided the population into four groups: African, colored, white, and Indian. Only those classified as white were entitled to the full set of civil and political rights in the RSA.

It is important to recognize that apartheid represented a comprehensive set of interwoven policies. From 1948, when the NP successfully took control of the South African government, through parts of the 1970s, apartheid was gradually imposed through a series of government acts. The Prohibition of Mixed Marriages Act and the Immorality Act represented early attempts to maintain racial purity by prohibiting intermarriage and sexual relations between the

races. The 1950 Population Registration Act formed the basis of the South African racial classification system, and the Group Area Act segregated residential and commercial areas by race. The 1956 Native Resettlement Act resulted in the forced relocation of millions of Africans (Beck 2000, 127). Each of these pieces of legislation augmented the existing pass laws that restricted the movement of nonwhites. In 1952, the government expanded the pass laws to include women. Primary, secondary, and—eventually—postsecondary education were also subject to racial segregation. Finally, the Promotion of Bantu Self Government Act, as mentioned above, completed the process of confining most nonwhites to a series of ten Bantustans.

Despite the repressive and degrading nature of apartheid, the ANC's initial policy focused on working within the white system. It took a series of events to convince the ANC and other opposition groups that nonviolent constitutionalist opposition should be abandoned in favor of guerrilla war. First, the Sharpeville massacre of 1960 demonstrated that the NP government was willing to respond to protests with violence. As a result of Sharpeville, 71 blacks were killed, and more than 200 blacks were injured (Davis 1987, 12). The riots that followed Sharpeville resulted in further government crackdowns on opposition groups.

Second, the decision by the government to ban the ANC and the PAC in the wake of the Sharpeville and the violence that followed destroyed any remaining opposition links to the government. The Unlawful Organizations Act of 1960 was a crushing setback for those members of the ANC who would have preferred to continue the current strategy of attempting to negotiate with the government while pursuing civil disobedience. Once the ANC was forced underground, it became clear that nonviolence would not produce the desired result of securing political rights for nonwhites within the existing government structure.

Although Sharpeville opened the door to violent resistance against apartheid, the Soweto

Students protest the mandatory use of the Dutch-based Afrikaans language in South African schools in Soweto on June 16, 1976. Police opened fire on the protesters when tear gas failed to curb them. At least six people (including four whites) were killed, and at least forty were injured in the day-long riot. (Bettmann/Corbis)

massacre made civil war inevitable. Before Soweto, MK conducted extremely limited operations against a relatively small number of government installations. In 1975, the white minister of Bantu education declared that social studies and math would be conducted in Afrikaans in all Bantu secondary schools (Beck 2000, 160). Is response, nearly 20,000 secondary students marched in protest against the government order on June 16, 1976. SAP personnel fired into the crowd of students, setting in motion a series of riots and crackdowns that resulted in nearly 200 deaths within a few days. Nearly 150 buildings and 150 vehicles were also destroyed (Davis 1987, 36). Hundreds more were killed during the remainder of 1976. The Soweto massacre also resulted in a flood of new

MK recruits. Many of these recruits were well-educated blacks who had become increasingly responsive to the Black Consciousness Movement (BCM) of the early 1970s.

Outcome
Conflict Status

The township revolts that began in Sharpeville in 1984 marked the beginning of the end for the apartheid regime. President Pieter Willem Botha imposed a state of emergency in parts of the RSA in July 1985 and a nationwide state of emergency in June 1986 (Beck 2000, 176). More than 30,000 people were detained as a result of Botha's orders. Many of those detained died in SAP custody from torture or general neglect.

The suspension of political rights associated with the state of emergency was partially successful in bringing the townships under government control.

Although the township revolts did not topple apartheid directly, they did serve to increase international attention to the plight of a majority of the South African people. Before the revolts, the Organization of Petroleum Exporting Countries (OPEC) was the first organization to impose significant sanctions against South Africa in the form of an oil embargo (Beck 2000, 156). South Africa used the high price of gold to circumvent the boycott, purchasing oil from Iran before the 1979 revolution. The commonwealth imposed sanctions on South Africa in 1985. In 1986, the United States passed the Comprehensive Anti-Apartheid Act over President Reagan's veto. Although Reagan refused to completely implement the act, he did place restrictions on technology transfer between the United States and South Africa. The European community also imposed sanctions on the apartheid regime in South Africa. The United Nations Security Council, however, refused to respond to calls from the General Assembly for the imposition of comprehensive economic sanctions against South Africa. Veto threats from the United States, the United Kingdom, and France prevented the UN from moving beyond the arms embargo mandated by Security Council Resolution 418 in 1977.

Economic sanctions, although important in furthering the economic isolation of South Africa, were not enough to end apartheid. As mentioned earlier, the role of international lending institutions, coupled with divestment on the part of some multinational corporations, began to cripple the South African economy (Beck 2000, 178). South African debt skyrocketed as international banks refused to refinance poorly performing loans. The overall economic decline, in turn, convinced many white-owned businesses in South Africa that it would be better to survive under majority rule than to go bankrupt under apartheid.

In 1989, F. W. de Klerk replaced Botha as the head of the NP. On February 2, 1990, de Klerk announced the release of Nelson Mandela from prison. The government also legalized the UDF, the ANC, the PAC, and the SACP. Throughout 1991, de Klerk eliminated most of the policies that collectively made up apartheid. One might have expected the ANC to take advantage of government weakness by attempting to forcibly remove the last vestiges of apartheid. The imminent collapse of the Soviet Union, coupled with ongoing battles with the Inkatha Freedom Party (IFP) and internal political wrangling over ANC policy, forced the rebels to the negotiating table. In December 1991, 228 delegates met in Johannesburg under the auspices of the Convention for a Democratic South Africa (CODESA) (Thompson 1995, 247). The PAC and the Azanian People's Organization (AZAPO) refused to join the negotiations.

The failure of a second round of CODESA talks threw the entire transition process into doubt. In addition, a massacre led by members of the IFP, supported by the SAP, reinforced ANC suspicions of NP sincerity at the negotiating table. A series of secret meetings, however, maintained critical communications during the crisis and set the stage for a return to the negotiating table (Beck 2000, 187). Despite attempts by white extremist groups to disrupt the negotiations, the participating parties were able to agree on an interim constitution in November 1993. South Africa's inaugural democratic elections were scheduled for April 26, 1994.

From April 26 to April 29, South Africans witnessed the first truly democratic elections in SAP history. The ANC garnered 67.2 percent of the vote, the NP secured 20.4 percent, and the IFP received 10.5 percent. Despite some irregularities, observers declared that the overall election was free and fair. On May 9, 1994, the South African National Assembly elected Nelson Mandela president.

Duration Tactics

The South African civil war lasted almost twenty years. There are several interrelated explanations for the conflict's long duration. First, although

The South African Truth and Reconciliation Commission

In 1993, South Africa promulgated an interim constitution designed in part to facilitate the transition between majority and minority in South Africa. It was clear to those who drafted the constitution that political change would not be enough to heal the damage caused by decades of political struggle. Chapter 16 of the interim constitution states:

> This Constitution provides a historic bridge between the past of a deeply divided society characterized by strife, conflict, untold suffering and injustice, and a future founded on the recognition of human rights, democracy and peaceful coexistence and development opportunities for all South Africans, irrespective of color, race, class, belief or sex.
> . . . In order to advance such reconciliation and reconstruction, amnesty shall be granted in respect of acts, omissions and offenses associated with political objectives and committed in the course of the conflicts of the past.

Ultimately, the South African Truth and Reconciliation Commission was established to trade truthfulness from all participants in the South African conflict for amnesty with respect to crimes that may have been committed. However, the ANC, former President de Klerk, and the Inkatha Freedom Party (IFP) mounted legal challenges against release of the findings of the commission. Both parties were concerned about the condemnations made in the commission's final report. The various parties were unable to reach a settlement that would allow publication of the report until January 2003 (Truth and Reconciliation Commission 2003).

The final report of the commission was critical of all sides in the conflict. With respect to the apartheid government, the commission found various criminal acts, including extrajudicial killing of political opponents and widespread torture (Truth and Reconciliation Commission 2003). The IFP was found responsible for acts of collusion with the government in its efforts to persecute the ANC—specifically, the IFP established a paramilitary hit squad in cooperation with the SADF that was responsible for attacks against civilian members of the ANC and the United Democratic Front (UDF). The Commission also found the ANC responsible for several human rights violations, including acts contrary to the Geneva Conventions and Protocol, which the ANC had agreed to follow (Truth and Reconciliation Commission of South Africa 2003; South African Interim Constitution 1993).

the South African government had success in limiting rebel activity, it was never able to completely decapitate the ANC or MK. Several key leaders, Oliver Tambo most noteworthy among them, were able to escape South Africa and secure sanctuary in other states. In the wake of the Soweto massacre, Tambo made the fateful decision to move the resistance movement back into Africa (from London). The new wave of government violence during and after Soweto provided MK with a source of new recruits.

Second, in a related fashion, the willingness of several states to allow MK bases in their territory prevented the SADF from achieving an early victory. Had the MK been forced to train inside South Africa, it almost certainly would have

been quickly defeated. Early government efforts to infiltrate the ANC and MK inside South Africa clearly demonstrate that rebels benefited from their ability to train at a distance. At the same time, however, MK reliance on bases outside South Africa made it much more difficult to gather a significant number of rebels inside the country, which served to lengthen the war.

Third, it took a significant amount of time for the international community to pressure the NP to abandon apartheid. For example, the United States, which was worried about the existing Communist foothold in Southern Africa, did not want to allow Africa's most developed state to fall under Communist control. Although it is doubtful that South Africa would have become a

Marxist state under ANC rule, the NP was quite effective at convincing the West that the ANC was part of the Communist threat. As a result, it took almost ten years for the first meaningful sanctions to be levied against South Africa. International lending institutions, as well as multinational corporations, also were slow to react. An abundance of natural resources and (at times) inexpensive labor acted as a magnet for multinational corporations.

Fourth, it took a great deal of time for Africans in South Africa to mobilize against apartheid. The government's monopoly on the media prevented many Africans, Indians, and coloreds from recognizing that a rebellion even existed. Poor access to education, low wages, and restrictions on freedom of movement created conditions under which most nonwhites were more concerned about day-to-day survival than about the broader liberation movement. As education opportunities for blacks increase, however, more individuals became receptive to efforts by the BCM and the UDF to raise awareness about political issues. The township revolts of the mid-1980s resulted in large part from the increase in African political awareness.

Finally, conflict both among the rebels and within the NP resulted in a significantly longer conflict. A series of mutinies within MK camps in 1984 demonstrated that the rebels were not always united. In total, the ANC executed at least thirty-four of its members for various offenses in the camps (SAPA 1996). The willingness of the IFP to collaborate with the South African Defense Force also lengthened the conflict by perpetuating black-on-black violence. (During the apartheid era, the military was called the South African Defense Force. After the transition to majority rule, the SADF was renamed the South African National Defense Force). Mangosuthu Buthelezi, leader of the IFP, believed that apartheid could be attacked from within the existing system by using the homeland governments to gain leverage with the NP. Whites were also intensely divided on issues related to apartheid. Extreme right-wing groups both in-

side and outside the NP attempted to disrupt the transition to multiracial democracy throughout the negotiation process.

External Military Intervention

The portion of the South African civil war that took place within the RSA was free from direct, armed external intervention. In fact, it was far more common during the South African civil war for the RSA to intervene directly in other countries (see earlier section, "Duration Tactics"). However, indirect intervention on the part of the Soviet Union was one of the keys to MK survival. The Soviet Union provided MK rebels with most of their weapons and funding. In addition, Soviet intelligence was critical to Umkhonto we Sizwe's ability to avoid detection, to strike government targets, and to gain information about SAP and SADF movements. Finally, the Soviet Union and its satellites in Eastern Europe provided advanced military training to hundreds of rebels. The anti-apartheid movement fit well with the Soviet strategy of assisting national liberation movements.

In contrast to the conflict within South Africa, there was direct military intervention by foreign powers outside the RSA. The most notorious example of foreign intervention occurred in the Angolan civil war. South Africa itself intervened directly in Angola beginning in August 1975. MPLA control of the majority of Angolan territory provided safe haven for the ANC–MK and the South West Africa People's Organization (SWAPO), which was fighting against South Africa for Namibian independence (Garztecki 2002, 35). By October 1975, the SANDF had advanced to within 100 miles of the Angolan capital.

In response to the South African offensive, the Soviet Union, which had earlier provided direct military support via Cuban troops, arranged for massive reinforcements from Cuba. Cuban troops allied with the MPLA were able to push the SADF into Namibia. In effect, Cuban intervention in Angola benefited the ANC and the SWAPO as much as it did the MPLA. In

1985, South Africa became party to the Lusaka Accord, which provided for an end to Angolan support of the ANC and SWAPO and a withdrawal of Cuban troops from Angola, in exchange for South African withdrawal from Angola and independence for Namibia. Despite this agreement, South Africa continued incursions into Angola as part of its "hot pursuit" policy against insurgents.

Conflict Management Efforts

In spite of the amount of international attention on the conflict in South Africa, there were few actual attempts to mediate the conflict. The bulk of international efforts were aimed at ending apartheid, which implied support for the rebels. The United Nations Security Council imposed an arms embargo on South Africa, and the General Assembly (GA) was quite active in establishing plans of action to end apartheid. The GA, beginning with Resolution 721 (VIII) of 1953, adopted annual resolutions condemning apartheid. The GA also established the Special Committee Against Apartheid and used parliamentary procedure to expel South Africa from the GA, over the objections of several Western states.

India did propose tripartite negotiations between itself, Pakistan, and the RSA over the issue of the treatment of Indians in South Africa in 1949. The proposed talks failed, however, after the passage of the Group Areas Act. The British Commonwealth sent the Eminent Persons Group to South Africa in 1986 in an attempt to bridge the gap between the ANC and the NP (Beck 2000, 176). However, the talks broke down once it became clear that the Eminent Persons Group would not suggest an end to commonwealth sanctions against South Africa without an end to the policy of apartheid.

Conclusion

The crumbling and ultimate collapse of apartheid have been compared to the crumbling of the Berlin Wall. Along with the wave of independence from colonial rule that swept through much of sub-Saharan Africa in the 1960s, the end of apartheid clearly stands as one of the most critical events in the history of modern Africa. The transition from white minority rule to relatively stable democracy is also a tremendous achievement on a continent where various forms of dictatorship and instability remain common. For the first time in multiple generations, the majority of South Africans have the opportunity to take advantage of the country's bountiful natural resources.

Despite South Africa's immense promise, however, democratic consolidation and political stability are by no means assured. Perhaps the most enduring legacy of the apartheid era is the degree of income equality that continues to plague the country. GDP per capita remains significantly higher among whites. In addition, the slow pace of land reform means that many Africans remain trapped in the homelands while whites continue to control the most productive land. One of the greatest potential sources of political instability in the RSA is that blacks will forcibly evict whites from the land. Future stability will depend on the ability of the government to foster income and territorial equality.

From a military perspective, the greatest challenge to South African stability is the integration of former MK rebels into the new South African Defense Force. Existing integration efforts have been fraught with difficulty, including difficulties associated with developing a list of MK personnel eligible for integration. In addition, many rebels who trained in the former Soviet bloc have had difficulty obtaining rank commensurate with their training and experience.

Trevor Rubenzer

Chronology

1910   Union of South Africa becomes an independent state within the British Commonwealth.

1912   South Africa Party (SAP) splits; National Party (NP) formed; South African native

National Congress (SANNC) formed; SANNC later renamed African National Congress (ANC).

1913   Land Act passes in spite of ANC protest; Africans are prohibited from purchasing land outside of native reserve areas and leasing land owned by whites.

1933   Afrikaner nationalists form a more reactionary version of the NP.

1948   National Party wins plurality of seats in elections, forms ruling coalition.

1949   Prohibition of Mixed Marriages Act is passed.

1950   Immorality Act prohibits interracial sexual relations; Population Registration Act provides for the classification of every South African by race; Group Areas Act divides residential and commercial areas by race; Suppression of Communism Act results in banning of South African Communist Party.

1953   Public Safety Act and Criminal Amendment Act provide broad emergency powers to the government, along with the ability to punish acts of protest.

1955   ANC adopts Freedom Charter.

1956   Native Resettlement Act eliminates remaining African property rights; millions of blacks are forcibly relocated.

1959   Bantu Self-Government Act restricts African political rights to the homelands; PAC forms.

March 21, 1960   PAC leads demonstration against pass laws in Sharpeville and other South African cities; police fire on protesters, killing seventy-one blacks and wounding more than 200.

April 8, 1960   Unlawful Organizations Act passes; ANC and PAC are banned; SAP arrests thousands of suspected ANC and PAC members.

June 1961   Umkhonto we Sizwe (MK) is established by the ANC national executive.

December 16, 1961   MK announces its existence with a series of bombings, coupled with the distribution of leaflets, in Johannesburg, Port Elizabeth, and Durban.

1962   Mandela sentenced to five years in prison for having previously left South Africa illegally.

June 1963   General Law Amendment Act allows the SAP to hold individuals for up to ninety days without reason.

June 12, 1963   Government announces arrest of 3,246 PAC members, essentially decapitating the organization.

July 1963   Rivonia raid results in the capture of key members of the ANC–MK leadership.

October 1963   Rivonia trial begins; Mandela ultimately sentenced to life in prison; Oliver Tambo becomes the "face" of the ANC; Tambo sets up ANC offices in London; little rebel activity for more than a decade.

1969   Bureau of State Security (BOSS) is created.

1975   ANC begins to form new cells inside South Africa.

November 11, 1975   MK is invited to form training bases in Angola.

January 1, 1976   UN establishes Centre Against Apartheid.

June 16, 1976   Soweto massacre; secondary school students gather in Soweto to protest the imposition of Afrikaans as the official language of instruction; SAP opens fire on protesters, more than 200 killed within a few days; hundreds of buildings and vehicles are destroyed; Soweto riots spread throughout South Africa during 1976–1977.

November–December 1976   MK forms first training bases in Angola; number and intensity of MK attacks increase; more than 150 separate attacks between 1976 and 1982.

November 4, 1977   UN Security Council imposes arms embargo on South Africa.

June 1, 1980   MK attacks South African Coal, Oil and Gas Corporation facilities; attacks cause more than 58 million rand in damage.

August 20, 1983   United Democratic Front (UDF) is launched.

1984   Township revolts begin in Sharpeville; rebels affiliated with the UDF or the BCM begin to take control of the townships.

March   Mozambique signs nonaggression pact with RSA, agrees to expel ANC in exchange for cessation of RSA support of Renamo.

March 21, 1985   SAP opens fire on unarmed blacks attending the twenty-fifth anniversary commemoration of the Sharpeville massacre; nineteen people are killed. Commonwealth imposes economic sanctions on South Africa.

July 1985   P. W. Botha declares state of emergency in township areas, extended to the entire RSA in June 1986.

July 26, 1985   UN Security Council passes nonbinding resolution encouraging member states to impose sanctions on South Africa.

June 12, 1986   Botha declares nationwide state of emergency; tens of thousands are arrested.

September 1986   U.S. Congress passes Comprehensive Anti-Apartheid Act over

President Reagan's veto; however, the act is never fully implemented.

1987 International lending institutions refuse to extend poorly performing South African loans. Multinational divestment intensifies.

January 1989 F. W. de Klerk assumes power.

February 2, 1990 De Klerk announces release of Mandela and legalization of ANC, PAC, SACP, and UDF; violence erupts between ANC–UDF and IFP; 700 people die in the conflict/

February 11, 1990 Mandela is released from prison after twenty-seven years.

August 1, 1990 MK suspends operations.

December 20, 1991 Formal negotiations take place between the government and eighteen other parties under the auspices of CODESA.

1992 Whites voice support for de Klerk's reform proposals in a general election.

May 1992 Second Round of CODESA talks fail to produce a result.

April 1993 Multiparty negotiations on South Africa's future resume.

June 25, 1993 Two thousand white extremists attack the Johannesburg World Trade Center (site of the negotiations). No injuries are reported.

July 1993 Negotiations result in a date of April 27, 1994, for South Africa's first democratic elections; IFP refuses to accept negotiations.

December 1993 RSA parliament approves negotiation results; de Klerk and Mandela are awarded Nobel Peace Prize.

April 19, 1994 Buthelezi agrees to IFP participation in South African elections in exchange for assurances of nondiscrimination.

April 26–29, 1994 Elections are held; ANC secures 67.2 percent of vote.

May 9, 1994 Newly constituted South African National Assembly chooses Nelson Mandela to be South Africa's first postapartheid president.

Glossary

Africanism: An ideology grounded in black nationalism. In South Africa, Africanists believed that the struggle against apartheid ought to be conducted by indigenous Africans. The Pan Africanist Congress (PAC) and the Black Consciousness Movement (BCM) were two of the principal proponents of Africanist thought in South Africa.

apartheid: Meaning "separateness" in Afrikaans, the policy implemented by the National Party from 1948–1994 that was designed to ensure white supremacy through the imposition of racial segregation, restrictions on political rights and freedoms, and separate education and development policies for nonwhites.

Bantustan: Homeland reserved for a specific Bantu-speaking ethnic group; also referred to simply as homelands.

grand apartheid: Policies designed to control the political and territorial rights of nonwhites in a manner that would ultimately lead to a white majority in South Africa.

import substitution industrialization (ISI): A development strategy that relies on encouraging domestic production in place of imports. Governments that favor ISI often impose heavy tariffs and quotas on imports in order to protect developing industry. In South Africa, international trade sanctions temporarily bolstered the South African economy by eliminating competition from foreign producers.

nonracialism: An ideology grounded in the idea that South Africa could exist as a multiracial state, including whites. All individuals, regardless of race, who opposed apartheid would be allowed to participate in the struggle for liberation.

pass laws: A series of government acts that restricted the movement of nonwhites outside the Bantustans. The pass laws initially applied only to men but were later extended to women.

petty apartheid: Policies designed to control the day-to-day life of nonwhites. For example, the Prohibition of Mixed Marriages Act restricted interracial marriage.

List of Acronyms

ANC: African National Congress
AZAPO: Azanian People's Organization
BCM: Black Consciousness Movement
BOSS: Bureau of State Security
CODESA: Convention for a Democratic South Africa
GA: General Assembly (UN)
GDP: gross domestic product
IFP: Inkatha Freedom Party
ISI: import substitution industrialization
MK: Umkhonto we Sizwe (Spear of the Nation)
MPLA: Popular Movement of Angolan Liberty (Movimento Popular de Libertacão de Angola)

NP: National Party
OPEC: Organization of Petroleum Exporting
     Countries
PAC: Pan Africanist Congress
RENAMO: Resistência Nacional de Mocambique
RSA: Republic of South Africa
SACP: South African Communist Party
SADF: South African Defense Force
SANDF: South African National Defense Force
SANNC: South African Native National Congress
SAP: South Africa Party
SAP: South African Police
SWAPO: South West Africa People's Organization
UDF: United Democratic Front
UNITA: National Union for the Total
     Independence of Angola (União Nacional
     para a Independência Total de Angola)
UP: United Party

References

African National Congress (ANC). 1980. "ANC Signs the Geneva Protocols." Press Release. www.anc.org.za/ancdocs/history/mk/geneva. html (accessed June 12, 2005).

African National Congress (ANC). Website. 1997. "Further Submissions and Response by the ANC to Questions Raised by the Commission for Truth and Reconciliation." www.anc.org. za/ancdocs/misc/trc2.html (accessed June 12, 2005).

African National Congress (ANC). Website. 2005. "The Freedom Charter." www.anc.org.za/ ancdocs/history/charter.html (accessed June 11, 2005).

Beck, Roger B. 2000. *The History of South Africa*. Westport, CT: Greenwood Press.

Davis, Stephen M. 1987. *Apartheid's Rebels: Inside South Africa's Hidden War*. New Haven, CT: Yale University Press.

Doyle, Michael W., and Nicholas Sambanis. 2000. "International Peacebuilding: A Theoretical and Quantitative Analysis." *American Political Science Review* 94(4).

Ellis, Stephen, and Tsepo Sechaba. 1992. *Comrades Against Apartheid: The ANC and the South African Communist Party in Exile*. Bloomington: Indiana University Press.

Feit, Edward. 1971. *Urban Revolt in South Africa 1960–1964: A Case Study*. Evanston, IL: Northwestern University Press.

Garztecki, Marek. 2002. "Angola: Recent History." In *Africa South of the Sahara*, edited by Katharine Murison, 34–40. London: Europa.

Harsch, Ernst. 1987. "South Africa: From Settlement to Union." In *The Anti-Apartheid Reader*, edited by David Mermelstein, 47–63. New York: Grove Press.

Heston, Alan, Robert Summers, and Bettina Aten. 2002. *Penn World Tables, Version 6.1*. Center for International Comparisons at the University of Pennsylvania (CICUP).

Kempton, Daniel R. 1989. *Soviet Strategy Toward Southern Africa: The National Liberation Movement Connection*. New York: Praeger.

Lieberfeld, Daniel. 1999. *Talking with the Enemy: Negotiation and Threat Perception in South Africa and Israel/Palestine*. Westport, CT: Praeger.

Marshall, Monty G., and Keith Jaggers. 2002. *Polity IV Dataset*. College Park, MD: Center for International Development and Conflict Management, University of Maryland. www. cidcm.umd.edu/inscr/polity/polreg.htm (accessed June 11, 2005).

Meli, Francis. 1989. *A History of the ANC: South Africa Belongs to Us*. Bloomington: Indiana University Press.

Motlhabi, Buti George. 1988. *Challenge to Apartheid: Toward a Morally Defensible Strategy*. Grand Rapids, MI: William B. Eerdman's Publishing Company.

Muthien, Yvonne. 1990. "Protest and Resistance in Cape Town, 1939–65." In *Repression and Resistance: Insider Accounts of Apartheid*, edited by Robin Cohen, Yvonne Muthien, and Abebe Zegeye. New York: Hans Zell.

Saunders, Christopher. 2002a. "Namibia: Recent History." In *Africa South of the Sahara*, edited by Katharine Murison, 726–31. London: Europa.

Saunders, Christopher. 2002b. "South Africa: Recent History." In *Africa South of the Sahara*, edited by Katharine Murison, 965–75. London: Europa.

Seekings, Jeremy. 2000. *The UDF: A History of the United Democratic Front in South Africa 1983–1991*. Athens: Ohio University Press.

South African Interim Constitution. 1993. www. oefre.unibe.ch/law/icl/sf10000_.html (accessed June 14, 2005).

South African Press Association (SAPA). 1996. "ANC Executed at Least 34 of Its Cadres in Angola: Mbeki." www.doj.gov.za/trc/media/ 1996/9608/s960822b.htm (accessed June 15, 2005).

Thompson, Leonard. 1995. *A History of South Africa.* New Haven, CT: Yale University Press.

Truth and Reconciliation Commission of South Africa. 2003. "Final Report" www.info.gov. za/otherdocs/2003/trc/ (accessed June 14, 2005).

Van Buren, Linda. 2002. "South Africa: Economy." In *Africa South of the Sahara,* edited by Katharine Murison, 975–81. London: Europa.

Williams, Rocky. 2002. "Integration or Absorption: The Creation of the South African National Defense Force, 1993–1999." *African Security Review* Vol. 11(2). www. iss.org.za/PUBS/ASR/11No2/Williams.html (accessed June 14, 2005).

Sri Lanka (1972–Present)

Introduction

Since the early 1970s, and more intensely since 1983, Sri Lanka's Sinhalese-dominated government has been locked in a secessionist conflict with elements of its Tamil minority. Although a military and political stalemate has supported a cease-fire since February 2002, a return to all-out war seems more likely than an agreement on a lasting peace. The war originated as Sri Lankan government policies and anti-Tamil riots cumulatively undermined the security of the Tamil population. In turn, the Sinhalese–Tamil conflict generated intra-Tamil and intra-Sinhalese conflicts. Both have produced far more death and suffering than the supposedly central interethnic conflict. Chances for an early end to the war were dashed by the rise of the radical and ferocious Liberation Tigers of Tamil Eelam (LTTE)—in which India's intervention was crucial. The Sinhalese–Tamil conflict is unlikely to end without the decline or reform of the LTTE, which maintains a stranglehold on the Tamil population of the contested regions. After reviewing background information on Sri Lanka, this article summarizes the history of the conflict. It then analyzes the sources of the conflict, the strategies and tactics employed by the two sides, and the barriers to resolving the conflict.

Country Background

The teardrop-shaped island of Sri Lanka lies 20–40 miles off the southern tip of India, across the Palk Strait. Its maximum north-south height is about 270 miles, and its maximum east-west width is about 170 miles. Much of the island—including much of the northern and eastern conflict zone—is thickly forested.

In 2003, the population was 19.3 million, up from 15.8 million in 1985. There are four major ethnic groups: The Sinhalese make up 74 percent of the population; the Sri Lankan Tamils, 12.6 percent; the Indian Tamils, 5.6 percent; and the Sri Lankan Muslims, 7.1 percent. (These proportions are from the last complete census, taken in 1981. They are not estimated to have changed much, although emigration may have produced some decline in the Sri Lankan Tamil share.) The Sinhalese and Tamils are most strongly distinguished by language and religion, but also by political history and culture. Sinhalese speak their own language (Sinhala), and are overwhelmingly Buddhist. The Sri Lankan and Indian Tamils and most Muslims are native Tamil speakers. The Sri Lankan and Indian Tamils are also overwhelmingly Hindu. On the basis of religion, the Muslims identify themselves as a distinct ethnic group (Kearney 1985, 899; Senaratne 1997, 21–24). In this chapter, Sri Lankan Tamils are referred to simply as Tamils, and Sri Lankan Muslims as Muslims, unless otherwise noted.

At the time of the 1981 census, prewar ethnic settlement patterns had changed little. Sri Lankan Tamils were and are concentrated in the north and to a lesser extent the east. Over half the

715

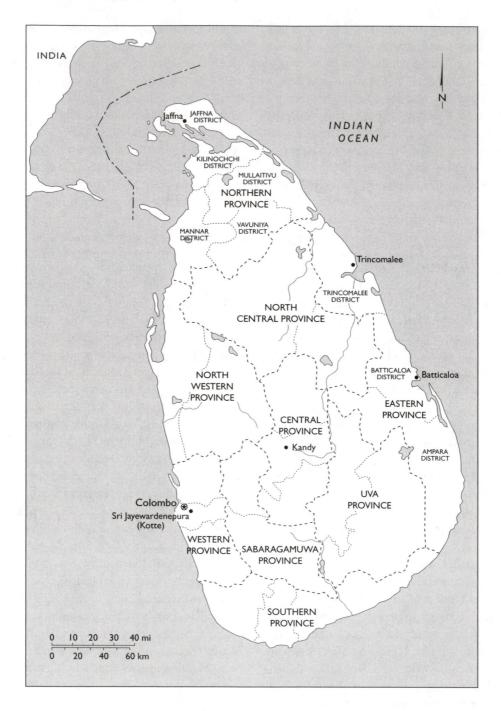

Sri Lankan Tamils are in the north, and the majority of these are in Jaffna district. The Indian Tamils are concentrated in the central highland districts and in the Sri Lankan Tamil-dominated northern districts. The Muslim population was concentrated in four heavily Sri Lankan Tamil districts—the east coast districts of Amparai (Muslim plurality), Batticaloa, and Trincomalee, and northern Mannar district (Kearney 1985, 899–902). Jaffna, Kilinochchi, Mannar, Mullaitivu, and Vavuniya districts together constitute the Northern Province, and Amparai, Batticaloa, and Trincomalee districts the Eastern Province. In the 1981 census, the Northern Province was 91.7 percent Tamil (including a small proportion of Indian Tamils), 3.2 percent Sinhalese, and 5.0 percent Muslim, and the Eastern Province was 42.4 percent Tamil (including a small proportion of Indian Tamils), 25.1 percent Sinhalese, and 32.5 percent Muslim. The war produced waves of Tamil, Sinhalese, and Muslim refugee flows into and out of the north and east, along with a separation of ethnic groups in the war-torn north and east. Initially, Tamils fled riots and pogroms in the Sinhalese-dominated south, going to the north or abroad. Later, the LTTE sought to cement control by driving Sinhalese and Muslims from the north and parts of the east; at the same time, many Tamils fled back south, abroad, or to displaced persons camps to escape the fighting and the brutal wartime regimes of the government forces and the LTTE.

Since independence in 1948, Sri Lanka has had functioning democratic institutions. Political violence has been common since the late 1970s and early 1980s, particularly around election times. Since 1979, legal rights have been formally restricted under various emergency security laws. Informally, the major combatants have violated rights on a huge scale.

In 2003, Sri Lankan per capita income, measured in terms of purchasing power, was about $3,000 (2003 dollars)—a level similar to that in China. From 1977, Sri Lanka opened up its economy, generating annual GDP growth of around 5 percent. Manufacturing and especially services have grown significantly, although 35 percent of the workforce remains employed in agriculture (Asian Development Bank 2005).

Conflict Background

Beginning in the tenth century, and particularly in the thirteenth century, Tamils from southern India invaded Sri Lanka and settled along the northern and eastern coasts. The Sinhalese population was driven back to the central highlands and the southern and western coasts, although significant Sinhalese communities remained in parts of the east. In the early sixteenth century, when Europeans began penetrating the region, there were a number of Tamil and Sinhalese kingdoms—Tamil in the north and east, and Sinhalese elsewhere. The Muslim population is descended from Arab, Indian Muslim, and Malay traders that settled on the island.

Under British rule (1815–1948), the country was increasingly run by English-speaking, largely Christianized, and culturally Anglicized local elites—later disparaged as "black Englishmen." They were mostly Sinhalese but also included many Tamils and other minorities. Sinhalese national identity is intertwined with Buddhism, which, having been largely expelled from its Indian birthplace, was viewed as having found a saving refuge in Sri Lanka. British rule was thus associated with threats to the two primary markers of Sinhalese ethnicity—the Sinhala language and Buddhism. Both because the British viewed Tamils as more politically reliable, and because Tamils tended to be better educated and more entrepreneurial, Tamils became disproportionately represented in the colonial administration, the professions, and commerce. The British also brought in Indian Tamils to work tea and rubber plantations in the hitherto Sinhalese-dominated central highlands. After independence in 1948, the Sinhalese sought to reassert their majority status, and the Sri Lankan Tamils sought to defend their positions, status, and identity. Although the Sri Lankan Tamils feared a tyranny of the Sinhalese majority, the Sinhalese feared domination by a combination of the local Tamils and the giant Tamil community of South India.

The first postindependence government was formed by the United National Party (UNP), the party of the Anglicized elite. The UNP was nonsectarian and secular in principle and technocratic in orientation. Nevertheless, its Citizenship Act of 1948 disenfranchised the Indian Tamils of the central highlands on the basis that they were Indians rather than natives. (In 1964, by agreement with India, about half of the "stateless" Indian Tamils were given citizenship. Still more became citizens in 1984. The process of granting citizenship to all resident Indian Tamils was completed in 2003.) This was resented by the Tamils of the north and east. Tamils also felt threatened by government irrigation programs to resettle poor peasants—overwhelmingly Sinhalese—in less densely populated north-central and eastern regions.

The year 1956 was Buddhism's 2,500-year anniversary. There was a great outpouring of Sinhalese Buddhist nationalism, and elections were won by a Sinhalese nationalist splinter of the UNP, the Sri Lankan Freedom Party (SLFP). The 1956 Language Act, in addition to making Sinhala the official language, required government employees to show Sinhala competence within three years. A nonviolent protest by Tamil legislators was attacked by a Sinhalese mob, leading to a week of interethnic rioting. In the following years, Sinhalese language proficiency requirements largely purged the civil service of Tamils. The 1956 elections also showed that the autonomy-oriented Federal Party had become the strongest Tamil party. The Federal Party's demands for regional self-rule did not clearly reject separatism; and from the mid-1950s, it claimed not only the Tamil-dominated Northern Province but also the ethnically heterogeneous Eastern Province as integral parts of the Tamils' traditional homelands. This combination of vagueness and far-reaching goals provoked both Tamils and Sinhalese.

In 1957, SLFP leader S.W.R.D. Bandaranaike and Federal Party leader S. Chelvanayakam tentatively agreed to allow limited regional autonomy and official use of the Tamil language in the north and east and to address Tamil grievances on the land settlement and citizenship issues. But the agreement broke down amid dueling protests over the language issue. This triggered another round of rioting, in which hundreds died—mostly Tamils. (Following the riots, a bill was passed authorizing the use of Tamil as an official language in the north and east. The necessary implementing legislation, though, was only

The Bandaranaike Family

S.W.R.D. Bandaranaike was the son of a knighted member of the local Anglicized elite. Returning to Ceylon from Oxford, Bandaranaike converted to Buddhism and got involved in politics. He founded the SLFP in 1951. Coming to power on rising Sinhalese Buddhist nationalism in 1956, Bandaranaike sought to reconcile the Language Act with a deal granting the Tamils limited language rights and autonomy. Following a backlash from his own movement and anti-Tamil rioting, Bandaranaike was assassinated in 1959. He was succeeded by his wife, S.R.D. Bandaranaike, the world's first female prime minister. She served as prime minister in 1960–1965, 1970–1977, and 1994–2000. In her first two terms, she continued to support the Sinhala-only language policy, along with related policies to increase Sinhalese representation in government, education, and skilled positions generally. The Bandaranaikes' daughter, Chandrika Bandaranaike Kumaratunga, was elected president in 1994 and appointed her mother to a third term as prime minister. Initially, Kumaratunga sought accommodation with the LTTE. After the LTTE broke off negotiations and returned to war in 1995, she became more skeptical about subsequent peace efforts. At a 1999 campaign rally, she was injured in an LTTE suicide bombing.

passed in 1966.) Soon after, Bandaranaike was assassinated for insufficient loyalty to the Sinhalese nationalist cause and was succeeded as SLFP leader by his wife, S.R.D. Bandaranaike. In response to the 1961 Tamil nonviolent campaign for language rights in state employment, state services, and education, the government banned the Federal Party and arrested its leaders. In 1968, SLFP-led opposition prevented creation of district councils, which had been agreed upon by the UNP and Tamil political leaders (De Silva 1981, 1986; Kearney 1967).

Influenced by international ideological trends as well as local frustrations, the 1970s saw a pronounced radicalization among both Sinhalese and Tamils. After the 1970 election, in April–June 1971, the radical Marxist–Sinhalese nationalist National Liberation Front (JVP) mounted an unsuccessful armed uprising. Thousands of police, troops, and rebels were involved in fighting across the Sinhalese parts of the country. The new 1972 constitution changed the country's name from Ceylon to Sri Lanka, retained Sinhalese as the official language, and recognized Buddhism as the majority religion. Mass protests by Tamils led to clashes and arrests of demonstrators. Throughout the 1970s, S.R.D. Bandaranaike's government nationalized many key industries and gave preference to Sinhalese in hiring. Starting in 1970, affirmative action policies in university admissions disproportionately reduced access for Tamils. This measure radicalized many younger Tamils.

In 1972, the first armed Tamil groups emerged—the Tamil New Tigers (renamed the LTTE in 1976) and what later became the Tamil Eelam Liberation Organization (TELO). Also in 1972, the Federal Party and other parties and organizations formed the Tamil United Front, which increasingly advanced independence as a goal. In 1976, renamed the Tamil United Liberation Front (TULF), its Vaddukodai Resolution demanded an independent Tamil state of Eelam and appeared to endorse the use of violence. The TULF didn't see that it was writing its own epitaph. The Tigers' most sensational early attack—a sign of things to come—was the 1975 murder of Jaffna Mayor A. Durraiapah, a prominent Tamil supporter of the SLFP (McGowan 1992, 149–77; O'Ballance 1989, 2–14; Senaratne 1997, 24–28, 56–61, 76).

In the 1977 elections, the UNP won a huge victory, while the TULF swept the Tamil-majority districts on an independence platform. UNP leader J. R. Jayawardene became prime minister and later president. Postelection violence between UNP and SLFP supporters spiraled into anti-Tamil riots across the island. Around 100 Tamils were killed. Jayawardene began to reverse the statist economic policies of previous SLFP governments and reached out to the West for assistance. Jayawardene also promised better treatment of Tamils. The new 1978 constitution provided for the use of the Tamil language in government services, but the atmosphere did not improve.

The deepening political disputes and anti-Tamil riots raised hackles in India. In India's Tamil Nadu province, political parties, civil society organizations, and notables helped to set up Sri Lankan Tamil militant bases. The Indian government, fearing secessionist tendencies among India's own Tamils and unhappy with Jayawardene's Western-oriented diplomacy, allowed the process to go forward. Tamil armed groups, like many other revolutionary groups of the time, also received training in Soviet-backed, Palestinian-run camps in Lebanon. Tamil attacks intensified from April 1978, when the LTTE killed four policemen in Jaffna. In September, the LTTE blew up a civilian airliner near Colombo. Continued attacks on police led the government to declare a state of emergency in Jaffna. As government forces heavy-handedly rooted about, the armed Tamil groups melted away. Many fled across the Palk Strait to India.

Tamil attacks again intensified from 1981, now focusing more on intimidating moderate Tamils. By this time, there were five significant Tamil armed groups or paramilitaries. Along with the LTTE and TELO, there were also the Eelam Revolutionary Organization of Students (EROS), the People's Liberation Organization of Tamil Eelam (PLOTE), and the Eelam People's Revolutionary Liberation Front (EPRLF). In 1980, District Development Councils had been created to devolve power from the central government. In the run-up to the 1981 council elections, Tamil paramilitary attacks on police and moderate Tamils triggered rioting in Jaffna by police and UNP supporters. Anti-Tamil riots again broke out but this time were stopped quickly by the government (Kearney 1985; O'Ballance 1989, 14–20; Senaratne 1997, 61–67; Singer 1996, 1147–49).

In 1982, the UNP government substituted a largely rigged referendum on retaining the 1977 parliament for the regular parliamentary elections—although its victory in the 1982 presidential election indicated that it probably would have retained a reduced majority. This disenfranchised younger voters, further radicalizing many of them. In July 1983, thirteen Sinhalese soldiers were killed in an LTTE ambush in Jaffna. The next day, soldiers retaliated by killing about fifty Tamil civilians in Jaffna. Anti-Tamil rioting then broke out in Colombo, apparently instigated to a large extent by UNP trade union operatives, and then spread out of control throughout the city and elsewhere on the island. For days, the Sri Lankan government and armed forces did not act forcefully to stop the rioting. Hundreds of Tamils died; thousands were wounded; more than 100,000 sought refuge in India; and tens of thousands migrated to the West. The massive violence of 1983 drove large numbers of moderate Tamils into the extremist camp. Soon afterward, the government banned the Marxist-nationalist JVP party, and TULF representatives in parliament were expelled for refusing to take a newly required oath of allegiance to a unified Sri Lanka.

The Indian government, worried about public opinion in Tamil Nadu, began to arm and train the Tamil paramilitaries. Hitherto small, clandestine safe havens and networks of support in Tamil Nadu were now developed on a much larger scale. The riots yielded a mass of new recruits for the Tamil paramilitaries, who were now funneled through the more sophisticated training routines being imparted by Indian intelligence. The estimated number of trained Tamil fighters rose from about 200 before the riots to about 5,000 a year later. The highly skilled expatriate Tamil communities in the West soon developed into formidable nodes of political organization, fund-raising, and even arms and drug smuggling (Gunaratna 1993; Senaratne 1997, 33–50, 67–72).

From 1983, larger and more frequent attacks by the LTTE and other Tamil paramilitaries were followed by more intense government counterinsurgency campaigns. In this brutal fighting, both Sinhalese and Tamil civilians were targeted and killed in larger numbers. Tamil moderates were more than ever before driven into the hands of the LTTE and lesser militant organizations. Indian intelligence continued to provide Tamil paramilitaries with bases, training, and arms. Tamil fighters, weapons, and supplies were then ferried across the Palk Strait. Also under Indian pressure, inconclusive negotiations between the Sri Lankan government and the Tamil paramilitaries were held in 1984 and 1985. The government rejected Tamil demands for an autonomous region including the Northern and Eastern Provinces.

In the heavily Tamil northern districts, government forces were increasingly confined to their bases. Jaffna and other northern towns fell under Tamil paramilitary control. In these areas, the paramilitaries controlled distinct territories from which they sought to extract resources and manpower. Public intimidation and frequently executions enforced social order, political discipline, and fiscal compliance. In the more ethnically divided eastern districts, Tamil forces had more limited sway in heavily Tamil areas and conducted guerrilla attacks from jungle bases.

While staging attacks against the Sri Lankan security forces and Sinhalese civilians and "disciplining" Tamil politicians and civilians, the armed Tamil groups simultaneously competed with each other to become the "sole legitimate representative" of the Tamil people—to use the 1970s euphemism for one-party dictatorship. The LTTE was most aggressive and successful. Soon after the 1983 riots, the LTTE was at work killing leaders of newly formed Tamil militant groups and forcibly absorbing their cadres. In 1986, the LTTE launched assaults on TELO and then on the EPRLF. Fighting between Tamil militant groups produced casualties comparable to those occurring in the fighting with government security forces—not to mention the much larger numbers of Tamil civilians killed in day-to-day "disciplining" efforts. (Through 1997, the LTTE alone is estimated to have killed about 1,500 members and supporters of other Tamil militant groups, whereas about 2,500 Tamils were killed fighting with government security forces. Another 40,000 or 50,000 Tamils died violently during this period. It is unknown how many of these were actual or alleged criminals killed by Tamil militants and how many were political killings of various stripes (Senaratne 1997, 75, 85).) By 1987, the LTTE was clearly the dominant militant group. Regionally, the LTTE controlled the northern Tamil heartlands, particularly the Jaffna peninsula, while the other armed groups were stronger in the east. This corresponded to intra-Tamil regional differences, with the Tamils of the homogeneous north more supportive of secession at all costs, and the Tamils of the ethnically divided east more open to some kind of federal compromise. None of the armed Tamil groups had much success in forcibly integrating either the Indian Tamils of the central highlands or the Muslims of the eastern provinces into the secessionist enterprise (Senaratne 1997, 73–87).

In April 1987, the LTTE killed more than 200 Sinhalese civilians in two bloody attacks. The next month, the Sri Lankan government—which had built up a larger military since the early 1980s—launched an all-out conventional offensive to regain lost territory. Under the threat of Indian military intervention, the Sri Lankan government was forced to end the offensive and accept a settlement dictated by the Indian government of Rajiv Gandhi—the Indo-Lankan Accord of July 29, 1987. This combined a cease-fire with a federal solution enforced by a 3,000-strong Indian Peacekeeping Force (IPKF). Sri Lankan security forces withdrew to their bases. The Tamil paramilitaries were to turn over their weapons to the IPKF, which occupied the Northern and Eastern Provinces. The Northern and Eastern Provinces were to be merged, with a later referendum in the Eastern Province to determine whether the merger would be permanent. Provincial Councils were to be created to allow a high degree of provincial autonomy, above all in the newly created, Tamil-dominated Northeast Province. In addition to policing this

Velupillai Prabhakaran

Born in 1954 in a small town on the Jaffna peninsula, Prabhakaran received a good education and was steeped in Tamil grievances and frustrations. In 1972, at age 18, he was a founder of the Tamil New Tigers, which renamed itself the LTTE four years later. Prabhakaran participated in the 1975 murder of Jaffna Mayor A. Durraiapah, a Tamil supporter of the SLFP. Public notices threatened the killing of any Tamils who opposed him. Prabhakaran later received training in India from Indian intelligence. Within the LTTE, Prabhakaran built a cult of personality. New recruits were carefully vetted and trained and took an oath of loyalty to Prabhakaran himself. All received cyanide pills and were expected to commit suicide rather than allow themselves to be interrogated (McGowan 1992, 183–84 ; O'Ballance 1989, 13–14). Over time, surprisingly large numbers have done so. In addition to maintaining secrecy and loyalty, Prabhakaran has proved to be a highly skilled organizer, military leader, and political strategist. He steadily built the LTTE into a sophisticated, flexible, and well-financed military and political organization. He was able to carry on protracted warfare with the Sri Lankan government, the competing Tamil parties and paramilitaries, and even the Indian armed forces. At the same time, he successfully mobilized varying levels of support from foreign governments, Tamil expatriate communities, and Western humanitarian nongovernmental organizations (NGOs). The 2002 cease-fire agreement, by creating at least the appearance of progress toward a negotiated peace, established Prabakharan as an internationally recognized leader with implicit immunity for as long as the "process" continues. In more than thirty years of armed struggle, he is the sole survivor.

agreement, India undertook to respect the territorial integrity of Sri Lanka and to prevent the Tamil paramilitaries from using Indian territory. With the exception of the LTTE, the Tamil paramilitary groups accepted the agreement and cooperated with the IPKF. The LTTE was forced to accept only because the Indian government, for a time, held LTTE leader Velupillai Prabhakaran under house arrest. The LTTE then made only a token show of turning over its weapons to the Indians (Senaratne 1997, 88–91).

As a deceptive calm descended on the north and east, the rest of Sri Lanka exploded. Mainstream Sinhalese opinion was shocked and outraged at India's forced intervention. Antigovernment demonstrations convulsed the cities. The Marxist–nationalist JVP, functioning underground since 1983, saw an opportunity to take power on the surge of aggrieved Sinhalese nationalism. Instead of attacking the police and armed forces as in 1971, the JVP tried to paralyze the civil administration and the economy by attacking UNP leaders, government personnel, and the country's transportation, communication, and utilities infrastructure, and by intimidating the civilian population into supporting strikes in key economic sectors. When the UNP sought to relegitimize itself by holding presidential and parliamentary elections in 1988–1989, the JVP attacked the opposition parties and intimidated voters. The JVP's all-out assault was reciprocated by government security forces, armed UNP elements, and later armed groups from opposition political parties. Civilians were caught in a storm of violence, much of its indiscriminate, which subsided only with the killing or capture of most of the JVP leadership at the end of 1989. Between 40,000 and 60,000 Sinhalese were killed during the JVP insurrection of 1987–1989 (Senaratne 1997, 103–44). This figure is roughly comparable to the total number of casualties in intra-Tamil conflicts. By comparison, the number of casualties directly due to Sinhalese–Tamil fighting is much smaller.

In the north and east, tensions between the LTTE and IPKF were immediately evident. LTTE supporters inflamed relations with the IPKF, and the Indians armed other Tamil paramilitaries as a counterweight to the LTTE. By October 1987, a new round of LTTE attacks on Sinhalese civilians in the north and east forced the IPKF into the Sri Lankan government's counterinsurgency role. The IPKF had to use heavy weapons to secure

Jaffna. Under the burden of policing the entire north and east, the Indian troop contingent ballooned to around 100,000. The LTTE was driven into the jungles and, in the Jaffna region, the villages and safehouses, but maintained guerrilla operations and imposed a heavy toll on the IPKF.

Other Tamil armed groups—the ENDLF, the EPRLF, and TELO—assumed the leadership of the newly consolidated Northeast Province. They were armed, trained, and pressed into policing and counterinsurgency roles alongside the IPKF. Yet two important factors prevented these groups from gaining enough legitimacy to marginalize the LTTE. First, the IPKF and its allied Tamil paramilitaries, like the Sri Lankan armed forces before them, alienated much of the Tamil populace with heavy-handed methods and poor discipline. Taking advantage of the opportunity, the LTTE frequently designed its operations to elicit maximum collateral damage to Tamil civilian life and property. Second, the ENDLF, the EPRLF, and TELO were widely perceived as corrupt instruments of Indian policy and hence as unreliable representatives of Sri Lankan Tamil interests.

The LTTE's final trump card was the JVP rebellion, which was a far greater threat to the Sri Lankan government. After elections were held in 1988–1989, the main grievance sustaining Sinhalese support for the JVP was the humiliating and apparently ineffective IPKF presence. In April 1989, the Sri Lankan government's appeal for negotiations was rejected by the JVP and accepted by the LTTE. The LTTE duly agreed to a cease-fire and negotiations, giving Sri Lankan President Premadasa an excuse to demand the withdrawal of the IPKF. In March 1990, the IPKF withdrew, having suffered more than 1,000 killed and 3,000 wounded. The LTTE immediately decimated the IPKF's armed Tamil proxies, in the process capturing the weapons stores left by the IPKF. In short, the LTTE emerged from the Indian intervention as a battle-tested, well-supplied organization, lacking any serious Tamil political rivals (IISS 1990, 176–78; Senaratne 1997, 92–101).

After finishing these intra-Tamil mopping-up operations, the LTTE dropped the pretense of negotiations and relaunched the war against the Sri Lankan government. After intense fighting, the Sri Lankan army was able to regain control over the east and much of the north, but the LTTE controlled the Jaffna peninsula. There, a sophisticated LTTE administration developed, enforcing order through a rudimentary police, judicial, penal, and tax system. The LTTE also maintained a significant but less hegemonic presence in the east, where it faced a more difficult environment—large Sinhalese and Muslim populations, a more effective Sri Lankan government and armed forces presence, and residual Tamil paramilitary rivals. From 1990–1994, heavy but indecisive fighting between government forces and the LTTE continued. Many Tamil civilians were killed, which helped to maintain local Tamil support for the LTTE. Meanwhile, the LTTE maintained a barrage of assassinations and terror attacks on Sinhalese civilians. LTTE suicide attacks killed President Premadasa in May 1993 and UNP presidential candidate G. Dissanayake in October 1994, along with dozens of other notables and bystanders.

Chandrika Bandaranaike Kumaratunga, daughter of S.W.R.D. and S.R.D. Bandaranaike, was elected president in 1994. Seeking a political solution, she offered greater devolution of power. Kumaratunga agreed to lift the blockade of the LTTE-controlled north amid a cease-fire and negotiations with the LTTE. She struggled to develop a plan to devolve power and then to push it through the parliament. At the same time, she built up the army's capabilities while trying to improve discipline. The LTTE, after initially declaring that it might accept a "substantive alternative" to independence, showed little interest in an autonomy deal. After using the brief lull to increase its strength and try to extract unilateral military concessions from the government, the LTTE returned to war in April 1995, with the sinking of two Sri Lankan naval vessels.

The Sri Lankan armed forces went on the offensive, taking control of the main contested cities of the north and east, including Jaffna. Rather than risk its strength in a frontal battle with government forces, the LTTE withdrew to the jungles to prosecute a low-intensity war. The LTTE was able to shoot down a number of military transports, sink a number of navy ships, and strike the oil storage facility at Colombo's airport. In January 1996, a little over a month after Jaffna fell to government forces, the LTTE exploded a huge bomb outside the central bank building in Colombo, killing close to 100 people and injuring more than 1,000. Similar attacks followed, including a truck-bomb attack on Sri Lanka's most sacred Buddhist temple, in Kandy. In January 1998, government-sponsored elections sought to return local government to Tamils. The LTTE responded by assassinating the newly-elected TULF mayor, S. Yogeswaran, along with other Tamil municipal officials. In December 1999, in an LTTE attack on a campaign rally that killed twenty-six, President Kumaratunga herself lost an eye (*Economist*, October 22, 1994, 41; *Economist*, February 7, 1998, 41; IISS 1996, 207–208).

Meanwhile, the Sri Lankan army had become overextended. By 1998, the LTTE was able to fight the Sri Lankan army to a standstill in large-unit engagements. In 1999–2000, the LTTE retook much of the Jaffna peninsula, although not Jaffna city. A military stalemate ensued. The LTTE continued its bloody campaign of suicide assassinations, killing both Sinhalese and moderate Tamil politicians. President Kumaratunga sought to press ahead with her autonomy plan, in which extensive powers would be devolved to the provinces. The Northern and Eastern Provinces would be consolidated pending a later referendum in the ethnically heterogeneous Eastern Province. Parliamentary resistance led to political stalemate. The LTTE conditioned negotiations on a withdrawal of government forces. In July 2001, thirteen LTTE fighters struck the country's main airport, destroying eight military planes and about half the jets of the national civilian air carrier, Air Lanka.

With President Kumaratunga now turning against concessions to the LTTE, the December 2001 parliamentary elections were won by the opposition UNP. In February 2002, Norwegian-brokered talks were opened amid a cease-fire and an end to the economic blockade of LTTE-held regions. The new prime minister, Ranil Wickremesinghe, was willing to give the LTTE a dominant political role in a regional autonomy compromise that would preserve Sri Lanka's territorial integrity. The LTTE agreed in principle to accept some kind of devolution of power to an interim administration in the north and east but refused to rule out independence.

The cease-fire left the LTTE as the de facto government in the areas it controlled, including most of the Kilinochchi and Mullaitivu districts in the North. The LTTE didn't agree to disarm but only to stop smuggling in additional military supplies to its forces. The Sri Lankan government agreed to disarm non-LTTE paramilitaries that it had hitherto supported while allowing LTTE political cadres to function openly in areas of the north and east controlled by the Sri Lankan armed forces. Both parties are obligated to cease all violations of civil liberties, including forced conscription, extortion, intimidation, and other "control" measures routinely used by the LTTE. From May 2002, both Wickremesinghe and Kumaratunga explicitly refused to allow a de facto LTTE-run state to be created as long as core issues of Sri Lanka's territorial integrity and the powers, structure, and governance practices of autonomous provincial institutions remained unsettled.

Nevertheless, the LTTE has taken advantage of the agreement precisely to consolidate its exclusive control over a de facto statelet. The LTTE continued to assassinate its political enemies, both Tamil and non-Tamil, while the Sri Lankan state withdrew its support from anti-LTTE Tamil groups. During the cease-fire, LTTE troop and supporter strength has risen rapidly—largely through forcible induction of teenagers. Peace and the end of the blockade also increased tax revenues in LTTE-controlled regions, compensating for eroding foreign revenue sources. In April 2003, following two clashes at sea that showed the LTTE resupplying its forces in contravention of the cease-fire agreement, the LTTE withdrew from talks with the Sri Lankan government—although it did not return to war. (As of June 2005, the Nordic-run Sri Lankan Monitoring Mission [SLMM] reported 3,006 LTTE violations of the agreement, as against 132 by the Sri Lankan government. The LTTE violations also have been much more severe, reflecting a policy of violently subjugating the civilian population of the north and east. Last, the SLMM numbers are significant underestimates, leaving out incidents that are unverified—including almost all of the many assassinations and killings carried out by the LTTE.)

The LTTE's immediate pretext for suspending talks was the government's refusal to withdraw the army from positions that guaranteed continued control of Jaffna city. In October 2003, however, it became clear that negotiations broke down over the powers and governance of the projected autonomous Northeast Province. As a condition for resuming peace talks, the LTTE demanded that an Interim Self-Governing Authority be created in the north and east prior to final status talks. This would give the LTTE control over local security forces and external finance and trade and thus over a functionally independent state administration. On the other hand, the Sri Lankan government is willing to offer substantial self-government but wants transparent, democratic governance that doesn't threaten its sovereignty and territorial integrity.

In November 2003, President Kumaratunga declared a state of emergency and suspended the UNP-controlled parliament, arguing that Wickremesinghe's cease-fire concessions were allowing the LTTE to set up a de facto state. Fresh parliamentary elections in April 2004 were narrowly won by Kumarantanga's SFLP–JVP alliance, which is far more skeptical that a negotiated settlement with the LTTE can lead to anything but the break-up of Sri Lanka. Through some combination of genuine support and crushing intimidation, the LTTE-backed Tamil National Alliance (TNA)—a coalition of Tamil parties that agreed to recognize the LTTE's vanguard role in representing the Tamils—swept most of the seats in heavily Tamil districts of the north and east. This departs from the LTTE's traditional strategy of violently opposing Tamil participation in elections. At the same time, the LTTE struggled to crush a rebellion by its eastern command, led by Colonel Karuna. The tsunami of December 26, 2004, took more than 30,000 lives in Sri Lanka and devastated large parts of the east coast. In 2006, more frequent and intense LTTE attacks and Sri Lankan army responses appeared to shatter the fragile peace efforts (*Economist*, November 8, 2003, 41, March 27, 2004, 43, February 26, 2005, 40; Ganguly 2004; IISS 2003, 279–84; SIPRI 2004, 107–108).

To summarize, the war started as a secessionist conflict, with elements of the Sri Lankan Tamil population taking up arms in pursuit of an independent state in the north and east. The war is commonly viewed as starting with the intensified Tamil paramilitary activity that followed the anti-Tamil riots of July 1983. However, armed, active Tamil paramilitaries began forming on a small scale from 1972. The scale and intensity of fighting grew gradually through the mid- to late 1970s and early 1980s before intensifying qualitatively from 1983. The most significant international intervention was that of India, initially in allowing Tamil armed groups to set up safe havens in cooperation with Tamil Nadu authorities in the late 1970s, then in actively arming and training the Tamil groups from the early 1980s, and finally in the abortive effort to use the IPKF to impose an autonomy settlement in 1987–1990. The modern Sinhalese–Tamil conflict echoes, in both popular and elite historical memories, the precolonial centuries of rivalry between the Sinhalese and Tamil kingdoms.

The Insurgents

Beginning in the early 1970s, a number of Tamil paramilitary organizations initiated an armed struggle against the Sri Lankan state. Over time, the LTTE took an exclusive, dominating position. By the early 1980s, the LTTE had emerged as the most formidable Tamil paramilitary group. By the time Indian forces were forcibly introduced in 1987, the LTTE had become the dominant paramilitary group. In 1987–1990, Indian efforts to enforce a compromise settlement, by building up more moderate and dependent Tamil militant organizations, were defeated by the LTTE; and after the IPKF withdrew in 1990, the LTTE virtually exterminated its Tamil rivals, becoming the only significant military force engaged in armed struggle against the Sri Lankan state. The LTTE has always carried on a dual struggle, fighting rival Tamil moderates and extremists as well as the Sri Lankan state. Its struggle against rival Tamils has been highly successful. This effort continues just as much to deny the Tamils an alternative representative as to deny the Sri Lankan government an alternative negotiating partner.

In the early and mid-1970s, the Sri Lankan military was small and poorly armed. This made it possible for the Tigers and other nascent Tamil paramilitaries to rely on local stocks of guns and ammunition and on supplies taken from Sri Lankan security forces. Beginning in the late 1970s, funds and arms were procured in India's Tamil Nadu province and smuggled across the Palk Strait. From 1983, Indian intelligence agencies provided extensive funding, training, and weapons supplies to Tamil militant organizations, including the LTTE.

In the early 1980s, the LTTE and other Tamil paramilitaries sought to diversify their sources of external support. They reinforced local ties in Tamil Nadu separate from those controlled by the Indian state. They developed fund-raising networks among the well-off Tamil communities of Western Europe, North America, and Australia. They also became involved in the drug trade. All of these sources, particularly the Tamil

Table 1: Sri Lanka's Sinhalese–Tamil Ethnic Conflict

War:	Liberation Tigers of Tamil Eelam (LTTE) and other Tamil paramilitaries vs. government
Dates:	Starting on small scale in 1972, intensifying from July 1983; ongoing, but at much reduced level since February 2002 cease-fire; intensifying again in 2006
Casualties:	Approximately 120,000, including 50,000 killed in intra-Sinhalese violence and tens of thousands more in intra-Tamil violence
Regime type prior to war:	Democracy
Regime type during war:	Democracy
Regime type after war:	War ongoing; still democracy
GDP per capita year war began:	US $305 in 1982 (1982 dollars)
GDP per capita 5 years after war:	US $347 in 1987 (1982 dollars)
Insurgents:	LTTE; before 1990, other Tamil paramilitaries
Issue:	Ethnic conflict over creation of independent Tamil state in Northern and Eastern Provinces of Sri Lanka
Rebel funding:	Rebels aided by Indian government and Tamil communities in India and the West, in varying degrees over time; also self-financed through drug smuggling, kidnapping, and extortion rackets.
Role of geography:	Rebels hid in jungles.
Role of resources:	None
Immediate outcome:	Escalating internal ethnic conflict
Outcome after 5 years:	Indian intervention, which intensified rather than ended conflict
Role of UN:	None
Role of regional organization:	None
Refugees:	As of 2003, 386,000 internally displaced, 122,000 refugees
Prospects for peace:	Unfavorable without more effective military and political actions against LTTE, or LTTE leadership change

Sources: CIA 2005; IISS 1985–1990; SIPRI 2004, 107; UNHCR 2004.

communities of the West, have proven more reliable than the Indian state. Thus, from the early 1980s, Tamil paramilitaries had access to heavier and more sophisticated weaponry as well as better communications equipment and supplies. This includes the famous cyanide capsules, which LTTE fighters carry with them in case they are captured and subject to interrogation.

From the mid-1990s and again after September 11, 2001, the Sri Lankan government has had some success in getting the United States and other governments to crack down on the Tamil diaspora fund-raising infrastructure. These efforts have been helped by the LTTE's growing reputation for ideological extremism, operational ferocity, and terrorism. Even for Tamils in Sri Lanka and abroad, the LTTE's negative characteristics have increasingly overshadowed those

of the Sri Lankan state. However, the LTTE continues to wipe out, marginalize, or absorb alternative Tamil political leaders and organizations. As long as Prabhakaran remains in control, it is also difficult to imagine Tamil political alternatives emerging from within the LTTE.

The LTTE has always used low-intensity warfare: guerrilla attacks on police and military units; political assassinations of Sinhalese, Tamil, and Muslim leaders; extortion and intimidation of Tamil "host" populations; terror attacks on Sinhalese and Muslim populations; and ethnic cleansing of Sinhalese and Muslim populations in the north and east. Since the mid-1980s, it has acquired the capability to mount conventional operations using large units, heavier weapons, and sophisticated tactics. Since the departure of the IPKF, its capabilities have in-

Tamil Tiger leader Velupillai Prabhakaran inspects his troops in the Wanni region in northern Sri Lanka on February 20, 2004. (AFP/Getty Images)

creased, its conventional operations have become more daring and successful, its ethnic cleansing efforts have become systematic, and its low-intensity attacks have become deadlier and more sensational.

The jungles of the north and east have provided good cover for guerrilla activity. This has been especially important during periods when the LTTE has been driven from Jaffna and other Tamil cities and towns, first by the IPKF and, from 1995, by the Sri Lankan military. During these periods, the LTTE preserved its organization and cadres against a superior enemy while sustaining guerrilla and terror operations. Later, the LTTE used jungle terrain to advantage in conventional operations. In 1999–2000, the LTTE was able to cut off and overrun an overextended enemy. This allowed the LTTE to retake much of the Jaffna peninsula.

Signature LTTE low-intensity tactics include suicide assassinations of major political leaders (e.g., Indian Prime Minister Rajiv Gandhi, Sri Lankan President Premadasa, and also the attempted assassination of President Kumaratunga); large-scale terrorist attacks (e.g., the April 1987 attacks in Colombo and Trincomalee, which killed more than 200, and the January 1996 bombing of the central bank, which killed 100 and wounded more than 1,000); and destructive attacks on high-value infrastructure and military targets (e.g., oil storage and refining facilities, military and civilian jets, military and civilian ships). The LTTE has been adept at using huge homemade land mines to destroy passing military and civilian vehicles. (The LTTE absorbed these and other methods—both directly and by example—from Palestinian terrorist groups and Hezbollah. Over time, its skill in their use has become second to none.)

The LTTE also has well-known organizational and strategic habits. Although its ferocity is legendary, it is reputed to be honest rather than corrupt. This has made the LTTE more acceptable to the Tamil population, even though the LTTE has violently suppressed all political alternatives. The LTTE has basically enserfed the Tamil population in the areas it controls, mostly in the north. It uses a combination of indoctrination and force to extract manpower and resources while exterminating any political or military rivals. Where its control is contested by the Sri Lankan armed forces and by Sinhalese and Muslim communities—as in most of the east— it does its best to impose a similar control in Tamil-populated areas and to expand those areas by terrorizing and "cleansing" Sinhalese and Muslims.

In its struggle against the Sri Lankan government, the LTTE has always been willing to agree to cease-fires and, where possible, has used them to obtain substantive concessions. Yet it has never renounced the objective of independence in all of the Northern and Eastern Provinces and has always backed out of previous agreements when the balance of power shifted in its favor. There is little reason to believe that the present cease-fire will hold once the LTTE feels it can achieve more by returning to open warfare (Singer 1996, 1149–50).

The tactics of the Sri Lankan state and armed forces have often played into the hands of the LTTE. During the prewar and early wartime periods, and above all in 1983, the Sri Lankan government, police, and military did not act decisively to protect Tamil civilians during riots. In some important cases, paramilitary, police, and military forces actually fomented and participated in riots. Police and military forces often responded to guerrilla attacks by targeting Tamil bystanders. Organized counterinsurgency and conventional offensives have often caused significant unnecessary civilian casualties. The extent of the "dirty war" against Tamils can also be gauged from what Sri Lankan security forces were willing to do to their fellow Sinhalese during the second JVP insurrection. Only from the mid-1980s did increased resources and training begin to build up more capable and disciplined

armed forces. Improved conventional performance is evident from the mid-1990s, although the LTTE was able to regain the conventional initiative as recently as 1999–2000. Given that Sri Lanka is an island, and that India withdrew support from 1987, it is remarkable that the LTTE has been able to maintain the financial and logistical base necessary to sustain its extensive and sophisticated capabilities.

Causes of the War

The potential for Sinhalese–Tamil conflict was rooted in ethnic differences and settlement patterns, along with collective aspirations, grievances, and inequalities deriving from the precolonial and colonial periods. The ethnic division is defined by religious and linguistic differences. The division is historically associated with different precolonial political and sociocultural histories, including centuries of elite-level conflict and rivalry. The colonial period, particularly the late period of British rule, can be said to have "modernized" the ethnic division, that is, to have increased social integration and interdependence to the point where the ethnic division became more strongly felt at the mass level. Eventually, waning colonialism added democracy and ethnic politics to the intensified interdependence and more strongly felt inequality. Political tensions—between Sinhalese asserting their majority status and Tamils defending their minority rights—were inevitable. Settlement patterns gave the ethnic division a territorial dimension. With Tamils an overwhelming majority on the Jaffna peninsula and in some other regions of the north and east, Tamil pursuit of minority rights had the potential to seek territorial self-determination, as opposed to integration on the basis of equality. The centuries-long history of separate Tamil kingdoms in the north and east provided obvious precedents.

As shown by the long period of peace following independence, large-scale violent conflict was far from a foregone conclusion. Two factors are primarily responsible for igniting the war.

First, the intrusive, sometimes aggressive policies and weak capacities of the Sri Lankan state were responsible for a cumulative assault on the economic and physical security of the Tamils. At least from 1956, and arguably as early as 1948, the Sinhalese electorate and leadership, in an effort to assert majority rights and to rectify ethnic inequalities, imposed significant economic and status losses on the Tamil minority. Tamils did not see any clear, enforceable limits to this slow-motion marginalization process. Tamil civilian leaders abetted the trend by insisting on far-reaching autonomy goals and territorial claims. Most importantly, the Sinhalese-dominated police and security forces were undisciplined, and the Sinhalese political leadership often lacked the will to stop anti-Tamil riots. In some cases, most importantly in 1983, government elements were complicit in starting the riots.

Second, the Indian intervention turned what might have been a smaller, shorter bout of ethnic violence into a more intense, interminable conflict. In the late 1970s, Indian governments allowed Tamil Nadu to be turned into a safe haven for political organization, fund-raising, training, and arms smuggling—with the active involvement of the Tamil Nadu authorities. Then, from 1983, Indian intelligence directly trained and supplied the Tamil paramilitaries. This process transformed small, poorly armed and trained bands into large, sophisticated paramilitary organizations. During this formative period of relative military vulnerability, Indian safe haven put the "vital organs" of the Tamil paramilitaries beyond the reach of the Sri Lankan security forces. The India-based infrastructure made it possible to capitalize on the effects of the 1983 riots, raising the insurgency to qualitatively new levels of intensity.

The Indian intervention is related to the broader issue of the expected balance of power. Suppose both sides perceive that one side has clear military superiority. Then, responsible leaderships should find it easier to make a deal that recognizes the prerogatives of the strong and the residual rights of the weak, while avoiding the potentially high costs of violent conflict. (This argument holds only when both sides possess leaderships that are accountable to their constituents or at least concerned with their well-being. Thus, a leadership concerned primarily with its own power and seeing competitive or diversionary gain in conflict, or one whose ideological extremism makes it unconcerned with the costs of achieving its goals, may calculate that an adverse balance of power is not a sufficient reason to avoid war. At least until the late 1970s, it can be argued that both the Sinhalese and the Tamil leaderships were concerned with minimizing the costs imposed on their respective ethnic constituencies.) On the other hand, if the balance of power is less clear, it will be easier for both sides to perceive a significant probability of military victory and a low probability of catastrophic defeat, and hence more difficult for both sides to make significant compromises. This should increase the probability of war. In retrospect, a high level of uncertainty seems to have existed prior to the 1987 introduction of the IPKF. Sinhalese formed the overwhelming majority, but Tamils counted on receiving aid from India or at least from the 50 million Tamils of South India. Each side could thus perceive that it had a good chance of insisting on its "minimum" conditions at a time when giving in to the other side seemed to promise unacceptable losses of rights and security. If the leaderships then in control could have seen into the far more catastrophic future, it seems likely that they would have chosen to avoid war by compromising on the outstanding political and economic issues. Indeed, the autonomy arrangements, which Sri Lankan governments have sought to implement unilaterally since the 1990s, roughly coincide with what mainstream Tamil parties demanded through the 1960s.

To summarize, ethnic division and settlement patterns and related expectations and grievances created the potential for territorially based ethnic conflict. This potential was ignited by the reckless policies and weak capacities of

Sinhalese-dominated governments. Sinhalese recklessness and Tamil resistance were stimulated by an unclear balance of power. Last, a limited conflict was transformed into a full-blown war when India provided passive safe haven and then active support to the nascent Tamil insurgency.

Outcome

The onset of war does not explain why war persists for a long time. It is very unusual for wars to last as long as the one in Sri Lanka. Typically, wars end either when one side wins a clear victory or when the war is fought to a clear stalemate. At such points, both sides tend to decide that they do not stand to gain by continuing the war. This leads to a formal or informal peace, which reflects the power balance revealed by the war and the associated changes in conditions. What has made Sri Lanka different? The short answer is the LTTE. The LTTE has dominated the Sri Lankan Tamils since the IPKF's withdrawal in 1990. Due to some combination of thirst for exclusive power and ideological extremism, the LTTE under Prabhakaran seems willing and able to continue the war indefinitely. These preferences and capacities, when put into the context of Sri Lanka's ethnic settlement patterns, make it virtually impossible for any Sri Lankan government to make concessions that might satisfy the LTTE.

From its beginnings, the LTTE has fought a two-front war, fighting the Sri Lankan government while trying to monopolize the Tamil political space. Since the withdrawal of the IPKF in 1990, the LTTE has succeeded in crushing or intimidating both moderate and extremist Tamil rivals. Without moderate and robust Tamil political alternatives, there can be no peace without the LTTE's agreement. At the same time, the LTTE's organizational and military capabilities—including the crucial international fundraising and procurement that the Sri Lankan state has been unable to disrupt—have made it possible to sustain the war through thick and thin. The LTTE military strategy and tactics are as follows. When the enemy seems to be gaining a conventional military advantage or seems willing to make valuable concessions—as with the Sri Lankan state and the IPKF from 1989 to 1990 and the Sri Lankan state from 1994 to 1995 and since 2001—the LTTE agrees to cease-fires and negotiations. During these lulls, the LTTE rearms and resupplies, continues its war against Tamil rivals, refuses to drop its core independence goals, and demands unilateral concessions from the Sri Lankan government. Then, when the balance of power appears to have moved sufficiently in its favor, the LTTE restarts the war, as in 1990 and 1995. The LTTE has thus been willing to continue the war indefinitely, despite both horrific costs for the Tamil population and credible and attractive compromise options. This shows that its leadership is possessed by some combination of ideological extremism and personal power seeking.

In retrospect, what role was played by India's intervention? From the late 1970s, Tamil Nadu and Indian governments provided safe havens. From the early 1980s, India provided significant aid to Tamil paramilitaries. As the Sri Lankan government in turn sought military aid from the United States, the United Kingdom, Israel, Pakistan, and China, Indian support for the Tamil paramilitaries increased. Initial Indian strategy was driven by internal politics in Tamil Nadu and then also by the center's hostility to any foreign involvement in the region. From the early 1980s, India pressured the Sri Lankan government to negotiate a federal solution. At the same time, India built up Tamil paramilitaries to maintain pressure on the Sri Lankan government, while seeking control over the paramilitaries. The April 1987 LTTE attacks intensified the war, leading to direct intervention. As part of the 1987 Indo-Lankan Accords, Indian forces were sent to Sri Lanka to enforce the autonomy agreement. There, until the withdrawal of Indian forces in 1990, they continued to support Tamil paramilitary rivals of the LTTE. However, Indian forces were not even able to defeat the

LTTE directly, much less through the feebler efforts of their Tamil proxies. Overall, India's involvement solidified the domination of the very radicals that India sought to marginalize. This perpetuated the conflict and made it more likely that it would lead to an independent Tamil state—the outcome that Indian strategists most fear. It is hard to think of a more vivid example of how the principal–agent problem, combined with myopia and miscalculation, can produce self-defeating outcomes.

Why didn't the LTTE more quickly restart the war after 2001, given that there seemed little chance for a negotiated peace? The LTTE perceived the local and especially the international environments as threatening. Since the mid-1990s, Sri Lankan governments have made greater efforts to cultivate moderate Tamil political alternatives and to implement local and provincial autonomy. Particularly since 9/11, greater international efforts have been made to cut off LTTE financing and procurement. International assistance also promises to improve the capabilities of the Sri Lankan military. Under these conditions, the LTTE leadership appeared to have calculated that it was wiser to freeze the conflict with the Sri Lankan state, while focusing its energies on denying internal political alternatives to the Sri Lankan Tamils and reducing its dependence on more vulnerable elements of its international support network. This explains the LTTE's unprecedented effort to corral rather than destroy the Tamil political parties—unified in the Tamil National Alliance—in recent elections. It adapted the LTTE to the more controlled contours of the cease-fire–era battlefield, where rhetoric and institutional position can more usefully supplement guns as mechanisms of intra-Tamil control. Such efforts helped to relieve pressure and regain legitimacy on the international diplomatic front. As of late 2006, however, renewed LTTE attacks have been reigniting full-scale war.

Why haven't successive Sri Lankan governments been willing to go beyond various autonomy formulas to grant independence? Funda-mentally, all sovereign states are loathe to cede territory. In Sri Lanka's case, there are important reinforcing factors. First, the LTTE and other Tamil political organizations have demanded the Eastern as well as the Northern Province, even though Sri Lankan Tamils have not constituted a clear majority of the Eastern Province's population in recent times. Given that the Muslim population of the Eastern Province (32.5 percent in 1981; probably about the same currently) fears for its future under Tamil rule, it supports continued affiliation with the Sri Lankan state. If the Sinhalese (25.1 percent in 1981; probably about the same currently) and Muslims are taken together, then a majority or at least a large minority opposes secession of the Eastern Province. More detail is helpful here. The Tamil population is concentrated in the central Batticaloa district of the Eastern Province. Muslims and Sinhalese together constitute large majorities in Trincomalee district to the north and Amparai district to the south. Government-sponsored irrigation projects significantly increased the Sinhalese share of the Eastern Province's population since independence (Manogaran 1987). However, this does not establish a presumptive Tamil historical claim to the entire province. The Tamil presence in the region is more recent than that of the Sinhalese and has been limited to the coastal areas near Batticaloa and Trincomalee. Second, the Muslims of the coastal areas have in recent times always been comparable in numbers to the Tamils. Last, the Sinhalese have always retained a presence in the interior and in some coastal areas of the East. It is not clear that irrigation-driven settlement of lightly populated interior regions, in which the country's dominant ethnic group has traditionally resided and is proportionately represented, constitutes a seizure of land that is inherently Tamil (De Silva 1995, 75–95). Thus, Sri Lankan governments have always insisted on an Eastern Province referendum, to determine whether the Eastern Province will remain joined to the Northern, or will function as a distinct administrative entity.

Second, Sinhalese elites and masses do not trust that Sri Lankan Tamils will be content even with the entire north and east. They fear that, once a Tamil state is consolidated in the North and East, pressure will shift to the Indian Tamil-populated central highlands, and that such aspirations will sooner or later receive support from the Tamils of South India. Third, the Indian state doesn't support an independent Tamil state. Such a state will tend to create secessionist pressure in the Tamil-populated regions of South India. Without support from the regional hegemon, India, no Tamil state is likely to develop—at least not unless the Sri Lankan armed forces are utterly defeated. Finally, there is the nature of the LTTE itself. Rather than compromise its power and goals, the LTTE has been willing to plunge the Sri Lankan Tamils into an endless nightmare, which over time has far exceeded the violence, discrimination, and hardships of the pre-1983 period. The LTTE has implacably murdered those—among Sinhalese, Tamils, Muslims, and its own cadres—that appear to stand in its way. How can such an organization be trusted to follow through on any compromise commitments, or even to rest content with a state encompassing both the Northern and Eastern Provinces?

Two incidents are particularly telling. Prabhakaran chose to fight the IPKF, and later, after the IPKF had withdrawn, assassinated Rajiv Gandhi. Fighting the IPKF meant giving up the most credible possible autonomy compromise to fight an enemy much more formidable than the Sri Lankan military. Later, the killing of the iconic Indian leader could easily have provoked another war with the regional hegemon—which from 1987 to 1990 came closer to wiping out the LTTE than the Sri Lankan state ever did. Nevertheless, Prabhakaran calculated that the policies were acceptable means of protecting his power and maximalist independence goals.

These considerations explain the recent stalemate: The Sri Lankan state is determined to go ahead with autonomy with or without the LTTE; the LTTE, at least until international conditions became less threatening, stalled on the Sinhalese–Tamil front and focused on the intra-Tamil front. What will happen in the future? Basically, there are three scenarios. The status quo might persist more or less indefinitely, with the LTTE calculating that a quasi-state in the areas it controls is preferable to a return to all-out war. Second, the LTTE may have calculated that power has shifted sufficiently to reward a return to war. Last, a moderate Tamil alternative might arise, either from outside or inside the LTTE, and this may promise a more successful movement toward autonomy. However, as long as Prabhakaran leads the LTTE, the last option is extremely unlikely to develop or to last. If such a compromise option appears to be developing, Prabhakaran can be expected to relaunch the war against the Sri Lankan state and the Sinhalese, in order to remarginalize Tamil moderates and provide cover for intra-Tamil extermination efforts. In 2006, Prabhakaran seems to have abandoned the façade of deadlocked negotiations and returned to war.

Conclusion

Relatively clear policy recommendations follow for the Sri Lankan state and the regional and international great powers. An autonomy solution must be implemented, along with efforts to develop and protect moderate Tamil alternatives to the LTTE. At the same time, international controls to limit LTTE access to funding and supplies, along with continued improvement of the Sri Lankan armed forces' discipline and fighting capacity, are most likely to deter the LTTE. The emergence of Tamil political alternatives along with a credible autonomy option will force the LTTE to choose between peace and political normalization or a return to more intense war against both the Sinhalese state and Tamil rivals. Judging by its previous behavior, the LTTE will almost certainly choose war. Even then, the ground will have been prepared to fight the LTTE under more advantageous conditions, that is, with both a more efficient Sri

Lankan military and serious Tamil political alternatives. It is in this context that leadership change, which is likely only with the death of Prabhakaran, becomes most important. True, this alone will not end the war. On the other hand, it seems just as clear that even a stronger Sri Lankan military and legitimate Tamil political alternatives will not make an autonomy solution stick as long as Prabhakaran controls the LTTE. Once all or part of the LTTE is controlled by leaders willing to compromise for the sake of those it supposedly represents, there will be an internal Tamil mechanism to enforce a compromise settlement (Ganguly 2004, 915–16; IISS 2003, 280–84).

Given the underlying ethnic cleavage and settlement patterns, the war seems likely to end in one of two ways. One is an LTTE military victory, delivering a Tamil state in the Northern and Eastern Provinces. The other is an autonomy settlement, depending on the Sri Lankan state's enduring military superiority combined with moderating "regime change" among the Tamils—either moderating leadership change within the LTTE, or the rise of effective moderate Tamil challengers to the LTTE. To support an autonomy settlement, the Sinhalese parties will also have to maintain greater political consensus, and the state better administrative and security capacities, than in the past. The Tamils need leaders who care more about the costs of war and less about personal power and ideological glory. And the Sinhalese-dominated state needs to be powerful enough to impose high costs in a continued war for independence while offering a palatable and credible autonomy alternative.

Shale Horowitz and Buddhika Jayamaha

Chronology
1948   Sri Lanka gains independence from British rule.
1956   New SLFP government supports making Buddhism the official religion and Sinhalese the official language. Autonomy-oriented Federal Party becomes most popular Tamil party.
1957–1959   Tentative agreement to provide limited language rights and autonomy to Tamils breaks down amid Sinhalese opposition and anti-Tamil riots. Prime Minister Bandaranaike is assassinated.
1972   New constitution maintains Sinhalese as sole official language, gives official status to Buddhism. Tamil United Front formed, and increasingly advances goal of independence—renamed Tamil United Liberation Front in 1976. Early development of violent paramilitary organizations produces rising wave of violence.
1977   Tamil United Liberation Front, running on a platform of Tamil independence, sweeps Tamil-majority districts. Tamil militant attacks and anti-Tamil rioting follow.
1981, 1983   Anti-Tamil riots again follow Tamil militant attacks.
1984   LTTE violence and government responses escalate, leading to increasing numbers of civilian casualties among both Tamils and Sinhalese.
1987   Indian Peacekeeping Force (IPKF) inserted to impose autonomy settlement.
1987–1990   War occurs between IPKF and LTTE, and between Sri Lankan government and JVP.
1990   IPKF withdraws, and war resumes between Sri Lankan government and LTTE.
1994–1995   Chandrika Kumaratunga elected president of Sri Lanka. Cease-fire and negotiations with the LTTE take place.
1995   LTTE resumes war. Sri Lankan armed forces go on the offensive.
1999–2000   LTTE retakes much of the Jaffna peninsula.
2002–2005   Norwegian-brokered cease-fire stops heavy fighting, but negotiations fail to make progress.
2006   LTTE attacks reignite war.

List of Acronyms
EPRLF: Eelam People's Revolutionary Liberation Front
EROS: Eelam Revolutionary Organization of Students
IPKF: Indian Peacekeeping Force
JVP: Janatha Vimukthi Peramuna (National Liberation Front)
LTTE: Liberation Tigers of Tamil Eelam
NGO: nongovernmental organization
PLOTE: People's Liberation Organization of Tamil Eelam
SLFP: Sri Lankan Freedom Party

SLMM: Sri Lankan Monitoring Mission
TELO: Tamil Eelam Liberation Organization
TNA: Tamil National Alliance
TULF: Tamil United Liberation Front
UNP: United National Party

References

Asian Development Bank. 2005. *Key Indicators of Developing Asian and Pacific Countries.* Manila: Asian Development Bank. adb.org/ Documents/Books/Key_Indicators/2004/pdf/ SRI.pdf.

Central Intelligence Agency (CIA). 2005. *World Factbook.* Washington, DC: CIA. www.odci. gov/cia/publications/factbook/geos/ce.html.

De Silva, K. M. 1981. *A History of Sri Lanka.* Berkeley: University of California Press.

De Silva, K. M. 1986. *Managing Ethnic Tensions in Multi-Ethnic Societies: Sri Lanka, 1880–1985.* Lanham, MD: University Press of America.

De Silva, K. M. 1995. *Regional Powers and Small State Security: India and Sri Lanka, 1977–90.* Baltimore, MD: Johns Hopkins University Press.

The Economist. 1994. October 22: 41.

The Economist. 1998. February 7: 41.

The Economist. 2003. November 8: 41.

The Economist. 2004. March 27: 41.

The Economist. 2005. February 26: 40.

Ganguly, Rajat. 2004. "Sri Lanka's Ethnic Conflict: At a Crossroads between Peace and War." *Third World Quarterly* 25(5): 903–18.

Gunaratna, Rohan. 1993. *Indian Intervention in Sri Lanka: The Role of India's Intelligence Agencies.* Colombo: South Asian Network on Conflict Research.

International Institute for Strategic Studies (IISS). 1990. *Strategic Survey.* (Various annual issues.)

London: Brassey's, and Oxford: Oxford University Press.

International Institute for Strategic Studies (IISS). *The Military Balance.* (Various annual issues.) Oxford: Oxford University Press.

Kearney, Robert N. 1967. *Communalism and Language in the Politics of Ceylon.* Durham, NC: Duke University Press.

Kearney, Robert N. 1985. "Ethnic Conflict and the Tamil Separatist Movement in Sri Lanka." *Asian Survey* 25(9): 898–917.

Manogaran, Chelvadurai. 1987. *Ethnic Conflict and Reconciliation in Sri Lanka.* Honolulu, HI: University of Hawaii Press.

McGowan, William. 1992. *Only Man Is Vile: The Tragedy of Sri Lanka.* New York: Farrar, Straus & Giroux.

O'Ballance, Edgar. 1989. *The Cyanide War: Tamil Insurrection in Sri Lanka, 1973–1988.* London: Brassey's.

Senaratne, Jagath. 1997. *Political Violence in Sri Lanka, 1977–1990: Riots, Insurrections, Counterinsurgencies, Foreign Intervention.* Amsterdam: VU University Press.

Singer, Marshall R. 1996. "Sri Lanka's Ethnic Conflict: Have Bombs Shattered Hopes for Peace?" *Asian Survey* 36(11): 1146–55.

Stockholm International Peace Research Institute (SIPRI). 2004. *SIPRI Yearbook 2004: Armaments, Disarmament, and International Security.* Oxford, UK: Oxford University Press.

United Nations High Commissioner for Refugees (UNHCR). 2004. *Background Paper on Refugees and Asylum-Seekers from Sri Lanka.* www.unhcr.ch/cgi-bin/texis/vtx/publ/ opendoc.pdf?tbl=RSDCOI&id=40d837f42& page=publ.

Sudan
(1983–2005)

Introduction

Civil wars have caused almost 20 million deaths over the past fifty years. On average, these wars have lasted over six years (Fearon and Laitin 2003). As many as 90 percent of casualities in civil wars are civilian (Cairns 1997). This is due in part to the heinous nature of civil conflict, in which both rebels and the government's military have been known to use tactics that deliberately target civilians (Azam and Hoeffler 2002). Unfortunately, the most recent civil war in Sudan (1983–2005) stands out as one of the longest and most devastating wars in the world.

The purpose of this article is to provide an in-depth analysis of this conflict. It begins by providing a background of the country, including a focus on its history, cultures, and previous conflicts. It then moves into a more detailed analysis of the conflict, focusing on the insurgent groups, geographical factors, tactics used by both the government and rebels, and the role of external actors. The final section provides an analysis of the conflict's outcome, including a discussion of future prospects for peace in Sudan. While this history of Sudan is one of severe suffering and turmoil, recent developments point toward a more peaceful future for the country.

Country Background

Sudan is a central African state that straddles the cultural and geographic divide of North and sub-Saharan Africa. It lies directly south of Egypt and borders eight other countries. With an estimated population of 40 million people covering nearly a million square miles (about a quarter of the size of the United States), Sudan is the largest country in Africa. Since gaining independence from Britain in 1956, Sudan has been enveloped in a costly civil war for all but ten years of its existence. The most recent struggle, begun in 1983, has cost more than 2 million lives and has displaced more than 4 million people (CIA 2005).

Sudan has two distinct major cultures, Arab and black African, which have different demographics, religions, historical backgrounds, and political preferences. The northern Sudanese states include the majority of the population (22 million), cover the majority of the country geographically, and include most of the major urban centers (GlobalSecurity.org 2005). Historically, the north was deeply influenced by Egypt during the time of the pharaohs. Later, Islamic and Arabic traders left their mark on the northern Sudanese, who primarily speak Arabic and practice Islam (Althaus 1999).

Compared to northern Sudan, the southern region of the country has experienced far more difficulties in the country's short history. The south, which has a population of around 6 million, has endured the brunt of the civil violence in the country (GlobalSecurity.org 2005). Southern Sudan has a very heterogeneous population;

with some 117 different languages and 50 ethnic groups, it resembles the traditional African heritage (Althaus 1999; Ministry of Guidance and National Information 1983). Due to decades of civil war and neglect by the northern government, southern Sudan has suffered from a severe lack of infrastructural development. The economy is predominantly a rural subsistence economy (GlobalSecurity.org 2005). Christian missionaries in the early 1900s converted many southerners to Christianity (around 10 percent today). However, most practice some form of traditional African religion.

Since gaining independence from Britain, the Sudanese people have consistently endured both repression and poverty. Other than brief periods of democracy (1956–1957, 1965–1968, and 1986–1988), Sudan has suffered under repressive regimes. According to the Polity IV index, which is a measure of a state's regime type, Sudan has been a solid nondemocracy for all but thirteen years from 1956 through 2002 (Marshall and Jaggers 2003). This includes the twelve years prior to the onset of the current civil war and all years during the conflict.

Poverty often walks hand in hand with repression, and Sudan is no exception. With a gross domestic product (GDP) per capita of less than US $300 at the beginning of the war and a current GDP per capita of US $433, Sudan is among the top 10 percent of poorest countries in the world (CIA 2005). Although it is not the primary cause of internal conflict, poverty has worked to fuel the flames of rebellion while making civilians the major victims of the struggle.

Conflict Background

One must examine both the history of British colonialism and the role of Islamic fundamentalism to understand civil war in Sudan. In the early nineteenth century, Sudan was governed by Egypt, which was part of the Ottoman Empire. Early fault lines developed in the country between the Arab northerners and the black African southerners, who stood on opposing sides of the slave trade. In 1879, British general Charles Gordon was tasked by the Egyptians with pacifying Sudan and ending the slave trade. In 1885, Gordon was killed trying to quell a revolt led by Muhammad Ahmad al Mahdi, who sought to revive and purify Islam in the state. Al Mahdi, who was successful in the revolution, and his successor, Khalifa Abdallah, established Sudanese nationalism with close ties to the Islamic faith in their thirteen-year rule (Glickman 2000).

Khalifa Abdallah was defeated in 1898 by Lord Kitchener and a British force, which led to the establishment of the Anglo-Egyptian Condominium (1898–1956). This Condominium generally capped internal violence. However, British policies worked to divide the country and can be blamed for much of the violence that followed their withdrawal from the state. These policies included the support of Islamic Sudanese nationalism in northern Sudan in order to prevent the spread of Egyptian influence and to protect British interest in the Suez Canal (Woodward 1990, 20–25). At the same time, the British worked to spread a distinctly African Sudanese identity in southern Sudan, which was safe from the spread of Islam under British occupation. Although the British cannot be blamed for initially establishing the ethnoreligious divide between the north and the south, the sixty years of their administration did little to quell the division and likely worked to further divide the country (Daly 1989, 22; Glickman 2000; Woodward 1990, 4–5, 77–78;). After the withdrawal of Britain in 1956, the south was immediately marginalized and repressed by the north-dominated national government (Daly 1989, 89; Woodward 1990, 107).

Although British policies likely widened the divide between the north and south, the root of the animosity in Sudan is Islamic fundamentalism in the north, which has consistently discriminated against non-Muslim southerners in its attempt to spread Islam throughout the country. The radical Islamist project attempted to establish a state governed under the Islamic laws of the shari'a and viewed jihad (holy war) as an acceptable strategy for pushing Islam throughout the state. Given the Islamic leadership's view of the universal transcendence of Islamic fundamentalism, there has historically been no possibility of integrating Sudan's diverse populations into a single pluralist state (Lowrie 1993). This view, of course, is unacceptable to non-Muslims in southern Sudan, whose struggle to resist religious repression led to the decades-long civil war in the country (Glickman 2000).

The most recent Sudanese civil war (1983–2005) was directly related to the first Sudanese civil war (1956–1972), which began in the first year of independence and lasted nearly sixteen years. The first conflict erupted when the Sudanese government attempted to enforce Arabic as the country's official language and Islam as the official religion. The conflict ended in 1972, when the government granted the south extensive autonomy (GlobalSecurity.org, 2005). This peace was to be short-lived. In 1982, the central government reneged on many of its promises of self-rule and imposed Islamic law on the whole country, which led to renewed violence the following year. Additionally, the discovery of vast reserves of oil in southern Sudan intensified the causes of rebellion (Althaus 1999; Glickman 2000). During the first Sudanese civil war (1956–1972), Chevron discovered oil in the area between the northern and southern regions. Seeing that the oil revenue was disproportionately benefiting the north, and distressed by the government's reneging on previous promises, southerners were anxious to start the rebellion anew. The rebel groups originally presented overthrowing the government as their fundamental goal. However, in later years of the conflict, southern

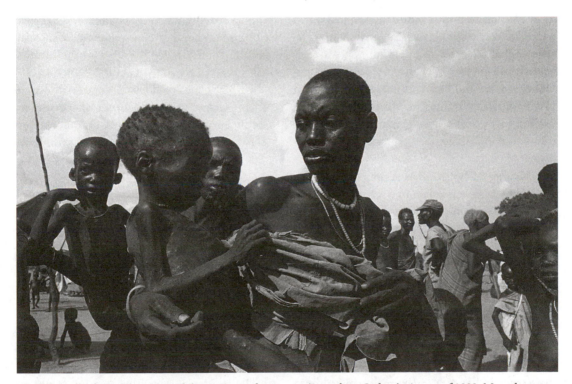

Civilians suffer from starvation and disease in a refugee camp in southern Sudan in August of 1998. More than two million people have died from fighting, disease, and hunger in the civil war that has ravaged Sudan since 1983. (Patrick Robert/Sygma/Corbis)

goals diverged; some wanted complete secession, and others sought regional autonomy, religious freedom, and profits from natural resource extraction, specifically oil (Fisher 1999).

Since the second civil war began in 1983, more 2 million people have died as a result of fighting, disease, and hunger. Another 6 million civilians fled the area, moving mostly to Kenya and Uganda (Althaus 1999). Much of this devastation was due to irresponsible government tactics. According to U.S. government and international human rights officials, the Islamic state in Sudan committed "gross human rights violations" and worked to aggravate wide-scale famine throughout the country (Locante, 1993). Besides deaths, Christian and other religious minorities saw their civil rights continually restricted during the course of the war. Amnesty International reported "disturbing accounts of extrajudicial executions, disappearances and torture" carried out by the Islamic government in the north (Locante 1993). During the war, non-Muslims in government-controlled areas were subject to shari'a, or Islamic law. Under the 1991 penal code, for example, all non-Muslims were banned from most jobs in the government, including the military and judiciary, could not testify against Muslims in courts, and were required to memorize the Qur'an to learn Muslim-based curriculum in the schools (Locante 1993).

The size of both the government's military and the rebel organizations grew over time owing to aid from outside forces. At the turn of the century, more than 50 percent of the government's budget was spent on military supplies (Jok and Hutchinson 1999, 136). Aid from countries such as Iraq, Iran, Saudi Arabia, and Libya also contributed to the growth of government forces (Glickman 2000). The exact size of the rebel organizations was difficult to measure, given that the insurgency was generally unorganized and heavily fractionalized, and alliances between rebel groups sometimes changed on a daily basis. The largest rebel organization in Sudan was the SPLA (Sudan People's Liberation Army). Led by John Garang, the SPLA had great success in the early years of the war. After eight years of fighting, it was able to drive the national army out of most of the south (Jok and Hutchinson 1999, 126). In August 1991, the SPLA was split into two warring factions by the Dinka and the Nuer, two of the largest ethnic groups in the south (Johnson 1998; Nyaba 1997). Later, the SPLA broke into three main factions: (1) the SPLA Torit faction, led by John Garang; (2) the SPLA Bahr-al-Gazal faction, led by Carabino Kuany Bol, and (3) the SSIM (South Sudan Independence Movement), led by Riek Machar. In 1997, the last of these three groups (the SSIM) concluded a peace agreement with the government, forming the UDSF (United Democratic Salvation Front) (Fisher 1999; Foek 1998). After forming this alliance, Machar's SSIM was able to plunder, steal, and destabilize the peace process while the government turned a blind eye due to the alliance (Foek 1998). Most reports considered the Garang-led SPLA faction the main rebel organization in Sudan; however, many other such organizations fell under the rebel group umbrella called the National Democratic Alliance (NDA), to which the SPLA belonged. These included the Sudan Alliance Forces, the Beja Congress Forces, and the New South Brigade (CSIS 2003).

The Cold War played an important role in the Sudanese civil wars, particularly the first war (1956–1978). Prior to the Six Days' War in 1967, the United Kingdom supported the Sudanese government. Following this war, Sudan was distanced from the West, whereas Soviets moved in to support the government (Cooper 2003). During the height of the Cold War, the U.S. government considered the dictatorship in Khartoum a key African ally due to their staunchly anti-communist stance. Since the 1989 military coup put a fundamentalist Islamic movement in power, Sudan has been considered a supporter of terrorism (Althaus 1999).

The most recent civil war has certainly not been confined to the Sudanese borders. Fleeing civilians in the south journeyed to the neigh-

Table 1: Civil War in Sudan

War:	SPLA and other factions vs. government
Dates:	November 1983–January 2005
Casualties:	2 million (1983–2005)
Regime type prior to war:	–7 (ranging from –10 [authoritarian] to 10 [democracy])
Regime type after war:	–6 in 2002, when war was ongoing (score ranges from –10 [authoritarian] to 10 [democracy])
GDP per capita year war began:	US $299.90 (constant 2000 dollars)
GDP per capita 5 years after war:	US $289.60 (constant 2000 dollars)
Insurgents:	SPLA (Sudan People's Liberation Army), several other factions
Issue:	Religion-based struggle for control of central government and/or secession
Rebel funding:	Funding from Ethiopia, Uganda, and Eritrea; indirect aid from the United States
Role of geography:	Large country with few paved roads has retarded government efforts to control rebel groups while encouraging inter-rebel fighting.
Role of resources:	Oil first exported in 1999 raised the stakes of the war.
Immediate outcome:	Peace agreement signed in January 2005.
Outcome after 5 years:	Tenuous peace; atrocities continue in Darfur region.
Role of UN:	Long-term humanitarian aid, currently considering peacekeeping forces.
Role of regional organization:	OAU active in 1990s working for peace; efforts led to 2005 agreement.
Refugees:	4 million since the start of fighting
Prospects for peace:	Favorable but tenuous

Sources: CIA 2005; Marshall and Jaggers 2003; World Development Indicators.

boring countries of Ethiopia, Kenya, Uganda, and Egypt in large numbers. In 1999, U.S. State Department officials estimated that some 350,000 people lived in refugee camps in Kenya and Uganda alone (Althaus 1999). Displacement of peoples resulted in what international humanitarian organizations call the "lost generation" of Sudan, because of the absence of educational opportunities and basic health care and the limited prospects for productive employment (Globalsecurity.org, 2005).

The Insurgents

In response to persistent northern efforts to unify the country by forcing Islam and the Arabic culture upon it, southern political organization and guerrilla movements arose in the early 1960s. The most significant of these groups, the Anya Nya guerrilla movement, appeared in 1962 and eventually became the SLM (Southern Sudan Liberation Movement) in 1971. Pressure from the SLM was a leading factor in the cre-

ation of the Addis Ababa Agreement in 1972, which ended the first Sudanese civil war by granting considerable autonomy to the south.

Although this agreement led to eleven years of peace, the root of the problem—northern efforts to establish an Islamic state—remained. Numeiri, the Sudanese government leader during this time, yielded to political pressure from the opposition Umma Party in 1983 by renewing the enforcement of shari'a throughout the country with the passage of the "September laws" (Woodward 1990, 157). These laws led to thousands of public punishments, including floggings, amputations, and executions of non-Islamic southerners (Langewiesche 1994, 27). In his efforts to punish southern rebels, in 1983 Numeiri sent Lieutenant Colonel John Garang to quell a mutiny of government soldiers in the south. Instead of following these orders, Garang encouraged a mutiny, garnered the support of the troops around him, and formed the Sudan People's Liberation Army, which later led to the Sudan People's Liberation Movement (SPLM).

The SPLM was the major force working to overthrow the Sudanese government during the second civil war.

Southern rebels in Sudan received political, military, and logistical support from neighboring countries such as Ethiopia, Uganda, and Eritrea during the civil war (Jok and Hutchinson 1999, 136). The United States also aided the rebels indirectly. In February 1998, for instance, the United States allocated $20 million in "nonlethal" military assistance to the governments that supported the SPLA rebel groups. Occasional CIA programs also aided the Sudanese rebels (Glickman 2000).

Geography

Sudan is the largest country in Africa, with a land area of nearly 1 million square miles. Bordering countries include Chad and the Central African Republic (west), Egypt and Libya (north), Ethiopia and Eritrea (east), and Kenya, Uganda, and Democratic Republic of the Congo (south). The Red Sea lies along nearly 500 miles of the northeastern border. The Nile River runs northward through the central part of the country, which includes nearly all of the Nile's great tributaries.

Like its peoples, Sudan's geography also falls along a north–south divide. Southern Sudan is a Texas-sized area of prairies, woodlands, shallow rivers, and marshes. The people residing in this area, who have more in common with people deep in Africa's heartland than with those in the northern part of the country, live traditional subsistence lifestyles off the land (Althaus 1999). Southern Sudan has no more than twenty-five miles of paved roads, and the vast majority of the region is without electricity or gas (Foek 1998). In northern Sudan, the geography is extremely diverse, ranging from uninhabitable deserts in areas to the west and east of the Nile, to mountains, clay plains, plateaus, and rich grasslands (Country Studies.com 2005).

Sudan's diverse geography played a key role in the most recent civil war. Rebel fighting followed a seasonal pattern, with heavy fighting during the dry season followed by a reduction in fighting during the months of heavy rainfall. The oscillation in rebel commitments between soldiering and farming encouraged disorganization and insubordination among rebel groups. These problems were compounded by the geographic isolation of many rebel units, which led to many independent warlords fighting among themselves as they attempted to overthrow the government (Jok and Hutchinson 1999, 135–36). The recent cultivation of the oil industry in Sudan also placed higher stakes on the civil war. In the last quarter of 1999, Sudan began exporting large amounts of oil from the southern areas via a pipeline extending from the south-central region of the country to Port Sudan along the Red Sea (CIA 2005). The extraction of oil from the south fueled the flames of war as southerners complained that the revenues benefited only the northern areas (Lacey 2005).

Tactics

Both rebel and government tactics acquired an increasing level of sophistication as the war progressed. Traditionally, SPLA forces practiced guerrilla tactics, including hit-and-run raids on government convoys, checkpoints, and towns in order to disrupt supply lines, destroy government equipment, and steal weapons, ammunition, cars, food, and medicines (Jok and Hutchinson 1999, 136; Vasagar 2004). Rebels were generally equipped with automatic weapons stolen from government forces (Foek 1998). In 1996 and 1997, rebel groups boosted their efforts by capturing a substantial number of tanks and armored cars from the Sudanese government (Human Rights Watch 1998). The rebellion also acquired such advanced weapons as Kalashnikov AK-47 assault rifles, rocket-propelled grenade launchers, antitank missiles, and Belgian-made automatic rifles, which rebels claim were stolen from government forces (Vasagar 2004). The improvement of rebel equipment gave rebel organizations better mobility and more consistent resupply capabilities (World Tribune.com 2002).

The recent flow of oil from southern Sudan also gave the rebels a new target. For instance, rebels bombed the newly built oil pipeline in September 1999, exactly twenty days after the first shipment of Sudanese oil was exported to Asia (Fisher 1999). Oil installations were under continuous attack in the later years of the war, despite SPLA warnings to oil companies operating in southern regions that it considered their operations to be military zones (*Agence France-Presse* 2001).

In recent years, foreign governments have played a key role, aiding rebels with more advanced weapons. Ethiopia provided T-55 tanks in the 1980s, and Uganda provided similar arms via the international arms market during the 1990s. Israel was criticized by the Sudanese government for supplying weapons and training to the SPLA, including a supply of antitank missiles via the Israeli embassy in Nairobi, Kenya (World Tribune.com 2002). Other supplies of arms and military assistance came from Eritrea and Uganda, which were firmly behind the effort to overthrow the current government (Human Rights Watch 1998). In addition to providing supplies, Ugandan troops were directly involved in antigovernment fighting, engaging the government on Sudanese territory on a number of occasions. The United States also indirectly supported the rebels by providing military support to Eritrea, Ethiopia, and Uganda (Human Rights Watch 1998).

The Sudanese government used a number of tactics to prevent its overthrow. One of its most successful tactics was to fan the flames of internal struggles within the rebel organization. The Sudanese government worked to frame the conflict as a struggle among southern tribes, while seeking peace with all groups individually (Jok and Hutchinson 1999, 128). In the later years of the war, the government worked through northern militia groups to fight the rebel organizations. The government-backed Janjaweed militia, for instance, continues to wreak havoc in the western region of Darfur (see sidebar, "Crisis in Darfur").

Government weapons came from a variety of sources. Recent arms suppliers included China, Iran, Yemen, South Africa, and former Soviet bloc states such as Kazakhstan. Before it was invaded by the United States in 2003, Iraq provided technical assistance and military training. Malaysia also played an indirect role by providing funds for arms purchases. Until 1995, France supported government forces by sharing satellite intelligence of SPLA movements, providing military training and technical assistance, and aiding the Sudanese government in negotiating access to neighboring Francophone states in order to stage attacks (Human Rights Watch 1998). The recent export of oil also helped the government establish links with arms suppliers. For instance, an agreement signed with Russia in 2002 gave Sudan rights to manufacture Russian battle tanks in exchange for oil concessions (Human Rights Watch 2003, 457).

Like the rebels' weaponry, government weapons, too, became more advanced over time. Recent acquisitions of large quantities of light and medium arms and ammunition, medium tanks, artillery, and air power drastically increased the government's ability to fight rebels. These weapons included MiG fighter planes, Mi–24 helicopter gunships, a modified version of the classic Soviet T-54 tank, and SCUD missiles (Human Rights Watch 1998). Overall, advanced weaponry such as night vision systems and nighttime aerial bombing gave the government a strong edge in military capability over the rebel organizations (World Tribune.com 2002).

Unfortunately, the rebels and the government had in common an utter disregard for civilian casualties. Beginning with the SPLA split between Dinka and Duer fighters in 1991, divisions between southern factions led to vicious attacks on civilian targets. For instance, in 1992 the SPLA-United alliance razed twenty-five Dinka villages, stealing cattle and killing many civilians, including young children (Jok and Hutchinson 1999, 131). Other tactics included extortion, rape, torture, and murder (Foek 1998). A recent report from the international medical organization Medicins Sans Frontieres (MSF) blamed warring parties on both sides for "appalling civilian mortality from infectious disease and violence" (MSF 2002). Such tactics included rape, murder, assault and the denial of access to humanitarian aid. Government forces were equally culpable in harming civilians. In 2003, for example, human rights groups accused the government of engaging in a scorched-earth policy in the Western Upper Nile of the South, killing or driving out civilians to make room for oil companies, whose revenues were used in part to fund the government forces (Cobb 2003). Unfortunately, disregard for civilian life made the innocent the biggest victims of the Sudanese civil war (Althaus 1999).

Crisis in Darfur

One of the most pressing issues facing Sudan and the international community today is the conflict in a northwest region of Sudan known as Darfur. Demanding that the Sudanese government stop arming the Arab groups in the region, address underdevelopment, and discontinue discrimination, two new rebel groups, the SLM (Sudan Liberation Movement) and later the JEM (Justice and Equality Movement) began a rebellion in February 2003 (IRINnews.org 2005). Unable to directly respond to the crisis itself due to the costly fighting in the south, the government responded by backing armed militias, known as the Janjaweed (U.S. Department of State 2004).

The government-backed Janjaweed militia pursued a scorched-earth policy in Darfur with widespread killing and raping of civilians and the razing of entire villages. For example, in February 2004, a band of militia members and government soldiers attacked the village of Taila, killing 67 people, abducting 16 girls, raping more than 93 females and displacing over 5,000 people (U.S. Department of State 2004). Overall, the violence in Darfur has caused around 180,000 deaths through violence, hunger, and disease, and more than 2 million have fled the region (Thomasson 2005). UN officials have referred to the crisis in Sudan as the world's worst humanitarian crisis (BBC 2005). U.S. Secretary of State Colin Powell, placing full blame on the Janjaweed and the Sudanese government, has called their actions nothing short of genocide (CNN.com 2004).

Recently, the international community has made moves to lessen the humanitarian suffering and work toward a tenuous peace in Darfur. For example, the AU (African Union) has deployed 2,300 troops to monitor the often broken cease-fire in the Darfur, while the UN WFP (World Food Program) works desperately to distribute food throughout the region. Despite these efforts, UN Secretary General Kofi Annan has pleaded adamantly for more international assistance, noting that the WFP faces a chronic shortage of funds (CNN.com 2005); the AU claims that an additional $466 million will be needed to sufficiently monitor the cease-fire (IRINnews.org 2005). Although failing to do much to disarm the Arab militia, the government of Sudan has also hindered efforts toward peace by denying visas to UN teams and blocking food and health aids from reaching its own people (U.S. Department of State 2004; Thomasson 2005). Ultimately, as Annan warns, a continued crisis in Darfur could help unravel the accord that ended the second Sudanese civil war in early 2005 (BBC 2005; CNN.com 2004; IRINnews.org 2005; Thomasson 2005; U.S. Department of State 2004).

Causes of the War

Most sources report that the conflict in Sudan was simply a fight between Sudan's Arab north and its black African south, or between northern Islam and southern Christian and animist faiths; however, scholars have recently begun to explain that the war was actually far more complicated (Althaus 1999). Scholars such as Douglas Johnson (2003, 5) have recently argued that the root cause of the Sudanese conflict was its traditions of governance rather than a conflict between Arabs and Africans. Beginning with Turkish conquerors in 1821, the governments of Sudan exploited the impoverished Muslim subjects in the north, who "passed on their losses to non-Muslims on the periphery." This tradition of exploitative governance resulted in what Johnson calls the "Sudanic state," which exploits all civilians, with the south bearing the brunt of this exploitation.

One of the most direct causes of the current divisions in Sudan can be traced to British decisions in the transitional period from colonialism to independent statehood. During this period, the British failed to consider southern needs in preparation for independence. Southern Sudanese leaders were not even invited to participate in the negotiations during the transitional period in the early 1950s. In the postcolonial government constructed in 1953, the Sudanization Committee included only six southern leaders from some 800 available senior administrative positions (Kasfir 1979, 369). This allowed the northern-dominated administration to use

The Lost Boys of Sudan

Good endings can come from bad beginnings, as an inspiring group of young Sudanese refugees known as the "Lost Boys" of Sudan (after the lost boys in *Peter Pan*) have come to show the world. Fleeing the violence of the second Sudanese civil war in the late 1980s, some 33,000 Sudanese children (mostly boys) fled their homes in the mid-1980s after their families were killed by government forces. These children, coming mostly from the Dinka or Nuer tribes of southern Sudan, journeyed hundreds of miles through the East African desert. Thousands miraculously survived the ordeal, finding refugee camps in Ethiopia and Kenya (Messina and Messina 2005).

To survive the journey, the Lost Boys became each other's families, with the older boys, many just 9 or 10 years old, caring for the younger ones. Many of these children died on the trek, from starvation, thirst, or animal attacks. To survive, the children often had to suck water from mud on the ground, eat leaves and the carcasses of dead animals, and cross crocodile-infested rivers. It is estimated that no more than 50 percent of the Lost Boys (around 10,000) survived the journey, finally finding safety with UN and Red Cross relief workers at the Kakuma refugee camp in 1992 (Walgren 1994).

In 1999, the UN Refugee Agency and the U.S. Department of State collaborated to bring 3,400 of the Lost Boys to the United States for permanent resettlement. Since then, they have been placed throughout the country in cities such as Omaha, Seattle, Richmond, and Grand Rapids. Upon arriving in America, boys under the age of 18 were assigned to foster homes and now attend school. Those over 18 had to go to work, where their low levels of skill forced them to take menial, low-paying jobs. Although the Lost Boys' transition to America has been rocky at times, overall their story is one of astonishing tragedy and perseverance (Crawley 2000).

the political machinery to force their Islamic agenda upon the entire state. Although southern opposition groups initially tried to redress their grievances within the framework of a unified Sudanese state, religious persecution left non-Muslims with few peaceful options for countering these policies (Bartkus 1999, 136; Wai 1981, 117).

In the early years of the Sudanese state, the northern government passed many measures to repress the non-Muslim population. For instance, in February 1962 the government expelled all Christian missionaries from the country and closed Christian schools (Gurdon 1989, 68). These measures, along with indiscriminate attacks on protesters in southern villages in late 1962, caused sporadic fighting and army mutinies in the south, which transitioned into a full-scale civil war (Hannum 1990, 311). Though the southern Sudanese had little chance of successfully overthrowing the government, the repressive policies of the government left them to choose between the lesser of two evils: Either endure escalating religious

and cultural persecution, or fight (Bartkus 1999, 137).

In the late 1960s and early 1970s, three key events led to peace. First, the 1969 coup placed Colonel Jaafar Numeiri in power, who then proposed that Sudan become a secular, socialist state. Second, bloody confrontations in 1971 between the Umma Party and the Ansar Brotherhood, two organizations consistently opposed to compromise with the south, reduced the power of Islamic fundamentalism in the government. Third, strong leadership by rebel leader Joseph Lagu overcame ethnic divisions and personal rivalries among the disparate rebel groups, bringing them together into the stronger Southern Sudanese Liberation Movement (Bartkus 1999, 137). These events led to the Addis Ababa Agreement of 1972, which provided for the demobilization of guerrillas and their reintegration into Sudanese society. More important, the agreement granted a great deal of religious and cultural autonomy to the south (see Bartkus 1999, 137–38, for more specific details of the agreement). Due to the enhanced political autonomy, southern factions were able to live in harmony during the eleven years following the agreement, expressing their disagreements through peaceful, political means (Johnson 1988, 6).

The autonomy and freedom delivered to the south by the northern government was short-lived, however. As Islamic fundamentalists, who opposed the 1972 Addis Ababa Agreement from the start, grew in political power, President Numeiri was forced to announce in late summer of 1983 that Sudan would once again become an Islamic state (Ottaway 1987, 891, 893). This announcement was followed by a series of decrees that came to be known as the September laws. These decrees severely restricted the rights of non-Muslims (Ottaway 1987; Woodward 1990, 111). During the first two years after the passage of these laws, thousands of public punishments, including floggings, amputations, and executions, were handed out after extrajudicial trials (Langewiesche 1994, 27). Once again, in 1983 Sudan plunged deep into a second civil war pitting non-Islamic southerners against the religious and cultural intolerance of Islamic fundamentalist leaders in Khartoum (Bartkus 1999, 141).

Outcome
Conflict Status

In the early years of the 1990s, the international community, led by Eritrea, Ethiopia, Uganda, and Kenya, led an effort to bring peace to Sudan. Under the auspices of the IGAD (Intergovernmental Authority for Development), these countries began their mission in 1993. Since then, results have been mixed. In 1994, the IGAD initiative pushed the 1994 DOP (Declaration of Principles) plan, which aimed to identify the elements necessary for a successful peace settlement. This agreement was not signed by the Sudanese government until 1997, after it had lost several major battles to SPLA forces. Also pushing the government toward peace was the National Democratic Alliance, an umbrella coalition of opposition parties in the north and the south created in 1995. The NDA included opposition groups such as the SPLA, DUP (Democratic Unionist Party), and Umma parties. By uniting rebel and opposition groups into one organization, the Sudanese civil war became more than ever a center–periphery fight rather than a north–south conflict (GlobalSecurity.org 2005).

In addition to signing the DOP plan in 1997, the Sudanese government signed a series of agreements with rebel organizations led by former Garang lieutenant Riek Machar. These included the Khartoum, Nuba Mountains, and Fashoda agreements. Like the IGAD initiative, these agreements called for a measure of autonomy for the south and the right of self-determination (GlobalSecurity.org 2005). Despite the agreements of the early and mid-1990s, the struggle in Sudan continued largely unabated in large areas of the country past the turn of the century.

Great humanitarian crises brought on by war and a drought in 2000–2001 caught the attention of the international community, which provided—and continues to provide—large amounts of humanitarian aid to Sudan to ward off mass starvation (GlobalSecurity.org 2005). Beyond natural disasters, the victimization of civilians by both the government and the rebels came to the attention of the international community in the last decade.

Beginning in early 2002, Sudan saw a series of important agreements that led to a more peaceful country. In June 2002, a round of peace talks began under the previous IGAD initiative. Led by international observer countries, including the United States, the United Kingdom, Norway, and Italy, these talks ended on July 20 with the signing of the Machakos Protocol. This agreement provided for a six-year interim period after which a referendum on self-determination would be held in the south, giving the region a clear choice between a united Sudan and separated states. The agreement also states that the Islamic shari'a law would continue only in the northern regions (GlobalSecurity.org 2005).

Later that summer (August 2002), a second round of talks began between the warring factions to discuss the sharing of power and wealth. This round brought together President Beshir and SPLA-leader John Garang in a historic meeting in Kampala. More important, the talks resulted in the signing of an MOU (Memorandum of Understanding) on October 15, 2002, which called for a complete cessation of fighting for three months. A third agreement in February 2003 strengthened the two sides' stand on the cessation of hostilities (GlobalSecurity.org 2005). This agreement called for the creation of a new international team to verify and monitor compliance with the agreement. These agreements were extremely important to Sudan's long-term stability, given previous studies finding that the inclusion of the international community in the peace negotiation process is crucial to its success (Walter 2002).

The last two years of the civil war brought a series of important agreements, which resulted in peace in much of the country. In January 2004, the government and rebels signed an accord on wealth sharing, which had become a major issue in later years of the fighting (especially since the export of oil in 1999). Later that year, on May 24, 2004, the warring parties signed three key protocols, which provided for six years of autonomy for southern Sudan, to be followed by a referendum on the political future of the region. Finally, in January 2005, a peace agreement signed by southern rebels and the government of Sudan marked the end of the twenty-one-year-long struggle (Crilly 2005). Signed by Sudan's Vice President Ali Osman Taha and SPLA leader John Garang, this agreement called for a permanent cease-fire between the two sides. Additionally, it placed Garang in the post of first vice-president in an important power-sharing deal.

Learning from the previous mistakes of the Rwandan civil war, neither side disbanded its armies under the agreement. This provides a deterrence against possible genocide and at the same time leaves the country in a state of tension, given that either side could quickly resume the conflict if the peace process hits a snag (Lacey 2005; Njorge and Makgabo 2005; Walter 2002). Despite government reports of repeated violations of the cease-fire by rebel factions, today the majority of Sudan rests in tenuous peace (IRINnews.org 2005).

Duration Tactics

Two key features of the second Sudanese civil war make it stand out among all civil wars. The first is the widespread atrocities against the civilian population perpetrated by both the government and rebel factions. The second is the duration of the war: twenty-one years. Several factors led to both the intensity and the long duration. One factor was the government's ability to keep southern rebels fighting among themselves. Jok and Hutchinson (1999, 135–36) explain that the Khartoum government skillfully played rebel forces against each other by allying with southern factions as they attempted to gain control of the rebel movement. This led to roughly balanced forces between the warring rebels, which further prolonged the conflict.

A second factor contributing to the duration of the war was the government's inability to handle the guerrilla tactics practiced by Garang's SPLA forces. Moreover, local support for rebel organizations helped them maintain supplies to continue fighting. A third factor was the government's unwillingness to bend in its efforts to extend Islamic law to the entire country. According to SPLA leader John Garang (1987), given the options between peace under Islamic law versus a prolonged and deadly struggle, most southern Sudanese felt that war was better than peace. Further, the government's history of reneging on promises led to an extremely low level of trust between the warring parties. This highlights the need for an international presence if peace in Sudan is to continue after the January 2005 agreement (Lacey 2005).

Finally, one can look at resources as a factor that contributed to the long duration of the civil war. After beginning exports of oil in June 1999, the Sudanese government initially claimed that the oil profits would be shared throughout the country and used to build roads, schools, and irrigation projects. The failure of the government to spread the oil wealth to the southern regions, however, strengthened the resolve of the rebel organizations (Fisher 1999). The discovery of oil also raised the stakes—that is, the victor would have control over a large supply of oil reserves; this made both sides more resolved in their struggle (Glickman 2000; Fearon and Laitin 2003).

External Intervention and Conflict Management Efforts

Until recently, the international community overall was neglectful of efforts to end the Sudanese civil war (Althaus 1999). Efforts in both the 1990s and the 2000s were almost exclusively diplomatic, with earlier efforts to promote peace coming exclusively from Sudan's African neighbors. Fortunately, recent efforts by the international community have made significant progress in promoting peace in the region. One of the most significant developments in the peace process in Sudan was a result of the September 11, 2001, terrorist attacks on the United States. Following these attacks, the Bush administration placed Sudan on the list of state sponsors of terrorism, making them susceptible to the same U.S. military intervention experienced by other states, including Afghanistan and Iraq (Matheson 2005). Under pressure from both African-American leaders and Christian activists in the United States, who noted the Islamic government's repression of religious rights, the Bush administration worked for peace in the country (Raghavan 2005). The main result of this pressure was to signal to the government of Sudan that military intervention on the side of the rebels was likely, making the government more apt to make concessions to the rebel organization. Ultimately, this pressure led to the agreement in early 2005.

In addition to pressure from the United States, which seemed to be the most significant

conflict management force, other actors in the international community played roles in promoting peace in the country. For instance, the United Nations is currently looking into the logistics of providing a peacekeeping force in Sudan to help make the January 2005 agreement a success. Other countries and organizations, such as South Africa and the African Union (AU), have committed to helping enforce this agreement (Lacey 2005). The vast majority of external efforts, however, have come in the form of humanitarian assistance. Responding to humanitarian crises such as famine in the 1980s, for instance, the UN and several dozen private relief agencies set up Operation Lifeline Sudan to channel food and other aid to the south. This operation, which was originally meant to be a short-term humanitarian fix, was in operation for nearly the entirety of the Sudanese civil war (Althaus 1999). More recent efforts, such as a donors' conference held by Norway in April 2005, are important international efforts to aid the peace process in Sudan.

Conclusion

After twenty-one continuous years of war, prospects for future peace in Sudan may finally be looking up. Although atrocities still continue in the Darfur region, the agreements signed recently bode well for a peaceful future. The root causes of the civil war, including religious repression, unequal distribution of wealth and power, and ethnic discrimination, which have been addressed in recent agreements, must continue to be at the forefront of Sudanese politics if peace is to continue in the country. Fortunately, the recently signed agreement follows policy advice from civil war scholars such as Walter (2002) by establishing a transition period (six years), merging the fighting forces, sharing the oil wealth, and dividing political offices. Specifically, the inclusion of SPLA leader John Garang as one of Mr. Bashir's vice presidents will provide previously the ignored southern groups with a strong voice in government, which should go a long way to reduce rebel grievances. A second positive sign for the future of peace in Sudan is the increased interest of the international community in establishing and sustaining peace in the country. Kenyan General Lazaro Sumbeiywo, for example, acted as chief mediator during the negotiations leading to the 2005 peace agreement. The efforts of Norway, which held a donors' conference in 2005 to bring significant developmental aid to Sudan during the transitional period, should also help in future efforts to sustain peace (Lacey 2005).

Although general optimism seems warranted regarding the prospects for future peace in Sudan, one might easily have reached the same conclusions at the end of the first Sudanese civil war in 1972. Currently, the most pressing issue in the country is the crisis in Darfur, which must come to a quick and peaceful end before the conflict spreads again throughout the country. If the political leaders have truly learned from the mistakes made during the tenure of peace following the first civil war, we should expect the country to become more peaceful and prosperous as time progresses. However, if strict Islamic fundamentalists are allowed to force their views upon the non-Islamic population in the south, once again we will likely see the country plunged into a long and devastating civil conflict.

Clayton Thyne

Chronology

1898–1856 Sudan is ruled by Anglo-Egyptian Condominium.

1956 Sudan gains independence from Britain.

1956–1972 First Sudanese civil war

1983 President Numayri declares the introduction of shari'a (Islamic law) and later martial law. Relations with non-Islamic south deteriorate.

1983–1984 Rebels begin to organize SPLA, led by John Garang.

April 1986 Sadiq al-Mahdi becomes prime minister after Numayri is deposed by a group of officers. Three years of chaotic government begin.

June 1989 Lieutentant General Omar Hasson al-Bashir (leader of National Salvation Revolution) takes power in a coup, dissolves parliament.

July 1992 Government offensive seizes southern territory, including SPLA headquarters at Torit.

February 1993 Government officials and rebels hold first talks in Uganda and Nigeria.

May 1994 IGAD, a regional conflict-solving body, urges self-determination for the south. Sudanese government quits talks.

March 1996 Presidential elections begin, Bashir wins.

April 1996 UN Security Council passes sanctions against Sudan for sponsoring terrorism.

May 1996 Bashir calls for national reconciliation and peace talks with rebels.

April 1997 Sudanese government signs deal with SSIM and other rebel groups, isolating SPLA.

October 1997 Government and SPLA begin peace talks in Kenya.

November 1997 U.S. government imposes economic sanctions against Sudan.

August 1998 United States launches missile attack on pharmaceutical plant in Khartoum.

December 1999 Bashir dissolves National Assembly, declares state of emergency.

February 2000 Talks resume but end five days later, after rebels accuse government of indiscriminate attacks on civilians.

December 2000 Bashir reelected for another five years in elections boycotted by main opposition parties.

September 2001 UN lifts sanctions against Sudan; U.S. sanctions continue.

February 2001 Islamist leader Hassan al-Turabi arrested after his party, the Popular National Congress, signs Memorandum of Understanding with SPLA.

March 2001 UN's World Food Program struggles to feed 3 million facing famine.

January 2002 Government and rebels sign a cease-fire agreement in Switzerland.

July 2002 Talks between Sudanese government and SPLM yield Machakos Protocol, addressing issues of religion and self-determination. Bashir meets rebel leader John Garang for the first time.

October 2002 Government and SPLM sign cease-fire during the latest round of peace talks.

February 2003 Rebels in Darfur rise against government, claiming the region is neglected by the government.

September–October 2003   Government and SPLA sign security deal, clearing the way for peace talks.

October 2003   PNC leader Turabi is released from detention, ban on PNC is lifted.

January 2004   Army moves to stop rebels in Darfur, hundreds of thousands of refugees flee from Darfur to Chad.

March 2004   UN accuses progovernment Arab Janjaweed militias of genocide in Darfur.

May 2004   Government and southern rebels agree on power-sharing protocols as part of peace plan.

January 2005   Garang and chief government negotiator Taha sign a comprehensive peace accord, ending the civil war.

April 2005   Donors at a conference in Norway pledge $4.5 billion to help southern Sudan.

List of Acronyms

AU: African Union
DOP: Declaration of Principles (1994)
DUP: Democratic Unionist Party
GDP: gross domestic product
IGAD: Intergovernmental Authority for Development
JEM: Justice and Equality Movement
MOU: Memorandum of Understanding (2002)
MSF: Medicins Sans Frontieres
NDA: National Democratic Alliance
OAU: Organization for African Unity
SLM: Southern Sudan Liberation Movement
SPLA: Sudan People's Liberation Army
SPLM: Sudan People's Liberation Movement
SSIM: South Sudan Independence Movement
SSLM: Southern Sudanese Liberation Movement
UDSF: United Democratic Salvation Front
WFP: World Food Program (UN)

References

Agence France-Presse. 2001. "Sudanese Rebels Claim Attack on Oil Regions of Sudan, Killing Dozens." January 27.

Althaus, Dudley. 1999. "Inside Sudan's Civil War." *Houston Chronicle.* www.chron.com/cs/CDA/plainstory.mpl/special/sudan/321650 (accessed February 3, 2005).

Azam, J. P., and A. Hoeffler. 2002. "Violence Against Civilians in Civil Wars: Looting or Terror?" *Journal of Peace Research,* 39(4): 461–85.

Bartkus, Viva Ona. 1999. *The Dynamic of Secession.* Cambridge, UK: Cambridge University Press.

British Broadcasting Corporation (BBC). 2005. *Q&A: Sudan's Darfur Conflict.* May 26. www.news.bbc.co.uk/1/hi/world/africa/3496731.stm (accessed July 3, 2005).

Cairns, Edmund (1997). *A Safer Future: Reducing the Human Cost of War.* Oxford, UK: Oxfam Publications.

Center for Strategic and International Studies (CSIS). 2003. *The Military Balance, 2003–2004.* www.csis.org/military (accessed July 2, 2005).

Central Intelligence Agency (CIA). 2005. *World Factbook: Sudan.* www.cia.gov/cia/publications/factbook/geos/su.html (accessed March 12, 2005).

CNN.com. 2004. *Powell Calls Sudan Killings Genocide.* September 9. www.cnn.com/2004/WORLD/africa/09/09/sudan.powell (accessed July 15, 2005).

CNN.com. 2005. *Annan: We Must Race to Save Darfur.* May 26. www.cnn.com/2005/WORLD/africa/05/26/sudan.annan.reut/index.html (accessed June 5, 2005).

Cobb, Charles, Jr. 2003. *Peace in Sudan, How Close?* www.allafrica.com/stories/200304250001.html (accessed April 2, 2005).

Cooper, Tom. 2003. *Sudan, Civil War Since 1955.* Air Combat Information Group. ttp://www.acig.org/artman/publish/article_180.shtml (accessed May 1, 2005).

Country Studies.com. 2005. *Sudan: Geography.* www.countrystudies.com/sudan/geography.html (accessed April 4, 2005).

Crawley, Mike. 2000. "'Lost Boys' of Sudan Find New Life in America." *Christian Science Monitor* 92(243).

Crilly, Rob. 2005. "Sudan May Face Renewed Civil War." *New Scotsman.* www.globalpolicy.org/security/issues/sudan/2005/0411developdraft.htm (accessed May 8, 2005).

Daly, M. W. 1989. "Islam, Secularism and Ethnic Identity in the Sudan." In *Religion and Political Power,* edited by Gustavo Benavides and M. W. Daly. Albany, NY: State University of New York Press.

Energy Information Administration. 2005. *Country Analysis Briefs: Sudan.* March. www.eia.doe.gov/emeu/cabs/sudan.html (accessed April 2, 2005).

Fearon, James D., and David D. Laitin. 2003. "Ethnicity, Insurgency, and Civil War." *American Political Science Review* 97(1): 75–90.

Fisher, Ian. 1999. "Oil Flowing in Sudan, Raising the Stakes in Its Civil War." *New York Times* (October 17).

Fisher, Jonah. 2005. "Sudan Militia Blocks Aid Delivery." *BBC News.* news.bbc.co.uk/2/hi/africa/4559279.stm (accessed: May 19, 2005).

Foek, Anton. 1998. "Sudan's Tragic Legacy of Civil War." *Humanist* 58(5).

Garang, John. 1987. *John Garang Speaks.* Edited by Mansour Khalid. London: KPI.

Glickman, H. 2000. "Islamism in Sudan's Civil War." *Orbis* 44(2): 267–81.

GlobalSecurity.org. 2005. "Sudan Civil War." www.globalsecurity.org/military/world/war/sudan.htm (accessed April 4, 2005).

Gurdon, Charles. 1989. "Instability and the State: Sudan." In *The State and Instability in the South,* edited by Caroline Thomas and Paikiasotby Saravananuttu. London: Macmillan.

Hannum, Hurst. 1990. *Autonomy, Sovereignty, and Self-Determination: The Accommodation of Conflicting Rights.* Philadelphia: University of Pennsylvania Press.

Human Rights Watch. 1998. "Global Trade, Local Impact: Arms Transfers to All Sides in the Civil War in Sudan," 10(4a). August. www.hrw.org/reports98/sudan/ (accessed March 4, 2005).

Human Rights Watch. 2003. *Sudan, Oil, and Human Rights.* New York: Human Rights Watch.

IRINnews.org. 2005. *Sudan: Annan Calls for Support to AU Mission in Darfur.* United Nations Office for the Coordination of Humanitarian Affairs. www.irinnews.org/frontpage.asp?SelectRegion=East_Africa&SelectCountry=Sudan (accessed May 2, 2005).

Johnson, Douglas. 2003. *The Root Causes of Sudan's Civil Wars.* Bloomington: Indiana University Press.

Johnson, Douglas. 1998. "The Sudan People's Liberation Army and the Problem of Factionalism." In *African Guerrillas,* edited by C. Clapham, 53–72. Oxford, UK: James Currey.

Johnson, Douglas H. 1988. *The Southern Sudan.* London: Minority Rights Group.

Jok, Madut, and Elaine Hutchinson. 1999. "Sudan's Prolonged Second Civil War and the Militarization of Nuer and Dinka Ethnic Identities." *African Studies Review* 42(2): 125–45.

Kasfir, Nelson. 1979. "Explaining Ethnic Political Participation." *World Politics* 32: 365–88.

Lacey, Marc. 2005. "Sudan and Southern Rebels Sign Pact to End Civil War." *New York Times* (January 1).

Langewiesche, William. 1994. "Turabi's Law." *The Atlantic Monthly* (August).

Locante, Joe. 1993. "Civil War Brings Suffering to Sudan." *Christianity Today* (May 17).

Lowrie, Arthur, ed. 1993. *Islam, Democracy, the State and the West: A Round Table with Dr. Hasan Turabi,* 13. Tampa, FL: World and Islam Studies Enterprise.

Marshall, Monty G., and Keith Jaggers. 2003. *Polity IV Project: Political Regime Characteristics and Transitions, 1800-2002.* www.cidcm.umd.edu/polity/ (accessed March 31, 2006).

Matheson, Ishbel. 2005. "Sudan Peace Pact Marks New Chapter." *BBC News.* news.bbc.co.uk/1/hi/world/africa/4157897.stm (accessed April 4, 2005).

Medicins Sans Frontieres. 2002. "MSF report blames war tactics for massive civilian mortality rate in Western Upper Nile". Press Release, April 29. www.msf.org/countries/page.cfm?articleid=ABD3E96E-45E6–4403-AA5E465AD82FEBC2 (accessed May 1, 2005).

Messina, James J., and Constance M. Messina. 2005. *Tools for Coping with Life's Stressors.* www.coping.org/wordauthors/lostboys/history.htm (accessed July 2005).

Ministry of Guidance and National Information. 1983. *Sudan Yearbook.* Khartoum, Sudan: Ministry of Guidance and National Information.

Njorge, Gladys, and Tumi Makgabo. 2005. "Historic Sudan Peace Accord Signed." CNN.com. www.cnn.com/2005/WORLD/africa/01/09/sudan.signing/ (accessed May 4, 2005).

Nyaba, A. 1997. *The Politics of Liberation in South Sudan: An Insider's View.* Kampala, Uganda: Fountain.

Ottaway, Marina. 1987. "Post-Numeiri Sudan: One Year On." *Third World Quarterly* 9.

Prendergast, John, and David Mozersky. 2004. "Love Thy Neighbor: Regional Intervention in Sudan's Civil War." *Harvard International Review,* 26(1). hir.harvard.edu/articles/1220/1/ (accessed May 20, 2005).

Raghavan, Sudarsan. 2005. "Pact Signed to End War in Sudan." *Philadelphia Inquirer.* www.philly.com/mld/inquirer/news/nation/10606385.htm (accessed August 8, 2005).

Reuters. 2005. *Annan: We Must Race to Save Darfur.* CNN.com. www.cnn.com/2005/WORLD/africa/05/26/sudan.annan.reut/index.html (accessed May 27, 2005).

Thomasson, Emma. 2005. "Hague Court Opens Probe into Crimes in Darfur." *Reuters* (June 6). www.reuters.com (accessed July 26, 2005).

United States Department of State. 2004. *Sudan: Ethnic Cleansing in Darfur.* April 7. Washington, DC. www.state.gov//documents/organization/31952.pdf (accessed July 26, 2005).

Vasagar, Jeevan. 2004. "Rage Finds an Outlet in Sudan's Rebel Camps." *The Guardian.* Available online: www.guardian.co.uk/sudan/story/0,14658,1314199,00.htm (accessed: April 20, 2005).

Wai, Dunstan. 1981. *The African-Arab Conflict in the Sudan.* London: Holmes and Meier.

Walgren, Judy. 1994. "The Lost Boys of Southern Sudan." *Africa Report* 39(3): 40–42.

Walter, Barbara. 2002. *Committing to Peace: The Successful Settlement of Civil Wars.* Princeton, NJ: Princeton University Press.

Woodward, Peter. 1990. *Sudan, 1898–1989: The Unstable State.* Boulder, CO: Lynne Rienner.

World Development Indicators. (WDI) Online. The World Bank Group. 80-devdata. worldbank.org.proxy.lib.uiowa.edu/dataonline (accessed December 26, 2005).

World Tribune.com. 2002. "Sudan Rebels Advance with New Weapons from Israel." Special to World Tribune.com: Middle East Newsline. October 4. 216.26.163.62/2002/af_sudan_10_04.html (accessed: April 4, 2005).

Tajikistan (1992–1997)

Introduction

The disintegration of the Soviet Union and Mikhail Gorbachev's policies of perestroika (restructuring) and glasnost (openness) encouraged the emergence of proreform and anti-Communist political movements in many Central Asian republics. In Tajikistan, one of the Soviet Union's far southeastern republics, Gorbachev's reforms helped to legitimize the demands by several new political parties and groups (opposition movements) for independence, democratic freedoms, regional autonomy, and economic reforms. Following Tajikistan's independence in 1991, these opposition movements were repressed by the neocommunist (government) forces, which led to demonstrations and riots. This civil strife finally led to regional conflict and civil war in 1992.

Following the eruption of civil war in Tajikistan in October 1992, fighting continued sporadically until 1997. Sambanis (2002, 220) lists the Tajikistan civil war as lasting from 1992 to 1994, in October of which a temporary cease-fire was signed, and by which time most of the serious fighting had ended. More frequently the civil war period is seen as 1992–1997. During these years, the temporary cease-fire was violated, and there were periods of intense conflict, until 1997, when an enduring peace accord was signed under UN auspices. The civil war resulted in the deaths of between 50,000 and 60,000 peo-

ple, created a million refugees (700,000 of whom were internally displaced refugees), and prompted large numbers of professionals and skilled workers to emigrate to Russia, Ukraine, and Belarus (see sidebar, "Refugees and Civil War"). Some 55,000 children were orphaned and thousands of women widowed; 26,000 families were left without their primary income earners (Akiner and Barnes 2001). Beyond this immediate human cost was the loss to critical infrastructure, electricity and communication services, and education and health facilities. An estimated 35,000 houses were destroyed, as were about 10 percent of school buildings (see sidebar, "Civil War Affects Civil Education"). In total, about 40 percent of the Tajikistan population was directly affected by the civil war, although some regional populations suffered disproportionately; the majority of those killed, for example, were ethnic Tajiks from the Gharm and Pamir regions.

Following peace talks led by the United Nations and the Organization for Cooperation and Security in Europe (OSCE), a peace accord was signed in June 1997 by the neocommunist and opposition parties. The accord created a National Reconciliation Commission (NRC) and set aside 30 percent of the executive positions in the presidential republic for representatives of the secular and Islamist movements that made up the United Tajik Opposition (UTO). The

Refugees and Civil War

Tajikistan's civil war resulted in almost a million refugees; 700,000 people were displaced within the republic itself, and a further 250,000 fled to neighboring countries such as Afghanistan, Russia, the Ukraine, Byelorussia, Uzbekistan, Turkmenistan, Kyrgyzstan, and Kazakhstan. However, some of these refugees never returned to Tajikistan, and they then required the assistance of the United Nations High Commissioner for Refugees (UNHCR).

For example, the UNHCR has been providing protection to 13,000 refugees in Turkmenistan since 1995. It has assisted the Turkmen government in integrating the refugees into local communities through language courses and vocational training. UNHCR has also given agricultural machinery, including tractors, bulldozers, and water pumps, to these refugees to enable them to become more self-sufficient.

In August 2005, a permanent solution was found for the refugees who had fled Tajikistan for Turkmenistan, when the government of Turkmenistan granted them citizenship. "We are extremely happy and grateful to the Turkmen government for this generous decision," said Annika Linden, chief of mission for the UNHCR in the Turkmen capital, Ashgabat (UNHCR 2005).

Russian troops and border guards previously stationed in Tajikistan were given permanent basing rights, whereas UTO military forces (around 5,000) were integrated into the Tajik army.

Since the cease-fire, low-level conflict between government forces and Islamist groups has continued, including a number of assassinations of political figures. On the whole, however, a return to civil war does not appear likely under the new political order (Akiner and Barnes 2001).

Country Background

Situated in Central Asia, Tajikistan shares its borders with Uzbekistan in the northwest, the Kyrgyz Republic in the north, China in the east, and Afghanistan in the south. Tajikistan is a mostly (93 percent) mountainous, landlocked country covering an area of 143,000 square kilometers. In fact, Tajikistan is home to some of the highest mountains in the world, which range from 1,000 feet to 27,000 feet. Nearly half of Tajikistan's territory is above 10,000 feet. Tajikistan's mountainous territory defines its main regions: Leninabad (the Fergana valley); the Karategin and Hissar valleys; Khatlon (Kulyab province); Gorno-Badakhshan (defined by the Pamir mountains) and Kurgan-Tyube. Its capital, Dushanbe, is located in the west of the country.

Tajikistan's population in 2006 was about 6.6 million people, most of whom live in rural areas. Additionally, 1 million Tajiks live in Uzbekistan and 4 million in Afghanistan. According to the 2000 census, the breakdown of key ethnic groups of the country is as follows: Tajik, 80 percent; Uzbek, 15 percent; Russian, 1 percent; Kyrgyz, 1 percent; others, 2.6 percent (CIA 2006). Prior to the civil war, Russians made up about 7 percent of the population. The vast majority (85 percent) of the population are Sunni Muslim; only about 5 percent are Shi'a Muslim.

Because two of central Asia's main rivers, the Amu Darya and the Syr Daryaiver, run through Tajikistan, the country is well endowed with water resources. This allows about 80 percent of Tajikistan's arable land to be irrigated and has contributed to Tajikistan's specialization in cotton production (about half of the total agricultural production). There is also substantial hydroelectric power generation, which provides surplus electricity for aluminum production.

Regime Type

The modern state of Tajikistan traces its origins to 1924, when the Soviet Union established it as an "independent" republic within Uzbekistan. In 1929, it became the Tajik Soviet Socialist Republic. Before real independence in 1991, Tajikistan was ruled as a one-party state by the Tajikistan Communist Party (TCP), primarily by elites

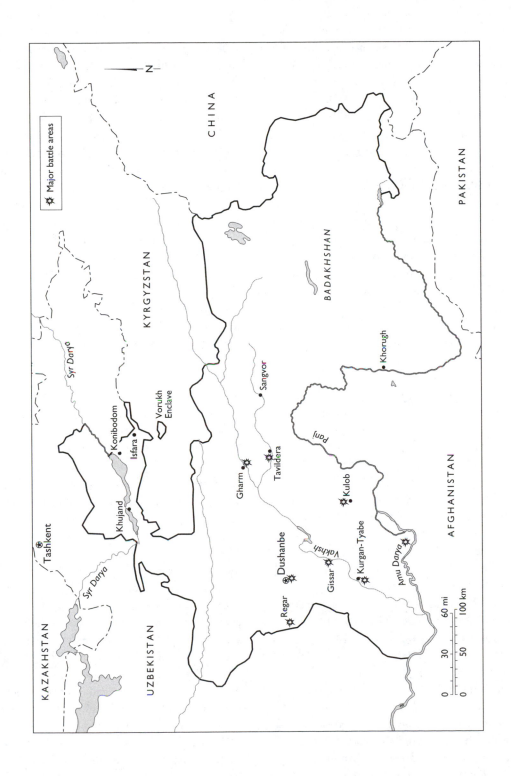

from the northern province of Leninabad but also with the support of the Kulyabis from the south, who were in charge of military affairs. Today, Tajikistan is a presidential republic with a bicameral legislature. The lower chamber has sixty-three deputies (forty-one directly elected, twenty-two proportionally elected), whereas the upper chamber has thirty-three deputies. Local councils indirectly elect twenty-five members, and the president appoints eight.

At independence in 1991 and before the civil war, Tajikistan was rated "partly free" (see Tables 1 and 2). Many members of the new parliament were parliamentarians who either had previously served under Soviet rule or had headed local and regional governments.

Although parliamentary elections were held during the civil war, international observers declined to monitor the 1994 elections because of continued fighting and the elections' boycott by opposition parties. Unsurprisingly, the elections resulted in a parliament dominated by the TCP, led by President Emomali Rahmonov. Over the course of the civil war, dozens of journalists were murdered; despite constitutional guarantees of freedom of speech and the press, independent journalists continued to face harassment and intimidation. For these reasons, the regime type of Tajikistan was rated "not free" in 1995, with a Polity IV rating of –6 (where a fully autocratic regime would score –10).

Following the 1997 peace accord, presidential elections were held in 1999 and parliamentary elections in 2000. Although these elections were peaceful, they were widely considered flawed and unfair. (This is according to the U.S. Department of State [2004], but it could also describe the most recent elections in Tajikistan in 2005.) The supporters of President Rahmonov (who were mostly former members of the old Soviet bureaucracy) limited the ability of the opposition, the UTO, to compete for power. The UTO alleged that the government did not allow some opposition candidates to be registered, excluded UTO representatives from election monitoring commissions, and engaged in widespread vote rigging.

In addition to concerns about the conduct of democratic elections, Tajikistan is still regarded as fairly autocratic because parliament has little true independence; real power lies with the president. According to the constitution, the president appoints and dismisses the prime minister, the government ministers, the regional, provincial, and city chairmen, and the chairman of the National Bank. The president also determines which government ministries to establish or abolish, the composition of the Constitutional Court, the Supreme Court, the High Economic Court, and state committees, as well as chairing the Security Council and the Council of Justice.

In 2003, President Rahmonov further consolidated his power by using a popular referendum to approve a package of constitutional amendments to increase the powers of the president—the most controversial of which (Article 65) allows the president to serve two seven-year terms instead of the one term agreed to under the 1997 peace accord. This constitutional change allows Rahmonov to seek a further two terms following the expiry of his current term in 2006. These retrograde steps in Tajikistan's democracy have contributed to a fall in its 2003 rating on the Polity IV variable to –3 (Marshall and Jaggers 2004).

Economic Situation

Tajikistan is one of the least wealthy countries in the world and the poorest nation within the Commonwealth of Independent States (CIS). The country's social development and economic indicators have only just begun to return to the levels seen before the onset of the civil war (see Table 2). Tajikistan's economic and social recovery also remains vulnerable to external events, such as the typhoid epidemic that struck the capital, Dushanbe, and Southern Tajikistan in 2002. Drought has reduced cereal harvests, whereas ongoing border and customs difficulties with neighboring countries have had a negative impact on cross-border trade.

Although gross domestic product (GDP) has begun to rise slowly since the 1997 peace accord, per capita GDP declined almost two-thirds between 1990 and 2000. Essential physical infrastructure—shelter, hospitals, schools, water systems, roads, bridges, and energy lines—were severely damaged in the civil war, whereas population displacement and massive destruction of property combined to create housing shortages and property disputes. The growth of the population from 5.3 million in 1990 to 6.6 million in 2006 has placed considerable demands on land and other resources. Because a significant proportion of the population is young, youth unemployment has also become a problem. In 1997, almost 60 percent of people aged sixteen to twenty-nine years were unemployed. More positively, life expectancy at birth remains higher than in many Central Asian republics, and the infant and under-five mortality rates are improving. Literacy was almost universal and well above other countries before the civil war (UNICEF 2005).

The Tajik economy is now in a period of adjustment. By the end of 2000, Tajikistan had achieved full currency convertibility, almost complete price liberalization, and significant progress in small-scale privatization. Institutional reforms—tax reform in 1998, the banking sector's restructuring, and the legal and regulatory development of markets—have helped Tajikistan's macroeconomic indicators improve. Growth rates have been as high as 10 percent, whereas inflation has stabilized at around 11.5 percent per annum. However, the country's external debt has increased substantially, and the economy remains heavily dependent on exports of cotton and aluminum. There are also a substantial underground economy and corruption because of the extensive criminal networks that have infiltrated much of Tajikistan's political and economic life. Tajikistan was ranked among the ten most corrupt countries surveyed by Transparency International in 2004 (Transparency International 2004).

Conflict Background

Although the disintegration of the Soviet Union encouraged Tajikistan's transition to declare independence in September 1991, it also helped precipitate the civil war that erupted between opposing political and regional factions in October 1992. The collapse of the Soviet Union meant the end of generous budget transfers to Tajikistan (equivalent to about 40 percent of GDP) and the end of ready markets for Tajikistan's goods. Consequently, Tajikistan's economic conditions rapidly deteriorated, leading to protests about the worsening living conditions and the need for economic and political reform.

At the same time, Gorbachev's policies of perestroika and glasnost suggested that these protests would be tolerated. By 1990, a number of political movements and parties opposed to the Communist regime had formed. They included the Rastokhez Popular Movement (RPM), the Democratic Party of Tajikistan (DPT), and the Islamic Renaissance Party of Tajikistan (IRP). These organizations and political parties, together with the La'li Badahshon and Nosiri Khusraw societies, formed what became known as the United Tajik Opposition (UTO), or "the opposition" for short. La'li Badahshon is a political party composed mostly of Pamiri people. It advocated greater autonomy for Badakhshan, a mountainous region in eastern Tajikistan.

Following the resignation of the head of the Tajik Communist Party, the democratic and Islamic opposition parties pressured the Tajik Legislature to suspend TCP activities and to declare the republic's independence, which it did on September 9, 1991. This, however, precipitated a strong Communist backlash. The Communists declared a state of emergency, reconstituted the TCP in parliament, and nominated Rahmon Nabiyev as president for the November elections. (Nabiyev had been the head of the TCP in Tajikistan before being removed by Gorbachev in 1985.) Opposition parties nominated a well-known film director, Davlat Khudonazarov, as their presidential candidate. Nevertheless, Nabiev was elected president of Tajikistan in November 1991 with 57 percent of the vote, against Khudonazarov's 37 percent.

An anticommunist demonstration takes place in Dushanbe, Tajikistan, on October 4, 1991. (Pascal Le Segretain/ Sygma/Corbis)

Following the November 1991 presidential election, the legitimacy of Nabiev's presidency began to be called into question as doubts about the conduct of the election were raised and further developments unfolded. Attempts by the ex-communists (Leninabadis and Kulyabis) to remove all opposition members from the parliament and government led to frequent public demonstrations in the capital, Dushanbe, between supporters of the government and the opposition parties. During March and April 1992, opposition supporters held a rally in front of the building of the Central Committee of the TCP. In response, the government launched its own rally in support of the president. In addition, the president created a number of "presidential guard" units, which were drawn from supporters from Kulyab but which also contained some criminal elements. These units were armed with 1,800 Kalashnikov automatic rifles. (These units would later form the basis of the Popular Front of Tajik-

istan [PFT], a political party that, when it came to power, engaged in criminal and violent activities.) On May 5, 1992, opposition supporters stormed the national television station as well as the presidential palace. In so doing, they gained access to the armory. Inevitably, this resulted in armed clashes between the two groups, which continued on the streets of Dushanbe until May 10.

The demonstrations and violence prompted talks between the two sides, which succeeded in reaching an agreement on the formation of a coalition government. The Government of National Reconciliation (GNR) saw several opposition leaders receive a number of key posts. Of eight members, four represented Pamir-Gharm and four Kulob-Leninobod. Leninabad, Kulyab, and the local Uzbeks all refused to recognize the GNR, however, which they declared unconstitutional.

Commanding little authority, the GNR was unable to prevent the civil unrest that followed.

Criminal activities increased as the system of law and order broke down, followed by the gradual disorganization of all municipal services and the economy in general. A released criminal, Sangak Safarov, established himself as a warlord at the head of the Popular Front, a coalition of Soviet-era political elites and criminal elements. The Popular Front attacked opposition sympathizers in the south part of the country. With the support of Uzbekistan, further attacks were launched on the approaches to Dushanbe and on the Regar and Gissar areas, which had small Uzbek populations.

The opposition responded by forming self-defense units—one of which, led by Said Nuri, succeeded in pushing the Popular Front back. In September 1992, a pro-opposition group of youth captured President Nabiev and forced him to resign at gunpoint. These events prompted a joint communiqué from the presidents of Russia, Kazakhstan, and Uzbekistan. The communiqué described the conflict as a threat to the entire Commonwealth of Independent States and stated that intervention would be necessary if the fighting could not be halted (Neumann and Solodovnik 1995).

In November 1992, the situation became untenable for the GNR, and they resigned en masse. Imomali Rahmonov was then appointed chairman of the Supreme Soviet's Executive Committee and proclaimed a civic truce. Despite the truce, the Popular Front (with the support of the Russian 201st Motorized Rifle Division and the Uzbek air force) continued to bomb opposition strongholds in Kofernihan and subsequently captured opposition positions. The Popular Front's military tactics include brutal reprisals against opposition sympathizers, especially those of Gharmi or Badakhshoni descent.

These attacks pushed opposition forces across the Panj River into Afghanistan and forced democratic and Islamic opposition leaders to take refuge in Moscow, Iran, Afghanistan, and Saudi Arabia. From their positions along the Tajik–Afghan border, opposition forces continued to fight, forcing hundreds of thousands of people to flee the country.

By the summer of 1993, the civil war had subsided considerably. Nevertheless, Russia's political and military leadership was of the view that a peace settlement was the only solution. The activities of the opposition groupings within the country and ongoing military tension along the border showed Russia that Tajikistan was far from stable and cast doubt on the ability of Rahmonov and his command to restore order. Consequently, in September 1993, Kazakhstan and Russia asked the UN to give the 25,000-strong Russian forces in Tajikistan a mandate to operate as a UN peacekeeping force. Even though this request was rejected by the UN, the director of the Russian Foreign Intelligence Service, Evgeni Primakov, managed to make direct contact with the Tajik opposition in the following months. By March 1994, Anatoli Adamishin, President Yeltsin's envoy to Tajikistan, had met with Akbar Turajonzoda in Teheran.

Although peace efforts continued throughout 1994, they had reached a stalemate by 1995. Then, in 1996, the Taliban captured Kabul, upsetting the regional geopolitical balance. Foreign governments became alarmed that the Taliban might also threaten Tajikistan and therefore began to encourage their respective allies within Tajikistan to begin negotiating an end to the civil war. Factions within Tajikistan also came to understand that ongoing civil conflict might lead to losing the country entirely. Foreign governments subsequently provided practical support to the peace process that sought to achieve a power-sharing compromise to govern the country. With both sides realizing that their ultimate interests were converging, the UN was able to "build a momentum for peace" (Akiner and Barnes 2001). The peace process culminated in the General Agreement on the Establishment of Peace and National Accord, which was signed in Moscow during June 1997 under UN, OSCE, and Russian auspices.

The Insurgents

Distinguishing between the rebels and government forces in the Tajikistan conflict is problematic because, at various stages of the conflict, both sides could be said to have rebelled against the official government. Both the rebels and government forces were essentially political groups formed around regional and historical attachments who could mobilize substantial armed support. Both sides in the Tajikistan conflict largely depended on support from foreign sponsors.

On one side were the old Communist sympathizers and elites from the Leninabad region, who joined with people from the Kulob region in the south, and eventually the Hissaris, to form a new alliance, the People's Front of Tajikistan (PFT). During the Soviet period, Kulobis were generally underrepresented in positions of national authority. As the conflict began, they were able to create armed groups and support the government. As the war continued, the Kulobis began to gain the balance of power in this "government alliance." By the end of the 1990s, the Kulobi faction had managed to marginalize the Leninabad elites and cement their own power under President Rahmonov. Russia and other Central Asian countries, principally Uzbekistan, supported the progovernment faction financially and militarily.

The opposition forces were a coalition of new opposition political parties that could be identified by their different ideologies—promoting national unity, democracy or Islamic values—and also by the regions that supported them (such as Gharm and Gorno-Badakhshan). The civil war should not, therefore, be seen simply in terms of an ideological struggle. Instead, the various ideological movements—communism, democracy, and Islamism—helped to reinforce people's sense of regional identity.

The first new opposition organization to appear was the Rastokhez Popular Movement, which appeared in 1988 and was composed mainly of Dushanbe-based intellectuals. The RPM's agenda was built on issues of national identity such as the promotion of national culture and recognition of the national language as

Table 1: Civil War in Tajikistan

War:	United Tajik Opposition (UTO) vs. government
Dates:	October 1992–June 1997
Casualties:	50,000–60,000
Regime type prior to war:	–2 (1991; ranging from –10 [authoritarian] to 10 [democracy])
Regime type after war:	–1 (2000; ranging from –10 [authoritarian] to 10 [democracy])
GDP per capita year war began:	US $496 (nominal, 1990)
GDP per capita 5 years after war:	US $252 (nominal, 2003)
Insurgents:	5,000 United Tajik Opposition (UTO) forces
Issue:	Postindependence ideological struggle
Rebel funding:	Regional clans, Iran, Pakistan
Role of geography:	Mountainous terrain reinforced regional rivalries
Role of resources:	Negligible
Immediate outcome:	National peace accord, power-sharing arrangements
Outcome after 5 years:	Relative peace, flawed parliamentary elections
Role of UN:	Established UNMOT, facilitated peace talks
Role of regional organization:	OSCE active in institution and democracy building, drafting constitution, and promotion of human rights
Refugees:	950,000 (700,000 internally displaced)
Prospects for peace:	Reasonable if economic and political reforms are implemented.

Sources: Marshall and Jaggers 2004; UNICEF 2005; World Bank 2005.

Table 2: Selected Country Indicators

Indicator	1990	1995	2000	2003
Regime type (Polity IV)	−2 (1991)	−6	−1	−3
Political rights (Freedom House)	5	7	6	6
Civil liberties (Freedom House)	5	7	6	5
Status (Freedom House)	Partly free	Not free	Not free	Not free
Population (million)	5.30	5.84	6.19	6.25
Percentage of under-fives suffering from stunting	..	36% (1995–2003)		
Life expectancy at birth	69	..	67	66
Net primary school enrollment/ attendance	..	80% (1996–2003)		
Share of government expenditure on education	4% (1992–2004)			
Share of government expenditure on health	2% (1992–2004)			
GDP (US $ billions, nominal)	2.63	..	1.06 (2001)	1.64
GDP per capita (US $)	496	..	171	252
Rate of inflation	153% (1990–2003)			
Military expenditure as share of GDP	0.4% (1992)	1.0%	..	1.3%
Armed forces personnel (thousands)	3 (1992)	18	7 (1999)	7
Share of government expenditure on defense	9% (1992–2004)			

Sources: Freedom House 2004; Marshall and Jaggers 2004; UNICEF 2005; World Bank 2005.

the state language. Then followed the formation of the Democratic Party of Tajikistan (DPT) in August 1990 and the Islamic Renaissance Party of Tajikistan (IRP) in October 1990. The DPT, as its name suggests, was opposed to Marxist ideology and a totalitarian system of government, aiming instead to introduce democracy, a market economy, and a fairer distribution of power. The IRP aimed for a greater role for Islam in the political life of Tajikistan. With its support base in the southwest part of the country, the IRP was the largest of the opposition parties. Jointly, these three parties formed the UTO.

The UTO forces were supported by Iran and to a lesser extent by Afghanistan and Pakistan.

Davlat Usmon, a UTO leader and former deputy prime minister of Tajikistan, revealed that sympathetic Tajik Afghan mujahideen commanders and a number of Islamic nongovernmental organizations (NGOs) supplied arms, ammunition, and financial support to the UTO. The former allowed the UTO to base themselves across the border in Afghanistan.

It also appears that militant Islamist interests in Pakistan and Saudi Arabia may also have supported the UTO. According to Akiner and Barnes (2001, 93), Pakistan helped Tajik Muslims by providing religious training to refugee children as well as by extending financial assistance through Islamic organizations. Pakistan allegedly gave covert military aid to the Tajik opposition via governmental and nongovernmental channels (Iji 2001, 369).

Tactics

The PFT's military tactics included brutal attacks on opposition sympathizers, especially those of Gharmi or Badakhshoni descent. Gharm and Pamir villages, which were opposition strongholds, were bombed by the Uzbek air force. With the support of the Russian 201st Motorized Rifle Division, which numbered about 25,000, the Popular Front managed to capture most of the areas still held by the opposition. According to Neumann and Solodovnik (1995), the 201st Motorized Rifle Division may have provided four tanks and six armored personnel carriers to the Kulyabi forces loyal to Nabiev, and these may have been decisive in their subjugation of Kurgan-Tyube.

Following the collapse of the GNR in 1992, opposition forces retreated across the Panj River into Afghanistan as well as into the difficult terrain of the interior of Gorno-Badahshon. From their positions along the Tajik-Afghan border, opposition forces continued sniping activity and minor attacks on border posts. The most serious of these occurred on July 13, 1993, when a border post with a contingent of 47 Russian soldiers was attacked; 24 guards were killed and another 18 wounded. In total, close to 300 people, including civilians, insurgents and border guards, were killed in this attack (Neumann and Solodovnik 1995).

Causes of the War

Although there is no consensus on the causes of the Tajikistan civil war, a number of internal (domestic) and external (geopolitical) factors have been suggested. At the domestic level, a set of political and economic grievances, reinforced by history and geography, worked against the emergence of a genuine Tajikistan national identity following its independence from the Soviet Union. Ethnic diversity and the mountainous terrain were contributing factors, while "lootable" natural resources do not appear to have played a role in the emergence of the conflict. External geopolitical factors—the security concerns of Russia and Uzbekistan—aggravated the slide into civil war.

Internal Factors
Regional Factionalism and Lack of Democratic Institutions

Regional factionalism was one of the primary domestic causes of Tajikistan's civil war. Both government and opposition forces had strong regional bases. The government (excommunist) forces were supported by the northern Leninabad and Kulob regions, whereas the UTO drew support from ethnic Tajiks in the Gharma and Qarateguine Valleys east of Dushanbe and from Pamiris who lived in Dushanbe. This regional factionalism was partly the product of Soviet policies and partly the result of Tajikistan's mountainous terrain, which reinforced a sense of regional, rather than national, identity.

Tajikistan was a direct creation of the Soviet Union, but it was created with little regard for the cultural and ethnic basis of the Tajik people. Although there were 1 million Tajiks when the country was formed in the 1920s, only 300,000 found themselves in the newly established state of Tajikistan. The rest were isolated within other national borders. For example, the cities of Bukhara and Samarqand (historically and culturally important to the Tajiks and the majority of whose population was Tajik) were located in the new state of Uzbekistan. This cultural fragmentation was then reinforced by the ongoing Soviet suppression of any emergent Tajik national identity.

The natural barriers provided by Tajikistan's mountain ranges also served to compartmentalize the different regions by making communication and contact between them difficult. This appears to confirm Collier and Hoeffler's (2000) model, which suggests a negative relationship between the degree of geographic dispersion of the population and civil war outbreaks. In other words, a highly concentrated population is associated with fewer civil war outbreaks, whereas a high degree of dispersion—as a result of geographic features such as mountain ranges—may contribute to a higher risk of conflict.

Applied to Tajikistan, this means that local politics and regional identity became more important than any sense of national identity. Indeed "identity regionalism" is a loose translation of the local term *mahalgaroi*—blood and geographical origin as a basis of group identity.

When the Leninabad region's elites ascended to top Communist Party and government positions in Tajikistan in the 1940s, they used mahalgaroi as a policy to maintain regional rivalries and their own position as the most economically developed, most politically privileged region during the Soviet era (Iji 2001, 359). Even following the collapse of the Soviet Union, the Leninabad region used their control of the political apparatus to channel as much as 70 percent of the country's budget into their own regions.

By contrast, many of Tajikistan's other regions suffered declines in GDP of as much as 60 percent as a result of the loss of Russian subsidies, a reduction in access to credit, a decline in customary markets, and an increase in corruption and crime. (Corruption—nepotism, theft, and bribery—had intensified in the 1980s to the extent that "mafias" were engaged in large-scale illegal economic activities, often with the covert participation of officials.) Such one-sided regional economic development only aggravated the regional and social tensions. For many opposition or antigovernment forces, the Soviet establishment was synonymous with Leninabad rule. When these opposition forces began to demand more equitable regional economic development, political reforms, and national unity, the Leninabad's hold on power and economic privilege were threatened.

A second aggravating factor in the slide into civil war was the undeveloped nature of Tajikistan's fledgling democracy following independence. The suddenness of the transition to independence meant that Tajikistan simply did not have the features essential to a well-developed democratic process: respect for human rights, a free media, an independent judiciary, and an acceptance of political competition through democratic political parties. Frustration at the unevenness of regional economic development and at widespread corruption led to grassroots protest in Dushanbe in February 1990. Faced with a power structure that seemed set on preserving these economic disparities, opposition forces were able to mobilize and focus demands for a truly national Tajikistan society based on democracy, the rule of law, and equality.

But when opposition demands for a more inclusive and democratic political regime moved from social protest to civil unrest, the ex-Communist leaders were not only unwilling to allow these new challenges to their political authority but also unable to prevent the ensuing civil conflict. This supports findings that countries in the middle of the autocracy–democracy spectrum are actually at greater risk of civil war than those at either extreme (Sambanis 2002, 223). Tajikistan—rated close to the middle of this scale in 1991—was not so autocratic that social protest was immediately repressed, but neither was it democratic enough to allow such protest to be seen as legitimate and to be managed in a democratic way.

Other Internal Factors

As already noted, Tajikistan's mountainous terrain limited the formation of a national identity and tended to reinforce regional animosities based on disparities in regional economic development. These regional animosities were also partly the result of ethnic divisions. Tajikistan is ethnically diverse, and the civil war in part divided it along ethnic lines. Ethnic Uzbeks living in Tajikistan constituted a powerful community of 23 percent of the population. A more even sharing of political and economic power clearly had negative implications for this ethnic group, which were concentrated in the Leninabad (Kulyab) and Kurgan-Tyube regions. The opposition forces were from areas more thoroughly

Tajik and less ethnically mixed (Dunn 1997). It is these regional animosities—a consequence, in part, of the terrain and the ethnic divisions—that defined the warring parties in the Tajikistan civil war.

External Factors: Geopolitics

External factors were also contributing causes of Tajikistan's civil war. The two main external actors were Uzbekistan and Russia, both of whom supported the Soviet-era Tajik government for their own reasons and intervened militarily. In this, they were aided by appeals from Leninabad (government) forces who realized that they would be unable to defeat the opposition alone.

Uzbekistan's president, Islam Karimov, privately feared that any coalition of Tajikistan's government and the Islamic-democratic opposition might be viewed as a model in his own republic (Akbarzadeh 1996). Karimov may also have feared potential territorial claims over Samarkand and Bukhara from forces seeking to regain their national identity. Publicly, however, Karimov played on fears of Islamic fundamentalism to justify military intervention.

The presence within Tajikistan of the Russian military unit, the 201st Motorized Rifle Division, also played a part in drawing Russia into the Tajikistan conflict. Faced with the prospect of cuts to the armed forces and no chance of service in Russia, the division's Russian-speaking officers (most of whom had been born in Tajikistan) managed to play on Russian perceptions that Islamic extremism would have a domino effect in the region, reaching Russia's southern borders (Plater-Zyberk 2004, 8). This threat seemed to be confirmed by an attack on a Russian border post in 1993 and is seen as having strengthened the resolve of Russia to remain militarily involved in Tajikistan (Sherr 1993). When asked why Russian soldiers were dying in Tajikistan, the Russian defense minister stated, "The borders of Tajikistan are the borders of Russia" (Plater-Zyberk 2004, 8). Thus, to secure the CIS generally and Russia in particular required patrolling the Tajik–Afghan border. A

further justification of Russian military support of the Khujandi–PFT alliance was that a mass exodus of Russians and Russian speakers from Tajikistan might be avoided.

Outcome
Conflict Status

The Tajikistan civil war was brought to a formal end on June 27, 1997, when President Rahmonov and UTO leader Said Abdullo Nuri signed the Tajik National Peace Accord in Moscow. The peace accord established a twenty-six-member National Reconciliation Commission, to be headed by an opposition representative but with seats split evenly between the government and the UTO. The NRC would implement the peace agreement, repatriate and assist refugees, and introduce legislation for fair parliamentary elections, as well as integrating UTO members into 30 percent of ministerial and departmental posts. As part of the peace accord, a general amnesty was declared for all participants in the conflict, and opposition soldiers were integrated into the regular army. Under the auspices of the United Nations Mission of Observers in Tajikistan (UNMOT) and the International Red Cross, a full exchange of prisoners was also to take place.

Following the initial transitional period of the peace accord, presidential and parliamentary elections took place in late 1999 and early 2000. With the departure of most international monitoring bodies, Tajikistan then faced the problems of reconstruction associated with all postconflict situations. This rebuilding process was not helped by the failure to implement all of the important provisions of the peace accord. The demobilization of opposition forces remained incomplete, and the government failed to meet the 30 percent quota of senior government posts to be awarded to the UTO.

Duration Tactics

The intervention of Russia, Uzbekistan, and Iran had a significant impact on the duration and ending of hostilities in Tajikistan because these states were the strongest external patrons of each side. Although Iran did not intervene militarily in the conflict, it did provide financial and political support to the Islamic opposition.

Until Uzbekistan and Russia became involved militarily, the confrontation between the Khujandi–PFT alliance and the opposition might not have escalated into civil war. This is because both the procommunists and the opposition forces fought one another as ill-organized militias bearing small arms, such that by the early autumn of 1992 neither side could prevail militarily. Once Uzbekistan and Russia intervened militarily, however, a low-level civil conflict developed into a full-scale civil war (Gretsky 2006).

The effect of such external support appears to have persuaded each side that it alone would prevail in the conflict. Consequently, both the government and the opposition parties engaged in peace negotiations only halfheartedly, with neither side seeing the other as legitimate. Russia was determined to continue to support the Rahmonov regime, which it had helped to install. It therefore endorsed the government's attempt to strengthen its own position by holding presidential and parliamentary elections in 1994 and 1995 (Jonson 1998).

It was not until the end of 1995, against the backdrop of a rising Taliban regime in Afghanistan, that both Russia and Iran became seriously interested in settling the conflict in Tajikistan. It was then that Moscow began to have doubts about the prospects for a military solution to the conflict. In the face of the UTO's advances on the battlefield, the disintegrating power of the Rahmonov regime, and the weakening capabilities of its own armed forces, Russia came to perceive the cost of further military involvement in Tajikistan to be too high. The fear of repeating the catastrophic Chechnyan scenario may also have influenced the Russians' change in position (Jonson 1998).

The role of Iran was also important in bringing the conflict to an end. In part, Iran may have appreciated that a Shi'a Muslim revolution, as had occurred in Iran, was unlikely in Tajikistan, where most Muslims were Sunni. Iran may also have been keen to close down any opportunities for the United States and Turkey to increase their influence in the region—a position Iran shared with Russia. Iran therefore had good reasons to encourage the peace process.

External Military Intervention

The two states to intervene militarily in the Tajikistan civil war were Russia and Uzbekistan. As indicated earlier, the Russian military unit, the 201st Motorized Rifle Division, was already present in Tajikistan when hostilities broke out. The division consists of the 92nd, 191st, and 149th motor rifle regiments, the 401 independent tank battalion, and self-propelled artillery and air defense missile regiments (Plater-Zyberg 2004, 4).

Russia was, in effect, responsible for the maintenance of security and order within Tajikistan, especially along the vulnerable Tajik–Afghan border. The Russian units' main mission was to secure the southern border of Tajikistan, which it shares with Afghanistan and across which opposition forces had been receiving substantial support. The military tactics used by the border forces have been described by Russian general staff personnel as similar to those used by the Soviet army in Afghanistan: reliance on base camps, forward deployment of combat helicopters, and counterinsurgency involving local collaborators (Neumann and Solodovnik 1995).

Military intervention by Uzbekistan also appears to have had a significant impact on the conflict. In the second half of 1992, Uzbekistan allowed the pro–Nabiev Popular Front forces to use its territory for military training and to launch attacks on Dushanbe (Akbarzadeh 1996). The use of Uzbekistan aircraft and tanks also appears to have been decisive in forcing the opposition forces across the border to Afghanistan, as well as encouraging the procommunist militia to force more than 100,000 Tajiks to seek refuge there.

Conflict Management Efforts

Although the main external actors in the Tajikistan civil war were eventually instrumental in initiating negotiations among the opposing sides, the substantial disagreement among them on the way negotiations should proceed risked deadlock. Here, the United Nations came to play an important role.

The UN defined its mandate as mediating between the two warring parties and legitimizing the Kulyabi–UTO peacekeeping formula. The UN was able to bring both sides to the negotiating table and also served as a line of communication between them. The UN secretary-general special envoy to Tajikistan, Ramiro Piriz-Ballón, set up four rounds of negotiations between the opposing sides between April 1994 and May 1995. Russia, Afghanistan, Iran, Kazakhstan, Kyrgyzstan, Pakistan, and Uzbekistan served as observers, and the OSCE and the OIC were also present at the talks (Iji 2001).

The first subsidiary-level talks were held in Moscow in April 1994. However, the Tajik government refused to accept the opposition's proposal for a cease-fire, despite repeated statements by the Russian deputy minister of defense that Tajiks themselves should find a political resolution to the civil war. The first-round talks did achieve agreement that any questions concerning an election or a new constitution would be held over for discussion until the final round of peace talks, under the auspices of the UN.

The subject of the second round of talks, held in June 1994 in Tehran, was a cease-fire. No cease-fire agreement was signed, however, because the government rejected several of the opposition's conditions. The opposition requested that all political prisoners be freed, that all politically motivated prosecutions be dropped, that the official ban on opposition parties be rescinded, and that restrictions on the media be removed.

At the third round, held in October 1994 in Islamabad, the parties did manage to sign the cease-fire agreement, allowing the UN to establish a mission of observers in Tajikistan (UNMOT). The mission's primary function was to observe the implementation of the agreement, but it also gave much-needed international exposure to the Tajik tragedy.

Although in the middle of peace talks, the government attempted to strengthen its position by proceeding with presidential elections and a referendum on the constitution on November 6. Rahmonov won the election, but opposition parties were excluded, and foreign observers considered the result to have been rigged.

A fourth round of peace talks took place in Almaty in May 1995. The agenda for the fourth round—agreed upon in the first round—included the topic of political and institutional reform. The opposition's reform package proposed the formation of a Council of National Unity, in which each side would have 40 percent of the seats; representatives from ethnic minorities would share the remaining seats. The government rejected the opposition's reform package, arguing that it had already introduced a number of political and economic reforms. It put forward a number of minor items unrelated to the round's formal agenda, including a permanent cease-fire and the repatriation of refugees.

Faced with stalemate, Piriz-Ballón suggested a number of compromises that were seemingly agreed to by both sides. At this point, the Russian deputy foreign minister intervened and persuaded the Tajik government to refuse to sign the compromise statement. As a consequence, the fourth round of the Tajik peace talks did not produce any substantial agreement on fundamental political and constitutional reforms. More seriously, the government's attempts at consolidating its own position slowed down the peace process, and by 1995 attention had shifted away from the negotiating table and back to the battlefield.

Peace talks remained deadlocked until 1996, when the Taliban captured Kabul. This development appears to have reinvigorated peace talks. Foreign governments, now concerned with spillover effects from Taliban rule, began to put increased pressure on their respective Tajik allies to find a political solution to the war. The Tajik factions also realized that continued warfare could threaten the future independence of the country and that the compromise power-sharing agreement proposed previously was preferable to losing the country entirely. With both sides moving closer to consensus, the UN was able to play a leading role as an international and neutral mediator in the peace negotiations. These concluded with the General Agreement on the Establishment of Peace and National Accord, signed in Moscow in June 1997. It should also be noted that the Organization for Security and Cooperation in Europe also played an important role. It provided assistance in such areas as institution and democracy building, the drafting of a constitution, and the promotion of human rights.

Having two sets of mediators involved in the Tajikistan conflict management process allowed the burden of peacemaking to be shared and helped to build consensus among the parties. Mediation is usually a complex process requiring a high level of resources; by sharing this burden both the UN and OSCE may have been more effective than either alone. As Hampson (1996, 233) has observed, "Third parties need other third parties."

Conclusion

Although the peace accord of 1997 signaled the end of civil conflict in Tajikistan, Tajikistan's hard-won peace and stability remain at risk. Radical fringe Islamist groups continue to express discontent, a spate of political assassinations has occurred, confrontations between the president and former warlords is ongoing, tensions with neighboring Afghanistan and Uzbekistan remain, and the dominance of the president's own small elite continues to fuel corruption, inefficiency, and economic deterioration (International Crisis Group 2004). The potential for further civil conflict in Tajikistan remains unless three issues are addressed: political reform, economic stagnation, and ethnoregional tension.

Political reform is necessary if the tensions between President Rahmonov and the opposition party, the IRP, are to be reduced. Although Rahmonov has openly accused members of the IRP of promoting extremist views, he has himself succeeded in changing the constitution so that his presidency could be extended for two more seven-year terms. The IRP, the only Islamic party with government participation in Central Asia, contends that Rahmonov's government is taking the same hard-line, anti-Islamic posture that led to civil war in 1992.

The parliamentary elections held in February 2005 were criticized by the Organization for Security and Cooperation in Europe, which said the elections fell short of the international standards for transparent and democratic elections (IRIN News Organization 2005). The OSCE said that prominent opposition leaders were barred from the polls, that four independent media outlets were closed before the elections, that a lack of information available to the public prevented voters from learning more about the candidates, that vote-counting procedures were suspect, and that voter turnout appeared to be unrealistically high, casting doubts over the reliability of the figures. Indeed, "[E]lections in Tajikistan remain simply a legitimizing ritual" (Marshall and Jaggers 2004).

Tajikistan also faces several economic problems, including corruption, high unemployment, high external debt, and limited structural reforms. Members of the country's security and police forces are alleged to have connections with organized crime groups involved in the drug trade (Freedom House 2005). Rampant illicit trafficking of Afghan opium and heroin through Tajikistan has meant increased levels of narcotics addiction; combined with poverty, it is creating a growing problem with prostitution and HIV/AIDS.

Females are especially disadvantaged in Tajikistan. The civil war stimulated increased violence against women and left many women the sole providers for their families. Discrimination against women in the workplace has increased because of high unemployment, and this has been accompanied by a contraction in girls' access to education. Poverty and the lack of free education has meant that almost one-fifth of Tajik children between the ages of five and fourteen must work to help support their families rather than attend school (see sidebar, "Civil War Affects Civil Education").

Although Tajikistan's economic and social problems are recognized by the government and civil society organizations, addressing them has been hampered by a lack of resources. Social and economic problems such as corruption, violent crime, and economic distortions threaten Tajikistan's stability and development. In turn, such problems allow more radical political forces to promote their own causes—and not necessarily through peaceful or democratic means.

The residual interregional tensions are a third area that must be addressed if a recurrence of the conflict is to be avoided. For example, the balance of power has shifted following the war in that the Kulobi elites have increased their control over national authorities and business enterprises. This shift can only exacerbate the sense of exclusion felt by those regions that do not enjoy the same levels of political and economic development. It has been suggested that the ongoing political and economic disparities among Tajikistan's regions will result in regional leaders' beginning to make devolutionary, or even secessionist, demands (Akiner and Barnes 2001).

It is also possible that Tajikistan's neighbors will use these internal regional tensions to once again justify intervention in Tajikistan's domestic affairs. For example, the Uzbekistan government may regard its own security as best achieved by installation of a client regime in Tajikistan. To this end, it may support moves by the Islamic Movement of Uzbekistan to create an Islamic rebellion within Tajikistan through its associations with Islamic militants in that country.

Civil War Affects Civil Education

It is estimated that the civil war destroyed about 20 percent of Tajikistan's schools, while many more lack sanitary facilities or heat. Heavy damage was inflicted on universities in Dushanbe and Kurgan-Tyube and on vocational schools in Dushanbe, Kofirnigan, and Khatlon. By World Bank estimates, the total loss to the education sector (furniture, equipment, and textbooks) was more than US $100 million.

But the effects of the civil war in Tajikistan have lingered long after the final shots were fired and will require more than simple reconstruction efforts. Half of Tajikistan's population is under eighteen years of age, two-thirds live in rural areas, and Tajikistan is no longer a place where children can get a free education. According to UNICEF, 18 percent of Tajik children between the ages of five and fourteen are forced to work to help support their families rather than attend and pay for school. Because of low pay, many teachers have sought other jobs. There are also severe shortages of textbooks and other school materials. With economic growth averaging 8 percent per annum over the past five years, however, poverty has been reduced, allowing the state to focus on social reform (Richter 1994; UNICEF 2005).

Despite these political, economic and social problems, it seems that there is still underlying consensus within Tajikistan that the trauma of the civil war should not be repeated, that peaceful development should be the only way forward. This consensus may not be enough by itself to ensure the stability of Tajikistan in the coming years, but it is at least a necessary first step.

John Wilson

Chronology

February 1990   Protests demanding the Communist regime implement economic and democratic reforms take place in Dushanbe, the capital of Tajikistan.

March 1990   Communist regime refuses permission for opposition parties to participate in elections.

August 1991   Head of Tajik Communist Party (TCP) resigns following failed coup against Gorbachev and demonstrations in Dushanbe.

September 9, 1991   Independence from the Soviet Union declared by Tajikistan; state of emergency declared and TCP banned.

October 1991   State of emergency rescinded; TCP reinstated.

November 1991   Presidential elections held; Soviet-era Nabiev elected head of new republic.

March 1992   Opposition proreform parties lead public demonstrations in the capital, Dushanbe.

April 1991   Antireform, progovernment forces form presidential guard units and are given 1,800 Kalashnikov automatic rifles.

May 1992   Opposition forces occupy national television station and the presidential palace; armed clashes between the government and opposition forces on the streets of Dushanbe until May 10.

May 1992   Government of National Reconciliation (GNR) is formed.

June 1992   The Popular Front, a coalition of Soviet-era political elites and criminal elements, attacks opposition sympathizers in the south of Tajikistan.

July 1992   Tajikistan signs a treaty of cooperation and assistance with Russia, enabling antigovernment forces to be cleared from Tajikistan by Russian forces.

November 1992   The GNR resigns; Imomali Rahmonov nominated as chairman of the Supreme Soviet's Executive Committee; civic truce proclaimed.

December 1992   Civic truce violated when the Popular Front—supported by the Russian 201st Motorized Rifle Division and the Uzbek air force—pushes opposition forces across the Panj River into Afghanistan.

July 13, 1993   Russian border post attacked by opposition forces, resulting in the death of 24 guards, 200 villagers, and 60 attackers.

November 1993   Russian diplomatic efforts begin; Tajik rebels resume fighting in Gorno-Badakhshan.

April 1994–May 1995   Four rounds of UN-sponsored talks held between the two sides. Russia, Afghanistan, Iran, Kazakhstan, Kyrgyzstan, Pakistan, and Uzbekistan serve as observers; OSCE and OIC are present.

October 1994   Cease-fire agreement signed in Islamabad; UN establishes a mission of military observers in Tajikistan (UNMOT).

November 1994   Rahmonov is elected president of Tajikistan, although opposition parties do not contest the election.

June 1995   Armed conflict continues in southern Tajikistan and on the Afghan border.

June 1996   Civil war escalates with Russian air attacks on opposition villages in south and central Tajikistan.

August–November 1996   Heavy fighting in central Tajikistan; rebels advance toward Dushanbe, threaten to take control of eastern parts of the country.

November 1996   Rahmonov signs new ceasefire agreement with opposition forces; National Reconciliation Council (NRC) is proposed to amend the constitution.

April 1997   Rahmonov wounded in assassination attempt, but UTO denies involvement.

June 27, 1997   Civil war officially ends with signing of General Agreement on Peace and National Accord in Tajikistan.

List of Acronyms

CIS: Commonwealth of Independent States
DPT: Democratic Party of Tajikistan
GDP: gross domestic product
GNR: Government of National Reconciliation
IRP: Islamic Renaissance Party of Tajikistan
NRC: National Reconciliation Commission
NGO: nongovernmental organization
OSCE: Organization for Security and Cooperation in Europe
PFT: Popular Front of Tajikistan
RPM: Rastokhez Popular Movement
TCP: Tajik Communist Party
UNHCR: United Nations High Commissioner for Refugees
UNMOT: United Nations Mission of Observers in Tajikistan
UTO: United Tajik Opposition

Glossary

autocracy: A form of government in which unlimited power is held by a single individual or a single party (one-party rule).

glasnost: A Russian word meaning "publicity" or "openness." One of Mikhail Gorbachev's policies introduced to the Soviet Union in 1985.

government forces: Ex–Communist Party members.

mahalgaroi: Loosely translated as "identity regionalism"; refers to groups whose main identity is based on blood and geographical origins and whose main loyalty is to the region.

mujahideen: Plural form of *mujahid*, from the Arabic for "struggler"; someone who engages in jihad, or struggle. Sometimes translated as "holy warrior" and more recently used to describe various armed fighters who subscribe to Islamist ideologies.

opposition; rebel forces; insurgents: A coalition of proreform and anticommunist political movements promoting national unity, democracy, or Islamic values.

perestroika: Russian for "restructuring"; refers to the economic transformation of the Soviet economy initiated by Mikhail Gorbachev in 1987.

Polity IV: An indicator of democratic development in which a rating of 10 means full democracy and –10 full autocracy.

Shi'a Muslims: Muslims who believe that Ali ibn Abu Talib (who was the Islamic prophet Muhammad's cousin) should have followed Muhammad as the direct successor and leader of the Muslims.

Sunni Muslims: The largest denomination of the Islam religion, Sunnis regard the first four caliphs as Rightly Guided Caliphs—caliphs who followed the tradition of the Prophet in terms of their lifestyles and styles of governance.

References

Akbarzadeh, Shahram. 1996. "Why Did Nationalism Fail in Tajikistan?" *Europe-Asia Studies* 48(7): 1105–29.

Akiner, Shirin. 2003. "Political Processes in Post-Soviet Central Asia," *Perspectives on Global Development and Technology,* 2(3/4).

Akiner, Shirin, and Catherine Barnes. 2001. *Tajikistan: Disintegration or Reconciliation?* London: The Royal Institute of International Affairs.

Central Intelligence Agency (CIA). 2006. *The World Fact Book: Tajikistan.* www.cia.gov/cia/publications/factbook/geos/ti.html (accessed November 24, 2006).

Collier, Paul, and Anke Hoeffler. 2000. *Greed and Grievance in Civil War.* Policy Research Working Paper Series 2355. Washington, DC: The World Bank.

Dunn, Michael Collins. 1997. "Great Games and Small: Afghanistan, Tajikistan and the New Geopolitics of Southwest Asia." *Middle East Policy* 5(2): 142–48.

Freedom House. 2005. *Freedom in the World: Tajikistan.* Country Report, 2005 Edition. . www.freedomhouse.org/template.cfm?page=22&year=2005&country=6844 (accessed November 24, 2006).

Gretsky, Sergei. 2006. *Civil War in Tajikistan: Causes, Developments and Prospects for Peace.* Washington, DC: The Eisenhower Institute. www.eisenhowerinstitute.org/programs/global partnerships/securityandterrorism/coalition/regionalrelations/ConflictBook/Gretsky.htm (accessed November 24, 2006).

Hampson, F. O. 1996. *Nurturing Peace: Why Peace Settlements Succeed or Fail.* Washington, DC: United States Institute of Peace Press.

Iji, Tetsuro. 2001. "Multiparty Mediation in Tajikistan: The 1997 Peace Agreement." *International Negotiation* 6(3): 357–385.

International Crisis Group. 2004. *Tajikistan's Politics: Confrontation or Consolidation?,* ICG Asia Report No. 33, May 19. www.crisisgroup.org/library/documents/asia/central_asia/040519_tajikistan_politics_confrontation_or_consolidation.pdf (accessed November 24, 2006).

International Monetary Fund. 2005. *Republic of Tajikistan: Selected Issues and Statistical Appendix,* IMF Country Report No. 05/131: April. www.imf.org/external/pubs/ft/scr/2005/cr05131.pdf (accessed November 24, 2006).

IRIN News Organization. 2005. "Tajikistan: OSCE Criticizes Parliamentary Polls." UN Office for the Coordination of Humanitarian Affairs, February 28. www.irinnews.org/report.asp?ReportID=45835 (accessed November 24, 2006).

Jonson, Lena, 1998. "The Tajik War: A Challenge to Russian Policy." Discussion Paper 74. London: The Royal Institute of International Affairs.

Marshall, Monty G., and Keith Jaggers. 2004. *Polity IV Country Report 2003: Tajikistan.* Center for International Development and Conflict Management. February. www.cidcm.umd.edu/inscr/polity/Taj1.htm (accessed November 24, 2006).

Neumann, Iver B., and Sergey V. Solodovnik. 1995. *Russian and CIS Peace Enforcement in Tajikistan,* Publication No. 1, Center for Russian Studies. December 31.

Plater-Zyberk, Henry. 2004. *Tajikistan: Waiting for a Storm*. Central Asian Series, 04/13, May. Conflict Studies Research Centre, Defence Academy of the United Kingdom.

Richter, Anthony. 1994. "Springtime in Tajikistan." *World Policy Journal* 11(2): 81–86.

Sambanis, Nicholas, 2002. "A Review of Recent Advances and Future Directions in the Quantitative Literature on Civil War." *Defence and Peace Economics* 13(3): 215–43.

Sherr, James. 1993. "Escalation of the Tajikistan Conflict." *Jane's Intelligence Review* (November): 514–16.

Transparency International. 2004. *Transparency International Corruption Perceptions Index 2004*. London: Transparency International. October 20. www.transparency.org/policy_research/surveys_indices/cpi/2004 (accessed November 24, 2006).

United Nations Humanitarian Commission for Refugees (UNHCR). 2005. "Over 10,000 Tajik Refugees to Become Citizens in Turkmenistan." August 10. www.unhcr.org/news/NEWS/42fa23954.html (accessed November 24, 2006).

United Nations International Children's Fund (UNICEF). 2005. *Statistics: Tajikistan*. www.unicef.org/infobycountry/Tajikistan_statistics.html#5 (accessed November 24, 2006).

United States Department of State. 2004. *Background Note: Tajikistan*. Bureau of European and Eurasian Affairs. October. www.state.gov/r/pa/ei/bgn/5775.htm (accessed November 24, 2006).

World Bank. 2005. *2005: World Development Indicators*. Washington, DC: The World Bank.

Turkey
(1984–1999 and 2004–Present)

Introduction

Turkey's Kurdish insurrection and its primary agent, the Kurdistan Workers Party (PKK), arose from a confluence of three principal forces, one historical, one political, and one circumstantial. The historical force was Turkey's ancient Kurdish population, whose nationalist ambitions predate the Turkish state itself. Described in Western literature as early as 401 BC by Xenophon, the Kurdish peoples have inhabited the Anatolian steppes since time out of memory. Although the Kurds have never organized as a modern nation-state, nationalist ambitions grew steadily in popularity and fervency throughout the twentieth century. The political force was a burgeoning socialist movement, replete with radical revolutionary elements. Although socialism arose purposefully during Turkey's political liberalization of the 1950s, its early form and character were relatively benign. By 1970s (a time of great political and economic upheaval in Turkey), socialist organizations were diverse and widespread; and although their popular appeal was still slim, they had organized cultivated revolutionary cells and promulgated militant agendas. The PKK would be born from the union of Kurdish nationalism and radical socialism. The circumstantial force was Turkey's military, who in September 1980 instigated a bloodless coup and declared martial law throughout much of the country. The PKK might have been content

to pursue redress through Turkey's legitimate political institutions, or to remain only a minor security threat, had it not been for the actions of the Turkish Armed Forces. To regain order from a state of near anarchy, sweeping arrests of dissidents ensued; and the PKK, feeling itself persecuted and seeing no further hope of accommodation through the (suspended) political process, resorted to armed insurrection.

The following war persisted virtually unabated to the present. Although two unilateral cease-fires were called by the PKK (1993–1994 and 1999–2004), neither was respected by either party and served only to lower the conflict's intensity. The insurrection also experienced increasing frustration on both sides, which served to steadily escalate the war's brutality. For its part, the Turkish government was widely accused of detaining civilians without charges, torturing suspects, carrying out extrajudicial executions, displacing populations, and making no serious efforts to address the "Kurdish question." The PKK, on the other hand, eventually resorted to terrorist tactics against Turkish interests at home and abroad, carrying out ferocious bombings, kidnappings, and assassinations against Turkish nationals, foreign tourists, military personnel, and numerous Kurdish civilians whom it considered government collaborators—at times attacking entire villages for "collaboration." Concerns over Turkey's treatment of the Kurds have complicated Turkey's admission to the European Union as well as its foreign relations and arms purchases. The PKK has earned Kurdish separatists an ignoble image, making it difficult for legitimate and peaceful Kurdish interest groups to gain sympathy. Not surprisingly, the PKK's tactics have caused it to be classified as a terrorist organization on both United States and European lists.

By 1999, more than 300,000 casualties had accumulated on both sides; deplorably, most were innocent civilians, and a significant number of whom (which will never be known) were neutral Kurds who discovered that neutrality and collaboration with one side or the other amounted to the same thing. More than 8,000 civilians were killed in PKK terrorist actions alone between 1984 and 1999. An unknown number were victims of mystery killings and disappearances attributed to Turkish police, intelligence, gendarmerie, and village guards acting on their own initiative. By 1999, the war's total cost exceeded an estimated US $200 billion. The war's tremendous human cost was also evident in the more than 300,000 Kurds made refugees by a conflict that frequently saw entire villages destroyed.

By spring 2004, normalcy had finally returned; shady MIT (National Intelligence Organization) agents no longer eavesdropped in local venues; police checkpoints and random personal searches were all but forgotten; PKK guerrillas no longer extorted "taxes" from Kurdish families or impressed their sons and daughters into service; Kurdish shepherds tended their flocks in pastures long cleared of land mines. But in May of that same year, the PKK ended their five-year cease-fire; civil war was declared anew. The repercussions of this for Turkey, the Kurds, and the PKK itself remain to be seen.

Country Background

The 1970s was a period of widespread political, social, and economic upheaval, which would see the decade end with parliamentary breakdown,

conditions of near anarchy, and a military coup to restore order. The country's already stagnating economy was severely hurt by oil shortages after 1973; by 1977, inflation exceeded 50 percent by some estimates, and unemployment had reached a staggering 30 percent (Glazer 1996). Turkey's industrial development slowed as oversea markets closed with increasing energy costs—Turkey's balance of trade reaching US $4 billion. The government's recovery efforts, which included energy conservation, import reductions, and two major devaluations of the Turkish lira, only reduced production further—and foreign investment was scant because of perceived government incompetence.

Amid this climate of rampant economic crises, radical political camps emerged on both ends of the spectrum, many of the more extreme parties forming strong-arm gangs. Politicized Islam led to sectarian violence (more than 100 Sunni and Alevi died in one day's violence in the town of Kahramanmaras in 1978, many of the Alevi having been burned alive). By the late 1970s, political strife had become increasing violent and by mid-1980 was claiming more than twenty lives a day (Glazer 1996).

In September 1980, following its inability to elect a new president, Turkey's parliamentary government was overthrown by the armed forces in a bloodless coup. The subsequent military government extended martial law, already in force in Istanbul and the Kurdish provinces, throughout the country. Following the coup, agitators, party leaders, student activists, and suspected militants of all political persuasions were arrested. Trade unions and political parties were abolished. By some estimates, as many as 30,000 people were arrested in the weeks following the coup—10,000 were still being held two years later (Glazer 1996).

In this climate of crackdown, Abdullah Öcalan and his followers fled the country and made contact with Palestinian militants in Lebanon's Bekaa valley, where they formally established the PKK and its first permanent training camps—convinced that the military coup

Table 1: Casualties Resulting from PKK Terrorism and Insurgency 1984–1998

Year	Major terrorist attacks	Civilians killed in major attacks	Civilians wounded in major attack	Civilians killed in other actions	Turkish security forces killed[†]	Terrorists and insurgents killed[‡]	Public and private facilities destroyed	Public and private facilities damaged
1984	-	-	-	20	24	11	0	0
1985	-	-	-	82	67	100	1	3
1986	-	-	-	74	43	64	7	3
1987	4	37	3	237	62	107	13	13
1988	2	38	0	81	50	103	13	22
1989	1	24	0	136	153	165	44	44
1990	0	0	0	178	169	350	12	17
1991	1	11	18	170	264	356	26	46
1992	3	70	59	761	755	1055	185	160
1993	6	176	37	1218	671	1699	255	263
1994	1	5	13	1082	1093	4114	134	239
1995	4	48	9	1085	584	2292	36	25
1996	4	35	23	*1000	419	3501	14	65
1997	2	11	19	*800	*300	n/a	60	92
1998	4	16	123	*600	*200	n/a	8	25
Total	32	471	304	7524	4854	13917	808	1017

Sources: Turkish Ministry of Foreign Affairs 2003; Facts on International Relations and Security Trends 2005; Institute for Counter-Terrorism Data 2005.

Notes: * Precise data for these years is unavailable.

† Includes military, police, and village guards.

‡ Includes terrorists killed in suicide bombings.

left them no political avenue to their goals, their only choice being armed revolution.

PKK insurgents first penetrated Turkish borders in 1984, just as civilian control was being restored. Although the ensuing conflict was financially very costly, it did not significantly affect Turkey's economic progress. Turkey's 1985 GDP was US $2.34 billion and had rocketed to US $154 billion by the first PKK-declared ceasefire in 1993.

Conflict Background

Although Turkey itself has not fought an interstate war since its war of independence (1919–1920), it is a frequent (and enthusiastic) participant in UN and NATO operations and has nearly gone to war with Greece on several occasions. Turkey maintains a high readiness for war, and its 514,000 men and women under arms represent the second-largest force contribution to NATO (the North Atlantic Treaty Organization) after the United States. The country's foreign policy, however, tends to be pragmatic and peace oriented. Turkey has consistently sought diplomatic solutions to achieving stability in its region of the world; a notable exception, however, is the Cyprus crisis.

In 1964, massacres of ethnic Turkish Cypriots by Greek Cypriots in favor of Cyprus's annexation by Greece were reported. Turkey threatened to intervene on behalf of the ethnic Turks in Cyprus but was warned in a letter from U.S. President Lyndon Johnson that should the Soviets oppose Turkey's intervention and enter the conflict against them, the United States would probably not come to their assistance. The so-called Johnson Letter provoked widespread resentment of the United States in Turkish public opinion, which persisted throughout the 1960s.

Turkey finally did intervene in Cyprus in 1974 (following a Greek-sponsored coup attempt on the island), deploying more than 40,000 troops and 200 tanks to the island and securing ethnic Turkish settlements in the north within a week. The United States countered with a trade embargo that lasted until 1978, which further strained U.S.–Turkish relations and exacerbated Turkey's struggling economy. As relations with the United States deteriorated, changes in Soviet policy gave Turkey the opportunity and incentive to improve relations with the Soviet Union.

In the end, the Cyprus intervention had little to do with the PKK's formation that same year; politically, it represents an event that distanced Turkey from the West and brought it closer to the Eastern bloc (until the 1980 coup); however, this did little to enhance leftist sympathies in Turkey. The intervention had broad popular support, low casualties, and came to a quick, satisfying conclusion—consistent with Ankara's military objectives. The war's most significant repercussions were the economic constraints imposed by U.S. sanctions—a significant trade partner, and (more importantly) a source of foreign aid. However, considering the economic impact of the 1973 energy crisis and the political impact of a hamstrung parliament and widespread urban violence, the Cyprus incident's economic effects must be viewed in context.

The Insurgents

Kurdish separatism is an intractable issue between Turks and Kurds and an issue shared by many of Turkey's neighbors. The Kurds are distributed among a number states: Turkey (14 million), Iran (6 million), Iraq (4–5 million), and Syria (fewer than 1 million), with smaller concentrations inhabiting Armenia and Azerbaijan. Although the Kurds are a linguistically and culturally distinct people inhabiting a largely contiguous area of land, their political aspirations

are complex. The rural Kurds—who comprise the population's majority—are organized around hierarchical clans who control their lands in a characteristically feudal arrangement. Disputes between these clans are common and frequently take on the character of bloody feuds. So, although the Kurds are ethnically homogeneous (the source of their nationalism), they are socially heterogeneous, with clan loyalty often overriding loyalty to any greater Kurdish nation (Cornell 2001). This has led others to accurately characterize Kurdish nationalism as akin to Arab nationalism in the early twentieth century; that is, however appealing the idea of a common national identity, the social reality makes its practical realization impossible. To further complicate matters, the PKK, the militant–political voice of Kurdish nationalism, espouses a Marxist-Leninist ideology that understandably disdains both Turkish hegemony in "Kurdistan" and the Kurd's own feudalistic social arrangement. Naturally, many Kurdish tribal leaders oppose the PKK's political ideology and are thus reluctant to support it.

The PKK itself is the militant incarnation of the political ideals of one man: Abdullah Öcalan, the PKK's charismatic founder and chief official. Öcalan was born in the Kurdish province of Sanlıurfa in 1949. After failing the entrance exam for Turkey's revered national military academy, he was accepted into Ankara University and studied political science. Öcalan was attracted to leftist political ideologies early in his university studies and became involved in the Marxist-Leninist and Maoist debate club the Revolutionary Youth Federation (Dev-Genc). These university debate clubs spawned many formal revolutionary organizations; one of these was the TPLA (Turkish People's Liberation Army), which intended to stage an armed socialist revolution in Turkey's impoverished Kurdish territories and which Öcalan later joined. The TPLA, however, did not see Kurdish liberation as separate from the country as a whole (viewing the southeastern territories as merely a logical starting point because of perceived social and economic repression in that region and favor-

Table 2: Civil War in Turkey

War:	PKK vs. government
Dates:	August 1984–September 1999 and May 2004–present
Casualties:	316,000
Regime type prior to war:	7 (ranging from –10 [authoritarian] to 10 [democracy])
Regime type after war:	7 (2003 data; ranging from –10 [authoritarian] to 10 [democracy])
GDP per capita year war began:	US $61.5 billion
GDP per capita 5 years after war:	Not applicable
Insurgents:	PKK (Kurdistan Workers Party)
Issue:	National liberation for ethnic Kurdish peoples in southeastern Anatolia
Rebel funding:	Organized crime, private sponsorship, occasional foreign aid.
Role of geography:	Mountainous Anatolian Plateau used for escape, headquarters, and training camps.
Role of resources:	Turkey's Kurdish territories have significant freshwater resources, including hydrological developments by the Turkish government.
Immediate outcome:	Turkish security forces quickly gained control, putting the PKK on the defensive.
Outcome after 5 years:	PKK expands its terrorist activities, begins soliciting aid from socialist states.
Role of UN:	None
Role of regional organization:	EU pressure on Turkey mitigated human rights abuses by security forces.
Refugees:	353,000; 26 percent repatriated since 1999 cease-fire.
Prospects for peace:	Unclear

Sources: CIA 2005; CSIS 2003.

able geography for armed insurrection). Öcalan, himself a Kurd and concerned more with Kurdish separatism itself, left the TPLA with a group of disciples, who called themselves the Apocu (Followers of "Apo," Abdullah Öcalan), and a preliminary plan for their own socialist–Kurdish revolution.

In 1974, Abdullah Öcalan, along with his brother Kesire Yildirim Öcalan and supporters Haki Karaer, Cemil Bayik, and Kemal Pir, founded the Kurdistan Workers Party as a Marxist-Leninist political party committed to establishing a socialist Kurdish state from the Kurdish portions of Turkey, Iraq, Iran, and Syria. Öcalan considered Turkey's Kurdish lands in the southeast to be Kurdistan's largest province and decided to focus his group's initial efforts there. Although they built up the membership, arms, and funding needed for a full-scale revolution, the PKK chose three Kurdish cities for its first wave of agitation: Diyarbakir, Şanliurfa, and Gaziantep (see map).

Diyarbakir had historical significance as the center of Kurdish revolts going back centuries. Şanliurfa had an entrenched feudal social structure, and its impoverished population had frequent conflicts with the government. Gaziantep was heavily industrialized and had a poor working class who, the PKK believed, would readily rally to their socialist cause (the PKK also established its first underground headquarters there at this time). In May 1977, the group came into conflict with another Kurdish socialist group, Sterka Sor (Red Star), which culminated in Karaer's assassination. This event marked a change in the PKK's composition and tactics. Following the attack, Abdullah Öcalan's brother, Kesire Yildirim, left the organization, and Öcalan organized counterassassinations of the Sterka Sor's members—effectively destroying the organization. Although the PKK strove to expand its membership and suppress its rivals, it also began trafficking illicit narcotics as a source of funding; Turkey itself, and the Kurdish territories

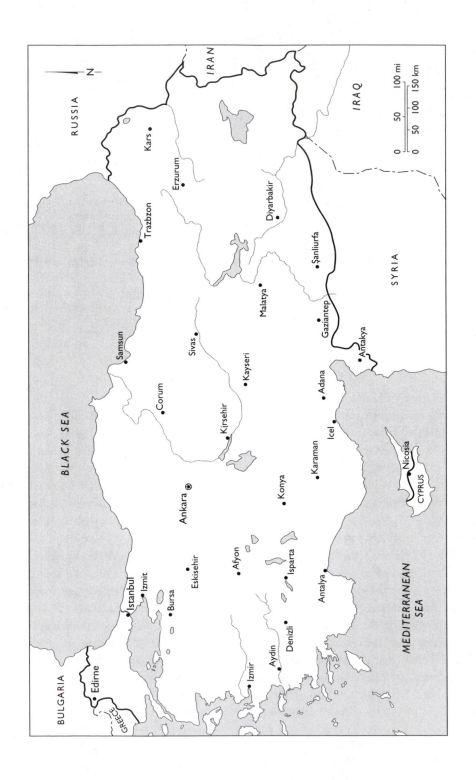

in particular, formed the principal clandestine drug route between Iran, Afghanistan, and European markets.

In November 1978, the Kurdistan Workers Party was officially formed. The PKK was organized around a president (Abdullah Öcalan) advised by a council of the presidency. A central committee forms the main decision-making body at the party level; individual provincial committees inform local committees, who organize individual cells. (The PKK's original structure remains relatively unchanged to this day, although since Öcalan's capture in 1999, there is no longer an office of the presidency; instead, the party is led by the council of the presidency.)

Because of their increasingly violent Communist agitation and criminal activities, several PKK members were arrested, and in 1979 Öcalan fled to Syria and thence to Lebanon. In Lebanon, Öcalan contacted Palestinian guerrillas and arranged for PKK militants to use their training facilities in Lebanon's Bekaa valley. Following the PKK's Second Party Congress, held in August of 1982, it was agreed that Palestinian-trained PKK guerrillas would begin infiltrating Turkey by late 1984 to initiate an armed uprising among Kurdish peasants.

Geography

Geography both helped and hindered PKK operations. The close proximity of ambivalent states allowed the PKK to withdraw to safety when pursued. Semipermanent mustering and supply bases were established in northern Iraq; and training camps, sometimes far abroad, allowed PKK militants to train in relative security—and in a socially isolated environment that facilitated ideological indoctrination. The disinterest of Turkey's southern neighbors and the simple remoteness of their Turkish borders meant that PKK rebels there were seldom confronted. The northern no-fly zone in Iraq (established at Turkey's behest to minimize Kurdish refugees during Operation Desert Storm in 1991) ensured that Iraq's government could not prosecute the PKK even if they had wanted to.

Although Turkey's military has from time to time crossed the Iraqi border to attack PKK bases or pursue militants, this tends to evoke chastisement from the international community. (Turkey's perennial ambitions for European Union admittance have tended to moderate its tactics in accord with what EU member states will tolerate.)

Most of the region called Northern Kurdistan is straddled by the craggy Taurus mountains, abutted by the Anatolian Plateau's semiarid steppes. The Tauruses dip into Northern Iraq and provide a natural border between the two countries. Vegetation is sparse and shrubby and provides little cover (although the PKK use what foliage exists to maximum effect when setting ambushes). The region experiences harsh winters, which, combined with absent vegetation, tend to reduce (but not arrest) the PKK's countryside guerrilla activity during the colder months. The Taurus mountains' high peaks and narrow passes help conceal PKK movements, and its guerrillas have constructed a complex system of independent caves for concealing themselves and caching supplies.

The same mountainous lands that give refuge to PKK guerrillas tend to hinder the very idea of Kurdish nationalism itself. The Taurus mountains have isolated the Kurds not unlike the Alps isolate the varied peoples of Switzerland. Rural Kurdish communities are remote from one another; their limited interaction over the centuries has fostered cultural idiosyncrasies and linguistic dialects among individual Kurdish enclaves. Many rural Kurds are still organized in feudalistic clans in which family loyalty is to the clan in general and the clan chieftain in particular, and to whom the idea of a Kurdish nation is remote to the point of meaninglessness. Some of these groups share centuries-old animosities that blind them to any idealistic notion of fraternity.

Tactics

PKK tactics, and those used by Turkey to confront them, have understandably evolved over the conflict's twenty-year history. Tactical changes and responses followed a typical pattern of measure and countermeasure. As the war's tactical evolution is best understood in the context of its various political and strategic developments, these too are discussed.

On the basis of tactical adaptation alone, the war can be divided into four phases according to the tactics employed and the strategic situation. The first phase (1984–1989) was characterized by relatively low-intensity fighting. The PKK was still a small organization with few militants and little support. The Turkish government did not take their threat seriously and opted for a defensive strategy that protected rural villages but failed to steal the PKK's initiative. The second phase (1989–1991) was characterized by a mature PKK—its membership enlarged, its arsenal cached, its training and tactics improved. Frequency and success of PKK attacks increased dramatically, and in response the government hurriedly developed an offense-oriented counterinsurgency program. Much of the countryside was under PKK influence (if not control), and attacks on major cities began. The third phase (1991–1996) was characterized by a maturing counterinsurgency program. Casualties during this phase were highest as the entrenched PKK was driven from its strongholds and the government slowly retook control. The PKK was forced to abandon its semipermanent bases in Turkey early on but operated effectively from foreign bases and roamed freely and fiercely at night. The Turkish military's first cross-border attacks took place, as did the first use of suicide bombings by the PKK. The fourth and final phase (1996–1999) was characterized by containment, with government control restored. Most of the heaviest fighting occured in northern Iraq, where the PKK still operated and trained recruits at remote bases. Finally, a ceasefire was called in 1999, with Abdullah Öcalan's arrest.

The first phase began in August 1984, when two groups of PKK guerrillas, under the command of Mazlum (Mahsun) Korkmaz, infiltrated Turkish territory from Syria. Their mission was threefold: first, to reconnoiter the Anatolian Plateau and Turkish security forces, attacking the latter as opportunity afforded; second, to form revolutionary committees and establish cells among the population; and third, to disseminate PKK propaganda. This initial PKK thrust would fail to achieve any of its objectives and would be forced to retreat to northern Iraq—pursued by Turkish border security.

In analyzing their failure, the PKK concluded that, as most of the guerrillas were university students, they did not understand local peoples, customs, or dialects; they were insufficiently trained and equipped to live in the rough Anatolian countryside; they had little information about the land or climate; they were insufficiently armed to fight the Turkish army; and they had inadequate logistics.

Following its defeats, the PKK held its third-party conference in August 1984 to reevaluate its strategy, tactics, and organization. It was decided that PKK military and political activities would be handled by two separate and specialized groups. PKK's armed component was designated the ARGK (Arteshen Rizgariya Gelli Kurdistan—the Kurdistan National Liberation Army). The ARGK adopted a formal military structure and chain of command: Its basic element, the group, consisted of seven to eleven soldiers; three groups formed a unit, and three units formed a platoon; three platoons formed a battalion, three battalions a brigade, and three brigades a regiment. By this time, the PKK had at least one complete regiment under arms (comprising between 1,700 and 2,800 militants), and thousands more sympathizers. The PKK's political component was designated ERNK (Eniya Rizgariya Netewa Kurdistan—Kurdistan People's Liberty Front). ERNK was tasked with some of the ARGK's support, such as recruitment and logistics, but focused on garnering finances and arousing public support for the organization, thus providing ARGK with intelligence, supplies, and refuge when in country. Once a support base was established in the countryside, ERNK would move into the cities to organize more robust regional supply chains.

The PKK's third Congress also addressed funding issues, and a "tax law" was drafted that allowed militants to extort money from Kurds to support their campaign—the taxes levied as "protection" money from wealthy Kurds. This would remain a source of funding throughout the organization's history, although it tended to hinge on PKK control of the cities and access to their inhabitants. Extortion efforts were later expanded to Kurdish businesspeople in Europe, many of whose murders abroad are believed to be the result of PKK extortion efforts. In addition to narcotics and extortion, the PKK also ran legitimate business and ostensible charities (particularly in Europe) devoted to Kurdish humanitarian relief.

Meanwhile, Turkish tactics were also evolving to deal with the embryonic revolution. Following initial PKK attacks in 1984, the Turkish prime minister, Turgut Özal, and his Motherland Party formed an institution of temporary "village guards." Select Kurds in particularly violent territories were trained as paramilitaries to protect the lives and property of their fellow villagers. The village guard system was a turning point in the government's fight against the PKK—although it also occasioned the first in a bloody series of conflict escalations. The village guards were intended to fight the PKK while building up government support among the Kurds, and there was even an expectation that the village guards would moderate the PKK's ambitions, as they would be faced with fighting fellow Kurds and, seeing that the government had Kurdish support, more willing to renounce violence. The PKK, however, showed no compunction in attacking the village guards themselves—and, as a retributive measure, retaliated against the guardsmen's families as well. (Through the PKK's deterrent policy of deliberately attacking civilian collaborators, its reputation as a terrorist organization began to grow.) By 1987, PKK forces were attacking entire villages for "collaborating" with the enemy.

The village guard strategy was defensive in nature, however. It sought only to protect lives and property, and to inhibit PKK recruitment activities in the villages themselves. That the Turkish government did not take any concerted military action against the PKK throughout the 1980s emphasizes the Özal administration's belief that the PKK were little more than brigands and were not a threat to the Turkish state. Indeed, unrest in the Kurdish provinces was attributed to economic and social underdevelopment. Moreover the Turkish Land Forces (TLF) themselves were trained, organized, positioned, and equipped to fight a conventional war (which was expected to be defensive in nature), anchoring NATO's right flank. The anticipated battlefield was not the Anatolian plateau but Turkey's northern borders with (Soviet) Armenia and Azerbaijan or its western border with Greece; force distribution and organization reflected this.

In response to escalating PKK violence, the government adopted a second defense-oriented

Table 3:
Kurdish Peoples Living Abroad

Country	Kurdish Population
Germany	500,000–600,000
France	100,000–120,000
Israell	100,000–120,000
Lebanon	80,000–85,000
The Netherlands	70,000–80,000
Switzerland	60,000–70,000
Belgium	50,000–60,000
Austria	50,000–60,000
Sweden	25,000–30,000
United Kingdom	20,000–25,000
Greece	20,000–25,000
United States	15,000–20,000
Denmark	8,000–10,000
Canada	6,000–7,000
Norway	4,000–5,000
Italy	3,000–4,000
Finland	2,000–3,000

Source: CIA 2005.

policy. Echoing strategies used by the United States in Vietnam to drain the Viet Cong's support base, entire Kurdish villages were forcibly relocated. These "evacuations" were intended to move endangered populations to better-controlled areas of the country. Initially, evacuated rural villages were moved to the major cities, but this radical change in environment often left pastoral Kurds bewildered and resentful. The first forced refugees tended to be poorly supported, and many became vagrants. International outcry and governmental attempts to minimize Kurdish malcontent resulted in compensation funds for deported people, state-managed refugee camps, and, later, state-built temporary housing. In all, more than 850 Kurdish hamlets and villages were forcibly evacuated and subsequently burned to deny their property to the PKK. However, the Turkish government stands accused in some cases of burning villages as a punitive measure in areas of PKK sympathy.

Although the village guard strategy did succeed at frustrating PKK operations in villages, it put little pressure on the organization itself. The PKK used this period to accumulate arms, train recruits, and gather foreign support and funding. Developing a specialization in ambush tactics, their preferred targets became soldiers on border patrol and TLF convoys on Turkey's southern highways. Border patrol garrisons themselves also made attractive targets because their small complement and remote locations made them easy to overwhelm.

By the early 1990s (beginning the war's second phase), the TLF was developing a respectable capability in counterinsurgency warfare. Having studied American tactics in Vietnam, the military concluded that U.S. failures resulted from the faulty strategy of killing insurgents faster than they could be replaced, rather than controlling territory. Instead of emulating Vietnam-style search-and-destroy missions, Turkey opted to station large numbers of soldiers in the countryside and develop a visible presence in Kurdish villages. One American tactic in which Turkey took particular interest was the use of helicopters

as air cavalry. Improved battlefield mobility being emphasized, fleets of helicopters rapidly transported soldiers to any area where PKK contact was made. Thus, the Turkish army could concentrate its forces in overwhelming numbers where and when needed, choosing the optimum times for their attacks. Like the United States, Turkey appreciated the value of helicopter gunships to support these operations. During this phase of the conflict, Turkey struggled to expanded and modernized its attack helicopter force of American-supplied AH-1 Cobra and AH-64 Apache gunships, though acquisition efforts were frustrated by effective pro-Kurdish lobbying in the U.S. Congress.

By 1996, operations against the PKK had moved out of the villages and into the surrounding hills and mountains. Direct military operations against PKK guerrillas became more common. The military's maturing night-fighting capability prevented PKK guerrillas and cadres from infiltrating villages; therefore, police forces and village guards became less involved in anti-PKK operations, and reports of civilian mistreatment decreased. By some assessments, village life returned to normal. Because large-scale military operations were now conducted away from populated areas, civilian casualties were minimized.

Turkish tactics during this fourth period emphasized open-country warfare and tended to favor combined arms operations, including commandos and infantry transported by helicopter (usually the UH-1 Iroquois or the UH-60 Black Hawk) or by armored personnel carriers (APCs) supported by attack helicopters. The multirole F-16s of the Turkish air force provided aerial bombardment and close air support. As Turkish air attacks increased, the PKK also began using FIM-92 Stinger missiles of German origin. The Stingers' battlefield effect was negligible, however, as they were seldom seen in fighting or captured in caches and were probably in very short supply.

This same year saw a dramatic change in PKK tactics that many interpreted as a sign of desperation: suicide bombings. Between 1996 and 1999, PKK terrorists carried out sixteen successful suicide attacks, killing twenty people. Targets varied from tourists to police headquarters to government and military facilities. Female suicide bombers were used for the first attacks—with explosives strapped to their bellies as if pregnant.

Meanwhile, by the mid-1990s Turkey had more than 70,000 village guards under arms, who served in a high-risk capacity but were paid an attractive salary (Ismet 1995). They were typically lightly armed with Russian or Turkish-made automatic rifles. Participation in the village guards was ostensibly voluntary, although recruiters often considered refusal to join as a sign of PKK sympathy or collaboration. Widespread allegations of corrupt village guards also began emerging. Some village guards being found guilty of consorting with the PKK, participating in their extortion and tax collecting activities, and even fighting alongside them. Other village guards being accused of extrajudicial violence against Kurdish villagers they believed to be PKK conspirators, which included unsupervised searches, interrogations, and occasional extrajudicial executions. It must be appreciated that, among widespread reports of civilian deaths and disappearances, it was often unclear which side was responsible.

In response to growing complaints of mistreatment, by 1994 the Turkish military issued its "Guide to Principles of Behaviors." Distributed specifically to soldiers in Turkey's southeast, the guide encouraged soldiers and officers to familiarize themselves with and respect local peoples and customs; among other things, the guide laid down strict guidelines for searches and interrogations, specifically prohibiting village guards from performing such activities unsupervised. Acknowledging that abuses were inevitable in a conflict of this kind, the Turkish government also established a fund to compensate civilians for any damage to property resulting from searches or collateral damage, later extended to compensate civilians whose property had been damaged

or destroyed by the PKK. Critics argue, however, that these guidelines were not consistently applied or enforced and compensation funds insufficient. Although breaching the 1994 principles was considered a violation of military discipline and law—risking dishonorable discharge, up to five years of hard labor, and forfeiture of future public office—the conviction rate equaled only about 3 percent of cases filed (U.S. Department of State 1997).

In 1996, the Turkish military and police began special training in human rights for new recruits and officers and enlisted personnel in the field. The Turkish military also adopted a policy of "appropriate force," whereby greater attention was paid to the size and composition of an enemy body and the proportional force of arms required to destroy it. As a result, collateral damage reportedly declined. To improve its army's image among Kurds, Turkey also began tasking its soldiers with "goodwill" missions, using the military construction corps to make visible infrastructural improvements in the Kurdish territories. In this way, Ankara intended to confront much of the region's underdevelopment (which many still believed was behind the rebellion) while putting a government face on these improvements to win the Kurdish people's hearts and minds.

Casualties on both sides of the fighting peaked in 1996 but declined as the PKK's popular support diminished and government forces took control of the countryside; at this point, the conflict entered its fourth phase. The PKK suffered a severe blow when Syria finally bowed to Turkish pressure and agreed to evict the PKK from its territory. Northern Iraq was considered too dangerous for the PKK leadership, so Abdullah Öcalan and his council went into hiding. Öcalan applied for political asylum across Europe but was consistently denied. His eventual capture by a joint Turkish, American, and Israeli effort forced the war's second cease-fire in 1999. Öcalan's highly central role in the PKK prevented the organization from functioning without him for some time.

Causes of the War

Turkey's Kurdish insurrection had no single cause, although historical circumstances played a key role. First was the ideological notion of Kurdish nationalism: that Kurds, being a linguistically and culturally distinct people, ought to be afforded self-government. These ideas were not new and followed the wave of nationalist movements that swept across Europe in the late nineteenth century, breaking upon Levantine shores by the World War I to inspire the Arab revolt. The Turkish state itself was originally conceived and fought for under nationalism's banner, with the Kurds embraced under the label "Mountain Turks." Among Kurds, nationalist sentiment was most pronounced among educated Kurds living in cities. Rural Kurds (who represent the population's majority) in their close-knit feudalistic clans found nationalism's claim of a monolithic Kurdish identity much less convincing, and clan leaders found such ideas threatening to their positions. So, although the Kurds are ethnically homogeneous (the source of their nationalism), they are socially heterogeneous, with clan loyalty often overriding loyalty to any greater Kurdish nation (Cornell 2001). Nevertheless, Kurdish nationalism's advocates have persisted throughout Turkey's history. Turkish politics has always had an undercurrent of Kurdish nationalism, though the nationalists themselves are divided over whether autonomy (greater self-government within the Turkish state) or separatism (seceding from the Turkish state altogether) is the appropriate solution.

The second ideological issue was the influence of leftist political ideology. Turkey's first military coup d'état (in 1960) was primarily a reaction to what the military perceived to be growing authoritarianism in the government. (When Turkey's democratically elected government tried to extend its influence to the military itself by interfering with promotions and appointments, the military's reaction was, in a sense, one of self-defense). Following the coup, the military junta drafted a new liberal constitution (Turkey's Second Republic) that allowed or-

ganizations on the extreme left (previously excluded) to form legal political parties. Although the Second Republic constitution did help expand the influence of radical ideologies, it should be remarked that leftist organizations have always been an extremely marginal element of Turkish politics. For example, in the 1980 elections, just prior to the September coup, only four of Turkey's seven Marxist-oriented parties managed to gather 1 percent of the national vote (Tartter 1996).

Turkey's economic problems throughout the 1970s made leftist economic theories and political ideologies more attractive to many Turks, particularly university students. Several student movements with Marxist, Leninist, or Maoist ideologies took part in revolutionary activities to bring about a socialist Turkish state. Among these organizations, one in particular, the Turkish People's Liberation Army (TPLA), was intent on starting a revolution in Turkey's southeast—the most underdeveloped part of the country—convinced that, if they were successful, other socialist states, particularly the Soviet Union, would come to their aid. Abdullah Öcalan was originally a member of the TPLA, but because they did not see Kurdish separatism as a distinct objective, Öcalan and many followers splintered from the group and formed their own organization combining Marxist-Leninist ideology with Kurdish nationalism.

This is where historical circumstances intervene. Öcalan might have been more willing to pursue his goals politically in the Turkish parliament had the entire country not had such little faith in it, or if the military had not intervened when it did and abolished political parties. Anatolia's southeast was attractive from a Marxist perspective because of its underdeveloped feudal countryside and industrializing cities with large burgeoning (and perceivably exploited) working class. Leninist ideology made Kurdish separatism all the more convincing and imperative, for it saw the Kurds as an exploited nation, imperially subjugated by the Turkish state. What was generally perceived as an ineffective government when Öcalan's following was formed came to be perceived as an oppressive, authoritarian, military, government by the time the PKK began guerrilla operations in earnest in 1984.

Outcome

Following Abdullah Öcalan's capture and the subsequent 1999 PKK cease-fire, many observers believed the conflict was over, at least in terms of its previous scale and intensity, but Turkey's bloody conflict with the PKK is still going on. Violence diminished during two unilateral cease-fires called by the PKK. The first (1993–1994) was intended to boost dwindling PKK moral in late 1992 following the increasing success of village guards and Turkey's military. The second PKK cease-fire was called by Öcalan after his capture by Turkish security forces in Kenya. During that cease-fire, the longest and most successful yet, the PKK changed its name to KADEK (Kurdistan Freedom and Democracy Congress) at its 2002 party conference and proclaimed a commitment to nonviolence in support of Kurdish rights—particularly to pursue its goals legitimately through Turkey's parliament. However, the KADEK surrendered neither their arms nor any of their members to Turkish justice; they retained their foreign bases and the ability to resume formal hostilities at any time. Although the KADEK claimed these conditions were necessary for purposes of self-defense, many saw this as an indication that the group was not fully committed to a peaceful, democratic solution. Moreover, during the cease-fire's intervening years, terrorist attacks continued sporadically in Turkish cities. Although KADEK never formally acknowledged complicity in any of them, their organization was linked to several (according to Turkish security). The KADEK changed its name to Kongra-Gel (KGK) in 2003 in an attempt to disassociate itself with alleged violence committed under the KADEK label, although Kongra-Gel has been linked to at least one terrorist attack since then.

Conflict Status

Charging that Ankara's concessions were symbolic and that meaningful change was not happening swiftly enough, in 2004 Kongra-Gel changed its name back to PKK and resumed guerrilla operations against Turkish security forces from its bases and training camps in northern Iraq, which had never been dismantled. Turkey's military implored the United States and the Iraqi government to put pressure on the PKK's Iraqi operations, but although the United States in particular concurred that the PKK needed to be dealt with, it did nothing, as its forces were occupied with suppressing Iraq's own insurgency. Finally, with tacit approval from the United States, Turkey quietly resumed its cross-border attacks against PKK bases in March 2005. The PKK presently has an estimated 4,000 to 5,000 militants, of which 500 are believed to be in Turkey, 500 in Iran and 4,000 in northern Iraq (U.S. Department of State 2005). The organization was expelled from Syria under a joint Turkish–Syrian agreement in October 1998 and still has thousands of sympathizers in Turkey and Europe.

Duration Tactics

Why has Turkey's Kurdish insurrection persisted (at various levels of intensity) for nineteen years? The first reason is the war's evolutionary nature; the conflict did not erupt spontaneously but escalated very gradually. This was partly because of the PKK's own beleaguered development. Although its goals and purposes seemed clear at the outset, putting these ideas into action was another matter. The PKK's Kurdish worker's revolution was confronted with a couple of false starts and constantly reevaluated and adjusted its tactics. The Turkish government was slow to react to the PKK threat and, by underestimating the PKK's early popularity and tenacity, was complacent in mounting a concerted opposition, thus giving the PKK's forces time to perfect its tactics while expanding its organization and sphere of influence.

Guerrilla fighters of the Kurdistan Workers Party (PKK) listen to instructions from their team commander in a camp near Arbil in northern Iraq on August 11, 2005. The Kurdish conflict in Turkey has claimed some thirty-seven thousand lives since 1984, when the PKK took up arms for Kurdish self-rule in southeastern Turkey. (Mustafa Ozer/AFP/Getty Images)

Even after the Turkish government seized the initiative, its prosecution of the PKK was impeded by the ease with which Kurdish fighters could melt away across Turkey's borders. Thus, the war degenerated into a stalemate in which, although the military tended to have control of the villages and much of the countryside, insurgents were still free to launch attacks from positions of relative safety and increase their reliance on terrorist tactics.

Throughout this, the PKK endeavored to improve its funding situation, finding a lucrative source in the smuggling of illicit narcotics (particularly opiates and hashish) into Europe. The PKK was organizationally well-suited to this task. Its operations were clandestine to begin with, and it was organized into isolated cells that could conceivably carry out any mission while benefiting from compartmentalized security. PKK militants roamed over a territory where drug smuggling was already pervasive, said territory being a major corridor for opium smuggled from Iran and Iraq to Europe. The PKK's logistical network, once established, could move narcotics as speedily and surreptitiously as it did arms and supplies. Clandestine cells in the cities often were devoted to drug processing, and their refined product was transported to İstanbul or other port cities and thence to Cyprus, a narcotics nexus for drugs entering Europe. No precise data exist on any of the PKK's illegal fund-raising activities, though the drug trade is believed to be its primary and most lucrative source of funding—one from which it continues to profit.

External Military Intervention

Although no foreign arms have intervened on the PKK's behalf (the cause of Kurdish separatism being no more popular in Syria, Iraq, and Iran than it is in Turkey), all three countries have disputes with Turkey on issues ranging from territorial claims to water rights to oil exploration. These three states have tended to pressure the Turkish government by contributing funds or arms to the PKK and by ignoring PKK bases in their respective territories.

Turkey's hydrological projects in southeast Anatolia are a particular bone of contention. Dams along the Euphrates River restrict Syria's and Iraq's freshwater supply, thus frustrating their own efforts to expand agriculture along the Euphrates. Syria in particular has a history of enthusiastically supporting anti-Turkish forces from Armenian terrorists to Kurdish guerrillas; and this support seems to be linked to progress or regress in Syria's ongoing water negotiations with Turkey.

Iran and Turkey share a pronounced ideological animosity. Turkey is a progressive, Western-oriented, secular Islamic republic; Iran is an Eastern-oriented Islamic theocracy—and each country strongly associates its politics with its national character. Although Iran ignored the PKK throughout much of the 1980s (finding their atheistic Marxist-Leninist orientation understandably unsavory), by the early 1990s the PKK was reforming its image. By that time, the PKK had begun to realize that far too many Kurds also found the PKK's atheistic ideology untenable, and thus the organization began to downplay the atheistic teachings of Marx and to pepper their propaganda with Islamist rhetoric. Their new goal of an Islamic Kurdish state was greeted by Tehran, and training facilities were constructed just across the Iranian border.

Overall, the tacit support the PKK received from Turkey's neighbors certainly extended the war. Although Turkey's military typically managed to secure the Turkish countryside, the guerrillas were always able to withdraw across borders into accommodating states. By the early 1990s, the PKK had no permanent or even semipermanent bases in Turkey itself; nearly all guerrilla operations were organized and staged from abroad.

The complacency and complicity of Turkey's neighbors certainly extended the war by a decade—one that witnessed the war's bloodiest actions on both sides, as well as its greatest humanitarian cost to so many neutral Kurds, to whom the war had brought nothing but persecution, misery, and death.

Conflict Managment Efforts

Conflict management efforts on the part of other governments, NGOs, or the UN have been minimal. Turkey has insisted throughout the conflict that the PKK is an internal security concern; unwilling to lend legitimacy to the PKK's activities, Turkey has repeatedly downplayed the conflict's guerrilla aspects, has emphasized the PKK as a terrorist organization, and has stated emphatically that government was winning the fight. Turkey has never participated in any cease-fire with the PKK or any form of negotiation and would regard any third party's intervention as legitimizing what the Turkish foreign ministry continues to call "the world's most notorious terrorist organization" (Turkish Ministry of Foreign Affairs 2003).

For its part, the PKK rejects the terrorist label, insisting that it does not attack civilians and that it conducts its war in strict accordance with the four Geneva Conventions (Öcalan 1995)—although the PKK's definition of *civilian* tends to be narrower than the Geneva Conventions permit, as it excludes elected and appointed (unarmed) representatives of the state in Kurdish provinces, and its attacks are consistently carried out with reckless disregard for civilian casualties.

However, foreign states (particularly the United States, Turkey's principal arms provider) and the EU have certainly influenced the conflict. Kurdish and human rights lobbies in the United States consistently seek to block sales and transfers to Turkey of arms that might be used in the Kurdish conflict. The EU has voiced particular concern over allegations of human rights abuses by Turkish security forces, and at Turkey's incursions into northern Iraq, which are considered violations of international law and the 1991 imposed northern no-fly zone. These objections certainly have positively affected the war's humanitarian aspects, for international pressure has resulted in better human rights training and an overall reduction in abuses. This likely served to improve the government's image in Kurdish eyes and frustrated PKK recruitment and propaganda efforts. However, the international condemnation evoked by Turkey's cross-border attacks has tended to restrain their frequency, duration, and intensity— which has likely served only to aid the PKK and prolong the war.

Conclusion

To consider the future of Turkey's violent struggle with the PKK is to consider two separate outcomes: the military consequences of the war itself and the future of Turkey's Kurdish peoples. The Middle East's Kurds are among its most ancient populations (described by Herodotus and Xenophon in the fifth century BC), but they have never in recorded history had a country of their own. For more than 2,500 years, they have lived as citizens of one mighty empire or another: the Persian, the Seleucid, the Persian (again), and finally the Ottoman.

After World War I, President Woodrow Wilson listed among his Fourteen Points the self-determination of all nations (including the Kurds), but British and French interests in territory and oil left the Kurds divided between the European postwar mandates. The Kurds fought alongside and supported Atatürk in Turkey's war of independence (1919–1920), not wishing their lands to come under Armenian or Russian control. However, they quickly fell victim to Turkey's assimilationist programs, which sought a singular and cohesive Westernized culture. For brief periods, speaking Kurdish and wearing Kurdish dress were imprisonable offenses in Turkey. Kurdish nationalists were active in Turkish politics from the republic's founding but divided when it came to appropriate goals. When leftist theories of armed revolution overlapped

the plight of Turkey's impoverished Kurds, all it took was a visionary, charismatic, and ruthless leader to cement them with Kurdish nationalist aspirations.

Turkey's constitution lists the state's territorial integrity as one of three "irrevocable" constitutional articles, and thus the government will make no concessions with respect to an independent Kurdish state, which convinced the PKK that armed insurrection was its only hope. After nearly a decade of guerrilla warfare and terrorism, however, the PKK was no closer to its goal. If any solution exists to the Kurdish question, it will likely come about only with a more cohesive Kurdish political unity.

Although the PKK recently resumed its insurgency, its guerrilla war shows little hope of succeeding if the newly formed Iraqi government or the resident United States military force works to drive the PKK from northern Iraq. Deprived of these bases, the militants have no other refuge from which to stage their attacks. How long it will take for the PKK to be removed from Iraq, however, depends on how quickly Iraq's own insurgency is suppressed. In the five years since the 1999 cease-fire, Turkey has striven to secure its southeastern provinces, making future attempts at infiltration unlikely. Unfortunately, it is likely that, even if the PKK's guerrilla forces are decisively defeated, its terrorist elements may long endure. The organization still has many cells throughout Turkish cities and maintains its involvement in organized crime.

As for the Kurds themselves, Turkey's fight with the PKK has given Kurdish separatism a bad name and has probably hindered what might otherwise have been a constructive dialogue between Turks and Kurds. One positive outcome, however, is that the conflict has induced the Turkish government to treat the Kurds and Kurdish culture with greater respect—if for no other reason than to retain their loyalty. The government's Southeast Anatolian Project (GAP), which is finally coming to fruition, should create more jobs and improve the region's standard of living, thus eliminating one of the war's key contributing factors.

What is most encouraging for the Kurdish people is that, over the years, the Turkish state has come to see itself differently—no longer as the political expression of the Turkish nation but as a modern civil consociation capable of embracing diverse peoples under a common rule of law. This transformation parallels nationalism's general decline the world over. As ethnopolitics loses its coherence for the Turks, perhaps in time it will for the Kurds as well.

Peter Finn

Chronology

1971   Turkish military takes power in Turkey's second coup; constitution is amended to limit civil rights.

1978   Martial Law is declared in thirteen southeastern Turkish provinces. Abdullah Öcalan establishes PKK.

1980   Turkish military instigates a bloodless coup; Kurdish nationalists suffer harsher repression as political parties are abolished and dissidents arrested.

1984   PKK begins guerrilla operations against Turkish government; military personnel and police forces are its primary targets. First phase of conflict begins, characterized by relatively low-intensity fighting.

1985   Village guards established in response to initial PKK attacks.

1988   Turkish government gives its governor-general of the Kurdish provinces authority to evacuate villages and deport the population.

1989   Turgut Özal is elected president. Second phase of conflict begins. PKK insurgency gains membership and momentum. Turkish military begins offense-orientated counterinsurgency program.

1990–1991   Operation Desert Shield/Desert Storm is mounted. Northern Iraqi Kurds revolt against Iraqi government; uprising is suppressed, thousands of Kurds flee to Turkey and Iran. Turkish military begins attacking PKK bases in northern Iraq. Third phase of conflict begins; Turkish counterinsurgency efforts gain momentum.

1992   Iraqi Kurds support the Turkish military and attack PKK bases in Northern Iraq.

1993–1994   PKK declares unilateral cease-fire and drops demands for Kurdish independence. After Turkish president Özal dies, negotiations end and conflict resumes. PKK begins to moderate Marxist-Leninist rhetoric for greater Muslim appeal. Turkey begins combined air and ground operations against PKK camps in Northern Iraq.

1994   Turkey begins air strikes against PKK bases in northern Iraq.

1996   First PKK suicide bombings occur. Turkey declares new security zone in northern Iraq. Conflict transitions into fourth phase.

1997   Turkey invades northern Iraq with more than 50,000 troops in ten-week-long Operation Hammer; an estimated 3,000 PKK guerrillas are killed.

1998–1999   Kurdish commandos arrest Abdullah Öcalan in Kenya. Turkish court sentences Öcalan to death. PKK declares a second cease-fire.

2004   PKK cease-fire keeps conflict intensity low, but is respected by neither side. PKK abrogates its second cease-fire; conflict resumes.

2005   Turkish forces recommence attacks against PKK bases in northern Iraq; their land forces make incursions into Iraq's northern territory in hot pursuit of PKK insurgents.

List of Acronyms

AH-1: Bell-Textron Cobra/Super Cobra/King Cobra

AH-64: Boeing Apache attack helicopter

APC: armored personnel carrier

ARGK: Kurdistan National Liberation Army

CHP: Cumhuriyet Halk Partisi (Republican People's Party)

Dev-Genc: Revolutionary Youth Federation

DHKP/C: Revolutionary People's Liberation Party/Front

DP: Democratic Party

ERNK: Eniya Rizgariya Netewa Kurdistan (Kurdistan People's Liberty Front)

EU: European Union

GAP: Güneydoğu Anadolu Projesim (Southeastern Anatolian Project)

GDP: gross domestic product

KADEK: Kurdistan Freedom and Democracy Congress

KGK: Kongra-Gel

MIT: Millî İstihbarat Teşkilatı (National
Intelligence Organization)
NATO: North Atlantic Treaty Organization
NGO: nongovernmental organization
PKK: Partiye Karkêran Kurdistan (Kurdistan
Workers Party)
TAF: Turkish Armed Forces
TPLA: Turkish People's Liberation Army
TLF: Turkish Land Forces
UH-1: Bell Iroquois utility helicopter (a.k.a.
Huey)

References

Bodnarchuk, Kari. 2000. *Kurdistan: Region Under Siege.* Minneapolis: Lerner.

Center for Strategic and International Studies (CSIS). 2003. *The Military Balance, 2003–2004.*

Central Intelligence Agency (CIA). 2005. *World Factbook: Kurdish Diaspora.* www.institutkurde.org

Cornell, Erik. 2001. *Turkey in the 21st Century.* Richmond, Surrey, UK: Curzon Press.

Criss, Nur Bilge. 1995. "The Nature of PKK Terrorism in Turkey." *Studies in Conflict and Terrorism* 8: 17–37.

Facts on International Relations and Security Trends (FIRST). 2005. first.sipri.org/ (accessed November 21, 2005).

Glazer, Steven. 1996. "Historical Setting." In *Turkey: A Country Study,* edited by Helen Metz, 1–68. Washington DC: Federal Research Division, Libarary of Congress.

Gunter, Michael. 1997. *The Kurds and the Future of Turkey.* New York: St. Martin's Press.

Institute for Counter-Terrorism. 2005. www.ict.org.il/ (accessed November 21, 2005).

Ismet, G. 1995. "The PKK: Freedom Fighters or Terrorists?" *American Kurdish Information Network* 7.

Kasaba, Reşat. 2001. "Kurds in Turkey: A Nationalist Movement." In *Ethnopolitical Warfare: Causes, Consequences, and Possible Solutions,* edited by Daniel Chirot and Martin Seligman, 163–78. Washington, DC: American Psychological Association.

O'Ballance, Edgar. 1973. *The Kurdish Revolt: 1961–1970.* London: Faber and Faber.

Olcott, Martha. 1999. "New States and New Identities: Religion and State Building in Central Asia." In *Ethnic Conflict and International Politics in the Middle East,* edited by Leonard Binder, 245–76. Gainsville, FL: University Press of Florida.

Öcalan, Abdullah. 1995. *PKK Statement to the United Nations.* Geneva, Switzerland: The Kurdistan Workers Party (PKK).

Tartter, Jean. 1996. "National Security." In *Turkey: A Country Study,* edited by Helen Metz, 307–73. Washington, DC: Federal Research Division, Library of Congress.

Taspinar, Omer. 2005. *Kurdish Nationalism and Political Islam in Turkey: Kemalist Identity in Transition.* New York: Routledge.

Turkish Ministry of Foreign Affairs. 2003. www.mfa.gav.tr/MFA/ForeignPolicy/Mainissues/Terrorism (accessed June 1, 2005).

U.S. Department of State. 1997. *U.S. Military Equipment and Human Rights Violations.* Report Submitted to the Senate Foreign Relations Committee, July 1. www.nisat.org/export_laws-regs%20linked/usa/report_on_turkey.htm (accessed November 15, 2006).

Uganda
(1986–Present)

Introduction

Uganda is situated in a region of Africa that has been directly affected by many recent and ongoing civil wars. The Democratic Republic of the Congo (DRC), Sudan, Burundi, Rwanda, and the Central African Republic have all experienced internal armed conflicts since the end of the Cold War. Uganda is a particularly tragic case. Once regarded by British colonial authorities as the "pearl of Africa," the country seems to have been caught in an endless cycle of internal violent struggles since its accession to independence in 1962. In the last forty years, governments in Kampala have been removed by military coups, by foreign invasion, and by armed rebellion.

Still, the International Monetary Fund (IMF) considers Uganda a positive model because its yearly economic growth rate rose to an average of 5 percent following monetary reform in 1987. Indeed, the website of the British Broadcasting Corporation (BBC News) presents Uganda as a country that "has rebounded from the abyss of civil war and economic catastrophe to become relatively peaceful, stable and prosperous" (BBC 2005). For many observers of economic development in Africa, Uganda represents something of a success story.

Country Background

The British connection with Uganda is an essential part of Uganda's history and current international relations. Following decades of contact with foreign traders and missionaries, much of the territory known today as Uganda became a British protectorate in 1894. In the context of the decolonization movements following World War II, the British granted internal self-government to Uganda in 1961. Prime Minister Milton Obote led the country to formal independence on October 9, 1962.

Political life in Uganda during the following years was marked by a struggle between supporters of a centralized state and supporters of a loose federation that recognized various tribal kingdoms. Backed by his largely Langi and Acholi soldiers from the north of Uganda, Obote eventually took over all government powers in February 1966 and then proceeded to appoint himself president in a new republic that abolished the traditional kingdoms. Despite Obote's attempts in the late 1960s to broaden his military-based rule by gaining popular support with the partial nationalization of major industries and banks, it was not long before his army commander, Idi Amin, staged a coup in January 1971 while Obote was attending a Commonwealth Conference in Singapore.

Over the next eight years, Idi Amin generally eliminated democratic institutions and ruled by decree. Many analysts consider that his reign of terror crippled the economy and forced "the state into little more than an instrument of plunder" (Brett 1995, 137). Economic decline, social disintegration, and massive human rights violations characterized the country during most of the 1970s (U.S. Department of State 2005a, 3). Although exiled activists threatened Amin throughout his reign, it was dissension within the army that ultimately led to his downfall. Having dealt with a mutiny in the late summer of 1978, Amin proceeded to send some units into northwest Tanzania. The Tanzanian army responded by expelling the invaders, joining up with Ugandan exiles, and then moving on to take Kampala in April 1979. Amin fled to Libya and later to Saudi Arabia, where he lived in exile until his death in July 2003.

Following the ousting of Amin, attempts to establish an interim government in Kampala were unsuccessful. Elections were eventually held at the end of 1980, and Milton Obote returned to power amid allegations of electoral fraud. Massive human rights violations continued under Obote's second term, and his security forces are accused of laying waste to much of the country in their campaign against the rebel National Resistance Army (NRA) led by Yoweri Museveni (U.S. Department of State 2005a, 3). The area north of Kampala known as the Luwero Triangle was the site of particularly brutal atrocities committed by Obote's forces.

Obote's rule finally came to an end when one of his army brigades, composed largely of Acholi fighters, took Kampala and established a military government. The leader of the new regime, General Tito Okello, promised to end the tribal rivalries and hold fair elections. However, human rights abuses continued as the Okello government ravaged the countryside in an attempt to destroy the NRA's support (U.S. Department of State 2005a, 3).

Ignoring a cease-fire he had signed in December 1985, Museveni and his NRA proceeded to seize power by force in Kampala on January 26,

1986. The political grouping created by Museveni, the National Resistance Movement (NRM), has controlled the government ever since. Museveni is credited with putting an end to the abuses of previous governments as well as initiating economic liberalization and reforms in accordance with the requests of the IMF, the World Bank, and donor governments. Most of Uganda's industry is related to agricultural production, and almost of all the country's foreign exchange earnings come from agricultural products. Coffee, of which Uganda is Africa's leading producer, accounted for about 19 percent of the country's exports in 2002, whereas fish accounted for 17 percent (U.S. Department of State 2005a, 3).

Although the government's economic performance has been applauded internationally, the political situation has raised some concerns. Since taking power in 1986, Museveni has pledged to rid the country of dictatorship, mismanagement, and the cycle of violence that characterized its postindependence history (Bøås 2004, 296). Given the social makeup of the country, Museveni believes multiparty democracy will only create political polarization that will be based on ethnic affiliation. His view is that industrialization and the creation of socioeconomic classes will eventually provide a solid base for party politics (Bøås 2004, 297; Museveni 2000, 95–96). The government has therefore been based on a "movement" system that severely restricts the activities of political parties. The current constitution, which was adopted in 1995, provides for an elected executive president, along with a relatively independent parliament and judiciary. The constitution was recently amended to remove the provision that limited the president to two five-year terms. Although it has been viewed with considerable skepticism by international observers, this amendment allowed President Museveni to be a candidate in the presidential elections that were held in February 2006. Museveni was declared the winner in the election, but his leadership style has been generally characterized as corrupt and unethical.

Democracy in Uganda

Dr. Kizza Besigye challenged President Museveni in the presidential elections of March 2001 and lost. He appealed to the Supreme Court, which ruled by majority decision that the fraud and violence during the elections were not sufficient to set aside the results. Besigye then fled into exile and returned in October 2005 to run again for president. Several days after his return, he was arrested on treason and rape charges and remanded to Luzira Prison near Kampala. His arrest provoked demonstrations and looting in Kampala. Although Bisegye was eventually released from prison after several weeks, human rights observers were concerned that the authorities would obstruct his campaign rallies because he was Museveni's main challenger in the first multiparty presidential elections in twenty-five years (Human Rights Watch 2005).

Conflict Background

Uganda's troubled postindependence history is intimately linked with continuous violence and conflict. Indeed, it is somewhat difficult to distinguish periods when rebel groups are active from periods when the insurgents are regrouping or reforming under different movements. Nevertheless, according to some conflict specialists, there have been three civil wars in Uganda up to the end of the Cold War: a one-month armed conflict in 1966 that resulted in 2,000 deaths, a twelve-month conflict in 1978–1979 that resulted in a similar number of deaths, and a seventy-two-month conflict in 1980–1986 that resulted in 300,000 deaths and around 347,000 displaced persons (Doyle and Sambanis 2000). These statistics should be supplemented by a new post-1986 civil war involving several anti-Museveni movements. Despite the relatively positive economic developments in Uganda since Museveni took power, continuous fighting has unfortunately drained much of the national budget. The recent conflict areas have been concentrated primarily in northern Uganda and the region around the Rwenzori Mountains in western Uganda.

According to the U.S. Department of State, the "vicious and cult-like" Lord's Resistance Army (LRA) continues to "murder and kidnap civilians" in northern Uganda (U.S. Department of State 2005a, 4). The rebel movement is estimated as having roughly 1,500 lightly armed troops, although many are child soldiers (IISS 2004, 248). Some analysts believe the number of LRA fighters may be as high as 4,000 (SIPRI 2004, 112.) The LRA faces Museveni's army, the Uganda People's Defense Force (UPDF), a relatively modern force that includes roughly 40,000–45,000 troops (IISS 2004, 248). The conflict in the north has resulted in massive population displacement. At more than 1.3 million people (USCRI 2005, 11; most other sources provide higher numbers), the estimates for displaced persons far exceed the numbers relating to earlier conflict periods. The situation in northern Uganda is such that war has become an integral part of the politics of daily life; the local population and soldiers live by and suffer from the economy of war (Bøås 2004, 286). More than half the population of the Gulu and Kitgum districts are living in camps made for displaced persons (most estimates are considerably higher; see, for example, World Vision 2004, 4). The creation of these government-organized temporary settlements has paradoxically contributed to the further impoverishment of locals. Fields that were once relatively fertile are now lying empty, and locals have become dependent on other sources of food and income generation (Bøås 2004, 286).

Uganda's northern neighbor, Sudan, has also been implicated in the LRA's insurgency. Since around 1994, Sudan has allegedly been aiding the LRA and conducting a proxy war against Kampala, partly motivated by Khartoum's perception that Museveni was aiding the Sudanese People's Liberation Army (SPLA) in their struggle against the Sudanese government (Prunier 2004, 365).

The spillover effect has not been limited to the northern borders of Uganda. Several rebel groups operating from the chaotic regions of eastern DRC have mounted attacks in the mountainous southwestern areas of Uganda. To

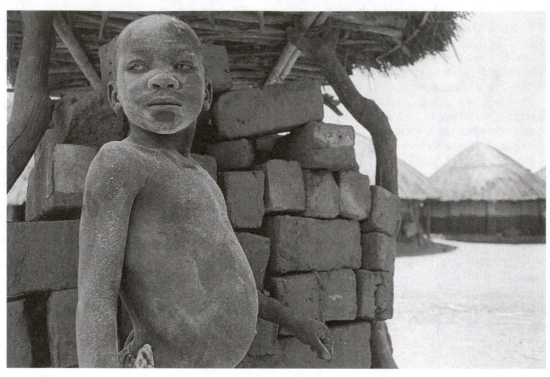

A child stands outside a hut in an internally displaced persons camp in northern Uganda in November 2004. Two decades of civil war in Uganda have led to chronic internal displacement. (Silvia Morara/Corbis)

the extent that these groups have benefited from foreign support, they have implicated the Kinshasa government and the possibility that it may have conducted a proxy war through Ugandan dissidents. This threat has motivated Kampala to send the UPDF across the border in controversial incursions into DRC. The engagement in the resource-rich eastern regions of DRC was slowly replaced by economic motivations.

Kigali has also recently been implicated in supporting these anti-Museveni armed groups based in eastern DRC, as the relations between Museveni and Rwanda's president Paul Kagame have soured. It should be remembered that Kagame, as leader of the Rwandan Patriotic Army, launched his exiled rebel forces from Uganda and managed to take power in Rwanda by July 1994 as the country spiraled out of control with genocidal mass killings. Although the forces of the new Kigali regime pursued the sol-

diers of the old regime in the eastern regions of ex-Zaire (DRC), the UPDF took advantage of the situation and attacked the anti-Museveni movements based on the border regions of ex-Zaire (Prunier 2004, 374). The September 1996 Rwandan military operation against the refugee camps in the South Kivu region eventually expanded such that the Rwandans found themselves operating with Ugandan troops against an alliance of rebel and governmental troops from the region. According to some analysts, the multistate attack on ex-Zaire turned the regional proxy conflicts into a continental problem (Prunier 2004, 374). By late 1998, the UPDF, along with Congolese rebels was even threatening to advance to Kinshasa before the air forces of Namibia, Angola, and Sudan began airlifting soldiers and bombing operations to help President Kabila's regime (Prunier 2004, 380). A peace agreement was signed in Sirte (Libya) be-

Table 1: Civil War in Uganda

War:	Various insurgent groups vs. government
Dates:	July 1986–present
Casualties:	more than 7,000
Regime type prior to war:	–7 (ranging from –10 [authoritarian] to 10 [democracy]); movement system that prohibits opposition political parties
Regime type after war:	Not applicable
GDP per capita year war began:	US $465 (estimated)
GDP per capita year after war:	US $465 (estimated)
Insurgents:	Lord's Resistance Army, Allied Democratic Forces, and others
Issue:	Alienation of northern Acholi, Islamic revolution
Rebel funding:	Diaspora, Sudan
Role of geography:	Rebels hide in bush and rough terrain.
Role of resources:	Not significant
Immediate outcome:	Not applicable
Outcome after 5 years:	Not applicable
Role of UN:	Humanitarian relief aid
Role of regional organization:	No direct role
Refugees:	703,500 (excluding 1,330,000 internally displaced persons)
Prospects for peace:	Favorable

Sources: Doyle and Sambanis 2000; Marshall and Jaggers 2002; SIPRI 2004, 112; USCRI 2005, 11; U.S. Department of State, 2005a.

tween Museveni and Kabila on April 17, 1999. Yet tensions have now risen between Kampala and Kigali following years of military cooperation and presence in the chaotic and resource-rich regions of DRC.

The Insurgents
The Rebel Groups

There have been numerous Ugandan rebel groups over the last decades, and it would be of limited use to describe all of them here. As the most prominent of the rebel movements that are currently active, the LRA is described in some detail following. The Holy Spirit Movement Force (HSMF) is also described because some observers claim that the LRA is related to or inspired by this earlier, sect-like, armed movement that was created in the wake of Museveni's seizure of power. Several other rebel groups are also covered to provide a fuller picture of the current difficulties in establishing a central government in Kampala that accommodates the

various ethnic or religious aspirations in modern-day Uganda.

The Holy Spirit Movement Force (HSMF)

This millenarian guerrilla movement was active during the period 1986–1987 as it fought the Museveni regime, mainly in northern Uganda. It was allegedly created on August 6, 1986, when the spirit Lakwena ordered a mystical young prophetess, Alice Auma, to stop healing the sick and to start raising an army for an antigovernment crusade (Bøås 2004, 289; Van Acker 2004, 346). Alice capitalized on powerful feelings of guilt, collective despair, and the need for spiritual cleansing to create a movement that contained elements of both a cult and a military organization (Brett 1995, 146). As members had to undergo ritual purification to be cleansed of past sins, the HSMF offered redemption to Acholi who believed they were being punished for atrocities committed by Acholi soldiers under Obote and Okello (Westbrook 2000, 3).

Operations guided by the Holy Spirit Tactics often disregarded basic military principles because soldiers were taught they had become invincible through the power of spiritual redemption (Van Acker 2004, 347). At a more practical level, the HSMF received arms in November 1986 from another rebel group, the Ugandan People's Democratic Army (UPDA; see section following) but later broke away with many of its soldiers (Brett 1995, 146). The bitter and disoriented Acholi soldiers of the HSMF eventually made their way south almost to Jinja in October 1987 before being stopped by the Uganda People's Defense Force (Prunier 2004, 366; Westbrook 2000, 2). Following this defeat some 80 kilometers east of Kampala, the wounded Alice took refuge in Kenya, and the movement has apparently ceased to exist.

The Lord's Resistance Army (LRA)

Some observers believe that the LRA is a new incarnation of the HSMF (Bøås 2004, 289; Prunier 2004, 366), whereas others see it as a distinct organization with both differences and similarities (Westbrook 2000, 4). The LRA is sometimes perceived as having vacillated between following Lakwena's beliefs, adopting Christian fundamentalist ideas, and incorporating Muslim rituals (Westbrook 2000, 4). This bizarre movement was created by Alice's cousin (or nephew), Joseph Kony, who claimed to have similar spiritual visions as he began to lead a small guerrilla war in almost impenetrable terrain in north Acholi near the Sudanese border (Prunier 2004, 366).

In its early years, the LRA seems to have used a version of the Holy Spirit Tactics, although it was less clearly articulated and its political vision was apparently more ambiguous (Van Acker 2004, 348). When the leadership of the UPDA signed a peace accord with the UPDF in 1988, several dissenting commanders left the UPDA and decided to join the LRA insurrection. In due course, they persuaded Kony to adopt guerrilla (or terror) tactics over Holy Spirit Tactics (Van Acker 2004, 348).

After the failure of talks with Minister Betty Bigombe in 1994, Kony was invited to Juba in south Sudan, where he allegedly obtained significant military aid from the Sudanese government following a symbolic acceptance of Islam by some of his fighters (e.g., name changes and some religious conversions). Sudan rapidly turned the motley group of rebels into a "coherent, well-supplied military enterprise" (Van Acker 2004, 338) that included more than 2,000 well-equipped troops (Prunier 2004, 366–67) that could contribute to its fight against the SPLA. However, the Sudanese army has occasionally been frustrated in its attempts to bolster the LRA; instead of pinning down the UPDF in key sectors or wearing it down with effective ambushes, the rebels have preferred to terrorize villages and murder civilians in Acholi (Van Acker 2004, 376).

It is therefore far from clear that much of the Acholi people support the LRA (Van Acker 2004, 352). Observers suspect that its support comes mainly from the diaspora Acholi (Bøås 2004, 290; Westbrook 2000, 5). More recently, the LRA's insurrection has shown signs of slowing down, as the rebels are becoming more officer heavy due to casualties, capture, and defections, as well as a lessened capacity to regenerate (ICG 2005, 2). This is partly the result of the protocol signed between Uganda and Sudan in 2002 that allows the UPDF to pursue the LRA into southern Sudan up to an agreed "red line" (Van Acker 2004, 352). As a result, the LRA no longer maintains a fixed headquarters in southern Sudan, even though command and control remains intact (ICG 2005, 3). In August 2006 it signed a truce with the government that will hopefully bring an end to one of Africa's most tragic conflicts.

The Ugandan National Liberation Army (UNLA)

This group consists of Okello's primarily Acholi soldiers who withdrew to Sudan following the NRA's victory in January 1986 (Westbrook 2000, 3).

The Uganda People's Democratic Movement/Army (UPDM/A)

Once the NRM took control of the entire country in April 1986, a relative peace was established until the UPDA (formed by Acholi exiles) launched an attack from Sudan in July 1986 (Westbrook 2000, 3). The UPDA was based in the refugee camps of southern Sudan, whereas the political leadership was entrenched in London; it apparently did not enjoy widespread support in Acholi. Yet former UNLA soldiers joined it after the fall of Gulu and Kitgum to the NRA; consequently, they greatly expanded the existing brigades (Van Acker 2004, 342).

The UPDA eventually came out of the bush following a peace agreement on June 3, 1988 (Brett 1995, 147). However, a large contingent of disenfranchised members stayed in the bush after the accord. Joseph Kony apparently joined the UPDA in early 1987 as a young "spiritual mobilizer" (Van Acker 2004, 347) before going on to form the LRA.

The Allied Democratic Forces (ADF)

Some observers believe this rebel group was created as a result of the proxy war between Sudan and Uganda; it is a coalition formed from a variety of anti-Museveni movements aided by Sudan (and DRC) and active on Uganda's western border with DRC (Hovil and Werker 2005, 13). Its roots are apparently found in a group of Islamic activists from the Tabliq movement who went underground after their release from prison in the 1990s (Bøås 2004, 293). They reappeared in February 1995 in the western district of Bunyoro, conducting military training with Sudanese help, but they escaped after an intervention by the UPDF. (Their peak period was in 2000, when they had an estimated 1,000 fighters who asserted their presence in areas such as Bundibugyo near the Rwenzori Mountains [Bøås 2004, 293].) The ADF was greatly weakened in 2002 (Prunier 2004, 381). Recent estimates place their strength at roughly 200 lightly armed fighters (IISS 2004, 377).

The Allied Democratic Movement (ADM)

This is a Baganda guerrilla movement created in London in January 1995 in the tradition of the Kabaka Yekka (a monarchist party of the 1960s) to fight Museveni's regime and restore the Baganda king (Prunier 2004, 361). It recruited primarily among the majority of Baganda who are Christians (Prunier 2004, 371).

The National Army for the Liberation of Uganda (NALU)

Created in 1988, this guerrilla movement follows in the tradition of the Rwenzururu movement created by the Bakonjo, who fought the British colonial authorities for autonomy from Bunyoro (western Uganda). The Rwenzururu leaders signed an armistice with the Obote regime in August 1982. Yet, one of the leaders, Amon Bazira, obtained help from Presidents Mobutu and Moi to start a revival of the movement after Museveni's rise to power in 1986. The new movement apparently never had the popular appeal of Rwenzururu, but it had enough financing to pose a threat to Museveni. It disappeared after Bazira was shot dead in Nairobi in 1992; many of its members allegedly joined the ADF.

The Ugandan Muslim Liberation Army (UMLA)

This Islamic anti-Museveni guerrilla group declared war on the Museveni regime in January 1995. It was apparently supported by the Baganda Muslims, who during the 1981–1986 bush war had provided key support to the NRA (Prunier 2004, 370). By recruiting among the minority of Baganda who were Muslim, along with non-Baganda Muslims throughout Uganda, the UMLA complemented the ADM and its Anglo-Protestant leaders in the overall Baganda struggle against Museveni (Prunier 2004, 371). Its first military operations were defeated near Lake Albert in February 1995, and the survivors fled near Bunia in ex-Zaire. In Bunia, they apparently made contact with Sudanese army officials supplying the Rwandan Interahamwe and the West Nile Bank Liberation Front (WBNLF; see following); the Sudanese allegedly began helping the UMLA and fusing it with the ADM (Prunier 2004, 372–73).

The West Nile Bank Liberation Front (WNBLF)

This anti-Museveni guerrilla movement was created in November 1994 in Faradje (in the former Zaire) by Juma Oris (a former commander under Idi Amin), following a secret deal between Khartoum and Kinshasa that allowed the Sudanese army to reorganize former Kakwa and Aringa soldiers on the Zairian side of the West Nile region (Prunier 2004, 367).

The rebels surrendered en masse to the UPDF during the 1997 fighting in northeast Zaire. Remnants were ambushed by the SPLA as they tried to join up with Sudanese forces in Yei (southern Sudan) in March 1997, while survivors of the ambush fled to the Sudanese army garrison in Juba (Prunier 2004, 376–77). The WNBLF faded away following the 1999 Sirte agreement, and their current strength is estimated at more than 1,000 soldiers (IISS 2004, 377).

The People's Redemption Army (PRA)

The NRM alleges that the PRA is a new Rwandan-backed rebel movement consisting of former ADF fighters, supporters of the opposition candidate in the 2001 presidential elections (Kizza Besigye), and dissatisfied soldiers (Bøås 2004, 294; Van Acker 2004, 353). This rebel group is allegedly led by Colonel Samson Mande and Colonel Anthony Kyakable, who are receiving Rwandan support to train forces in Ituri together with the ADF (Bøås 2004, 294).

Geography

Uganda is endowed with ample fertile land, regular rainfall, and mineral deposits. This is one of the main reasons it appeared destined for rapid economic growth following the colonial period. Unfortunately, this potential has not been realized, and the rich and varied landscape that was once admired by locals and foreigners alike has now ironically facilitated the activities of insurgents.

With Lake Victoria and the Victoria Nile River, which flows through the country, Uganda has plenty of water sources. The country enjoys a tropical climate that is tempered by an average altitude of 1,000 meters. Mountain ranges are found in the extreme west and east of the country. At 5,109 meters, Mount Stanley in the Rwenzori Mountains is the country's highest peak. In between the mountain ranges are lush and fertile fields on the shores of Lake Victoria. The land varies considerably in the northeast, where it becomes semidesert.

The Acholi region of northern Uganda does not hold any known reserves of key strategic resources, but this may change as the oil wealth of southern Sudan is unlocked following the 2004 peace agreement between Khartoum and the SPLA. To date, all three of the Acholi-inhabited districts (Gulu, Kitgum, and Pader) have been marginalized from mainstream development (Van Acker 2004, 336).

The current armed conflict has been taking place primarily in the districts of Kitgum and Gulu, with several recent attacks in the neighboring Pader and Lira districts. As the largest district in Uganda (16,136 square kilometers), Kitgum shares a long border with Sudan. Its seasons are basically divided into rainy and dry periods. During the rainy periods, tall, green grasses and thick brush characterize the landscape. The population, essentially rural, is estimated at close to half a million people. Gulu district is situated to the southwest of Kitgum, and it shares a small border with Sudan. The elevations of the land range from 351 to 1,341 meters. Its population is almost as large as the one in Kitgum (Westbrook 2000, 2).

The operational capacity of the insurgents in the north has clearly been helped by the proximity of Sudan, a large country with its own internal conflicts and somewhat uncontrolled border regions. To the extent that the northern parts of Uganda are relatively far from the capital, which

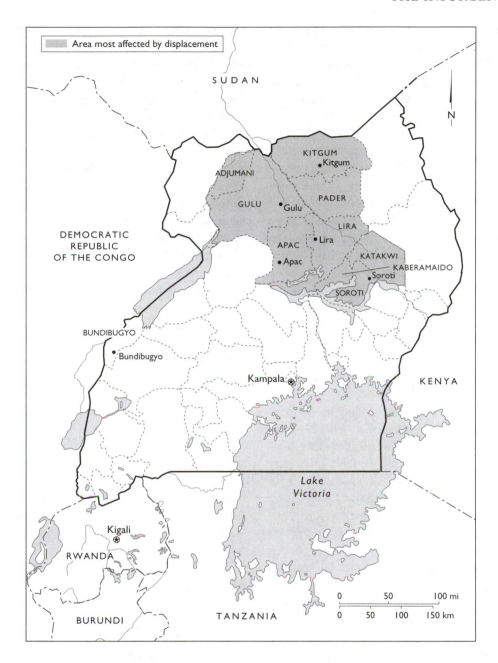

is situated in traditional Baganda territory, the geographic distances have helped the rebels maintain a prolonged insurrection. Another striking feature of the Acholi-inhabited northern region is that it appears "empty," owing to the existence of protected camps where villagers are assembled by force and supposedly provided with government protection (Van Acker 2004, 343). Like many governments in similar situations, Kampala has pursued this policy to make it more difficult for the insurgents to hide among the civilians.

The civil war in Uganda has also recently affected areas outside the underdeveloped north and particularly the southwestern regions near the Rwenzori Mountains. It is clear that the ADF chose western Uganda as a base of operations partly because of the mountainous terrain (Bøås 2004, 293) and lush forests. The proximity of DRC's chaotic provinces is clearly a factor that facilitates the activities of insurgent groups.

Tactics

Over the years, the LRA has become notorious for the mutilation and summary execution of civilians, as well as the abduction of children for use as foot soldiers (Van Acker 2004, 335). The LRA remains committed to terror tactics, and it is not concerned about controlling territory. Indeed, the suffering of Acholi civilians at the hands of the LRA is characterized by attacks on villages and looting, along with mutilation and mass abductions (ICG 2005, 2). An estimated 20,000 children have been violently abducted to serve in its ranks (World Vision 2004, 4). Movement of LRA commanders between Uganda and Sudan has been common in order to evade capture and to reorganize (ICG 2005, 5).

The LRA allegedly began wholesale kidnapping after the failed 1994 talks with Bigombe (Van Acker 2004, 337). Given that the LRA is essentially an Acholi resistance movement, it may seem strange that Acholi civilians are its main victims. This is part of the difficulty in understanding the political objectives of the rebel group. Most analysts agree that Kony and his commanders have not been particularly clear in their political objectives. It appears that the LRA is simply trying to wreak havoc with brutal attacks that portray the government as incapable of protecting the internally displaced persons (ICG 2005, 1). To achieve these ends, LRA attacks are generally carried out by small groups using machetes and light arms. The rebel group sustains itself by stealing food, punishing collaboration with the government, prolonging a de facto state of emergency, and maintaining visibility with spectacular actions (ICG 2005, 2).

In dealing with this unusual and senselessly violent insurgency, the government has alternated between applying military pressure on the rebels, thinning out their ranks with amnesty offers, and reviving the political process through negotiations (Van Acker 2004, 337). In terms of protecting civilians, the government has assembled people into camps that are protected by local home guards (Van Acker 2004, 343). To many observers, the camps indicate the existence of a de facto state of emergency. Yet many Acholi perceive them to be a method of earmarking the north as a labor reserve for sugar cane and tea plantations. Indeed, Acholi often express fears of hidden government intentions relating to land ownership (Van Acker 2004, 343).

Although the government has established protected camps for the villagers, it also encourages former fighters to turn themselves in at a regional reception center (ICG 2005, 3). In the past, it has been reported that rebels who did not receive external assistance had to live off the local population and eventually turned into gangs that rob civilians (Brett 1995, 149). This is one of the important issues that must be addressed in order to resolve the current conflict in the north.

In the western parts of Uganda, the ADF leadership and membership have remained relatively obscure over the years, thereby helping to keep their internal and external contacts safe from intelligence agents. The obscurity also adds a mythological dimension to the ADF (Bøås 2004, 292). By operating in non-Acholi territory that is considered the heartland of the NRM, the ADF's strongest asset is that it raises questions about the legitimacy of Museveni's new Uganda (Bøås 2004, 293).

Faced with insurrections in the north and to the west, Kampala has sought to modernize its military with the purchase of new equipment. For example, the UPDF can now count on main battle tanks (152 T-54/55), fighter jets (six MiG-21, five MiG-23) and helicopter gunships (six Mi–24) acquired in recent years (IISS 2004, 248). Although these purchases are intended ostensibly to make the army more effective in general combat operations, at least two complications should be noted. At slightly over 2 percent of GDP, the amount of military spending has risen over the last few years to levels that have attracted some concern from key Western donors (Bøås 2004, 343). The spending has also been linked to military corruption, which has had a negative impact on the UPDF's ability to put down the insurrections. Indeed, many examples of military procurement have not resulted in the increased combat advantage sought by the UPDF. Top defense officials, including Museveni's half-brother Major General Salim Saleh, have been implicated in the associated corruption scandals (Tangri and Mwenda 2003, 540–43).

Causes of the War

The almost constant internal armed conflicts that have plagued Uganda since independence are undoubtedly caused by a variety of factors. Yet several recurring themes can be pointed out. Although many civil wars on the African continent have been the result of secessionist movements and ideological or religious differences, Uganda's civil wars are best characterized as the result of ethnic differences and their connected political and economic tensions. A succession of repressive regimes since the British pulled out in 1962 has only added to the country's inability to build a national cohesive bond that unites the competing ethnic groups.

The fact that the country does not have a common language understood by the majority of its inhabitants is a reflection of the divisions between the numerous ethnic groups. Swahili has been promoted at various periods as a unifying African language, yet it has not developed as Uganda's national language (Ofcansky 1996, 72–73). The country's official language is English, and it is used essentially in urban circles related to government, media, commerce, and academia. The majority of inhabitants, however, do not speak English: Instead, they communicate in more than thirty distinct languages and dialects (Kasozi 1994, 227–34). Without a common language, it is clearly difficult for political leaders to

communicate directly to the entire population and for the country to develop a sense of shared history and political aspirations that can lead to national integration. The traditional ethnic allegiances are consequently easier to exploit by opportunistic elites.

Deep cultural cleavages exist between the Bantu central and southwest parts of the country and the Nilotic northern parts (Bøås 2004, 285). For example, northern Ugandans, who served as a reservoir for cheap labor and British colonial soldiers, resent the perceived preferential treatment accorded to the southern Baganda population (Van Acker 2004, 341). Some argue that the Acholi were relatively marginal to early British colonial rule and that they were largely viewed as a tribe of inferior order (Bøås 2004, 287). These types of dynamics are present throughout the country with the various ethnic groups. The overall result is a national political culture in which there is a perception that an ethnic group's best survival strategy is to displace the ruling ethnic group and seize power.

Indeed, for much of its history since independence, military force in Uganda has not been subject to genuine control by civilian authorities (Brett 1995, 129). Furthermore, frequent changes in the composition of the military have resulted in the regular rotation of low-skilled persons from specific ethnic groups in and out of civilian life (Van Acker 2004, 338–39). Some commentators point to Idi Amin's 1972 order for Acholi and Langi soldiers to return to barracks, only to be massacred, as the event that "firmly introduced competitive retaliation on an ethnic basis" (Van Acker 2004, 340).

In terms of the current civil war, it is necessary to set the violence in the context of the NRA's victory after a six-year bush war. Acholi soldiers were disproportionately represented in President Obote's armies in the 1960s and 1980s. Many Ugandans consequently blamed the Acholi for the atrocities committed in the Luwero Triangle northwest of Kampala during Museveni's bush war against Obote. Given their prominence in Obote's armies, as well as their active participation in the battles against the NRA when it was taking control of the country, the Acholi were in a difficult situation following Museveni's victory in 1986. After taking power, Museveni immediately ordered all Acholi to hand in their weapons; memories of the retributive actions of Idi Amin in the early 1970s resulted in many young Acholi preferring to keep their weapons and to take to the bush (Bøås 2004, 287–88). Over the ensuing months, members of the formerly well-disciplined NRA avenged themselves upon their former enemies by plundering, murdering, and raping the civilian population in Acholi (Bøås 2004, 287–88). It is against this background that the HSMF was created. The human rights abuses by the NRA in northern Uganda had undoubtedly driven many people into the bush during the initial stages (Brett 1995, 147).

For all the progressive official statements on national harmony, elements within the NRM have tended to blame the Acholi community for the unrest that followed Museveni's 1986 victory, claiming that they never fully accepted his authority because they were deprived of the ability to loot other Ugandans. From this perspective, the causes of the war are largely resource based, with tribal opportunism playing a key role in access to wealth (Westbrook 2000, 6).

It is difficult to apportion blame in a context that involves interethnic tensions within a country. Yet some factors are relatively clear. To the extent that the current armed conflict involves mainly the Acholi people, it should be noted that the economies of the two Acholi districts of Kitgum and Gulu are severely underdeveloped, even by Ugandan standards (Westbrook 2000, 2). Acholi has become a chronic conflict zone partly because of the Acholi's perception that they are excluded from the Ugandan polity (Bøås 2004, 284). From the mass killings by the NRA in 1986 to the characterization of the war as an "Acholi problem," and more recently the use of the displaced persons' camps and the widespread problem of stolen cattle (Westbrook 2000, 7), the collective grievances of the Acholi

reflect considerable mistrust between the north and Kampala. For example, Museveni received less than 20 percent of the people's vote in Acholi during the 1996 presidential elections, even though he won with a large majority throughout Uganda (Westbrook 2000, 4).

Alleged discrimination in terms of the benefits from economic development has aggravated the Acholi sense of exclusion. Some observers argue that the product of economic growth following the monetary reform of 1987 has been distributed in an uneven manner (Oloka-Onyango 2000, 34–35), with most going to NRM officials and cronies while other Ugandans have been left with comparatively little (Bøås 2004, 284; Prunier 2004, 372). This uneven distribution of wealth following a period of relative prosperity adds to the ethnic marginalization that has plagued the country since independence.

Even in terms of humanitarian assistance, the perception of discriminatory treatment is still present. The government has often been accused of not meeting the basic needs of the displaced persons in the protected camps of the north; poor sanitation, limited clean water, congestion, and rampant disease have all attracted international attention (ICG 2005, 11). Acholi complain that the effects of the war have also hit them in another disproportionate manner: The Karamojong in northeast Uganda have conducted frequent armed cattle raids against their Acholi neighbors (Knighton 2003, 427). Indeed, the violent conflicts involving pastoralists in the region are believed to be aggravated by cattle rustling and small arms proliferation through cross-border smuggling (Knighton 2003, 429).

Other, more controversial factors should be considered in an assessment of the causes of civil war in Uganda. Arms proliferation in the region, particularly as a result of the wars in Sudan and DRC, has contributed to the problems of violence in Uganda (Van Acker 2004, 345). Moreover, Sudan's support for the LRA is an important factor, although it has apparently been reduced (ICG 2005, 4), and latest reports suggest it is coming to an end (*New Vision* 2005a). At a more individual level, a number of officials, both military and civilian, have clearly benefited from supplying the war effort (Westbrook 2000, 7) and may not be interested in encouraging a cessation of hostilities.

The most controversial aspect of national politics in Uganda has arguably been the twenty-year ban on multiparty elections. Museveni consistently argued that the manipulation of ethnic identities by party politics had contributed to the turmoil of the 1970s and 1980s (Bøås 2004, 297). In associating a multiparty system with violence, the NRM suggested it was the sole guarantor of the social revolution needed to end the cycle of violence that dominated the country's history since independence. This image of chaos and violence as the alternative to Museveni's Uganda is regularly used to link political opposition to rebel movements (Bøås 2004, 298). For example, following the defeat of Kizza Besigye, the opposition candidate in the 2001 presidential elections, the NRM attempted to associate his supporters with the insurgency (Bøås 2004, 294). After two decades in power, Museveni's movement appears to be uneasy in addressing political dissent in a manner consistent with international human rights standards. This problem arguably reflects one of the key causes of Uganda's current civil war.

Outcome
Conflict Status

The current civil war in Uganda has been going on for twenty years. A few comments on the outcome of some of the political violence in the mid-1960s are useful in understanding why it has been difficult to bring peace to the country. Although it was put down with the help of the British military, the 1964 mutiny indicated that a northern group (the soldiers came predominantly from Acholi, Teso, Lango, and West Nile) could exert considerable influence on national politics (Brett 1995, 135). Idi Amin became deputy commander of the army following the

reinstatement of those involved in the uprising. A year later, he was made army commander as Obote responded to accusations that both men were involved in gold and ivory smuggling from Zaire (Brett 1995, 135). Obote then proceeded to abrogate Buganda's autonomy, repealed the constitution, and sent army units to attack the kabaka's palace, forcing the Baganda king into exile. Obote proclaimed himself president as elections were cancelled. A lesson learned for many observers was that force had paid off in the short term. In terms of the country's political future, the army high command had been drawn into partisan politics, thereby damaging any faith in the country's nascent democracy (Brett 1995, 136). The stage was set for the violent political developments of the following decades: A few years later, Idi Amin turned the state into an instrument of extortion and sectional domination. In other words, Ugandan society was decaying as brute force was used for private benefit (Brett 1995, 152).

After twenty years of insurrection in the northern regions of Uganda, the unhealthy political problem just described has contributed to a grave humanitarian crisis. Uganda presently holds the fourth-largest internally displaced population of the world (USCRI 2005, 11). The humanitarian plight of civilians is characterized by a phenomenon known as "night commuters": children who flee their villages every night to sleep in the cities to avoid abduction (World Vision 2004, 5). Their numbers are estimated to be around 32,000–52,000 (U.S. Department of State 2005b, 2). The problem of population displacement is such that United Nations officials consider the crisis to be one of the worst in the world today.

Duration Tactics

Because the LRA does not have the means to overthrow the government in Kampala, it is fighting what may be termed a protracted war. It seeks to wear down the UPDF and gain strength over time. To the extent that Sudan has tried to undermine the government in Kampala, it has been accused of encouraging prolonged insurrections within the borders of its southern neighbor.

There is another dimension that has probably contributed to the prolongation of the armed conflict. Many sources have alleged that military corruption results in considerable financial gain for army officers and government officials (e.g., Tangri and Mwenda 2003, 539). The implication is that this dynamic of corruption within the UPDF and the NRM is a significant factor in the duration of the civil war.

External Military Intervention

Over the last decade, Sudan, DRC, and Chad have all sent troops on combat operations in the border regions where Ugandan rebel groups have been present. To the extent that Sudan and DRC have led proxy wars against Uganda by assisting anti-Museveni rebel movements, the country's most recent civil war is clearly affected by external military intervention. The extent of Sudan's support for the LRA can be debated, yet there is little doubt that it has contributed in prolonging an insurrection that many thought would have dissipated years ago.

In terms of a foreign military presence that may play a constructive role in the future, the African Union and the United Nations need to consider how observers might be deployed to assembly points pursuant to a cease-fire (ICG 2005, 12). Similarly, it has been suggested that, as the United Nations Mission in the Sudan (UNMIS) deploys 10,000 peacekeepers to Uganda's northern neighbor, the Security Council could ask it to observe LRA movements and report LRA locations (ICG 2005, 12).

Conflict Management Efforts

There have been significant conflict management efforts by national and local leaders since armed opposition groups began challenging Museveni's government in 1986. These efforts have resulted in deals whereby some rebel groups have abandoned their struggles and integrated with national political and military structures. The ef-

Uganda in the Democratic Republic of the Congo

In a decision rendered in December 2005, the International Court of Justice ruled that Uganda had "violated the principle of non-use of force in international relations and the principle of non-intervention" by occupying the Ituri region in eastern DRC and by "actively extending military, logistic, economic and financial support to irregular forces having operated on the territory of the DRC." According to the court, these actions could not be justified by the principle of self-defense. The court also found that the Ugandan army committed "acts of killing, torture and other forms of inhumane treatment of the Congolese civilian population, destroyed villages and civilian buildings, failed to distinguish between civilian and military targets and to protect the civilian population in fighting with other combatants, trained child soldiers, incited ethnic conflict." Although it did not consider that "Uganda's military intervention was carried out in order to obtain access to Congolese resources," the court stated that it had "ample persuasive evidence to conclude that officers and soldiers of the UPDF, including the most high-ranking officers, were involved in the looting, plundering and exploitation of the DRC's natural resources" (ICJ 2005).

forts to negotiate with the LRA have also recently been assisted by key Western states, resulting in a truce that was signed in August 2006.

For more than a decade, Museveni has authorized one of his northern ministers, Betty Bigombe, to pursue direct talks with Kony. Although she had not met directly with him, she visited southern Sudan in 2004. In April 2005, via cellular phones, Kony and Bigombe held the "most comprehensive set of discussions" dealing with cease-fire modalities, aspects of an overall peace deal, and concerns about obstacles to progress; yet fighting continued in Kitgum, Gulu and Pader, despite the contacts between Kony and Bigombe (ICG 2005, 4). (There was concern that Museveni needed to make his offers public and halt military actions in order to give the process a chance to succeed [ICG 2005, 4]. Along with the recent truce, there have been some other positive results: On May 13, 2005, the Amnesty Commission began to run a national disarmament, demobilization, and reintegration program aimed at helping former rebels to return to civilian life (ICG 2005, 8). This project is funded largely by the Multi-Country Demobilization and Reintegration Program that is managed by the World Bank.

In terms of more direct international involvement, a "quartet of interested countries" has been formed, with the Netherlands, the United Kingdom, and Norway joined since 2005 by the United States. They are trying to promote the peace process. Yet the most prominent example of international involvement has been the recent indictments filed by the prosecutor of the International Criminal Court (ICC) against five LRA leaders, including Kony and his deputy Vincent Otti (ICC 2005, 1). Local Acholis and diplomats in Kampala are divided on this issue; some feel that justice must be done and that LRA leaders should be prosecuted, whereas others believe that prosecutions will ruin peace efforts and lead to new atrocities (ICG 2005, 9). Although it is likely that the threat of warrants has contributed in applying pressure on the LRA to negotiate and on Sudan to reduce overt support, the effect is unclear now that the indictments have been issued and made public.

Conclusion

The LRA insurgency in the north of Uganda was largely a product of Acholi alienation since 1986. To varying degrees, there is potential for this kind of antagonistic relationship to develop between Kampala and other ethnic groups in various parts of the country. This is one reason why it is important to make sure that the twenty-year-old rebellion in the north has actually ended following the recent truce agreement between the LRA and the government.

A comprehensive settlement strategy concerning the northern insurgency should include integration packages for destitute LRA members so that they can be reintegrate into society, better governance initiatives that promote the well-being of locals, a stronger humanitarian safety net for the displaced persons, and, more generally, a planning process that normalizes the region and gives northerners more say in government (ICG 2005, 5). Some of these elements may be complicated by the government's international commitments relating to the ICC's decision to prosecute key LRA members. Just as the future of the ICC depends partly on the success of its first prosecution attempts, it also needs to show sensitivity to the peace process. It can play a positive role, for example, by helping to identify who exactly is assisting the LRA and providing it with sanctuary and supplies in southern Sudan (ICG 2005, 9).

From a military viewpoint, the UPDF needs to improve its counterinsurgency operations by operating in smaller units and using more sophisticated communications and night vision equipment, along with improving its mobility (ICG 2005, 6). Effective counterinsurgency tactics need to be buttressed by efforts to improve relations with locals, whom the UPDF often accuses of aiding the rebels. As in any peace-support operation, the government has to realize that the "territory" to be captured is "the hearts and minds" of the locals and that this task requires considerable human resources (IISS 2004, 5). Although enhancing the capacity of the local defense units that protect the displaced persons' camps will improve the situation of civilians (ICG 2005, 6), the larger strategy should consider that an agropastoralist society cannot function if the population is confined to protected camps (Van Acker 2004, 357). This is the dilemma facing Museveni as he tries to increase his political legitimacy in the north part of Uganda.

Indeed, Uganda's recent history suggests that Kampala's legitimacy to govern the alienated north will depend on its ability to maintain a respectable human rights record. As documented in numerous reports by international NGOs, abusive procedures during arrests and detention have contributed to an absence of trust among locals (Van Acker 2004, 356).

Yet respect for human rights standards alone will not necessarily solve the problems that have repeatedly led to civil war in Uganda. The treatment of civilians should be placed in a wider perspective that considers the regional political complexities. Uganda is located in a part of the world where the viability of states is complicated by the porous nature of national borders. The DRC, for example, is perhaps an extreme example of a state that exerts limited control over its geographic frontiers. The problem is accentuated because ethnic solidarities across the borders are sometimes stronger than formal citizenship affiliations. This transnational factor can be used to mobilize ethnic solidarity networks by emphasizing feelings of political neglect (Prunier 2004, 383). It is in this way that some of the unstable states in the region, including Uganda, have seen their local problems transformed into regional problems.

From this standpoint, the spread of Islam is one of the factors that have guided Khartoum's support for anti-Museveni movements. Even though some Ugandans have been pushed to Islamic groups because of social and economic marginalization rather than any desire to adopt the shari'a system (Prunier 2004, 382), the effects of militant Islam in Uganda should not be ignored.

In order to ensure that the insurgency in the north has finally ended, pressure is needed on Sudan to make sure that Kony has no option but to negotiate and bring his long rebellion to a definite close (ICG 2005, 2). The recent signing of a protocol providing for the Sudanese armed forces and the SPLA to join in the hunt for the LRA is an indication that Sudan decided to cooperate more fully with international efforts to bring an end to the LRA's insurgency (New Vision 2005a). With such positive developments, the LRA's days are numbered. Indeed, the truce it has accepted appears to have put an end to the country's civil war and will allow all of Uganda

to develop so that it can perhaps one day fulfill its potential to be a "pearl of Africa."

Michael Barutciski

Chronology

October 9, 1962   Uganda becomes independent.

February 1966   Milton Obote suspends constitution.

January 1971   Idi Amin overthrows Obote.

August 1972   Amin orders expulsion of Asians from Uganda.

July 1976   Israeli commandos raid Entebbe Airport to rescue hostages taken by Palestinian terrorists.

April 1979   Amin overthrown by Tanzanian army and Ugandan rebels.

December 1980   Obote returns to power after winning elections.

July 1985   Obote overthrown by Acholi army officers, who set up Military Council.

January 1986   Yoweri Museveni and his NRA take Kampala and overthrow Military Council.

April 1986   NRA controls all of Uganda.

July 1986   UPDA rebels launch attack against NRA from Sudan.

October 1987   HSMF defeated by NRA 80 kilometers from Kampala.

March 1988   UPDA signs peace accord.

April 1991   Operation North launched against LRA.

February 1994   Negotiations between Betty Bigombe and LRA break down.

May 1996   Museveni wins presidential elections.

March 2001   Museveni wins presidential elections. Sudan signs protocol allowing Ugandan troops to engage LRA in southern Sudan. Operation Iron Fist launched against LRA.

June 2003   Ugandan troops withdraw from DRC.

February 2004   LRA attacks a displaced persons' camp, killing more than 300 civilians.

August 2005   Constitutional amendment passed allowing incumbent president to hold office for more than two terms.

October 2005   ICC announces warrants of arrest issued against LRA commanders.

February 2006   Museveni wins presidential elections.

August 2006   Truce signed between LRA and government.

List of Acronyms

ADF: Allied Democratic Forces
ADM: Allied Democratic Movement
DRC: Democratic Republic of the Congo
HSMF: Holy Spirit Movement Force
ICC: International Criminal Court
IMF: International Monetary Fund
LRA: Lord's Resistance Army
NALU: National Army for the Liberation of Uganda
NGO: nongovernmental organization
NRA/M: National Resistance Army/Movement
PRA: People's Redemption Army
UMLA: Ugandan Muslim Liberation Army
UNLA: Ugandan National Liberation Army
UPDF: Uganda People's Defense Force
UPDM/A: Ugandan People's Democratic Movement/Army
UNMIS: United Nations Mission in the Sudan
SPLA: Sudanese People's Liberation Army
WNBLF: West Nile Bank Liberation Front

Glossary

Acholi: A people and a territory in northern Uganda.
Baganda: The people of Bugunda.
Buganda: The traditional territory of the Baganda people, in the center of the country around Kampala.
kabaka: The king of Buganda.

References

Amnesty International (AI). 2005. *Annual Report.* London: Amnesty International Publications.
BBC News. 2005. *Online Country Profile: Uganda.* news.bbc.co.uk/1/hi/world/africa/country_profiles/1069166.stm.(accessed November 22, 2006)
Bøås, Morten. 2004. "Uganda in the Regional War Zone: Meta-Narratives, Pasts and Presents." *Journal of Contemporary African Studies* 22: 283–303.
Brett, E. A. 1995. "Neutralizing the Use of Force in Uganda: The Role of the Military in Politics." *The Journal of Modern African Studies* 33: 129–52.
Brett, E. A. 1998. "Responding to Poverty in Uganda: Structures, Policies and Prospects." *Journal of International Affairs* 52: 313–27.
Dicklitch, Susan, and Doreen Lwanga. 2003. "The Politics of Being No-Political: Human Rights Organizations and the Creation of a Positive Human Rights Culture in Uganda." *Human Rights Quarterly* 25: 482–509.

Doyle, Michael W., and Nicholas Sambanis. 2000. "International Peacebuilding: A Theoretical and Quantitative Analysis." *The American Political Science Review* 94(4). Data set notes at http:33www.worldbank.org/research/conflict/papers/peacebuilding/datanotes_final.pdf (accessed February 18, 2005).
Hovil, Lucy, and Eric Werker. 2005. "Portrait of a Failed Rebellion: An Account of Rational, Suboptimal Violence in Western Uganda." *Rationality and Society* 17: 5–34.
Human Rights Watch. 2005. *Uprooted and Forgotten: Impunity and Human Rights Abuses in Northern Uganda.* New York: HRW Publications.
Integrated Regional Information Networks (IRIN). 2005a. *UN Says No Sign of LRA in the East.* Geneva, Switzerland: UN Office for the Coordination of Humanitarian Affairs. November 10.
Integrated Regional Information Networks (IRIN). 2005b. *Uganda: LRA Rebels Ask for Peace Talks with Government.* Geneva, Switzerland: UN Office for the Coordination of Humanitarian Affairs. November 30.
Internal Displacement Monitoring Centre (IDMC). 2005. *Uganda: Relief Efforts Hampered in One of the World's Worst Internal Displacement Crises.* Geneva, Switzerland. December 12.
International Court of Justice (ICJ). 2005. *Armed Activities on the Territory of the Congo (DRC) v. Uganda.* Press release. The Hague, Netherlands: ICJ. December 19. www.icj-cij.org/icjwww/idocket/ico/icoframe.htm.
International Criminal Court (ICC). 2005. *Warrant of Arrest Unsealed against Five LRA Commanders.* Press release. The Hague, Netherlands: ICC. October 14.
International Crisis Group (ICG). 2005. *Building a Comprehensive Peace Strategy for Northern Uganda.* Africa Briefing No. 27. Brussels, Belgium. June 23.
International Institute for Strategic Studies (IISS). 2004. *The Military Balance 2004–2005.* Oxford, UK: Oxford University Press.
Kaiser, Tania. 2005. "Participating in Development? Refugee Protection, Politics and Developmental Approaches to Refugee Management in Uganda." *Third World Quarterly* 26: 351–67.
Kasozi, Abdu K. 1986. *The Spread of Islam in Uganda.* Nairobi, Kenya: Oxford University Press.

Kasozi, Abdu K. 1994. *The Social Origins of Violence in Uganda: 1964–1985.* Montreal, Canada: McGill-Queen's University Press.

Knighton, Ben. 2003. "The State as Raider among the Karamojong." *Africa* 73: 427–55.

Marshall, Monty G., and Keith Jaggers. 2003. *Polity IV Dataset.* College Park, MD: Center for International Development and Conflict Management, University of Maryland. www.cidcm.umd.edu/inscr/polity/Gua1.htm (accessed February 18, 2005).

Musveni, Yoweri K. 2000. *What Is Africa's Problem?* Minneapolis: Minnesota University Press.

New Vision. 2005a. "Three Forces to Attack Kony Rebels." Kampala, Uganda. November 21. www.newvision.co.ug/D/8/13/466905 (accessed January 5, 2006).

New Vision. 2005b. "LRA Talks Still On, Says Bigombe." Kampala, Uganda. December 9. www.newvision.co.ug/D/8/16/470167 (accessed January 5, 2006).

Ofcansky, Thomas P. 1996. *Uganda: Tarnished Pearl of Africa.* Boulder, CO: Westview Press.

Oloka-Onyango, J. 2000. "Poverty, Human Rights and the Quest for Sustainable Human Development in Structurally-Adjusted Uganda." *Netherlands Quarterly of Human Rights* 18: 23–44.

Oloka-Onyango, J. (ed.). 2001. *Constitutionalism in Africa: Creating Opportunities, Facing Challenges.* Kampala, Uganda: Fountain.

Prunier, Gérard. 2004. "Rebel Movements and Proxy Warfare: Uganda, Sudan and the Congo." *African Affairs* 103: 359–83.

Sathyamurthy, T.V. 1986. *The Political Development of Uganda: 1900–1986.* Aldershot: Gower.

Stockholm International Peace Research Institute (SIPRI). 2004. *SIPRI Yearbook.* Oxford, UK: Oxford University Press.

Tangri, Roger, and Andrew Mwenda. 2003. "Military Corruption and Ugandan Politics Since the Late 1990s." *Review of African Political Economy* 98: 539–52.

U.S. Committee for Refugees and Immigrants (USCRI). 2005. *World Refugee Survey 2005.* www.refugees.org/article.aspx?id=1342& subm=19&ssm=29&area=Investigate.

U.S. Department of State. 2005a. *Background Note: Uganda.* www.state.gov/r/pa/ei/bgn/2963.htm (accessed June 10, 2005).

U.S. Department of State. 2005b. *Country Reports on Human Rights Practices 2004—Uganda.* www.state.gov/g/drl/rls/hrrpt/2004/41632.htm (accessed June 10, 2005).

Van Acker, Frank. 2004. "Uganda and the Lord's Resistance Army: The New Order No One Ordered." *African Affairs* 103: 335–57.

Westbrook, David. 2000. "The Torment of Northern Uganda: A Legacy of Missed Opportunities." *Online Journal for Peace and Conflict Resolution* (June): 1–12.

World Vision. 2004. *Pawn of Politics: Children, Conflict and Peace in Northern Uganda.* Kampala, Uganda: World Vision Uganda.

Yemen
(1962–1970)

Introduction

Certainly before the civil war but also during and afterward, North Yemen was among the poorest and most undeveloped countries in the world. Leading up to the 1962 revolution that overthrew the 1,000-year-old theocratic government system, North Yemen was, by dint of both government policy and geography, isolated to the extreme, with minimal links not only to Western states but also to Arab countries. Some little trade originated in the country's rudimentary ports, but the economy was by and large based entirely on subsistence agriculture, which, coupled with its almost nonexistent transport and communications infrastructure, left its population in a state of severe poverty. Such government administration as existed was almost entirely restricted to resource extraction among the cities and large towns, whereas large sections of the country—primarily the mountains and deserts of the north and east—were controlled by a multitude of warring tribes and effectively outside the control of the central government.

To complicate matters, its inhabitants suffered from the singular misfortune of residing on what amounted to the battleground of the Arab cold war (Kerr 1971). Although many of the grievances that led up to the 1962 revolution were real and reflected homegrown conflicts within Yemeni society, the "civil war," for its first five years at least, was fought mainly by Egyptian

troops on the side of the fledgling republic and with Saudi funding among the supporters of the ousted royal family. What might have been yet another relatively minor armed conflict in an unstable regional backwater was transformed into something totally different by regional geopolitics, as the struggle between royalists and republicans became a battle by proxy in which "a fiery front dividing the whole Arab World" pitted the Arab monarchies against the revolutionary republics (Dresch 2000, 89–91). The war, which resulted in some 200,000 deaths and the devastation of large swaths of the countryside, was prolonged and perpetuated by external intervention. Despite multiple attempts at mediation under the sponsorship of both third parties and the participants themselves, the war itself did not so much end as die out after the departure of Egyptian troops in the aftermath of the 1967 Arab-Israeli war and the subsequent ending of Saudi subsidies to the royalist forces. The final reconciliation, achieved by Yemeni politicians under Saudi auspices in 1970, maintained the republic but produced a weak state with low levels of administrative capacity and minimal physical control over its own territory.

Country Background

Yemen as a geographic region has existed for millenia, and when the former northern and southern republics united in 1990 to form the current Republic of Yemen, they brought into political existence a country based on the model of a modern state that comprised much of historical geographic Yemen. This article focuses on the civil war waged in what was the northern republic from 1962 to 1970.

Administration of geographical Yemen has long been notoriously difficult. Its mountainous terrain provided refuge for heterodox interpretations of Islam and enabled the resident tribes to maintain a high degree of autonomy, resulting in near endemic tribal conflict. It was in this context at the end of the ninth century that several of the tribes of the north invited a well-respected Zaydi (a branch of Shi'a Islam) jurist to take up residence as imam in the city of Saada to act as a mediator between the tribes, which formed the starting point of the Zaydi Imamate. The institution and doctrine of the imamate remained essentially constant throughout the subsequent 1,000 years (Stookey 1978, 79).

During the first half of the twentieth century, Yemen remained one of the most insular societies in the world. The country's awkward mountainous geography made it difficult for the major European powers (not to mention local authorities) to subdue its tribesmen and administer the territory. In any event, there were not sufficient incentives for the great powers to bear this cost: Yemen had neither lucrative natural resources (small deposits of oil were only discovered in the 1980s) nor key strategic sites. After the withdrawal of the Turks at the end of World War I, the contemporary imam, Yahya bin Muhammad of the Hamid al-Din Dynasty, embarked on a campaign of territorial acquisition. This campaign broke the power of the strongest tribal confederation of the Red Sea coast and brought grudging acquiescence from many of the tribes of the north and east. This expansionary drive came to a halt, however, in the 1930s. After losing a war with Saudi forces, the imam signed the Treaty of Taif in 1934 that ceded to the fledgling Saudi kingdom some of his northern territories,

which would become prominent rebel staging grounds during the civil war. In the same year, the imam signed the Treaty of Sanaa with Britain, accepting the status quo and recognizing implicitly the lines of territorial demarcation agreed to by the British and Ottomans in 1905.

Government policy kept Yemen as isolated from the external world as possible. Furthermore, geography and a disinclination on the part of the imams to invest in basic transport and communications infrastructure meant that the different regions of the country were isolated from one another as well, resulting in a low volume of internal commercial and intellectual exchange (Stookey 1978, 184). Such government administration as existed was essentially extractive in the lowlands and on the coast (generally populated by Sunni Muslims of the Shafai school) but mostly nonexistent in the predominantly Zaydi highlands, where the tribes were sufficiently strong to set their own terms for taxation—that is, minimal when they were paid at all (Peterson 1982, 38–39). Fearing arbitrary tax laws and property confiscation, the small merchant class that existed avoided capital investments in Yemen proper and instead sent profits to Aden and elsewhere. The population was dispersed among approximately 50,000 small hamlets with an average settlement size of fewer than 100 people practicing subsistence agriculture, which employed at least three-quarters of the labor force (Peterson 1982, 13). No statistics were kept, and estimating the size of the economy at the beginning of the revolution would entail wild guesswork. Rough estimates from the end of the war showed the economy producing $100–$150 per capita in 1970 prices, or $350–$500 per capita at current prices, but given the sizable amount of guesswork and poor data quality, these figures should be read as indicative of magnitude.

Yemen has experienced autocratic rule of varying degrees of severity throughout the twentieth century. The prerevolutionary imamate was an absolute monarchy, with pretensions to but not the capacity for totalitarianism (polity = –6). The republican regime that took power in 1962 lurched between liberal democratic ideals and autocratic practice, varying frequently according to the strategic needs of the republic's Egyptian allies (polity = 0 in 1962 but deteriorated to –3 by 1966). The republican regime that emerged from the civil war was subject to subsequent destabilizing events in the form of border conflicts, internal dissent, and coups, which erased any slim chance there may have been that the constitution adopted at the end of 1970 would in fact produce a democratic regime (polity = –3 in 1970, which deteriorated to –4 by 1974).

The revolutionary regime that took power in 1962 was initially modeled closely on the Egyptian system. A revolutionary command council soon gave way to de facto presidential rule under Abdullah al-Sallal, but the strength of the president vis-à-vis his prime minister and his cabinet waxed and waned according to Egyptian needs and the plethora of "temporary" and "permanent" constitutions issued during the Egyptian period. Sallal was deposed bloodlessly shortly after the Egyptian withdrawal in late 1967, at which point a three-man republican council took over and vacillated between a collective executive and a military dictatorship.

The postwar regime was similar in practice to the republican system in place at the end of the war, with a few modifications. The settlement terms in 1970 expanded the republican council and added a royalist, as well as allocating a minority of seats in an appointed consultative council to the former rebels. The collective executive was retained in the 1970 constitution, although the appointed council gave way to an elected legislature, whose members took office in 1971. A weak and deadlocked government eventually fell to a military coup in 1974, the assassination of the new president in 1977, the assassination of the subsequent president shortly thereafter in 1978 by elements of the southern republic, and the rise to the presidency of Ali Abdullah Salih in 1978.

Conflict Background

The Yemeni civil war, which began the night of the coup against the imam on September 26, 1962, and ended formally with the negotiation of the national reconciliation pact in May 1970, was among the most destructive civil wars of the post–World War II era, in which as many as 200,000 people, approximately 5 percent of the population, were killed (Halliday 1974, 118). Although the war began with a revolution that enjoyed at least some initial popular enthusiasm, it was not a revolution to which large components of the population subscribed wholeheartedly. Meanwhile, an underlayer of religious and tribal tension certainly existed, in which many (but not all) Zaydi tribes lined up behind the ousted imam, and most Shafais supported the revolution, if not the particular republican governments in place, which tended to reproduce patterns of Zaydi dominance of key positions of power.

Finally, it was an ideological war to the degree that at least some republicans were fighting for "change" or "progress" and at least some royalists were fighting to protect a traditional religious institution they considered legitimate. What proportion of either side actually fought on behalf of a deeply held ideology is debatable, but if nothing else, Yemen provided the battleground for other peoples' ideological wars in that it was the venue for the Arab cold war, which pitted the revolutionary republics (Egypt in particular) against the conservative monarchies (headed by Saudi Arabia). Republican forces, which began the war with approximately 6,000 poorly trained regulars and never exceeded many more than 10,000 troops (O'Ballance 1971, 86, 136, 199), were dwarfed by the size of their Egyptian allies, whose forces several times reached 70,000 soldiers (O'Ballance 1971, 155; Stookey 1978, 238; Zabarah 1982, 74). On the royalist side, the six to seven "armies" scattered throughout the north and east counted up to approximately 2,000 semitrained soldiers each (i.e., "regular" royalist forces numbered at most 14,000 troops and probably considerably less at any given time, as the constituent soldiers faded in and out of the fighting). The vast bulk of the royalist forces consisted of tribal irregulars, which constituted up to 30,000 and 80,000 fighters from those Hashid and Bakil tribes that sided with the imam, and whose services of questionable reliability were bought by funds provided almost entirely by Saudi Arabia (O'Ballance 1971, 141, 142 fn. 1). Only after key geopolitical changes in 1967 (the Egyptian loss in the 1967 war with Israel and subsequent withdrawal from Yemen, and the emergence of a revolutionary Marxist regime in the former British possessions in the south) did the Saudi–Egyptian rivalry give way to an eventual settlement as republican forces managed to outlast their royalist opponents, who melted away in the absence of Saudi subsidies.

In the leadup to the 1962 revolution, the imamate was far from a stable institution, with coup attempts in 1948 and 1955. Some religious scholars opposed the centralization of power in the hands of the royal family and the transformation of the imamate from an elected (by them) institution to a hereditary one, and members of other notable families who had previously provided key administrators and candidates for the imamate itself shared these grievances. Some army officers and disaffected intellectuals, meanwhile, despaired of the backwardness of the country and began to argue (circumspectly) for government reform. From the latter group arose the Free Yemeni Party in 1944, a socially conservative organization that began to advocate constitutionalism from its base in Aden and whose leaders would play key roles in subsequent coup attempts and in the republican regime.

By 1962, Yemen was a hot spot of tension and intrigues. The imam, having endured numerous assassination attempts, was in ill health and increasingly unable to undertake his day-to-day administrative responsibilities. The crown prince, meanwhile, had provided ineffective leadership when previously called upon. The officer corps was increasingly politicized, in part because of the increasing use of Egyptian military trainers who took it upon themselves to offer "ideological training" as well. A group of fifteen lieutenants had formed a Free Officers Organization (modeled after the Egyptian Free Officers) in December 1961 (Peterson 1982, 86), and approximately a fifth of the 400 officers were Nasserist activists (Halliday 1974, 114). The imam was subject to a venomous propaganda assault from Cairo-based radio broadcasts. The tribes were estranged, and some elements of Hashid were alienated. It was within this environment that Imam Ahmad, defying expectations, died peacefully in his sleep on September 19. Badr ascended to the imamate, but his reign lasted only a week amid the numerous conspiracies. A group of army officers moved against the imam on the night of September 26, the next day (prematurely) announcing Badr's death and proclaiming the birth of the Yemen Arab Republic.

The Insurgents

For most of the duration of the war, two administrations—a republican one centered in the capital of Sanaa and a royalist one centered around the imam and the royal family in the mountains of the north—claimed to represent the true government of Yemen, although in practice this was a legalistic claim on the part of both administrations, neither of which actually administered much government machinery at all. Nonetheless, republican forces controlled the capital for the duration of the war, and they were recognized as the legitimate representative of Yemen by the United Nations within three months of the revolution in December 1962.

The rebels comprised the supporters of the imam, commonly referred to as the royalists. Although it was unclear where noncombatants stood in terms of their support for the imamate or the republic, the core of the support for the imam came from the constituent tribes of the two great tribal confederations in the north,

Table 1: Civil War in Yemen

War:	Royalists vs. republicans
Dates:	September 1962–May 1970
Casualties:	200,000
Regime type prior to war:	–6 (ranging from –10 [authoritarian] to 10 [democracy])
Regime type after war:	–3 (ranging from –10 [authoritarian] to 10 [democracy])
GDP per capita year war began:	Less than US $500 (1996 prices)
GDP per capita 5 years after war:	Less than US $500 (1996 prices)
Insurgents:	Royalists (supporters of the ousted imam)
Issue:	Ideological struggle for central government; proxy war between regional powers
Rebel funding:	Foreign aid (principally Saudi)
Role of geography:	Rebels based in the mountains
Role of resources:	No significant natural resources
Immediate outcome:	Saudi-brokered settlement favorable to government
Outcome after 5 years:	Coup and military government
Role of UN:	Failed mediation and peacekeeping mission
Role of regional organization:	Arab League sporadically active
Refugees:	Some internal displacement
Prospects for peace:	Continued instability

Hashid and Bakil (though a not insignificant portion of Hashid sided with the republic). Most of the tribesmen were Zaydis, and so the imam could in theory invoke religious doctrine to call upon their support. Many continued to view the imamate as the legitimate form of authority beyond the tribe, which was one of the factors that enabled the long-running effort at counterrevolution (Stookey 1978, 211–12). Although this may have been sufficient incentive for some of the tribesmen, and whereas many were opposed to what they saw as an invasion by a foreign army (the Egyptian forces), it was clear relatively early on that the large majority fought for material incentives—either for the chance to sack republican-controlled population centers, to despoil Egyptian soldiers, or usually for money or war materiel. On many occasions, the tribesmen offered their services to the highest bidder, and they often switched sides on a temporary basis to maximize their gains (O'Ballance 1971, 90). It was sometimes boasted (or decried, depending on who one asked) that the tribes were "royalist by day and republican by night" (Halliday 1974, 130, 141 fn. 18).

Although some funds and material support came from other conservative Middle Eastern and Islamic states (initially Jordan and Pakistan and later Iran), and although Britain decidedly looked the other way as major royalist supply routes emanated from the south, the vast bulk of the funds provided came from the Saudis. With no natural resources of which to speak and a rural population base living off of subsistence agriculture that produced little surplus that could be taxed, the royalist forces were almost entirely dependent on Saudi funding. The Saudi government, in turn, used this leverage to direct the royalist campaign in ways consistent with Saudi needs.

The royal family was spread loosely throughout the mountains of the north to prosecute the war but were only in sporadic contact and were, regardless, divided into factions. Although all members proclaimed loyalty to Badr as the legal imam, he was not a popular choice. Royalist inability to institute direct administration over its territory and the tribes that lived there persisted throughout the war. Taxes were collected sporadically at best, and movement within tribal

Royalist forces man a recoilless gun on the crest of Algenat Alout in January 1964. (Keystone Features/Getty Images)

territory took place only as the tribes permitted (Stookey 1978, 239–43).

Geography

Yemen's rugged topography was one of the key factors contributing to the persistence of the civil war. Given the mountainous nature of the terrain to the north, the population was scattered and isolated, public infrastructure in the form of roads and telecommunications was practically nonexistent, and the maneuverability of a conventional army was fraught with logistic problems. During the first few weeks of the war, republican forces consolidated their hold over the Shafai-majority coastal areas (the Tihama) and the triangle between the major cities of Sanaa, Taizz, and Hodayda, where there was essentially no fighting (Dresch 2000, 96). Meanwhile, royalist forces, most often based in caves,

organized themselves in the mountains of the north. From these starting points, the war swung back and forth according to whichever side happened to be waging an offensive campaign (Halliday 1974, 121), although the core republican and royalist territories were set within the first few months after the revolution.

Parallel to the Tihama, the mountains and highlands of the north and east on which the war was fought are composed of broken, difficult terrain. The sheer ruggedness of the rocky mountains throughout Yemen's history had acted as a protective natural barrier to foreign invasions as well as a buffer against the central government. It was also here, primarily in the abundant caves, that the royalist commanders made their bases of operation, although republican forces maintained a few isolated garrisons, most notably in Saada. The imam himself, for

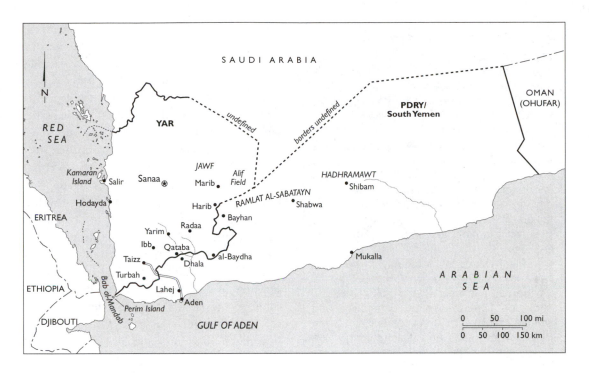

his headquarters, chose a series of caves at Mount Qara in the northwest mountains (forty miles southwest of Saada), where he stayed until being forced to relocate in August 1964. Prince Hassan Hamid al-Din took caves near Amlah (twenty miles east of Saada) for his base, and various other princes spread throughout the northern and eastern regions of the Jawf and Marib. Najran, across the border in Saudi Arabia, became a political and military rallying point for the royalists (O'Ballance 1971, 83–84).

Despite initial successes, it became clear that the conventional army sent by Egypt was ill equipped to fight a war in the mountains. Supply routes were logistically complicated and under constant threat of ambush, and the mountains themselves provided ample shelter and hiding places for royalist forces that quickly adopted guerrilla tactics. The Egyptians turned increasingly to the use of heavy bombers, but the caves provided both shelter and concealment from aerial raids. Further, one set of caves could often serve essentially as well as another, which meant that the capture of one of the headquarters would merely inconvenience royalist leaders rather than cripple them.

Tactics

The most intense fighting occurred in the initial stages of the war, as both sides attempted to achieve quick, decisive, and total victory in the military and consequently political sense. After this first period, however, the civil war evolved into one of guerrilla tactics on the part of the royalists and counterinsurgency efforts on the part of the republicans and their Egyptian allies. Traditionally, imams called upon tribal warriors for short campaigns on an ad hoc basis, sometimes against foreign invaders, sometimes under the veneer of jihad, but often

The Tribal System in Yemen

The idea of tribes and tribesmen usually conjures images of nomadic livestock herders or Bedouin living in tents in the desert, but the overwhelming majority of tribesmen in Yemen are in fact sedentary farmers who control their own land. This tribal control over the land and the self-reliance that came as a product of subsistence farming have been important in the maintenance of tribal autonomy in Yemen; the tribesmen have maintained political power because they have been both farmers and warriors (Adra 1985, 275–76).

Tribal values focus broadly on cooperation with one's own group (often defined by the particular situation) and autonomy, emphasizing honor, courage, generosity, and self-sufficiency. The large (primarily Zaydi) tribes of the north and east (primarily collected into the Hashid and Bakil confederations, regionally dominant since pre-Islamic times) could form large coalitions for collective action, whereas coordinated activity was more difficult to achieve among the (usually Shafai) tribes of the coast and lowlands (Adra 1985; Dresch 1989; Stookey 1978, 168–84).

The imams were rarely able to subdue the tribes, especially in the highlands, and ruled via a combination of persuasion, bribery, hostage taking, and using one tribe to discipline another. When the civil war broke out, most of the Zaydi tribesmen sided with the imam (although important elements of Hashid fought with the republic), but from the beginning the royalist campaign was hampered by constant bargaining with tribal leaders over the use of tribesmen as warriors and the fees and wages needed to maintain their "armies" in the field and the loyalty of their soldiers.

with strong material inducements in the form of direct payments or license to sack enemy cities (as happened to the capital after the attempted coup in 1948).

Tribesmen followed their own shaykhs, and large forces were inevitably fractious coalitions liable to splinter in short order. Hence, absent rapid progress or other inducements, the imams could not hope to maintain the cohesion of a large body of warriors, much less a standing army. Small wonder, then, that the initial royalist strategy was to drive straight for the capital to "cut off the head of the snake," bypassing other republican-held territory and population centers along the way. When the attempt to storm Sanaa failed, and especially after the Egyptian offensive of 1963 pushed the imam's supporters firmly back into the mountains, the royalists turned increasingly to guerrilla tactics that, at any rate, were sufficiently familiar to the tribesmen that they could be undertaken with minimal additional military training or discipline. The terrain and the tribesmen, who were the country's most effective fighters, determined the nature of the military tactics (Wenner 1967, 59). In general, aside from a small force assembled under Muhammad bin Hussein, the royalists had no regular army and relied almost totally on tribal forces, acting as guerrillas, the composition of which were subject to negotiation with their respective shaykhs for each contemplated operation (Stookey 1978, 243).

Royalist forces subsisted primarily on small arms, usually Saudi-supplied rifles, supplemented by whatever heavier weapons they could capture from the Egyptians or extract from the Saudis. Meanwhile, republican forces, which up through 1967 essentially meant the Egyptian Expeditionary Force (Yemeni republican troops were generally acknowledged to be ineffective, while tribal auxiliaries were notably unreliable), had access to the full weight of the Soviet-supplied Egyptian armed forces, which included tanks, armored troop carriers, MiGs, and heavy bombers. The nature of the terrain and the enemy they faced, however, substantially nullified the advantage in arms. The tribesmen learned to ambush the tanks and troop carriers in the mountain passes, which regardless were difficult to traverse. Fighter jets were an unnecessary luxury against an insurgency that had no air force. And although bombing raids frightened the tribesmen (initially) and devastated fields, there was little of intrinsic military value to target, and royalist forces could take cover in the caves and move about by night.

Despite initial successes, it became clear as the war dragged on that militarily the Egyptians were unable to cope with Yemeni conditions, as the increasing reliance on air raids attests (Halliday 1974, 127). Although the Ramadan Offensive of 1963 was a military success, it was precisely so because it was the campaign that most closely approximated a conventional ground war. Once they had pushed the royalists back into the mountains, however, their conventional superiority lost much of its edge, and the Egyptians soon began resorting to counterinsurgency tactics. Troops directed fire into the countryside "at the least excuse" and relied on "vicious air strikes" to deter attacks from hostile tribesmen (O'Ballance 1971. 108). In pursuit of the same goal, the republicans reinstituted a new version of the hostage system (imamic practice for keeping order in the countryside included taking hostages from shaykhs as pledges of good conduct) by encouraging the shaykhs to send their sons to Sanaa for school, whereas Egyptian forces sometimes dispensed with the euphemisms and simply took hostages to keep local tribes docile (O'Ballance 1971, 90–93). As the war continued, however, an uneasy stalemate set in, in which republican forces could disrupt royalist supply lines and vice-versa. It was in this context that Egyptian commanders began signing unauthorized local truces with royalist forces to allow supply chains through, which was highly embarrassing to the Egyptian high command (Wenner 1967, 212).

Causes of the War

The revolution of 1962 and subsequent civil war was brought about by domestic conflicts and enabled by external intervention. Internally, Yemen suffered from a number of growing conflicts: between liberal reformers and defenders of the status quo, between the urban population and the rural tribesmen, and between Zaydi and Shafai

Muslims. Although Yemeni in origin, these conflicts were magnified by regional geopolitics, and it is almost certainly without question that these external influences transformed what might have been a relatively limited event into a highly destructive and long-lasting civil war.

Laying aside the relatively small Ismaili and Jewish communities in Yemen, the population was divided almost evenly between Sunni Muslims following the Shafai school of law and Shi'a Muslims following the Zaydi branch. Although doctrinal differences exist, divisions between the two sects were primarily political, as "the average person in Yemen understands very little, if anything, of the doctrinal differences" (Wenner 1967, 35). Zaydis, as cosectarians of the imam, received preferred status over Shafais, who were not recruited for responsible positions in the administration or the armed forces (Stookey 1978, 172–73) and suffered from discrimination and harassment by Zaydi officials (Peterson 1982, 77).

Overlying the sectarian cleavage was the tribal system in Yemen, which tended to reinforce Zaydi dominance. Tribalism was particularly robust in the mountains of the north, where most of the tribesmen were Zaydi. The tribal system became much weaker in the lowlands and along the coast, where most Shafais lived. Although Shafai tribes existed (constituting approximately one-fifth of the tribes in Yemen), they were generally much weaker and less able to act collectively than the Zaydi tribes of the north, particularly those of the Hashid and Bakil confederations. Further, many of the inhabitants of the cities in the lowlands and the coast did not participate in the tribal system, so political divisions between the sects were further strengthened by this urban–rural division (Wenner 1967, 38–39). What small merchant community existed did so in the cities and was primarily Shafai. Yemen under the imams was far from a developmental state, and taxes and duties were designed to extract resources rather than encourage industry or commerce. It is therefore unsurprising that prominent Shafai merchants were among the key financial backers of the reformers and later the revolutionaries.

Yemen had long been poor and had long been tribal, yet the imamate had persisted for a millenium. What was different was the rest of the world, which had continued to develop and had left Yemen behind. The imams had long maintained a policy of isolationism, perhaps out of unaffected concern for the spiritual well-being of their subjects, but also certainly to preserve their (legally, if not practically) absolutist prerogatives. Yet, following a pattern that repeated itself throughout the Arab states, the imams in the twentieth century began to open Yemen very cautiously to the outside world, seeking to borrow selectively from the military and technological progress that occurred beyond its borders while keeping out cultural and political influences that could upset the status quo. As was the case in the other Arab states, however, it proved a practical impossibility to import science and technology without its attendant political and intellectual baggage.

It was within the context of the Imam's campaign to build up the power of the central government against domestic opposition (i.e., the tribes) and the power of the state against stronger regional entities (i.e., Saudi Arabia and Britain) that Yahya sent the first group of cadets to Iraq for military training in 1936, although the military coup that erupted shortly thereafter caused him to recall the cadets before the end of their training period—despite this cautionary step, these students produced "an inordinate number" of participants in the 1948 and 1955 coups, the assassination attempt of 1961, and the president and several ministers of the first republican government (Peterson 1982, 78; Stookey 1978, 190–91). There had been some mild interactions with outside powers previously, but this mission was to mark the beginning of a long and ambivalent attempt by the imams to enhance their coercive capabilities by building up the army, but with the incompatible aim of keeping the army too weak to challenge their au-

thority. The imams would later acquire military hardware from outside powers but then leave it languishing to rust in crates at the airport or disassemble and hide key components for fear that it could fall into the wrong hands, presumably those of the military, for whom it was ostensibly intended.

Those Yemenis who were able to go abroad—the military cadets, but also those who evaded emigration restrictions to work in the Gulf or Aden—were exposed to startling contrasts provided by life outside the imam's jurisdiction. The comparison was not even with the industrial countries of Europe, but with the developing countries of the Arab world. Yet this may have made the contrasts all the more troubling: The economic, social, and political conditions in these countries were significantly better than those found in Yemen and furthermore had been built up in other Arab and Muslim societies (Stookey 1978, 191). Many Yemenis, especially Shafais who had migrated for work, returned frustrated at the stagnation in Yemen and began to participate directly in political dissent, and those Yemenis who were able to leave the country for education were particularly likely to join the various opposition movements that began sprouting up (Peterson 1982, 72). There was an increased demand for reform among the young and educated, which the old adminstrative apparatus could not absorb. The country lacked basic infrastructure, and there were no tangible economic developments; and "since the Imam seemed unwilling to move in the direction of reform, the entire system appeared inert" (Zabarah 1982, 43).

It was in this domestic context that the revolutionary movements that had been springing up in the Arab world began to exert influence. Essentially begun by the 1952 Free Officers coup in Egypt, revolutionary Arab nationalism made "remarkable inroads" in Yemen during the reign of Imam Ahmad (Zabarah 1982, 37). Yet Yemen as the regional backwater was far from the locus of the geopolitical struggle, which was focused in the north between "progressive" and "conservative" regimes (Kerr 1971, 1–10). Yemen was certainly counted among the conservative states, and Imam Ahmad was subject to varying degrees of vilification by the *Voice of the Arabs* broadcast from Egypt. Despite this, the imam in 1956 signed the Arab Solidarity Pact, designed to counter the 1955 Baghdad Pact between Britain and several regional states, with Egypt and Saudi Arabia (both of whom cited the pact as justification for their intervention in the civil war), which among other things sent Yemeni cadets to Egypt for training and brought Egyptian instructors to Yemen. Although the older, Iraqi-trained officers might have been willing to reform the imamate, the new junior officers were exposed to more revolutionary ideas by their instructors, and at least some of the new officers were receptive to these ideas (Stookey 1978, 255). After Egypt and Syria united to form the short-lived United Arab Republic in 1958, Imam Ahmad confederated with them. Yet once Egypt terminated the confederation at the end of 1961, the imamate was targeted again.

After Imam Ahmad died in his sleep on the night of September 19, Badr took over the imamate and appointed himself prime minister in order to undertake a series of reforms. Whether or not he seriously intended to reform the imamate, and whether or not these reforms would have been more successful than his earlier disastrous attempts, turned out to be a moot point when a group of army officers moved against him a week later on the night of September 26. Had this particular group not done so, however, it was likely that another eventually would have; there were several cliques of officers contemplating a coup, as well as subversive groups among Hashid and Bakil (most of which did not know of each other) (O'Ballance 1971, 68). The revolutionaries were comprised of a loose coalition of the urban population: army officers, Shafai merchants, young intellectuals, Free Yemenis, and dissident expatriates. The army officers of course provided the coercive capacity, whereas the merchants provided planning and funds and helped smuggle arms and ammunition (Stookey 1978, 225–28).

Within this context, Egyptian influence proved quite important. A large body of the officer corps had formed a Nasserist society, and many were attempting to emulate the Free Officers model that had overthrown the Egyptian monarchy (Halliday 1974, 114). An Egyptian foothold in the Arabian peninsula would be geopolitically advantageous, as it would put Egypt in a position to threaten the conservative regimes there or to take control of the vast oil wealth on the peninsula. Whatever the motive, the Egyptian ambassador was either involved in, or at least had intricate knowledge of, many of the various plots against the imam. Egyptian paratroops were landing in the capital within a day of the proclamation of the republic, and war materiel was landing in the port of Hodayda within two days, and these ships must have been at sea while the coup was taking place (O'Ballance 1971, 67, 84).

Outcome

The civil war that followed the 1962 revolution lasted until 1970, although the outcome was basically established after the republican government was able to survive the departure of the Egyptian armed forces that had done most of the fighting and to break the siege of Sanaa in 1968, which turned out to be the last major push royalist forces were able to muster. After the loss in the 1967 war with Israel, Egypt withdrew its troops from Yemen and left the republican government to fend for itself (although timely assistance from the Soviet Union, the newly independent South Yemen, and Algeria helped to fill part of the gap). With the Egyptian withdrawal, the primary rationale for continued Saudi subsidization of the royalist campaign disappeared. Replacing it was a concern over the radical regime that took power upon independence in South Yemen, and Saudi interests now dictated a rapprochement with whatever government existed in the north in order to contain the south.

Conflict Status

As part of the agreement reached at the Arab League summit meeting at Khartoum in August/September 1967, the Egyptians agreed to withdraw from Yemen, while the Saudis agreed to cut off funding to the royalists, on which both governments made good (in contrast to numerous prior agreements). After the failed last campaign to seize the capital, royalist forces disintegrated quickly as no more funds came in to pay for the tribal irregulars. Sporadic fighting continued for another two years, but republican and royalist representatives (excluding the royal family) were eventually convened in Jiddah in March of 1970, where they were able to reach an agreement on national reconciliation on March 28.

The agreement amalgamated the two governments, but on an unequal basis. Members of the royal family were barred from participating, and the republic survived, with approximately the same governing institutions as had existed since shortly after the Egyptians withdrew. The appointed National Assembly was expanded from forty-five to sixty-three seats, with the additional eighteen seats going to royalist appointees. The republican council, which served as a four-man collective executive under its chair, was expanded to include a royalist. Royalists took up a minority of positions in the council of ministers and ambassadorial postings, and some provisions were made for local administration staying in the hands of whichever side controlled the territory at the time. A conference of "tribal and national" authorities was to be convened, and one of its tasks was to adopt provisions for regional autonomy. After the reconciliation agreement, a permanent constitution was drawn up, submitted for public comment, and promulgated on December 28, 1970. It sought to erect effective barriers against autocracy, provided a bill of rights, stressed the importance of Islam, and made mention of "custom" in an attempt to reassure the tribes (Halliday 1974, 138; Peterson 1982, 130; Stookey 1978, 254; Zabarah 1982, 108).

Duration Tactics

Internal strife may have caused the 1962 revolution, but external intervention enabled the civil war. Had the events of September 26 occurred without subsequent Egyptian support, it is entirely possible that the imam could have rallied the tribes against the coup plotters, as had happened in 1948 and 1955. Yet, given the Egyptian intervention "to protect the revolution" and the Saudi counterintervention, the 1962 overthrow of the Imam occurred in a fundamentally different political context.

The civil war itself went through three major stages. The most intense fighting occurred from 1962 to 1965, when both sides sought a complete political and military victory. From then until the 1967, the war was in stalemate, with numerous attempts to negotiate an Egyptian–Saudi understanding (the Yemenis were consulted only minimally), and growing dissidence among republicans. The final stage began after the Egyptian defeat in the 1967 war with Israel, after which Egypt withdrew from Yemen and Saudi Arabia ceased funding the royalists. After the last major royalist offensive failed to capture Sanaa, sporadic fighting continued (without serious threat to the republican government) until the reconciliation agreement of 1970 (Halliday 1974, 121).

The country went back and forth between offensive and counteroffensive, and meanwhile, the republic itself went through a large number of constitutions, where institutional changes tended to follow from Egyptian dictates. Although Nasser and Faysal attempted to settle the civil war between themselves on a number of occasions, the agreements generally came to little. The war had certainly reached a stalemate by February 1966, when Britain released a defense white paper that announced that it would withdraw from Aden and the Federation of South Arabia (i.e., its protectorates in what would become South Yemen) by 1968. Whereas an attempt at a settlement (possibly in good faith) was then under negotiation, the British announcement caused Nasser to redouble his commitment to the republic in order to be well positioned to influence whatever new political entity took shape there (O'Ballance 1971, 157). Only after the loss of the war with Israel did Nasser decide to withdraw from Yemen, and then only in a package deal in which Saudi Arabia and Kuwait would cover revenues lost due to the closure of the Suez Canal. As Saudi interests shifted from maintaining a buffer against the Egyptians to containing the radical regime that emerged in South Yemen, attempts at settlement increasingly began to favor conservative trends in the republic as a more realistic option than continuing to prop up the imam.

External Military Intervention

The Yemeni civil war was indelibly linked with foreign intervention. Even had the September revolution caught all outside parties unawares, the rapid deployment by Egypt (and subsequent counterintervention by the Saudi-led conservative monarchies) ensured that what might otherwise have been a relatively mild affair became a long-running, extremely destructive proxy battle (Zabarah 1982, 72, 95). The Egyptian intervention protected the nascent republic from what probably would have been rapid defeat by the northern tribes (Halliday 1974, 120), and only overall Egyptian direction of all levels of the republican government and military held the country together in the early days of the revolution (Peterson 1982, 89).

Though the civil war in Yemen pitted revolutionary republics against conservative monarchies in broad terms, in practice it meant a war fought by Egyptian troops on one side and Saudi money on the other. Nasser seized on the September revolution as an opportunity to regain the initiative in Arab affairs in the wake of the Syrian secession from the United Arab Republic: "[H]is army intervened as the champion of revolutionary progress, while Saudi Arabia and Jordan . . . were put in an an ultra-reactionary light in the eyes of their own peoples. Both Syria and Iraq recognized the revolutionaries, but could exert no influence on Yemen and could take no

credit" (Kerr 1971, 40–41). Whether or not prestige or ideology really were the key motivating factors, the vast oil wealth of the sparsely populated peninsula certainly added to the appeal of a foothold in Yemen.

The Saudis, meanwhile, decided that an Egyptian-backed revolution on their borders constituted a mortal threat, especially given early republican pronouncements that "Yemen considers itself at war with Saudi Arabia" and proclamations of intent to create a Republic of the Arabian Peninsula (Dresch 2000, 91; Wenner 1967, 194). Saudi forces were incapable of defending the kingdom's border against the Egyptian army, and Egyptian aircraft made unopposed bombing sorties into Saudi territory. Saudi counterintervention, in other words, was essentially defensive, and it soon developed that their only effective buffer was the ability of the royalist forces to stave off the Egyptian military, which at times bombed Saudi towns and cities (O'Ballance 1971, 87; Stookey 1978, 247; Wenner 1967, 200 fn. 22).

Events in Yemen did not fail to arouse the interests of the superpowers. The Soviet Union and the eastern bloc countries supported the republic with arms shipments, training, and economic assistance (Zabarah 1982, 79). Although most of this aid did not actually trickle down to the Yemenis themselves—having first been filtered through their Egyptian allies—Soviet aid became relatively more important after the Egyptian withdrawal beginning in late 1967 and was instrumental in helping republican forces withstand the siege of Sanaa.

The United States was uneasy about Soviet aid to the republic and expressed concern about threats to Saudi Arabia, with which it had a special relationship due to the massive oil reserves found in the kingdom. Early in the war, the Kennedy administration promised to support Saudi territorial integrity, and this promise was later backed up by shows of force and military aid, as when in early January 1963 the United States dispatched jet fighters, a destroyer, and paratroopers to Saudi Arabia in response to

Money in Yemen

Yemen under the imams was among the poorest countries on earth—a situation that persists today. The extremely primitive nature of the economy was compounded by the (non)administration of the state's finances. The imams were notoriously tightfisted with state and personal revenues (the distinction barely existed), but it would have been unclear how large the state's financial reserves were, for no statistics, fiscal or otherwise, were kept (O'Ballance 1971, 34–35; Peterson 1982, 70–71).

In addition to a lack of even basic statistics about the population and economy, Yemen had no banking system (nor any banks) and no monetary system. Transactions were conducted in cash, using the Maria Theresa thaler as the currency. The thaler was a heavy silver coin minted in Europe (though later struck from European molds in Yemen) that fluctuated according to the world price in silver. Anecdotes abound on the difficulty and nuisance of using this particular form of currency: Merchants needed to keep huge sacks of the coins to conduct their transactions, government employees had to go to the treasury with a camel or donkey to collect their wages, and dues to international organizations such as the United Nations were paid on the order of tons of coins (at prices prevailing at the time, a pound of the coins was worth approximately $10 to $15 US) (O'Ballance 1971, 34; Stookey 1978, 202).

Egyptian bombing raids on Saudi territory (Wenner 1967, 205), and later in 1965, when both the United States and Britain began shipping large consignments of fighter jets and other military equipment to the kingdom (Zabarah 1982, 99). Despite these shows of support for Saudi Arabia and concern over increasing amounts of Soviet aid flowing to republican forces, the United States recognized the republic on December 19, 1962 (United Nations recognition followed the day after), possibly in an attempt to disassociate itself from "feudal regimes," possibly to scare its conservative allies into re-

form, and possibly to grant Nasser the option to withdraw gracefully. In any event, it became clear later that American recognition was part of a tacit agreement with Egypt in which the latter was to withdraw from Yemen in return for recognition of the republic and cessation of Saudi aid to the royalists, although the sincerity of Egyptian intentions was subsequently put to doubt (Wenner 1967, 203).

After Egyptian troops began arriving in republican-held territory, Egyptian officers quickly took control of most substantial elements of the military campaign, as well as administration of the country. Almost from the beginning, the Egyptian Expeditionary Force "fought the war as foreign invaders rather than as allies of the young republic" (Halliday 1974, 127), which caused considerable resentment among the erstwhile tribal forces they used as irregulars as well as among more independent-minded politicians, who increasingly joined dissident groups and attended conferences aimed at national reconciliation convened independently. Egypt maintained control of aid inflows, which meant that most of what was earmarked for the republic by other Arab or Soviet bloc countries was actually used or distributed by Egypt itself (O'Ballance 1971, 107, 163–64). The president of the republic, Abdullah al-Sallal, was called to Cairo frequently for "consultations" and was sometimes detained there when his presence in Yemen was problematic for Egyptian strategy (as, for instance, when he was kept in Cairo for approximately a year in 1965–1966). Other key politicians were frequently detained in a similar fashion, to be released when it served Egyptian interests.

Royalist forces, meanwhile, were heavily dependent on Saudi funding and support, and this aid varied in volume according to whether or not an attempted settlement was in the works or if royalist maneuvering displeased the Saudi government sufficiently. Aid came in "massive doses" of money and arms when it appeared necessary, but supplies tended to slack off whenever Saudi Arabia believed it necessary to permit

Egyptian forces the opportunity to extract themselves from Yemen (Stookey 1978, 247; Zabarah 1982, 75–76).

The war dragged on longer than Nasser may have calculated initially, and insofar as Yemen was "a testing ground for the struggle for influence between the forces of revolution and conservatism," Egypt became mired in what was sometimes called "Nasser's Vietnam" (Kerr 1971, 111). Egyptian troop totals expanded and contracted over the course of the war in line with changes in Egyptian strategy. More than 3,000 troops had landed within a few days of the revolution, and by the end of 1962, 15,000–20,000 soldiers were stationed there. The number climbed to 30,000 by the middle of 1963 in the context of the Ramadan Offensive and by mid-1964 reached 50,000. More than 70,000 Egyptian soldiers were in Yemen in August 1965, after which Egyptian troops began to withdraw under the stipulations of the Jiddah Agreement. After the British announcement in February 1966 that it would be evacuating the south by 1968, Egyptian strategy again changed as its reduced force of 20,000 soldiers mostly withdrew into the Sanaa-Taizz-Hodayda triangle to wait out the British (and the royalists). Troop totals again rose and by the end of 1966 reached 60,000–70,000. Egypt began withdrawing its soldiers in the leadup to the war with Israel in 1967 and just before the war in June had perhaps 15,000 troops in Yemen. After the loss, troop levels rose again slightly to 25,000 at the beginning of July but were finally withdrawn according to the conditions of the Khartoum Agreement beginning in October 1967. Troop figures are scattered throughout a wide variety of sources. The strengths of the Egyptian Expeditionary Force were not published, and given its dispersion through Yemen and troop rotations, the total number was often difficult to assess accurately (O'Ballance 1971, 97). Figures cited (and intervening totals) can be found in Dresch (2000, 90), Halliday (1974, 118), O'Ballance (1971, 84, 97–98, 128, 155–57, 168, 182–83), Wenner (1967, 198, 206–207, 210), and Zabarah (1982, 74, 99).

Saudi policy at this point began to shift. The Soviet Union, Syria, and Algeria began to fill some of the gap left by the departing Egyptians in terms of arms and money; the Federation of South Arabia had collapsed, and the radical National Liberation Front had taken over in what became South Yemen (and in fact began sending volunteers to fight alongside the republicans and to help in forming increasingly radicalized popular militias). The imam and the royal family were becoming liabilities, and Saudi policy shifted from support for the royalists to willingness to deal with conservative elements among the republicans to help contain South Yemen (Stookey 1978, 252).

Conflict Management Efforts

Initial mediation efforts took the form of a letter from President John F. Kennedy to the leaders of Saudi Arabia, Egypt, Jordan, and the republican government (but not to the imam, whose government still enjoyed official American recognition) in late November 1962, proposing that Egypt would withdraw all its troops and materiel from Yemen, while the Saudi, Jordanian, and British-protected South Arabian Federation governments would cease all assistance to royalist forces. Both Saudi Arabia and Egypt rejected the initiative the next day, however (Wenner 1967, 199–200). This initial effort thwarted, Kennedy sent a mission under Ellsworth Bunker to the region in March 1963, while the United Nations sent its own mission under Ralph Bunche. Neither made any attempts to see royalist representatives, and it was within this context that Egypt drastically increased the number of troops in Yemen during the Ramadan Offensive (probably to present a fait accompli to the missions). By mid-April, however, Bunker was able to extract a commitment from both Saudi Arabia and Egypt to establish a "disengagement." The secretary-general of the United Nations, U Thant, was subsequently able to announce the agreement to the Security Council on April 30, 1963, in which Saudi Arabia pledged to cease all aid to the imam, and Egypt agreed to a phased withdrawal of its troops and not to take punitive action against royalist forces or breach Saudi territory. The two countries and the republican government consented to the creation of a team of United Nations observers, the costs of which would be born equally by Egypt and Saudi Arabia (Wenner 1967, 206–207).

An advance team of the United Nations Yemen Observer Mission (UNYOM) arrived in mid-June, although actual operations did not begin until the beginning of July. It was to be constituted as a 200-member force, although it was significantly smaller in practice, with as few as twenty-five members. It was "far too small to carry out even an observation role properly," especially since it was tasked with ensuring that no Saudi aid crossed the long Saudi–Yemeni frontier and that no new Egyptian troops entered to replace those departing (O'Ballance 1971, 103–105; Wenner 1967, 208). In mid-August, the commander of the force resigned, complaining of inadequate support, managerial incompetence of the Secretariat, neglect of his reports, and an unrealistic attitude toward UNYOM's capabilities (UNYOM, for instance, was prohibited from any contact with royalist forces until late August). In early November, U Thant announced that Egypt and Saudi Arabia were willing to continue funding an extended mandate, and regular two-month extensions under a series of commanders followed until the mandate was finally allowed to expire in early September 1964 (Wenner 1967, 208–10).

After the failure of the UNYOM mission, attempts at negotiation came either from within the Arab world or from within Yemen itself. Unfortunately, the Arab League, at least early on in the civil war, was unable to play a useful role in conflict mediation because it was itself rent by the geopolitical jockeying of its various member states:

> By the end of January 1963 . . . members of the League had fallen into a long and complex pattern of quarrels. Iraq refused to recognize Kuwait, and on this account had recalled its ambassadors from all other League members.

Egypt had never recognized the Syrian regime, and had broken off diplomatic relations with Jordan. After the Yemeni republican revolution, diplomatic relations between Saudi Arabia and Egypt were broken off as well. Egypt, Iraq, Syria, and Lebanon recognized the Yemeni republicans; Saudi Arabia and Jordan still recognized the royalists (Kerr 1971, 40).

Yet inter-Arab relations appeared on the mend by the time of the Arab League summit meeting in Cairo in January of 1964, and then direct Egyptian–Saudi negotiations at the second summit meeting in Alexandria in September produced a plan similar to the United Nations disengagement plan but with a joint Saudi–Egyptian force playing UNYOM's role. The two countries agreed to "replace" the leaders of the opposing factions and create a new government. As a result of this agreement, representatives of the two factions met at Erkwit in Sudan from October 30 to November 4. The participants announced that a National Congress would take place in late November, to be attended by tribal, religious, and military leaders (O'Ballance 1971, 131; Wenner 1967, 215). None of these steps had any practical effect, however, and the cease-fire broke down almost immediately (Wenner 1967, 214–15; Zabarah 1982, 97).

The civil war continued in the wake of the failure of the Erkwit Conference, punctuated by growing republican dissent and occasional attempts to convene peace conferences outside the reach of the republican government or the Egyptian forces. The next attempt at outside mediation, again between Egypt and Saudi Arabia, occurred in late August 1965, when Nasser flew to Jiddah to meet with King Faysal. The Jiddah Peace Plan, announced August 24, contained a number of points that, at least initially, both Egypt and Saudi Arabia appeared intent on implementing. As before, there was to be an Egyptian withdrawal (this time phased over a ten-month period) in exchange for the Saudis withholding all military assistance to the royalists. A transitional council comprised of fifty members of all national interests would decide on a temporary system of government and prepare a national plebiscite to determine which form of government Yemenis wanted. A joint Saudi–Egyptian committee would supervise the borders and ports to ensure that no further military assistance reached either side (Wenner 1967, 219–21).

The council, composed of twenty-five royalist and twenty-five republican representatives (with liasons from Egypt and Saudi Arabia), convened in Harad on November 23 and deadlocked almost immediately. Part of the problem, again, was that this was a peace plan authored at the behest of the Egyptian and Saudi heads of state and designed to meet their objectives first and foremost. "Nobody consulted the Yemenis at Jiddah. No one even seemed to consider what the Yemenis might think, except to assume that whatever Nasser and Faysal agreed upon would be acceptable to republicans and royalists" (Kerr 1971, 108). The conference broke for Ramadan in late December and adjourned until February 20, 1966, though in fact it never reconvened. More Egyptian troops and equipment began to arrive in early January, and in late February Nasser announced that Egypt would stay as long as necessary (O'Ballance 1971, 154; Wenner 1967, 221–23).

The Yemeni civil war again reverted to a stalemate, which ultimately was not broken until the 1967 Arab-Israeli War in June. At the Arab League summit begun in late August in Khartoum, Nasser agreed to withdraw his troops, after which Faysal agreed to end the subsidies paid to the royalists. Egypt began its withdrawal by mid-October and completed it soon thereafter. The last Saudi aid to the royalists had ceased by March of 1968, after the failure of the siege of Sanaa (O'Ballance 1971, 186–87, 200).

Over the course of 1968 and 1969, conservative elements within the republic were able to dismantle leftist power bases and began to negotiate a final rapprochement with some of the key tribal shaykhs (Halliday 1974, 137). Yemeni republican delegates to an Islamic Conference being held in Jiddah in March 1970 were subsequently able, under Saudi auspices, to meet with senior royalists (excluding the royal family) to reach agreement on national reconciliation, which was announced March 28 and which was to mark an end to polemics and a final cease-fire (Halliday 1974, 138; Stookey 1978, 255; Zabarah 1982, 108).

Conclusion

By the time the civil war was over, Yemen had been relegated to the familiar position of regional backwater—the Saudi–Egyptian geopolitical struggle had ceased, and the rest of the world had long since ceased to care. The new government inherited a wasted economy, a weak security apparatus, and minimal administrative capacity. The state remained impoverished, and the government was unable to meet its own budgetary needs without foreign assistance (Peterson 1982, 16; Stookey 1978, 258–62).

Given its poverty and weakness, it was little wonder that Yemen suffered from significant political instability, including a coup in 1974, an assassinated president in 1977, and another one in 1978. Though Yemen did achieve some degree of political stability under President Ali Abdullah Salih from 1978 on, it only rarely entered Western consciousness as something other than a political curio as "one of the two Yemens." Although Yemen did attain positive coverage when the northern and southern republics united in 1990 and subsequently held reasonably respectable parliamentary elections in 1993, the short civil war of 1994 served as a reminder that Yemen was a far from stable place. The country lapsed into the background again until the bombing of an American destroyer in Aden in 2000 and the September 2001 attacks on the World Trade Center put Yemen back on the map as a potential ally in (or site for) the "war on terror."

The contemporary campaign against extremist groups—either transnational or homegrown offshoots—is often fought in poor countries that are either failed or in danger of failing. The focus has expanded beyond particularly salient sites, such as Afghanistan, to include less well-known countries, for example, in and around the horn of Africa (Burrowes 2005), where the focus has shifted increasingly to state building: improving the capacity of governments to actually govern the territories they claim. Many people, particularly those tasked with selling the war on terror to their own publics, cite poverty and lack of freedom as the key sources of militancy. To the degree that this claim is true, a policy of propping up friendly dictators is unlikely to produce long-term security gains. Countries such as Yemen—impoverished, insecure, and difficult to administer—will continue for the foreseeable future to be venues for the war on terror. Success will probably be defined in terms of security outcomes, but whether this security comes from police crackdowns or from tangible economic and political development will likely determine how long this security will last.

Daniel Corstange

Chronology

September 19, 1962   Imam Ahmad dies. Crown Prince Muhammad al-Badr succeeds to the imamate.

September 26, 1962   Military coup d'état overthrows imamate.

September 27, 1962   Yemen Arab Republic is declared; Egyptian troops begin to arrive.

November 27, 1962   Kennedy peace proposals are announced but rejected the next day.

December 19, 1962   United States recognizes the republic; UN recognition follows the next day.

July 1963   United Nations Yemen Observation Mission arrives in Yemen.

August 26, 1964   Imam's headquarters captured, but imam escapes.

September 4, 1964   United Nations Yemen Observation Mission withdraws.

September 1964   Direct negotiations occur between Egypt and Saudi Arabia for the first time at the Second Arab League Summit Conference in Alexandria.

October 30–November 4, 1964   Erkwit Conference is held.

April 30–May 5, 1965   Khamir National Peace Conference is held.

August 24, 1965   Jiddah peace plan agreed upon between Egypt and Saudi Arabia.

November 23–December 24, 1965   Harad Conference is held.

February 20, 1966   Britain issues defense white paper announcing its withdrawal from Aden and the Federation of South Arabia by 1968.

June 1967   June War: Israeli forces occupy Egypt's Sinai Peninsula.

August 31, 1967   Egyptian–Saudi agreement reached at Khartoum Summit Conference.

November 3, 1967   Sallal leaves for exile and is formally deposed two days later.

November 30, 1967   National Liberation Front assumes power in South Yemen.

December 1, 1967–February 8, 1968   Siege of Sanaa.

March 28, 1970   Royalist–republican negotiations culminate in a national reconciliation pact.

July 1970   Saudi Arabia and Yemen establish normal diplomatic relations.

December 28, 1970   Permanent constitution promulgated.

March 1971   First popular elections in Yemeni history are held for the Consultative Council.

References

Adra, N. (1985). "The Concept of Tribe in Rural Yemen." In *Arab Society: Social Science Perspectives,* edited by S. E. Ibrahim and N. S. Hopkins, 275–85. Cairo, Egypt: American University in Cairo Press.

Bidwell, R. 1983. *The Two Yemens.* Boulder, CO: Westview Press.

Burrowes, R. D. 1987. *The Yemen Arab Republic: The Politics of Development, 1962–1986.* Boulder, CO: Westview Press.

Burrowes, R. D. 2005. "Yemen: Political Economy and the Effort Against Terrorism." In *Battling Terrorism in the Horn of Africa,* edited by R. I. Rotberg, 141–72. Washington, DC: Brookings Institution Press.

Carapico, S. 1998. *Civil Society in Yemen.* New York: Cambridge University Press.

Dresch, P. 1989. *Tribes, Government, and History in Yemen.* Oxford, UK: Clarendon Press.

Dresch, P. 2000. *A History of Modern Yemen.* Cambridge, UK: Cambridge University Press.

Halliday, F. 1974. *Arabia Without Sultans.* New York: Vintage Books.

Kerr, M. H. 1971. *The Arab Cold War: Gamal 'abd al-Nasir and His Rivals, 1958–1970,* 3rd ed. New York: Oxford University Press.

O'Ballance, E. 1971. *The War in the Yemen.* London: Faber and Faber.

Peterson, J. E. 1982. *Yemen: The Search for a Modern State.* London: Croom Helm.

Stookey, R. W. 1978. *Yemen: The Politics of the Yemen Arab Republic.* Boulder, CO: Westview Press.

Wenner, M. 1967. *Modern Yemen 1918–1966.* Baltimore: Johns Hopkins University Press.

Zabarah, M. A. 1982. *Yemen: Traditionalism vs. Modernity.* New York: Praeger.

Zimbabwe
(1972–1979)

Introduction

Between 1972 and 1979, black African nationalists fought the white-ruled Rhodesian government for control of the country now known as Zimbabwe. The Rhodesian/Zimbabwean civil war could be variously described as an ethnic conflict (white Africans versus black Africans), an ideological battle for control of the state (procapitalist government versus socialist rebels), or a war against a repressive regime. Yet to reduce this conflict to any one of these paradigms would be to obscure a complex reality that touched on all these themes and others; for example, the importance of geography, transnationalization of conflict, foreign intervention, mediation, and international attempts at conflict management.

Ultimately, the nationalists were successful in bringing about majority rule and ending the reign of an oppressive regime that had become an international pariah. However, the legacy of the conflict would include an armed, organized, and ethnically divided African society that would fall back into conflict four years later, and the entrenchment of a one-party state under President Robert Mugabe that would become increasingly authoritarian over time. That a civil war fought along ethnic lines would lead to renewed ethnic conflict within the victorious coalition highlights the complexity and danger of activating ethnicity as an organizational strategy and a source of political identity.

Country Background

Zimbabwe is a landlocked country in southern Africa situated between South Africa, Botswana, Mozambique, and Zambia. Before the colonial period, two main ethnic groups resided in the country: the Shona, who make up roughly 82 percent of the population, and the Ndebele, who constitute another 14 percent. The Ndebele, who are concentrated in the southwestern regions of the country, migrated up from South Africa during the 1830s, conquered the Shona, and established a kingdom across much of the area of modern-day Zimbabwe.

Geographically, Zimbabwe is relatively flat in the west and mountainous in the east, near the border with Mozambique. The Zambezi River marks the border with Zambia, and the Limpopo River defines the southern frontier with South Africa. Most people are employed in agriculture, with the main cash crops being tobacco and cotton, although mining activity (gold, coal, copper, nickel) makes up a significant share of the economy.

Although Robert Moffatt was the first British citizen to reach the country in 1854, he was followed by his son-in-law, the famous explorer David Livingstone. Christian missionaries soon began to arrive, and news of the natural and mineral wealth of Zimbabwe reached England. Cecil Rhodes (see sidebar, "Cecil Rhodes"), who had made a fortune in South Africa's Kimberly mines, soon became interested in Zimbabwe for economic reasons, and under the British South African Company took the country in the name of the British Empire in 1890, after which it was named Southern Rhodesia (Zambia was called Northern Rhodesia). Although it soon became apparent that mining prospects were limited, hundreds of British settlers took residence in Rhodesia after the colonial government made generous land offers.

The conflict in Zimbabwe pitted the white settler government against black African guerrilla fighters. Before the conflict, black Africans had been systematically disenfranchised by the minority white government through strict requirements on voter eligibility that barred all but a handful of black citizens from the polls. The expropriation of land resources by settlers also limited black economic prospects. At the end of the war, universal franchise was granted with significant power-sharing guarantees for the white population, and in 1980 Robert Mugabe, head of the Zimbabwe African National Union, became the country's first black African head of state. However, despite the euphoria that followed the first election, Mugabe quickly moved to impose one-party rule and silence his opponents, including Africans who had fought with him during the civil war. During the most intense phase of the conflict, from 1976 to 1979, thousands of white settlers emigrated from Zimbabwe, taking much of their wealth and expertise with them, causing GDP (gross domestic product) to fall substantially. Since 1980, frequent attacks on white farms and mismanagement of redistributed lands have led to food shortages and famine.

Cecil Rhodes

The name *Zimbabwe* is a Shona term meaning "Stone House" or "House of the Chief," referring to ruins that mark the capital of the ancient kingdom of Great Zimbabwe. However, until liberation from white rule in 1980, the country was referred to as Rhodesia after the political and business leader, Cecil Rhodes, who conquered the area for Great Britain. It was also called Southern Rhodesia before present-day Zambia, formerly known as Northern Rhodesia, gained independence.

Cecil Rhodes is undoubtedly one of the most important and controversial figures in African colonial history. Rhodes was born in England in 1853 but moved to South Africa in 1870 to reunite with his brother. While in South Africa, Rhodes successfully invested in diamond mining—he was a cofounder of the DeBeers mining company—and rose to prominence in the region as a successful entrepreneur. In addition to his business success, he became an influential figure in the British colonial government, eventually becoming prime minister of the Cape Colony.

Rhodes's interest in the region that is now known as Zimbabwe was partly for his own commercial interests and partly due to his belief in the expansion of the British Empire. His writings suggest that he firmly believed in the superiority of European, and particularly British, culture, and he supported British efforts to acquire continuous holdings from Cape Town to Cairo. Under suspicious circumstances, in 1888 Rhodes convinced the Ndebele king, Lobengula, to grant him mining concessions in the area, but his intention to take the region for the British Crown quickly became clear. Under the British South Africa Company, Rhodes received a royal charter in 1889, with which he raised his own private army, invaded Mashonaland and Matabeleland, and deposed Lobengula (who later died of smallpox). His conquests took him farther north as well, into modern-day Zambia. Lured by Rhodes's promise of mining and farming wealth, white settlers quickly took holdings in the new colony, displacing the black African population and sowing the seeds of future conflict.

Rhodes's poor health was a constant problem for him. He died of heart failure in 1902 at the age of forty-nine. As part of his will, Rhodes established the prestigious Rhodes Scholarship, which, unlike the country he conquered, still bears his name (Roberts 1987).

The legacy of the war continues to shape Zimbabwean politics. Most important, although the conflict succeeded in putting an end to a discriminatory system that denied black Africans their basic human rights, ethnic relations have never fully healed. To this day, black African resentment over decades of ill treatment and the continued economic dominance of the white minority sporadically boils over into violence. Moreover, relations between the Shona and the Ndebele minority are often strained.

Conflict Background

Dissatisfaction with white settler rule and the acquisition of the most productive agricultural lands by British settlers led to a mass uprising by both the Ndebele and the Shona in 1896. This conflict, known as the First Chimurenga, or uprising, would inspire the Second Chimurenga, from the mid-1960s through the end of white rule in 1980. The unequal distribution of land was perhaps the most contentious issue during both chimurengas and remains a hot political issue to this day. Whites, who made up a small fraction of the population, owned most of the land and settled in the most agriculturally productive regions of the country.

Not only did the white settlers dominate in agriculture, mining, and urban enterprises, they also dominated the colonial government, despite their status as a small minority. By the early 1960s, black nationalist parties demanding majority rule and land redistribution began to turn to violent tactics, beginning with acts of sabotage and rioting. Although Great Britain was growing sympathetic to the idea of independence and greater African representation, the white settler government, led by the Rhodesian Front (RF) prime minister, Ian Smith, was not willing to compromise. In 1965, the Rhodesian government made a unilateral declaration of independence, freeing itself from British rule but retaining white dominance over the government.

From the mid- to late 1960s, two main rebel factions, the Zimbabwe African National Union (ZANU) and the Zimbabwe African People's Union (ZAPU), fought against the Rhodesian government. ZANU was concentrated in the north and east of the country and made extensive use of bases in neighboring Mozambique. ZAPU fought from bases in Zambia and Botswana and concentrated its efforts in the southwestern parts of Zimbabwe. The rebel factions were split along ethnic lines, with ZAPU drawing its support mainly from Ndebele regions and ZANU being a largely Shona party. Although there were attempts to unify the parties in later stages of the conflict, these efforts were short lived and of limited success.

The first shots were fired on April 28, 1966, when a small group of guerrillas crossed the Zambia–Rhodesia border and engaged the Rhodesian Security Forces (RSF) in the town of Sinoia. However, major guerrilla offensives did not begin until late 1972, when ZANU conducted a number of strikes in the northeast. The fighting escalated over the next few years, with the most intense fighting occurring during the final years of the conflict. The rebels were not successful in taking control of significant parts of Zimbabwe, but they were able to cause serious disruption across the country, eventually forcing the government to grant most of their demands as embodied in the Lancaster House Agreement of 1980.

Norma Kriger (1992) estimates that by the end of the war, there were roughly 20,000 ZANU and 8,000 ZAPU guerrillas. She also writes that between December 1972 and early 1979, more than 6,000 rebels had been killed, along with 760 Rhodesian security personnel, 3,845 black civilians, and 310 white civilians. In addition to the dead, the conflict caused tens of thousands of refugees to flee to nearby countries, where refugee camps became a source of rebel supplies, recruits, and subsequent targets for RSF cross-border offensives.

There were efforts at peace before the implementation of a final agreement. In 1978, the white regime signed an agreement to form a coalition government with the United African

Table 1: Civil War in Zimbabwe

War:	ZAPU and ZANU rebels vs. government
Dates:	December 1972–December 1979
Casualties:	27,000
Regime type prior to war:	4 (ranging from −10 [authoritarian] to 10 [democracy])
Regime type after war:	5 (ranging from −10 [authoritarian] to 10 [democracy])
GDP per capita year war began:	US $1,481 (constant 1990)
GDP per capita 5 years after war:	US $1,466 (constant 1990)
Insurgents:	ZANU (Zimbabwe African National Union), ZAPU (Zimbabwe African People's Union)
Issue:	Ideological/ethnic struggle for control of central government
Rebel funding:	Soviet and Chinese aid, revolutionary taxation
Role of geography:	Safe havens in bordering countries (Zambia, Mozambique, Botswana)
Role of resources:	Conflict over distribution of farmland
Immediate outcome:	UK-brokered peace settlement leading to 1980 elections, ZANU leader Robert Mugabe elected president
Outcome after 5 years:	Renewed conflict between ZAPU and ZANU partisans
Role of UN:	Facilitated peace talks; no peacekeepers
Role of regional organization:	None; frontline states participated in multilateral talks.
Refugees:	198,000
Prospects for peace:	Unfavorable

Sources: Heston, Summers, and Aten 2006; Polity IV Project 2006.

National Congress (UANC), with Bishop Abel Muzorewa as the new Prime Minister. However, this agreement was rejected by ZANU and ZAPU, who saw Muzorewa's "black" government as a front, with real political power still in the hands of whites. The war officially ended in a negotiated settlement of December 21, 1979. Under pressure from neighboring states, the United Kingdom, and the United States, the parties to the conflict came to an agreement that granted universal suffrage, in effect ending white settler rule. However, substantial constitutional guarantees were given to ensure the protection of white economic and political interests, along with their physical safety.

The Insurgents

The primary rebel organizations were the military wings of ZAPU and ZANU: the Zimbabwean People's Revolutionary Army (ZIPRA) and the Zimbabwean African National Liberation Army (ZANLA), respectively. Following the banning of ZAPU as a legitimate civic or-

ganization in 1962, the party moved to more militant tactics, and ZIPRA was founded in Zambia under the leadership of Joshua Nkomo. Nkomo was born in 1918, was educated at missionary schools, and attended the University of Fort Hare in South Africa. Studying at the first university open to black Africans on the continent, Nkomo was part of a cohort that included many of the most significant figures in the various African independence movements, among them Kenneth Kaunda (later president of Zambia), Nelson Mandela (later president of South Africa), Seretse Khama (later president of Botswana), and Julius Nyerere (later president of Tanzania), as well as two individuals who would form the core leadership of the Zimbabwean nationalist movement, Herbert Chitepo and Robert Mugabe.

In 1963, ZANU split from ZAPU under the political leadership of Ndabiningi Sithole. Although the split may be attributed to personal animosities within the leadership, over time the split has come to be understood as motivated by ethnic cleavages within ZAPU. Although ethnic

Table 2: Refugees from Zimbabwe in the Frontline States

	1975	1976	1977	1978	1979
Botswana	80	1,100	4,000	17,760	22,530
Mozambique	14,500	30,000	42,400	100,000	150,000
Zambia	N/A	120	30,000	45,320	25,000

Sources: United Nations High Commissioner for Refugees. Data for earlier periods not available.

lines of division were never absolutely clear in practice, ZAPU was mostly composed of ethnic Ndebele, and ZANU was predominantly Shona. Another group, the largely nonviolent United African National Congress, led by Archbishop Abel Muzorewa, was much more moderate than the radical ZANU and ZAPU. Before the final peace agreement, Muzorewa would be asked to head the Rhodesian government, although most black Africans dismissed this government as merely a black façade of the white regime.

In the early years (1964–1977), rebels relied upon a mixture of popular mobilization and coercive recruitment. Political rallies espousing socialism and black nationalism drew several thousand people into the cause. Press-ganging and abductions were also common recruitment tactics employed by both ZIPRA and ZANLA forces (Kriger 1992). However, large-scale coercive recruitment had been largely abandoned by 1977. To begin with, there was international outrage over the practice, and it failed to generate loyal soldiers. Specifically, Preston (2004) argues that international media portrayal of two events—ZANLA's abduction of hundreds of children from a Catholic missionary school in 1973 and ZIPRA's similar raid on the Manama secondary school in 1977—brought international condemnation. Once under arms, unwilling soldiers would often desert at the first opportunity, in many instances providing intelligence to the RSF about their former captors. Several of these "turned" rebels wound up in the RSF, including in the elite counterinsurgency force, the Selous Scouts (see sidebar, "The Selous Scouts").

Another reason coercive recruiting tactics were abandoned is that the deteriorating economic sit-

uation in Rhodesia/Zimbabwe—the product of the ongoing insurgency and international sanctions against Rhodesia—made joining rebel forces more attractive to young Zimbabweans. Preston notes also that between 1975 and 1978, real GDP decreased by 12 percent, with an even larger drop (20 percent) in real wages. Further, by 1976 Rhodesia/Zimbabwe was graduating 50,000 black African students per year with no job prospects and no access to farmable land. Indeed, an *Economist* report on the Manama incident demonstrates that the alleged "kidnappings" may have been facilitated by this economic logic:

> The Rhodesian government says they [the recruits] were forced to go at gunpoint: the Botswana government says that 384 youngsters who arrived all claimed to have left Rhodesia willingly. The Rhodesian argument is strengthened by the fact that 10 children, together with two teachers, returned home saying they had escaped. The Botswanan argument is strengthened by the fact that so few managed to get away. It would be hard for four armed men to conduct nearly 400 young people between the ages of 12 and 21 through 12 miles of bush at night if most of them had not been willing to go (*Economist*, 1977a).

The article then goes on to quote several teachers at the academy who reported that students were planning to join the insurgency anyway, due to a lack of employment opportunities. Moreover, constant attacks on rural infrastructure, especially the educational, health care, and freshwater supply systems were generating as many as 50,000 refugees a year (Preston 2004). These highly politicized populations were fertile ground for rebel recruiting efforts.

The Selous Scouts

Cunning, highly mobile, multiethnic, and with unparalleled bush fighting skills, the Selous Scouts were the most feared of all Rhodesian state forces. However, the Selous Scouts came to represent the failure of a counterinsurgency doctrine concerned more with military superiority than with winning the "hearts and minds" of the population. Although responsible for the most significant state victories of the campaign, their often brutal tactics ultimately eroded any remaining support for the government in rural Zimbabwe.

In response to an escalation of insurgent activities in December 1972, the Selous Scouts were formed in 1973 under the direction of Captain Ron Reid-Daly. Reid-Daly had joined the military in 1951 as a member of the Rhodesia Squadron of the British Special Air Services (SAS). His formative experiences as a counterinsurgency specialist came during the British campaign against Communist insurgents in the then British-controlled Federation of Malaya (present-day Malaysia).

The Selous Scouts were a mixed-race fighting force composed of highly motivated volunteers and "turned" guerrilla fighters. There is little argument about their combat capabilities. Skilled at clandestine operations and tracking, the Selous Scouts were responsible for an estimated two-thirds of all enemy combatant deaths. Moreover, the Selous Scouts conducted attacks on guerrilla bases in Mozambique and Zambia, including a 1979 attack on ZIPRA headquarters in Lusaka, Zambia, that nearly ended in the death of Joshua Nkomo.

Despite their formidable military capacity, the Selous Scouts were not successful in developing rural support for the Rhodesian government. Most corrosive to their attempts was their use of pseudoguerrilla (also called pseudoterrorist) tactics, which consisted of black African operatives posing as guerrillas to infiltrate rural villages and gather intelligence. In practice, this tactic required all other Rhodesian state forces in the area to evacuate, leaving local populations defenseless against ZIPRA and ZANLA forces. Moreover, Scout units attempted also to discredit guerrilla forces by engaging in acts of intimidation and brutality against villagers.

Outside support was crucial to both ZIPRA and ZANLA and fit patterns representative of the broader struggles of the Cold War and the independence movement in Africa. Self-avowedly socialist (or Marxist, depending on the perspective of the foreign observer) and anti-colonial, both ZIPRA and ZANLA benefited from support from communist countries and other African states. ZIPRA benefited from training and financial support from newly independent African states (e.g., Algeria, Tanzania, Ghana), as well as the Soviet Union and Cuba. Reflecting the competition over leadership of the Communist revolution in the developing world, China offered support to ZANLA in the form of training, weaponry, and operating finances. These ideological differences were also evident in the forces' strategic doctrines. Following the Soviet line on national liberation, ZIPRA focused its energies more on arming and training a fighting force to engage the RSF in large-scale, conventional battles. ZANLA, influenced by the Maoist doctrine of sustained peasant rebellion, focused its efforts on undermining the institutions of the state through guerrilla tactics. Operationally, this difference led to a striking asymmetry of force within the country: As of 1977, ZIPRA had some 500 fighters in country; ZANLA counted 3,500 (*Economist,* 1977b).

For the government, South Africa would become a key ally upon which it relied for resources and support. South African police and security forces began operating within Rhodesia/Zimbabwe in 1967, reinforcing Rhodesian forces. Moreover, South African economic aid accounted for 50 percent of the Rhodesian state defense budget. Undoubtedly, the aid of neighboring states served to prolong the war by bolstering the resources of both sides.

"Revolutionary taxation," or the confiscation of goods from rural villages, was common to both ZIPRA and ZANLA and was another key source of finances. In the case of Rhodesia/Zimbabwe, there is some debate over the degree to which these rebel groups enjoyed popular support in rural areas and whether or not material support for the rebels was voluntary or amounted to little more than extortion. Kriger (1992) has argued at length that ZIPRA and ZANLA were successful despite their general inability to develop popular support. Partly, this lack of mass support stemmed from the belief that peaceful compromise was preferable to an armed confrontation; also, however, many tribal chiefs who had considerable influence over ordinary people had been bought off by the government. This latter issue led both ZANLA and ZIPRA forces to target the traditional chiefs, who were seen as cooperating with an oppressive regime.

Geography

The geography of Zimbabwe is dominated by two biomes: Moving from west to east, semiarid and sparsely populated savannah gives way to a more densely populated subtropical climate that follows a monsoon pattern, with dense forests and dry months occurring in the winter (summer in the northern Hemisphere). Zimbabwe is largely flat; its most mountainous region is the Eastern Highlands, a range that makes up Rhodesia/Zimbabwe's natural border with Mozambique.

The effects of waging guerrilla war in dense forests were evident. First, Zimbabwe's geography, in addition to patterns of land tenure, created a highly dispersed rural population. With the rural population spread rather thinly over the countryside, Rhodesian state forces were unable to keep remote villages from interacting with rebels. Local knowledge of rural areas clearly favored the indigenous African population over the white settlers as well. Second, the presence of dense forests mitigated many of the advantages in heavy arms and vehicles enjoyed by Rhodesian state forces. This was especially the case during the monsoon season, when rebels were able to take advantage of reduced visibility and diminished state capacity for aerial reconnaissance.

Rhodesian state forces responded in two ways. The first was to concentrate rural populations in protected villages (PVs), ostensibly to separate local populations from rebel forces and better "protect" remote communities from rebel forces. By January 1978, between 350,000 and 700,000 rural Africans had been relocated to some 234 PVs (Beckett 2001). In effect, the PVs were a means of keeping the rural population under control. The second was to develop and train special units in bush fighting and tracking. In 1973, the Rhodesian state formed the Selous Scouts, a mixed-race force composed of highly trained volunteers. For a variety of reasons to be discussed shortly, their tactics were often counterproductive to the goal of building political support for the Rhodesian state, although they were highly effective from a military perspective (see sidebar, "The Selous Scouts").

More salient to the conflict was Rhodesia/Zimbabwe's immediate neighborhood. Bordered to the north, east, and west by newly independent, black African–ruled states and to the south by white-dominated South Africa, both the Rhodesian state and rebel groups benefited from foreign intervention. For ZANU and ZAPU rebels, the benefits came in the form of access to safe havens across the Zambezi River in Zambia (for ZIPRA) and the Mozambican border (for ZANLA). Mozambique would become especially important after the Portuguese government ceded control to Frelimo (Front for the Liberation of Mozambique) in 1974. These borders had the added benefit of being composed of natural boundaries (the Zambezi River and mountains near Mozambique) that impeded the mobility of counterinsurgency forces in these areas. To a lesser extent, ZIPRA forces made use of Botswanan territory to avoid the cordon sanitaire, an 864-kilometer corridor of heavily mined territory along the Zambian and Mozambican borders. Despite massive cost to the Rhodesian state (estimated at more than $2 billion), the cordon sanitaire never managed to halt the flow of rebels into Rhodesian/Zimbabwean

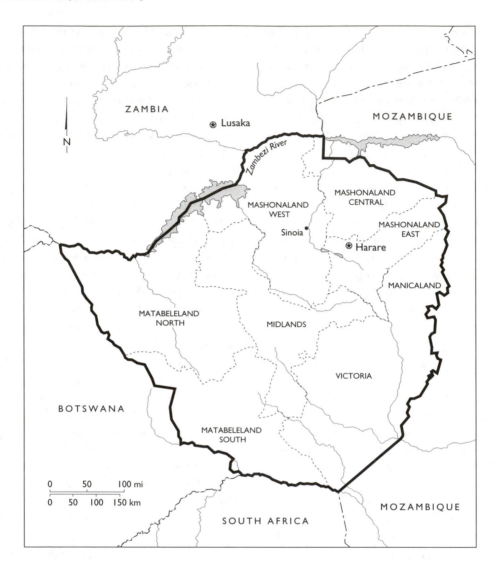

territory. Rebel camps across the border proved invaluable to the insurgency, as rebel units could escape the full force of state repression efforts.

To characterize these havens as entirely safe, however, would be inaccurate. Rebel operations in neighboring countries invited cross-border attacks by Rhodesian security forces and brought about political complications with host governments. Initially, there were limited attacks on external bases by the Selous Scouts, who worked to infiltrate rebel units. But by 1978, attacks on Mozambican and Zambian soil were more extensive, with raids extending as far as Harare. In one infamous incident, the RSF attacked the Nyadzonia refugee camp in Mozambique, claiming that the camp was sheltering insurgents. However, reports of mass civilian casualties prompted an international outcry and condemnation of the action as violating Mozambican sovereignty.

Moreover, operations in neighboring countries brought rebel groups into political quarrels with host governments. The clearest example of this was Kaunda's 1975 expulsion of the Sithole-led ZANU rebels from Zambia following the assassination of ZANU war council chairman Herbert Chitepo. Chitepo's assassination followed brutal infighting between the

ZANU leadership and rank-and-file field cadres. The infighting, which involved bloody purges of cadres dominated by the Karanga (a clan within the Shona tribe), resulted in a split within ZANU and the rise of Robert Mugabe to a position of leadership. The frontline states (Zambia, Mozambique, Botswana, and Tanzania) also had a big role in shaping political developments within the rebel movement. Importantly, these sanctuary governments used the threat of expulsion to force the ZANU and ZAPU factions into a united cause known as the Popular Front (PF). In practice, however, the ZANU and ZAPU components never fully integrated, and internal bickering within the PF meant that it never became a coherent organization. Although the ZANU-PF and ZAPU-PF were formally united and negotiated with the government together, rivalries within the PF prevented a unified black movement. The frontline states would also become instrumental in the peace process as they grew weary of continued fighting along their borders and pushed for compromise.

On balance, access to these cross-border havens was crucial to the rebel war effort, which likely would have been unsuccessful in their absence. Up until the time of the Lancaster House Agreement, rebel forces were still unable to prevent Rhodesian security forces from moving freely across the country; moreover, the rebels had been largely unsuccessful at securing support and protection from rural populations (Kriger 1992). Unable to project conventional military authority on Rhodesian/Zimbabwean territory, the rebels' only lifeline was their access to these havens. This reliance on foreign support, however, had the drawback of limiting the rebel's autonomy from external influence on their tactics and operations.

Tactics

From a tactical perspective, the Rhodesian/Zimbabwean civil war can be broken into three phases: 1972–1975, 1976–1977, and 1978–1979. In many respects, these phases are more similar than different: Rebel forces employed guerrilla tactics and sabotage throughout, whereas the RSF continuously pursued a policy of isolating rebels from rural populations and using pseudoinsurgent infiltrators to compromise rebel units. However, the three phases can be distinguished according to: (a) the dominant form of insurgent activity, and (b) the geographic extent of penetration into Rhodesian/Zimbabwean territory.

For the black African nationalists, their tactics were based on undermining the Rhodesian economy and minimizing direct engagement of the RSF until the final stages of the war. From the perspective of the white settler government, the civil war demonstrated several of the axioms that are foundational to modern counterinsurgency policy: the importance of accurate intelligence and bush fighting capabilities, the necessity of controlling border regions, and most importantly, the centrality of winning the "hearts and minds" of local populations. Unfortunately for the white settler state, this final lesson was learned through failure.

The first phase of the war, 1972–1975, consisted primarily of ZIPRA and ZANLA forces engaging in attacks on isolated communities and intimidation of local black African authorities, particularly tribal chiefs who had been co-opted by the white government. During this period, ZANLA guerrilla forces were responsible for the majority of rebel offensives. Usually organized in groups of fourteen to twenty, ZANLA infiltrators would target remote farms and ranches, often killing black African farmhands (to intimidate others from working with whites) and destroying irrigation and cattle dip systems. Comparatively, violence against white farmers was rare, with rebels focusing their attention on economic infrastructure.

The widening of the second front along the Mozambican border and the diminished role of South African defense forces in 1976–1977 defined the second phase of the war. Although ZANLA forces had been active in Mozambique since 1972, this offensive did not intensify until

Mozambique achieved independence from Portugal and the Mugabe-led ZANU-PF was expelled from Zambia in 1975. This had two effects. First, it intensified the war in Mashonaland and Manikaland, drawing the attention of security forces away from the Zambian border. Also, the move into more densely populated areas allowed the rebels to intensify attacks on the transportation system, with the primary targets being rural buses and private vehicles (Beckett 2001).

The final phase of the war, 1978–1979, was defined by the widening of the rebel offensive and the employment of regular, armored rebel forces on the part of ZIPRA, and heavier engagement of the RSF on Rhodesian/Zimbabwean soil. As mentioned earlier, ZIPRA had made a decision to develop regular forces (as opposed to guerrilla units) in the belief that the war would eventually be won on a conventional battlefield. Prior to the third phase, nationalist guerrillas depended on small arms supplied by the Soviet Union (in the case of ZIPRA) and China (ZANLA), including automatic rifles (AK-47, AK-74) and smaller sidearms (9mm Makarov pistols) (Sibanda 2005). Improvised gasoline bombs and Soviet and Chinese antipersonnel mines constituted the majority of rebel ordnance. In contrast to these earlier phases, during the later years the rebels began utilizing Soviet field artillery (105mm guns) and heavy 82mm mortars, as well as regular infantry units, in attacks on RSF garrisons and white-controlled towns (Brickhill 1995). At the same time, irregular (i.e., guerrilla) forces were for the first time protected from aerial bombings by antiaircraft guns and mobile surface-to-air missiles.

The experience of the RSF highlights the problem of basing counterinsurgency policy on military, rather than political, concerns. Militarily, the RSF was able to repulse large-scale rebel operations and racked up large body counts and highly favorable kill ratios (between six and fourteen rebel casualties for every one RSF casualty). Most military personnel were deployed defending static positions such as government installations, railways, PVs, and white-owned farms. This meant that only a small fraction of the RSF was involved in frequent armed encounters. To overcome the deficiencies of manpower that arose from this defensive posture, the RSF developed two primary offensive instruments: the Selous Scouts, who were tasked primarily with intelligence gathering but were utilized as strike forces in the later stages of conflict, and airborne, tactical response units known as Fire Forces. The Fire Forces were elite units consisting of light bombers and helicopter-borne troops. Once intelligence on rebel locations was received, these units could be deployed quickly and enjoyed aerial superiority up until the last phase of the war. The Selous Scouts and the Fire Forces were responsible for 75 percent of all rebel casualties (Beckett 2001).

Though the RSF was well-trained and enjoyed a superiority of firepower and numbers, its ultimate failing as a counterinsurgency force lay in its incorrect assessment that the rebel movement was primarily a military problem rather than a political one for the Rhodesian government. This emphasis can be illustrated with two examples. First, the PV (protected village) strategy for separating the rebels from the local population also had the effect of separating black Africans from their agricultural livelihoods and restricting their movements. Moreover, conditions in the PVs were not unlike those in refugee camps, with chronic supply shortages and sanitation problems. For these reasons, PVs became fertile ground for rebel recruitment and in some instances became rebel sanctuaries (Sibanda 2005). The second example was the fact that, although the counterinsurgency campaign was being waged in the countryside, the Rhodesian government emphasized increased political representation for black Africans without addressing the issue of land reform, in which ordinary rural dwellers had a clearer interest. Ultimately, the RSF found that the counterinsurgency campaign could not be won militarily without concrete attempts to ad-

A Rhodesian government soldier holds villagers at gunpoint as he interrogates them about antigovernment guerrilla activity in southern Rhodesia in September 1977. Rhodesia assumed the name Zimbabwe in 1980. (J. Ross Baughman/AP/Wide World Photos)

dress the underlying political and economic sources of support for rebel forces.

Causes of the War

Disentangling the causes of the Rhodesian/Zimbabwean civil war requires separating the conflict from its overlapping anticolonial and Cold War contexts. As has been discussed in previous sections, the civil war was motivated by three principal factors: (1) the economic and political domination of a sizable black African majority by the white African settler minority, (2) an anticolonial conflict between perceived agents of European domination and wrongfully subjugated peoples, and finally (3) a conflict between the market-oriented Rhodesian government and Marxist nationalist groups. In fact, these three explanations are not in tension. Rather, the first cause explains the nature of grievances among the rebel population and its basis of popular support, whereas the second and third causes

help to explain the timing of the conflict and the nature and extent of international involvement.

Land and political representation were at the heart of the struggle in Zimbabwe, as they constituted the primary grievances over which the rebels fought. The Land Tenure Act of 1930 granted the minority white settlers 49 million acres of land and the majority African population just 21 million acres. White settler lands, moreover, were in the most productive and fertile regions of the country. Politically, Africans were greatly underrepresented in government as well. Although the white settler government formally espoused the principle of "racial partnership," barriers to political participation by blacks, particularly voter eligibility requirements based upon education and income, ensured that most Blacks could not vote and that the legislature consisted of no more than a handful of black representatives. As if economic and political discrimination were not enough, discriminatory policies similar to those in place in South

Africa riled ordinary Africans. As one observer remarked,

> Whites in Southern Rhodesia saw themselves as gods. To protect themselves from being desecrated by Africans, so they thought, they put in place rigid separatism in hospitals, hotels, schools, swimming pools, restaurants, toilets and buses. Africans were always served in stores after Whites. At Post Offices, entrances and counters were separate and were not allowed to partake of European alcoholic drinks or beer, even wine for that matter (Quoted in Sibanda 2005, 40).

After World War II, pressure for decolonization and national self-determination mounted—both within Africa and in the colonial centers—which explains the timing of demands for majority rule. Although the United Kingdom formally ruled Southern Rhodesia, the white settler government had considerable autonomy in governing the country. Beginning in the late 1950s, the Southern Rhodesia African National Congress (SRANC), which was headed by a former trade unionist, Joshua Nkomo, pressed for greater rights for the black majority and eventually took up the cause of universal adult suffrage, which meant an end to white rule. The party demanded that the British colonial government grant majority rule before full independence, although the white minority government was adamantly against the idea. In principle, the British government was sympathetic to the cause of black self-rule, although in practice, implementing expanded rights for the majority population was extremely difficult because of the objections of the settlers.

Widespread protests during Febuary 1959 led to the banning of the SRANC and the tightening of security in Rhodesia. The following year, SRANC members reorganized under the banner of the National Democratic Party (NDP). Peaceful demonstrations organized by the NDP provoked a police backlash and widespread rioting in July 1960, followed by a larger clampdown on dissent. Then, in December 1961, the government banned the NDP as well,

causing many in the African nationalist movement to question the efficacy of nonviolent protest. Leaders began to contemplate a war. Within ten days of the banning of the NDP, Nkomo and his followers established the Zimbabwe African People's Union (ZAPU), which would subsequently become a major actor in the guerrilla campaign against the Rhodesian security forces. Although ZAPU was banned soon after its founding, its leaders simply went underground or into exile. In preparation for an insurgency, the party began to seek out small arms and send fighters to the Soviet Union for military training; recruitment drives also began in neighboring Zambia. Thereafter, the party began to gravitate more and more toward Marxist ideals, and it drew inspiration from successful models of revolution in Russia, Cuba, and China.

The white settlers were becoming uneasy about stirring African nationalist sentiment, both within Rhodesia as well as across the African continent. In the elections of December 1962, an almost entirely white electorate voted for the ultraconservative party, the Rhodesian Front (RF), to form the government. Headed by Ian Smith, the Rhodesian Front demanded that Britain grant independence to Rhodesia under the current constitution, which guaranteed minority rule. The British, however, were opposed to granting independence without substantial constitutional reforms designed to grant greater political rights to black Africans. The issue came to a head in 1965, when the Smith government issued a unilateral declaration of independence, thereby freeing Rhodesia from British rule and preempting meaningful constitutional reform. Although Britain rejected the declaration, the Rhodesian government viewed itself as ruling an independent nation.

Black Zimbabweans and newly independent African governments across the continent were outraged by the move, and support for a violent struggle mounted. Neighboring Zambia agreed to host rebel factions on its soil to dislodge the minority government. ZANU's military wing,

ZANLA, instigated the first clashes with the RSF at Sinoia on April 28, 1966, a day that is still commemorated as Chimurenga Day in Zimbabwe.

Outcome
Conflict Status

There were several failed attempts to end the civil war in Zimbabwe. Three negotiated settlements failed in talks before a final deal was struck. Despite the rhetoric of the black nationalists and the uncompromising public declarations of the Rhodesian Front, negotiations began early in the conflict, demonstrating both sides' willingness to find a peaceful solution to the war. The first negotiations were held at Victoria Falls in 1975 but failed quickly, as Smith was still confident of a military victory. The U.S. secretary of state, Henry Kissinger, brokered the second round of negotiations and submitted a settlement plan, but the rebels rejected it on the grounds that it allowed whites to maintain control of key military posts. The next attempt at peace, the Anglo-American initiative, came to an end when Smith struck a side deal with the UANC to allow new elections with black participation. Although Bishop Abel Muzorewa won these elections in 1978 and officially became prime minister, the military was still controlled by whites, and so ZANU-PF and ZAPU-PF rejected the deal.

The civil war in Zimbabwe officially ended with the signing of the Lancaster House Agreement on December 21, 1979. The agreement was signed by the leaders of the Popular Front factions, with Robert Mugabe representing ZANU-PF and Joshua Nkomo representing ZAPU-PF. On the government side, Bishop Muzorewa was the official representative of the Zimbabwean state, although Ian Smith played an active role in the negotiations. With Margaret Thatcher as the new British prime minister, the UK played a much more active role in these final negotiations.

The Lancaster House Agreement was brokered by the British government, who appointed an interim governor, Lord Christopher Soames, to direct the transition period. It was agreed that elections would be held the following year under the principle of majority rule. However, to get them to agree to the plan, whites would retain 20 seats in the 100-member parliament. It was also agreed that land reform would eventually take place, but the protection of white property would be guaranteed, and fair compensation would be given. Furthermore, during the implementation of the agreement and the 1980 elections, British Commonwealth forces would be on the ground to smooth the transition process and prevent the reignition of fighting.

The elections gave Mugabe and the ZANU a landslide victory. However, to assuage the concerns of the other parties, Mugabe appointed whites to cabinet positions and gave ZAPU leaders, including Nkomo, positions in the administration as well. This "honeymoon" would be short-lived. During the mid-1980s, Mugabe moved to purge his rivals, including his former allies in the ZAPU. Former ZAPU fighters again took up arms, along with other opposition parties, but this uprising was short-lived, and several thousand ethnic Ndebele were slaughtered in Matabeleland. With ZAPU out of the way, Mugabe turned his attention to white farmers. Having held power for more than twenty-five years, Mugabe has periodically encouraged attacks on white farms and the confiscation of farmland for redistribution, mainly to his own supporters.

Duration Tactics

The war lasted from 1972 to late 1979, although rebel forces had engaged in low-level fighting since at least 1966. As mentioned previously, the ability of rebel forces to maintain bases in neighboring countries from which they recruited and trained soldiers was critical to their longevity. Without the protection of the frontline states, the vastly superior RSF would have militarily defeated the rebel movement in its initial phases. Although the rebels enjoyed some sympathy within the local population, the Rhodesian state was adept at co-opting local leaders, gathering intelligence, and disrupting rebel activities. The

RSF's ability to directly engage rebels with its superior military forces, however, was largely confined to its own territory. Limited strikes did occur across the border, especially in Zambia and Mozambique, but the RSF was neither willing nor able to invade these countries with the bulk of its military forces.

The war certainly took a heavy toll on the white government and the settlers. White residents fled the country as the war escalated. Furthermore, international condemnation and sanctions severely harmed the Zimbabwean economy. The assistance of South Africa was critical to the continued functioning of the government—it could not have held out until 1980 without military support from South Africa and access to its markets. Whites certainly viewed black rebel forces as a threat to their livelihoods and even their continued existence in Africa; therefore, they were quite resolute in protecting their interests.

Pressure from the frontline states and from South Africa was critical in pushing the warring parties to the negotiating table. Zambia and Mozambique were hit especially hard by the fighting. Cross-border strikes threatened local citizens in these countries, and the war was an economic disaster for them, particularly for landlocked Zambia, which had lost access to ports on the Indian Ocean. South Africa put pressure on Ian Smith to negotiate as well, fearing that Soviet, Cuban, and Chinese influence in the region would increase the longer the war continued. For similar reasons, the United States also became interested in a quick resolution to the conflict.

However, as Walter (2002, Ch 6) notes, although international pressure was important in forcing both sides to the negotiating table, it was by no means sufficient in getting them to come to an agreement. The government and the rebels attempted negotiations several times since at least 1975, although a final peace would not be agreed to until Lancaster House. Walter (2002) argues that both sides were concerned about their physical safety during and after the implementation of the peace agreement, and that British commitment to protect both sides was critical. The PF factions feared that if they gave up their external bases and arms, they would be vulnerable to attack by the government. White settlers feared that, were blacks to gain control of the military after a peace accord, they would be subject to reprisals. Therefore, negotiations failed repeatedly until there was a firm commitment on the part of the British to guarantee the security of both demobilized rebels and white Zimbabweans. The British showed their resolve to maintain the peace by their positioning of troops in Zimbabwe and the appointment of Soames as governor.

External Military Intervention

For ZANU–ZANLA and ZAPU–ZIPRA, external support was critical in two respects. First, Soviet and Chinese aid provided them with weapons and training that allowed them a fighting chance against the better-equipped RSF. Second, the assistance of neighboring governments was critical for defensive reasons, as it allowed the rebels a relatively safe place to regroup. For the Rhodesian government, international ostracism coupled with economic sanctions made it clear that the regime could not survive for long. The support of South Africa, also dominated by whites, was critical to the long-term viability of the government. However, for both the rebels and the government, reliance on external support had its costs as well. It meant that external actors with their own agendas easily manipulated them. For example, the frontline states reluctantly pushed ZANU and ZAPU into an agreement to form the PF; pressure from these states also forced the rebels into negotiations with the government despite their ambivalence about doing so. Furthermore, the government's reliance on South Africa for economic and military assistance made it vulnerable to pressure to negotiate on terms that were not entirely its own.

Conflict Management Efforts

Just as external actors were critical to the initiation and continuation of the war, they were also key to negotiation success. External patrons demanded an end to the war for their own reasons and were able to bring both sides to the table to discuss peace. The United States also pressed for peace and facilitated negotiations, but its role in the final settlement was relatively limited. The UK clearly facilitated the final peace negotiation. The British mediated the Lancaster House Agreement, assumed control over Zimbabwe during the transition period, and provided extensive security guarantees to both sides during the transfer of power.

Conclusion

The civil war in Zimbabwe draws attention to the legacy of colonialism in Africa. Zimbabwe was one of the last outposts of European dominance over African populations, and the white government drew considerable fire from the international community for its racial intolerance. However, the sad irony of the war is that, although black Zimbabweans loathed the white government for its racist policies, the liberation movement was itself divided along ethnic lines. Early on in the conflict, the Ndebele and the Shona formed rival factions, and after the war the Shona-led ZANU established a one-party state.

The war also highlights the importance of external actors to "civil" conflicts. In Zimbabwe, as in several other wars, both the government and the rebels relied heavily upon external patrons for support. Furthermore, the rebels, lacking territory of their own, benefited from external bases in neighboring countries into which the government could not extend its reach. Also important were international sanctions and opprobrium, which imposed heavy costs on the government. However, external support also meant that the warring parties were never completely free from interference by outside actors; although they gained important resources, both the Rhodesian government and the rebels lost a degree of autonomy in directing their own policies. External influences were also important in prompting both sides to negotiate, and the UK was vital to the success of the final peace deal.

Although Zimbabwe and its neighbor, South Africa, are unique in that a small minority of European settlers dominated a largely black African state, the lessons learned in these conflicts are applicable to conflicts elsewhere. In many multiethnic countries, a particular ethnic group dominates the central government. When political power and economic opportunities are distributed according to ethnic characteristics, disadvantaged groups have strong incentives to rebel. Therefore, efforts to grant political representation and economic opportunities to broad segments of society are vital to ensuring lasting peace.

Cullen S. Hendrix and Idean Salehyan

Chronology

1961 Constitutional talks between United Kingdom and South Rhodesia end in the promulgation of a new constitution based on a qualified franchise (repudiating the promise of universal franchise, as was canonized in the 1923 constitution), with majority home rule not guaranteed for another fifteen years. The National Democratic Party, a black African party organized around the expansion of suffrage, rejects the new constitution and is subsequently banned.

December 1962 Zimbabwean African People's Union (ZAPU) founded under leadership of Joshua Nkomo. The party is immediately banned, forcing party leadership into exile in Zambia.

1963 Zimbabwean African National Union (ZANU) splits from ZAPU under leadership of Ndabiningi Sithole.

1965 Ian Smith's Rhodesian Front government declares independence from Great Britain.

1966 United Nations imposes sanctions against Rhodesia's apartheid regime. Guerrillas based in Zambia engage Rhodesian Security Forces at the Battle of Sinoia, first battle of conflict.

1972 ZANLA guerrillas begin infiltrating from bases in Mozambique; war begins.

1973 Rhodesian Security Forces launch Operation Hurricane against ZANLA bases in Mozambique.

1974   Portugal cedes power to Marxist Frelimo government in Mozambique. Frontline ZANU soldiers rebel against ZANU political leadership, leading to mass executions and infighting.

1975   South African government withdraws majority of police and security forces from Rhodesian territory; covert operations continue under the name Operation Polo. ZANU war council chairman Herbert Chipeto is assassinated by car bomb under murky circumstances. Robert Mugabe assumes control of ZANU.

1976   Nkomo and Mugabe agree to form alliance known as Patriotic Front; alliance is never fully integrated militarily. U.S. Secretary of State Henry Kissinger and South African Prime Minister John Vorster open Geneva Conference; Rhodesian government rejects United Kingdom's offer to appoint transitional government.

1978   Rhodesian government announces internal settlement agreement providing for a transitional government with Ian Smith as prime minister but with other portfolios shared between white and black ministers. Fighting intensifies.

1979   New constitution for Zimbabwe/Rhodesia is adopted; United Africa National Council (UANC) leader Bishop Abel Muzorewa is elected nation's first black African prime minister. Lancaster House conference convened under mediation of Lord Carrington, UK Secretary of State for Foreign and Commonwealth Affairs, and is attended by representatives of UANC, ZAPU, and ZANU. Agreement is reached on a cease-fire, with new elections to be held in 1980.

1980   Patriotic Front alliance breaks to contest elections. ZANU leader Mugabe defeats Nkomo (ZAPU), Muzorewa (UANC), and Sithole (ZANU) and becomes the nation's first internationally recognized president with formal independence from United Kingdom.

List of Acronyms

GDP: gross domestic product
Frelimo: Front for the Liberation of Mozambique
NDP: National Democratic Party
PF: Popular Front (sometimes listed by faction, ZANU-PF and ZAPU-PF)
PV: protected village
RF: Rhodesian Front
RSF: Rhodesian Security Forces
SRANC: Southern Rhodesia African National Congress
UANC: United African National Congress
ZANLA: Zimbabwe African National Liberation Army
ZANU: Zimbabwe African National Union
ZAPU: Zimbabwe African People's Union
ZIPRA: Zimbabwe People's Revolutionary Army

Glossary

chimurenga: "Uprising"; refers to the black struggle against white rule.

frontline states: Countries that harbored ZANU and ZAPU: Zambia, Mozambique, Botswana, and Tanzania.

Lancaster House Agreement: Peace agreement (1979) that ended the Zimbabwean civil war.

Mugabe, Robert: Head of the Zimbabwe African National Union; later became the first black head of state in Zimbabwe.

Ndebele: One of the two major ethnic groups in Zimbabwe. ZAPU supporters were largely from the Ndebele group.

Nkomo, Joshua: Head of the Zimbabwe People's Revolutionary Army.

Shona: One of the two major ethnic groups in Zimbabwe. ZANU supporters were largely from the Shona ethnic group.

Smith, Ian: Rhodesian Front prime minister of Zimbabwe during the civil war.

References

Beckett, Ian F. W. 2001. *Modern Insurgencies and Counter-Insurgencies: Guerrillas and Their Opponents Since 1750*. London: Routledge.

Brickhill, Jeremy. 1995. "Daring to Storm the Heavens: The Military Strategy of ZAPU, 1976–1979." In *Soldiers in Zimbabwe's Lieration War*, edited by Ngwabi Bhebe and Terence Ranger. London: James Currey.

Economist. 1977a. "Willing or Unwilling?" Section: International (February 5): 68.

Economist. 1977b. "Rhodesia: A Siding Near the War's End." Section: International (December 3): 76.

Heston, Alan, Robert Summers, and Bettina Aten. 2006. *Penn World Table Version 6.2*. Center for International Comparisons of Production, Income and Prices. Philadelphia: University of Pennsylvania.

Kriger, Norma. 1992. *Zimbabwe's Guerrilla War: Peasant Voices*. Cambridge, UK: Cambridge University Press.

Meredith, Martin. 2005. *Our Votes, Our Guns: Robert Mugabe and the Tragedy of Zimbabwe.* New York: Public Affairs.

Mugabe, Robert Gabriel. 1983. *Our War of Liberation.* Gwere, Zimbabwe: Mambo Press.

Nkomo, Joshua. 1984. *Nkomo: The Story of My Life.* London: Metheun.

Polity IV Project. 2006. *Regime Characteristics and Transitions, 1800–2004.* Center for International Development and Conflict Management. College Park: University of Maryland.

Preston, Matthew. 2004. "Stalemate and the Termination of Civil War: Rhodesia Reassessed." *Journal of Peace Research* 41: 65–83.

Ranger, Terence, 1985. *Peasant Consciousness and Guerrilla War in Zimbabwe: A Comparative Study.* London: James Currey.

Roberts, Brian. 1987. *Cecil Rhodes: Flawed Colossus.* London: Hamilton.

Sibanda, Eliakim M. 2005. *The Zimbabwean African People's Union, 1961–1987.* Trenton, NJ: Africa World Press.

Smith, Ian Douglas. 1997. *The Great Betrayal: The Memoirs of Ian Douglas Smith.* London: Blake.

Tungamiri, Josiah. 1995. "Recruitment into ZANLA: Building Up a War Machine." In *Soldiers in Zimbabwe's Liberation War,* edited by Ngwabi Bhebe and Terence Ranger. London: James Curry.

United Nations High Commissioner for Refugees. Various years. *UNHCR Statistical Yearbook.* Geneva:UNHCR Population Data Unit.

Walter, Barbara. 2002. *Committing to Peace: the Successful Settlement of Civil Wars.* Princeton, NJ: Princeton University Press.

CIVIL WARS CHRONOLOGY

Civil Wars and Important International and Security Events 1945–2006

1945
February
Soviet leader Joseph Stalin, British Prime Minister Winston Churchill, and U.S. President Franklin Roosevelt meet in Yalta to discuss postwar arrangements.

May
Victory in Europe Day (VE Day).

July
United States conducts the world's first nuclear test. U.S. president Harry Truman, British prime minister Clement Atlee, and Stalin meet at Potsdam to further discuss postwar arrangements. Conference ends the following month.

August
United States drops first atomic bomb on Hiroshima, Japan. Soviet Union declares war on Japan. United States drops second atomic bomb on Nagasaki. Japan surrenders unconditionally to the Allies. Indonesia declares independence.

October
United Nations is founded.

1946
April
Syria declares independence.

July
The Philippines becomes independent.

December
French Fourth Republic is established.

1947
August
Pakistan and India obtain independence.

October
First Kashmir War between India and Pakistan starts; ends in January 1949.

1948
January
Indian leader Mahatma Gandhi is assassinated.

February
Sri Lanka gains independence.

March
Full-scale civil war starts in Costa Rica, continues until April 1948. Belgium, Britain, France, Luxembourg, and The Netherlands sign Treaty of Brussels.

April
Charter of the Organization of American States is signed; Organization of American States (OAS) is established.

May

Israel is declared an independent state. Arab states invade Israel. Israel signs separate armistices in 1949.

June

Berlin blockade starts. Blockade ends in May 1949.

August

Republic of Korea (ROK, South Korea) is established.

September

Democratic People's Republic of Korea (DPRK, North Korea) is established.

1949
January

Karen separatist insurgency and civil war in Burma (Myanmar) starts.

April

Republic of Ireland is established. North Atlantic Treaty is signed. North Atlantic Treaty Organization (NATO) is formed.

May

Federal Republic of Germany (West Germany) is established.

August

Soviet Union detonates its first atomic bomb.

October

People's Republic of China (PRC, China) is established.

German Democratic Republic (East Germany) is established.

December

Nationalist Party of China (KMT), defeated in Chinese civil war, flees to Taiwan and establishes Taipei as new capital of Republic of China (ROC).

1950
February

China and the Soviet Union sign Treaty of Friendship, Alliance, and Mutual Assistance.

June

Korean War breaks out.

1951
August

U.S.–Philippines Mutual Defense Treaty is signed.

September

Australia–New Zealand–United States (ANZUS) Treaty is signed. Treaty of Mutual Cooperation and Security between Japan and the United States is signed.

1952
February

Turkey joins NATO.

April

Under the Treaty of San Francisco, the United States ends its occupation of Japan, Japan gains its full independence.

1953

March

Stalin dies.

July

Korean War ends.

October

U.S.–South Korea Mutual Defense Treaty is signed.

1954
May

French forces at Dien Bien Phu surrender to the Viet Minh.

June

Civil war and insurgency in Guatemala start.

August

First Taiwan Straits crisis starts. China stops shelling Quemoy and Matsu islands in May 1955. Second (1958–1959) and third (1995–1996) crises follow.

July

Japanese Self-Defense Forces are founded.

At Geneva Conference, Vietnam is divided into North Vietnam and South Vietnam.

September

Australia, France, Great Britain, New Zealand, Pakistan, the Philippines, Thailand, and the United States sign Southeast Asia Treaty Organization (SEATO). SEATO is disbanded in 1977.

December

Mutual Defense Treaty between the United States and Taiwan is signed.

1955
February

Baghdad Pact is signed. Iraq, Turkey, Iran, Pakistan, and Britain are members of the pact.

May

West Germany joins NATO.

Warsaw Treaty Organization (WTO) is established.

1956
March

Pakistan becomes an Islamic republic.

July

Egypt announces nationalization of the Suez Canal Company.

October

Israel invades the Sinai Peninsula.

Britain and France bomb Egypt to force it to reopen Suez Canal.

November

Soviet Union sends troops into Hungary, crushing Hungarian reform movement.

UN General Assembly adopts resolution calling for Britain, France, and Israel to withdraw from Egypt.

December

Communist revolution and civil war start in Cuba. Japan becomes a member of the UN.

1957
January

Israel withdraws from Sinai Peninsula.

March

Egypt reopens Suez Canal.

Treaty of Rome is signed. European Economic Community (EEC) is established.

August

Federation of Malaya obtains independence.

1958
May

Internal strife in Lebanon and first Lebanese civil war starts (this ends in June 1959).

North American Aerospace Defense Command is created.

October

Fifth Republic constitution of France is introduced.

1959
January

Cuban President Fulgencio Batista is overthrown by Fidel Castro's force. United States recognizes new Cuban government of Castro.

1960

February

France detonates its first atomic bomb.

May

U.S. U2 spy plane is shot down by the Soviet Union.

July

Congo (Zaire) experiences secession, anarchy, civil war, and the Belgian Congo crisis until mid-1964.

August

Cyprus obtains independence.

October

Nigeria obtains independence.

1961

January

United States breaks off diplomatic relations with Cuba.

April

Cuban exiles fail to overthrow Castro at Bay of Pigs.

May

Republic of South Africa comes into existence.

July

Soviet Union and North Korea sign Treaty of Friendship, Cooperation and Mutual Assistance.

China and North Korea sign Treaty of Friendship, Cooperation and Mutual Assistance.

August

Berlin Wall is built.

September

Coup is staged in Syria; the country's withdrawal from United Arab Republic (UAR) is announced.

December

Castro declares Cuba a Communist country.

India invades Goa.

1962

January

Cuba's membership in the OAS is suspended.

March

The war between Algeria and France ends.

July

Algeria is pronounced independent.

August

Jamaica gains independence.
Trinidad and Tobago gain independence.

September

Military coup takes place in North Yemen, followed by civil war. Egyptian forces complete their withdrawal in October 1967 when royalists no longer pose a threat to the republican government.

October

Cuban missile crisis. China–India war over territorial disputes starts. India declares a unilateral cease-fire in November 1962.

1963

January

France and Germany sign treaty on Franco-German cooperation (also known as the Elysee Treaty).

June

The United States and the Soviet Union sign Memorandum of Understanding to establish direct "hotline" communications link between the two nations for use in a crisis.

August

United States, Britain, and the Soviet Union sign Partial Test Ban Treaty (PTBT).

September

Anya-Nya terrorists attack the Sudanese government; first civil war in Sudan takes place. Cease-fire ends military hostilities in March 1972.

November

President John F. Kennedy is assassinated.

December

Civil war breaks out in Cyprus. Withdrawal of Greek and Turkish forces is completed in February 1968.

1964
January

China and France establish diplomatic relations.

April

Military coup in Laos is followed by the second Laotian civil war. Peace conference in February 1973 leads to formation of provisional government.

August

U.S. destroyers report attacks by North Vietnam in Gulf of Tonkin.

October

China successfully detonates its first atomic bomb.

1965
March

First American combat troops arrive in South Vietnam.

April

Rebellion starts in the Dominican Republic. Elections supervised by the OAS are held in June 1966.

June

Japan and South Korea sign Treaty on Basic Relations.

August

Second Indo-Pakistani War. Cease-fire is accepted by both countries the following month.

November

Fighting begins on the border between Chad and Sudan after rebellion is instigated in the eastern province of Ouadai. Sporadic fighting continues until late 1972, when rebellion collapses.

1966
March

French President Charles de Gaulle announces France's complete withdrawal from NATO's military command.

May

Chinese leader Mao Zedong launches Cultural Revolution. China explodes its first hydrogen bomb. Guyana gains independence.

October

Military encounter occurs between Guyana and Venezuela over Venezuela's occupation of Guyana's portion of Ankoko Island.

November

Cuban-assisted guerrilla insurgency occurs in Bolivia; ends in July 1970.

1967
May

Biafra declares secession and independence from Nigeria. Nigerian forces invade in July 1967; Biafran forces surrender in January 1970.

June

Six Days' War between Israel and Arab starts.

Soviet Union drops diplomatic relations with Israel after Six Days' War.

August

Association of Southeast Asian Nations (ASEAN) is established by Indonesia, Malaysia, the Philippines, Singapore, and Thailand.

1968
January

Political liberalization (Prague Spring) starts in Czechoslovakia.

Communist forces launch Tet offensive in South Vietnam.

July

Nuclear Non-Proliferation Treaty (NPT) is signed.

August

Troops of Warsaw Pact countries (except Romania), led by the Soviet Union, invade Czechoslovakia to end political liberalization.

October

Strenuous government efforts to quell Kurdish rebel activity in Iraq leads to serious fighting until January 1970.

1969
March

Military clash occurs between Chinese and Soviet troops over disputed Damansky/Zhenbao Island.

August

British troops are deployed in Northern Ireland.

1970
April

United States invades Cambodia.

October

October Crisis of Québec, Canada, occurs when members of the Front de libération de Québec kidnap British trade comissioner James Cross and Minister of Labor and Vice Premier of Québec Pierre Laporte. Canadian prime minister Pierre Trudeau uses the War Measures Act to increase police power.

Fiji obtains independence.

1971
February

South Vietnamese troops invade Laos with U.S. help.

March

Pakistan sends troops to East Pakistan to suppress an uprising.

August

India and Soviet Union sign Treaty of Peace, Friendship and Cooperation.

October

China joins UN and Taiwan is expelled.

December

Bangladesh is established after Pakistani forces surrender in East Pakistan.

1972
January

Pakistan withdraws from the Commonwealth.

February

President Richard Nixon visits China.

March

Bangladesh and India sign Treaty of Friendship.

May

Strategic Arms Limitation Talks (SALT I) take place. Treaty between United States and Soviet Union is signed limiting antiballistic missile (ABM) systems.

July

Simla Agreement on Bilateral Relations between India and Pakistan is signed.

September

Arab terrorists kill Israeli athletes at Olympic Games in Munich.

Martial law is announced by Philippine President Ferdinand Marcos.

1973
January

Denmark, Ireland, and United Kingdom enter European Economic Community.

Ferdinand Marcos becomes president for life of the Philippines.

United States signs peace treaty ending its involvement in Vietnam.

March

Last U.S. soldiers leave Vietnam.

June

Conference on Security and Cooperation in Europe is formally opened in Helsinki.

September

Military coup led by Augusto Pinochet overthrows democratically elected government of Chile.

October

Yom Kippur War between Israel and Arab starts.

1974
March

Kurdish rebellion under Mullah Mustafa Barazani resumes in Iraq; fighting breaks out. Rebellion is quelled; Iraq proclaims amnesty for Kurds, who are surrounded by April 1, 1975.

July

Turkey lands forces in Cyprus.

Treaty between United States and Soviet Union is signed limiting underground nuclear weapons tests.

November

Irish Republican Army (IRA) bombs Birmingham pub.

1975
March

Shah decrees Iran a one-party state; by 1976, civil disorder is widespread.

April

Lebanese civil war starts; ends in October 1990.

Pol Pot takes power in Cambodia and establishes Democratic Republic of Kampuchea in 1976. "Killing fields" experienced by Cambodians.

Communist forces capture Saigon; South Vietnam surrenders.

November

Angola obtains independence.

Spanish dictator Francisco Franco dies; Prince Juan Carlos becomes king and head of state.

East Timor declares independence.

December

Indonesia invades East Timor.

1976
January

Spain and United States sign Treaty of Friendship and Cooperation.

May

Kurds attack Iraqi forces; conflict continues until the fall of Saddam Hussein.

June

Soweto riots occur in South Africa.

September

Mao Zedong dies.

1977
January

Civil conflict in El Salvador and the Salvadoran Civil War take place until late 1992.

July

Deng Xiaoping is restored to his offices in China.

September

Panama and United States sign treaty on status of Panama Canal.

Fifteen countries sign Nuclear Non-Proliferation Pact.

November

Egyptian President Anwar Sadat visits Israel.

1978
January

Armed conflict in Chad erupts. New government is established in June 1982.

March

Israeli forces invade Lebanon.

September

Egypt and Israel sign Camp David peace accords.

December

Crisis occurs between Argentina and Chile over Beagle Channel. Act of Montevideo is signed the following month to ease tensions.

Vietnam invades Cambodia, overthrows Pol Pot regime.

1979
January

China and United States establish diplomatic relations. Shah of Iran leaves the country for exile.

February

Ayatollah Khomeini becomes religious leader of Iran.

China–Vietnam war starts; ends the following month.

March

Egyptian–Israeli peace treaty is signed in Washington.

April

Yusufu Lule is sworn in as president of Uganda after fall of Idi Amin. Civil war starts in December 1981, continues until 1994.

June

SALT II, treaty between United States and Soviet Union on the limitation of strategic offensive arms, is signed.

October

South Korean President Park Chung Hee is assassinated.

November

Radical students invade U.S. embassy in Iran, take Americans hostage.

December

Soviet Union invades Afghanistan.

1980
January

Egypt and Israel establish diplomatic relations.

April

United States drops diplomatic relations with Iran.

May

Kwangju Uprising in South Korea is suppressed.

September

Iraq invades Iran. Eight-year-long Iran–Iraq war begins.

October

Syria signs Treaty of Friendship and Cooperation with Soviet Union.

1981
January

American hostages in Teheran are released after 444 days in captivity.

Greece enters European Community.

June

Israel attacks and destroys Iraqi nuclear reactor near Baghdad.

September

Belize gains independence.

October

Egyptian President Anwar Sadat is assassinated; Hosni Mubarak becomes president of Egypt.

December

Wojciech Jaruzelski declares martial law in Poland.

1982
April

Argentina invades the Falkland Islands.

May

Spain joins NATO.

June

Israel invades South Lebanon.

Argentine troops in the Falkland Islands surrender to British forces.

July

Liberation Tigers of Tamil Eelam begin a campaign of violence against regime in Sri Lanka.

1983
January

Colombia, Mexico, Panama, and Venezuela initiate Contadora Group.

March

President Ronald Reagan proposes Strategic Defense Initiative.

May

Accord is signed on Israel's withdrawal from Lebanon.

September

Korean Air Lines jet (KAL 007) shot down by Soviet fighter plane.

October

Suicide bombing of American and French barracks in Beirut takes place.

United States invades Grenada.

First democratic election is held in Argentina after seven years of military rule.

1984
January

Brunei obtains independence.

October

Indian Prime Minister Indira Gandhi is assassinated.

December

Britain and China sign Sino-British Joint Declaration about the future of Hong Kong.

1985
February

New Zealand declines to allow U.S. guided missile destroyer to visit, under its antinuclear policy.

March

Mikhail Gorbachev becomes general secretary of Soviet Communist Party.

May

Argentina and Chile sign treaty at the Vatican over island disputes in the Beagle Channel.

July

In New Zealand, agents of French secret service sink *Rainbow Warrior*, flagship of environmental group Greenpeace.

November

Argentina and Brazil signed the Foz de Iguazú Declaration.

1986
January

Portugal and Spain enter the European Community.

February

Single European Act (SEA) is signed.

Philippines dictator Ferdinand Marcos is ousted.

April

United States launches air attack on Libya.

December

Foreign ministers of Argentina, Brazil, Colombia, Mexico, Panama, Peru, Uruguay, and Venezuela meet to establish body for political consultation and coordination, later called the Rio Group.

1987

September

Fighting breaks out in northern region of Curette, People's Republic of the Congo, between government forces and supporters of a former army officer; rebellion ends in July 1988.

November

Bomb explodes on Korean Air Flight 858.

December

Treaty between United States and Soviet Union is signed on elimination of intermediate- and short-range missiles.

1988

July

USS *Vincennes* shoots down Iran Air Flight 655.

August

Pakistan President Mohammad Zia ul-Haq dies in a plane crash, which also kills U.S. ambassador.

December

Pan Am Flight 103 crashes after a bomb explodes.

1989

January

Free Trade Agreement (FTA) between Canada and United States takes effect.

Cuban troops begin to withdraw from Angola.

February

Last Soviet troops leave Kabul, Afghanistan.

June

Iranian religious leader Ayatollah Khomeini dies.

Chinese government uses military to suppress democratic movement in Beijing.

Solidarity wins first free election in Poland.

November

Berlin Wall is opened.

In Czechoslovakia, Velvet Revolution begins, peacefully overthrows Communist government.

December

United States invades Panama.

Libyan-trained rebels invade Liberia from Côte d'Ivoire (Ivory Coast).

President Nicolae Ceausescu is overthrown and executed in Romania.

1990

January

Panama leader General Manuel Noriega is captured by U.S. forces.

February

South African President Frederik Willem de Klerk declares failure of apartheid; Nelson Mandela is released from Victor Verster prison.

West and East Germany reach agreement for two-stage plan of reunification.

Argentina and Britain resume diplomatic relations.

March

Patricio Aylwin becomes first democratically elected Chilean president since 1973.

April

Trinidad, Tobago, and Venezuela sign Delimitation Treaty to settle territorial dispute over the Gulf of Paria.

May

North and South Yemen are united into a single state, the Republic of Yemen.

August

Iraq invades Kuwait.

October

East Germany is absorbed into the Federal Republic of Germany.

November

Treaty on Conventional Armed Forces in Europe (CFE Treaty) is signed by NATO and Warsaw Pact states.

UN Security Council passes Resolution 678 requiring Iraqi leader Saddam Hussein to withdraw his forces from Kuwait by January 15, 1991.

1991

February

Czechoslovakia, Hungary, and Poland form the Visegrad Group.

Kuwait is liberated by U.S.-led coalition.

May

Lebanon and Syria sign Treaty of Brotherhood, Cooperation and Coordination.

June

Slovenia and Croatia declare independence from Yugoslavia.

Boris Yeltsin wins first popular presidential election in Russian Federation.

July

Warsaw Treaty Organization is officially dissolved.

Strategic Arms Reduction Treaty (START I) between the United States and the Soviet Union is signed.

August

State Emergency Committee stages unsuccessful coup in the Soviet Union.

September

Soviet Union recognizes independence of Estonia, Latvia, and Lithuania.

October

Agreement reached at Paris conference regarding peace and democracy in Cambodia.

November

Djibouti Civil War starts; continues until July 1993.

December

Commonwealth of Independent States is founded. Gorbachev resigns as president of Soviet Union. Supreme Soviet officially dissolves Soviet Union.

1992

February

Treaty on European Union (EU; also known as the Maastricht Treaty) is signed.

U.S. president George Bush and Yeltsin hold first meeting since dissolution of the Soviet Union.

March

Bosnia declares independence from Yugoslavia.

June

UN conference on the environment and development (Earth Summit) is held.

July

Cease-fire to halt fighting in Tajikistan is negotiated but soon fails; civil war continues sporadically until June 1997.

September

First democratic election in Angola is held.

October

Peace agreement of Mozambique is signed, ending long civil war.

December

Kim Young-sam wins presidential election in South Korea.

U.S. troops are sent to Somalia.

1993

January

Czechoslovakia is divided into two independent sovereign states, Slovakia and the Czech Republic.

Treaty between United States and Russia on Further Reduction and Limitation of Strategic Offensive Arms (START II) is signed.

February

Terrorist bomb explodes in World Trade Center in New York.

May

Elections are held in Cambodia under supervision of UN Transitional Authority in Cambodia (UNTAC).

July

In Japanese general election, politicians form first non-Liberal Democratic Party (LDP) government, ending thirty-eight-year dominance of LDP in Japanese politics.

September

Israel and Palestine signed Oslo Accords.

October

In Somalia, eighteen U.S. soldiers and hundreds of Somalis are killed in a gun battle.

In Russia, conflict occurs between forces under Yeltsin and opponents in Russian parliament.

November

Armed clashes occur in Yemen; conflict escalates in January 1994. The civil war ends in July 1994. Official ceremony held for the creation of Eurocorps in Strasbourg.

1994
January

North American Free Trade Agreement (NAFTA) takes effect, includes United States, Canada, and Mexico.

April

Rwanda President Juvenal Habyarimana and Burundi President Cyprian Ntayamira are killed in plane crash. Genocide follows in Rwanda. First multiracial election is held in South Africa.

May

Nelson Mandela becomes first black president of South Africa.

July

North Korean leader Kim Il Sung dies. His son, Kim Jong Il, succeeds him.

Israel and Jordan sign Washington Declaration.

First meeting of ASEAN Regional Forum takes place.

October

United States and North Korea sign Agreed Framework, ending first Korean Peninsula nuclear crisis.

Israel and Jordan sign peace treaty.

December

First Chechen War starts; ends in 1996.

1995
January

Mercado Commun del Sur (MERCOSUR), customs union between Argentina, Brazil, Paraguay, and Uruguay, takes effect.

Austria, Finland, and Sweden join the EU.

Chinese President Jiang Zemin spells out mainland's stance in Eight-Point Offer to Taiwan.

July

President Bill Clinton announces normalization of U.S. relations with Vietnam.

Muslim civilians are massacred in Srebrenica, a UN "safe area," after its capture by Bosnia Serbs.

October

Second referendum on Quebec's independence is held (the first was held in 1980). Proposal of secession is defeated.

November

Israeli Prime Minister Yitzhak Rabin is assassinated.

December

General Framework Agreement for Peace in Bosnia and Herzegovina (also known as Dayton Peace Accords) is signed.

1996
March

First direct presidential election is held in Taiwan.

September

Comprehensive Test Ban Treaty (CTBT) is opened for signature.

Taliban storm presidential palace in Kabul, capital of Afghanistan.

October

First New Zealand general election under Mixed Member Proportional (MMP) electoral system takes place.

November

Switzerland joins NATO's Partnership for Peace.

1997
May

NATO and Russia sign NATO–Russia Founding Act.

July

Britain hands over sovereignty of Hong Kong to China.

October

Burnham Truce marks end of armed struggle by Bougainville separatists in Papua New Guinea. Permanent cease-fire is signed in April 1998.

1998
April

British and Irish governments and various Northern Ireland political parties sign Belfast Agreement (also known as the Good Friday Agreement).

May

India announces it has conducted a series of nuclear tests.

Indonesian President Thojib Suharto resigns.

Pakistan announces it has conducted nuclear tests.

August

U.S. embassies in Kenya and Tanzania are bombed by terrorists.

Real Irish Republican Army (RIRA) commits Omagh bombing in Northern Ireland.

October

Israel and Palestine sign Wye River Accords.

Former Chilean dictator Augusto Pinochet is arrested in London for crimes against humanity and human rights violations. He is released in 2000.

1999
February

Rambouillet talks held to address conflict in Kosovo but break up the following month.

India and Pakistan sign Lahore Agreement.

March

Czech Republic, Hungary, and Poland join NATO. NATO starts bombing Serbia to force it to withdraw from Kosovo.

June

Slobodan Milosevic accepts autonomy plan of Kosovo; Serbian forces withdraw.

September

Peacekeeping troops led by Australia are sent to East Timor to restore order and stop violence.

October

General Pervaiz Musharraf leads military coup and takes control of Pakistan.

Russian ground forces advance into Chechnya.

December

China and Vietnam sign Vietnam–China Treaty on Land Border.

Yeltsin resigns and names Vladimir Putin acting president; Putin is elected president in March 2000.

2000
February

North Korea and Russia sign new Treaty of Friendship.

March

Chen Shui-bian wins Taiwan presidential election.

May

Coup is staged in Fiji. Two previous coups occurred in 1987.

Israeli troops withdraw from Lebanon.

October

Milosevic is overthrown in Serbia.

2001

January

Joseph Estrada stands down as president of the Philippines.

February

Treaty of Nice is signed.

April

Black Sea Naval Co-operation Task Group (BLACKSEAFOR) Agreement is signed in Istanbul.

U.S.–Chinese relations are tense after collision of Chinese fighter and American surveillance plane.

Milosevic is transferred to International Criminal Tribunal for the former Yugoslavia.

September

Terrorists attack targets in the United States, including the World Trade Center in New York City and the Pentagon.

November

Northern Alliance seizes Kabul in Afghanistan. Alliance had received support from the United States.

Maoist guerrillas launched forty-eight simultaneous attacks on the police and army in Nepal, killing hundreds.

December

Terrorists attack Indian Parliament in New Delhi.

United States grants China permanent normal trade relations status.

2002

January

United European currency (the Euro) replaces national currency of twelve EU states.

In State of the Union address, President George W. Bush calls Iran, Iraq, and North Korea "the axis of evil."

April

Cease-fire negotiations are concluded in Angola; Angola civil war ends.

May

NATO-Russia Council is established.

East Timor gains independence.

President Bush and President Putin sign Strategic Offensive Reductions Treaty (SORT).

June

United States formally withdraws from Anti-Ballistic Missile (ABM) Treaty.

September

Fighting breaks out between Ivory Coast government and rebel soldiers.

Switzerland joins UN.

Bush administration releases National Security Strategy for the United States of America.

October

Two bombs explode in town of Kuta on island of Bali, Indonesia.

Chechen terrorists kidnap hostages in Moscow; three days later, Russians use force to end crisis.

November

China and Association of Southeast Asian Nations sign code of conduct in South China Sea to maintain peace and stability.

UN Security Council passes Resolution 1441, forcing Iraq to disarm.

December

Bush administration releases National Strategy to Combat Weapons of Mass Destruction.

Chile and United States sign the U.S.-Chile Free Trade Agreement.

2003
January

North Korea withdraws from Nuclear Non-Proliferation Treaty.

March

Forces led by the United States invade Iraq.

April

Forces seized control of Baghdad. North Korea admits it has nuclear weapons.

May

President Bush declares major combat phase in Iraq has ended.

July

Inter-American Convention against Terrorism takes effect.

August

Peace agreement ends fourteen years of civil war in Liberia, prompts resignation of former President Charles Taylor, who is exiled to Nigeria.

Negotiated cease-fire between Maoist guerillas and government forces in Nepal breaks down.

October

Malaysian Prime Minister Mahathir Mohamad resigns after twenty-two years in power.

December

Saddam Hussein is captured in Iraq.

2004
March

Terrorist bombings take place in Madrid.

Bulgaria, Estonia, Latvia, Lithuania, Romania, Slovakia, and Slovenia formally become members of NATO.

May

Cyprus, the Czech Republic, Estonia, Hungary, Latvia, Lithuania, Malta, Poland, the Slovak Republic, and Slovenia join the EU.

June

United States transfers sovereignty of Iraq to interim government.

July

International Court of Justice says barrier Israel is building to seal off West Bank violates international law.

U.S. Senate Intelligence Committee releases critical report on the CIA's prewar estimates on Iraq. An inquiry report is critical of prewar British intelligence on Iraq. Independent National Commission on Terrorist Attacks Upon the United States releases its findings: that the United States had failed to understand the gravity of threat posed by radical Islamists.

August

Extensive fighting between Shi'ite cleric Muqtada al-Sadr's Mehdi Army militia and U.S. and Iraqi forces in Najaf region of Iraq.

Traces of explosives are found in the wreckage of two aircraft that crashed almost simultaneously after departing from Moscow.

September

Chechen terrorists seize school in Beslan, North Ossetia.

November

George W. Bush is reelected president of the United States.

Major U.S.-led offensive is launched against insurgents in Falluja, Iraq.

2005
January

Elections for a Transitional National Assembly in Iraq are held.

February

In Nepal, King Gyanendra dismisses Prime Minister Sher Bahadur Deuba and his government, declares a state of emergency, and assumes direct power.

North Korea says it is suspending its participation in talks over its nuclear program.

Former Prime Minister of Lebanon Rafik Hariri is killed in Beirut. Cabinet of Prime Minister Omar Karami resigns after anti-Syrian rallies are sparked by the assassination. Calls increase for Syrian troop withdrawal.

April

Iraqi parliament selects Kurdish leader Jalal Talabani as president. Ibrahim Jaafari, a Shi'a, is named prime minister. Syria says it has withdrawn all its military forces from Lebanon as demanded by the UN.

May

European Constitution is rejected in a referendum held in France.

June

European Constitution is rejected in a referendum held in the Netherlands.

July

Four terrorist bombings occur in London. More attempted bombings occur later in month.

August

State of emergency is declared in Sri Lanka after Foreign Minister Lakshman Kadirgamar is assassinated.

Israel evacuates settlers from twenty-five settlements in Gaza Strip and West Bank.

Iraqi draft constitution is read to National Assembly.

September

Japan's Prime Minister Junichiro Koizumi is reelected.

October

Bombs explode on the island of Bali, Indonesia.

November

Suicide bombers attack three hotels in Jordan.

December

Iraqis go to the polls to choose first full-term government and parliament since the U.S.-led invasion.

2006

January

Ehud Olmert assumes powers of Israel's Prime Minister Ariel Sharon.

Upsurge of violence occurs in Iraq.

Hamas performs well in Palestinian parliamentary elections.

February

International protests sparked by publication of cartoons depicting the prophet Muhammad.

April

Rebels seeking to oust President Idriss Deby of Chad battle government forces on outskirts of N'Djamena, the capital. Chad cuts diplomatic ties with Sudan, accusing it of backing rebels.

May

Government in Khartoum, the capital of Sudan, and main rebel faction in Darfur sign peace accord; however, two smaller rebel groups reject the deal.

July

As major Israeli offensive is under way in Gaza Strip, Hezbollah fighters based in southern Lebanon attack an Israeli military checkpoint, capturing two soldiers. In response, Israel launches invasion of southern Lebanon that continues for the next five weeks. North Korean missile tests prompt an international outcry.

September

A ceremony to transfer operational command from U.S.-led forces to Iraq's new army is postponed.

October

North Korea claims it has tested a nuclear weapon.

November

Saddam Hussein is found guilty of crimes against humanity and is sentenced to death. The Democratic party wins control of the U.S. Senate and House of Representatives in midterm elections. These election results are influenced by the ongoing violence and destruction in Iraq.

Paul Bellamy
(The views expressed are those of the author and not necessarily those of his employer)

Index

North Atlantic Treaty
Organization (NATO)
(continued)
expansion and deployment of,
38
Turkey's military force
contribution to, 775
North Kalimantan National Army
(TKNU), 431
North Korea. See Korea, North
North Korean People's Army, 462,
464
North Korean Workers' Party,
463
North Yemen. See Yemen
Northern Alliance, 97, 861–862
Northern Ireland, 854, 861
Northern People's Congress
(NPC), 577–578
Northern Rhodesia. See Zambia
Norway, 747–748, 805
Norwegian People's Aid, 135
Nosiri Khusraw society, 29, 757
NPA. See New People's Army
NPC. See Northern People's
Congress
NPFL-CRC. See National
Patriotic Front of Liberia-
Central Revolutionary
Council
NPLF. See National Patriotic Front
of Liberia
NPP. See National Patriotic Party
NRA. See National Resistance
Army (Uganda); National
Revolutionary Army
NRC. See National Reconciliation
Commission
NRM. See National Resistance
Movement
Ntare V Ndizeye (King of
Burundi), 208, 212
Ntayamira, Cyprian, 860
Nuclear Non-Proliferation Treaty
(NPT), 26, 854–855
Nuers, 6
Nujoma, Sam, 304
Numeiri, Jaafar, 739, 744–745,
748
Núñez Méndez, Jairo, 276
Nur, Adan Abdullahi, 681
Nuri, Said Abdullo, 759, 764
Nyamwisi, Mbusa, 296
Nyerere, Julius, 832

Nyima, Gedhun Choekyi, 255

OAS. See Organization of
American States
OAU. See Organization of African
Unity
O'Ballance, Edgar, 476–477, 480,
483, 486, 823
Obasanjo, Olusegun, 582
Obote, Milton, 662, 791–792, 795,
801, 803, 806
Öcalan, Abdullah, 39–40, 774,
776–777, 779–780, 783–785,
789
Öcalan, Kesire Yildirim, 39, 777
OCHA. See United Nations Office
for the Coordination of
Humanitarian Affairs
October 10 Agreement, 258–260
Office of the High Representative
(OHR), 192–193
Ogaden National Liberation Front
(ONLF), 352, 361–362
Ogaden region and peoples,
74–75, 351–354. See also
Ethiopia
OHR. See Office of the High
Representative
OIC. See Organization of the
Islamic Conference
Oil
in Angola, 125
in Azerbaijan, 145, 156–157
the Chechen conflict and, 42
in Colombia, 275
in Ethiopia, 73, 363
in Indonesia, 425–426
the Iraqi conflict and, 12
in the Middle East, 57–58
in Nigeria, 73, 567, 571, 579
Organization of Petroleum
Exporting Countries (see
Organization of Petroleum
Exporting Countries)
as revenue source for
insurgents, 62
secessionist rebellion and the
presence of, 18
in Sudan, 73, 737–738, 740–741,
746–747
Ojukwu, Chukwuemeka
Odumegwu, 18, 70, 570–571,
573, 577, 579–580, 582–583
Okello, Tito, 792, 795–796

Olmert, Ehud, 59, 864
ONLF. See Ogaden National
Liberation Front
ONUMOZ. See United Nations
Operation in Mozambique
ONUSAL. See United Nations
Observer Mission in El
Salvador
OPEC. See Organization of
Petroleum Exporting
Countries
Operation Flash, 315, 323
Operation Lifeline Sudan, 747
Operation Polo, 412
Operation Production, 516
Operation Provide Comfort, 454
Operation Storm, 315, 323
OPM. See Free Papua Movement
(Organisasi Papua Merdeka)
ORDEN. See National Democratic
Organization
Organizacion Politico Militar
(Military-Political
Organization—OPM), 279
Organization for Economic
Cooperation and
Development (OECD), 12
Organization for Security and
Cooperation in Europe
(OSCE), 35, 156, 648, 753,
759, 767
Organization of African Unity
(OAU)
Biafra, actions regarding, 575,
580
Burundi, actions regarding,
210
colonial borders, inviolability of,
684
the Congo, actions regarding,
305
Ethiopia, actions regarding, 355,
359, 363
Ethiopia and the founding of,
353
Liberia, actions regarding, 504,
505
Rwanda, actions regarding, 655,
663, 666
Somalia, actions regarding, 678,
690–691
See also African Union
Organization of American States
(OAS), 340, 560–561, 849